United States Professional Tennis Association

Our History, Our Members and Our Contribution to the Sport

Acclaim Press
MORLEY, MISSOURI

Acclaim Press
— Your Next Great Book —

P.O. Box 238
Morley, MO 63767
(573) 472-9800
www.acclaimpress.com

Chuck Gill, USPTA President
John Embree, USPTA CEO/Executive Director
Julie Myers, Project Coordinator

Publishing Consultant: Keith Ellebrecht
Editor: Charles A. Francis
Book Design: Devon Burroughs
Cover Design: M. Frene Melton

ISBN: 978-1-942613-63-3 / 1-942613-63-6
Library of Congress Control Number: 2017900442

First Printing: 2017
Printed in the United States of America
10 9 8 7 6 5 4 3 2 1

This publication was produced using available information.
The publisher regrets it cannot assume responsibility for errors or omissions.

Contents

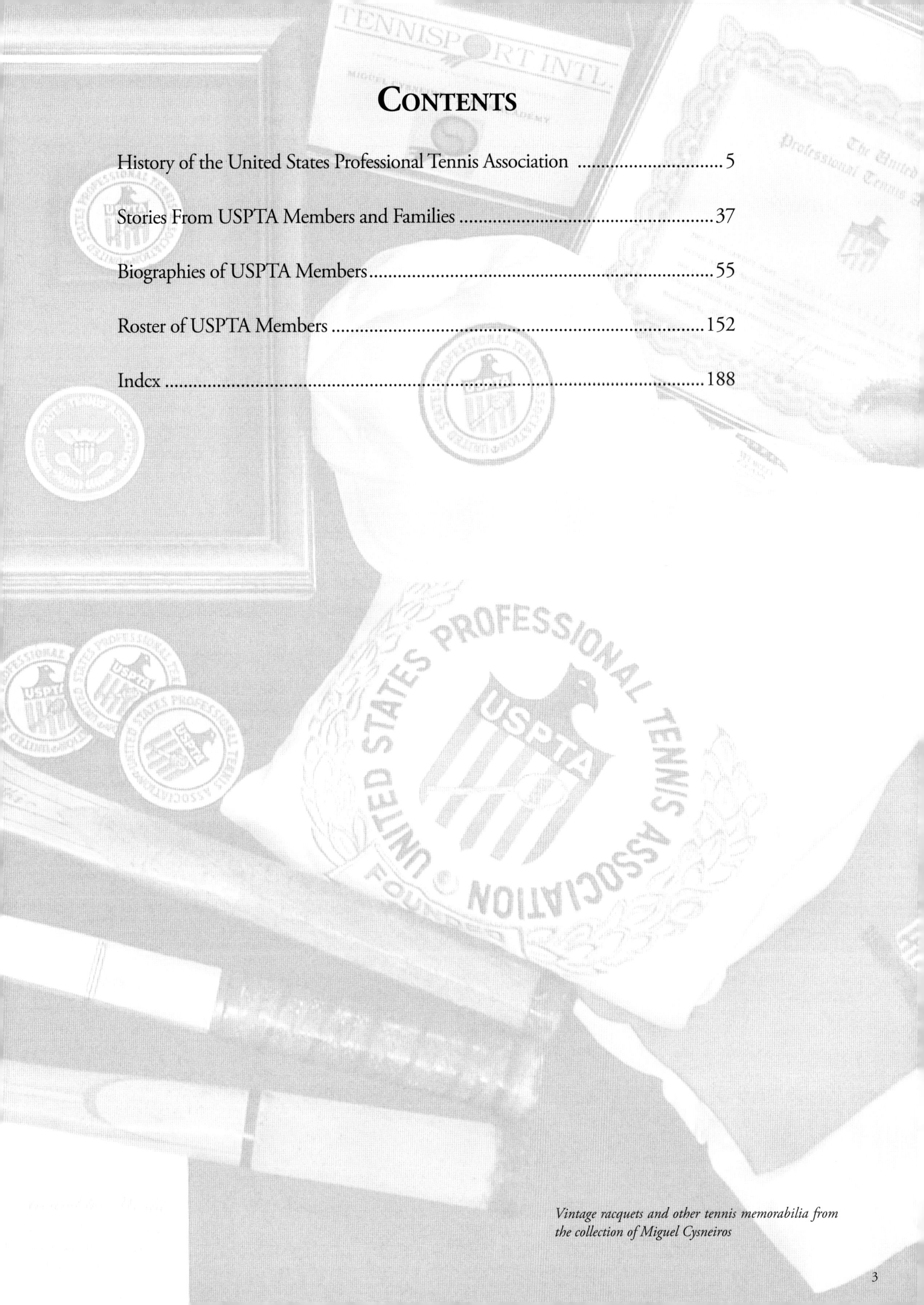

Vintage racquets and other tennis memorabilia from the collection of Miguel Cysneiros

United States Professional Tennis Association, Inc.

Elevating the standards of tennis-teaching professionals and coaches

USPTA members,

For nearly 90 years, the United States Professional Tennis Association has existed to provide education and networking opportunities for tennis-teaching professionals. From the original goal to "further the best interests of the game of tennis, especially through the professional players and instructors of the sport" to our current mission, "to elevate the standards of tennis-teaching professionals and coaches," USPTA has always been about the teaching pro. The passionate leaders of the Association have worked hard throughout the decades to provide opportunities, benefits and programs for its members. This book honors their immense contributions, as we look forward to the future of our sport!

As you read through these pages, you'll see that the Association has gone through many periods of change. This year, 2017, marks the beginning of a new era for USPTA. After more than 25 years in Houston, the World Headquarters is returning to Florida to our new home in Lake Nona, adjacent to the USTA National Campus and the "home of American tennis." Exciting times are ahead for our professionals as we continue to work more closely with our allied associations, the United States Tennis Association and Club Managers Association of America, while also bringing other racquet sports associations into the fold.

This book celebrates the diverse history of the USPTA and you, the member. I would like to thank those of you who have contributed your personal histories to this publication, as well as our national board, executive committee and national staff who continue to make the USPTA the great association it is. We hope you enjoy looking through this book, reading about our growth, and learning more about pros like yourself.

Chuck Gill
USPTA President, 2016-2017

3535 Briarpark Drive, Suite 202 • Houston, TX 77042

800-877-8248 • 713-978-7782 • 713-978-7780 fax • uspta@uspta.org • uspta.com

History of the United States Professional Tennis Association

Notable PLTA members, clockwise from top left: Bobby Riggs, Pauline Betz Addie, Pancho Segura, Alice Marble, Jack Kramer, Sarah Cook.

History Shows Growth of a Profession, The Start of an Industry

This article, written by Dan Soine, former USPTA Public Relations Coordinator, was originally published in the December 1998 issue of ADDvantage *magazine. It has been modified from the original to include current history.*

Some of the material was adapted from "Tennis: A Professional Guide," no longer in publication. The 326-page manual features a history of professional tennis, tennis skills, strategy, match preparation, biomechanics, tournament organization, rules and more.

On Sept. 23, 1927, a small group of tennis professionals gathered in an upper-story room of the Spalding building in New York City. Their mission: to bridge the gap between the amateur ranks and a respectable career as a tennis professional.

Little did they know their plan would materialize into today's United States Professional Tennis Association, a worldwide organization of more than 15,000 teaching professionals dedicated to promoting the sport and raising the standards of their profession.

First serves

Among the pioneers at that initial planning meeting were George Agutter, the first head professional at the renown West Side Tennis Club in Forest Hills, N.Y.; James Burns; William Croker, head professional at Longwood Cricket Club in Boston; Ed Faulkner; Henry Geidel; Paul Heston; Walter Kinsella; Frank Lafforgue; Harry McNeal; James Reid; H.L. Richards; Vinnie Richards; Harvey Snodgrass and Charles Wood.

They met to organize a national body that would work to further the best interests of the game of tennis, especially through the professional players and instructors of the sport. Although tennis was introduced to the United States in 1874, it was not until the years following World War I that tennis became popular enough to warrant professional instructors, and the majority of these instructors were located on the East Coast.

When the group emerged from its first meeting, the Professional Lawn Tennis Association (PLTA) of the United States was born. The group sent out the following notice to all recognized tennis professionals:

"For some time there has been a very strong feeling among lawn tennis professionals that there is a need for some organization to protect and promote their interests, and to assist them in obtaining a proper and recognized status in the tennis world. A meeting was held on September 23 and it was decided to form an Association ... An initiation fee of $10 will be charged to all new members. Dues are to be $5 annually.

"An executive committee has been elected and a constitution adopted. It is the desire of this executive committee to have all tennis professionals of accepted standards become members of this Association. As one of these, you are cordially invited to fill out the enclosed application blank for membership."

Pro active

As the years passed, America's greatest tennis players and teachers belonged to the PLTA, including Jack Kramer, Tony Trabert, Fred Perry, Don Budge, Bobby Riggs, Pancho Segura, Bill Tilden, Ellsworth Vines, Frank Parker, Vinnie Richards, Bruce Barnes and Welby Van Horn.

As early as the 1940s, the organization also began to attract famous women members, including Pauline Betz Addie, Alice Marble and Sarah Cooke.

These women and men were the cream of the tennis crop, and their professional tours captured the imagination of thousands of fans around the world.

During this period, the PLTA membership was limited primarily to the eastern United States. The association offered few benefits other than a membership directory, annual meetings and an opportunity to meet others in the profession.

The Spalding building in New York City was the site of Association's first meeting.

Frank Sedgman, Pancho Segura, Jack Kramer, Vic Hossack, Don Budge, Pancho Gonzales (1950)

In the late 1940s, membership increased to more than 200 of the nation's top professionals. The group added benefits such as a job placement service, two meetings a year and a model professional contract for members to use with their clubs.

Vinnie Richards was one of USPTA's founding members.

In following years, the PLTA acquired an official song, "I'm in the PLTA now!," and members were involved in three movies, *Topflite Tennis, Great Moments of Great Matches with the World's Greatest Pros; Tennis by Contrast, Comparative Games of Riggs, Budge, Perry, Stoefen and Tilden*; and *Mixed Troubles*, a tennis comedy starring Mickey Rooney, Walter Pidgeon, Pauline Betz and Sarah Palfrey Cooke.

In 1957, the association changed its name to the United States Professional Lawn Tennis Association (USPLTA). Membership grew to more than 550 professionals in eight geographic regions under the presidency of William Lufler in the early 1960s.

The open tennis explosion in 1968 brought professional players into their heyday, and the industry grew by leaps and bounds. The first national certification exams were administered in 1969 under then President Jack Barnaby, modeled after those already in use by several of the association's divisions. Over the years, it was molded under the direction of George Bacso, former USPTA director of certification and academies, into the extensive exam it is today.

The establishment of professional standards through the Certification Exam caught the attention of teaching professionals interested in a tennis career path, and membership began to grow. During the 1960s and early '70s, USPLTA expanded west and added its last eight divisions. It made its final name change to USPTA in the early '70s.

Professional tennis comes of age

From the 1920s to the 1950s, professional tennis events consisted mainly of head-to-head tours featuring the likes of Bill Tilden, Ellsworth Vines, Fred Perry, Don Budge, Bobby Riggs and Jack Kramer. These professional tours "barnstormed" throughout Middle America with portable courts, gradually educating and preparing a tennis public outside of the East Coast.

The professional tours captivated the public, but professional players were shunned by the national governing body, the U.S. Lawn Tennis Association (USLTA). The USLTA realized that the success of the pro tennis tours would mean the loss of the power USLTA gained from organizing amateur events. Thus, professional players were excluded from USLTA tennis tournaments, including the U.S. National Championships. This was also the case in England, where professional players were excluded from playing Wimbledon at the All England Club.

Beginning in the late 1960s, Texas oil tycoon Lamar Hunt signed more and more top amateur players to professional contracts with World Championship Tennis (WCT). WCT blossomed at the country's new indoor sports arenas, and was fueled by the growth of televised sports and the introduction of the tie-breaker, which allowed television networks to better determine the length of a match.

Before the 1960s and the success of WCT, only a few players at a time had ever turned professional – the money did not exist for more. Fearful that too many of the top players were turning professional and that Wimbledon would cease to be the world's premier tennis tournament, the All England Club, together with the British and U.S. national governing bodies, forced "open" tennis on the International Lawn Tennis Federation in 1968. Finally, amateurs and professionals were allowed to compete together. The major federations had little choice since they all depended on the financial success of their major tournaments, and this financial success hinged on the attendance of the top players.

The success of WCT also paved the way for the formation of the current men's pro tour – the ATP Tour. When the national federations found that their top national players were choosing WCT events over their national tournaments, the ILTF attempted to exert sanctioning power over the players. Although one national federation alone could not compete with WCT, all of them together, as the ILTF, could affect a player's potential welfare considerably by suspending him or her from ILTF tournaments. As the national federa-

USPLTA officers, 1958. Clockwise, from bottom center: Louis Ballato, Mickey Phillips, Thomas Byrne, Lillian Martin, George Agutter, James A. Bernson, Herb Walker, Richard Barrow, Claudia Long and Arthur F. Condon.

Arthur Ashe and George Bacso

tions were fighting with WCT and reaffirming their commitment to ILTF, the players themselves saw an opportunity to have a voice in running the pro game. In 1972, several prominent players met in Forest Hills to lay the foundation for an association of players – the Association of Tennis Professionals (ATP).

While the ATP (and later the women's WTA) represented the needs and desires of professional players on the world's expanding pro circuit, USPTA focused on the needs and aspirations of club teaching professionals, instructors and coaches. The ATP, WTA and USPTA continue to work together to represent the entire spectrum of professional tennis, from club pros to touring pros.

The positive association between USPTA and the pro tours continues today. Former tour players often join USPTA following their touring years in order to develop club management skills and contacts needed to start a new career. Or vice versa – current USPTA teaching pros sometimes try their luck on the pro tour depending on their success in regional and national events.

USPTA teaching professionals work hand-in-hand with pro tournament organizers to run tennis clinics and special events at many ATP and WTA events throughout the United States. USPTA speakers have also taught business and other professionals skills at several ATP/WTA Professional Courses. These courses provide career transition services to retiring players.

Endorsement history

The Association's first endorsement began in 1973 with the USPTA Pro Penn tennis ball. This relationship continued until December 2013, the longest-running endorsement in the tennis industry.

USPTA president Sheldon Caldwell signs a licensing agreement with Yonex while Bill Tym (right) and a representative from Yonex watch.

Prince's Jim Baugh and USPTA President Tim Heckler in front of the USPTA headquarters in Sarasota, Fla., 1982. Prince became the official racquet of the USPTA in that year.

The earliest racquet endorsement was with TAD/Davis in the early to mid-1970s. This was short lived and cash value to the Association was insignificant. However, the racquet endorsement program continued to grow:

- Yonex became the official racquet in 1977.
- Prince became the official racquet in 1982. This was a groundbreaking endorsement for both companies since Prince was the only oversized racquet in the world at that time.
- Wilson became the official racquet in 1993.
- HEAD was the official racquet for USPTA from 2003 to 2013.
- From 2014 to mid-2016, Prince was the official racquet as well as ball, string and accessories.
- In August 2016, Wilson became the official tennis equipment supplier of the USPTA. This includes racquets, balls, strings, grip, bags, 10 and Under Tennis equipment, stringing machines, and platform tennis paddles and balls.

Earlier string endorsements included Ashaway, Gamma, Prince, Wilson and HEAD.

USPTA entered the shoe endorsement business in 1973, with companies such as Converse, Nike, Spalding, Pro Penn and Asahi. Various endorsements included shoes as well as clothing: Prince, Wilson and Lotto; while some covered apparel only: Living Legend. The Fromuth/Nike footwear and apparel endorsement began in 2006 and the deal was recently extended through 2021.

There have been numerous miscellaneous endorsements over the years, including Subaru Cars, Matchmate ball machines, SmartShield Sunscreen, American Airlines, Bollé sunglasses and Excel sport drinks.

Building a profession

A World Headquarters building was just a dream in the formative years of USPTA. Over time, the national office moved from Huntsville, Ala., to The Colony Beach and Tennis Resort near Sarasota, Fla., then to Saddlebrook Resort near Tampa, Fla.

In 1990, USPTA took the next step in its development as an association. After years of saving, it purchased a two-story office building in Houston to house its World Headquarters. The fully computerized, state-of-the-art USPTA offices brought member services to an even higher level. USPTA's ownership of the building served as a source of financial stability, in addition to building member pride in the organization. It also had two tennis courts used for certification testing as well as filming needs.

But Florida was calling, and in June 2016, USPTA announced that it would break ground for its soon-to-be new home in Lake Nona, Fla., site of the USTA's Home of American Tennis in the Lake Nona Sports & Performance District. The association will relocate to its new headquarters in late spring 2017. The single-story, 10,000-square-foot building will house a technologically driven office space and lab for learning and training. In addition, the space features an in-house multimedia studio that will allow for TV-quality production for educational content.

From 1974 to 1981, the membership increased from 1,000 to 2,500. It has since leaped from 2,500 to more than 15,000 members.

As the number of members grew, so did the number of membership benefits. Today, USPTA offers on-court liability insurance, an endorsee-supported retirement plan, home and auto insurance, extensive continuing education, online tools, prize-money tournaments, influence with club owners and managers, a national public relations program and a variety of product packages, to name a few.

Roy Emerson joined the USPTA in 1981.

Some of the most successful teachers, coaches and players joined USPTA's membership ranks throughout the 1970s, '80s, '90s and into the 2000s. Some standouts include Arthur Ashe, Nick Bollettieri, Vic Braden, Peter Burwash, Mary

USPTA staff at the USPTA National Office in Sarasota, FL

Artist's conception of USPTA World Headquarters in Lake Nona, Fla., to open spring 2017

Carillo, Alex Olmedo, Cliff Drysdale, Chris Evert, Vitas Gerulaitis, Jack Groppel, Tim and Tom Gullikson, Billie Jean King, Jim Loehr, Dennis Ralston, Pam Shriver, Stan Smith, Fred Stolle, Bill Tym, Gigi Fernandez, Taylor Dent, Roy Emerson, Rod Laver, Patrick McEnroe, Tracy Austin, Katrina Adams, Emilio Sanchez and many others.

In the early 1980s, the women members organized, their numbers began to grow, and they acquired stronger leadership roles. Kathy Woods served as the first woman president of the association from 1994-1996. Minority professionals also became more involved in the tennis profession and USPTA formed multicultural committees at the divisional and national levels.

In 1981, the Japan Professional Tennis Association invited USPTA and Fred Stolle to conduct a tennis academy in Tokyo and became the first foreign tennis organization to join USPTA. Other allied associations USPTA has worked with include the Asociacion de Profesores & Instructores de Tenis de Mexico, A.C., the British Professional Tennis Coaches' Association and the Tennis Coaches of South Africa.

The USPTA Multimedia Department produces "On Court with USPTA," a tennis instructional series for the Tennis Channel.

USPTA president Sheldon Caldwell (left) and Executive Director Bill Tym (right) pose with club president Dr. Murph Klauber at the USPTA's announcment of the selection of The Colony Beach and Tennis Resort at Longboat Key, FL.

Nick Bollettieri, Donald Dell and Bill Tym at the 1978 National Convention

USPTA World Headquarters, Houston 2014

Current international relationships exist with Tennis Coaches Australia Victoria and Registro Profesional de Tenis, as well as the JPTA. In addition, a USPTA China Division was formed in 2010. USPTA now boasts members from more than 80 countries.

In 2015, the USPTA incorporated the Professional Platform Tennis Association, adding a new certification type to the membership.

There have been many changes in the association and in the tennis industry since Sept. 23, 1927. New racquets, new pro stars and new teaching methods continue to touch millions of tennis enthusiasts worldwide.

Nevertheless, one constant remains – the dedication of thousands of USPTA teaching professionals who continue to shape the way people learn and play the game.

USPTA President Tim Heckler and Mr. Matsumoto, Vice President of the JPTA, signing the letter of intent to become the first foreign tennis organization to join the USPTA, 1982.

Bill Tym (left) and Fred Stolle conduct a coaches workshop in Japan for the Japanese Professional Tennis Association.

In 2015, the USPTA began certifying platform tennis professionals. Anton Mavrin and Patricio Misitrano taught a special course at Wee Burn Country Club in Darien, Conn., 2015.

USPTA TIMELINE

1927 Professional Lawn Tennis Association of the United States was formed
1957 Association name changed to United States Professional Lawn Tennis Association
1969 First certification exams were administered
1970 Association name changed to United States Professional Tennis Association
1974 Ray Bovett, first full-time executive director
1974 First national office in Houston
1975 Bill Tym becomes second full-time executive director after the death of Bovett. USPTA has 1,000 members.
1975 National office moves with Tym to space outside of Chattanooga, Tenn.
1977 USPTA celebrates 50th anniversary and launch of *ADDvantage*, USPTA's own magazine, under president Sheldon Caldwell.
1978 USPTA strikes endorsement agreement with Colony Beach & Tennis Resort near Sarasota, Fla., to move its headquarters there. Michael Fryer hired as executive director. Membership is up to 2,000.
1982 Tim Heckler becomes executive director/CEO
1982 Japan Professional Tennis Association becomes first international division
1983 USPTA moves headquarters to Saddlebrook Resort
1983 Computerization of USPTA begins
1984 Membership totals 4,000
1990 USPTA begins original free grassroots lesson program, Tennis Across America
1990 USPTA moves its headquarters back to Houston and its own building
1992 Membership grows to 10,000
1993 USPTA officially opens its Hall of Fame with induction of the late Arthur Ashe
1994 USPTA introduces Little Tennis®, a new program targeting young players from 3 to 10

Tim Heckler served as USPTA's CEO for 30 years.

1995 USPTA launches www.uspta.com
1997 USPTA offers free personal websites to every member
1999 USPTA launches Find-a-Pro service
2002 USPTA celebrates 75th anniversary
2003 USPTA launches TV show "On Court with USPTA" that airs on the Tennis Channel
2004 USPTA introduces Player Development Program
2007 USPTA has 14,500 members
2010 USPTA China Division is formed
2012 Tim Heckler retires as CEO and John Embree assumes the reins
2015 USPTA has 15,000 members
2015 USPTA begins certifying platform tennis instructors
2016 USPTA breaks ground on new World Headquarters in Lake Nona, Fla.
2017 USPTA relocates to Lake Nona, Fla.

Aerial view of The Colony Beach and Tennis Resort, home of the USPTA Headquarters, 1979-1984

USPTA Past National Presidents

George Agutter (1927-35) was a charter member and the USPLTA's first president, serving seven terms. He was a teaching professional at West Side Tennis Club at Forest Hills in New York City. He previously worked at the Queen's Club in London.

Edwin Faulkner (1936-37) was a charter member of the association and also served as president of the Middle States Division. He coached tennis at Swarthmore College in Delaware County for 41 years. He was named head coach of the Spanish Davis Cup team in 1923, and from 1924 to 1926, he coached the United States to three consecutive Davis Cup victories.

Henry Geidel (1938-39) was a charter member and also served as secretary of the association. He was the tennis and squash coach for the Nassau Country Club on Long Island, where he worked for more than 32 years.

James Pressly (1940-41) was the fourth president of the association and he was a club pro for Jupiter Island Club in Florida and Bedford Golf and Tennis Club in New York for more than 30 years. He was a captain in the U.S. Army during WWII. Before he was a teaching professional, Pressly earned a master's degree in history from Columbia University. All five of his children played college tennis on scholarships, and two went on to earn national titles.

Charles Wood (1942-46) was a charter member of the PLTA and was the first amateur to turn professional. He played in the first National Professional Tennis Championships in 1927 and won the National Professional doubles title in 1933 and 1936. He was the owner and manager of the Coral Beach Club in Palm Beach, Fla., for many years.

Frank Rericha (1947) served as executive secretary of the association from 1945-1946 before serving as president. He was the tennis professional for Greenwich Country Club in Greenwich, Conn., for many years and then later worked at the Wilmington Country Club.

George Seewagen (1948-53, 1962-63) was the only member to serve as president twice. He was the tennis coach at St. John's University for 49 years. He also was the tennis professional at Jackson Heights Tennis Club and the 7th Regiment Tennis Club, and he coached the ELTA Junior Davis Cup Squad.

Mercer Beasley (1954) coached at Tulane, Princeton, Lawrenceville School and the University of Miami, and taught tennis at private clubs in Milwaukee, Pasadena and Chicago. He authored the book, "How to Play Tennis: The Beasley System," in 1933, which was a highly influential book that emphasized accuracy and consistent play.

Thomas Byrne (1955-56) was a USPTA member for 44 years. Prior to serving as national president, he was the Eastern Division's president from 1954-55. He was the professional at Travers Island, N.Y., for many years.

Arthur Condon (1957-58) was the professional for Old York Road Country Club in Jenkintown, Pa., and Northeast Harbor Tennis Club in Northeast Harbor, Maine.

Ralph Chambers (1959-61) was recognized in 2000 as USPTA's longest serving member – 72 years. He coached Army Men's Tennis from 1933 to 1946. In 1965 he received the Joseph D. Deitz Bowl Award.

Bill Lufler (1963-66) was a collegiate coach at Presbyterian College, the University of Miami and the University of South Florida. He was the head professional at West Side Tennis Club in Forest Hills, N.Y., and St. Petersburg Tennis Center and Safety Harbor Spa and Resort in Florida. Under his direction as president of USPTA, the Association adopted stricter admission standards and encouraged better communication among those in the profession. He was a USPTA member for 65 years.

Milton Phillips (1967-68) also served as the association's secretary. He was a tennis professional at Schuyler Meadow Club in Loudonville, N.Y.

Jack Barnaby (1969-70) was a USPTA member for 47 years. He was the winningest coach in the history of Harvard University, coaching from 1932 to 1976. He was inducted posthumously into the USPTA New England Hall of Fame in 2013. Barnaby was instrumental in the creation of the first USPTA Certification Exam in the mid-1970s.

Dave Muir (1971-72) has been a USPTA member for 53 years. In 2015 he received the USPTA George Bacso Lifetime Achievement Award. Muir has coached some of the top teaching pros in the Chicago area today, several national champions, and Illinois High School Champions. He continues to be an integral part of the local USTA Competition Training Center Program, being a CTC coach for the last 20 years. Muir also served as president of the USPTA Midwest Division, and he was the head coach of the USTA Competition Training Center at Homewood-Flossmoor from 1988-2009.

Ted Withall (1973) has been a USPTA member for 64 years. He is a Master Professional and he served as the Florida Division president in 1967. He founded the H.V. Kaltenborn Junior League in Stony Brook, N.Y. (1958-61) and the Arvida Trophy League, and adult competitive league for clubs from Palm Beach to Fort Lauderdale, Fla. (1958-70).

Les Longshore Jr. (1974) was a professional tennis player, coach, umpire, English teacher and distance runner. He was a cofounder of the Southern Professional Tennis Association and the Birmingham Track Club. He ran in every Vulcan Run marathon and completed 37 marathons, the last in 2002 at age 76. He was a USPTA member for 50 years.

Tex Schwab (1975) introduced during his presidency the first filing system of membership data – it was recorded on note cards and kept in small cardboard boxes. There were approximately 1,000 members at the time. He was a USPTA member for 42 years.

Sheldon Caldwell (1976-78) was the "father of ADDvantage magazine," which was first published in 1977. As president, his goal was to recruit more members into USPTA, and also to improve the way the association communicated with the members and the industry.

Alex Gordon (1976) served as president during a very turbulent time in USPTA's history. Under his leadership, the board was completely revised and the USPTA began to experience unprecedented growth and progress. As a coach, he was first hired on as head professional at Hotel Del Coronado in San Diego in 1946. He taught there for 10 years and then returned again in 1960 and remained there until 1976. The San Diego resident passed away during his term as president. The Alex Gordon Professional of the Year award was named in his honor, and he was inducted posthumously into the USPTA Hall of Fame in 2007.

George Bacso (1978-80) was USPTA's Director of Certification and Academies for many years. He traveled the world conducting Certification Exams, Tennis Teachers' Courses and Certification Training Courses (PTCA I). Bacso was instrumental in developing the current USPTA certification process and worked with USPTA's national tester network. He also served several years as the president of the USPTA Eastern Division. He received the USTA National Education Merit Award and the national USPTA Professional of the Year Award. Bacso also received the inaugural George Bacso Lifetime Achievement Award in 1998, and he held a Master Professional rating. He was inducted into the USPTA Hall of Fame in 1994.

Tim Heckler (1980-82) was USPTA's CEO for 30 years, from 1982-2012. Prior to that, he served on the national USPTA executive committee and board of directors. He was USPTA Professional of the Year in 1979 and a Master Professional. As CEO, Heckler guided the Association through a period in which it increased its membership fivefold and its annual income tenfold, established USPTA as the foremost organization of teaching professionals in the world, and revolutionized USPTA's operations through computerization. He was inducted into the USPTA Hall of Fame in 2000.

Bill Tym (1982-84) served as USPTA's executive director from 1975-78 and helped create a standardized certification test. Tym was named USPTA Professional of the Year in 1982, College Coach of the Year in 1989, and Touring Coach of the Year in 1997 and 2002. He also received the George Bacso Lifetime Achievement Award from the USPTA in 2001 and the International Tennis Hall of Fame Tennis Educational Merit Award in 1981. He was inducted into the USPTA Hall of Fame in 2007.

Mike Eikenberry (1984-86) has been a USPTA member for 45 years and he earned the George Bacso Lifetime Achievement Award in 2009. As president, it was his recommendation that USPTA investigate the use of computers by the national office.

Jim Reffkin (1986-88) has been the director of tennis for the city of Tucson's Parks and Recreation Department and the Reffkin Tennis Center (renamed in his honor in 2009) for 40 years. He was named USPTA Professional of the Year in 1996 and he was inducted into the USTA Southwest Section Hall of Fame in 2005.

Rod Dulany (1988-90) became director of tennis at Washington Golf and Country Club in 1972 and served in this capacity for the next 30 years. He was the first Junior Tennis Council Chair for the USTA/Mid-Atlantic Section, and later served as section's president and delegate to the USTA from 1991-1998. Dulany was president of the USPTA/Mid-Atlantic Division from 1977-1980 and served on the USPTA Executive Committee from 1976-1996 and the national USPTA Board of Directors from 1984-1992. Dulany is a USPTA Master Professional and was named the USPTA Professional of the Year in 1980.

Jack Justice (1990-92) has been a USPTA member since 1969. He also served as president and secretary of USPTA's Southern Division, was on the USTA National Junior Tennis League Committee, and was a USTA clinician and umpire. In 1988, Justice co-authored USPTA's "How to Hire a Tennis Professional," an employment assistance manual that outlines 10 important steps in the hiring process.

Gordon Collins (1992-94) has been a USPTA member since 1976. He served as president of the Northern California Division from 1981-83 and he was the division's Professional of the Year in 1980, 1981 and 1983. Collins is the tennis director at Bay Club Courtside in Los Gatos, Calif. He also serves as a director on the USTA Norcal Board.

Kathy Woods (1994-96) has the distinguished honor of being the first and only woman to serve the association as national president. She is the director of tennis at the USTA National Campus in Lake Nona, Fla., and has been a certified teaching professional for nearly three decades. In 1996, Woods was honored with the prestigious Educational Merit Award by the International Tennis Association for outstanding service to tennis at the national level.

Kurt Kamperman (1996-97) is the USTA's chief executive for Community Tennis and the USTA National Campus, and has led the USTA's efforts to increase tennis participation in the United States. He previously was president of the Tennis Industry Association. Kamperman is a USPTA Master Professional and has been a member for more than 30 years.

Will Hoag (1997-99) has been the director of tennis at Coral Ridge Country Club, owned by the Robert Trent Jones family, in Fort Lauderdale, Fla., since 1973. He became a member of USPTA in 1972, is a Master Professional, and he was named USPTA Professional of the Year in 2002.

Joe Thompson (1999-2003) is a USPTA Master Professional and the 1998 USPTA Professional of the Year. He was the director of tennis for Rolling Hills Country Club in Golden, Colo., for 30 years, and he has been a USPTA member since 1976.

David T. Porter, Ed.D. (2003-05) is the head tennis coach at Brigham Young University Hawaii. He is a USPTA Master Professional and was named USPTA Professional of the Year in 2012. He has been a Head Tester since 1988, served on the National Board from 1994-2007 and has been a member since 1986.

Ron Woods (2005-07) has been involved in tennis for more than 50 years and has been a USPTA member since 1967. He was on the USPTA national board for 13 years. As a player, he attended the University of Houston on a tennis scholarship. Woods was the director of tennis at the Corpus Christi Country Club from 1970 to 2001, and then went on to serve as the executive director for the USPTA Texas Division for several years.

Harry Gilbert (2007-09) is the head professional at Waccabuc Country Club in Westchester County, N.Y., during the summer and is director of tennis at the Hammock Beach Resort in Palm Coast, Fla., during the winter. He has been a USPTA member since 1981. He served on the Florida Division Board of Directors for eight years, including a three-year term as president. He was named Florida Division Professional of the Year in 1992 and 1994.

Tom Daglis (2009-13) is a USPTA Master Professional. He was the 2003 George Bacso Tester of the Year, and in 2006, he received the USPTA Professional of the Year Award. He was also inducted into the USPTA Southern Hall of Fame.

Tom McGraw (2013-15) is the tennis director at the Port Royal Club in Naples, Fla. McGraw has been teaching tennis since 1979 and a USPTA member since 1980. He earned his Master Professional status in 2008. He previously served as president of the USPTA Southern Division and USTA Kentucky Vice President concurrently.

USPTA Master Professionals

Larry Abrams
Lee Adams
Janet Adkisson
Greg Alexander
Bob Anderman
Kirk Anderson
Jorge Andrew
Jim Annesi
George Bacso *
Mike Baldwin
Rosie Bareis
Jack Barnaby *
Van Barry
Sanford Baruch *
Sheryl Behne
Craig Bell
Lorenzo Beltrame
Marvin Benzing
Jay Bewley
Nick Bollettieri
Bill Bond *
Donnia Bondallian
Chip Brooks
Dave Brown
Bunny Bruning
Fred Burdick
Harry Burrus *
Peter Burwash
Shelly Caldwell *
Jorge Capestany
Allan Carvell *
Mark Centrella
Manuel Cervantes
Michael Chamberlain
Howard Chodak
Holly Chomyn
Chris Chopra
Will Cleveland
Steve Contardi
Jim Cox *
Alan Cutler
Tom Daglis
Peter Daub
Jim Davies *
Jim Davis
Robert Davis
Ken DeHart
Rosemary DeHoog
Becky Desmond
Kim Dillard
Joseph Dinoffer
Rod Dulany
Larry Dupleich
David Dvorak
Fred Earle III
Fred Earle Jr. *
Todd Ellenbecker
Doug Eng
John Foley
Dexter Fong
Jack Foster
Ty Fuller
Paul Gagon
Ed Garcia
David Gary
Nicolaus Getz
Florin Giuglescu
Barry Goldsmith
Sylvia Gothard
Tommy Gray
Ian Griffin
Jack Groppel
Spike Gurney
David Hagler
Jay Hardman
Feisal Hassan
Jeff Hawes
Tim Heckler *
Allan Henry *
Don Henson
Will Hoag
Bob Holm *
Gary Horvath
Glen Howe
John Ingram
Dean Ives
Gordon Johnson
Jack Justice
Kurt Kamperman
Leo Katz
Dick King
Dave Kozlowski
Jim Krimbill
Chuck Kuhle
Jo Ann Kurz
Anna Kuykendall
Ron Lague
Phil Lancaster
Don Leary *
Darryl Lewis
Larry Lineberry
Jim Loehr
Les Longshore Jr. *
Angel Lopez
Bob Love
Charles Lundgren *
Rick Macci
Doug MacCurdy
Paul MacDonald
Paul Marcum
Patrick Mason
Jay Massart
Ken McAllister
Tom McGraw
Mark McMahon
Ed McQuillin
Luis Mediero
Michael Mercier
David Minihan
Bal Moore
Gardnar Mulloy *
Avis Murray
Jack Newman
Dan O'Connell
Mike O'Connell
Stan Oley
Desmond Oon
Ajay Pant
Jim Parker
Guy Parks
Jimmy Pitkanen
Joseph Pizzat
David Porter
Dave Power
Ben Press *
Warren Pretorius
Hank Quinn *
Adrian Rattenbury
Mark Rearden
Ron Rebhuhn *
Jim Reffkin
Allie Ritzenberg
Albert Rogers *
Hans Romer
Raul Saad
Emilio Sanchez Vicario
Mark Savage
Nick Saviano
Paula Scheb
Brett Schwartz
Diane Selke
Ed Serues *
James Shaughnessy
Len Simard
Dave Sivertson
Sean Sloane
Dean Snyder
Randy Stephens
Tom Sweitzer
Keith Swindoll
R J Tessier
Joseph Thompson
John Trinity
Gary Trost
Bill Tym
Mike Van Zutphen
Fernando Velasco
John Verde
Rick Vetter
Tommy Wade
Betty Walsh
Russ Warner
Hugh Waters
Doug Welsh
Pat Whitworth
Glenn William
Ted Withall
Ron Woods
Ron Woods
Rod Workman
Paul Xanthos *
David Zeutas-Broer

*Deceased

USPTA HALL OF FAME GRAND INDUCTEES

This is the Association's highest honor afforded any person, national or international, living or deceased. Inductees have given exemplary service to the tennis-teaching profession. Inductees must have momentous international and/or national tennis industry or teaching service, be well known by name to teaching professionals in the country in which they reside and fulfill various other requirements.

Peter Burwash, *inducted in 2016*

USPTA Master Professional Peter Burwash is the founder and president of Peter Burwash International, which for 41 years has been the world's largest tennis management company, operating in 32 countries. PBI was named "One of the Ten Best-Managed Companies in America" by author James O'Toole in his book, "Vanguard Management." He is a featured international speaker for Fortune 500 companies and the author of 11 books, including "The Key to Great Leadership." As a player, he competed on the AT Professional Tennis Tour from 1968 to 1974, won 19 international singles and doubles titles and was a former Canadian No. 1 and Davis Cup Player.

Burwash is an International Tennis Hall of Fame Educational Merit Award winner and was named "one of the One Hundred Most Influential Forces in Twentieth Century Tennis." He was inducted into the University of Toronto Sports Hall of Fame in 2004, Northern California Tennis Hall of Fame in 2010, Tennis Industry Hall of Fame in 2015, and Hawaii Tennis Hall of Fame in 2015.

Tom Gullikson, *inducted in 2015*

Tom Gullikson is a legendary player and coach who has taught Grand Slam champions and helped grow the game of tennis. Gullikson and his twin brother, Tim, played collegiate tennis together at Northern Illinois University, where they still rank as two of the top student-athletes at the university. At the professional level, Gullikson won 16 top-level doubles titles – 10 of them with Tim. His career-high rankings were world No. 34 in singles and No. 9 in doubles, both in 1984. Gullikson earned his only Grand Slam title in 1984 at the U.S. Open, taking home the mixed doubles championship with partner Manuela Maleeva.

Gullikson became one of the original members of the USTA Player Development Program, coaching players such as Todd Martin, Jennifer Capriati and Andy Roddick. He served as Director of Coaching for the program from 1997 to 2001. He also served as the U.S. Davis Cup Captain from 1994 to 1999. He captained the teams that won the Davis Cup in 1995 and were runners-up in 1997. In 1996, he coached the U.S. men's Olympic tennis team, and guided Andre Agassi to winning the Olympic Gold Medal in Atlanta. Gullikson later returned to the USTA where he is now the lead national coach for men's tennis with USTA Player Development. A USPTA member for more than 28 years, Gullikson has been generous with his time to share his expertise with other tennis-teaching professionals.

Dennis Van der Meer, *inducted in 2015*

Dennis Van der Meer was a pioneer in creating a standard for tennis-teaching instruction. He began playing tennis at an early age while living in Namibia in southern Africa with his missionary father and mother. After a stint with the Davis Cup at the age of 19, Van der Meer found his calling to teach tennis. He made a name for himself in Johannesburg, South Africa, before he quickly developed a large following in the U.S. Eventually he started to coach professional players, including Margaret Court and Billie Jean King, who he coached during the famous "Battle of the Sexes" match with Bobby Riggs in 1973. Van der Meer founded the Professional Tennis Registry in 1976. He was instrumental in developing the TennisUniversity course manual, which became the first of PTR's instructional series of books and supplements. He became one of the first registered coaches of both the ATP and WTA, and he has coached hundreds of nationally and internationally ranked professional and junior players throughout his career, including world champions in singles and doubles.

A USPTA member for 54 years, Van der Meer is a believer in the concept of tennis for everyone. He also developed courses and manuals for teaching wheelchair tennis and adaptive techniques.

Nick Bollettieri, *inducted in 2013*

Nick Bollettieri of Bradenton, Fla., has been one of the most influential people in tennis. A year after becoming a USPTA member, he founded the

Nick Bollettieri Tennis Academy (now known as IMG Academy) in Florida in 1978, which was the first full-time tennis boarding school to combine intense training on court with custom-designed academic curriculum. His approach led to 10 No. 1 players in the world: Andre Agassi, Boris Becker, Jim Courier, Martina Hingis, Jelena Jankovic, Marcelo Rios, Monica Seles, Maria Sharapova and Venus and Serena Williams.

Vic Braden, *inducted in 2013*

Vic Braden has impacted tennis as a player, teaching professional and broadcaster. He was the founder/director of the Vic Braden Tennis College in Coto de Caza, Calif., co-founder of Vic Braden Tennis College at Star Island Resort in Kissimmee, Fla., and co-founder of Vic Braden Tennis College in St. George, Utah. He and Jack Kramer co-founded the Jack Kramer Tennis Club in Palos Verdes, Calif. Since joining the USPTA in 1984, he authored numerous books including *Tennis for the Future, Teaching Children Tennis the Vic Braden Way, Quick Fixes* and *Mental Tennis.* As a professional player, he was invited to play in the World Tennis Championships three times.

Steve Wilkinson, *inducted in 2013*

Steve Wilkinson of Saint Peter, Minn., was the head men's coach at Gustavus Adolphus College for 39 years from 1971-2009 and is the winningest coach in the history of men's collegiate tennis with 923 victories. He coached 46 players to 87 all-American honors (including current ATP tour player Eric Butorac). He founded the Tennis and Life clinics/camps more than 25 years ago and dedicated his time and effort to improving tennis performance of youth and adults while teaching life lessons that can be used off the court. He was a USPTA member from 1972 to 2015.

Doris Hart, *inducted in 2012*

Doris Hart is one of three players, all women, to have a "boxed set" of Grand Slam titles every possible title (singles, same-sex doubles, and mixed doubles) from all four Grand Slam events. The others are Margaret Court and Martina Navratilova. She won 35 Grand Slam titles during her career. Six of her titles were in women's singles, 14 in women's doubles, and 15 in mixed doubles. Hart retired from the tour in 1955 the same year she joined USPTA to become a tennis-teaching professional. She was inducted into the International Tennis Hall of Fame in 1969. She is the first woman inducted into USPTA's Hall of Fame.

Pancho Segura, *inducted in 2012*

Pancho Segura is a former leading tennis player of the 1940s and 1950s, both as an amateur and a professional. In 1950 and 1952, he was the World Co-No. 1 player. He was born in Guayaquil, Ecuador, but moved to the United States in the late 1930s. He is the only player to have won the U.S. Pro Tennis Championship title on three different surfaces (which he did consecutively from 1950-1952). He joined USPTA in 1946, and was widely credited with helping develop the young Jimmy Connors. He was inducted into the International Tennis Hall of Fame in 1984.

Randy Snow, *inducted in 2010*

Randy Snow became the first Paralympic athlete inducted into the U.S. Olympic Hall of Fame in 2004. He was a silver medalist in the 1,500-meter wheelchair race at the 1984 Summer Olympics. He won gold medals in both singles and doubles with Brad Parks at the 1992 Summer Paralympics in Barcelona. He also won the U.S. Open Wheelchair singles titles 10 times and doubles six times.

A USPTA member for 17 years, Snow was considered a pioneer and an innovator in the wheelchair industry and helped improve the designs for athletes and improve the lives of many disabled people. He devoted his time to giving back and sharing the game of tennis.

Welby Van Horn, *inducted in 2008*

Welby Van Horn's career as a coach has spawned institutions such as the Welby Van Horn Tennis Academy in Boca Raton, Fla., and Welby Van Horn tennis programs in a number of locations. The teaching system he developed is still used today and it is featured in his book "The Secrets of the Tennis Master."

Van Horn was a star player and contemporary of other world-class players and USPTA members, including Fred Perry, Bobby Riggs, Bill Tilden and Bruce Barnes. When he was 19 years old, he reached the finals of the 1939 U.S. Nationals. One of the high points of his playing career was his crushing defeat of the great Bill Tilden during a match between U.S. and British Empire service teams at Wimbledon in 1945. Van Horn also won the United States Pro Championship (a USPTA event) in 1945.

Bill Tym, *inducted in 2007*

Bill Tym, a USPTA Master Professional and past USPTA national president, has been involved in tennis as a coach, player and administrator for half a century. He coached the Vanderbilt University men's tennis team to its first NCAA tournament. As a player, Tym was a Southeastern Conference singles champion at the University of Florida. He also competed on the international tour and won 10 national and international titles. As executive director of USPTA, Tym helped create a standardized certification test. Tym was named USPTA Professional of the Year in 1982, College Coach of the Year in 1989, and Touring Coach of the Year in 1997 and 2002. He also received the George Bacso Lifetime Achievement Award from the USPTA in 2001 and the International Tennis Hall of Fame Tennis Educational Merit Award in 1981.

Alex Gordon, *inducted in 2007*

Alex Gordon made great contributions to the game of tennis as a coach, player and USPTA member. As a coach, he was first hired on as head professional at Hotel Del Coronado in San Diego in 1946. He taught there for 10 years and then returned again in 1960 and remained there until 1976. As a player, he attended UCLA and was captain of the men's tennis team and the No. 1 singles player. He was also the two-time Southern California Interscholastic doubles champion. Gordon was the USPTA national 45 doubles champion in 1969, '71 and '72 (with Ben Press).

Gordon was the president of the USPTA San Diego Division in 1969-1974. He was also president of the USPTA national Board of Directors in 1976, but passed away during his presidency. He is credited with holding the Association together in the 1970s, when it struggled with internal political turmoil. For that and his other contributions, the Alex Gordon Professional of the Year award was named in his honor.

Clarence Mabry, *inducted in 2006*

Clarence Mabry was both a respected player and tennis-teaching professional. As a player, he was nationally ranked and a state champion, winning the Southwest Conference singles and doubles title while at the University of Texas at Austin in 1946. In 1955 he established the Trinity University's men's tennis team and went on to develop a nationally recognized program. He led them to the NCAA championship in 1972, and for 18 of his 19 years as coach, his team ranked in the top four NCAA teams, giving him an impressive win-loss record of 319-36.

Mabry's other honors include induction into the Intercollegiate Tennis Association Men's Tennis Collegiate Hall of Fame, Texas Tennis Hall of Fame, San Antonio Hall of Fame, Trinity University Hall of Fame and the University of Texas Hall of Honor.

Tut Bartzen, *inducted in 2003*

Tut Bartzen was one of America's top amateur tennis players, ranked in the U.S. top 10 from 1953-62. He was unflappable on clay courts, achieved a national ranking of No. 2 in 1959 and reached as high as No. 3 in 1961. He was 15-0 as a Davis Cup player and also served twice as assistant captain. He competed with players like Rod Laver, Roy Emerson and Chuck McKinley and won.

Bartzen joined USPTA in 1961 and a year later turned professional as a player and became a tennis professional at the Colonial Country Club in Fort Worth. After the 1998-99 season and 25 years as head men's tennis coach, Bartzen retired from Texas Christian University. Starting with a group of walk-ons and one scholarship, Bartzen experienced all but one winning season. With a winning record of better than 70 percent, his team finished in the nation's top 20 all but three times between 1977 and 1998.

Tim Gullikson, *inducted in 2001*

Tim Gullikson, a USPTA member from 1989 until his death in 1996, was a teaching professional, playing professional and coach to other world-class playing professionals, including Pete Sampras, who he coached to six Grand

Slam singles titles. As a USPTA member, Gullikson was generous with his time as a speaker at educational events and a promoter of the association.

Gullikson and his brother Tom were doubles partners in high school and college, and then club teaching professionals before joining the pro tour in 1976. Tim Gullikson was the ATP's Newcomer of the Year in 1977 and reached 11 finals and won 16 doubles titles. Ten of those came when playing with Tom, with whom he reached the doubles final at Wimbledon in 1983.

Tim Heckler, *inducted in 2000*

Tim Heckler was USPTA's CEO for 30 years, from 1982-2012. Prior to that, he served on the national USPTA executive committee and board of directors before being elected USPTA president in 1980. He was USPTA Professional of the Year in 1979 and a Master Professional.

As CEO, Heckler guided the Association through a period in which it increased its membership fivefold and its annual income tenfold, established USPTA as the foremost organization of teaching professionals in the world, and revolutionized USPTA's operations through computerization.

While attending Lamar University in Beaumont, Texas, on a tennis scholarship, he played the international circuit, including Wimbledon in 1959 and 1961, and the US Open in 1960. Heckler assumed a full-time tennis-teaching position in 1970 at Houston's Westwood Country Club, and was elected president of USPTA's Texas Division in 1974. In 1973 he was the consultant to and tennis director for the Bobby Riggs vs. Billie Jean King "Match of the Century" held in the Houston Astrodome.

Paul Xanthos, *inducted in 1999*

The late Paul Xanthos amassed a 550-94 win-loss record during a 28-year career as tennis coach of Los Angeles Pierce College. During Xanthos' tenure at Pierce College, he led teams to 23 conference championships, and experienced winning streaks of 96, 50, 37 and 27 wins in a row.

Xanthos wrote numerous articles and books on tennis, and conducted tennis seminars worldwide. He was a charter member of the USPTA Education and Research Committee, and was instrumental in founding the USTA's National Tennis Teachers Conference.

His awards include the USTA Award of Merit in 1974, the USPTA California Division Coach of the Year in 1981-84, and the Intercollegiate Tennis Association's Community College Coach of the Year in 1988. In 1994, he was named USPTA Coach of the Year and was also inducted into the ITA Hall of Fame. Xanthos was a USPTA honorary member and Master Professional.

George Bacso, *inducted in 1994*

The late George Bacso served as USPTA's Director of Certification and Academies. In this capacity, he traveled the world conducting Certification Exams, Tennis Teachers' Courses and Certification Training Courses. He was also a popular speaker and clinician in the United States. Bacso was instrumental in developing the current USPTA certification process and worked with USPTA's national tester network.

From 1978 to 1980, he served as USPTA's national president. He also served several years as the president of the USPTA Eastern Division. He received the USTA National Education Merit Award and the national USPTA Professional of the Year Award. Bacso also received the inaugural George Bacso Lifetime Achievement Award in 1998, and he held a Master Professional rating.

Arthur Ashe, *inducted in 1993*

The late Arthur Ashe was the first inductee into the USPTA Hall of Fame. Ashe's tennis accomplishments, including Wimbledon and US Open titles, earned him the world's No. 1 ranking on two separate occasions 1968 and 1975. He was instrumental in the founding of the ATP Tour and the National Junior Tennis League.

Ashe, who died of AIDS complications in 1993, is also well remembered for his off-court activities, including his outspoken support of the anti-apartheid movement in South Africa, a writing career that earned him an Emmy award and his publicized battle with AIDS. He was also active in bringing inner-city children into the sport of tennis through programs such as USPTA's Tennis Across America.

USPTA Members Donate Millions Through Lessons for Life

In November 1998, long-time USPTA member and USPTA Director of Certification and Academies George Bacso lost his battle with cancer. He was a legend in the association and impacted many lives and careers of USPTA Professionals. George's birthday was in October, so to honor him, USPTA named October "Tennis Against Cancer Month" and announced that the association was joining the fight against cancer through a new "Lessons for Life" fundraiser benefitting the American Cancer Society. Each USPTA member was asked to conduct one lesson or clinic and donate the fees to the ACS.

But USPTA members, being the creative, generous and passionate people that they are, did so much more. In addition to donating lesson fees, members also made monetary donations and organized special events to raise even more money.

After USPTA Professional Brenda Mertz was diagnosed with breast cancer in 1998, she welcomed the opportunity to participate in Lessons for Life.

"When I found out USPTA would be teaming with the American Cancer Society to stomp out this disease, I couldn't wait to get started," she said. "I didn't realize it would be one of the easiest things I'd ever done. Every single person I asked to take a lesson said yes."

Her first event raised $1,200. Mertz has held a one-day event every year since, and now 17 years later, she has raised more than $168,000.

Lessons for Life was modeled after the Missouri Valley Division's program by the same name, which began in 1996. Kim Bastable was the division's executive administrator at the time. She said the idea was developed as a way for pros to show pride in their community and to give back in a team effort that would reflect good will on the tennis community.

Russ Warner, 1999 president of the division and chairman of Lessons for Life, said, "I'm happy that USPTA has embraced a national charity. We are always trying both to help people and to spread the good word about USPTA. This program has been very successful in the Missouri Valley and now on the national level, and we look forward to better things to come."

That first year, more than $55,000 was raised for the ACS. At the 2000 USPTA World Conference, the ACS presented the USPTA with an achievement award that recognized USPTA members' efforts to raise money to help find a cure for cancer.

Over the next two years, USPTA members continued to hold events and donate money to the ACS.

Father and son USPTA members Stan and Craig Willeford taught side by side for 12 hours at Four Seasons Tennis Club in Sherman, Texas. They gave lessons to more than 50 players and raised $1,115.

"Before the event started, we set a goal of raising $700," Craig Willeford said. "But about 12 hours before the lesson marathon, the phone just kept ringing and ringing. We were extremely excited to know that so many people wanted to contribute to the cause."

USPTA Professional Wayne Street, along with other teaching pros around Petaluma, Calif., held a "Tennis Against Cancer: Y2K and Beyond" event that raised $12,000. They contributed lessons to a silent auction and organized a half-day round robin for 56 people. The event also had a barbecue lunch, fashion show and raffle that included a mountain bike, bottle of wine and a 1978 BMW.

One of the most creative fundraisers was part of the event at Courtside Tennis Club in Naples, Fla., which raised $12,000 with the help of 17 pros. Volunteers filled a Volkswagen Beetle with tennis balls and sold guesses as to the number.

Brenda Mertz (right) with Olivia Theiler, a leukemia survivor who is one of the beneficiaries of money raised through the "Lessons for Life" program

First "Lessons for Life" event, held at Pelican Bay Community Courts in Naples, FL, Oct. 23, 1998. The 7th, 8th and 9th persons from the left, respectively, are Michelle Young (daughter of Brenda Mertz), Brenda Mertz and Jim Mertz.

"Lessons for Life" event, 2016

While Lessons for Life continued to increase its donations to ACS, it did not recognize the charitable contributions of USPTA members who raised money for other causes. Therefore, in 2002, USPTA made Lessons for Life an umbrella program that recognized the contributions by members to any legitimate charity.

Paula Scheb of the Florida Division was chairwoman of Lessons for Life at that time. "We are so excited about making Lessons for Life inclusive of every member's charitable work," she said. "Many of us have contributed to the same fundraisers for years, and we've added many more. The industry and public will be impressed with the amazing contributions, big and small, that really add up."

That year, USPTA members raised more than $2.5 million for charity. Beneficiaries included American Cancer Society, Cystic Fibrosis Foundation, Juvenile Diabetes Research Foundation, Tim & Tom Gullikson Foundation, Mothers Against Drunk Driving, Scripps Stevens Cancer Center and many smaller, local charities.

"Lessons for Life shows all the great things tennis professionals do for their communities and for people," Warner said. "That's been our whole goal for this program."

Also in 2002, the USPTA added a silent auction to the World Conference lineup, with the proceeds being donated to the USPTA Foundation and being added to the Lessons for Life grand total. Past items have included autographed racquets, resort stays and clothing. That first year, the auction raised $5,363.

In 2005, $8,197,249 was raised for charity – the largest amount in one year by Lessons for Life since its inception. This was the year Hurricane Katrina devastated the Gulf Coast, and many of the fundraisers and donations were to benefit those affected.

USPTA and Rally for the Cure joined forces in 2009 to raise awareness in the fight against breast cancer through tennis and Lessons for Life. Rally for the Cure provided tools and materials for USPTA tennis-teaching professionals interested in running a Lessons for Life charity tennis event in support of Rally for the Cure.

USPTA teamed up with ThanksUSA in 2012 as part of the "Tennis Thanks The Troops" campaign to encourage USPTA members to raise funds for families of military personnel, specifically by providing scholarships. These events are usually held near Memorial Day and Veterans Day and count toward the Lessons for Life total.

Over the years, USPTA members continued to donate their time and money, with annual contributions in the millions. By the end of 2015, USPTA members raised nearly $55.5 million for local and national charities through Lessons for Life since its inception.

USPTA annually recognizes a USPTA member at the World Conference who has done the most to raise money for charities through tennis events. While the award spotlights individuals who have raised large amounts of money, it also honors those hosting the most creative, original or unique tennis event to raise money for charities. To have an event counted toward Lessons for Life, USPTA members need to register their events at uspta.com/About > Programs > Lessons for Life.

USPTA Marked Diamond Anniversary in 2002

(The following articles were published in ADDvantage magazine throughout the year in 2002 to celebrate USPTA's 75th anniversary.)

USPTA officially celebrated its diamond anniversary during the 2002 World Conference on Tennis at Bally's Las Vegas, Sept. 21-28. More than 1,500 teaching professionals, industry leaders, media and others took part.

Also in 2002, USPTA celebrated the 25th anniversary of *ADDvantage*, the Association's monthly trade publication. The magazine is a mix of member contributions, industry news and photos and staff contributions.

Racquets, Eagles and Stars. Oh My!

Logos used to create Association's image through 75 years

February 2002 — USPTA's founders and early members combined their love of tennis with patriotism to create symbols to identify the Professional Lawn Tennis Association of the United States.

The earliest USPTA logos were a combination of red, white and blue and featured bold stripes like those on the American flag. The first one included a shield atop two crossed racquets. The shield included the identifying letters "PLTA of U.S." A later version was identical in design, with the exception of a name change that switched the initials U.S., creating the acronym "USPLTA."

Early version of logo

The Association later simplified its logo, using two crossed racquets and three balls placed within a circle. The letters "USPLTA" were placed at the inside top of the circle, just above the crossed racquets.

The most recognizable and widely used USPTA logo is probably the shield that contains the eagle, red and white stripes and a single tennis racquet. The shield also includes the Association's complete name, which in most cases has been difficult to read on a small logo. A modified version of this logo uses only the initials "USPTA."

"Circle" version of logo

The single racquet logo was developed after USPTA tried to trademark a similar design with two crossed racquets. The trademark application was rejected because a man in Maryland had already registered the use of the crossed racquet design. Although a trademark had been established for the crossed racquets, USPTA was never challenged on its use of the concept, but it wanted to protect the use and uniqueness of its own logo, its name and initials, so the single racquet shield became the official logo.

The "A" logo was developed some time after the eagle shield and was designed to emphasize the "A" and the "professionalism" of USPTA members. This logo was used on *ADDvantage* magazine, various advertisements, USPTA merchandise and letterhead.

"A" logo

Another popular USPTA image is that of its 60th anniversary seal. It was developed in 1987 and includes a variation of the eagle shield surrounded by the Association's name and a wreath. Because of its formal appearance and use on previous USPTA letterhead, business cards and other merchandise, many members considered this to be the Association's primary logo prior to 1997.

"Eagle" logo, featuring complete name of Association and a single racquet

USPTA's newest logo was designed in response to an industry call for an updated USPTA image. A slide presented at the Tennis Industry Association's Forum more than seven years ago displayed various tennis industry logos side by side. USPTA's anniversary seal was among them, and the Association received feedback from several prominent industry leaders who said that while the seal served its purpose in various formats, it did not clearly identify USPTA and was not easily recognized in smaller sizes. Also, when the USPTA seal or crest appeared alongside other industry logos such as those for USTA, ATP and the WTA Tour,

1987 logo

it was noticeably out of date and was not as streamlined as the other professionally designed images.

With the help of some industry friends, USPTA looked at hundreds of potential logos, keeping in mind that a clean, uncluttered logo with a broad appeal was the goal. It had to be flexible enough to include both the initials and the entire name of the organization, and be presented in a form that could be used in a variety of circumstances.

Current USPTA logo

USPTA has been identified with many logos throughout the years, and still uses several trademarked emblems for a variety of formats and media. There has never been a designated "official" logo. Instead, USPTA has changed with the tennis industry and has adapted its logos to suit a variety of needs and design applications.

Renowned Players Grace USPTA Championships

May 2002 — USPTA's International Championships are as old as the Association itself, with the first being played in 1927. In the early years, the organization represented both professional coaches and players. The official tournament's champions list illustrates this with an impressive list of professional players – including Bill Tilden, Jack Kramer and Pancho Segura — who have claimed the title.

Vinnie Richards, a prolific tournament winner and a founding member of the Professional Lawn Tennis Association of the United States (PLTA), won the Association's first two tournaments and the fourth and seventh. However, Bill Tilden got in on the action early, too, and was the National Professional Champion in 1931 and '35. Two years after becoming the first player to achieve a Grand Slam and one year after turning pro, Don Budge added his name to the PLTA champions list in 1940 by defeating Fred Perry, then again in '42 by defeating Bobby Riggs.

Perry and Riggs would challenge for the title again and win, Perry twice and Riggs three times. Jack Kramer also owned the title in 1948.

"It is a policy of the PLTA to run an active national tournament each year and since the first in 1927 both the quality and interest have increased on a considerable scale," reported the 1945-46 PLTA Official Guide. However, there were years when the tournament wasn't held, such as 1944, when enough players were not available (presumably because of the war effort); and 1952-61.

Many of the most well-known professional players among the men, including Kramer, Riggs and Budge, were PLTA members. Although women professionals such as Pauline Betz Addie, Alice Marble and Sarah Cooke joined PLTA in the '40s and were very popular touring players, the Association's first women's tournament wasn't held until 1969.

The men's tournament continued to produce excitement. PLTA's 1951 Official Guide and Yearbook announced the 1950 champ this way: "A new star blazes across the pro tennis horizon in the person of Francisco "Pancho" Segura – surprise winner of the 1950 National Professional Championship at Cleveland. Runner-up in the dramatic final match: Frank Kovacs." Segura and Kovacs had beaten Kramer and Riggs in the semifinals, and the singles and doubles field split a total purse of $10,000. Segura would go on to win again in '51 and '56.

For some years, the PLTA sanctioned additional tournaments, including the National Professional Clay Championships, other surface-specific tournaments, the annual fall and spring tournaments, regional championships and circuits. While the major annual tournament was open to nonmembers, not all sanctioned tournaments were. The first annual fall tournament, played at Cresthaven Yacht and Country Club in Whitestone, Long Island, was described in the 1948 yearbook like this:

"Thirty members of PLTA entered the tournament, which was closed to fully paid-up PLTA members ... The tournament was designed to give the PLTA pros a chance to get together, play each other, have dinner parties, talk over their mutual problems, and in general get to know each other better. And that is certainly what took place." In 1964, the Association began holding national team championships for competition between the divisions. There were 11 divisions at the time: Eastern, Florida, Mid-Atlantic, Middle States, Midwest, New England, Northwest, Southern and, recently added, San Diego, Texas and California. New England and Florida dominated the early years, accounting for four of the first six team-match championships. Members of the 1968 winning Midwest team were given blazers and USPLTA emblems.

Though the USPLTA Championships were open to nonmembers, very often it was Association members who were vying for the national championship title. In 1967 – 10 years after the PLTA moved the U.S. from the back of its name to the front to become the USPLTA – "The men's singles had an unprecedented draw of 53 players, thanks to the heroic efforts of Tournament Director Ted Withall," according to the 1968 yearbook. The total purse was $5,000, and the men's open champion was member Sam Giammalva of Houston, who defeated member Warren Woodcock, a teaching pro in Florida and New Jersey. Giammalva also teamed with member Jason Morton of Fort Lauderdale, Fla., for the doubles title.

In the late 1960s, senior age divisions were added to the men's tournament, and women played their first USPLTA Championships at the Frontier Hotel in Las Vegas in 1969. Ann Rockwell of the Bonanza Country Club in Las Vegas defeated nonmember Linda Van der Meer for the open singles title. Rockwell teamed with another Las Vegas pro, Jo Schwickert, to defeat Van der Meer and another nonmember, Valerie Scott, in open doubles.

The championships continued to progress because of changes in the industry and the Association. 1968 marked the beginning of the open era of tennis, and in 1983 the USPTA Executive Committee made a dramatic change to the championships.

Members had continued to compete against nonmembers in the championships, though many of the nonmembers competing were playing professionals who were no longer represented in the industry by USPTA. Prize money was raised through USPTA, especially through national sponsorships and endorsements, and member dues supported the overall project. Many believed that USPTA's resources should be reserved for the benefit of USPTA members. The Executive Committee voted that only USPTA members would be eligible to compete in USPTA tournaments beginning in 1984.

The USPTA International Championships have remained highly competitive. Accomplished and experienced players from many backgrounds have made their marks on the championships. Peter Doohan, Jim Parker, Pat Serret, Viktoria Beggs, Kim Barry and Cammy MacGregor are just a few. Seventy-five years later, the tournament continues to be a highlight of the World Conference on Tennis, held each year in September.

USPTA Has Built ADDvantage Over Past 25 Years

By Jill Phipps, USPTA staff writer

April 2002 -- Starting out true to its name, *ADDvantage* already had 50 candles on its birthday cake when this milestone magazine greeted the tennis world in January 1977.

The cover of the first issue pictured a tennis-court birthday cake, with 50 candles all aglow, celebrating the golden anniversary of the United States Professional Tennis Association.

The USPTA and its new magazine shared a bright future, and still do today.

Although both have seen significant changes over the years, history is repeating itself as the USPTA celebrates its 75th anniversary and *ADDvantage* marks its 25th year.

As 1977 unfolded, the USPTA was looking forward to hosting its national convention in Las Vegas. The World Conference on Tennis, as it is now called, is returning to the city of excitement in 2002.

Sheldon Caldwell was USPTA President in 1976-78 and was the founder of ADDvantage magazine.

In this new century, the USPTA is growing, boosting its educational standards, expanding its services and renewing its commitment to make a difference in the lives of its members – just as it was 25 years ago.

Sheldon Caldwell, president of the USPTA from 1976 to 1978 and founder of *ADDvantage,* was passionate about the need for a tennis professionals' magazine.

Caldwell worked hard to turn his vision into reality. In 1976, he began trying to sell his idea for a magazine to the board of directors and spent several months raising enough advertising to get it off the ground.

Caldwell, who had seen the USPTA grow from a few hundred mostly Eastern pros since the late 1950s, would later write that some had said the Association would never be able to afford a magazine. But he had also heard time and again that "We'll never really be national" or "We'll never be able to get people to test for membership."

Those achievements came to pass through the hard work of devoted leaders, he pointed out. And so did the magazine.

The January/February 1977 issue marked the debut of *addvantage* (the "add" was lowercase then) as a bimonthly publication. USPTA members received the National Newsletter and later the USPTA News Journal in alternating months.

It was an ambitious young magazine, with a circulation of 6,000 – more than double the ranks of the Association at that time.

All USPTA members received the magazine free and other professionals were given a one-year complimentary subscription. It went to all members of the U.S. Track and Court Builders Association, the National Indoor Tennis Association and USTA clubs.

The president's message in the first issue began with these words: "Looking back on our 50 years of achievements is a source of pride to the USPTA. But we are more concerned with the challenge of the future. That is why 1977 is a kickoff year, as much as it is an anniversary year."

Caldwell was proud to announce that the year's first activity was also "perhaps the most exciting in our existence.

"The magazine is, and will be, dedicated to raising and maintaining the standards of professional teaching in tennis," he wrote in that column, called "A look ahead." "We have a very simple goal for each issue," he had explained. "To help the professional tennis teacher become a more complete professional; a more complete person. *Addvantage* will be a service magazine, an aid to the professional."

But Caldwell also saw the publication as part of the ongoing effort to make the USPTA stronger and more active than ever.

"We were very anxious to grow, to have a national center like we (now) have in Houston," Caldwell said in a recent phone interview. The 70-year-old past president is semi-retired and lives in St. Petersburg, Fla.

Although USPTA put out a newsletter periodically, "We had no voice that was out there," Caldwell said. "I thought *ADDvantage* would be somewhat of a coffee table magazine. I thought it would reach a lot more people than we were reaching without it."

Caldwell, who speaks his mind, said he wanted *ADDvantage* to consistently take a strong editorial stance on issues that affected the entire tennis industry. In his opinion, it became more

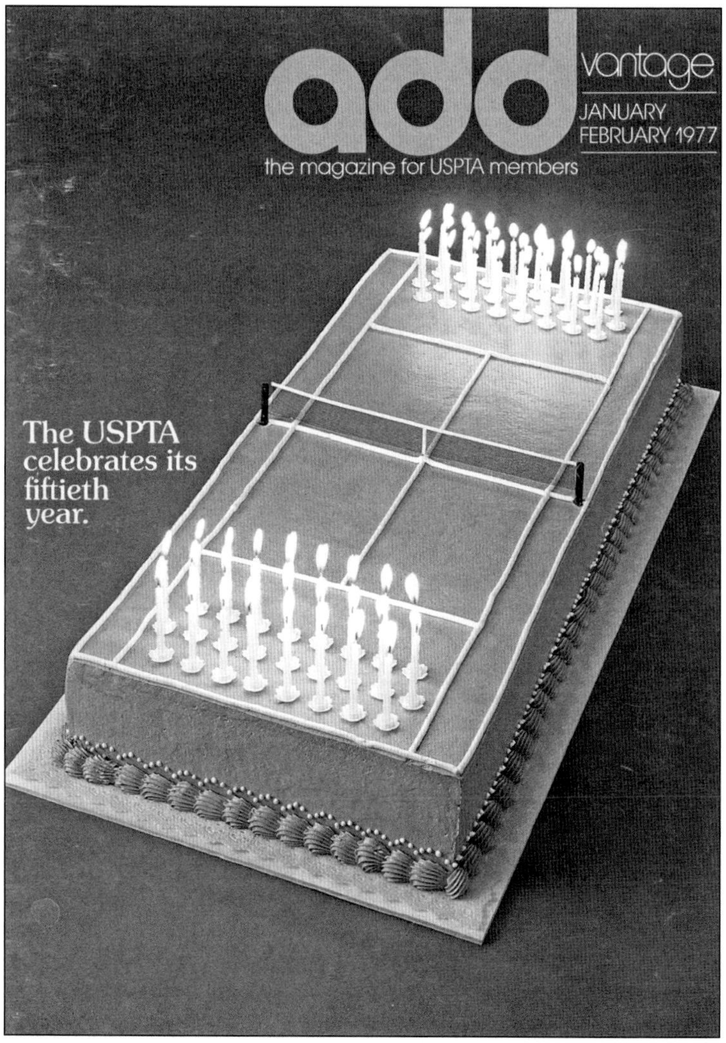

The first issue ADDvantage celebrates USPTA's 50th anniversary in 1977

of a trade magazine for members, and "there's nothing wrong with that."

"I think it has served the Association well," Caldwell said. "It has gone on to be a voice in USPTA, an aid to its members, and has contributed to our growth and well-being. It is a visible, acceptable publication for the general public."

Caldwell said he personally keeps an eye on the "industry action" section of the magazine to see if he knows anybody mentioned in the news briefs.

The magazine has, of course, changed over the years. It became a monthly publication in 1989, and the USPTA News Journal was retired. More color was added and a new logo adopted.

For the first nine years of publication, every magazine cover was a photo illustration that cleverly incorporated one or more tennis balls.

Some of the covers were created strictly for the visual effect, others were seasonal and some were tied into story themes. Tennis balls were cradled in everything from a coconut ("Crack the nut for profit") to a baseball mitt ("The power serve.")

"They were artfully prepared," Caldwell said of the memorable covers. The idea came from Group One, the Cleveland, Ohio production company that designed and printed the magazine.

USPTA contributed articles to the magazine. But the production company had editorial control.

The tennis ball covers continued until the national office took over coordination of the magazine in 1986. At that time, the USPTA still depended on a printer to do much of the layout.

Since 1995, USPTA has had total creative control over *ADDvantage* by producing it in house with desktop publishing software. This means that all layout, photo scanning and other graphics are produced and placed by the staff. Even many of the photos, including those featured in USPTA ads, are shot with a digital camera. And, much of the written copy, with the exception of member articles and editorials, is created and edited by various USPTA staff members.

"I am delighted it has reached its 25th anniversary still intact," Caldwell said. "A great deal of that I contribute to (Chief Executive Officer) Tim (Heckler) and the national office."

Longtime, Lauded Members Look Back on 75 years

By Jill Hathaway Phipps, USPTA staff writer

March 2002 — John Huber was 20 years old when a small group of tennis professionals formed the Professional Lawn Tennis Association of the United States in 1927.

But he did not join the group until 1970, when he was 64 and retired from the insurance industry.

"I wanted to join because of the publicity, the activity, the fact that they were the best … like the PGA," Huber said. "That connection (the USPTA) is good to have behind you; I knew I needed that for lessons."

In 1970, the Association had already changed its name to United States Professional Lawn Tennis Association, and was about to change it again by dropping "Lawn" from the name. It had fewer than 1,000 members.

Huber, like USPTA, came on strong in his later years.

The 95-year-old Huber is one of the oldest active pros in the USPTA, which has grown to more than 12,500 members.

This resident of Newbury, N.H., still – officially – teaches one day a week at a local club and gives an occasional lesson even

New England Teaching Pro Association meeting, 1962. Kneeling, L-R: Bill Power, Dan Hart, Henry Majkut, unidentified, John L. Foley, Cory Wynn, Jack Kenney. Standing: Dave Drury, Charlie Swanson, Frank Fiala, Jack Barnaby, Herb Stead, Sheldon Caldwell, Skip Howard, Ed Serues, Ralph Chambers.

when he's not working. "I may be up there practicing and give somebody a lesson for free," he said. "That's my life – tennis and stocks."

Huber has been a top player in USTA national age-division competition, and will be inducted this June into the New England Tennis Hall of Fame by USA Tennis New England.

Huber gets frustrated when he can't find anyone his age to compete against at USPTA conventions. He knows there are a lot of good senior players among his fellow teaching pros.

He can't help asking: "Why the heck did they stop at age 70 or 72?"

But the USPTA is still going strong at 75, fueled by the dedication and experience of its eclectic membership.

Some of Huber's contemporaries, in their 80s and 90s, joined more than 50 or even 60 years ago.

Their high-profile ranks include brothers Bill and Frank Kenney, who served as private pros for presidential families and other famous figures; Pauline Betz Addie, a four-time U.S. Nationals (now U.S. Open) and Wimbledon champ; and Jack Barnaby, the winningest coach in the history of Harvard University.

These longtime members have seen the USPTA change a great deal in terms of growth, educational requirements and technology. But they, like many of their counterparts today, joined because they wanted to be part of a united effort to promote the interests of tennis professionals.

For the Kenney brothers, it was also a matter of family tradition. Their older brother, father, uncle and two cousins were all teaching pros and members of the Association.

Bill Kenney, an 84-year-old resident of Michigan City, Ind., joined the PLTA in 1934.

"There wasn't too much organization to it. I guess it's changed quite a bit," Bill said, adding, "I think they're going in the right direction."

Bill, who served as head tennis pro at the Philadelphia Cricket Club for 29 years, considers himself lucky because he had a retirement plan. "It's tough nowadays for pros in a private club with all the expenses."

He also was a private pro for Edmund Lynch, the latter-half namesake of the Merrill Lynch investment company, and his family in Long Island, N.Y.

Frank Kenney, who joined the PLTA in 1939, recalled that his brother used to travel with Lynch on his yacht to play at clubs. Their father, who joined the PLTA shortly after it was formed, worked as a private pro for Harold S. Vanderbilt.

A lot of pros in the late 1930s and '40s worked for prominent families and their guests, said Frank, an 83-year-old resident of Newport, R.I.

"I met a lot of nice people – ambassadors, presidents and senators," Frank said. "I taught Jacqueline Kennedy how to play tennis in Newport. She lived here.

"I was very friendly with the president (John F. Kennedy), but he didn't play that much tennis. I knew him as a senator," Frank said.

He spent his winters in Palm Beach, Fla., where pros would play doubles with club members on Sunday afternoons.

"I've had a great life," Frank said. "The only thing is, back in those days there wasn't any pension. And there weren't many pros."

Frank said he believes the PLTA had about 60 members when he joined. There was no certification test then, but "you had to be an assistant pro for two years before you joined." He also remembers a $10 initiation fee.

"I think the USPTA has come a long way and I think they do a good job," Frank said.

In the 1950s, "It was a low-key organization, certainly not what it is today," said Charlotte Barnaby. Her husband, Jack, joined the PLTA in 1954 and served as president from 1969 to 1970. "He was sort of interested in bringing it to life again," she said.

Jack Barnaby, who coached winning teams at Harvard from 1932 to 1976, loved teaching and "was very interested in bringing tennis professionals into an accepted way of life," Charlotte Barnaby said. "In that era, coaches were on the lowest rung of the ladder."

Just prior to going to print with this magazine, Barnaby died on February 12. According to his wife, he still loved the game until he passed away, and watched it on television when he could.

Pauline Betz Addie was among the famous female players who joined the PLTA in the early 1940s. "Everybody liked the idea of being part of an association," she said. Her son, Rusty Addie, also is a USPTA pro.

Pauline Betz Addie

Although she doesn't teach much anymore, "It's nice to meet with other pros and get their views on things," Addie said.

The 82-year-old resident of Bethesda, Md., still plays doubles in a country club league. Asked if playing against a tennis legend is a bit intimidating for her opponents, she quipped, "They can stand it.

"Tennis is still an important part of my life, and always will be," Addie said. At this point in life, though, "You have to pick your partners and opponents more carefully than you used to."

USPTA National Award Winners

George Bacso Lifetime Achievement Award

2016 Ben Press
2015 David Muir
2008 Tim Heckler
2002 Paul Xanthos
2001 Bill Tym
1999 Mike Eikenberry
1998 George Bacso

Alex Gordon Award for the USPTA Professional of the Year

2016 Kirk Anderson
2015 Jorge Capestany
2014 Randy Mattingley
2013 Avis Murray
2012 David T. Porter, Ed.D.
2011 Feisal Hassan
2010 Ron Woods
2009 Robert Greene Jr.
2008 Tom Sweitzer
2007 John Joyce
2006 Tom Daglis
2005 Rick Macci
2004 Steve Diamond
2003 Jim Loehr
2002 Will Hoag
2001 Dave Kozlowski
2000 Mark McMahon
1999 Chip Brooks
1998 Joseph Thompson
1997 Luis Mediero
1996 Jim Reffkin
1995 Angel Lopez
1994 Kurt Kamperman
1993 Jim Davis
1992 Bill Bond
1991 Nick Bollettieri
1990 Peter Burwash
1989 Vic Braden
1988 Spike Gurney
1987 Jack Groppel
1986 Sean Sloane
1985 Dave Sivertson
1984 George Bacso
1983 Paul Gagon
1982 Bill Tym
1981 Ken McAllister
1980 Rod Dulany
1979 Tim Heckler
1978 Rob Danner/Bill Thompson
1977 Joe Dennis
1976 Fernando Velasco

USPTA President's Paul Waldman Award

2016 Fred Viancos
2015 Warren Lem
2014 Paul Waldman
2011 Ben Press / Steve Wilkinson
2007 Townsend Gilbert
2002 John Huber
1997 Charlie McCleary
1996 Eve Kraft
1995 James Evert

USPTA Star Award

2016 Patrick LaSalle
2015 Trenton Corvino
2014 Kevin Clark
2013 David Pack
2012 Catherine Thomas
2011 Fitz Paccione
2009 Shelley Susman/Brian Egelhoff
2008 David Boon
2007 Jane Hines
2006 Chris Michalowski/Tony Reyes
2005 John "Jack" Foster/Robert Reed
2004 Ronald Elizondo/Anna Hazlett
2003 Britt Feldhausen

Players of the Year

2016
Stefano Ianni (male)
Agata Cioroch (female)
Franco Mata (over 35)
Jeff Cohen (over 45)
Mike Fedderly (over 55)

2015
Adrians Zguns (male)
Carrie Kalapala (female)
Paulo Barros (over 35)
Trish Riddell (over 40)
Kamil Kuchta (over 45)
Steve Brady (over 50)
Ruth Hessert (over 50)
Gewan Maharaj (over 60)
Mike Barnes (over 65)

2014
Paulo Barros (male)
Marina McCollom (female)
Paulo Barros (over 35)
Jeff Cohen (over 45)
Kathy Vick (over 45)
Kie Foreman (over 50)
Gewan Maharaj (over 60)
Geoffrey Moore (over 65)
James Ridgley (over 75)

2013
James Daly (male)
Ristine Olson (female)
Juan Garcia (over 35)
Oren Motevassel (over 40)
Jeff Cohen (over 45)
Julie Farina (over 45)
Kie Foreman (over 50)
Kathy Vick (over 50)
Sal Castillo (over 55)
Kathy Barnes (over 55)

2012
James Daly (male)
Agata Cioroch (female)
Jonas Lundblad (over 35)
Robin Keener (over 35)
Jeff Cohen (over 45)
Kathy Vick (over 45)
Kimm Ketelsen (over 55)

2011
Tony Larson (male)
Amy Alcini (female)
Kamil Kuchta (over 35)
Robin Keener (over 35)
Vincent Horcasitas (over 45)
Kathy Vick (over 45)
Gewan Maharaj (over 55, co-winner)
Kimm Ketelsen (over 55, co-winner)
Binki Thalheimer (over 55)

2010
Cory Ross (male)
Marina McCollom (female)
Guillaume Gauthier (over 35)
Robin Keener (over 35)
Pat Serret (over 45)
Kathy Vick (over 45)
Cliff Price (over 55)
Elizabeth Leach Bohac (over 55)

2009
Cory Ross (male)
Marina McCollom (female)
Jeff F. Cohen (over 35)
Robin Keener (over 35)
Pat Serret (over 45)
Sheila Chirocosta (over 45)
Cliff Price (over 55)
Laura Thomson (over 55)

2008
Adrians Zguns (male)
Marina McCollom (female)
Jeff F. Cohen (over 35)
Robin Keener (over 35)
Pat Serret (over 45)
Kathy Vick (over 45)
Gewan Maharaj (over 55)
Sue Bramlette (over 55)

2007
Paulo Barros (male)
Julie Cass (female)
Anders Eriksson (over 35)
Sophie Amiach (over 35)
Val Wilder (over 45)
Viktoria Beggs (over 45)
Brian Cheney (over 55)
Sue Bramlette (over 55)

2006
Paulo Barros (male)
Christina Oldock (female)
Jeff Cohen (over 35)
Julie Cass (over 35)
Val Wilder (over 45)
Kathy Vick (over 45)
Tommy Connell (over 55)
Avis Murray (over 55)

2005
Anders Eriksson (male)
Julie Cass (female)
Kevin Pope (over 35)
Robin Keener (over 35)
Val Wilder/Jason Morton (co-winners, over 45)
Kathy Vick (over 45)

Men's Open Singles Champ Mario Martinez (L) and Women's Open Singles Champion Robin Coverdale, 1988, Palm Springs, CA

2004
Anders Eriksson (male)
Julie Cass (female)
Mark Harrison (over 35)
Robin Keener (over 35)
Brian Cheney/Jim Parker (co-winners, over 45)
Sue Bramlette/Kathy Vick (co-winners, over 45)

2003
Anders Eriksson (male)
Julie Cass (female)
Andrew Stoner (over 35)
Robin Keener (over 35)
Glenn Williams (over 45)
Sabita Maharaj (over 45)

2002
Carl Clark (male)
Julie Cass (female)
Jeff Greenwald (over 35)
Christine Sheldon (over 35)
Bob Litwin (over 45)
Trish Faulkner (over 45)

2001
Guillaume Gauthier (male)
Kasey Gladding (female)
Pat Serret (over 35)
Christy Wing (over 35)
Brian Cheney/Jim Parker (co-winners, over 45)
Trish Faulkner (over 45)

2000
Mario Tabares (male)
Kasey Gladding (female)
Pat Serret (over 35)
Kathy Vick (over 35)
Gewan Maharaj (over 45)
Suella Steel (over 45)

1999
Ken Kuperstein (male)
Tracie Currie (female)
Pat Serret (over 35)
Lisa Seemann (over 35)
Jimmy Parker (over 45)
Judy Louie (over 45)

1998
Scott Stewart (male)
Tracy Houk (female)
Pat Serret/Frank Swope (co-winners, over 35)
Tracy Houk (over 35)
Bob McKinley (over 45)
Patricia Faulkner (over 45)

1997
Greg Neuhart (male)
Kim Barry (female)
Wayne Pickard (over 35)
Susan Bramlette (over 35)
Tommy Connell (over 45)
Carol Baily (over 45)

1996
Pat Serret (male)
Beverly Bowes-Hackney (female)
Mike Fedderly (over 35)
Karen Sather (over 35)
Gewan Maharaj (over 45)
Avis Murray (over 45)

1995
Sean Brawley (male)
Mary Norwood (female)
David Mathews (over 35)
Judy Louie (over 35)
Cliff Price (over 45)

1994
Peter Doohan (male)
Kim Barry (female)
Sal Castillo/Bob McKinley (co-winners, over 35)
Sue Bartlett (over 35)
Howard Hunt (over 45)

1993
Mark Fairchilds/Brian Joelson (co-winners, male)
Pamela Casale-Telford/Jami Yonekura (co-winners, female)
Sal Castillo/Tommy Connell (co-winners, over 35)
Susan Dillinger (over 35)
Arthur Thomson (over 45)

1992
Young Min Kwon/Pat Serret (co-winners, male)
Kim Barry/Tracy Houk-Kuhn (co-winners, female)
Armistead Neely (over 35)
Betty Walsh/Carol Baily (co-winners, over 35)
Steve Wilkinson (over 45)

1991
Tim Wilkison (male)
Kim Barry (female)
Claude England/Armistead Nealy (co-winners, over 35)
Bill Tym (over 45)

1990
Pat Serret (male)
Lisa Seemann/Michele Sniffen (co-winners, female)
Juan Diaz (over 35)
Jeanette Paddock (over 35)
Tommy Bartlett (over 45)

1989
Mario Martinez (male)
Robin Coverdale/Vikki Beggs (co-winners, female)
Joe Lyden (over 35)
Tommy Bartlett/Ed Serues (co-winners, over 45)

1988
Vikki Beggs (female)
Jorge Andrew (over 35)
Tommy Bartlett (over 45)

1987
Jeanette Paddock (female)
Brian Cheney (under 45)
Roald Flater (over 45)

1986
Judy Courtney (female)
Juan Nunez (under 45)
Tommy Bartlett (over 45)

1985
Judy Courtney (female)
Juan Nunez (under 45)
Tommy Bartlett (over 45)

USPTA President Tom McGraw (left) with Peter Smith, 2014 USPTA Steve Wilkinson College Coach of the Year, 2014, New York

1984
Gene Russo (male) /Tommy Bartlett (over 45)

1983
Jim Parker (male) /Tommy Bartlett (over 45)

1982
Chris Parker (female) /Charles Oliver (over 45)

1981
Richard Johnson (male) /Bob Davis (over 45)

1980
Armistead Neely (male)

1979
Tommy Bartlett (male)

1978
Charleen Grafton (female)

1977
Alan Cheeseboro (male)

1976
Dell Sylvia (male)

Steve Wilkinson College Coach of the Year

2016 Kim Gidley
2015 Rolando Vargas
2014 John-Paul Connell
Peter Smith
2013 Paul Settles
2012 Ron Albers
2011 Peter Smith
Mike Gennette
2010 Kendell Hale
2009 Billy Chadwick
2008 Bill Macom
2007 Michael Center
2006 Steve Wilkinson
2005 Peter Burling
2004 Matt Knoll
2003 David T. Porter
2002 David T. Porter
2001 Craig Tiley
2000 Paul Kostin
1999 Billy Pate
1998 Andy Brandi
1997 Norma Taylor
1996 John Peterson
1995 Bernard "Tut" Bartzen
1994 Paul Xanthos
1993 Jim Moortgat
1992 Bal Moore
1991 John Officer
1990 Mike DePalmer
1989 Bill Tym
1988 Andy Brandi
1987 Tommy Bartlett/Frank Brennan
1986 Chuck Kriese
1985 Frank Brennan
1984 Paul Xanthos
1983 Tommy Bartlett
1982 Ron Woods
1981 Chuck Kriese
1980 Robert Bayliss
1979 Dan Magill
1978 Dell Sylvia
1977 Alice Tym

Tim Gullikson Touring Coach of the Year

2016 Dion Crupi
2015 Craig O'Shannessy
2014 Nick Saviano
2013 Philip Farmer
2012 Jonas Lundblad
2011 Kendall Brooks
2010 Dave Licker
2009 Adrian Chirici
2008 Meredith Geiger-Walton
2007 Kari Yerg
2006 Francisco Montana
2005 Bob McKinley
2004 Craig Tiley
2003 Craig Kardon
2002 Bill Tym
2001 Chris Bovett
2000 Rick Macci
1999 Raul Saad
1998 Butch Walts
1997 Bill Tym
1995 David Harley Smith
1994 Mervyn Webster
1993 Nick Saviano
1992 Armand Molino
1991 Craig Kardon

High School Coach of the Year

2016 Dick Johnson
2015 Reedy Toney
2014 Clete Browder
2013 Randy Stephens
2012 William Wickenheisser
2011 Jackie Mueller Egelhoff
2010 Vance VanPelt II
2009 Lawrence Eyre
2008 Laurie Martin
2007 David Steinbach/Gordon Hammond (co-winners)
2006 Beth Miller
2005 Dale Eshelbrenner
2004 Dan T. Holden Jr.
2003 Mark Faber, boys Anni Miller, girls
2002 Claudia Coleman/Elliot Lovi (co-winners)
2001 Preston Jackson Jr.
2000 Anne Meigs
1999 Scott Enge/Anni Miller (co-winners)
1998 Scott Enge/David Steinbach (co-winners)
1997 Sam Levy
1996 Anni Miller
1995 Anne Beasley Cook
1994 Jay Kramer
1993 Betty Sue Hagerman
1992 Robert Charles Krueger
1991 Elliot Lovi

Facility Manager of the Year

2016 Dan Miles
2015 Richard Macey (large facility)
Ryan George (small facility)
2014 C.J. "Joe" Bendy Jr. (large facility)
Larry Savvides (small facility)
2013 Tom Sweitzer (large facility)Fernando Velasco (small facility)
2012 Trent Schiek (large facility)
Dee Henry (small facility)
2011 Derrick Barnett (large facility)
Raul Saad (small facility)
2010 Rod Heckelman
2009 Michael Mahoney
2008 J.J. Sehlke
2007 Mike Doty
2006 Nick Johnson
2005 Brad Ellinger/Mike Woody (co-winners)
2004 Steve Matlaga
2003 Bob King/Michael McCarthy (co-winners)
2002 Bob Staehle (private)/Ed Prudhomme (public)
2001 Glen Howe
2000 Greg Lappin

Industry Excellence Award

2016 Jeff Bearup
2015 Lane Evans
2014 Jeff Rothstein
2013 Gerry Maingot
2012 Ken Sumrow
2011 Matthew Boughton
2010 Emily Schaefer
2009 Angelo Rossetti/Ettore Rossetti
2008 Stephen Tscherne
2007 Sue Burke
2006 Joe Dinoffer
2005 Punam Kersten

2004 Dave Gary
2003 Bryan Nibert
2002 Alan Cutler
2001 Ken Veney
2000 Daniel Bonfigli
1999 Feisal Hassan
1998 Kevin Young
1997 Mike Lange
1996 Gerry, Clare, Matt, Mike and James Springer
1995 Mary Herrick
1994 Tim Barnes

George Bacso Tester of the Year
2016 J. Weston Reese
2015 Tom Ingram
2014 Kyle LaCroix
2013 Jack Foster
2012 Feisal Hassan
2011 Ben Rakusin
2010 David T. Porter
2009 Glen Howe
2008 Mike Lange
2007 Tommy Wade
2006 Gary Trost
2005 Tommy Wade
2004 Tommy Wade
2003 Tom Daglis
2002 Tom Ingram
2001 R.J. Tessier
2000 Jack Justice
1999 Don Henson
1998 George Bacso

Division of the Year
2016 Texas
2015 Texas – large division
New England – small division
2014 Texas – large division
Southwest – small division
2013 Texas – large division
Southwest – small division
2012 Texas – large division
Southwest – small division
2011 Texas – large division
Southwest – small division
2010 Texas – large division
Missouri Valley – small division
2009 Texas – large division
Southwest – small division
2008 Texas
2007 Texas
2006 Texas
2005 Texas
2004 Texas
2003 Midwest
2002 Midwest
2001 Texas
2000 Florida
1999 Texas
1998 Texas
1997 Midwest
1996 Florida
1995 Midwest
1994 Southern
1993 Midwest
1992 Midwest
1991 Southern
1990 Northern California
1989 Intermountain
1988 Midwest
1987 Midwest
1986 Midwest
1985 Florida
1984 Southern
1983 Midwest
1982 Southern
1981 Southern
1980 Southern
1979 Midwest
1978 Southwest

Sheldon Caldwall congratulates Jack Michalko, representing the Southwest Division, 1978 Division of the Year.

1977 Southwest
1976 Midwest

Most Improved Division
2012 Southern
2010 Missouri Valley
2009 New England
2008 Missouri Valley
2007 New England
2006 Southern
2005 Southwest
2004 Florida
2003 New England
2002 Southern
2001 Southwest

Newsletter of the Year
2016 Midwest
2015 Texas
2014 Southern
2013 Midwest
2012 Southern
2011 Southern
2010 Southern
2009 Southern
2008 Texas
2007 Southern
2006 Intermountain
2005 Midwest
2004 New England
2003 Florida
2002 Southern
2001 Midwest
2000 California
1999 Florida
1998 New England
1997 Florida
1996 Midwest
1995 Midwest
1994 Midwest
1993 Midwest
1992 Intermountain
1991 Midwest
1990 Intermountain
1989 Midwest and Intermountain
1988 Intermountain
1987 Southern
1986 Florida and Southern
1985 Florida
1984 Midwest
1983 Southern
1982 Texas and Southern
1981 Mid-Atlantic
1980 Texas
1979 Southern
1978 Southern
1977 Southern
1976 Midwest

USTA/USPTA Community Service Award
2016 Aki Takayama-Wolfson
2015 Lisa Gilbride
2014 Tim & Peanut Harper
2013 Mark Faber
2012 Geoff Griffin
2011 Michael Andrews
2010 Paul Garron
2009 Tom Fey
2008 Jorge Andrew
2007 Craig S. Jones
2006 Chris Michalowski
2005 Ben Press
2004 Paul Allam
2003 Mike Woody
2002 Kenneth W. Sumrow
2001 Marilyn Crandall
2000 Steve Gallagher
1999 Larry C. Hampton
1998 Gregory T. Aten
1997 Robert Ruzanic
1996 Mervyn Webster
1995 Everett "B.B." Brown
1994 Deborah Gavin
1993 Paula Scheb
1992 Kirk Anderson
1991 Scott R. Schultz
1990 Jim Murphy
1989 Edward D. McQuillin
1988 Jack Justice
1987 Randy Chamberlain
1986 Ulysses (Pete) Brown
1985 James Newton Cox

Education merit award for 10 years of continuing-education participation
2016
Nelson Alapi
Doug Eng
Trish Faulkner
Mike Gennette
Marc Majdick
Ajay Pant
Patrik Segfeldt
Charlotte Wylie

2015
Karl Akkerman
Ron Dyson
Warren Lem
Bill Mecca
Jeff Rothstein
Keith Swindoll

2014
Tim Irwin
Angela Koumaris
Christin Thurston

2013
Jeff Cohen
Chuck Gill

2012
Nick Bollettieri
Richard Centerbar
Steve Diamond
Jerri DiCamillo
Charlie Gundi
Patrick Hanssen
Nick Hummel
Jim Laughlin
Bradley Leu
Jack Michalko
Robin Newman
Warren Pretorius
Jim Sciarro
David Steinbach
Christopher Stevens
Gary Trost
Martin Vinokur, Ph.D.

2011
David Hardy
Simon Harrington
Warren Lem
Fernando Mateu
Bill Mecca
Joe Roediger
Ian Thomson
Craig Wells
Pat Whitworth
Ron Woods

2010
Patricia Anderson
Jorge Capestany
Tom Daglis
Ken DeHart
Harry Gilbert
Tim Heckler
Will Hoag
Alvin Hom
Tom Ingram
Randy Mattingley
Daniel Moster
Mark Savage
Joseph Thompson
Ron Woods
2009
Mark Faber
John Yandell

2008
Fred Burdick
Patrick Kearns
Tom McGraw

2007
Rosie Bareis
Bunny Bruning
Alan Cutler
Mark Fairchilds
Michael Friedman
Jeff Hawes
Thomas Jaeger
Patrick Kearns
Stan Oley
Anne Pamplin-Evenson
Fred Viancos

2006
Jack Foster

2005
Don Henson
Pat Whitworth

2004
Holger Nickel

2003
Jorge Andrew
Daniel Burgess
Joseph Dinoffer
J. Townsend Gilbert
Feisal Hassan
Barbara Johnston
R. J. Tessier
William Rork Thompson

2002
Lee Ann Berning
Tommy Connell
Michael Lange
Paul MacDonald
Kevin McCarthy
Jose Morales
Tom Sweitzer
Michael Woody

Education merit award for 20 years of continuing-education participation

2016 Rosie Bareis
Bunny Bruning
Alan Cutler
Stan Oley
Anne Pamplin-Evenson
Fred Viancos
2015 Jack Foster
2014 Pat Whitworth
2012 Daniel Burgess
Feisal Hassan
Barbara Johnston Hill

Lessons for Life Individual Award

2016 Ettore and Angelo Rossetti
2015 Suzanne LaBelle
2014 Bill Riddle
2013 Matt Grayson
2012 Kyle Kaneshiro
Dave Neuhart
2011 Fernando Velasco

2010 Ken Sumrow
2009 David Altshuler

Tennis Across America Individual Award

2015 Ron Woods
2014 Jason Holland
2013 John McWilliams
2012 Jackie Roe
2011 Bill Mecca
2010 Ron Woods
2009 Jacques A.P. Faulise

Diversity Award

2016 Ronald Elizondo
2015 Dale Evans
2014 Christopher Tran
2013 Cindy Benzon
2012 Angel Lopez
2011 Ira Peskowitz

U30 Award

2016 Ryan McDaniel
2015 Jeremiah De Jose

Top Education Participants

2015 Josh Jorgensen
2014 Levander Kelley
2013 Josh Jorgensen
2012 Josh Jorgensen

Two-time Tennis Across America Individual Award winner Ron Woods (right) with Gerry Maingot, Bob Mapes and Vic Braden at a 1991 Tennis Across America clinic.

HONORARY MEMBERS

Katrina Adams
Pauline Betz Addie *
Jack M Barnaby *
George E. Barnes *
Bill Bell *
Steven Bellamy
Asher J. Birnbaum
Mike Blanchard *
Vic Braden *
George H.W. Bush
Mary Carillo
Ralph E. Chambers *
Natalie Cohen *
Robert B. Colwell *
Robert A. Cookson *
Hunter L. Delatour Jr.*
Fred A. Earle Jr.*
Walter E. Elcock *
Jimmy A. Evert *
Allen Fox, Ph.D.
J. Howard Frazer
John Gardiner *
Lucy S. Garvin
Sam Giammalva
Abe Golden *
Dick Gould
J. Randolph Gregson *
Jane Brown Grimes
Alex Guerry *
Gladys Heldman *
Mervin A. Heller Jr.*
Slew E. Hester Jr.*
Franklin R. Johnson
Gordon D. Jorgensen *
Robert J. Kelleher *
Billie Jean King
Don Klotz *
Eve F. Kraft *
Jack Kramer *
Robert Lansdorp
Rod Laver
Julia A. Levering
Claudia Long *
Clarence Mabry *
George R. MacCall *
Dan Magill *
Stanley Malless *
David R. Markin
Harry Marmion *
Alastair B. Martin *
Mark McCormack *
Hilary Paul McGuire
Walter Montenegro *
Ed Moosbrugger *
Jason Morton *
Bill Mott *
Chet Murphy
Chuck Norris
Desmond Oon, Ph.D.
Fred Perry *
Anne M. Pittman *
Bill Price *
Marvin P Richmond *
Ted R. Schroeder *
Alan G. Schwartz
Pancho Segura
Sam Shore *
Pam Shriver
Stan Smith
Randy Snow *
Lester M. Snyder Jr.*
Tony Trabert
Edward A. Turville *
Welby Van Horn *
Jon Vegosen
Paul Waldman *
Martina Widjaja
Roy Wilder *
Paul J. Xanthos *

*Deceased

USPTA member Paul Christian (left) and CEO Tim Heckler (right) welcome President George H.W. Bush as an Honorary USPTA Member (1998).

Stories From USPTA Members and Families

Steve Denton working with kids at a Tennis Across America event in Corpus Christi, TX, 1998

Early Professional Lawn Tennis in America

Submitted by Richard Hillway

Only months after Major Walter Clopton Wingfield in London had patented a portable (usually outdoor) tennis court on Feb. 23, 1874 and published the first-ever lawn tennis rules' booklet two days later, thereby inventing the game of lawn tennis (now called tennis), the game became popular worldwide. As with all sports, professionals emerged early in lawn tennis. Professionals who had already been teaching real (court) tennis and rackets became the first lawn tennis pros. Examples of nineteenth century lawn tennis professionals were: in England, George Lambert (Marylebone Cricket Club) and Tom Fleming (Maida Vale Club); on the French Riviera, Irishman Thomas Burke and in America, Tom Pettitt (Newport Casino) and Robert Moore (Tuxedo Park). For decades, the professionals were separated from the amateur "gentlemen," given an inferior social status, not called "Mr.," excluded from the club members' locker rooms and porches, and kept out of all amateur tournaments such as Wimbledon and the U.S. Nationals. No wonder none of the respectable, well-to-do amateurs wanted to turn professional at that time.

There were no lawn tennis tournaments for professionals in either Europe or America for many years. Occasionally, there were exhibition matches played between amateurs and professionals who, prior to the 1920's, were "teaching pros." Englishman Tom Pettitt had come to America in 1876 at age 17 and, after the Newport Casino opened in 1880, became their first professional of court and lawn tennis. The initial U.S. singles champion, Richard D. Sears of Boston (U.S. champ 1881-87), played several exhibition matches against Pettitt. A few took place in 1886. At the Longwood Cricket Club on May 14, Sears won 4-6, 6-3, 6-3, 7-5. That match was described in *The American Cricketer* as "about as pretty a display of the beauties of lawn tennis as was ever seen in this country." At Nahant, near Boston, James Dwight, the "father of American lawn tennis," only lost five games to Pettitt in a 3-set win. On Aug. 27, at the Newport Casino, Sears again easily defeated Pettitt. And on Oct. 7, 1886 Dwight and Sears teamed up to beat Pettitt and his partner in doubles at Longwood in five sets. Such public matches pairing amateurs against professionals were later outlawed by the USNLTA.

The First Professional Match in America

In the Nov. 20, 1927 issue of *American Lawn Tennis*, the earliest American professional tennis matches were described by William M. Fischer, whose wonderful personal library of early tennis books now resides at St. John's University. Fischer wrote, "... the first professional lawn tennis contest in America was held at Newport, RI on Aug. 19, 1889. The players were George Kerr, the Irish professional, and Thomas Pettitt, the court tennis champion." Pettitt had traveled to England in 1885 where he became the world's court tennis champion and Kerr had visited America from Ireland to challenge for that crown. Kerr was successful and defended his title for 12 years. He was also the lawn tennis professional at the Fitzwilliam Lawn Tennis Club in Dublin, Ireland for 23 year. While in America, Kerr defeated Pettitt in lawn tennis at Newport, 6-3, 6-1, 6-1. At Springfield, MA on Sept. 21, Pettitt turned the tables and won 6-4, 2-6, 6-3, 6-4. Kerr then won the odd match at Longwood, Boston, of Sept. 25, 6-3, 3-6, 6-4.

The First-Ever, City-to-City, Professional Tennis Tour Took Place in America

Charles (Cash and Carry) Pyle, an American sports and motion picture promoter who represented athletes such as footballer

Vintage racquets and other tennis memorabilia from the collection of Miguel Cysneiros

Red Grange, contracted six important tennis players to play four months of matches across the U.S. and Canada. They played 40 dates at 39 cities. The tour started in New York and the Northeast, traveled west through Chicago, Vancouver and Seattle, down the west coast through San Francisco and L.A., east through cities such as Dallas, New Orleans and Havana, and played its last match in Providence. The first matches were on Oct. 9, 1926 and the last on Feb. 14, 1927. Most nights consisted of four matches--two out of three sets in men's and women's singles, followed by one set of men's and mixed doubles. The star of the troupe was the French lady and six-time Wimbledon singles winner who had lost only one match in eight years of international competition, Suzanne Lenglen. Twenty-seven years old, she traveled with her mother, maid, masseuse and 11 trunks. Her tour rival was the Californian, Mary K. Browne, 35, who had been the U.S. champion in three events during 1912-14. The star male player was Vinnie Richards, 23, who had won the U.S. doubles five times (once as a 15-year-old with partner Bill Tilden in 1918) and the 1924 Olympic singles and doubles. His three opponents were Howard Kinsey of San Francisco who had reached three finals in the 1926 Wimbledon; teaching pro and former top 10 American from California, Harvey Snodgrass and French Davis Cupper, Paul Feret. Charles Wood filled in three times and Wes Wesbrook once. The crowds were good with the largest, New York (13,000), Cleveland (10,000) and Los Angeles (9,000) and the smallest, San Antonio and Dallas (1000 each) and Wichita (500). Pyle had failed to draft Bill Johnston and then Bill Tilden before recruiting Richards, and Helen Wills and Molla Mallory before accepting Browne. Vinnie Richards missed five of the 40 matches due to illness, Suzanne Lenglen failed to play the last four matches due to tonsillitis and Feret missed the last three when recruited by the French military. Lenglen lost only two sets in her 36 singles matches with Browne and Richards finished with 28 wins and three losses in singles. Lenglen had been guaranteed $50,000 plus a percentage of the gate and so earned close to $100,000; Brown, $35,000 plus 5%; Richards at least $35,000; Kinsey, $20,000; Snodgrass, $12,000; Feret, $10,000 and Pyle about $50,000 to $75,000. Lenglen and Richards told how much they preferred the pro game where they earned their pay to "shamateurism" which couldn't support them. This first tennis tour of premier plays gave professional tennis more recognition than it had ever received in the past.

The Beginnings of the Professional Lawn Tennis Association Which Later Became the USPTA

After the Pyle tour had ended in early 1927, Vinnie Richards and Howard Kinsey, to earn a better living, saw the need for American tennis professionals to create an organization and a major tournament. Along with teaching pros, they took the lead in founding America's first professional tennis association. They met on Sept. 23, 1927 in an upper story room of Spalding & Bros. Sporting Goods New York store at 105 Nassau Street. H. Levon Richards chaired the meeting attended by George Agutter, James Burns, William J. Croker, Edwin Faulkner, Henry A. Geidel, Paul Heston, Walter A. Kinsella, Frank Lafforgue, Harry A. McNeal, James Reid, Vincent Richards, Harvey Snodgrass and Charles M. Wood. They created the Professional Lawn Tennis Association of the US. Its purpose was to protect and promote the interests of all professional coaches and players in its association and to help them to obtain a recognized status in the lawn tennis world. More meetings were held and annual dues were set at $5 with an initiation fee of $10. A constitution was drawn up and adopted. An executive committee was elected which invited all lawn tennis professionals to become members. The executive committee consisted George Agutter, chairman, head pro of the West Side Tennis Club, Forest Hills, NY; Harry A. McNeal, treasurer-secretary, The Heights Casino, Brooklyn, NY; Walter A. Kinsella, The Fraternity Club, NY; Howard O. Kinsey, California Tennis Club, San Francisco, CA and William J. Croker, pro at the Longwood Cricket Club, Boston, MA. The association worked to improve courts and playing conditions and to provide competent instruction to meet the growing demand of new players. Professionals looking for teaching jobs and clubs looking for professionals were encouraged to contact the PLTA. The earliest presidents of the association follow. George Agutter served as president for nine years, followed by two-year terms for Ed Faulkner, Henry Geidel, James G. Pressly and then Charles M. Wood from 1941 through 1945 during the war, after which came Frank J. Rericha for one year and George Sweewagen.

The First American Professional Tennis Tournaments

The first professional tennis tournament held in America was played at the Palm Beach Tennis Club in Palm Beach, FL and finished on Tuesday, March 22, 1927. In the final match, Paul Heston defeated George Agutter. At the time, both players were employed by the Palm Beach club for the winter months.

However, America's first major professional tennis championship was directed by Doc Kelton and located on the Notlek Tennis Courts (clay courts), 119th Street and Riverside Drive in New York, on Friday through Sunday, Sept. 23-25, 1927. The PLTA was formed during the evening of that tournament's first day and many tournament participants attended that meeting.

Sixteen professional tennis players, mostly teaching pros, competed in the first PLTA tennis tournament. They were Vincent Richards from New York, the first important American touring pro and the foremost professional player at that time; Howard Kinsey, star player from the California Tennis Club who had won the 1924 U.S. doubles with his brother; Charles M. Wood, former national indoor junior champion and pro at the Fairview Country Club; Paul Heston of Washington, SC who in the spring of 1927 had competed in the world's professional championship at Cannes; Edwin Faulkner of the Germantown Cricket Club who had trained Jean Borotra for the last Davis Cup matches; George Agutter, West Side Tennis Club professional and his assistant, Warren Kruger; Louis Volpe Jr., a 17-year-old who had been a professional for two years in Newton Center, MA; William Ganley, a former Seabright star and professional squash player; Otto Glockler, pro of the Chevy Chase Club in Washington DC; H.W. Hagemann of the Salem Country Club in Peabody, MA; James P. Reid of the Crescent Athletic Club in Brooklyn; John Collom, the Baltimore Country Club professional; Julius Boise, pro at the Allegheny Country Club of Sewickley, PA; Captain Calerian J. Yavorsky, professional at the Nipnichsen Club and former amateur champion of South Russia and Charles Haggett.

In the tournament, the favorites came through. In the semifinals, Richards defeated Wood 6-0, 6-1, 6-2 while Kinsey beat Heston 6-0, 6-4, 6-3. More than a thousand spectators watched top-seeded Vinnie Richards defeat second-seeded Howard Kinsey in the final, 11-9, 6-4, 6-3. From a total purse of $2000, Richards won $1000, Kinsey $700 and the losing semi-finalists, $150 each.

This first major pro tournament became an annual event. It was called the U.S. Pro Championships. Here follow some of the significant players who won the event and the number of times each did so--Vinnie Richards, four; Karel Kozeluh of Czechoslovakia, two; Bill Tilden, two; Fred Perry, two; Ellsworth Vines, one; Don Budge, two; Bobby Riggs, three; Jack Kramer, one; Pancho Segura, three; Pancho Gonzales, eight; Ken Rosewall, three; Rod Laver, five; Jimmy Connors, one; Bjorn Borg, three and Ivan Lendl, three.

The Significant One-on-One Professional Tours

From 1926 through the 1950's, America was blessed by one-on-one professional city-to-city tours where the reigning world's top professional played nightly against, in most cases, the world's amateur king who had just turned pro. Bill Tilden had been the first amateur champion to turn professional (December 1930) and go on tour, but after that, most reigning amateur male champions turned professional, one by one. The tours were great for spectators since it was as if Federer and Djokovic or Nadal played head-to-head matches perhaps a hundred times during a year. During the 1960's, the one-on-one tours were replaced by pro tournaments in many locations. By 1968 open tennis had been adopted worldwide through the efforts of Wimbledon officials as Herman David and American administrators as Bob Kelleher. Pros could now play in the tournaments previously confined to amateurs. This erased the need for one-on-one tours. The important promoters of the pro tours and events from 1930 to the 1960's were, in order, Bill Tilden, Jack Harris of Chicago and Wilson Sporting Goods Co., Bobby Riggs and Jack Kramer. Here are the most significant one-on-one tours followed by the number of matches won by each player. The asterisks stand for preliminary matches played as the undercard for a more important rivalry.

1928 – Karel Kozeluh d. Vinnie Richards – 15-5.
1931 – Bill Tilden d. Karel Kozeluh – 63-13.
1934 – Ellsworth Vines d. Bill Tilden (age 41) – 47-26.
1935 – Bill Tilden d. George Lott – 73-27.
1937 – Ellsworth Vines d. Fred Perry – 32-29.
1938 – Ellsworth Vines d. Fred Perry – 49-35.
1939 – Don Budge d. Ellsworth Vines – 22-17.
1939 – Don Budge d. Fred Perry – 18-11.
1941 – Don Budge d. Bill Tilden (age 48) – 51-7.
1946 – Bobby Riggs d. Don Budge – 23-21.
1948 – Jack Kramer d. Bobby Riggs – 69-20.
*1948 – Dinny Pails d. Pancho Segura – 41.31.
1950 – Jack Kramer d. Pancho Gonzales – 96-27.
*1950 – Pancho Seguara d. Frank Parker – easily, once winning 20 in a row.
1951 – Jack Kramer d. Pancho Segura – 64-28.
*1951 – Pauline Betz Addie d. Gussy Moran – 64-28.
1953 – Jack Kramer d. Frank Sedgman – 54-41.
*1953 – Pancho Segura d. Ken McGregory – 71-25.
1954 – Pancho Gonzales d. Frank Sedgman – 30-21.
1956 – Pancho Gonzales d. Tony Trabert – 74-27.
*1956 – Pancho Segura d. Rex Hartwig – 56-22.
1957 – Pancho Gonzales d. Ken Rosewall – 50-26.
1958 – Pancho Gonzales d. Lew Hoad – 51-36.
*1958 – Troy Trabert d. Pancho Segura – 34-31.

The PLTA changed to the USPLTA in 1957 and shifted again to its present title, USPTA during the 1971-72 administration of president David Muir. This was at least three years before the USLTA became the USTA in 1975. (It had been the USNLTA until 1920.)

Special Olympics... Skill-Courage-Sharing-Joy

By Robin Newman, USPTA

(The following article was originally published in Base Lines, *a publication of the USPTA Florida Division, December 1991/January 1992 issue.)*

The execution of their strokes might not be perfect. Their shot placement is sometimes not accurate. But their determination and drive is incredible! They strive to be the best they can be.

Who are these special athletes? None other than the 1991 United States Special Olympics women's Tennis Team: Victoria "Tori" Pole, Valentina "Tina" Monk and Tabatha "Tabby"Towns all from Hollywood, Florida.

When I received a telephone call in January asking if I would be interested in coaching three of the Florida contenders for the 1991 International Special Olympics, I thought about it for only

Special Olympics tennis competitors, September 1991. Clockwise from top left: Valentina "Tina" Monk, Tabatha "Tabby" Towns, Coach Robin Newman and Victoria "Tori" Pole.

a few seconds before I knew that it would be a fulfilling and challenging task, especially since it had to do with teaching and tennis.

I have been teaching middle school and high school physical education since 1972 and have been involved in tennis since 1985 after attending a USTA Schools Program workshop given by Barbara Braustein. Needless to say, I was hooked on teaching tennis! Not only did I become actively involved in the USTA Schools Program but in 1987 I became a USPTA Teaching Professional.

These three athletes became involved in the Special Olympics Program through their school, the Quest Center, a school for special children and adults in Hollywood, Florida. Their interest in tennis started to develop three years ago when Beverly Dollard, the parent of one of their classmates wanted to see tennis offered to her son and his friends. Because of her interest, dedication and determination, a tennis program for special athletes was offered through the Department of Recreation in Miramar, Florida and thus started Tori, Tina and Tabby's involvement in tennis. Because of the support of their parents, friends and coaches, the girls decided to pursue tennis in the Special Olympics.

Since its creation in1968, using funds from the Joseph P. Kennedy, Jr. Foundation, the Special Olympics has grown to include more than one million participants in the United States and in 91 foreign countries. The program culminates in August of the year before the regular Olympic Games and includes the following events: tennis, basketball, bowling, diving, floor hockey, frisbee throwing, gymnastics, ice skating, poly hockey, soccer, softball, track and field, volleyball and wheelchair events. There are also demonstration events in badminton, cross-country running, dance, equestrian events, field hockey, golf and rhythmic exercises.

Local games take place in more than 10,000 communities around the world. In Florida alone, over 12,000 athletes participated in 61 countries. In order for athletes to have been competitors at the International Special Olympics that were held in Minneapolis, St. Paul, from July 19 through July 27, 1991, they had to have competed on the county, district and state Special Olympics.

Each athlete at the Special Olympics is placed in a division of equal competitive abilities. I couldn't have been any prouder of the women because each of them placed in their division. Tina placed sixth for skills competition, Tori placed sixth for singles competition and Tabby won a gold medal for skills competition and a gold medal for singles competition.

Coaching Tori, Tina and Tabby has been one of the most rewarding experiences in my teaching career. If I was down, after a hard day teaching, they always had a way of cheering me up. Their love was unconditional and they always had hugs and smiles for me. I have never taught individuals who have had the drive and dedication that these three athletes did. They always gave it their best and even when they were frustrated, they would try again, and again, and again!

When I handed each of the women a new Prince tennis racket, the look on their faces and the appreciation was beyond words. We all should take a lesson from these three athletes because they are so sincere in everything they do and expect nothing in return.

As far as I am concerned, Tori, Tina and Tabby, have all won the Olympic Gold and have lived up to the Special Olympic Pledge "Let me win, if I cannot win, let me be brave in the attempt!" On each of the medals the following words are inscribed ...

"Skill-courage-Sharing-Joy!"

New Orleans World Conference Provides Setting for Reunion with Godfather

By Sam Parfitt

In 1990, my twin sister and I were christened in a rural Norfolk village church, in the east of England. Our godfather, Andy Durham, was one of the only ones who managed to beat the snow and attend the event! An American, Andy had come over to England to coach tennis, and he ran coach education courses with my father, Murray Parfitt.

That christening was the last time we saw Andy, as he moved back to the States. But my father talked so fondly of their friendship and of Andy's enthusiastic tennis coaching that I always felt a connection, especially as I began to fall in love with the sport.

As a boy, my Dad gave me the tennis book Andy had written, and I still remember the book's diagrams of Andy playing a forehand with perfect technique and modeling the correct body angles of the serve. I would read the book night after night!

Murray Parfitt (left) holding son Sam, with Sam's godfather, Andy Durham and his daughter, at Sam's christening.

Sam Parfitt (left) reunites with godfather Andy Durham at the 2015 USPTA conference in New Orleans.

Tennis became my life and I moved to the United States in 2009 to play division one college tennis.

In 2015, at the age of 25, after I had graduated from my time as a collegiate player in Tennessee, I began my USPTA coaching certification. As an excited new member of the USPTA, I decided to attend the world conference in New Orleans. I found Andy online and told him I'd be at the conference. To my excitement, he said he would be too!

I arrived to a packed hall in New Orleans, sat down and glanced at a man standing just feet away to my left. Could it be him?! All I had to go on were the memories of reading his book. The brown-haired, spectacled tennis player, dressed in immaculate tennis attire, with perfect forehand technique from the pages I read as a boy.

This man certainly looked kind, as my Dad said he was. Perhaps it was him.

The talk ended, and I approached my godfather! We met for the first time in twenty-five years and we got on famously! It was an incredible week and I realized everything my father had told me about him was true! He, like my father, is a true gentleman, and scholar of the game. What a special few days it was. Andy is now part of an expert team I have set up for a new non-profit called The True Athlete Project. It is so fulfilling to be connected after all these years. Thank you USPTA!

How Legendary USPTA Coaches Helped Make My Dreams Come True

By Jim Morton

As a young boy growing up in a farm town in rural Ohio, I always believed that one day I would be a professional athlete. I loved sports and played as many organized sports as I could throughout High School. Basketball and football were my favorites, but as a 5-foot-6, 145-pound athlete, my options seemed to be limited and my goal nearly impossible.

However, it was in seventh grade when my dream took a new direction. I decided to give up baseball and play on the middle school tennis team because of a kind, young English teacher named Bob Kader, now a USPTA Pro. At the time, he had just taken up the game and volunteered to coach the team. Coach Kader saw something in me and when I moved on to High School he made sure the tennis coach and USPTA Pro Arnold Bradshaw would notice my potential too. It wasn't long before Coach Bradshaw came over to the courts and offered me encouragement to keep working on my game. Coach Bradshaw was already on his way to becoming a legendary coach, his boys' high school teams becoming the best in the state of Ohio winning over 480 matches during his tenure.

In the summer between my junior and senior year, Coach Bradshaw invited me to spend a week with him at his summer position as the Head Professional at a country club. This was where my dream started to become a reality! After helping to brush courts and string racquets, I was allowed to feed balls to some of the tiny tots; this is when I could see a clear path for tennis becoming my sport for a lifetime. After graduating from high school, Coach Bradshaw helped me secure a tennis scholarship to Lakeland Community College where I played for two seasons before moving on to Hiram College where I finished out my college career as the MVP of the team.

After graduation from Hiram College, I was fortunate to be offered a job as a "tennis professional" at a suburban Cleveland Yacht Club with two courts. Dreams do come true — I would be a Pro at tennis. Although I did my best at the position, it wasn't long before I realized I needed more than just being paid to be a true professional. So after the summer I packed my car and drove to Clearwater, Florida to stay with a friend and to pursue a career as a tennis professional.

While going from club to club, I came across an elderly man hitting with another gentleman at a local resort. Both were dressed immaculately in all white tennis attire and after they finished, I approached them and introduced myself. It was my great fortune that both were tennis professionals and one was the head professional at the resort. Upon talking to them, I found out that the head professional was in need of a court man who could string racquets and possibly serve as an extra pro during the busier times during the season. I quickly accepted the position and started work the very next day.

I had no idea of how lucky I was at the time to get this position but within a few weeks I found out that I was now working for Bill Lufler the legendary coach and the first president of the USPTA. The other gentleman was Tom Wright, his protégé, who was the head professional at Forest Hills, where the U.S. Open used to be played before moving to Flushing Meadows.

Bill, or "Pro" as everyone called him, was the epitome of a tennis professional. From his all white tennis attire to the way he meticulously taught every pupil, he set an example of what it meant to be a true tennis professional. To teach me how to teach the game the proper way, Pro would have me stand behind him as he fed his pupils and listen to what he was saying to each student, occasionally asking me questions of what I saw in the students' strokes. Before long he trusted me enough to feed the balls to the students while he stood on the other side of the net, near the student, so that he could demonstrate the point he was trying to teach.

After working for a couple of winter seasons for Pro, he recommended me for an Assistant Pro position with Tom Wright, who was working at a country club in Connecticut. Fortunately Tom, also a USPTA Pro, hired me and through him I was able to continue my education on how to be a complete tennis professional. He guided me on the aspects of managing a club job. He taught me how to always consider the majority at a club, emphasizing fairness to all, and to be passionate in my teaching. He even taught me how to write a tennis newsletter. After one season with Tom, he helped me get my first head professional job at a club in Connecticut.

It was while in this position, having apprenticed with two USPTA Professionals and been guided into the sport as a young boy by my early USPTA coaches, that I realized the common connection. Being a professional and continuing to grow as a professional was linked to becoming a Certified Member of the USPTA! So I registered for the test, studied the material and became a certified USPTA PROFESSIONAL. Dreams really do come true!

Arthur Ashe Was First an Intermountain USPTA Member

By John Williams

In a past issue of ADDvantage magazine there was an article about the 25th anniversary Arthur Ashe's induction into the International Tennis Hall of Fame. It also noted that Arthur became a member of the USPTA in 1985.

It was actually the Intermountain USPTA that inducted Arthur Ashe as an honorary member first. Arthur was a player spokesman for Head Sports, which at the time was based in Boulder. He continued his long relationship with Head Sports right up to his passing in 1993. Arthur was coming to Boulder on one of his many trips back to meet with the corporate staff at Head Sports. I was a member of their National Advisory Staff and so I was told about his upcoming trip.

At the next Intermountain USPTA meeting, I suggested the idea of inducting Arthur into our division as an Honorary Member. Everyone was in overwhelming agreement with the idea. Then a discussion ensued about what we might give him to honor the moment. Someone suggested a plaque; another suggested a group photo with Arthur and all of us. Someone said "do you think he will put the plaque or photo next to his Wimbledon or U.S. Open trophy?" The point was well made. After much discussion we finally settled on a plan. All of this with the approval of the National USPTA Office

We arranged a luncheon at Boulder Country Club where I was the Director of Tennis. Arthur had agreed to give a brief speech. The room was packed with USPTA pros, Head Sports staff and other invited guests. At the end of Arthur's talk, Randy Ross came to the podium. He told Arthur that he was being inducted as an honorary member of our division. To commemorate the event we wanted to give him something special. With that, Arthur Ashe was inducted into the Intermountain USPTA with the fine cowboy hat that you see in this picture. Arthur laughed and said it was an honor; he would enjoy both the hat and the story that went with it. Pictured with Arthur are two young trim tennis pros, Rob Scott and yours truly in the white Fred Perry sweater behind them.

Arthur was more than a world-renowned tennis star; he was a champion of many causes. Not the least of which was the Arthur Ashe Foundation for the Defeat of AIDS. This was the terrible disease that he contracted from a blood transfusion before they screened for such things. His efforts helped to change the minds of people worldwide about the AIDS epidemic. One of his goals was to make the world understand that this was a health concern, not a lifestyle issue. Whereas his mission was a success, the disease took his life on February 6, 1993. My wife Laurie was the National Promotions Manager for Head Sports at the time. Arthur was to speak at an event for Head at the Super Show in Atlanta. Because his health was failing he could not attend and instead Laurie had a video made that was played during the event. Immediately afterwards they were told Arthur had passed. Laurie was privileged and honored to attend the funeral in Richmond, Virginia.

It is a source of pride to say that I knew Arthur through my days with Head Sports and as a younger player when I had the

Arthur Ashe, John Williams and Rob Scott

opportunity to practice with him. I spoke with him in 1992 when I played in the Tennis Magazine Tournament at the West Side Tennis Club in Forest Hills, N.Y. Arthur gave yet another speech and because this was during the U.S. Open, he had to leave for one of his many commitments. As he turned and walked away I looked at him and thought, "I wonder if this is the last time I will see him." Alas it was.

"Words cannot suffice to capture a career as glorious, a life as fully lived, or a commitment to justice as firm and as fair as was his." New York Mayor David N. Dinkins

RAFAEL FUENTES HONORED

Submitted by Tim Wallace

Tennis players from across California's high desert came together in 2016 to present retired tennis pro Rafael Fuentes a lifetime achievement award in honor of his astounding resume as a player and instructor.

Born in a small rural town in El Salvador, he lived with his mother, father, and 11 siblings. Fuentes's first encounter with the sport of tennis was when his mother brought home a fuzzy white ball one day. She told her children she thought it was a golf ball. After the family moved to the capital, San Salvador, he began his tennis career as ball boy at the local tennis club. Just a few years later he became a National Champion for the first time, eventually garnering five such titles, in two different countries. After his illustrious playing career he continued as a teaching professional for 46 years.

Fuentes was Head Tennis Pro at El Panama Hilton Hotel in the Republic of Panama from 1963 to 1971. He then took his career to the United Stated where he served as Tennis Pro at the Midtown Tennis Club in Manhattan, N.Y., from 1971 to 1975. He next served as the Tennis Pro at Transworld Oil

Rafael Fuentes (center) receives a Lifetime Achievement Award from the High Desert Tennis Association.

Rafael Fuentes with one of his many trophies won as a player

America, Inc. in Manhattan from 1975 to 1989, becoming a citizen of the United States in 1980. In 1989, he became the Tennis Pro for Transworld Oil Ltd. in Bermuda, where he stayed until 2009.

Mr. Fuentes has been a member of the USPTA since 1972, has attended eight World Tennis Conferences and has given instruction in 18 different countries. He is an accomplished tournament player and was the National Tennis Open Champion of Panama in 1964, 1965, 1966, and 1968, and was a finalist in 1963 and 1967. Rafael also held the title of National Tennis Open Champion of El Salvador in 1968 and was a finalist in 1969. He played USPTA tournaments in New York, New Jersey, Florida, Nevada, California, and Mexico. He also played deep into the Central American Tennis Tournaments in Costa Rica, Colombia, and Puerto Rico in 1965.

He currently resides in Victorville, Calif., with his wife, where he is a member of the Spring Valley Lake Country Club.

TRIBUTE TO SUE DOYLE THE GURU OF TENNIS IN KEENE, NH

Submitted by Tina Spicher

Keene is a town in southwestern New Hampshire – population 23,000. In the early 1970s a group of tennis enthusiasts, including Sue Doyle, decided to build an indoor tennis club – not a business, just for them, to play tennis whenever they want, year round.

Every September, Sue runs the Keene City Tennis Tournament. In 2010 Sue and I (Tina Spicher) won the women's doubles. That same day we acknowledged Sue for her contribution to our community through tennis and shared our appreciation with her. She

Sue Doyle (seated), with Tina Spicher (standing) thanking Sue for her contribution to the tennis community

was presented with a framed photo showing her name on a brick at the International Tennis Hall of Fame and Museum in Newport, R.I., now a part of the Legends Walk at the Hall of Fame. The Keene tennis community purchased this brick. The contributions from the community to purchase the brick for Sue were overwhelming. The brick simply says, "Sue Doyle – Thank You –Keene, N.H."

Sue is a natural born leader. People love and respect her from the get-go. She has been the tennis pro at our indoor club since 1972. She's been a USPTA certified tennis teaching professional for 24 years. She's tireless. Sue was the tennis pro at our local country club for 28 years. They even named their courts after her. She's been honored twice as annual Cheshire County Sportsman of the year. She coached girls' high school tennis since 1978 and now volunteers, assisting and guiding the coach. She continues to be the pro of choice at our indoor club. Sue runs elementary and junior group lessons and ran a summer tennis camp for 13 years. She runs clinics and coaches three women's USTA league teams. Now you see why everyone who wants to or has hit a tennis ball in Keene knows Sue Doyle.

Sue has also had successes in playing USTA league tennis. She's been on women's 4.5 teams, three that made it to nationals. Sue and Susan Fratus have been ranked No. 1 in New England senior women's doubles, three times. She and her long time tennis partner, Bob Whitehouse (USPTA), have been ranked No. 1 in New England senior mixed doubles, four times.

In 1995 Sue told me I should join the USPTA. I did, and found it an impressive accomplishment and honorable organization. Sue changed my life for the better that day she said to me, "join the USPTA."

TRIBUTE TO TOM MAUCH

Submitted by Jerry Hubbard

I've been a USPTA Elite professional since 1977, and was a full-time teaching pro through 1987, when I changed careers and became a minister. I've stayed involved in tennis over the years, though, albeit part-time, coaching and teaching lessons off and on, mostly at Punahou School here in Honolulu, where the bulk of my career in tennis has been. I've maintained by USPTA credentials, though, and have seriously considered getting back into teaching and coaching when I retire from my current position. I'm also a USTA member, and have been playing in the 60s tournaments for the last few years.

I'm writing to honor long-time USPTA member Tom Mauch. Tom is 85 now, and lives in Murietta, Calif., but the bulk of his tennis career was here in Hawaii. What he did for tennis in Hawaii is, in many ways, unparalleled. I say this from first-hand experience, since I actually worked for him longer than anyone else (1973-76, 1980-87) during his years at Punahou (1966-92, if I remember correctly). Tom was more than a boss to me, though. He was more of a father figure, and in more recent years, a trusted advisor and friend.

In my estimation, his entrepreneurial spirit and forward-thinking attitude broke ground for tennis here in the islands. He arrived here in 1966, but had visited the year before at the invitation of former Punahou School tennis coach Elston Wyatt. Tom and his wife, Marian, and daughter Melinda, were from Berkeley, Calif., but left everything to move here to become the tennis pro for Punahou School. I wasn't here at that time, but remember the stories that people like former USTA (Hawaii division) president Sam Caldwell and Muriel Osborne (winner of several gold balls) told me, how no one thought you could make a living being a tennis pro, especially at Punahou, where it rained so much. But Tom defied the naysayers, and showed kids and adults alike how to squeegee off a court in minutes, using a team approach which I've never seen replicated, even at the U.S. Open. Besides the students and staff at Punahou, Tom would also bring in tourists from the burgeoning hotel industry in Waikiki, busing them up to Punahou himself in his '68 VW van during off-times at school. Long before anyone else, Tom advocated that Waikiki should take advantage of the tennis boom, which eventually resulted in the Ilikai Hotel installing seven courts (including the first-ever roof-top courts) in 1975. Other hotels and resorts in the islands followed suit during that time period (e.g., the Mauna Kea Beach Hotel, on the Big Island), but it was Tom's ideas that led the way.

Tennis had long been part of the sports program at Punahou, but on a very different scale, since tennis was generally more of a "country club sport" at that time of history. Tom's arrival, though, coincided with tennis moving into the open era, in 1968. In spite of the much more limited communications that existed in those days, Tom brought in players like Pancho Gonzales for exhibition events, as well as the U.S. Davis Cup team, in 1968, which included Jim Osborne, Jr., the only player from Hawaii ever to play Davis Cup. In fact, one of the exhibitions was held indoors at McKinley High School's gym (which was bigger than Punahou's, at the time), which Tom thought up at the last minute, since it was so rainy outside.

Tom had a rare combination of being a stickler for having his students "perfect the basics," but doing so in creative, fun-filled ways. I can't confirm this, but I think he was the first pro in Hawaii to use ball machines for lessons. We had six metal ball machines that were actually manufactured by a company in Ohio that made ball machines for baseball teams. We used to put up to five machines at a time on a court during group lessons, and kids would take turns hitting forehands, then backhands, then volleys, and even overhead smashes, in succession. As I've reflected on those days, it sometimes makes me cringe, thinking about how easy it would've been for a kid to shank a ball and hit another student in the eye. But interestingly enough, we never had any serious injuries, and a lot of that was due to Tom's organizational skills, and how well he managed groups. On the one hand, he was a "drill sergeant," and insisted on good behavior, good form, and staying in line. On the other hand, he was a genius at taking a group of kids with varying ages and ability levels, and helping each student improve, even if it was just a little, in every lesson. In fact, Tom's analytical skills were amazing. He was not only able to assess (i.e., to diagnose) a student's area of greatest need, but give him/her a pointer on how to improve. What's amazing to me is how Tom did this for each student in a group, in every group, every day. He didn't even know a lot of the kids all that well, but in a matter of minutes, was able to analyze their strokes, and give them a tip to help them leave feeling encouraged. In later years, I discovered that I had picked up some of these same skills, and used Tom's example as a benchmark when I was overseeing and training young college guys who taught under me at Punahou (circa 2003-08). Current Punahou School tennis director (and long-time USPTA member) Bernard Gusman, USPTA member and division tester Lee Couillard and I would bemoan the lack of analytical skills in younger pros, and expressed thanks for men like Tom, who set the standard for us, way "back in the day."

Tom was probably most well known for his grassroots approach to teaching tennis. Tom must've taught thousands of kids at Punahou over the years, which explains why Punahou dominated Hawaii high school tennis (and still does). Believe it or not, Tom was largely a self-taught player, but gleaned a lot from Dennis Van der Meer (who used to live and teach in Berkeley, where Tom was from) on how to teach tennis, prior to coming to Hawaii. In all the years I worked with Tom, he rarely spent a lot of time working with advanced juniors. His forte was working with beginners and intermediate players, helping them to get to where they could really enjoy tennis, on their own. Yet, I could name scores of junior players from Hawaii who grew up in Tom's group lessons, who went on to not only be top high school players, but played in college, and even beyond. Moreover, there were lots of other former students of Tom's who still play tennis today, and have beautiful, classic strokes. There was a tall, blonde girl from Maui (I forget her name now) who actually came to Oahu at Tom's invitation and lived with him and his family one summer, who went on to play pro tennis in the early days of the women's tour. Tom also worked with many other promising local juniors, but never made a big deal about it.

Tom not only worked with scores of kids from Punahou, but with the blessings of then-Punahou president John Fox (also an avid tennis player), he opened up the program there to all kinds of kids, not only from the nearby community, but across the island. He and local attorney Rick Fried (who still plays national-level tennis in his age group, the 70s) actually created a company called, "Tennis For Everyone," which I'm sure Rick could give you all kinds of interesting details on. During my first summer teaching under him at Punahou (in 1973), I can remember busloads of kids from Kalihi, Waianae, etc., coming in for free clinics on Saturday mornings. In those days, a soda was still 25¢, but I remember seeing Tom feeding his own quarters (from a big money bag) into the two side-by-side soda machines, so that each kid not only got a free lesson that day, but a free soda. Tom was a good businessman, to be sure, but he also had a paternalistic side to him, sort of like the stereotype plantation-owner from Hawaii's yesteryear, who cared about kids. Some teens would call him "Mauch the Grouch," because of how strict he could be, but he wasn't always a grouch. I knew him on many different levels, and most recently, as a fellow Christian minister. God changes people's lives for the better, and Tom changed a lot after he became a born-again Christian in the early 1980s. FYI, even at his age, he still serves in a volunteer capacity at the church he attends in Murietta, Calif., and also lectures at the nearby Calvary Chapel Bible College regularly. I hope I have that kind of energy into my 80s!

Clearly, Bernard Gusman has taken Punahou's tennis program to new levels during his tenure, and has brought his own innovations to help modernize how the game is now taught and coached, worldwide. Yet, as in many other fields of business, Punahou's program stands on the shoulders of those who've gone before us, and Tom Mauch's efforts cannot go unrecognized. I'm sure others, such as Lee Couillard (who essentially took my place at Punahou, after I entered full-time ministry), Rick Fried, and other old-timers can provide many more stories. Regardless of the field, not everyone appreciates pioneers during their lifetime, and it would be nice for the USTA to acknowledge Tom for the trail-blazing he did so many years ago for tennis here in Hawaii.

ONE OF FIRST USPTA PROS OVERCAME OBSTACLES TO PREVAIL IN TENNIS AND LIFE

Submitted by Carol Gilliford, daughter-in-law of Winnie Gilliford

Winnie Gilliford was a prominent, well-respected name in the Philadelphia tennis world. She taught individual players and coached teams of all sizes, ages and abilities for 57 years. Although she enjoyed a long and illustrious career in the Philadelphia area, it wasn't always a smooth journey.

Winnie Gilliford

Winnie Gilliford was born on October 16, 1919, with spina bifida and spent her life with a her right leg much smaller than her left, which required that she wear special built-up sneakers and shoes to compensate. She also had chronic back pain. Later in life she battled bladder and breast cancer. This might have discouraged a less staunch individual but her mother had the philosophy of "raising the child not the disability" and Winnie always said that "any success that I achieved in my lifetime can be attributed to her influence. There wasn't anything that she thought I couldn't try." So at a young age, Winnie was exposed to physically challenging sports and encouraged to try everything. She learned early that a regimen of exercise and therapy could minimize her disabilities. At age 13, she took up tennis as physical therapy.

Winnie joined the USPTA in 1963 and was the 19th woman to join the new organization. Because of being a single mother, she worked seven days a week as a club tennis professional for many years to give her three sons a stable home life.

Throughout her teaching career, her "people skills" and tennis prowess became legendary in the Philadelphia area. One former pupil said, "She possesses all the qualities of royalty — beauty, grace, patience, endurance and savvy." Winnie's ability to diagnose a tennis problem and articulate a solution had students flocking to her for lessons.

Winnie started her tennis career at Martin's Dam Club where she made it her responsibility to introduce players to one another and to arrange games with people of more or less equal abilities. An amazing ability to remember names and faces, and an understanding of players' ability levels helped to endear her to everyone.

After 16 years at Martin's Dam, Winnie was wooed away to the historic Merion Cricket Club to serve as the Head Professional and Athletic Director, a prestigious job for anyone, but a bright feather in the cap of a woman. Winnie took great pride in being part of the recorded history of Merion. The club had never hired a female head professional for any of its racquet sports, and still has not since Winnie's retirement. She served at the Merion Cricket Club for eight years, retiring in 1984.

In addition to Winnie's club assignments, which included being the first professional at Waynesborough Country Club and six years coaching Haverford Tennis Club, she also has coached suburban Philadelphia college and high school teams, beginning with Eastern College (now Eastern University) men and women. Following her retirement from Merion, she coached the Villa Maria Academy tennis team for 10 years, with one-year stints coaching Linden Hall girls and Radnor High School boys.

After a long Tennis Head Professional career, Winnie started teaching wheelchair-bound and physically challenged students the game of tennis. One of her students was born with no thumbs, so she adapted the grip on the racquet so that the student could hold it between her index and second fingers.

Winnie showed through her positive attitude and love of tennis that anyone, regardless of their physical challenges, can learn to play the only game with "love" in it.

Winnie found time after retirement to write a book called: "Winnie's Wisdom: Great Tennis Truths From An 'Old' Pro."

Winnie was honored many times over the years for her civic work and for her dedication to the tennis work she did with her physically challenged pupils. Her awards and accolades included being written up in the Philadelphia Inquirer Newspaper and being recognized by the USPTA with the President's Award.

The Rollie Mueller Family Three Generations of USPTA Tennis Professionals

Submitted by Jackie Mueller Egelhoff

A pioneer of tennis in Wisconsin is Rollie Mueller. Born in Milwaukee in 1918. Even though Rollie learned the game at a young age at a local park and went on to play on his high school team, Rollie's life was service to the game of tennis. At age 21 he became a tennis professional. In 1945 he bought and managed The Washington Tennis Club where he introduced the game to his two daughters and many others. He organized the County Parks Program, organized the first meeting of Wisconsin teaching pros and served on The USPTA Midwest executive board in the 1950s. He was president of the Wisconsin Tennis Association and was an active member for many years. Rollie was an active USTA umpire for more that 40 years. The Rollie Mueller family was USTA Midwest Family of the Year in 1978. In 1988 he received his 40-year USPTA service award, serving 42 years overall.

Daughter, Barbara Mueller, USPTA tennis professional for 40 years, is teaching at the Moorland Tennis Center, for the Oconomowoc Park and Recreation and the Advantage Wisconsin Adaptive/Wheelchair tennis programs. Barbara was a highly ranked, international player with over 55 singles and doubles national titles. Barbara is a former coach of the Ohio State Women's tennis team. Barbara was the USPTA Midwest Player of the Year in 1994. She was inducted into The USTA Midwest Hall of Fame in 2008.

Daughter Jackie Mueller Egelhoff, USPTA tennis professional is the Manager/Head Pro at The River Tennis Club in Milwaukee, Wis. Jackie is the Homestead High School boys' and girls' varsity coach since 1980. She is co-director of Advantage Wisconsin Adaptive/Wheelchair tennis programs since 1990. Jackie received the USPTA National High School Coach award in 2011.

L-R: Barbara Mueller, Jackie Mueller Egelhoff and Brian Egelhoff, the second and third generation of tennis professionals. Jackie holds a plaque honoring patriarch Rollie Mueller.

Bill Tym (left) and Rollie Mueller at a USPTA convention, 1975

Grandson, Brian Egelhoff, USPTA tennis professional is a teaching pro in Mequon, Wis. Brian is the co-director of The Advantage Wisconsin Adaptive/Wheelchair tennis programs since 1990. He received the Wisconsin Tennis Association Rollie Mueller Presidents Award in 1997, the USPTA Midwest Fay Tooley Award and the USPTA National Star Award in 2009.

TENNIS ALL IN THE EDLES FAMILY

By Mark Winters

(The following article appeared in the May 8, 2007 edition of the Long Beach, Calif. Press-Telegram)

Special to the Press-Telegram

In Long Beach tennis circles, many are aware of the unobtrusive role played by Dominador Edles and his wife, Florence.

Over the years their accomplishments are impressive. Never having been interested in claim, it's ironic that the Edles family's (including sons Joe and Mike and daughter Becky Edles-Rye) commitment was recognized when they were named the 2006 Southern California Tennis Association Family of the Year.

"We were very excited," Dominador said. "It was really a thrill. The whole family is involved with tennis all the time."

Joe, the Director of Tennis at Pinehurst Country Club in Denver, came to the award presentation at the Traus Stadium Clubhouse-UCLA.

"It was the first time we were all together (without spouses and children) in a long time," he said. "It was like when we were kids."

Earning the honor involves dedication and making a difference locally.

Dominador and Florence, both retired, have had a long-time passion for the game. While in the service, Dominador became an All-Navy tennis player.

Later, he was a machinist at MacDonnell/Douglas. Florence, an elementary school teacher in the Philippines, enjoyed a part-time career in catalogue sales at Sears while raising the children.

"When I was a kid, I was a ball boy in the Philippines," Dominador said. "I taught myself to play on a wall. When I was in the Navy, I played when I got off the ship. Later, I would always take the kids to the park.

"Since my wife retired, she has become a good player. She is really talented."

"We really didn't know mom played," Joe admitted. "She was always taking care of us."

Dominador and Florence spent almost 10 years helping the Long Beach Tennis Patrons succeed. Whether it was the Saturday morning workouts, clinics or tournaments, they were in the forefront, making sure youngsters had an opportunity to become better.

"The Patrons used Long Beach City College, El Dorado Park, Billie Jean King Tennis Center (formerly called Recreation Park)," Edles-Rye said. "The pros worked with juniors on stroke development, footwork and match play. They came from various facilities in Long Beach and really made a difference.

"The camaraderie among the juniors, pros and parents was fantastic. I should also mention the kindness of people like Dr. Ben

The Edles family (from left), Joe, Becky, Dominador, Florence and Michael, after being named Family of the Year by the Southern California Tennis Association.

Parks and Jack Lynch, who would pick up the Edles kids from across town and bring us to weekly workouts on the eastside."

Florence Edles shows her form while participating in the 2012 Michael Chang Clinic

The setting nurtured friendships.

"The parents did a lot of carpooling to tournaments in Southern California because first matches often began at 8 a.m. and the last ones were scheduled at 4 or 5 p.m." Edles-Rye said. "My mother was always carpooling Long Beach kids. She would feed them, too.

"When the Long Beach Junior Tournament took place (in March), she arranged housing for players who didn't live in the area."

While Dominador and Florence are thrilled with the SCTA honor, they are more comfortable talking about their children. Quickly, they point out that they have benefited from being involved in tennis. Joe played at SMU, Mike at UC Irvine and Becky at San Diego State.

2016 update: A fourth generation of the family, Becky Edles-Rye's son Rob, played collegiate tennis at Whitman College before serving as assistant coach at Coe College from 2010-12 and head coach at Knox College 2013-14. Rob finished his second year as assistant tournament director of the Michael Chang Tennis Classic. Mike Edles' daughter Ellie played collegiate tennis at UC–Davis, was assistant coach for two years at Cal Poly–San Luis Obispo and is currently assistant tennis coach at Middlebury College in Vermont.

And matriarch Florence? At the age of 88, she still plays tennis 2–3 times a week.

Transition from USPLTA to USPTA

By Mary P. Johnsen

This protege of Hazel Hotchkiss Wightman and Bill Hinchliff (Yale) joined the U.S. Professional Lawn Tennis Assn. in 1968. Being one of the very few female members, I was soon elected secretary of the Eastern PLTA group and found myself digging out the association records from paper bags stored in Mickey Phillip's closet.

Tex Schwab, head man, ran a travel company. At that time there were no paid officers, only volunteers, and some of us were overloaded. I worked full time and managed a household with four sons while being on the board, on the testing committee with George Bacso and lecture circuit with Charlie Lundgren. It occurred to me that the organization needed a full-time professional staff.

Having first met Don Dell when he was at Yale, I presumed to run the concept of an all-new association or an overhauled USPLTA by him. He stated that the overhaul was in his opinion the best approach due to the strength and longevity of the name.

My Army officer husband was reassigned to the Pentagon (1971) so I turned over the records and took an observer's seat to watch as exactly what should have happened did.

In 1972 when I was head pro at the Fairfax Racquet Club, I met a young man named John Embree. Later, when conducting a convention for the International Racquet Sports Association, I dealt with the same John Embree when he was the director of racquet sports at the Hilton Hotel in New Orleans. The fond relationship has lasted for over 40 years.

Henry Tiberio A 93-year-old Treasure at Beverly Golf & Tennis

(The following article was published in 2015 "Senior Tennis" and written by editor Dick Ernst. It has been updated by the editor.)

Former USTA New England president Harry Kirsch says, "Henry Tiberio is rightfully one of the most respected individuals in the New England tennis community. He made a major contribution to our game not only as an outstanding competitor but as a tennis teacher, coach, tournament director and organizer. For the past three years he won the U.S. National Grass Court tournament in the over 90 competition in both singles and doubles. His tennis prowess was exceeded only by his courage and determination in the 2015 final, when he upset the favorite, Fred Kowaleski, on his ninth match point in a dramatic third-set tiebreaker."

Henry Tiberio was about 15 years of age when his rowing team paused for a break near the tennis courts at Lake Quannapowitt in Wakefield (MA). The instant he caught sight of New England's Nos. 1 and 3 tennis players trading shots, Tiberio was mesmerized. He lingered for 45 minutes, long enough to be kicked off the team.

Now 93, Tiberio's love of tennis is still going strong. The Beverly resident has been a certified teaching pro of the U.S. Professional Tennis Association since 1974, has compiled dozens of USTA New England No. 1 rankings in singles and doubles and has several national top 10 singles rankings in various age divisions. He was inducted into the USTA New England Tennis Hall of Fame in 1997.

When not competing, Tiberio has coordinated USTA senior and super senior leagues at Bass River Tennis Club in Beverly, often giving lessons and working with seniors. He also has run men's round robins, singles clinics and senior socials and does racquet stringing and grip work.

Mike LaPierre, general manager of Bass River Tennis, relates how he has "really come to admire and appreciate Henry's passion for the game; he works tirelessly to develop programs and encourages everyone to enjoy the game and to strive to improve. He loves to compete himself and likes to see others play competitive matches. Henry inspires me every day to work hard for tennis. As I tell him all the time, I hope to be just like him when I grow up."

Ed LeDuc, the team coordinator who has taught at Bass River since 1974, has known Tiberio for more than 30 years. "Henry is

totally, absolutely dedicated to the game," noting that "his greatest asset as a player is his ability to still run like a deer while keeping the ball in play.

"He's always thinking about tennis, playing tennis, encouraging others to play and filling in with every group he can. He knows all the USTA results, he follows every match on TV and he generally has an all-encompassing obsession with tennis." LeDuc added: "He's very attentive to his work and is always on the ball. He's just astonishing."

Ninety-three year old Irving Levine of Rehoboth (MS) has played doubles with Henry for about 20 years. Irv notes that Henry has a good serve, solid backcourt and midcourt games, and an uncanny ability to anticipate shots and respond accordingly. Levine also notes that Tiberio "is very polite, but underneath it all is a fierce competitor. All of us who've been working all our lives had to play tennis as an aside. For years, he's been developing all these senior leagues and following them very carefully. He's giving back to the game through service."

After that day at the lake in Wakefield, Henry dedicated himself to becoming as good as the players he admired. Even by running around every backhand to hit a forehand, he played No. 1 for Wakefield High in his senior year. At Duke University, he was a top intramural player who also played doubles for the Blue Devils varsity team.

Tiberio continued to play while earning a master's degree from Boston University, serving in the U.S. Navy and raising a son and three daughters with Fran, his wife of 65 years. He worked for the Massachusetts Department of Social Services for 36 years until his retirement in 1985. Since then, tennis has become his second career. "It was tough, all those years of working with child abuse and neglect," Tiberio said. "I don't know what I would have done without tennis. But for this work and caring about kids and their families in need, I received the governor's award for meritorious service."

Tiberio won his first local tournament in a five-set duel in Greenfield (MA) in 1951 and earned a career high No. 11 ranking in New England in Open Men's singles. However, he said the turning point in his playing career was winning a 50-and-over tournament at age 59 and going on to achieve the top ranking in that age division later in the year. "I got a lot of confidence from that win," but Tiberio claims his best memory was a straight-set loss to Bobby Riggs in a national amateur tourney held at the International Tennis Hall of Fame in Newport (RI) in the 1970s.

Henry adds "in that match we were supposed to play on grass, but it rained so they moved us indoors. It was a very hot and humid day, and there was no air conditioning, but I played as hard as I could. At one point, Bobby hit a drop shot that I got with my backhand and sliced crosscourt. I was pleased when he applauded my winner, but the match was over quickly."

A 5'6" right-handed Tiberio still plays the grinding, backcourt game that he honed on clay courts during his youth-although he acknowledges that the greatest weapon in ultra-senior tennis is the drop shot. He has never required surgery and does not wear braces, and favors the forgiving playing surfaces of clay and grass. "It's mostly about health at our age," he said, "because we're not going to learn anymore."

A Beverly resident for 65 years, the old United Shoe CC, now known as Beverly Golf & Tennis, will always hold a special place in Tiberio's heart. First and foremost, it was where he met the love of his life, Fran, who caught his eye almost as quickly as the 12 pristine clay courts that line McKay Street. Over the years he's spent countless hours on those baselines with everyone from Fran to his several grandchildren. He vividly recalls the glory days when Beverly was the perennial host for the Massachusetts state championship.

"Back then the only other club that had 12 clay courts was Longwood," Tiberio says with a wistful smile surveying the courts, "now we are down to 10, thanks to the needs of the golf division. There was an area right over there where Bud Collins and the other writers would sit and report on all the matches. I think it is absolutely great what Michael LaPierre has been able to do over here."

Tiberio won his first national title, the USTA national Men's 85 Clay Court Championship at Pinehurst, N.C., in 2007. While he has never taken a tennis lesson himself, Tiberio remains committed to helping others improve their games. In addition to his part-time teaching duties at Bass River, Henry formerly coached the Hamilton-Wenham Regional High School girls team and intramurals for Wenham Middle School. Today, Henry enjoys working with the senior and super senior teams at Bass River which he calls "the center of senior tennis," although the club offers tennis programs for all ages and abilities.

"Our seniors are too good for me to coach, so I just keep after them for inspiration," he said. "I get a lot of satisfaction when our teams go to nationals. I tell them to bring the word across the nation that New England has good players. It was different when we didn't have indoor courts for winter play, but now New England players are true contenders."

It is Tiberio, however, who inspires all who embrace tennis as the sport for a lifetime. He has been training for clay and grass court tournaments this past summer with his ultimate goal of beating his career-best No. 3 national ranking achieved in the 70's division. Henry notes that there is always a new kid coming up and in a few more years, that could be me all over again. Three years into the 90's division Tiberio has been awarded the National Team Doubles No. 1 Certificate for 2012, 2013 and 2014.

LET'S DO OUR JOB COMPLETELY

By Bill Tym

(The following article appeared in the USPTA National Newsletter November/December 1982 and was submitted by Bill Tym.)

I love the game of tennis. For the past 30 years it has been good to me, whether I was involved in playing, coaching, or administration. Time prohibits my detailing how much I have gained from the game.

As with most things we hold dear and cherish, there is one major aspect of the game that annoys me. My pet peeve is to observe obnoxious or unacceptable behavior on court. Competition is very often a two-edged sword. One minute it brings out the best in us, but just as quickly, it can bring out the worst.

In my travels around the country I've realized that there is too little of the best and too much of the worst (and not just on TV). Court behavior has been a popular topic since men were competing in long white pants. Unfortunately, it is like the weather — an academic topic everyone talks about it, but nobody seems to be able to do anything about it.

This is not for the lack of trying. The USTA adopted an ingenious point penalty system several years ago. But more often than not the point penalty system has proven ineffective because of its lack of quick and consistent enforcement. Tournament officials have attempted to monitor frequent unprofessional behavior of playing pros by levying fines on violators after they have acted inappropriately. In some severe cases, players have been suspended from tournament play for a period of time. These well meaning methods failed to cure the problem they are merely controlling it to varying degrees.

We must go back to the origin of the problem in order to cure it effectively. That is where USPTA Professionals come into the picture. Only we have the power, the influence and the opportunity to eliminate this problem. More important, I believe that we have the responsibility and obligation to deal with this problem.

The current method of policing the matches and penalizing the perpetrators is negative and ineffective in the long run. Unacceptable or non-productive behavior on court will ultimately be eliminated through enlightened and effective coaching by well-trained and responsible teaching professionals.

Each student reflects his professional training on court. I agree that the top moneymakers in the game have an influence on your young players. However, nobody has a greater influence on a player than his or her coach or professional. It is easy to blame a student's bad behavior on parents, other players, and the system. Let's have the courage to be honest **WE** are responsible! Just as we are responsible for a student's stroke technique and footwork, we are equally responsible for his or her actions on the court. If our goal is to help each student reach his/her potential, then each student must learn to control his emotions as well as he controls his racquet.

The well-coached, or enlightened student understands the implications of negative behavior on court. He realizes that his ultimate potential is reached through discipline and control

control of the ball and control of the mind. Any student who strives toward his potential knows that psychological and physi-

Jack Kramer (left) and Bill Tym enjoy a light moment at a National Tennis Trade Show in Anaheim, CA.

ological control are linked closely together at the highest levels of the game.

Frustration is not the result of missing a shot. Frustration is the result of not being able to diagnose the problem and then correct it. I firmly believe that there are no emotional players and composed players-there are only well trained players and poorly trained players.

Although I readily accept my responsibility as a coach and professional, I do believe that the non-coaching rule in tennis prevents us from doing our job completely. The non-coaching rule in tennis today is one of the greatest roadblocks to eliminating the behavior problem. It is also ridiculous because it is unenforceable.

In other sports, coaches take an active role during competition. Ironically, the only time coaching is actively allowed in tennis is during Davis Cup competition. By the time a player reaches Davis Cup level, he probably doesn't need any coaching! He needs it most at an early stage of development when direction and support are most effective, when frustration lies close to the surface and dealing with each problem that arises is a new experience.

If coaching is acceptable at the Davis Cup level, let's be consistent and make it acceptable at all levels of competition. I'm not suggesting a change in the basic rules because no major change is necessary. The 90-second break between the odd games is an ideal time to allow coaching.

With this simple change of rules we could take two giant steps forward. We, as coaches, could eventually eliminate the unacceptable court behavior that now spoils the game, and by doing so, help our players reach their potential much more rapidly.

PAM AND DAVID LIPPY BEST MATCH EVER!"

Submitted by Pam Lippy, USPTA Elite Professional

Our story began on a very frigid Cleveland, Ohio, winter night in December 1996. There was an annual fundraising event that

Pam and David Lippy

showcased bachelors and bachelorettes. Each participant was required to make a $100 donation and write a personal bio for the all to read in the Ad book. The guests paid an entry fee to attend the event and purchased raffle tickets in the hopes of winning a date with one of the eligible bachelor or bachelorettes! The purpose of the event was to raise money for a worthy cause, providing tuition assistance for under privileged children to attend summer camp.

I was a "single 30-something teaching-tennis professional." Instead of making a financial donation, the event coordinators allowed me to donate $100 worth of tennis lessons to the silent auction! I wanted my bio to describe me without reading like a personal ad (these were still the days of print advertising)!

My bio read:

NEEDED IMMEDIATELY: A NON-SMOKING MIXED DOUBLES PARTNER! HE MUST HAVE NET HEIGHT AND BE ABLE TO SWING A RACQUET! GAME PLAN IS SMASHING SERVES AND BIG RETURNS! VICTORY CELEBRATION IS TO WINE AND DINE! THE BALL IS IN YOUR COURT!

The enchanted evening went by very quickly and at the end of the night the lucky winners were drawn! Over 30 bachelor and bachelorettes drew names out of numbered boxes. Smiles and pleasantries were exchanged by all. As the evening wrapped up, the participants were given the numbered box that corresponded to their individual bio. The excitement continued as I returned home and found five raffle cards in my box from one of the bachelors. On one of the cards was a hand written message saying that he played tennis!

I picked up the phone and called him to thank him for his generous donation to a very worthy cause. I also asked him to be my guest in a co-ed group lesson I was teaching that weekend. He gladly accepted!

Twenty years later, we are still a non-smoking mixed doubles team! We have added two tennis stars to our home court. We cause quite a racquet on the local circuit and continue to serve love!

LITERATURE FOR TENNIS LOVERS BY USPTA PROS

Some USPTA members can use a keyboard as well as they can a racquet. Enjoy this excerpt from a published work by a USPTA professional.

SPLENDOR ON THE GRASS

By Peter Fiore

(The following short story was published in the book "Keep the Ball in Front of You," 2013, Mushroom Press)

A morning in early September. Bright skies, sparkling air. Driving up Ocean Avenue from our B&B in Avon-on-the-Sea to Sea Bright, New Jersey, where I have an 11 o'clock match at the Sea Bright Lawn Tennis Club, the third oldest in the country, against Michael Ely in The National Men's 65 Grass Court Championships. Like driving thru parts of Greenwich or Newport. Long plush lawns and baronial houses. Three years ago the guys at Rockaway, where the 60's Grasscourts are held, were still telling stories of seeing the smoke rising from The Towers on the edge of the flat landscape on a morning so much like this and wondering if they should stay and play, or go home.

You never forget these things.

Ely is a Sea Bright Lawn Tennis Club member who lives in Calistoga, California, a relief if you subscribe to Henry's theory that the further a player travels, the better he is. He's visiting, maybe spending a month by the ocean, on the grass. "You shouldn't have any problem with him," Claude Green tells me. I haven't seen Claude in 25 years when he'd thrashed me, love and one, on the grass at Forest Hills. Still, when Ely called at 10:30 and said he was out at the Open, I was annoyed. I'd known lots of players like Ely on the circuit and in the clubs. Smug in their own arrogance, addicted to their whims. I'd made sure to eat early enough so as not to have a load of coffee and eggs bouncing around my belly when I stepped on the court, got myself mentally and physically ready to play at a certain time and even though I knew the winner had to play again at 3, I was eager to play the match. I'd been practicing on the grass, and my body felt light and strong, ready to go. I was eager for the ball. Now I had to sit around and watch, stretch and fidget.

A great veranda, the length of the clubhouse, looks out onto the grass courts. A gabled roof and a large clock at the highest peak. Pictures on the walls inside date back to the 20s—Big Bill, Little Billie Johnston, Elsworth Vines and Jack Kramer when they were young and had wings on their feet. I found a fig tree in the back and plucked off a couple to keep up my energy level. They were dark and firm, almost ripe.

We'd all done a lot of waiting in Maryland for the Atlantic Coast Cup matches in July. More matches than available courts. We were scheduled for 1:30 and didn't get on till close to 4. We stretched, told old war stories and watched. I told the guys about waiting to play American Tennis Association matches 30 years ago in Crotona Park in the Bronx. You waited hours to play and then, if you won, had to play matches back to back. Once I played three in the same day. Ken Murphy, the Tournament Director here at Sea Bright for the last seven years, a small martinet of a man with a friendly outlook, gets Mark Forrester, my 3 o'clock, to start at 2. I grabbed a turkey on a Portuguese roll, ate half and offered the other to Henry who was showering after his first round loss to Bob Anderson. A couple of Eastern players told me I had a good chance against Forrester, that he was mainly a clay court player. I was anything but, though I'd started out as a retriever in the Bronx when I began playing 33 years ago. But balls hardly bounced waist high on grass and the bounce was often unpredictable so you always wanted to be moving in, forcing the issue with underspin to make the ball stay even lower. The grass suited my attacking style of play just fine.

Who's your second match against?" Henry asked.

"A fellow named Mark Forrester from Moorestown."

"He's a real good player."

Henry reminded me Forrester was the number one seed at Morristown and played second singles for Middle States in Maryland, where Henry and I'd been teammates. Mark had taken a set from Gus Castillo who'd beaten Henry love and three and played the tour back in his day. I remembered Forrester had lost in the first round at Morristown to Dennis Lynch who'd traveled down from New Hampshire with his wicked backhand. They'd played on the court next to the one I was losing two and five to Roy Anderson, a former number one player from Princeton. There'd been a lot of friendly talk drifting over from that match but I'd had my hands full with Roy to notice much of the way Mark played.

Mark Forrester is a distinguished looking former Ivy Leaguer or maybe he went to Fordham—about 5' 8" or 9," maybe 160 lbs. and absolutely trim. He could be a country lawyer, a poet-doctor, or somebody's favorite grandfather. He has a strong upper body. On the grass I quickly see he has a clay court mentality. He hardly ventures near the net and though his groundies are solid when I hit him a hard slice off my forehand, he has trouble picking it up. He moves well side to side and his easy manner helps me relax. I take most of my warm-ups at the net, I don't plan on spending much time on the baseline. I'd recently come across a quote from Bobby Riggs that stuck in my head. "You should only hit 2 or 3 ground strokes per point," he's reported to have said. That's fine by me. Later, on one of the changeovers, I repeated it to Mark and he told me Riggs had bet against himself in the Billie Jean King match and actually threw the match.

"At heart Riggs was a riverboat gambler disguised in white shorts."

"What a disguise. He was a great tennis player."

Mark wins the toss and decides to serve. I choose the side with the sun so I don't have to serve the first time into it. I actually prefer to receive first, allowing me to play my way into the match and go for the early break. On the first point I get a second serve to my forehand and hit a drop shot winner. Four points later the opening break is mine on a forehand volley into the open court. On my serve I hit a high percentage of first serves into Mark's backhand, in close to his body and then punch away the volley or wait in no man's land for a ball I can hit the forehand vertical slice cross-court or the inside-out sweep—the shot my doubles partner, Larry Greller, says separates me from other players—into the backhand corner. The drop shot always lurks. Later on in the match Mark's returns would have more bite and penetration but early on he coughs up a lot. I go up 4-0, 5-2. I'm playing right on the edge of my athletic ability, doing what I do best. Moving quickly to set up my forehand in the middle of the court, volleying crisply and not missing overheads. I'm even diving for shots, picking one up just before it hits the turf and dropping it off the top of the net into Mark's court.

"Look how good you are!" Mark says.

"That's a beer I owe you."

On the changeover Mark tells me how when he played Gus Castillo in Maryland, he'd compliment his good shots in Spanish. Mark says, "Gus grunted, 'No hablo.' He wasn't any fun." We switch sides and Mark breaks me for 3-5, after a number of stressful deuces and ads. He's stepping into my serves and following his returns to net. Maybe I'm getting a little tired but I know I have to break him right back or face dire consequences.

Grass courts are moveable. Grounds crews will regularly move a court ten feet to the side and another six to eight feet in, to prevent the baselines from getting too much wear—the baselines at the Germantown Cricket Club by this time of year have become batter's boxes, completely worn down to the soil. A grounds keeper will then spray the old lines a lime green to blend in with the grass so as not to be confused with the chalk lines of the court being played on. But you still see where they were. Such was the case of Court 11. Earlier in the match, on a game point, Mark had hit an inside out forehand approach which raised the chalk in my backhand corner. On the changeover he showed me how his ball might have raised the chalk from an old line outside the court. "Those old lines can be distracting," he'd said.

But I'd been using those old lines six feet inside the baseline as benchmarks to position myself on the returns. Now I step inside them and when Mark tries to advance he finds the ball on him before he has time to get set up for the volley and this gives me room to pass on the next shot. All second serves are attacked relentlessly. I move almost three steps to my left, advertising my forehand, and Mark knows if he doesn't get the ball wide to my forehand or squeeze it into the small space on my backhand—both high risk second serves—he'll have to deal with a hard slice into his backhand corner or a drop to his forehand. This strategy will produce double faults at any level, and sure enough at 30-all Marks hits the second serve wide of the center service line. One more forehand return ends the first set.

But it's taken an enormous mental and physical effort. And I feel depleted.

Usually when I warm up my serve, I hit one underhand serve just to let my opponent know I have it. I had forgotten to do so for this match. And so at the beginning of the second set, I hold up my left hand with the ball in it and announce, "This doesn't count." Mark's a little puzzled and then I throw over the underhand serve, "I just wanted you to know I have it and I may use it." Mark nods in appreciation. It's wonderful being out in the sun, on the sweet smelling grass, with such a companion. Three points later when I do throw in the underhand serve and it squirts out to Mark's left and takes him off the court, he hits the most delicate, soft and unplayable angle that I've ever seen.

The ball goes over the net in both directions, I think, and clap my hands silently on my racket strings in Mark's direction.

He smothers my next serve and I net the volley and Mark has broken me again. This time he backs it up with four very busy serves and very quickly I'm wondering how I'll have anything left for the third set. And the urgency of that moment helps me hold.

Then we trade breaks till 5-all.

At one point I see Larry, standing by the fence watching. The next time I retrieve balls in his direction, I give him the score and say, "I can't hold serve." And before the words are out of my mouth, I remember eight year old Oliver, one of my students at

Sedgewood, saying, "I can't hit my forehand," and my reply, "Not, I can't. I'm having trouble hitting my forehand. It turns the negative into a problem to be solved."

You bring everything to the court.

Melanie Meyers, another student from Sedgewood, had an extra ticket for the first Wednesday of the Open and offered it to me. The lines were impossible, the food tasteless and expensive, but what I remembered most was the way the top players served, loading up the arm and snapping the wrist as they pushed up off the court. As I got tired, my service motion had tightened up. I make a mental note to become more spaghetti-like, let that arm fly and get up on my toes. And I move my grip a hair past an Eastern backhand to get a denser spin. Enough first first serves are effective to get the game, and now Mark has to serve at 5-6.

On the changeover, I towel off, take some water and look out over the green symetrical courts and the other players all in white turning themselves into birds, dipping and soaring as they chase down the yellow balls. I'd been wearing a white hat with the USTA logo in red and blue and "Eastern" printed in blue below the logo. We 'd all received one in Maryland. Gordon Aydelott's invitation to play on Eastern's team actually started this run. The commitment to play also meant the commitment to practice, and I sought out Larry and Henry all summer. Worked out on the grass at the Westchester Country Club thanks to Bid Goswami, the pro who also coaches the Columbia men's team. Played tournaments at some of the neatest venues in the East—the Morristown Field Club and the Arlington Players Club. And now here I was on the brink of something I couldn't put into words.

The hat weighs a couple pounds by now. I pick thru my bag and find a K-Swiss hat Larry Feldman, another student from Sedgewood, had given me along with a bag that contained two pair of shoes, one of which I was wearing, a pair of navy tennis shorts and a white tee shirt with matching trim. Larry always told me he had a friend at K-Swiss and it wasn't necessary to pay him for these. Let's win this one for Larry, I think as I get up to resume play.

Walking back to get the balls for Mark, I hear an argument from the court behind us between Jim Rauch from Annandale, New Jersey. and Alex Fuleki from Parrish, Florida. Rauch, a small round man, is yelling to Bill Poist, a large round man and Fuleki's doubles partner, his hands above his head. "Two and a half hours and not one call did I get on the baseline! Come on!!!" I turn back to the court, those things happen. I'd practiced with Fuleki the previous afternoon and thought he'd called a thin line.

"What's all the commotion about?" Mark asks.

"Bad line calls."

"Too bad."

Mark's first serve is high to my backhand and I can't get enough racket on the ball to get it over the net. 15-love. Then I get a second serve to my forehand but don't hit it with enough authority and Mark sends his backhand down the line. I'm in no man's land but I think I can get to it and then my feet give out beneath me and I go sprawling. Luckily the racket has also leaped free of any body parts. Mark rushes to the net.

"Are you all right?"

"Thanks, I' m fine."

"The Flying Fiore, that's who you are! The Flying Fiore!!"

I can't help but smile as I pick myself up off the court. This is my fourth fall of the match, but the others had been intentional lunges for balls slightly out of reach. This was a flat-out fall, I 'd hit the grass before I could blink…but nothing hurt. On the next point Mark hits an inside out forehand to my backhand corner, but I get there quickly, bend my knees and unload a topspin square-out down the line, two feet from Mark who is unable to play the ball, the hardest I've hit all match.

"Whooa! Where did that come from?"

Somewhere inside of me, I think. Mark hits the second serve long for 30-all. Then I roll the forehand return cross court at an unplayable angle. Match Point. Mark kicks the serve high to my backhand and the ball flies long. I look in under the brim of my hat at another second serve to my forehand and hit it down the line. Mark sends up a fairly deep lob which I hit into the open court. On match point I'm waiting for the serve to my backhand with a forehand grip. I get around the ball and slide it down the line. Mark gives me another ball in the middle of the court which I sweep into his backhand.

And then it's over. Mark's backhand sails wide and just like that, it's over.

Mark jogged to the net. He was smiling. We shook hands with both hands holding hands.

"That was a great match."

"I haven't played that well in years…ever, and you were an absolute pleasure to be on the court with."

"Yes, you too."

We sat in our chairs and breathed it all in. We knew we'd been some place special. The fragrance of the grass—like summer itself—the watery dreamlike sunlight . The joy of running and hitting. The revelation that our partnership had brought out the best in both of us. That this is why we played. Mark sighs and says, almost to himself, "A great afternoon of tennis." I don't ever remember pumping a fist or a fist being pumped. And I didn't understand how big a win this was until I looked up Mark's record on line two days later. It was as long as your arm and he'd been 17 in the country last year. I was happy not to know this when we were playing. Henry would agree. Mark went on to win the consolation and the next morning Ted Hoehn, the No. 5 seed, took me out 2 and love. So who was the winner? Mark got an extra three matches to play.

I took off my shoes and socks and we walked back across the grass together.

Biographies of USPTA Members

The biographies on the following pages were submitted by USPTA members. Neither the USPTA nor the publisher are responsible for the accuracy of the statements made in the biographies.

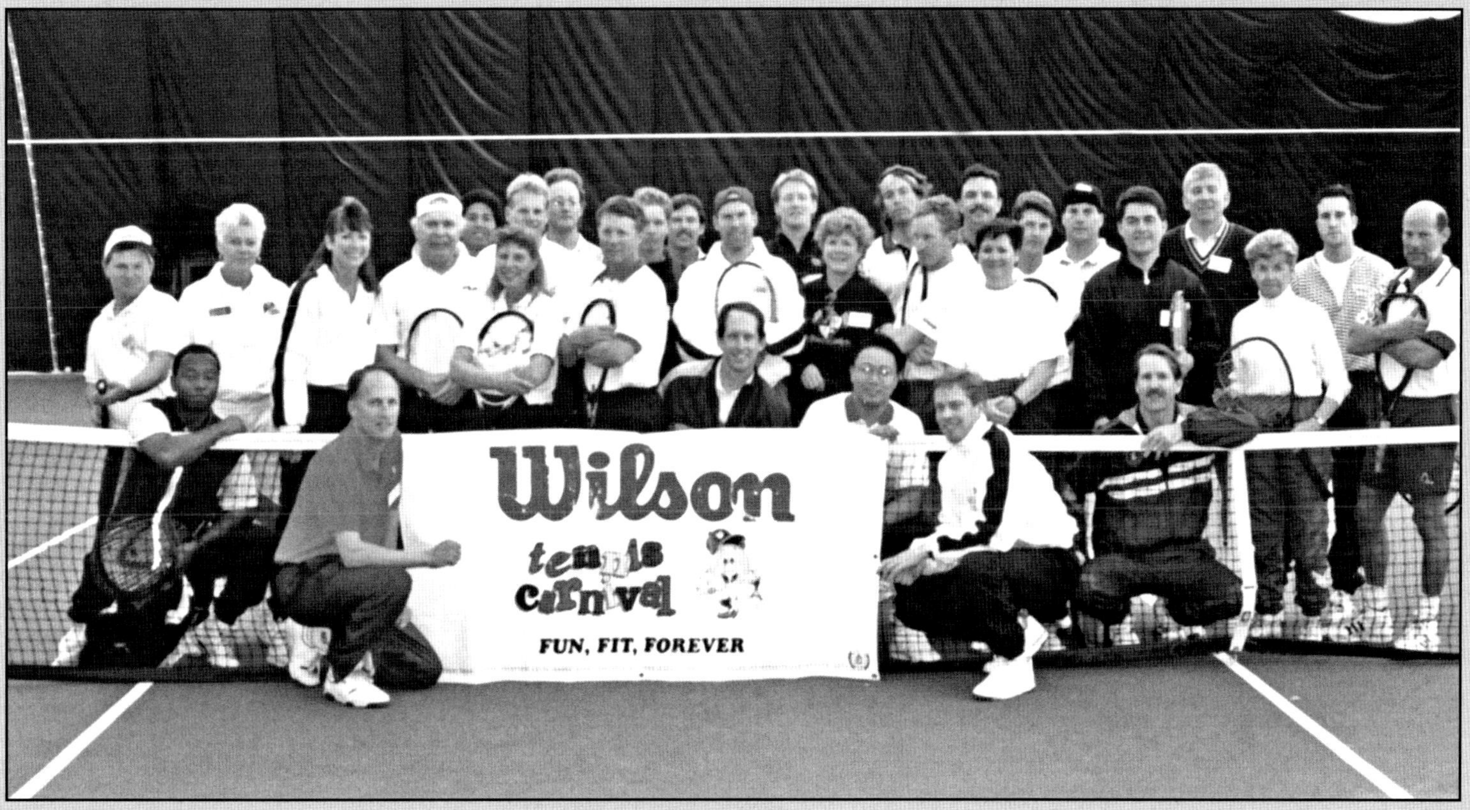

USPTA Pros at the 1995 Intermountain Division Convention

TRENT AARON says Chuck Cooper gave me my first tennis lesson when I was 6 years old, but I did not really take up the game until I was 11. I played some junior tournaments, mostly in the summers, and competed on two high school teams. While playing No. 1 singles for Kentucky Country Day, I met my college tennis coach, Jack Ebel, who offered me a scholarship to Transylvania University with a handshake agreement that he could get me accepted to this academically rigorous school.

I began my college career playing No. 2 singles and No. 1 doubles with Frank Wolny from Germany. I made it to the quarterfinals of the singles in our conference and the finals in doubles, which allowed us to be invited to the NAIA national tournament in Kansas City. In my final two years of college I played No.1 singles and won our conference singles competition individually once and as a team twice.

After college I decided to travel the world and compete on the Satellite tour. After about nine months on the tour, I met an older player, Sylvano Simonne, in Asia. He encouraged me to read Jim Loehr's book *The Mental Game of Tennis*. I also entered a Challenger event in Singapore and had my first real tennis-induced altered state of consciousness, otherwise known as "The Zone." From this experience I earned five ATP doubles points and a world ranking of 950.

After about a year and a half of the Satellites, I returned to the United States and moved to Southern California to earn my master's degree in clinical psychology with an emphasis in family and marriage counseling from Pepperdine University. Since then I have taken advantage of the year-round tennis climate and stiff competition that exists in SoCal. I have been ranked as high as No. 15 in singles and been to the finals of the Open Sectionals in doubles.

On the international level, I began traveling again in 1999 after resigning from a two-year stint as the head men's tennis coach at Loyola Marymount University. I have re-climbed the ATP rankings as high as No. 990 in doubles and am focused on an international singles breakthrough. I am currently No. 176 in the USTA National Men's Open singles rankings. The past three seasons in an effort to improve my clay court skills I have played for No. 1 for German Team in Bad Camberg, Germany, where we have moved up to and held the league in the prestigious Reganali division. Likewise I won the Hessen state 40's German title becoming an American Hessen Miester.

Some pros who have shared their knowledge with me are Robert Lansdorp, Frank McDonald, Chris Post, Del Purcell, Steve Stefanki, Susan and Larry Kline, and Ken and Courtney Hance. But I attribute much of my success to two coaches, John Hillebrand and Pete Fisher, who have worked with me over the past seven years. For 14 years John coached Jimmy Pugh, who achieved a career high world ranking of 37 in singles and won eight grand slams in doubles. Pete was the original mentor of Pete Sampras. In my mind, Jimmy and Pete are the most successful male players to come out of L.A. in the late '80s and '90s.

Pete Fisher continues to work with me on my serve, and I have recently had a breakthrough about the level of physical strength it takes to make it on the ATP tour. These days I am focused on getting more ambidextrous as well as constantly improving my posture with the Egoscue Method and two-handled tennis. Playing Natural Tennis gives me a full body and full brain workout but I can teach one-handled (as well as two-handled) tennis quite well. I have big plans of opening a training facility for posture alignment and fitness training near my home in San Pedro and am looking for a space to do so. This year I became a minority owner of Natural Tennis and have developed the technology to convert one-handle tennis racquets to Natural (two-handled) tennis racquets. Finally, I must mention and thank the Battistones for our 14-year relationship. Brian, Dann and Mark have shared their skills and knowledge and as my preferred training and traveling partners their tenacious work ethic and extremely good nature have hopefully rubbed off on me.

I am still climbing my own mountains as a player, but I also love teaching others who want to maximize their tennis potential

LAILA ABDALA says, "I love my job at Coronado Tennis Center." Laila is a USPTA Elite, Certified Cardio Tennis Instructor. She holds a MA in Sport Counseling and is a Certified Mental Toughness Specialist. She is the Coronado Middle School Tennis Coach. She is a Junior Team Tennis Coordinator. She is a SunDevil for life and a Rafa Nadal fan. She has been a Pac-10 Finalist and FedCup Player for Mexico. Laila uses a one-handed backhand. Laila says, "I wear a lot of sunscreen."

LARRY ABRAMS has been a member in good standing since 1976. He was President, USPTA New England on USPTA Executive Committee and USPTA New England Division Convention Chairman (1986–1990); received USPTA New England Long Term Service Award (1989), NELTA Joseph Dietz Service Award and USPTA New England Professional of the Year (1985 and 1987). Larry obtained Master Professional status Oct. 1, 1989, was USPTA New England Tester of the Year (1988, 1989, 1990).

Larry was co-ranked No. 9 USPTA 40 singles (1985), No. 3 ranked NELTA JV MXD (1986), No. 3 ranked Maine Tennis Association MXD and No. 2 ranked Maine Tennis Association Men's Doubles (1977–1978).

He has been published in *Tennis Magazine, Tennis Directory* and *Racquetball Illustrated.*

Larry was Assistant Tournament Director, Northern California Amateur Championships-Pebble Beach, CA (1975); Assistant Tournament Director, Almaden Wine International Senior Circuit-Pebble Beach, CA (1976–1977) and Assistant to Tournament Director Jim Westhall, ATP Volvo International Tournament Stratton Mountain, Vermont and the first year New Haven, CT, (1987–1990).

Larry was part of promotional team that brought Federation Cup USA vs. Russia to Stowe, Vermont (2007).

He volunteered to provide free junior tennis develop clinics and school programs throughout Vermont, California and St. Croix, U.S. Virgin Islands.

MAURICIO ACHONDO, tennis director at Twin Arbors Athletic Club, coordinates a fully-staffed, year-round tennis program while maintaining an active and successful competitive schedule.

Mauricio was named the USPTA Northern California Division Assistant Professional of the Year in 1989 and in 1997 was nominated for USPTA Regional Pro of the Year.

He earned a full scholarship to Stephen F. Austin State in Texas in 1983 where he a member of the NCAA Div. II All-American Team for singles/doubles and was ITCA Rolex National Singles Champion. He played in over 20 tournaments on the ATP Tour in 1988.

As a coach, over two dozen of his players have earned NCAA scholarships.

At Twin Arbors, Achondo coordinates a fully-staffed, year-round tennis program while coordinating all club events — including sanctioned tournaments — while managing 11 inter-club competitive teams, teaching private and group lessons and holding junior and adult workouts.

ALINA ACKENBOM is USPTA Elite-certified Tennis Professional. Since 1997 Alina has been directing tennis programs at Camp Friendship in Palmyra, VA, which attracts students from all over the world. In 2011 Alina launched Friendship Tennis Academy, dedicated to providing tennis instruction to junior and adult players.

In 2012 Alina joined QuickStart of Central Virginia (QCV), a non-profit organization that promotes, develops and grows tennis in 21 counties in central Virginia. Alina serves as president of QCV. In 2014 Alina joined USTA Mid-Atlantic Junior Development Committee.

Alina is originally from Russia where she learned to play tennis at Olympic School of tennis in Ufa, Russia. She was a nationally ranked junior player competing in numerous national and international tournaments. Alina holds a Master degree in Education from University of Ufa, Russia.

Alina believes one can teach a lot of valuable life skills through the sport of tennis.

A. LEE ADAMS served as the Tennis Professional at the Chevy Chase Club from 1977–2016 (40 years). He previously served as the Head Tennis Professional at the Cleveland Racquet Club (1970–1973) and the Chagrin Valley Racquet Club (1974–1976). Lee served as a Davis Cup Official in 1973. Lee's playing experience includes National Junior, NCAA, USPTA and USTA Championships, earning USTA National Rankings in both singles and doubles. In 2007 Lee, paired with Bill Rublee, reached the finals of the USPTA International 50 and over Championships. Lee served as President of the Middle Atlantic Professional Tennis Association (1983 and 1984) and earned the USPTA rating of Master Professional in 1989. Other honors include Greater Washington Professional of the Year (1982 and 1985), Maryland Professional of the Year (1984 and 2015) and Middle Atlantic Division Professional of the Year (1983).

JANET HOPPS ADKISSON is a member of Intercollegiate Women's Tennis Hall of Fame - ranked in top 10 USTA five times (No. 5, No. 1 in doubles, World top 15, World No. 2 mixed doubles and Wimbledon semi-finalist, two events (1960). Also a member of SU Hall of Fame, Washington Hall of Fame, Pacific Northwest Tennis Hall of Fame with tour wins – 22 doubles titles, nine singles, eight mixed and International Captain for USA (1958–1960).

She ran a tennis camp business (1970–1994), junior camps (1984–1994), consulted on building three clubs. She has coached several top ranking juniors, coached Seattle University Men's/Women's teams (1984–1994) and NAIA Top 10 twice nationally.

USPA offices Janet has held: Secretary-Treasurer/V.P. Head Tester and First Woman Division President in 1979. Janet received her Master Pro rating (1989).

Janet was named by *Sports Illustrated* in Top 500 Athletes of the state of Washington of the century.

Janet and William have seven children and nine grandchildren.

MIKE ALCOTT, USPTA Elite Pro since 1994. Grew up playing tennis on Long Island, NY. Was the youngest camper at sleep away camp in Pennsylvania at age 8. Moved to Texas and played three years in high school at Buna High School and lettered every year. Awarded walk-on scholarship to Lamar University. Began teaching tennis at the Houston Country Club in 1993 and became certified in 1994. In 1999 began teaching at Westside Tennis Club in Houston, TX, where he became involved in working with the events we hosted, such as the US Men's Clay Championships, Davis Cup tie between U.S. and Spain, and the End of the Year Masters Cup in 2003. In 2004 became Head Tennis Pro at The Briar Club and has been teaching lessons there since.

SUSAN ALLSHOUSE, Director of Palm Beach Tennis Associates Inc. in Boynton Beach, FL, has been in the tennis industry for 40+ years. Actively involved in teaching TIP using the ROGY format of play, she also serves as a volunteer for the USTA serving on the Schools Committee and as a member of the Player Development Workshop Faculty. For the USTA Florida Section, she sits on the Board of Directors as Chair of the Youth Tennis Council and the Youth Recreation Tennis Committee, and as a member of the Foundation Grant Committee. One of her proudest achievements is working with Special Olympics Florida and receiving the award for Outstanding Volunteer for Miami Dade County in 2014. With a passion for Youth Tennis, Susan received the USPTA Florida Division/USTA Florida Section 2014 Service Award for leadership and vision in promoting our organizations.

J.D. ALMOND, USPTA Elite Pro, became a tennis professional in 1990. "I was lucky enough to have a tennis professional take a chance on me at a country club in northern Virginia," he says. J.D. has been General Manager at Tuckahoe Recreation Club in McLean, VA, since 2007. He coaches players and teaches group lessons at Sudley Swim and Tennis Club in Manassas, VA, since 1995.

J.D. spends time outside tennis as a father, mentor and coach for his two sons. He enjoys playing on a classic baseball team. "Baseball is my first love and playing baseball as it was played in 1860s gives me a new appreciation for the game." You will find J.D. on a field with the Chesapeake, Potomac and Old Dominion Base Ball Clubs.

He has a master's degree in Sport Facility Management and Sport Coaching from the US Sports Academy in Daphne, AL. J.D. received his undergraduate degree in Business Management and Marketing from Longwood College in Farmerville, VA, in 1987. As a student at Longwood, he competed on the men's varsity tennis team as a walk-on. He was named the MVP in 1986.

In 1999, J.D. received the USPTA Mid-Atlantic High School Coach of the Year Award. He received the Delaney Athletic Conference Tennis Coach of the Year Award in 1995, '96, '98, '99 and 2000, and was 1992 and '93 Concorde District Coach of the Year. In 12 years as a head tennis coach, J.D. has won over 100 matches. In addition to coaching in high school, J.D. coached at the college level with George Mason University. He coached the women's tennis team in 2003-04.

J.D. was married to Sarbra in 2002 and they have two sons, Wyatt Christopher born in 2007 and their other son, Christopher Deyan, born in 2009, was adopted from Bulgaria in the spring of 2012.

DAVID ALTSHULER says his best work as a USPTA professional is his work in raising money for children battling cancer at the Dana Farber Cancer Institute in Boston, MA. The treatment center for children is known as the Jimmy Fund Clinic. He started this fundraiser, known as The Jimmy Fund Tennis Classic in 1990, just one year after he became a certified USPTA tennis professional. This event is held annually on the last Friday in June. To date he has raised just over $980,000. And next year should pass the million dollar mark. He says it is by far the best work that he has ever done and he can only hope that it has made a difference in the lives of these children as they battle this deadly disease. This is truly the work that he is most passionate about. He was honored to receive the first USPTA Lessons For Life Award in 2008 at the national convention held at Marco Island. The USPTA has been a great supporter of this event and his heartfelt thanks go out to them for their gracious generosity over the years. The battle to find a cure continues and hopefully we will see one in the not too distant future.

ARTHUR ANASTOPOULO started playing at the age of 11, spending many hours hitting on the wall and being mentored by Pat and Jack Adams at the Jack Adams tennis center in Charleston.

Arthur worked for the City of Charleston Dept. of Recreation as courts attendant at the age of 12. Arthur was a great all-around athlete playing basketball and had scholarship offers to play college basketball but chose tennis. Arthur had over 100 full scholarship offers to play tennis but chose the University of South Carolina, his home state.

He is one of South Carolina's and the University of South Carolina's most accomplished tennis players. Arthur turned professional in June 1980.

He played the U.S. overseas circuits. During his professional career he played in two Grand Slam events. He returned to South Carolina in 1984 and entered the University of South Carolina School of Law. After finishing his first year of law school he was offered and accepted the head tennis pro position for the city of Charleston and earned his USPTA teaching professional certification.

Arthur was inducted to AHEPA Athletic Hall of Fame, received the key to the City of Charleston, named SCPTA pro of the year in South Carolina and honored as one of the top 25 tennis directors in the nation by Reebok sporting goods.

Arthur and Vangie married in 1986. They have two boys (A.J. and Gus).

BOB ANDERMAN is a New York City native, graduating from Forest Hills High School in 1958. He received a BA and MA from the University of Maryland in 1968 and 1970, respectively.

Anderson has won many national and international tournaments and has held the No. 1 ranking in the USTA many times.

He began his teaching career in 1954. Highlights include head pro and owner of Tennis World, director and designer of the Quince Orchard Tennis and Swim Club, Director of Tennis at Norbeck Country Club, Director of Tennis Columbia Association, tennis pro Circle D, high school tennis coach, secretary of the Maryland Tennis Association and the Mid-Atlantic Division of USPTA, Mid-Atlantic Pro of the Year and Player of the Year and Maryland Pro of the Year.

KIRK ANDERSON is the Director of Coaching Education for the U.S. Tennis Association. He is a USPTA Master Professional and has taught tennis since 1969 in parks, camps, resorts and clubs. He has been at the USTA National office for 20 years and served as one of the original Schools Directors in the Midwest section for six years.

Anderson serves on the ITF Tennis Participation Task Force, the Aspen Institute Project Play initiative and the Special Olympics North America Development Committee. He has published dozens of tennis related articles and authored or co-authored nine books. He was project leader for the six online Coach Youth Tennis courses. Anderson directs a faculty of 67 teaching professionals who have conducted Recreational Coach and 10 and Under Workshops for nearly 100,000 coaches.

Anderson received the International Tennis Hall of Fame Educational Merit award and named Person of the Year by *Racquet Sports Industry* magazine. He was the 2016 USPTA Professional of the Year.

JORGE ANDREW has been the Director of Tennis Operations for the Lexington County Recreation Commission in Lexington, SC, since 2002. He oversees two large state-of-the-art tennis facilities with a total of 51 courts. Jorge is a USPTA Master Professional and PTR International Master Professional, the second person in the world to accomplish the highest certification in both teaching associations. He is also a member of the USTA South Carolina Hall of Fame since 2012.

In 2006 Jorge was named "USPTA Southern Professional of the Year." In 2008 he received the USTA/USPTA Community Service Award. Andrew was USPTA Southern Secretary/Treasurer from 2007 to 2008, and USPTA South Carolina President from 2003 to 2006.

Jorge is former Venezuelan Davis Cup player and captain. He played on the professional tour for more than 10 years, including appearances at all four Grand Slams tournaments. His highest ATP singles ranking was 61st in singles and 69th in doubles.

BRUCE ANGELI, Principal of Bruce C. Angeli LLC, a diversified holding company, has been actively playing tennis since college. He is also the author of "Late Call – Healthy Tennis for the Older Young at Heart," available on Amazon in either Kindle or soft cover formats. Although having taught tennis both in England while in the USAF and back in the U.S. as a civilian, he became USPTA certified in 2009 and is an Elite Professional. In 2001

Bruce Angeli with Domi Cibulkova

he was a 40+ singles finalist in the Connecticut Tennis Classic. He remains active in USTA 4.5 league play as a doubles specialist and coach and currently teaches in the mid-Fairfield County area of Connecticut. One of his proudest tennis achievements is when every high school student he taught made their individual school's tennis team. He holds a Bachelor of Science degree from Emerson College as well as being a licensed commercial pilot with an instrument rating.

NEIL R. ARCHER, USPTA Elite Professional, was introduced to the sport by his father in 1970, ranked as a junior USTA player in Northern California, he eventually played for Butte Community College. Taking a break for 10 years, he returned as a student of the

"modern" game. First professional teaching gig was at Yuba City Racquet Club in northern California. He quickly involved himself in the USPTA with a mission to make teaching pros aware of changes in the game and effect changes into the "modern" teaching of techniques. He rose through the board of Northern Cal's USPTA, eventually earning the Presidential seat. Head Teaching Pro at Millennium Sports Club, Rancho Solano and Head Teaching Professional at Wailea Tennis Club, Maui HI. Currently he's an independent professional on Maui. He wants to thank his wife, Tina, for her sacrifice and support. Dick "Archie" Archer, his dad, "you are my greatest inspiration." ALOHA.

BILL ARICK – 1986 was a life-changing year. At the youthful age of 44 he drove to Portsmouth, VA, and spent a couple days under the critical scrutiny of seasoned USPTA Professionals. He and 20 other hopefuls had their knowledge and proficiency evaluated in business, playing skills and (of course!) all areas of tennis instruction. As the evaluations concluded, he felt like he'd just completed and defended his doctoral degree project, completed his Army Basic Training and OCS and played Connors, Nastase, and McEnroe in the finals of all four Grand Slams in one day. HE BECAME A USPTA PROFESSIONAL and "proud" of it! He has been able to utilize this unique distinction as an avocation through 30 years as the Pro and Director of Tennis at Breton Bay Golf & Country Club in Leonardtown, MD.

In that position and working with Recreation & Parks, the USPTA has provided tennis training and activities for as many as 350 children and adolescents and 200 adults annually. Over 50 high school age program participants have been awarded All Southern Maryland Athletic Conference honors, seven have earned the Most Valuable Conference Player award and at least four players have received college (tennis) scholarships. Most important of all, many of the youth participants have grown to become community, government and military leaders; joining many of adult players who have played before and continue to play into (their) 60s, 70s and 80s! As for me at 73, my court time is mostly playing and watching the youth and adult players learning and playing this lifetime sport, thanks to the opportunity the USPTA gave to me 30 years ago. KEEP PLAYING TENNIS!

WILLIAM "BILL" R. ARONSON is a member of PSIA, PTR AND USPTA. He attended University of Utah (BS in Psychology – 1983); MS and CAGS (1986, counseling athletes), CSPP Fresno (Ph.D., Psychology, 1996), Plymouth State University, NH

(MBA, 2009) and Internship at University of Rochester (APA 1996).

He was Captain in USAF and a former Harry Hopman Tennis Professional. Bill was administrator of Sport Science (USTA). He served as Springfield College Head Men's Tennis Coach. At University of Lowell he was Head Women's Tennis coach. He was also an ITF Clinician. Bill was coach of Maccabiah Games, Uruguay and Australia.

ERICK BAER competed as a top junior in Southern California. In college, his D-I team was nationally ranked seventh. At one point, he was ranked 4th nationally in singles by the USPTA. He once competed in the main draw of the US Open.

Erick was the tennis director at North Ranch Country Club for 17 years. A few years ago, he won the National Senior Hard Court Doubles Championships. Erick likes to gently push his students to be more efficient, be in better shape and to use the latest techniques. We can all enjoy getting better at tennis.

MICHAEL BALDWIN, SR played Varsity Tennis at FSU, 1962, '63. Wrote Master's Thesis on equipment and beginning tennis players, 1969. Received Master's Degree from FSU, 1970. Began professional tennis coaching at The Breakers, Palm Beach, FL, 1974. Built

Centre Courts, Palm Beach, FL, 1979. 1984 was the year for me. Florida Division First Vice President, 19th USPTA Master Professional 1984. USPTA Florida Division Professional of the year, 1984. No. 1 ranked Mens 35 Doubles 1984. Martin Downs named No. 3 rated private tennis club in the U.S. by World Tennis Magazine, 1984. Purchased The Trails Racquet Club in Ormond Beach, FL, 1984. Director of The Outstanding Public Tennis Facility, Patch Reef Park, Boca Raton, FL, 1989. I RETIRED in 2005. North Carolina Community Service Award USPTA North Carolina 2014. Boys' Varsity Tennis Coach, Community School of Naples, FL, 2015–16. I AM STILL RETIRED, "Living the Dream." Tennis has been the Sport for a Lifetime for me!

MITCH BARNES has 30+ years tennis teaching/coaching, including extensive time spent working with national and international level high performance players.

Mitch is owner of MB Management, which provides coaching/teaching to adults,

juniors and sports management. Mitch is a former Head Coach for the High Performance Junior program at Competition Training Center USTA Hawaii Pacific Section. Mitch has served on the Board of Directors of USPTA

Hawaii Division and USTA Hawaii Pacific Section.

Prior to working with USTA, Mitch directed programs for Nick Bollettieri Tennis Academy in Japan, 38 courts tennis academy training juniors and professional players. Mitch was tennis director for Peter Burwash International, a tennis management organization providing tennis professionals to clubs and resorts worldwide. Mitch holds the highest tested certifications with U.S. Professional Tennis Association and Professional Tennis Registry. Mitch also has completed USTA's Sport Science exams level 1 – Foundations of Coaching, level 2A – Motor Learning & Sport Psychology, Level 2B - Sports Physiology & Nutrition and Level 2C - Sports Medicine & Biomechanics.

Mitch has conducted clinics for coaches, adults and juniors throughout Asia; he speaks both English and Japanese. His company has worked with various sports and racquet clubs in Japan providing designs, management and programming. Mitch resides in Honolulu with his wife, Mayumi, and his son, Matthew, currently attending high school at Hawaii Baptist Academy and competing regularly in both singles/doubles tournaments and playing USTA's Junior Team Tennis.

DR. MARTIN G. BAROCH, "Dr.MGB," is owner of Martin Baroch Tennis Academy & Human Performance Center based in Zurich area of Switzerland since 2002 and also globally active tennis coach, educator and consultant. After coaching beginnings in his native Czech Republic's capital Prague (former Czechoslovakia) in the '80s and beginning of '90s, Baroch spent almost 10 years in the Swiss Olympic Training Center in Leukerbad in the Swiss Alps. He has provided coaching and consulting services at professional tournaments and worldwide junior events since the late '80s. Among others he worked with Petr Korda, many players who reached top 100 positions on WTA ranking top juniors as well as world-class Alpine skiers. Baroch, founder of the Czech Professional Tennis Association (CPTA in 1992) and its Education Director, was a long-time USPTA International Head Tester and member of the USPTA National Education Committee; he holds Master Degree in Tennis Coaching from Charles University in Prague and is also certified professional with the Swiss Professional Tennis Association, ICI and PTR.

Baroch, a medical doctor by education, developed and constantly updates his own fully scalable tennis teaching system ©"Dynamic Total Body Tennis" using specially developed DTBT Foam Ball equipment, runs his own educational tennis social network MyTennisWorld.net (since 2007) and produced a worldwide distributed tennis documentary "A Tennis Champion is Born" (1995). In 2003 he explained to the tennis world in the "Last 20% Decide It All" the importance and also the associated challenges (mainly mental) of the full body engagement in all tennis strokes. Here he proved as sub-optimal the official methodologies of many national and international tennis associations. This information and his other seminars presented worldwide (on three continents) over the past two decades caused sustainable change and corrections in the tennis teaching and coaching by the world's leading tennis coaches as well as international and national tennis organizations and subsequently influenced the stroke production in professional and top-level junior tennis. Lately, he developed with TENNIS 3.0 the benchmark for sustainable tennis stroke development. His DVDs released by USPTA: "Technical, tactical and developmental aspects of serves and volleys," "Hip and shoulder activity determine stroke effectiveness and injury probability" and "Dynamic Total Body Tennis – future of the game" are building certain cornerstones of modern tennis training.

In his early years, Baroch, while acting as a conditioning coach for Czech Petr Korda, developed "Medicine Ball Stroke-like Throwing" warm-up and trainings form, which is widely used worldwide today. "Dr.MGB" also calls his own a 300,000+ photo database documenting strokes of practically all leading tennis players of the past 20+ years.

MARIO "MAR" BARRETTE attended Maisonneuve College and majored in marketing in 1976. He played varsity tennis while at Maisonneuve College. He coached at the Quebec Summer Games in 1973 and 1977.

Mario is a certified instructor in tennis, racquetball and squash and has coached for over 35 years.

He was head pro at the Richard Thomson School in Collingwood from 1982 to 1985. In 1979 and 1998 he was the pro at the Inn and Tennis Club at Manitou. Marion was Racquets Director for the Fitness Institute in Mississauga. Barrette was the host instructor at the Rogers Cup in Montreal in 2003.

In 1990 he co-produced the TV series "Tennis, Sport of a Lifetime."

Mario's daughter is Marissa.

DAN BARRIE, Tennis Director at Bahrain Tennis Academy (BTA) in the Kingdom of Bahrain, has been teaching professionally for 20 years. Commencing his teaching career in his native Melbourne, Australia, Dan became locally certified before obtaining USPTA certification in 1999.

In 2000 Dan moved to Bahrain with a vision of raising the standard of tennis there. He obtained USPTA Elite Professional status in 2005 and went on to establish BTA in 2009. During this period he also spent time as Tennis Director at Indian Head Camp, PA and was a hitting partner to professional players, including Rafael Nadal, at the Dubai Tennis Championships.

After regularly attending World Conferences, Dan became the first teaching pro in Bahrain to introduce the ITF's 10 and Under Tennis programs. BTA remains the only academy fully supporting the concept in both training and tournaments. He was also first to introduce Cardio Tennis to the Kingdom.

MIKE BAUGH is currently the Head Tennis Pro at Gateway Golf & Country Club and Head Boys' and Girls' Tennis Coach for Gateway Charter High School in Ft. Myers, FL. Originally from southern Indiana, Mike played for the University of Evansville and

Oakland City University before graduating with a degree in Biology '06 and a Master's in '06. He is the USPTA District 14 Vice President, USPTA U30 National & Florida Marketing Project Team Head, USPTA Florida Social Media Committee member, a part of the USPTA Adaptive Tennis National Committee and FHSTCA Region 14 Director. Mike is also an ambassador for ThanksUSA's Tennis Thanks the Troops scholarship program.

Mike is a Cardio Licensed Provider, USRSA Master Racquet Technician, FHSTCA Master Coach and AHLEI Certified Guest Service Professional.

He was awarded the 2015 USPTA Florida District 14 Pro of the Year award and one of three recipients of the Welsh Winner Circle Scholarship!

JONATHAN K. "J-BECK" BECKER graduated in 2011 from Tyler Junior College '13 (Certificate in Professional Tennis Management) and will graduate from Liberty University in 2018 (BS in Biblical and Educational Studies).

Amateur highlights include Super Champ Qualified in TX, Boy's 14U and 16U divisions. 2010 Texas Section Jr. Team Tennis Sportsmanship Award Winner. 2014 East Texas Major Zone Men's Open Doubles Champion. Ranked as high as 5 in 2014 USTA Texas Men's Open Doubles Ranking. Finished 2014 inside top 20 in USTA Texas Men's Open Doubles Ranking.

Professionally has been Assistant Tennis Professional at Tyler Tennis and Swim Club from 2010 to 2012. Began and currently oversees tennis programs for the city of Jacksonville, TX, from 2013-present. Full-time Assistant Tennis Professional at Cascades Country Club, 2015–2016. Head Assistant Professional at Crown Colony Country Club, 2016. 2014 NETXCTA Board Member and serves on USPTA Texas U30 Recruting Committee.

VIKTORIA "VIKKI" AND ALEXI BEGGS passed the USPTA exam in Carlsbad, CA, in 1986 per the directive of Pancho Segura. Alexi was working for Pancho at LaCosta Spa and Tennis Resort. Pancho mandated his teaching staff become USPTA members. Vikki was playing on the WTA tour and while visiting Alexi, decided to join her in taking the exam. Today they are still active members in the USPTA and are grateful for the many benefits they have received over the years. Examples include having Pancho Segura as my coach and mentor, a stimulating career, the opportunity to travel worldwide and the most wonderful plus a fantastic group of fellow USPTA professionals.

Vikki is a Sports Psychologist, Licensed Mental Health Counselor (L.M.H.C.), State of Florida (MH 4754), National Board of Certified Counselors member.

Career highlights include: USPTA National and World Ranked No. 1 Ladies Singles, USPTA National and World Ranked No. 1 Ladies Doubles with sister Alexi, USPTA National Player of the Year, ITF World Ranked No. 1 Ladies Singles and Ladies Doubles with sister Alexi, USTA Nationally Ranked old Balls in Singles and Doubles, WTA World Ranked.

JUSTIN BEHM was a Baltimore (MD) County High School Champion (1988) and played in Maryland State High School Championships and was 4th place in boys' singles (1988). In 1989 he was a member of Washington College Mens Tennis Team which won the Middle Atlantic States Athletic Collegiate and placed 4th at NCAA Div. III Championships.

From 1989–1993 he was a member of Towson State University Mens Tennis Team which placed second in the East Coast Conference (1990), NCAA Div. I.

Justin is an Elite Professional, being a USPTA member since 1992.

He was Assistant Professional at Ulhrondella Club, Baltimore County, MD, (1988–1995). From 1995-present he is on Pro Staff at Towson, MD, Orchard Indoor Club and from 1996-present, Director of Tennis at Baltimore County's Eagle's Nest Country Club.

In 2005, Justin was ranked No. 1 USTA Maryland Men's 35's Singles.

Justin, wife Julie, son Will and daughter Paige reside in Phoenix, MD.

DUDLEY BELL joined USPTA in 1959 and has been an active member 57 years. He has attended every National Convention except four. Sons David and Peter are also USPTA members. In 1996 the Bells were award USTA New England Family of the Year.

He has coached eight sports, 25 years in tennis and has qualified for six trips to NAIA Tennis Nationals in Kansas City, MO.

He developed the First Tennis Management Bachelors Degree curriculum, directing the program from 1986 through his 1996 retirement. He continues teaching tennis each fall semester. Dudley was a summer professional (40 years) including 25 years at C.C. of Pittsfield, MA.

He was a two-term President of New England Division and Board Member for 25 years.

Lyndon State honored him by naming the Dudley Bell Tennis Center and Museum on campus. Dudley was inducted into LSC Athletic Hall of Fame (1986), New England Basketball Hall of Fame (2009) and recently inducted into Vermont Senior Hall of Fame.

BILL BELSER, the tennis director at Providence Plantation Racquet and Swim Club, is a 30-year Elite USPTA Pro. He has coached all levels from beginners to Grand Slam Champions including Andy Roddick, Greg Rusedski and Aranxta Sanchez-Vicario.

Bill taught tennis all over the world, including Spain, Germany and Austria. He has coached on the pro tour, including at all four Grand Slams for over 15 years.

Bill teaches physical, aggressive and smart tennis, combining the knowledge he has learned from over 35 years of working with the best coaches and players to have played the game.

Three of Bill's players held the record for the fastest serve on the pro tour at one point in their career.

"Bill's ability to teach the serve is second to none. His understanding of the modern game and how to teach it, especially the techniques and mechanics of all the strokes, is extraordinary. He has a unique gift that enables him to bring out the best in his players," Thai Kwiatkowski, former No. 1 on collegerecruiting.com and No. 1 ranked NCAA player, DI.

Bill has presented at numerous international tennis conferences. He is fluent in English, German and Spanish

GERRY BERKHEIMER, Tennis Director at The Jungle Club in Vero Beach, FL–21 years. Has 33 years with the USPTA as an Elite Pro and 40 years total in the tennis business.

Gerry has taught over 20,000 kids and 11,000 adults in his career in clubs, camps, resorts, college and schools; hundreds into high school, college play and beyond. As a player, 2016 is his 51st year and he has celebrated over 339 trophies.

Gerry was No. 1 at Tennessee High School, No. 1 at Carson-Newman College and was a collegiate All-American in singles and doubles. No. 2 in Florida in 1986 in the 25's, No. 1 in the Kentucky Open division in 1990/1991 and was No. 1 in the Florida 45's in 2002.

He started a crisis center, Bristol, TN, 1972; taught tennis to prisoners and worked with foster care kids in Lexington, KY, 1988–1992, and 20 years mentoring Youth Guidance kids in Vero Beach, 1995–2015.

Gerry is an eight-gallon blood donor.

LEE ANN BERNING has been a partner of Wildwood Racquet Club in Fort Wayne, IN since 2000. A USPTA Elite Professional, Lee Ann became the Head Tennis Professional at Wildwood in 1991. Her service to the tennis industry has been extensive, including becoming the first female president in USPTA Midwest Division history and has served on USPTA national committees. She has spoken at several USPTA Midwest Conferences as well as the USPTA World Conference in 1996. Lee Ann has been awarded several professional distinctions including the Indiana USPTA Professional of the Year in 1993 and 1995 and was named the USPTA Midwest Professional of the Year in 2002.

Lee Ann Berning has served as a USTA Indiana District President, USTA Midwest Committee member, USTA Midwest Management Committee member and has served on a number of USTA national committees. She has been a featured speaker at several USTA tennis conferences including the 2002 and 2003 USTA National Tennis Teacher's Conference. She was the recipient of the 1997 USTA Midwest Cap Leighton Award citing her service to the community beyond her livelihood.

In addition, Lee Ann has been inducted into the Valparaiso University Athletic Hall of Fame, the Indiana High School Coaches Hall of Fame. She holds a master's in Administration from Indiana University.

JAY BEWLEY has been the Director of Racquet Sports at Baltimore Country Club since 2003 and has almost 30 years of experience coaching and managing racquet programs. He has been involved on numerous boards and loves giving back to the game that has given him so much. He became a Master Professional at the age of 34, has his Ph.D. in Marketing and Masters in Counseling. Jay is married with 2 daughters.

ASHER J. BIRNBAUM, an honorary member of USPTA for 50 years, founder and original editor/publisher of Tennis Magazine, which became the official monthly publication of USPTA, editor and publisher of USPTA Annual Directory (1970–1972). During the 1960s, involved with USPTA Presidents Bill Lufler and Dave Muir in negotiating unification of disparate regional pro tennis groups into national USPTA organization. Founder of Indoor Tennis Association (now known as the International Health, Racquet and Sportsclub Association). Founding member of US. Tennis Court and Track Builders Association (now known as American Sports Builders Association). Founder of Tennis Horizons (adult tennis clinics in several countries, including a site in Guadalajara, Mexico, led by USPTA tennis pro Ian Crookenden). Tournament promoter, including a Jack Kramer pro tour event in 1966; Australian pros vs. amateur members of the US Davis Cup team–under special sanction from ILTF and USLTA–at Northwestern University, in memory of Olen Parks, director of Wilson Sports tennis division, in 1968 and World Championship Tennis events in Chicago, Milwaukee and New Orleans, from 1969 to 1974. Co-founder of the U.S. Table Tennis Hall of Fame. Active member of the Northbrook (IL) Racquet Club.

DEBBY BLACKBURN, a USPTA member since 1977 holds an Elite Professional certification. Her teaching positions have been varied, to include affiliations with country clubs, community recreation centers, public park facilities, and military bases throughout North Carolina, Arizona and Virginia.

Debby received a Bachelor of Science degree in Elementary Education from Longwood University. Concurrently, she was a member of the Varsity Tennis squad playing the No. 1 doubles position and fluctuating between the No. 1 and No. 2 slots in singles. Her senior year she was honored to be chosen as one of "America's Outstanding College Athletes."

Following her intercollegiate career, she played many North Carolina state sanctioned tournaments achieving rankings in singles and doubles within the top five for several years.

Her other interests include physical fitness, golf, skiing, woodworking and home improvement DIY projects. Debby is married to George, a retired USMC Vietnam Veteran currently employed with MetLife in Cary, NC.

MICHAEL S. BLASS played varsity basketball and ran 440 and mile relay on the high school track team. He graduated from University of North Carolina-Chapel Hill, received doctor of dental surgery degree from Emory University School of Dentistry and practiced adult restorative dentistry in Atlanta (1965–2001). He was associate professor at Emory University School of Dentistry, guest lecturer at University of Pennsylvania School of Dentistry and conducted research for 36 years. He was an elected member of the American Academy of Crown and Bridge Prosthodontics and Honorable Fellow and Life Member of Georgia and American Dental Associations.

Eleanor and Michael Blass

Michael started playing tennis at age 34 and by 40 was playing USTA senior tournaments in doubles and singles, continuing until age 65. He always held a Georgia state ranking in both and in 1992 was ranked No. 2 in Georgia in doubles with best friend/partner, Georgia Tennis Hall of Fame member Joe Becknell, tennis partner for 25 years.

After retiring from dentistry, Michael began teaching tennis full time. He became a staff member at Canton's BridgeMill Tennis Club, where in 2001 a court was dedicated to him, "in appreciation for [his] passion for tennis and dedication to helping those who play." He became a USPTA-certified professional at age 70 and honorary member of the Modern Tennis Methodology Coaches Association in 2015.

Michael has coached many teams to City Championships in ALTA, including two winning women's teams at the AA-1 level.

At 74, Michael teaches six hours of private lessons, five days a week, to players ages 8 to 75. In lieu of payments, students make contributions to the tax-free foundation, Michael Blass Junior Tennis Foundation. Its mission is to support juniors by providing opportunities to develop physically and mentally through tennis. The foundation gives back by providing free private lessons to deserving juniors who desire to excel, but would not be able to experience tennis without financial assistance.

He and his childhood sweetheart, Eleanor (passed away December 2014 after a three-year battle with pancreatic cancer), raised three children.

CHUCK BLECKINGER was taught tennis at an early age when his father, Joe, purchased property that was The Oshkosh Tennis Club. Joe resurrected the courts, reinvented The East Side Tennis Club and ran the Wisconsin Open for Years.

In November 1998 Chuck was inducted in The Fox Valley Tennis Hall Of Fame. In junior tournaments in the 1950s dominating the State Boys 15's and 18's divisions earned him No. 1 ranking in the state in both age divisions.

Joe Bleckinger with children Chuck (left) and Bonnie in front of his business, Joe's Sports Shop

On the Oshkosh High School Boys Tennis Team, Chuck was undefeated in three years of high school play with a 63-0 record and became the first Fox Valley player to win three WIAA state singles titles in 1959, 1960 and 1961. He led the Oshkosh High School to the state team title in 1961 and was a member of Wisconsin's 1960 Junior Davis Cup Team.

Chuck earned a tennis scholarship at Tulane University and played the No. 1 or No. 2 singles spots for four years, winning a Southwest Conference Championship at No. 2 Singles.

He was one of the state's top men's players between 1961-66 and won three Wisconsin State Open Championships and State Closed Title during that period.

Chuck Bleckinger (back row, right end) with one of his junior teams, the Titans

As a senior competitor Chuck won the 50 and over singles title for State of California in 1996, Pacific Coast Seniors Champion in 1997 and Northern California Grand Prix, also winning four Central California Championships.

In 2013 he won the Fiesta Bowl singles, his first National Title in Phoenix, AZ.

Chuck has taught tennis in The East Bay since 1970, currently coaching a junior tennis team. Once a week he teaches a free tennis class for kids and adults.

DONALD BLY is often called the Godfather of West Coast tennis. He has coached for 40+ years, including current employment of Director of Tennis for City of Inglewood, CA, for 30 years. In this capacity he provides leadership and supervision of park staff, volunteers and complete coordination of all related activity at five tennis centers. He retired in 2010, but continues to coordinate these activities at the parks.

When Don had a stroke a few years ago, he returned to the court and upholds his winning legacy in tournaments, weekly matches with friends and/or newcomers.

Coach Bly's accomplishments include: Board of Directors for National Public Parks for 15 years; National Tournament Winner of Multiple Events (ATA, National Public Parks, USTA and more); started Inglewood Youth association; implemented tennis programs at all Inglewood High Schools, Ashwood Park, Rodgers Park, North Inglewood Park, Ed Vincent Park, Darby Park. He teaches classes and clinics to mentally challenged kids in groups of 20 per week, individual and group lessons for juniors and adults. He received SCTA Service Awards in 1988, 1998, 1999 and 2004. He directs, plans and hosts Inglewood 1, 2 and 3 Tournament, L.A. Metropolitan Tournament, LA BCD Tournament, LA Public Parks Tournament, LA Junior Metro Tournament and more.

Don is a Graduate of Van Der Meer Tennis College (1972 and 1984) and Vic Braden US Tennis Academy (1974). He holds memberships in USTA, SCTA, ATA, USPTA, National Foundation of Wheelchair Tennis, Professional Tennis Registry, Black Tennis Pro Registry, US Racquet Stringer Association, Board of Nat'l Public Parks (15 years); is High Performance Tennis Coach, Co-Founder of ACT–1996, Clinitioner for PTR and Co-Founder of NJTL–1971.

Don is a Lifetime Member of All Southern California Black Tennis Clubs - American Tennis Association, Pacific Coast Championships - Hall of Fame, Rancho Cienega Tennis Club and Harvard Tennis Club.

GARY BODENMILLER has been involved in the tennis profession for nearly 50 years. He is the owner/operator of Eastside Tennis and Fitness Club in Detroit.

Gary has received numerous awards from USPTA including Midwest Professional of the Year, past runner-up of the USPTA National Industry Excellence Award, Midwest Rookie of the Year and Midwest Faye Tooley Award. A former national clinician for USTA, he has shared his expertise throughout the Midwest and at the National Tennis Teacher's Conference in New York. He was the director of Chicago Tennis Workshop for 29 years and director of Detroit Tennis Workshop for 40 years. These two workshops have had a direct influence over thousands of high school tennis coaches and their players in both Michigan and Illinois.

Gary has written many articles that have appeared in several professional tennis and industry magazines and is the published author of two tennis books. He is a member of the Michigan High School Tennis Coaches Hall of Fame and is recognized as a world class collector of tennis memorabilia, some of which is on display at the Tennis Hall of Fame and the Wimbledon Museum.

RICHARD "DICK" BOHRNSTEDT, a No. 1 ranked junior in Southern California, 1968 U.S. Junior Davis Cup Team and semifinalist in US National Junior Hardcourts.

Dick is a two time All-American at USC, Southern California Intercollegiate Doubles champion w/Marcelo Lara in 1971, semifinals in 1972 US National Amateur Indoor singles, RU in doubles with Raul Ramirez, 1973, Rd. of 16 in Wimbledon doubles w/Bill Brown. WTT w/San Francisco Golden Gaters in 1974-75. 1976, Winner of California State Open, Alabama Open (Mobile), American Express Western Challenger Circuit. 1977, Rd of 16 Wimbledon doubles w/Mike Machette, Rd of 16 Australian Open (Dec) singles. Ranked No. 10 in U.S. doubles (1972), No. 30 in U.S. singles (1973), No. 98 in ATP World singles (1977).

Dick was Director of Tennis at Racket Club of Irvine (1979–1983); Head Pro, Los Angeles Tennis Club (1984–1988); Director of Tennis at Tennis Club Monarch Beach (1988–1995); Tennis Pro, Palisades Tennis Club, Newport Beach, CA (1996–2015).

ALEX BOSE, founder of Bose Tennis, knows what it means to train and compete at the highest level in the professional tennis world. He trained at the Nick Bollettieri Tennis Academy (now IMG Academy) from 1991 to 1999, playing in over 30 countries and reaching the top 25 in the ITF Junior World rankings. Bose climbed into the top 500 on the ATP World Tour before leading Duke University to the No. 2 NCAA Division I ranking in 2001.

Since 2003, Bose Tennis has been a leading tennis full service company striving to help clients reach their goals with hard work, integrity and respect. Bose is a USTA Tournament Director and is certified at the highest professional coaching level by the USPTA and USPTR. In 2014 he was named USPTA District Professional of the Year, Florida Division.

Alex Bose with children Maddox (left) and Sophie

Alex is father to Irish twins, Maddox and Sophie, who already love playing tennis.

LYNN BOTTGER began her career at The Grand Cypress' world-class resort in 1990 as a tennis pro and has served as Director of Tennis since 1995, consistently earning an annual ranking among the Top 50 BEST Tennis Resorts/Academies Worldwide. As Director, she has served as host site to numerous high profile events, i.e., USTA Florida's statewide, USPTA's worldwide and PTR's worldwide annual conferences, Fantasy Tennis Camps and co-host to FSU's Collegiate Clay Court Championships.

Lynn's been very active in her community, providing free weekly tennis lessons to underprivileged families for years and assisting many charities, either serving on the board and/or as Tournament Director, raising millions of dollars.

Prior to this, Lynn graduated from Bowdoin College (top 10 nationally ranked Liberal Arts College) with a degree in psychology/education, where she co-captained their winning varsity tennis team and worked as assistant tennis pro at Essex County Club three summers.

FUN FACT: My first tennis coach, Avis Murray, received USPTA Tennis Pro of the Year the year we hosted USPTA's annual World Conference at Hyatt Regency Grand Cypress – how cool was that ?!

YURI BOUDAGIAN, founder/owner of Yuri's Tennis School in San Francisco Bay Area, January 1996 – current. Following own motto - Passion, Intensity, Results! Head Tennis Pro at Metropolitan Club SF, June 2006 - current. USTA NorCal Coach at Player Development Camps. One of few ethnic Armenian USPTA Pros born on June 22, 1966 in Baku - capital city of Azerbaijan on the warm Caspian Sea shores - one of tennis hotbeds in Soviet Union.

Yuri Boudagian (right) with Ken DeHart at a USPTA conference, 2014

Yuri Boudagian with some of the awards won during his career

Absolutely fell in love with the sport, passionate about its dramatic history, and everything about tennis. Constantly following it up with continuing education!

Married for 29 years to sweetheart Tatiana Boudagian (Umanskiy). Most proud parent of 13-year-old twins, Daniel and Tiffany - excellent Honor Roll 8th grade students; as well as their successful tennis coach - both twins committed Jr. Tour players, representing Team NorCal and Olympic Club as Jr. Merit Members! Team NorCal was 2016 Zonal Champion, bringing home the first gold medals for the 14 BG team in more than a decade.

MATTHEW BOUGHTON played high school tennis at Austin High School, qualifying for State his senior year. He played in college at at RCC and was undefeated in regular season singles and doubles matches over a two-year period, twice advancing to the NJCAA National tournament. He was four-time all conference.

Matthew has been Tennis Director and head pro at Eau Claire YMCA for the past eight years. Previously was Junior Tennis coordinator for four years. Matthew is the NJTL and CTA lead person. Prior to starting the new CTA he served on Chippewa Valley CTA as a consultant for four years. He is on the USTA Northern Board of Directors, USTA Northern Player Id committee, USTA Northern Player comp committee, USTA Northern JTT committee, and USTA National JTT committee. He co-chairs USPTA Midwest U30 committee and is USPTA Wisconsin Vice President. In 2011 he was awarded USPTA Industry in Excellence Award and USPTA Wisconsin Pro of the Year. In 2012 his facility was awarded USTA Northern Organization of the year. In 2013 was awarded USPTA Wisconsin Pro of the Year and USTA Junior Team Tennis organizer of the year.

Matthew and Sara Boughton have two daughters, Gracie Noel Boughton and Jillian Rose Boughton.

GARY BOURGEOIS, currently Head Men's and Women's Tennis Coach at Mississippi Gulf Coast Community College in Perkingston, MS. He has been a member of the USPTA since 1989 and in player development for 34 years. His tennis resume includes developing players in resorts and clubs around the world as well as directing satellite academies for the Nick Bollettieri Tennis Academy in Austria and California. He was also Director of Tennis for the Department of Defense in Europe at the Armed Forces Recreation Center in Garmisch, Germany. He was also Director of the European Tennis Training Center at Hotel Olivi in Malcenie, Italy. He also coached on the ITF World Tour and the WTA Tour. He has been Head Men's and Women's Tennis Coach since 2004 and has been named "Coach of The Year" on nine different occasions by the MACJC, the Mississippi Association of Coaches, the USPTA and most recently in 2016 he was named the National Region III Men's Coach of the year by the ITA. The former Southern Miss quarterback has a Bachelor Degree of Science and is a USPTA Elite Professional.

DAN BOWERS was All American at National High School level, No. 1 all time career doubles at Northern Illinois University. He had No. 3 career victories in singles and No. 3 in combined victories.

Dan placed third place in doubles, USTA National Grass Courts with Branden Black and was awarded Bronze Ball in 2006, Men's 30's.

He became a USPTA member in 1993. Dan has been Head Pro to the Director of Tennis at Hillwood Country Club, Nashville, TN, for the last 23 years.

BEVERLY BOWES-HACKNEY, who played professionally on the Women's Tennis Association (WTA) Tour for 10 years - where she was ranked among the top 50 players in the world, is the Director of Tennis at River-Place Country Club.

Bowes-Hackney had a storied junior career in Chicago, before accepting a scholarship offer to play tennis at The University of Texas (UT). As a Longhorn, she was an All-American, the 1987 Southwest Conference Player of the Year, and recorded a career record of 100-21. After a successful career on the WTA Tour, Bowes-Hackney settled into south Florida where she worked for the USTA national junior program as well as the Evert Tennis Academy. In 2000, Bowes-Hackney became the head coach of the women's tennis team at Southern Methodist University and later an assistant coach with the women's team at UT.

ARNOLD BRADSHAW has been a member of USPTA since 1970. He played in three NAIA Championships for Edinboro, PA. During his playing career he was ranked No. 1 in the Alleghany Mountain Tennis Association (35 singles and doubles). He was ranked No. 1 in Northeast Ohio 45 Singles.

Arnold coached the Geneva High School (OH) Boys Varsity Tennis Team, which he started in 1966 until he retired in 1993. Their 28 season record is 483-44. The Northeast Ohio Conference record is 346-4. Fifteen GHS alumni are certified tennis pros and several have won national age group titles.

Arnold was featured in Faces In The Crowd in *Sports Illustrated* (1975) and on ESPN (1993). He was voted into the Inaugural Hall of Fame for Edinboro and is in the Ohio Tennis Coaches Hall of Fame. He was voted Tennis Pro of the Year in *Lowcountry Magazine*, Hilton Head, SC.

As a teacher, summers were free to go to other places for summer tennis programs: Lake Mohonk Mountain House, New Paltz, NY; Kahkwa Club, Erie, PA; Camp Mah-Kee-Nac, Lenox, MA; Carolina Country Club, Spartanburg, SC; and Madison Country Club, Madison, OH. After retirement two summers were spent at Easton Racket Club, Easton, CT.

This amazing tennis journey has been traveled with wife, Kathy, by his side for 46 years. Sons Ben and Abe played on the GHS team. In the state of Ohio, Tony Trabert gives a tennis award which is given their senior year - Ben

(1988) Abe (1993). Ben played tennis at Clemson and Edinboro and Abe played at the US Naval Academy. Arnold and Ben played Father-Son tennis and in 1988 they won the Ohio Father-Son Championship and went on to play in the Equitable Tournament at the US Open. In 2001 they were ranked 16 in the nation.

Arnold and Kathy presently live in Alabama where he continues to teach tennis at O'Connor Tennis Center, where Ben is head pro.

PAT BREEN is currently the Head Racquet Sports Director at The Peninsula Club in Millsboro, DE, an instructor for Cape Carousel after school program and runs a community tennis program at The Villages of Five Points in Lewes, DE.

Pat spent 22 years as a collegiate tennis coach, serving as head coach at Longwood University, University of Louisiana at Monroe, Samford and Georgia Southern. At Longwood he led a successful transition from NCAA Division II to Division I. At Samford he developed two NCAA Top 50 Division I nationally-ranked players, won two conference titles and twice broke into the Division I Top 50 national team rankings.

A two-time All-American at Abraham Baldwin College and member of a national junior college championship team, Pat was inducted into Abraham Baldwin's Athletic Hall of Fame in 2009. He completed his collegiate playing career at McNeese State, a Top 25 nationally-ranked team.

CHERYL (FROH) BROMLEY grew up in Sheboygan, WI, playing varsity tennis for South High School and the University of Wisconsin-La Crosse where she received All American honors for tennis. Cheryl has over 35 years of teaching experience working with all ages and she enjoys competing in USTA leagues.

After college, Cheryl was the Resident Tennis Pro at Topnotch Resort & Spa in Stowe, VT. She then started her own business, Paradise Tennis, which featured summer tennis camps for children. She also coached the Stowe High School girls' tennis team to seven State Championship titles.

Cheryl next relocated to Hillsboro Beach, FL, where she was the Director of Marketing, Croquet and Summer Tennis.

Currently, Cheryl is thrilled to be a part of the Sports Core Tennis staff in Kohler, WI, a five-star, five-diamond resort in the Midwest. She has been a member of the USPTA since 1985.

DAVID A. BROWN joined USPTA in 1973, became an Elite Pro in 1982, and Master Professional in 1992. His mentors were George Bacso and Joe Thompson.

Service to the industry includes Division President (Intermountain 1988), District President (South Florida 1992–1997), USTA Florida Community Coordinator 1998–2002, President Greater Volusia Tennis Network (Florida) 2006–2010, President Greater Volusia Tennis League (Florida) 2014–2016.

As a professional, Dave coached major college tennis at Colorado State University and served as Director of Tennis at several prominent clubs, including the Harvest House in Boulder, CO, the Florida Tennis Center in Daytona Beach, FL, and Plantation Bay in Ormond Beach, FL.

As a player, Dave was a standout in high school and college and graduated from St. Mary's College in California. He has held USPTA state, sectional and national rankings in singles, doubles and USTA national Father/Son doubles with his son, Aaron.

Notable awards include USPTA Intermountain Pro of the Year 1988; USPTA/USTA Service Award 2002; USPTA Florida District Pro of the Year 2005, '06, '08, '09, '14; USTA Florida Father/Son Champions 2011; USTA Florida Family of the Year 2011; USTA Florida Prestigious Merit Award 2015 for promoting and developing tennis in the state of Florida.

NORVELL BROWN has been a tennis instructor for both the East Side Competitive Tennis Club and Tennis at Brooklyn Union Tennis Club in Washington, DC. Relocating to Durham, NC, he became tennis coach at various high schools, including the North Carolina School of Science and Mathematics. He received the USPTA Southern Division High School Coach of the year award in 1996, the "Junior Tennis Council Award" from the NC Tennis Association in 1997 and the "1999 NJTL Chapter of the Year" from the USTA/ Southern Tennis Association. In 2003 he accepted the position of Tennis Director at the Carrboro Recreation and Parks Department. He is the founder of the Durham/Orange Community Tennis Association. In 2005 he was employed as Tennis Director at the Woodcroft Swim and Tennis Club. He decided to go into semi-retirement to write and publish his book "A Tennis Guide for the High School Rookie Coach."

CARI BUCK has over 25 years of experience in the tennis industry. With over 19 years of service to the USPTA, she has held teaching positions in Cape Cod, MA, southern Florida, Maui and Southern California. She has also worked as a sales rep for a tennis apparel manufacturer, an assistant to an ATP Tournament Director and for the last nine years has worked at Tennis Channel where she is now manager of Client Services. Currently Buck serves as the President of the USPTA California Division and is a member of the USPTA National Executive Committee. She is very active in the wheelchair tennis community, both on and off the court, as a coach and as a member of the USTA National Wheelchair Tennis Committee. One of her proudest achievements is having her family named as the USTA National Family of the Year in 1985.

KATHY BURKE joined the USPTA in 1976 as a tennis professional at McLean Indoor Tennis Center, McLean, VA. When McLean Indoor opened a club in Williamsport, MD,

Kathy moved there with her husband to direct and manage the new tennis and racquetball facility. In 1980 she returned to North Carolina to teach and coach tennis. While staying active with the USPTA and USTA, Kathy served as tennis coach and member of the faculty at Saint Mary's School in Raleigh, NC. 2016 marks Kathy's 40th anniversary as a member of the USPTA.

RICHARD CALLWOOD grew up playing tennis in the United Kingdom. Upon moving to the U.S. he attended SUNY Purchase College, New York. He double majored in Math/Computer Science BA and Economics BA. Richard then pursued a graduate degree attending Fordham University, New York. Economics MA

Richard's teaching accreditation includes Elite Pro with the USPTA and P-1 with USPTR.

Richard has been teaching tennis for over 27 years. He taught tennis for 20 years at Saw Mill Club, Mt. Kisco, NY. Richard was the Head Professional at Lakeside Field Club, North Salem, NY, for a number of years. Richard has taught and traveled worldwide with high profile business executives and their families. He is currently teaching at Armonk Tennis Club Armonk, NY.

Richard enjoys playing tournaments and has been ranked as high as No. 45 nationally in the U.S. in both singles and doubles.

BRANDON CARLSON has served the Bryan/College Station, TX, tennis community for the last four years as the Head Tennis Professional for the City of College Station Parks and Recreation program. His tennis journey started as a junior in the Dallas/Fort Worth Metroplex just over 20 years ago. He played countless USTA sanctioned ZAT, Champs and Super Champs tournaments throughout Texas and he was able to land his first job managing a pro shop and stringing racquets at the Hilton DFW Lakes Sports Club. He attended college at the University of the Ozarks in Clarksville, AR, where he was a four-year letterman on the Division III team and he was selected as an ESPN The Magazine Academic All-American his senior year. Since then, he has attained his USPTA certification in 2008, and he has enjoyed teaching and managing the program in College Station.

ANDREW CARTER has been devoted to the sport of tennis for over 30 years as a member of both the USPTA and PTR. Carter graduated from Tyler Junior College in 1985 with a tennis-teaching degree as an Associate in Applied Science, Recreation Leadership. Early in his career, Carter distinguished himself by teaching tennis for Nick Bollettieri and Harry Hopman. In 1988, he co-founded Carter Tennis Networks, a tennis operation company in Austin, TX, which managed several tennis clubs. For 13 years, Carter has been a Tournament Director for the USTA Pro Circuit, as well as a member of the Wilson Advisory Staff since 1998. In 2012, Carter's love for the sport led him to create the World Tennis Museum, an online museum that features coveted tennis memorabilia. Presently, Carter is the Director of Tennis at the Harlingen Country Club in south Texas, a position he has held since 1996. He is married to Beth, who has been a good sport about traveling to tennis tournaments for their family vacations, and has a son Taylor.

STAN CARTER is a certified Elite Professional in the California Division. Stan has been a board member since 2005 and serves as 2nd vice-president. He has been teaching tennis as his second career for 17 years. Stan played competitively as a junior and through high school.

Stan continues to learn by attending all of the USPTA educational forums held monthly, quarterly and yearly. Stan has many mentors assisting him and learns something every time he attends an event, watches another coach or is on the court teaching a student.

Stan Carter with one of the junior tennis teams he has coached

After years of on-the-court teaching experience, he found a home at the La Canada Flintridge Country Club. He is enjoying his third year there with James Panagopoulos, Director of Tennis. He teaches private and group lessons seven days a week, and is the LCFCC director of USTA Jr. Team Tennis.

ROBERT F. CAVANAGH started his career as High School Tennis, Basketball Team Capt. and co-Capt. He played on 3rd Army Tennis Team-won Army Championship/Semi Finalist–doubles (1970). Robert winner of Bahama's Doubles Tournament and International Collegiate Pro/Am Doubles Tournament (1994).

Robert has taught children from ages 2 to adults, handicapped and non-handicapped individuals, High School State Champions and pro tour players (46 years). He also has taught Adult Tennis Clinics for Rockland County, NY (21 years), CDTA (12 years) and Hunterdon County, NJ (four years). He has run tournaments in singles and doubles for Section I and USTA.

Robert was the Recipient of Coaching Award for Contributions to H.S. Tennis-Section I, New Jersey.

He has a Elite USPTA rating (27 years) and is a certified Tester.

He is on the Board of Directors-Asian American Tennis Association-Rockland County, NY.

Robert is currently co-owner of the HOOT ART GALLERY in Placitas, NM.

MARK CENTRELLA, born in Wilmington, DE, graduated from Archmere Academy (1991) and from University of Delaware (1995) with a Bachelor of Science in Accounting. He was a High School Singles state champion and Division I Varsity collegiate player at University of Delaware.

He is a USPTA Master Professional, Chair of the National Master Professional Committee, Head Tester for the Middle States, President of Middle States (2003–2007), Middle States Tester of the Year (2004, 2011), Middle States Pro of the Year (2004), Middle States Rookie of the Year (1995). USTA Honors – Middle States Pro of the Year (2012), Delaware District Pro of the Year (1998 and 2012) and Producer of Winning Doubles with Mark, DVD.

Mark and Katie have three children: Siena (2009), Amelia (2012) and Marco (2014).

DEBBIE CERELL-WEINBERG – A member of the USPTA since 2009. Born and raised in the New York tri-state area, she began playing tennis at the age of 8. She enjoys all aspects of the game for overall health, fitness and well-being. After working in Manhattan for a period of time, Debbie and her family relocated to Florida. She attended many tennis workshops and became certified in 2009 as a USTA Recreational Coach. In 2010 she became certified in Cardio Tennis and 10 and Under Junior Development. She has taught, inspired and motivated many young children and adults to excel in their tennis and fitness skills. Through care and understanding of different learning abilities, she has taught tennis to help others overcome physical and emotional challenges. Being able to help others is a great joy. In 2013, Debbie became a certified Tennis Professional with the USPTA and continues to work with children and adults for their tennis best.

MANUEL S. CERVANTES, born in Guadalajara, Jalisco, Mexico, Nov. 26, 1958, started tennis at 9 years of age. He has experienced tennis from all angles, junior tournaments regionally and nationally, college tennis in the U.S. for North Central Texas College and Truman University in Missouri. Professionally, he played from age 16 and again at ages 23-37, achieving a ranking of No. 12 in Mexico's professional circuit in 1987 in the Men's Professional Division. Manuel has coached top juniors, college players, and professionals for over 30 years. He achieved his USPTA Master Professional Certification in 2003.

Manuel has undergraduate degrees in Physics (1982) and Metallurgical Engineering (1986), as well as graduate studies in Engineering and Business from University of Texas at El Paso.

Manuel authored the book *What Tennis Pros Don't Teach (WTPDT), Wisdom Tennis 101* published in 2015 in all formats.

Currently, Manuel works as High-Performance Coach in NW Arkansas and lives with his wife Carmen, daughter Anasazi and her Pyrenees/Labrador StellaLuna!

A.J. CHABRIA, started his journey in tennis during the tennis boom of the 1970s, courtesy of his father and grandfather, who loved the game endlessly. He grew up as a happy junior player, making it to some national tournaments and the main draw of the Easter Bowl. After college tennis at Oglethorpe University, he played some open and pro circuit events, then fell in love with teaching and coaching while in graduate school and playing progams.

After helping at an academy program and a high school team, served almost five years as head professional at Marin Country Club in Novato, CA, then moved to Dallas, TX, to be tennis director at Lakewood Country Club.

At Lakewood, one of the oldest clubs in Texas, he has enjoyed a vibrant and expanding membership who have helped the game of tennis grow by leaps and bounds. They accomplished an award-winning renovation to the facility and have quickly become one of the most successful programs in the area.

He has served as President of the Board of the Dallas Professional Tennis Association and as Master Racquet Technician, tester and playtester for the USRSA. Has served as tour editor for TennisPlayer.net, covering several exhibitions, Davis Cup ties, Grand Slams and ATP events as a credentialed media member. He enjoys writing almost as much as the game itself.

Over the years, he has been fortunate to serve as advisory staff for Dunlop, Donnay, Völkl and Babolat and was a host and player involved in an exhibition with US Davis Cup hero, John McEnroe. With the help of his son and some juniors he has coached, he feels blessed to share his love for the game with children and teens in a free program he runs at various local courts.

Eternally grateful for the wonderful game of tennis.

MICHAEL CHAMBERLAIN has been Director of Tennis at The Racquet Club of Memphis since 2012. As Director he oversees the state's largest junior program, the state's largest indoor court facility, as well as the club's 2,000 members.

Michael is the Tournament Director of the USTA National G18 Clay Court Championships, the USPTA National Indoor Championships, as well as tournament director of several other high level USTA adult and junior events. Michael serves on several USTA and USPTA tennis committees including USTA Southern Junior Competition Committee and USPTA National Tournament Committee. Michael was named the USTA TN Professional of the Year in 2012 and USPTA TN Professional of the Year in 2013. Michael holds a bachelor's degree in Business and a MBA from the University of Memphis, and is a certified Master Professional with the USPTA. He is also published in numerous magazines and given multiple lectures around the country.

SUSAN CHANDLER grew up in Sarasota, FL, and played in the juniors in the '60s and '70s with Chris Evert, Betsy Nagelson, Jennifer Capriati, Wendy Overton, Mary Pierce and others. She was ranked in the top 10 in the U.S. in the 16 and under and 18 and under. At 17 she turned professional and went on the Women's Pro Circuit and was amongst the Virginia Slims Women. She played at Wimbledon, the French Open, Canadian Nationals and the US Open while it was at Forest Hills on grass.

Susan Chandler (right) with father Richard Vinton (center) and brother John Vinton, 2013

Florida 18-under Intersectional team, 1970. Left column, from top: Chris Evert, Susan Vinton (Chandler), Susan Epstein. Center: Patty Reese. Right column: Alice Richardson, Carol Grovesnor and Karen Benson

In the summer of 1972 she beat Kerry Harris in England, who was ranked No. 11 in the world at the time.

She had several coaches, among them Ken Wagstaff and Doris Hart. Dr. Richard Vinton, my father, also coached me and was my mentor and a major influence on my life. He wouldn't allow me to use a two-handed backhand even though Chris Evert was making it famous. He wanted me to learn every shot in the book so I could be an all court player. He also coached Jane Lutz in Sarasota, who is now ranked No. 1 in the world in the 85's women's division.

Susan earned her USPTA certification when she was in her early 20s while married to USPTA pro Gewan Maharaj. After she stopped playing professionally she began working for Nick Bollettieri and All American Sports, Mt. Kisco, NY. They travelled to different resorts in Florida, Massachusetts and Puerto Rico. They worked during a summer at the Rockefeller's home in New York. She taught at Topnotch at Stowe, Stowe, VT. She moved to Montreal in 1984, taught there and was the Canadian National Women's 35's singles champion. In 1992 Susan moved to Boca Raton, FL, where she raised her four children. In 2002 she began teaching at Addison Reserve in Delray Beach where she coached Victoria Duval for four years when she was 9 years old. In 2007 Susan began working at The Oaks in Boca Raton and then at The Ocean Club in Ocean Ridge, FL. Today she enjoys playing regularly and teaches privately.

JOSE CHIPE was born in 1947 in Guayaquil, Ecuador. After studying Electrical Engineering at Escuela Politecnica del Litoral for three years, he immigrated to the U.S. and completed his degree at Manhattan College, where he played varsity soccer. In 1968 he began teaching himself to play tennis by reading instructional books and watching films of match play at the public library.

Upon completing his master's in Environmental Engineering at Manhattan, he was sent to Rio de Janeiro, Brazil to work for the WHO as a water quality specialist. It was there he changed life course and was named head pro of the British American Club in Rio. He and his family remained in Brazil until 1989, at which time he returned to the U.S. and began teaching for Blairwood Health Fitness Club of Louisville, KY. He is certified by the USPTR as a Professional 1 and USPTA as an Elite Professional and has been a member of the latter for 25 years. He was the Kentucky State Verifier for 10 years.

"I certainly enjoy teaching tennis, which I consider a calling, not just a profession. My philosophy is that tennis is a sport for a life time with no real age limit. I provide my students with knowledge to live a healthy physical and mental life."

JEFF CHRISTIANSON, USPTA Elite Professional, Master's Degree in Health Psychology, former No. 2 Singles and No. 1 Doubles at Santa Clara University, All Wcc At Santa Clara University, ranked No. 2 Northern California Men's 30 Doubles.

Tennis Professional at Braemar Country Club, Tarzana, CA, 1996 to present. Brought Fright Night Junior Halloween Event to Braemar Tennis Club – Braemar's Largest Junior Event of the Year – one year had 200+ kids.

Formerly Men's Varsity Coach Santa Clara University and also taught at San Jose Swim and Racket Club (1993–1996) and Courtside Tennis Club in Los Gatos, CA.

Quarterfinalist Men's Doubles in USTA Men's 30 and USPTA Men's Open, Captain Varsity Tennis (Santa Clara University and Harvard High School Teams), Member of three Braemar CC National USTA Teams (1999, 2005, 2011).

Generally coaches ages from 5-95 – Part of the belief that tennis is "The Sport of a Lifetime" and can be a great part of everyone's health and wellness. Lucky to have worked with many great pros and directors.

CARL CLARK is the Director of Tennis at Hallbrook Country Club in Leawood, KS, after 15-year tenure as the Head Tennis Professional at The Country Club of Virginia in Richmond. He is a former world ranked doubles player and played college tennis at the University of Virginia. He currently holds 13 USTA National titles and over 50 Virginia State titles. Carl was a singles finalist in the ITF World Senior Championships in 2012 and a doubles finalist in 2014. Carl has represented the U.S. in the prestigious Potter Cup senior event in Barcelona, Spain, for four of the past six years. He was named the USPTA National Player of the Year in 2002 and has served as an officer for the USPTA Mid-Atlantic section for over 10 years. Carl has been a USPTA member for over 25 years.

JOHN CLEARY has been Director of Tennis at Lakewood Country Club in Rockville, MD, since 2011. He oversees all aspects of tennis operations, which serve the club's 650 member families.

John was previously employed from 2001–2011, as

the Director of Tennis at Norbeck Country Club, Rockville, MD, where he was also Assistant Professional from 1996–2001. From 1994–1996, John was Assistant Professional at Sportsplex in New Windsor, NY.

John's service to the USPTA includes being a Mid-Atlantic Division Board Member from 2000–2015, serving as Division President from 2011–2013. He earned USPTA Mid-Atlantic Professional of the Year Award for 2011, is a five-time winner of the USPTA Maryland Professional of the Year and earned USPTA Mid-Atlantic 35's Player of the Year honors in 2005.

As a college player, John was captain of the Division I men's tennis team at Marist College, while playing in No. 1 and No. 2 singles positions. At Marist, John earned a Bachelor of Arts degree in communications.

One of John's most memorable tennis experiences came while serving as a ball boy at the US Open from 1990 to 1993. He had the opportunity to be on the court with such tennis legends as McEnroe, Sampras, Lendl, Connors, Agassi, Graf, Navratilova and many others.

WILL CLEVELAND, originally from Dayton, OH, came to Ft. Wayne, IN's Wildwood Racquet Club in 1988 as general manager and is a partner. He holds a degree in economics from Wright State University where he served as men's and women's tennis coach from 1979–1983, coaching two NCAA national tennis championship participants and one AIAW All-American. He was recognized as a Master Professional by the U.S. Professional Tennis Association in 1994.

Will has served the tennis industry in a number of capacities. He is a former past president of the Northern Indiana Tennis Association, a USTA Zonal Coach, NTRP Sectional Verifier and received the 1991 USTA Midwest's Cap Leighton Award for his work in community tennis. In addition Will has served the USPTA as a past president of the USPTA Indiana District, a national certification tester for the USPTA and a speaker at USPTA Midwest and World Conferences. He was recognized as the 1992 USPTA Indiana Professional of the Year and was the first recipient of the USPTA Midwest Division Facility Manager of the Year Award in 1999. He was inducted into the USPTA Midwest Division Hall of Fame in 2012.

BERTAN CIKIGIL has enjoyed a 45-year career as professional in some of the most prestigious country clubs in America. The hallmark of his success includes expertly marketed creative concepts and program see today in some of the best-know club environments in America. His work continues onward today.

GARY CIMPERMAN was the 2014 USPTA Southern Assistant Tennis Pro of the Year, 2015 USPTA Southern Under-30 Pro of the Year and received the 2015 ITPA Paul Arber Young Coaches award – Honorable Mention.

Gary is a TIA Cardio Tennis Trainer. He was the USPTA Southern U30 Event Chairman, 2013–15. He was a featured speaker at 2014 USPTA Georgia State workshop and in 2015 at USPTA Southern Conference in Charlotte, NC. In 2015 he was the PTR Touring Pro for Couples, Negril, Jamaica. Gary has been published in USPTA *Southern Standard, Tennis View Magazine* and TheTennisReview.net.

He was a 2015 US Tennis Congress Faculty Member and founder of www.readtheracquet.com.

BEN COFER has been Owner/General Manager of Pinewoods Health and Racquet Club in Torrington, CT, since 2009. He also owned West River Tennis and Fitness Center in Londonderry, VT, since 1998. Before Vermont, he worked at clubs in Syracuse, NY, Cincinnati, OH, and Washington, DC.

He has been involved in the indoor tennis club business for 30+ years in positions including staff tennis professional, head tennis professional, director of tennis and club owner.

Bob has been a member of USPTA at the highest level for 30 years. He has taught several junior tennis players to Top 50 Rankings in New England. Bob is a proven player as he was the No. 1 player on his college tennis team, State University College at Oswego, NY, in the 1980s and more recently has been ranked in the Top Ten in New England in singles in his division every year since 2002. He achieved his highest rankings ever in 2009, 2010 and 2013 as he was ranked No. 2 in New England in the Men's 45 and Over Singles Division and in 2014 when he was No. 2 in New England in the 4.5 Men's Singles Division.

Bob is married to Enizete Cofer and has two daughters, Angelica and Sabrina.

CHUCK COLEMAN grew up in La Grange, IL. Began playing just before entering high school in 1969. Starting at the bottom of the Frosh-Sophomore team, worked up to No. 2 singles on the varsity as a senior. Entered the University of Redlands at age 17 in 1973, graduating in 1977. Once again, worked up the ladder, starting near the bottom and becoming a starter at No. 6 singles as a junior. Redlands was a powerhouse in those days. Played the NAIA tournament in Kansas City in 1976, where they finished second. That was a disappointment for many, as Redlands had previously won the event several times. When Gustavus Adolphus' Coach Steve Wilkinson became the winningest coach in college tennis, he broke the record previously held by Redlands' Coach Jim Verdieck.

Ranked only once, No. 6 in Northern California's Class A group. Bachelor's degree in Business, Mathematics minor. Teaching credential, High School Mathematics. Master's degree, Physical Education. Master's thesis topic was feedback's effect on speed and accuracy in the forehand. Currently hold 203 units of education from USPTA. Joined Oscar Wegner's MTMCA group several years ago and learned many new concepts there. Favorite saying: "Sportsmanship might not be No. 1, but it's way ahead of whatever is in second place."

CLAUDIA COLEMAN has been a USPTA professional since 2000. She attended John Curtis Christian School (K–12th) where she

was six-time MVP, Singles Regional Champion, Doubles Regional Champion and Mixed Doubles Regional and State Champion.

She is a former Division I college player for Louisiana Tech University and University of New Orleans. In 1999 she graduated from UNO with a BA degree in Graphic Design. After college, she played Southern tournaments in the women's open division where she finished as high as No. 23 in the South.

Since becoming a USPTA professional, she has been a pro at Woodlake Tennis & Swim Club, New Orleans Country Club and New Orleans City Park. As the high school coach at Metairie Park Country Day School for seven years, the girls won two consecutive State Championships and were state runners-up four times; the boys won four consecutive State Championships and state runners-up. She is a two-time USPTA High School Coach of the Year-Southern Division and USPTA National High School Coach of the Year.

She was assistant coach of the USTA Competitive Training Center and a NOMATA (New Orleans Metropolitan Area Tennis Association) volunteer member/USPTA Representative. Another honor was the NOMATA Tennis Professional of the Year award.

DR. D. KEITH COLEMAN has been involved in the coaching and teaching profession for 40 years. He began his career as the Assistant Director of The Don Budge Tennis Campus in 1977. He received Elite Professional status with the USPTA in 2004. Keith received the certification of Competitive Coach from the International Coaches Institute at the Sanchez-Casal Academy in 2014. He was the Director of Tennis and Head Pro at the Ocean City Tennis Center (Maryland) from 2004–2014. Dr. Coleman held tennis pro jobs at the Village Tennis Center (Louisville, KY), the Natick Racket Club (Natick, MA), and Sea Colony Tennis Resort (Bethany Beach, DE).

He holds a Doctorate in Psychology and currently teaches in the Ph.D. program in Pastoral Counseling at Neumann University (Aston, PA). He is the owner of neuro-tennis.com and a leader in developing neuroscience based approaches to teaching tennis.

GEORGE J. COLLIER competed on Pro Tennis and Challenger Circuit, 1970s and 1980s. He was Tournament Advisor, 1976, for All Army Tennis Championships.

George is presently Director of Tennis at SOS Club in Modesto, CA. From 1999 to 2005, he was Associate Tennis Professional, Stanford University. From 1984 to 1987, he was Director of Tennis, Golden Gate Park, San Francisco. In 1987 he was Volunteer High School Coach of the Year. From 1987 to 1991, he was Director of Tennis, Oakdale Golf and Country Club. George was a 1982 Member Wilson Advisory Staff. From 1984 to 1987 he was an Assistant Director of Rec. and Parks Department, San Francisco, CA.

George and Nancy have been married 40 years. They have a son, daughter and four grandchildren.

LORETTA CONWAY, Vice President of Steamboat Tennis and Court Sports, LLC and Business Development Director for the Tennis Center at Steamboat, has been a USPTA certified professional since 1994. Loretta has a rich history in community tennis, including serving as the Director of Community Tennis for USTA FL, from 1998–2002, working for USTA NorCal from 2003–2007 and acting as the Executive Director for Youth Tennis Advantage in the San Francisco Bay Area from 2007–2010. Loretta has been a member of the National USTA Adjunct Faculty since 2000. Loretta and her husband, Bill Conway, will be taking over the management of the Tennis Center at Steamboat Springs in October 2016.

JUAN CORONEL, born and raised in the Republic of Panama, learned tennis under the tutelage of Stanley Loney in Rainbow City, Canal Zone. Early in his career he distinguished himself as top junior and open player, representing Panama in international competitions. Juan came to the U.S. on a tennis scholarship attending Hampton Institute, in Hampton, VA, majoring in Speech Pathology and Audiology. Member of the 1976 NCAA Division II national champions, the Hampton Pirates.

A U.S. citizen since the 1980s, Juan has over 35 years as a very successful tennis professional working with juniors, as well as professionals on the WTA and ATP professional tours. Juan traveled the world as a circuit player and a coach being based in Monte Carlo for years. Juan served as the Davis Cup Coach in 2003 for Panama. This engaging Panamanian is fluent in four languages—English, Spanish, Portuguese and Italian.

JULIAN COUSINS has been coaching sports since 1992 when he qualified as a tennis coach with the USPTA. Julian trained at the world famous Bollettieri Academy which gave him a tremendous insight into the technical knowledge, practical and communication skills required to coach effectively. Since then he has continued his sports training with the USPTA to a very high qualified status. Together with his experience of 10 full ski seasons and involvement in the travel industry, he can offer a full range of great value coaching and sporting experiences. Julian is grateful for his education with the USPTA!

DANY CHRISTIAN COUTURE, born Feb. 19, 1958 in Montreal, Quebec, Canada,

was tossed his first tennis balls by his coach at age 7, played his first tournament at 8 and won the Laval Catholic High School tennis title in 1975. He finished his junior tennis career in 1975, earning a top ranking in Canada.

Dany attended the University of Alabama and earned his business degree in 1979. Shortly thereafter, he turned professional in 1979.

Dany played on tour for three years as a professional. Dany has brought the game of tennis to appreciative audiences and has coached and played in over 20 countries around the world. In 1989, Dany co-produced the TV Series "Tennis, Sport of a Lifetime."

Presently, Dany is a tennis consultant and a performance enhancement consultant based in Toronto, Canada. Dany also participates in a continuing series of network television and radio appearances throughout North America. Dany is married to his wife Nicole and has a daughter Sabrina with their three dogs and four cats.

JOHN S. CRAIG has been involved in tennis for 35+ years. He discovered tennis at the age of 15 and quickly embraced tennis as his primary sports interest. After moving from Connecticut to California, John started in both singles and doubles for Palomar College for two years and then earned a position as a walk-on at San Diego State University.

John began teaching tennis at the age of 19, when he conducted junior lessons for Escondido, CA. He was appointed Club Tennis Pro for The Courtyard in Escondido at the age of 20. While studying and competing in college, John coached the San Pasqual High School team to a league championship. He was also a Tennis Pro at the Rancho Bernardo Inn Tennis College for three years. The Rancho Bernardo Inn Tennis College was recipient of the "America's 50 Greatest Tennis Resorts" award for 20+ consecutive years by *Tennis Magazine*.

From 1986 to 1990, John was Director of Tennis at the John Wayne Tennis Club in Newport Beach, CA. He developed and managed instructional, competitive and social programs for a large, active and highly competitive membership that included notable members such as Rod Laver, Roy Emerson, Phil Dent and other touring professionals. He was also Resident Tennis Pro at the Four Seasons Resort & Hotel in Newport Beach for five years.

In 2010 he established and directed The Edge Tennis Academy in Newport Beach, CA. The academy developed numerous juniors who have established junior rankings and competed at high school varsity and collegiate levels.

In addition to tennis, John enjoys working on computers. He won the USPTA International Personal Website Contest in 2009 with a variety of creative features on his website.

John is happily married with a 9 year-old daughter.

JOE CSANDLI was a staple in central Florida for 30+ years. Joe was Head Pro at Winter Park Racquet Club for 14 years, but many of the tennis community will remember him at Orlando Tennis Club (OTC) downtown, where he was Head Pro for 15 years.

Joe will be a member of the USPTA for 40 years in 2016. In fact, Tim Heckler was his good friend and USPTA tester! He is very proud that he spent 20+ years raising money for the American Cancer Society and Cystic Fibrosis Society through charity tennis tournaments. Joe also started the Citrus Tennis Classic. Joe has been ranked No. 2 in the state in men's 35 over doubles and No. 1 with his son Kris in Father–Son Doubles.

Before moving to Orlando, Joe taught in Cocoa Beach, FL, where he was instrumental in pioneering the USTA Junior Team Tennis county-wide program. As a reward for having so many kids join the USTA, Joe was awarded lifetime membership to the USTA. He also spent time in Houston, TX, as Director of Tennis at John Newcomb's Quail Valley Racquet Club. He has numerous awards from the USTA: "volunteer of the year," Central Florida "USPTA Pro of the Year" and USTA school program "Clinician of the Year." Joe played college tennis at Lamar University in Beaumont, TX, lettering all four years.

Joe is now retired and lives in Altamonte Springs, FL, with wife Bette. He still plays competitive tennis and mountain bikes.

BRYCE CUNNINGHAM, a native of Australia, has stellar international coaching and tennis program management experience. Bryce's love for tennis started early in his youth. As a junior, he trained at the Chris Evert and Bollettieri Academies and went on to play internationally on the ITF circuit. Following his days as a tour player, Bryce earned his USPTA Elite Professional Certification, Tennis Australia Level 1 Certification as well as certification as a personal trainer. While still in Australia, he served as Head Tennis Professional at Tiebreak Tennis Academy in Coffs Harbour, directing the adult and junior programs as well as summer camps.

In 2008 Bryce moved to the U.S., joined the team at Cliff Drysdale Tennis and quickly moved up the ranks to Program Director and Camp Director at the award-winning tennis center at The Ritz-Carlton Key Biscayne, Miami, before taking over the Bluewater Bay Tennis Center in Niceville, FL, as Director. Under Cunningham's leadership, the facility has been voted "Best Tennis Center" in NW Florida by *Emerald Coast Magazine*. After leaving Bluewater Bay, Bryce is now the Director of Tennis at the world renowned Omni La Costa Resort in Carlsbad, CA, and oversees the tennis program year round. Omni La Costa Resort was also voted 2016 USPTA Club of the Year for the San Diego Division under his management.

DR. JOSEPH S. CURCIO, a retired Ph.D. Clinical Biochemist, attended St. Johns University, Monmouth University and Rutgers University.

He is a Certified Pro (9 years) of the United States Professional Tennis Association, a Certified Instructor (17 year) with Professional Tennis Registry and USTA Certified Official, ITA/Collegiate, Referee, 12 years.

Joseph is the Head Tennis Professional, The Oahu Club, Honolulu, HI (2005-present). Previously he was associated with Bollettieri Tennis Academy, Advanced Men's Tennis, Bradenton, FL, and Shadowbrook Tennis Club, Tennis Professional, Bonita Springs, FL.

He was the Lipton International Tennis Tournament Chairman of Credentials, Miami, FL, and Key Biscayne Yacht Club Tennis Chairman, Key Biscayne, FL.

Babolat: Tennis Racquet and Equipment Sponsored, 11 years.

USPTA Published Article, "Tennis Quality Assurance" ADDvantage Magazine, November 2011.

MIGUEL D. CYSNEIROS, Certified Elite Professional and member since 1982, (Master Pro candidate) PTR Professional (5A), TPA-Canada, Portuguese Federation- APTT, USRSA certified, USTA member. Canadian citizen lives in Oakville Ontario, Canada. Celebrates 40 years as career tennis professional, player, coach and entrepreneur. High School grad in Portugal, attended Ryerson University, Toronto, Marketing & Business Management. Speaks four languages.

Board member, Tennis Collectors of America - TCA, Prince Advisory Board and Pro-Shop dealer in Canada and Portugal for 35 years.

Eighth year as Tennis Director at Tecumseh Tennis Club, Ontario, runs MC Tennis Academy. Leads renovation of facilities, programs and membership from 150 to 450 active members, top coaching program in the area. Volunteers for club board, hosts community Family Days with 90 participants yearly.

Junior member of National Tennis Center, Lisbon, Portugal. Ranked top 50 Open in Portugal and Canada. Manager, tennis director & head professional at international resorts, tennis clubs and events in U.S., Portugal, Canada, France, Mexico and Bahamas, in eight countries and three continents!

Founded Tennisport Intl., Professional Tennis Services, Protennis and M. Cysneiros Tennis Academy. Consultant in planning six top resorts and clubs, over 50 tennis courts, in Europe and Canada. Tennis Director at five star tennis resorts, and owner, MC Tennis Academy, Hotel Vila Vita Park, Vilalara Thalassa & Tennis Club Montechoro, Algarve, Portugal 1990–2000.

Founder, T Director at Queen's Quay Racquet Club and Lambton Golf & CC in Toronto, Canada '80-'90. Started MCTA Performance team, coaching top 15 state, national ranked players, winning over 100 state and national titles, earning U.S. university scholarships, 2000-07.

Founder and Owner of "Classic Racquets from Around the World," top museum-collection in Canada, amongst the best in the world, includes 2,000 racquets and memorabilia, featured in 12 exhibitions. Tells 150 years of international tennis history, racquet and equipment evolution and contribution of many players who made that history.

Sons Michael and David, former top five ranked juniors, Open ranked players, in Canada and Portugal, both certified coaches, Head Pros at prestigious Beaumaris Yatch Club, Ontario. Michael played for Brock U, Canada, David played for DI U Montana on scholarship.

Dedication: To the thousands of wonderful people, my students who made my professional life so rewarding, friends and professionals around the world, be in touch!

In memoriam: To my father Fernao D. Cysneiros, an enthusiastic man, energetic ranked tennis player.

Full credits: in thankful appreciation to my longtime best supporter, sweetheart and wife Cindy, met in Paradise (Island), Bahamas, 37 years ago.

RICH DADICH, Elite Professional, has been a USPTA member since 1972.

He was Tennis Coach/Psychology Faculty at Penn State University, McKeesport, PA, campus (1970–1971); Instructor/Counselor, Tony Trabert Tennis Camp, Ojai, CA (1972); Tennis Director, Pima County Parks and Recreation Dept, Tucson, AZ (1973–1977); Head Pro, Tucson National Golf Club, Tucson AZ (1977–1980); Tennis Coach/Psychology Faculty, University of Dubuque, Dubuque, IA (1981); Manager/Head Pro, Lubbock Municipal Tennis Center, Lubbock, TX, (1982–2000), which was named "Outstanding Public Facility" by USTA–1986; and Tennis Pro, Hillcrest Golf and Country Club, Lubbock, TX, (2002–2015).

Rich was named "Master Racquet Technician" by the U.S. Racquet Stringers Association USTA Umpire and Referee. He has officiated WTA, ATP Events, Davis Cup and Big 12 Collegiate Events.

BORIS (BORISLAV) DAMJANOVIC was born Sept. 8, 1954 in Palace of King Nikola (Mirko) Petrovic in Podgorica. He lived in St. Stefan and was working as a professional tennis coach in famous Deluxe Hotels City, St. Stefan, in castle Milocer. He is proficient and has knowledge of several languages (English, Germany, Russian, Italian and little bit French).

He finished Faculty of physical education in 1976 in Croatia for tennis teaching and in 1977 was licensed for tennis coaching in Serbia, Novi Sad. Boris has been a tennis player junior and senior, national and international and a coach for 46 years. Since 1976 he is the top athlete of Yugoslavia - Monetenegro for tennis. Boris has been a USPTA professional member since 1986. He was international world tennis judge on Davis Cup in former Yugoslavia. In last 10 years he is VIP for Davis Cup and Fed Cup team of Serbia.

Boris is married and has four daughters: Milica, Milena, Ana, Aleksandra and grandson Niksa.

BOB DAVIS, USPTA 1972 Member and 1987 awarded Master Professional. Other USPTA awards: 1981 National Player of Year over 45, 1982 Mid-Atlantic Player of Year and Maryland Player of Year, 1987 Maryland Professional of Year. Tennis letters at Classen High School, Oklahoma City two years and

RWV Tennis Courts

University of Oklahoma three years. Graduated from OU in 1942 with BS in EE.

While a one-year member of Bethesda, MD, Edgemoor Tennis Club, he earned low USLTA amateur singles and doubles rankings. Bob served on Board of USPTA Mid-Atlantic Division and as Greater Washington Tennis Association VP and Men's three Interclub Leagues Chairman. He headed volunteers in four-court design, construction and operations of Prince George's Country Club; six-court Cheveriy Swim and Racquet Club; 10-court NASA/GSFC Goddard Tennis Club. As consultant, headed renovation of Rockville College 10-hard courts. In 1981, he served as Director of Tennis at Country Club of Woodmore while working full time at GSFC as Aerospace Design Engineer/Manager on Multimission Spacecraft and Payloads and on the On-Orbit Solar Maximum Repair Mission. Bob worked for about 30-years to get first-class Junior Champions Training Center for Prince Georges County, which was finally built in College Park, MD, on MNCPPC leased park land with private capital. Taught lessons to many girls and boys who made low state, district, national and international rankings; many got college scholarships and later became tennis-teaching professionals. Robert was the recipient of the 2016 USPTA/Mid-Atlantic Division Hall of Fame Award.

Bob has published a 100-page color picture/text book, *Developing a Private Tennis Facility: How I Designed, Built & Operated My First-Class Home/Tennis Court at Low Cost*. He is still writing tennis technical books and tips.

MAX DAVIS, born in Athens, GA, graduated from W.J. Woodham High School in 1976. He attended USC-Coastal Carolina (1982), attaining Bachelor of Arts in Interdisciplinary Studies, Coastal Carolina University (1995) - Bachelor of Science in Physical Education, The University of Tennessee (December 1997)- Master of Science in Education, Major: Human Performance and Sports Concentration, Sports Administration.

Max is certified as USPTR Professional Level, (1982) Hilton Head Island, SC, and USPTA Elite Level (1986) Denver, CO.

His teaching highlights (1982 through present) include Director of Tennis (Present) Sheraton BWP- Myrtle Beach, SC; Director of Tennis Myrtle Beach Hilton; Director of Tennis, Racquet Club of Jackson, TN; Director of Tennis, Homestead Swim and Tennis, Colorado; Head Tennis Professional, Lakewood Country Club, Colorado and Junior Development Coordinator, Sea Pines Plantation, South Carolina

Max is currently the owner and president of NRSM, INC. established in 1999 in Myrtle Beach, SC, to provide high quality sports products and resurfacing services throughout the U.S.

JAIME De CARVALHO, emigrating from Brazil in 1964 and becoming a USPTA certified professional the following year, has had a distinguished 57-year career teaching children, women and men of all abilities. Before leaving Brazil, he was the Director of the Sao Paolo Tennis Federation and Head Coach of the Brazilian Pan American and Brazilian Davis Cup Teams.

He taught at the Westside Tennis Club in Forrest Hills, NY, and the Upper Ridgewood Tennis Club in New Jersey before becoming the Head Pro at the Bronxville Field Club in New York where he taught for 31 years. He was the Assistant Coach for the University of Virginia men's tennis team from 1997 to 2001.

Jaime's honors include being an original Head Tennis Advisory Staff member, Coach of the Year by the U.S. Squash Tennis Association in 1978, and Professional of the Year by the USPTA's Eastern Division in 1995.

ANTHONY "TONY" A. DERITIS started teaching tennis in 1969, coaching the team at Bishop Neumann High School. He taught for the city of Philadelphia Recreation Department, Upper Main Line YMCA, and Vic Seixas Tennis, Inc. He served as assistant supervisor of ballboys and ballgirls at the International Professional Tennis Championships when it was held in Philadelphia; was a tennis shop owner; was instrumental in the resurgence of one public parks club and co-founded another.

After moving to Florida, he worked as Tennis Director at Bay Beach Racquet Club, Fort Myers Beach (coached Lee County Women's B league champions), taught for the NJTL at STARS Recreation Center, and helped coach at Evangelical Christian School. Anthony was ranked in Florida in Men's 35 and 55 singles.

Anthony first joined the USPTA in 1977. After a brief hiatus in the late '80s, he rejoined the USPTA in 1990 and joined the PTR in 1990.

Tony is married (50 years in May), four children, 11 grandchildren, seven great-grandchildren.

BECKY DESMOND retired in 2014, after teaching art for 52 years, in the Downingtown (Pennsylvania) school system. She also coached the high school tennis teams for 42 years. As director, she expanded the community's summer tennis program to 115 participants, and five facilities, and established similar programs in several neighboring towns. After 12 years as head pro at a country club, she returned to head Downingtown's local public tennis programs.

She continues coaching several USTA league teams, which include players of all ages and still serves on boards and committees of USTA-Middle States and Philadelphia Area Tennis District.

Becky, a former president with the USPTA-Middle States Section, continues to be active with that organization. She earned the USPTA Master Professional rating in 1995 and co-authored the USTA book, *Coaching Tennis Successfully*. Becky received the International Tennis Hall of Fame's Educational Merit Award in 1998.

STEVE DIAMOND, a USPTA Elite Pro, has been a full-time teaching professional since 1979. He received the 2004 Alex Gordon Award as the USPTA National Professional of the Year and in 2015 he was inducted into the USPTA Eastern Division Hall of Fame. He is a two-time president of the USPTA's Eastern Division; only a few have ever served more than one term as president. Steve was also the Eastern Division Professional of the Year in 1990 and 1999.

Steve has been the Director of Tennis at the Green Brook Country Club in North Caldwell, NJ, during the summer months, since 1991.

As a player, Steve and partner Gina Genovese won the Lipton National Mixed Doubles Tournament in 1978 and the USTA Eastern Section ranked him and partner Rayni Borinsky No. 1 in mixed doubles in 1982. He played No. 1 singles for Rider University from 1976 to 1978.

JUAN DIAZ was born in Havana, Cuba, on Oct. 19, 1950. He graduated from Plant High School, Tampa, FL, in 1970 and obtained a Bachelor of Art from University of Florida in 1975.

While at University of Florida he won No. 1 singles (1975) and doubles (1973) titles at SEC Championships.

Juan played Singles at the US Open Championships, 1976. He ranked No. 1 in 35's and over USTA in doubles 1986 and ranked No. 2 in 35's and over USTA in singles 1987.

Juan was a member of the US Team at Italia Cup 1986, runner-up and winning team in 1987.

MILLIE DIDIO is Senior Teaching Pro at The Tennis Club of Hastings and former Director of Adult Programs. She also holds seasonal positions as Assistant Director at Ardsley Swim and Tennis and Staff Pro for Lifetime Racquet Sports, Inc. Prior to that she was Staff Pro at Orienta Beach Club, Whippoorwill Country Club and Kela Tennis, all in Westchester County, NY.

Three time MVP All County first singles tennis player and Suffolk County singles semi-finalist for Northport High School. Two Time Academic All American Softball Player for Division I UConn. Played on the ITF/WTA professional tour two different times, and in between had a law career. On most recent tour she achieved a national ranking in singles of 106 and an ETA ranking of 2 in singles and won the 2011 USTA Waterbury Hardcourt Championship in women's open singles and player alternate for the 2008 US Open Qualifiers in singles.

GEORGE F. DIEFFENBACH was born and raised in Williamsport, PA, competed in the MSTA section as a junior, competed for Williamsport HS and earned four varsity letters for the University of Pittsburgh. He earned a BS, MEd, and Ed.D. from Pitt. He was the Pitt head tennis coach from 1975–2012. His team records were men 189-157, women 318-274. Dieffenbach has earned district, sectional and national USTA rankings. He has been a head pro and director of tennis at numerous clubs. George currently lives with his wife and children in Pittsburgh, Pa. A 20-year USTA member, he currently teaches at the Laurie Ann West Community Center and Meadow Park in Ohara Twp, PA. He is also a competitive runner racing from one mile to the marathon. George loves teaching proper tennis biomechanics and a confident mental game and strategy.

JAI DiLOUIE is a five-time USTA National Junior Champion, three-time NCAA Div. I All American, two-time member of USTA Jr. Davis Cup Team and USTA U21 Men's Amateur Hardcourt Champion.

Jai attained ATP Top 100 Singles Ranking (1980–1984). He was SMU Women's Head Coach of Conference Champions (1988) as first year coach. In 1989 and 1990, Jai was L.T.A. Men's National Coach. In 1991 he was I.T.F. Men's Professional Team Coach. He was a USA (full time) National Coach (1993–2010).

Jai and wife Khuyen have a daughter, Ava.

JOE DINOFFER has conducted clinics and exhibitions in over 50 countries, personally logging over 30,000 hours of instruction in English, Spanish, and German. A Master Professional in both the USPTA and PTR, Joe received the prestigious 2006 USPTA Tennis Industry Excellence Award, and was named USPTA Texas Division Pro of the Year for 2012.

Joe has written seven books, more than 20 DVDs, has authored more than 250 published articles and has also had numerous instructional tips airing on the Tennis Channel. Plus, Joe's YouTube channel has more than 300 video clips with over 40,000 views each month. As a member of the Head/Penn Advisory Staff and National Speaker Bureau, Joe is a frequent speaker at national and international tennis conferences, having conducted over 300 workshops since 1995.

He is also the founder of Oncourt Offcourt, Ltd., the world leader in creative tennis products for the teaching professional and coach.

NATALIZIA DIROMA (AKA NATALIE DIROMA) was born in Italy in 1964. Her amateur highlights include USPTA Women's National Champion in Las Vegas, 2002, Ranked No. 1, USTA Southern Section (1997–2000) Singles and Doubles, ranked National Top 10 (1998–2002) Single and Doubles and Southern Senior Cup Single and Doubles Player for nine years.

Natalie is actively participating in various ProAm charity events: Pro-Am—Wexford, Hilton Head Island, SC; Pro-Am—Roswell Country Club, Atlanta, GA; Pro-Am—Atlanta, GA; Pro-Am St Ives Country Club for Charity Guild of St Ives, Atlanta, GA.

She is currently Residential Head Pro at South Carolina Yacht Club (Hilton Head Island, SC) and was Director of Adult Tennis Programs for over 10 years at Sea Pines Resort in Hilton Head, SC, (2001–2012).

Natalie worked with Nick Bollettieri and Van Der Meer Tennis Center, Hilton Head Island, SC, as Tennis Professional and Club Assistant Administrator.

Natalie is married and living in Hilton Head Island.

RITA DOTSON is director of junior tennis and staff professional at the Roger Scott Tennis Center. She has served as President of the 501(c)3 not-for-profit organization Tennis-4-Everyone since 2001.

Dotson received B.S. and M.S. degrees in Health, Leisure and Sports and Sports Science from the University of West Florida. She is an active volunteer in the community. She received the USTA 10 & Under Tennis Award from the USTA and is an advocated for 10 & Under Tennis, Junior Team Tennis and L9 and L8 Entry Level Tournaments.

As a player she was ranked 6th is Florida Region 1 40 Doubles.

EMMA DOYLE is an internationally renowned professional speaker from Melbourne, Australia. She has been a proud member of the USPTA since 1998.

Emma is the director of ACE Coach, which is a consultancy business that has impacted over 100,000 players and coaches over the past 20 years. She coached for eight years on the world tour helping numerous female players reach career high singles and doubles rankings inside top 120 WTA.

After representing Middle Tennessee State University as the No. 1 player, Emma went on to coach Australian junior Fed Cup teams and was a former National Women's Selector. She is a Tennis Australia High Performance Coach, Talent Development Coach and the lead learning facilitator for Tennis Australia's coach education courses.

Emma's mission is to empower more female players and coaches in our industry and to inspire, improve and impact the communication, coordination and confidence of people around the world.

SUSAN "SUE" DOYLE began teaching tennis at age 15. She was a high school and middle school art teacher 10 years.

Sue has been a member of USPTA for 24 years, 1998 USPTA NE Northern Pro of the Year and received 2nd Annual Cheshire County Sportsman of the Year Award. She has a "Brick" at the International Tennis Hall of Fame (donated by the Keene Tennis Community.) She played four times in the NE 65 Mixed Doubles No. 1 and three times in the NE 55 Women's Doubles No. 1.

She has been Tennis Pro at Keene Country Club for 28 years, 12 years as girls tennis coach at Monadnock Regional High School, Volunteer coach with girls tennis team at Keene HS for the past 15 years. Sue has run the Keene City Championships for the past 30 years and a Memorial Tournament for the past six years. She has been tennis pro at the Racquet Club since 1972 and has coached two league teams since 1975.

She has made three trips to Nationals with senior 4.5 teams. She is an Addy Cup and Intersectional Team Player from New England. Sue was founder and director of Keene Tennis Camp for 13 years.

ROD DULANY has been a part of the tennis industry for the last 40+ years. He served as the Director of Tennis at Washington Golf and Country Club, was joint owner of Westwinds Tennis and Fitness Club, Executive Director of USTA/Mid-Atlantic Section and Director of Tennis at the Ocean City Tennis Center.

Rod also served in various capacities in both the USPTA and the USTA. During his years of service within the USPTA, he was President of the USPTA/Mid Atlantic Division from 1977–1980. At the national level, he was on the Executive Committee for 20 years. During this time Rod sat on the National USPTA Board of Directors for eight years and from 1998–2000 served as National President of the USPTA.

Rod served on over 14 National USTA Committees as well as five years as President of USTA/Mid-Atlantic Section and two years as the Delegate to USTA.

He achieved Master Professional status and was elected to both the Mid-Atlantic Tennis Hall of Fame and the USPTA Mid-Atlantic Tennis Hall of Fame. In 1980 Rod was voted the National USPTA Professional of the Year.

MAX DUNAEV, originally from Moscow, Russia, at 36, is USPTA Elite Professional since 2005. Nationally ranked he made finals of ITF junior events and moved to U.S. at age 17. Max earned All-America Athlete honors at Tyler Junior College. At Division I University of Texas at San Antonio he made all-conference player in singles and doubles, helped the team capture two conference titles and graduated with a degree in International Business.

As a teaching professional Max represented Sonterra Country Club as Head Professional, competed in USTA open tournaments capturing five titles in one year including Houston Coca-Cola Open. Later he trained best players in the world while coaching for Roddick Total Tennis and Macci Tennis Academies.

Max plus his beautiful better half Andrea and two wonderful sons, Maxim and Xavier, reside in Delray Beach, FL. He works as Head Professional at Fountains Country Club and coaches for TDK Tennis.

TIMOTHY "TIM" NEAL DUNFORD'S amateur highlights include All Conference-All Academic (2001-03), Coaches Choice Award 2003.

Professionally, was Assistant Men's and Women's Tennis Coach at Mount Olive College; D-II (NC)/2007-09. Men's team achieved the highest ranking in the program's history of 30th Nationally and the Women's team reached the NCAA Tournament as an at-large. Head Men's and Women's Tennis Coach at Thiel College; D-III (PA)/2010–13/ No tennis program since 2005. Tim built both programs. In 2013, Men's team broke the record for most wins in a season 14 (previous eight), most consecutive wins with six (previous four), most wins in conference play with five (previous four) and best winning percentage and overall record with .736/14-5 (previous .615/8-5). Head Men's Tennis Coach at The College of Wooster; D-III (Ohio)/2013–14/Wooster had not had a winning season since 2009 and not won a conference match since 2009. The year Tim was there, they went 10-9 and won a conference match. They beat several teams they had lost to previously and had wins over two D-II teams. Tim is currently Director of Tennis at Albion College; D-III (MI)/his first season with players he recruited. Tim looks forward to turning these programs around and putting them at the top of the MIAA.

Tim credits the loving support of parents, Harvey and Leda Dunford; brother, Chris Dunford and non-related brother/best friend, Bruce Davis. Last but not least, former coach/ best friend, Brandon Padgett.

ANDY DURHAM, raised in rural Indiana, working on the farm and playing on a Hall of Fame undefeated high school team, his first taste of teaching came after graduating from Purdue and teaching 4th grade.

To further learn the game he spent two years learning his trade on the Penn Circuit, post Wimbledon grass court tournaments, eventually winning the Laver/Emerson Mixed Doubles Championship.

As the student makes the teacher, he was entirely fortunate to work with students who became world class players. Working in the U.S. and then in U.K. where he developed the "Masterclass" for tennis pros, was Director of Tennis at the first American style tennis club in London, trained and tested hundreds of pros for the PTR and passing all the requirements to be a Registered Professional in U.K. Speaking engagements for the LTA, monthly articles in Tennis World and publications for the LTA and a book, *Play to Win: Tennis,* led to becoming selected as the Director of the Exhibition court at the 1992 Federation Cup in Nottingham, England.

JULIE DYBENDAHL, USPTA Professional, USPTR Level 3 Junior Development Certified, ITPA Tennis Performance Trainer, initially specialized in kids' coaching, using the coloured ball structure since 2003 and was awarded the role of Tennis Australia Hotshots Ambassador in 2009.

She learned most of her coaching in Europe in what is known as the "mini tennis" system.

Coaching venues include Wimbledon, West Middlesex and Manchester, UK; Sydney, Australia, Sanctuary Cove, QLD, Australia, Tallahassee, FL.

Since relocating to the U.S. (2013), Julie has attained USPTA and USPTR certifications for teaching adults and high level junior development training.

Attaining Tennis Performance Trainer with ITPA and Mental Toughness certification with Human Performance Institute, these certifications complement her USPTA certification attained in 2014.

Julie is a highly accomplished tennis player playing at 5.0 level in USTA rating system. She is ranked in Top 10 in the world as a ladies doubles player in the 45-year-old category and currently Top 20 in the same category of singles play.

FRED "FRITZ" A. EARLE III was born Jan. 9, 1934 in Modesto, CA. Graduating from Modesto High School (1951), he attended Modesto Junior College, AA, (1951-53), UCLA, BS, (graduated 1955) and graduate school earning General Secondary Teaching Credential (1956).

Fred was National Junior College Championship team member (1952, 1953) and UCLA 1954 NCAA championship team member.

He owned and managed Modesto Swim and Racquet Club from 1956 to 1988 with his father, Fred, and Ken Walts.

Fred was one of the first 18 Master Professionals in USPTA.

Fred was Director of Tennis at Carmel Country Club in Charlotte from 1987 until 2002. He retired from active club direction and teaching in 2002.

He is married to North Carolina Tennis Hall of Fame coach and player Beverly. Fred and Beverly run free summer tennis program and volunteer coaches for high school boys and girls tennis teams.

GLEN EASTRIDGE graduated from Courtland High School (Virginia), 1982. Graduated in 1988 with a Bachelor of Science (Physical Education Major/Coaching Minor) and 1990 Master of Science in Education (Physical Education Major/Higher Education Minor), both at James Madison University.

Glen ranked 11 in Mid Atlantic USTA region Men's 30 Singles and ranked 20 in Mid Atlantic USTA region Men's Open Doubles.

He was Mary Baldwin College Women's Head Coach (1991-95), George Mason University Men's and Women's Assistant Coach (1996-98), Kutztown University Men's and Women's Head Coach (1998-99), Eastern Mennonite High School (VA) Boys Head Coach (1987–1990) (four VIC Conference championship teams/1990 VIC Coach of the Year), Hanover High School (New Hampshire) Girls Head Coach (2003–14) (three state team championships/one individual state doubles champion team/one New England Championships doubles champion team).

Glen is a New Hampshire Interscholastic Athletic Association (NHIAA) Tennis Committee member (since 2012).

He and wife Shelagh have a daughter, Hannah.

JOE EDLES grew up playing tennis in Southern California and held top 10 national rankings in 14, 16 and 18's divisions, was named to

US Junior Davis Cup squad, collegiate All-American at Southern Methodist University in Dallas, Texas, earning a BA, Sociology.

In Colorado, USPTA Elite Professional Joe is currently Head Pro at Greenwood Athletic and Tennis Club, Greenwood Village, was at Mount Vernon Country Club, Meadowcreek Racquet Club, Denver Country Club and Pinehurst Country Club 20 years as Director of Tennis. In Illinois he taught at Champaign Country Club, The Racquet Club.

Ranked No. 1 in open doubles in Colorado with a USTA No. 1 ranking, 40-and-over singles, Intermountain Section. USPTA national champion in the 40-and-over, No. 1 national ranking, singles and doubles, Joe was president of Intermountain Division, Pro of the Year and national chairperson for Multicultural Committee, Division and District and Nominating circuit tournaments.

In 2007, his parents, sister, brother and he were awarded USTA Tennis Family of the Year, Southern California Section.

MIKE EDLES, 20th season as head coach, UCI Women's Tennis Team, winning record in 15 of 19 seasons and Big West Conference tournament final 12 times.

Coach Edles' most recent team-records include Big West regular season title and a third trip to the NCAA Tournament in 2013. Awarded Big West Coach of the Year award five times after posting a perfect conference record for the second time in his career, posting a 20-match win streak, leading the squad to its highest-ever national ranking of No. 23. Other coach of the Year awards: ITA/Southwest Region, Wilson/ITA West Region and has led several teams to year-end national rankings.

Edles, a four-year player, UCI and NCAA All-America earned a B.A. in economics. Other head coaching positions with numerous win records and awards: Cal State Bakersfield, Chapman University, Cal State Hayward, plus head women's coach at Boise State. Daughter Ellie played four years at UC Davis on a full tennis scholarship.

BECKY EDLES-RYE grew up Southern California in a tennis playing family. Brothers Joe and Mike are USPTA Elite Pros, mom Florence still plays weekly at 88, dad Dominador played tennis for US Navy and headed the 2007 SCTA Family of the Year Award. Son Rob is also USPTA certified and played four years for Whitman College collegiate tennis.

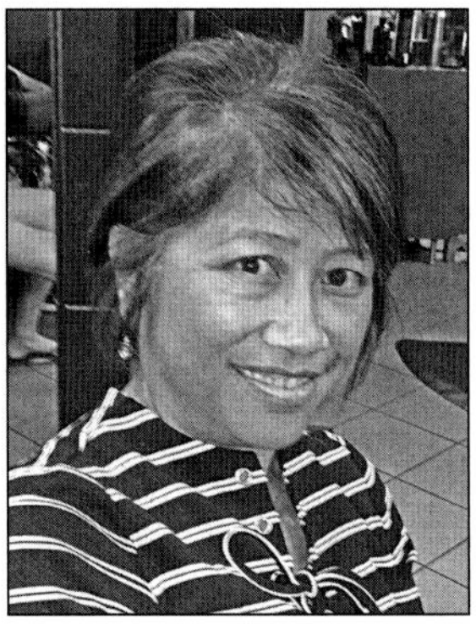

Becky was a ranked junior, played collegiate tennis at Long Beach City College, San Diego State University and is a USPTA Elite Pro. For SCTA, USTA Southern California she was the USTA Schools Director/Community Tennis Development and since 2002 is the Executive Director of the Orange County Community Tennis Association.

BRIAN EGELHOFF, former ranked junior player, is a teaching pro at the Elite Sports Club in Mequon, WI, since the 1990s. He is also the co-director/instructor of the Advantage Wisconsin Adaptive/ Wheelchair tennis programs for 25 years. Brian, USPTA (Wheelchair certified) has personally coached internationally ranked wheelchair players as well as recreational players. He is presently instructing adaptive tennis at the JCC Rainbow camp and working with veterans.

Brian was an assistant pro for a USTA Native American Midwest Tennis Program and presently teaches tennis in before and after middle school programs in the Mequon-Thiensville school district and in the summers teaches tennis for the Mequon-Thiensville Recreation Dept.

Currently he is serving on the USTA Midwest Adaptive Tennis committee, which is increasing awareness in the Midwest of Adaptive/Wheelchair programs. Brian has received the WTA's Rollie Mueller Presidents award in 1997, the USPTA Midwest Division's Fay Tooley Award in 2009 and was the 2009 USPTA National Star Award recipient.

JACKIE MUELLER EGELHOFF, former nationally ranked player, is the Manager/ Head Tennis Pro at The River Tennis Club in River Hills, WI, since 1984. She was Miss Wisconsin Tennis in 1964. Jackie is the Homestead High School Varsity Tennis Coach of the boys and girls teams since 1980. The girls' teams won five consecutive state championships. The boys' teams have five runner-up finishes. She was inducted into the Wisconsin High School Tennis Coaches Hall of Fame in 2015.

Jackie was The Wisconsin High School Coach of the Year three times; NFHS 2010 State Coach of the Year and 2010 USPTA Midwest HS Coach of the Year. She received The USTA Midwest, Cap Leighton award in 1997, the WTA, Bill Letwin award in 1991 and the WTA Rollie Mueller Presidents award in 1997. Jackie was the 2011 USPTA National High School Coach of the Year.

Jackie, USPTA (Wheelchair Certified) with son, Brian, created and teaches the Advantage Wisconsin Adaptive/ Wheelchair Tennis Programs and has been directing them for 25 years. She ran The National Indoor Wheelchair Championships for two years and has coached beginners to U.S. and ITF ranked wheelchair players. Currently she is on the Board of Directors of the Wisconsin Adaptive Sports Association and is working with veterans.

TODD ELLENBECKER is a physical therapist and clinic director of Physiotherapy Associates Scottsdale Sports Clinic in Scottsdale, AZ, and is the Vice President of Medical Services for the ATP World Tour. He received his degree in physical therapy

from the University of Wisconsin-LaCrosse in 1985 and a master's degree in exercise physiology from Arizona State University in 1989. He completed his Doctor of Physical Therapy from MGH–Institute of Health Professions in 2006. He is a certified sports clinical specialist and orthopaedic clinical specialist by the APTA. He is a certified strength and conditioning specialist by the NSCA. He is a certified USPTA tennis-teaching Master Professional, and served as Chairman of the USTA National Sport Science Committee for 14 years and is a current member. Todd is also the National Director of Clinical Research for Physiotherapy Associates. In 2008 Todd was the recipient of Samuel Hardy Educational Merit award from the International Tennis Hall of Fame.

MARK ELLIOTT, USPTA Elite Tennis Professional, has been a coach of the Chinese National Team, Chinese Davis Cup and Federation Cup head coach, teacher, director of tennis, host of tournaments, owner and part owner of clubs.

Mark Elliott (right) with Kiersten Fairchilds

Highlights of his career include: 1968 Mark played Pacific Northwest Circuit as Amateur. In 1972 he played the Professional Circuit in New Zealand, winning numerous tournaments including National Mixed Doubles Champion. From 1972–1974 he played US Open, Australian Open, and various other Professional Tennis Events in England, France, Germany, Holland and the Netherlands.

In 1985 was NorCal Coach of the Year/ Coached USTA Junior Wimbledon Team (1980/1987).

In 1987/1989 Seascape Racquet Club - Part Owner and Tennis Professional. Taught numerous Tennis Professionals, instrumental in bringing the Cal Open Tennis Tournament to Aptos, direct liaison with USTA. WTA and ATP governing boards, ran club member and junior events.

From 1999–2001 Kapalua Resort - Director of Tennis for the Ritz Carlton and Kapalua Bay Hotel. Hosted National 16–18 Boys and Girls Tournaments

JOHN EMBREE was named CEO and Executive Director for the USPTA starting in October 2012. He has held a wide variety of influential tennis industry roles for more than 30 years. They include serving as President of Prince Sports, The Americas; President of Balle de Match LLC; and spent 17 years at Wilson Sporting Goods Co. where he held a variety of positions including Vice President/ General Manager, Racquet Sports Division for six and one half years. Prior to joining the USPTA in October, 2012, he launched a tennis consulting practice in 2010 to assist endemic brands, associations and new corporate entities in maximizing their impact in the tennis marketplace. His client list included the USTA, Intercollegiate Tennis Association, Peter Burwash International, OTG (Off the Grid) Technologies, and Donnay USA.

In April, 2014, Embree was named to be on the Board of Governors of the International Tennis Hall of Fame in Newport, RI and has served on many national USTA committees since 1980, including the USTA Nominating Committee in 2005-2006, the Vice Chair of USTA Professional Circuits Committee from 2009-2010. He recently completed a two-year stint on the USTA 10 and Under Tennis Committee and is serving on the Local Play and Competition Committee for 2015/2016. He is also serving on the USTA Adult Implementation task force and has been named to serve on the USTA Sportsmanship task force for 2015-2016. During 2014, he helped the ITA with its College Match Format Task force and now serves on the ITA Hall of Fame Selection Committee.

In addition, he served as Presidential appointee of the Board of Directors of USTA Middle States section, was a board member over three years for the Arthur Ashe Tennis and Learning Center in Philadelphia, is a member of TIA Board of Directors and Executive Committee, past member of the Board of Directors of American College of Sports Medicine Foundation, and past President of the Chicago Tennis Patrons Foundation. One of his proudest achievements in tennis was the creation of the USTA Adult League Tennis program in 1980, when he served as the first USTA Adult League Tennis Administrator for two years. He earned a bachelor's degree from Washington & Lee University in Lexington, VA, and was inducted into the W&L Athletic Hall of Fame in 2005.

DOUG ENG, Ed.D., Ph.D., is a USPTA Master Professional and PTR International Master Professional, one of 10 worldwide to hold both honors. Doug has taught tennis for 29 years, including 20 as a college coach and headed several junior academies. Doug is a USTA High Performance Coach and has coached over 200 ranked players. He was named Best of Boston in 2010 by Boston Magazine and has won four divisional pro of the year honors from USPTA and PTR including both in 2008. In July 2013, Doug received the US Olympic Committee Doc Counsilman Award 2012 Coach of the Year for science and technology in Colorado Springs. Doug was President of USPTA New England, 2014–2015 and was co-chair of USPTA National Education Committee and College Curriculum committee, 2012–2013. He was President of PTR New England, 1994–2001. Doug has written nearly 100 articles on sport science, techniques and tactical analytics. Has additional certifications from NSCA (CSCS), IPTA (CTPT), Etcheberry Experience and Academia Sanchez-Casal. He has spoken at many USPTA, USTA ITA and PTR conferences, including the PTR Italy Forum and Australian Open Grand Slam Coaches Conference. He has trained and certified 2,000 coaches as a tester for both PTR, USPTA and workshop leader for USTA.

CLAUDE ENGLAND is a USPTA Elite Pro with 40+ years of teaching experience and 50+ years of playing competitive tournament tennis.

Currently, he is Director of Tennis at Woodholme Country Club in Baltimore, MD. Claude was born in New Zealand where he completed his high

school education and played junior tennis. A three-time National Champion he won 17+ under singles and doubles titles in 1972 and 19+ under singles title in 1974.

He represented New Zealand in International Junior Events, competing for the Linton Cup in Sydney, Australia in 1974 and the Junior Davis Cup (Galea Cup) in Italy in 1975. Claude graduated from the University of Maryland, attending on a tennis and soccer scholarship from 1975–1978. He was winner of the prestigious John W. Guckeyson Award for excellence in two sports, 1977.

A former ATP Touring professional (1978–1983), Claude achieved a world ranking of 235, competing worldwide in the U.S., South America, Asia, Australia and New Zealand. After touring he settled in Baltimore, MD, and began his full-time teaching career.

One of his proudest directing and teaching achievements was being the Director of Tennis at Chestnut Ridge Country Club in Baltimore, MD, for 27 years, (1984–2011).

Claude has continued to compete in Senior Age group tennis highlighted by: USPTA National Mens 35+ Singles Champion (1990–1991), USPTA Mens 35+ Player of the Year Award (1991), represented the U.S. in International Team Competition in Australia, Paraguay, Spain and Austria, played No. 1 singles in the victorious USA Dubler Cup in Paraguay 2000 and No. 2 singles on the second place Dubler Cup team in Austria 2001, ranked No. 1 USTA Mens 40+ singles (1998–1999), winner of USTA Mens 45+ National Singles Clay Court Championship (2000), 30+ Maryland State Titles and 30+ Mid-Atlantic Titles.

LANE EVANS has been a tennis teaching professional for almost 35 years, 27 of them as a USPTA member. Lane is a USPTA Elite Professional. He is certified as both a Fitness Trainer and Senior Fitness Specialist with the International Sports Science Association and is designated ITPA CTPS and MTPS degrees. He is also a USPTA tester.

He is Chairman of the USPTA National Sports Science Committee and the USPTA National Fitness & Wellness Committee. He is also on the USPTA National Tester Committee.

Awards: 2011—USPTA NC Professional of the Year and USTA NC Walt Stamer Senior Male Player of the Year. 2014—Fred Burdick "Pride of the South" award. 2014—USPTA/TIA Industry Excellence award and USTA NC "Carlton Harris Tennis Professional of the Year." 2015—"Alan Henry USPTA Southern Professional of the Year." 2015—five time "Top 10" Education Point Achiever-USPTA.

SUSAN A. EVANS played college tennis at the University of Iowa where she obtained a Marketing BBA in 1991. She played both singles and doubles for all four years.

Susan is an USPTA Elite Tennis Professional. She was the 2014 USPTA National Clay Court Women's 40 Doubles Champion and Singles Runner-up and the 2015 USPTA Women's 40's and Over Doubles Player of the Year.

She is the founder, owner and operator of Susan's Adventures, LLC – Island Tennis and Sunshine Bikes Tours.

MIKE FASH was born in Wimbledon in 1940 and as a junior was coached by the renowned British Davis Cup player and coach, Tony Mottram. Mike played junior tournaments in England and some in Europe. He joined the BBC, traveling extensively making documentaries. This made it difficult to continue tournament tennis.

Mike immigrated to the U.S. in 1980 to continue his movie career, came to L.A. and joined the USPTA.

He played at the Marina City Club near Santa Monica and then moved to the Desert and joined the Indian Wells Tennis Garden. Although retired, under the Director of Tennis Tom Fey, he now assists with the USPTA charity events, Kid's Day at the BNP Paribas Open, etc.

Mike ended his movie career as a Professor at USC Film School, lives in La Quinta, CA, and has a son and two daughters.

TRISH FAULKNER, originally from Sydney, Australia, has lived in the U.S. since 1965. Trish became a U.S. citizen in 2000.

As an Australian Junior champion, Trish was a tour player from 1962–1971. Trish began teaching tennis in Michigan for many years, eventually owning an indoor facility. Trish also played one year for the Detroit Loves World Team Tennis team. In 1974 Trish began working for the Women's Tennis Association as Head Tour Director and in 1983 Trish moved to Florida and worked full time for the WTA. In 1984 Trish was appointed the Marketing Director for the Women's Professional Tour. In 1988 Trish left the WTA and formed Triosports International, a sports marketing corporation which owned or operated four of the Virginia Slims Tour events for five years. In 1991, Trish returned to managing tennis facilities in Florida as the Director of Tennis at St. Andrews Country Club for three years.

Since 1994 Trish has been Director of Tennis at BallenIsles Country Club, in Palm Beach Gardens, FL. Trish has run over 100 USTA tournaments, three ITF World Senior Events in 1997, 2001 and 2014 with more than 48 nations and 2000 players.

Trish has been a member of the USPTA since 1967. She has served on the Women's Committee, the D&I Committee and the Florida Board. In 2015 Trish took over as President of the Florida Division. She co-wrote the "Complete Idiot's Guide to Tennis."

Trish has won numerous awards from the USPTA - female player of the year award, (twice), Special Service Award and has been ranked No. 1 in singles and doubles in the USTA senior rankings for many years, winning 38 gold balls. Trish received the Key to the City of Palm Beach Gardens in 2002 and was inducted into the Florida Tennis Hall of Fame in 2005. In 2001 Trish won the ITF World Singles and Team titles in Australia. Trish was named Sports Contributor of the Year for the Palm Beach County Sports Commission in 2016.

Trish has two sons, Grant and Scott, daughter-in-law Zamira and three grandchildren – Sydney, Emma and Ronan.

PAUL FEIN is a 45-year USPTA teaching pro-coach with an Elite rating, former top 10 men's open singles and top 5 doubles New England player and current No. 1 Super-Senior player. A tennis writer, Fein received nearly 40 writing awards and authored three books, "Tennis Confidential," "You Can Quote Me on That" and "Tennis Confidential II"—all ranked No. 1 among tennis books on Amazon.

Paul Fein with Martina Hingis

He founded-directed 1971–74 Springfield Satellite Tournament, one of the world's augural five Satellite tournaments, and commended by World Tennis magazine. He was catalyst-strategist to help save and re-open Forest Park's eight public clay courts in 1981; president, Springfield Tennis Club and Springfield Tennis Council; 2010 USTWA Vice-president. Awards include 1991 Tennis Week magazine's International Tennis Writer of the Year; 1987 Springfield Tennis Opportunity Program Community Service Award; 1988 NELTA Media Award (Sportswriter, Springfield Sunday Republican); 2003 USPTA New England Western Professional of the Year.

MARILYN S. FEINSTEIN, Elite Pro; 30-year USPTA member. Taught by her mother, Thelma "Tybie" Thall Sommer (Tennis Pro; in the USATT Hall of Fame; Lifetime Achievement Award Winner, winning two World Championships in Table Tennis). Marilyn was ranked as a junior in the Southwest; played varsity for the No. 1 college team, ASU; taught at several Connecticut clubs and was Assistant Coach for Yale University's Women's Team. As President of New Haven Tennis Association, she created a unique Team Tennis League, tripling their membership. In 1990 she helped Xerox Corporation become a founding corporate sponsor of the Volvo International Men's Tennis Championships in New Haven. Currently teaching in Colorado, she also does Peak Performance Coaching in work, sports and relationships. She and her mother are writing a book, "You Don't Have to Be the Best to Beat the Best: How to Create the Zone for Peak Performance in Sports and Life."

JOE FELICE played and was captain of the Penn State University Tennis Team where he graduated in 1967. He was commissioned in the U.S. Army where he was a member of the U.S. Army Tennis Team in 1969.

Joe started his Professional Career in 1969 at Franklin Racquet Club in Southfield, MI. In the Detroit area, he was Tennis Director at Franklin Racquet Club, Grosse Point Hunt Club and Beverly Hills Racquet Club. Also, Joe owned and operated Irish Hills Tennis Camp at Hillsdale College in Hillsdale, Michigan for 10 years. He was 1977 USPTA Midwest Pro of the Year.

Joe moved to Albuquerque, NM, in 1981, where he was Tennis Director at Tennis Club of Albuquerque for one year before becoming Tennis Director at Albuquerque Country Club for 25 years. In 1990 the Joe Felice Family was named the Southwest Section Family of the Year. Since 2006 Joe has been teaching and captaining USTA League Teams at Sierra Vista West Tennis Center. From 1989–2004 he was Head NTRP Verifier for the USTA Southwest Section. In 2014 he was the Southwest Section League Captain of the Year, captaining 23 teams and playing on 10 teams. In 2015 Joe received the Outstanding Tournament Enrichment Award from the Northern New Mexico District.

Joe has been a USPTA Elite Professional since 1971. He has been a member of the Head/Penn Advisory Staff for 37 years. Joe has been a highly ranked player in both USTA and USPTA rankings. Joe was President of the Northern New Mexico Tennis Association during 2014 and 2015.

BORIS FETBROYT is a USPTA Elite Professional and former Division I All-American tennis player for the University of Maryland Terrapins in 2009. He was only the third All-American in school history behind the great John Lucas and Andy Orban. After graduating Maryland, Boris went on to get his master's in Sports Management at Drexel University as well as becoming a teaching professional at the Country Club of Fairfax. After four years at the Country Club of Fairfax, Boris went on and became the Head Tennis and Paddle Professional at Baltimore Country Club. Boris considers USPTA Master Professional and current Director of Racquets at Baltimore Country Club Jay Bewley as his mentor. Recently Boris was awarded the Mid-Atlantic Under 30 Pro of the Year Award.

ANDY FINDLAY, originally from London, England, graduated from Mercyhurst Univ., Erie, PA, in 1981 with 3.4 QPA, an 81-32 singles record and a 72-27 doubles count. He was a four-time, first team All-American and Academic All-American. Also, Andy successfully coached the Mercyhurst men from 1982–1986 and Edinboro Univ. from 1992–2003. Currently, he is the Head Pro at Pennbriar A.C. Club and Lake Shore C.C. in Erie. In May 2004, Andy was inducted into the Mercyhurst Athletic Hall of Fame. Additionally, Andy owns and operates the www.intensetenniscamps.com in Slippery Rock, PA.

Andy is the lead coach for the USTA STC in Pittsburgh, has attended 43 national workshop, works as an RTC coach and coaches at the USTA National Team Championships in Mobile, AL.

In 1991, with Dennis Ranalli, the duo was ranked No. 1 in USTA MS. This pair currently represents the section as No. 1 doubles in USTA team age-group events.

JON FISCHER spent over 40 years teaching in Southeastern Michigan. A USPTA member since 1971, Jon spent 15 years as a tester and was named the USPTA Michigan Professional of the Year, (1973) and (1990). Jon developed numerous nationally ranked players and played a major role in the development of Lisa Bonder who reached No. 9 in the world in 1984. Jon spent 17 years as the Director of Tennis at the Travis Pointe Country Club. Jon was also the Junior Director for the Franklin Racquet Club and the Head Professional for the Huron Valley Tennis Club. Jon strung over 30,000 racquets and served in many capacities for the USTA and USPTA. A graduate of the University of Michigan, Jon lived and breathed everything Michigan. Go Blue! Jon passed away in the fall of 2014.

ROALD FLATER, member of USTA and USPTA Elite Pro for 40 years, started playing at age 9 in Norway and Sweden in Junior Tournaments. He has played competitive tennis tournaments for 80 years and still plays nationally and internationally.

Roald has ranked No. 1 in every age class division in Colorado and Intermountain, 38-80 in singles and/or doubles for 45 years since 1962. He won US National Public Parks Championship (1984 and 2012). He won the Gardnar Mulloy International World Cup for USA (2007), Christchurch, New Zealand as part of US Team.

He was elected USPTA National Player of the Year over 45 (1987), 10 times was elected USPTA Intermountain Player of the Year over 45 and elected Colorado CTA Senior Player of the Year over 50 (2002).

USA team that won the Gardnar Mulloy International World Cup championship in 2007. L-R: Tony Franco, Bill Tully, Roald Flater and Graydon Nichols.

Roald was elected to Colorado Tennis Hall of Fame in 2008.

He has coached boys and girls tennis teams as well as several high-ranking junior girls.

Roald and Sheryl have three daughters, four grandchildren and one great-granddaughter.

LORI IRENE FLICK played in No. 1 position at Greenwood High School (2007–2010), she was on the team for six years. Lori earned the all Region and MVP award all four years. She played for Women's Tennis Team at Lander University (2001–2014) and earned an Academic Tennis Award in 2013.

Lori currently is Stoney Point Teaching Professional at "The Links" on Lake Greenwood, SC; Greenwood High School (Region AAAA School) Head Girls' Tennis Coach and Tennis Instructor at Lander University.

Lori won 9.0 Mixed Doubles Team state final (2015) and held No. 1 Rank position in Womens' Open for SC USTA (2014 and 2015).

She was named to Peach Belt Conference Presidential Honor Roll all four years at Lander University and named ITA Scholar Athlete for 2014.

JOHN L. FOLEY has been a USPTA Pro since 1962. He has taught at Abenaqui in Rye, NH; The Indoor Court in East Providence, RI; The Worcester Tennis Club in Worcester, MA; The Sippican Club in Marion, MA; and the Essex County Club in Manchester By The Sea, MA.

At present, he is in his 51st year at the North Shore Tennis and Squash Club in Salem, MA.

In 2009 the club was renamed the John L. Foley Tennis Center at NSTSC in his honor.

He earned the Master Pro Classification in 2000 and was inducted into the USPTA/NE Hall Of Fame in 2015.

Over the years, he has served as Sec./Treasurer and Vice President of the NEPTA. He also served on many committees in the association.

In 1966, according to the Sony Corporation of New York, John was the first tennis pro to purchase a Sony video recorder for tennis instruction.

In the '70s/'80s, he gave many exhibitions as "Racket Man" for various charities. Many of these were with Bobby Riggs.

John collects tennis memorabilia and has an extensive book and racket collection.

DEXTER FONG is Tennis Director at California Family Fitness/Elk Grove, CA. Earned his BS degree in 1971, both MA degree and California Teaching Credential in 1973. Certified USPTA Master Professional since 1994, he served as Nor Cal division secretary, treasurer, VP, Regional VP, Nor Cal and National Diversity Committees. He is certified as a USTA High Performance Player Development Coach. He coordinated USPTA high school tennis coaches workshops from 1989–1999 in the Sacramento region.

Working for the City of Sacramento, Dexter changed the local tennis scene, bringing numerous USTA programs to the Sacramento region from 1970s to 1990s. With encouragement from the USTA, Dexter brought USTA Summer Junior team tennis to Sacramento in the 1980s, which is now the highest profile program in the area. He organized and directed the Sacramento USTA/NJTL chapter, providing free and low cost tennis to thousands of children for over 20 years. He advocated for the rehabilitation and construction of tennis courts and programs throughout the Sacramento region, which was eventually named one of the top 50 tennis cities in America by *Tennis Magazine*. He was a co-founder with Doug Atkinson, creating one of five pilot USTA Junior Area/Competition Training Centers in the nation. He spearheaded the first USTA Schools program on the West Coast with USTA staffer Lindsay Berman and when encouraged by the late Craig Stephens, Dexter served as the founding chair of the USTA Recreation Tennis Committee and later served on both the USTA Diversity and Junior Tennis Committees.

In 30 years serving the Sacramento Area Tennis Association, Dexter created and managed the growth of both Junior and Adult Grand Prix Tournament programs, the Tennis Little League Program and a Tournament Grants Program awarding scholarship money to deserving competitors.

As a coach, Dexter's USTA junior teams won numerous Sacramento region and Northern California titles as well as the State (Gar Glenny Cup) title. One of his USTA zonal teams placed first and his Intersectional Girls 18s team placed third nationally. His high school and community college teams won numerous conference titles. Dexter was selected to coach the 2006, 2007 and 2008 Northern California Pacific Cup teams. Many of his private students have earned high sectional and national rankings and tennis scholarships to various universities including UOP, UC Davis, San Luis Obispo, University of Hawaii, BYU Hawaii, Northwestern University, Eastern New Mexico among others. Two students earned NCAA National Championship team titles at BYU Hawaii and UC Santa Cruz respectively.

He's especially proud of the 1988 USTA Community Service Award, 1988 Service To Tennis Award from Billie Jean King, 1990 Wilson Staff Pro of Year, 1992 USPTA Pro of the Year, 1993 USPTA Contribution to Tennis, 1993 *Tennis Magazine* "America's Top Tennis Teachers," USTA/ITA Service To Tennis and 2006 MPC Service Award.

CHRISTER FRANCKE received Trainer 1, 2 and 3 education from NTF - Norwegian Tennis Federation. He is a USPTA Elite Professional (highest) and member in good standing with PTR and CPTA. Christer has attended several symposiums and workshops in the U.S. and Europe for many years.

As a tennis player he won Norwegian Championships in 1998 and has won more than 30 National Grand Prix tournaments, being ranked No. 1 in the country during many years.

As a coach Christer won the PTR Championship in 1993. He was a Member of The Norwegian Davis Cup Team from 1991–1993. Francke played Team Tennis for KTEV Kelkheim, Frankfurt 1990–2000.

Since 1999 Christer has been an expert TV commentator for Eurosport Television AS. He has been working for other Norwegian TV Channels such as NRK and Canal+/C More.

Until today Christer has been coach for several Norwegian Junior Champions in Norway and has many years of experience as Head Professional Coach in Oslo, Norway.

JANET FRENCH was inducted to Denison University Athletic Hall of Fame. She held USTA National Ranking in singles/doubles for 25 years, starting at age 60.

Janet, a 40-year member of USPTA, was Executive Director of District Tennis Association (1976–1990), volunteering for another 15 years including 12 years as National Ranking Chairman. Janet taught for Oak Park YMCA and Oak Brook Polo Club. She has received several honors from Midwest USPTA including the Fay Tooley Award and is a member of Chicago Tennis Hall of Fame.

Husband Paul has been a member of Oak Park Tennis Club since 1943. Children Ann, and Linda all are four-year high school tennis players. All had athletic scholarships for badminton. Linda is a two-time Olympian in badminton. Ann is in UW Madison Athletic Hall of Fame.

RAFAEL FUENTES served as Head Tennis Pro at El Panama Hilton Hotel in the Republic of Panama from 1963 to 1971. In addition he served as tennis pro at The Midtown Tennis Club in Manhattan, NY, from 1971 to 1975 and for Transworld Oil Ltd. in Bermuda from 1989 to 2009. Fuentes has been a member of the USPTA since 1972. He has attended eight World Tennis Conferences and has given tennis instruction in 18 different countries.

Fuentes is an accomplished tournament player. He was the National Tennis Open Champion of Panama in 1964, 1965, 1966 and 1968. He was a finalist in 1963 and 1967. Fuentes was also the National Tennis Open Champion of El Salvador in 1968 and Finalist in 1969. Also, he played deep into the Central American Tennis Tournaments in Costa Rica, Columbia and Puerto Rico in 1965.

TY FULLER, longtime Georgia tennis pro, recently retired from coaching after 50 years in the profession. Fuller started coaching in 1963 in Massachusetts and worked in the New England area at various clubs for about 10 years. In 1971, after a meeting with tennis commentator, Bud Collins, and pro, Arthur Ashe, he did a stint for the U.S. State Department touring around West Africa setting up tennis programs at various schools and universities.

Ty Fuller receiving his USPTA Master Professional certification in Sept. 1992 from USPTA President Gordon Collins.

In 1973, Fuller moved to Atlanta area and was tennis director and club manager at Dunwoody Radisson Inn. He remained there before starting Dunwoody Tennis School on Spalding Drive, which ran for 30 years. During his coaching tenure, many of his ALTA and USTA league teams won city titles. Fuller helped develop over 50 young tennis players into regional, as well as sectional, champions. Several students followed him into the coaching profession.

A tennis clinic and exhibition were conducted at the Atlanta Federal Penitentiary June 16, 1984 by four members of the Atlanta Professional Tennis Association. Kneeling, L-R: Ty Fuller, Randy Stephens, Sam Vanderbirt and Jim Edenfield.

Photo taken at the National Womens Indoor Tournament held at the Winchester Indoor Tennis Center in Woburn, MA, in 1965. Ty Fuller is third from right, next to Billie Jean Moffitt. Bud Collins, famous tennis commentator, is standing to the far left.

Over the years, he created many innovative instructional programs such as Tennis to Music, Tennis for Tykes and a TV series that aired on both Georgia Cable and CBS Atlanta. Additionally, Fuller donated time developing programs for the physically disabled, prison inmates and Atlanta's schools. In 2007, he was named "Pro of the Year" by the Georgia Professional Tennis Association, an organization he helped form in 1977. As a player, his USTA Senior League Team won city titles in 2010 and 2013 and a State Championship in 2005.

In 1992, Fuller reached the elite level of Master Professional and in 2016 he will be celebrating his 50th year as a certified USPTA member.

UMESH GADASALLI'S tennis experience spans three decades and includes competing at the junior and collegiate levels. Over the past 20 years, his dedication and passion for the game has enabled him to coach kids and adults, beginners, intermediate juniors, high school/college, USTA teams and tournament level players.

As a USPTA teaching professional, Umesh utilizes an athlete centered, collaborative coaching style. His knowledge about the game, ability to communicate analytical concepts to players of all abilities, utilizing multiple learning/teaching modalities, and his patient, encouraging coaching style keeps his sessions fun and interactive. Umesh's coaching methodology was honed by working directly with USPTA Master Professional Mike Van Zutphen and USPTA Professional John Huebner. He is formally trained in the Principles of Coaching and in Coach Effective Training program (CET, a cognitive-behavior approach) and is an accredited interscholastic coach by NFHS. As a result, Umesh's students gain self-confidence, develop positive character traits, experience a constructive sports outcome and develop overall self-efficacy.

Currently Umesh is a private lesson specialist with Lifetime Activities Inc. Previously Umesh completed coaching assignments at three SF/Bay Area high schools. Previously he was a head instructor with Arizona Tennis Association and was an assistant professional at Mesa Country Club. Umesh studied Economics in Wisconsin and Finance at U.C. Berkeley. Umesh's other interests include astronomy, business/finance, gastronomy, natural history, nature photography, international travel, World Affairs Council and volunteering.

MARIANO GALLO, born in Iquitos, Peru, and was a member of the Peruvian National Junior Team. Represented Peru in the 12, 14 and 16 year old divisions. Won numerous Junior competitions in Peru, and won an International Men's Doubles championship against Ecuador.

Moved to the U.S. in 1980 and became a tennis teaching professional at the Beverly Hills Hotel, under the great Alex Olmedo, Wimbledon and Davis Cup hero. Taught there from 1980 to 1986.

Owner of his own tennis academy since 1990 and was the head tennis professional for the City of Murrieta, CA, from 1990 to 2008. Became a USPTA Certified Tennis Instructor in 2009. Served as tennis advisor to the Murrieta Valley High School Tennis Team in 1994 and for the Special Olympics Team of the Temecula Valley in 1997. USTA Local League Champion Team member in 2013.

MICHAEL GAN began playing tennis with his sister/brother on his parents' driveway in Baton Rouge, LA, in 1974, back in the day with wooden rackets and no portable tennis nets. He was a self taught player with God-given talent whom he gives all the credit, along with his parents who paid for tennis shoes, rackets, strings, tournaments, etc., all the way up to his college days and beyond. The first match he ever saw on TV was Jimmy Connors vs. Arthur Ashe in the 1975 Wimbledon final. Jimmy Connors became his tennis inspiration from that point on, along with many other greats both male and female. Michael earned a state ranking as high as 6 in Louisiana as a junior player. He also attained a regional and state doubles championship at Catholic High School with his partner Len Lopoo. He played all positions his freshman year of college tennis for Southeastern Louisiana University in Hammond, LA. He began his teaching career as an assistant pro at opening of Bay Oaks Country Club in Clear Lake, TX, in 1989. His career includes the ranks as an assistant professional, head professional and director of operations at various facilities.

Michael Gan (standing, far right) with his USTA Texas Zonals team

In 2012 Michael created Tennis His Way + free volunteer tennis lessons to introduce homeschooled families to the game of tennis with lessons and learning tools to further help them move into the sport of tennis.

Michael is USPTA certified, was formerly USTA official certified, USTA ball boy certified for the 1992 Davis Cup, former USTA clinician for schools, a PTR affiliate and has coached all levels of players including wheelchair, nationals, team tennis, adult teams, collegiate players and ATP touring pros.

Michael has worked with many great tennis coaches over the years including: Steve Carter, Mike Estep, Larry Haugness, Jim Hunter, Craig Bell, Darren Boyd, Conrad Cowan, Joe Prather, Dave Ware, Bill Norfolk, Conrad Cowan, Allison Oneida, Damien Spizzo, Kendall Brooks, and many more over the years.

Michael's teaching and coaching awards include: The 2015 USTA/USPTA Charlie McCleary Award. USPTA Certified tennis teaching professional. USTA Texas Sectional/Zonals coach 2009/2013/2014/2015. USTA Southwest Section Girls 18's Fed Cup Coach 2006/2007. Prince Plugged in Academy travel Coach (El Paso Youth Tennis Center- 2005/2006/2007). 25 years experience in Teaching/Coaching and 36 years of playing experience. 2007 USTA Facility of the Year Award (New York City).

Currently Michael is offering private instruction through Michael Gan Tennis at various locations in the Dallas/Ft Worth area. "Jesus Christ has been my guide and helper along with many other peers during this long journey. I am blessed."

DUDLEY GAYLE has been a tennis enthusiast since his teenage years; an active player since the early 1960's, served as a USTA umpire for 12 years and is currently a Site Director at New York Junior Tennis and Learning since 1997. As an umpire, he served as District Director, was nominated for the Nicholas Powell Award in 1998, was awarded the Jack Stahr Award in 2000 and received the Grass Roots Official of the Year Award in 2003. He was also presented with the Presidential Sports Award for tennis by President Nixon in 1973.

He served as president of the St. Nicholas Tennis Club for two terms, and was also affiliated with the Haffen Tennis Club and the Liberty Racquet Club.

He is a life member of the USTA and the American Tennis Association, where he served as a member of the Budget Committee for two years.

He earned a BBA degree from Bernard Baruch College and was a New York City senior accountant for 25 years.

KATHLEEN GIBSON was MVP, Senior College; No. 1 College (1964-65); No. 2 Singles and No. 2 Doubles, Pittsburgh (1968); No. 19 Singles – Middle States Ranking (1968). She was a Singles Quarter Finalist at National Public Parks Tournament, St. Louis, MO (1966).

Kathleen is an Elite Professional since 1989, USPTA Certification in 1988. Assistant Pro at Beaver Brook Tennis Club (1986–2001) Jr. Program Director, clinics, privates and Jr. and High School Programs at Danbury, CT.

She was Racket Tester for *Tennis Magazine* (1992), National Player Development Instructor (1992), taught with Renee Richards – Advanced Jr. Program (1994-96) and Head Woman Pro—New Milford Tennis and Swim Club (2001–2014).

Kathleen continues to teach privately in Spring Hill, FL, and New Milford, CT.

She married Steve Toman in 2010 after being a widow for 10 years. She has six daughters; five have made their high school team.

CHUCK GILL has been Director of Tennis at Ibis Golf and Country Club in West Palm Beach, FL, since 1995. As Director of Sports since 2007, he oversees all aspects of the club's tennis, fitness, spa and aquatics operations, serving the club's 3,500+ members.

He previously was employed as director of tennis at clubs in Boca Raton, FL, and Stowe, VT, and as camp director, All American Sports Camp, at Palmas Del Mar in Puerto Rico.

Gill's role in the USPTA has included service on the Florida Division's board of directors from 1995-2005 and as president in 2002-03. From 2009-2011 he was a vice president on the USPTA National Board, serving as Chairman of the Convention Committee, the Tournament Committee, and Co-Chair of the Budget and Finance Committee. He is currently president of the National Board and he chairs the Endorsement Task Force and Strategic Planning Committee.

Gill was named the USPTA Florida Division Professional of the Year in 2002 and the Northern New England Pro of the Year in 1986. He was also honored as Florida Division's Tester of the Year in 2005, and received two Special Recognitions for Career Development by earning over 90 hours of continuing education credits.

He is also active as a USTA volunteer where he serves on the board of the USTA Florida Section and is a member of the USTA National 10-under committee. In 2012, Gill was chosen to join the USTA National Tennis Center Professional Advisory Staff, which is a group of 20 teaching pros who provide their expertise in helping with the US Open fan experience each year in New York.

In addition, he is a member of the Florida Chapter of CMAA and actively attends both national and regional education on trends in the private club industry. He has accumulated over 85 hours of educational credits.

Gill is a member of the professional advisory staff of Prince Racquet Sports. He previously served on the Board of Directors for the Tim and Tom Gullikson Foundation, which provides support for brain tumor patients and their families.

He has been involved with many "Lessons for Life" charity events, serving as Co-Chair of the Cystic Fibrosis "Love Affair" in 1995 and 1996, which raised over $150,000 for CF. He is actively involved with the Tim and Tom Gullikson Foundation, where he has helped organize and host 15 tennis and golf pro/ams between 1999 and 2007, raising over $1.4 million for the Gullikson Foundation.

As a player, Gill's past USPTA rankings include No. 3 in men's 40s singles (1998), No. 9 in men's 45 singles (2003) and No. 3 in men's 45 doubles (2005), and co-ranked No. 1 in men's 50 singles and doubles (2007). He was a frequent competitor on the Florida Grand Prix circuit where he has been ranked as high as 3 in singles and 1 in doubles in various age groups. In 2006, he captured his first national title when he and partner Glenn Williams of Memphis, Tenn., won the 50-over doubles championship at the 2007 World Conference. He followed up that spring by teaming with Kendall Lyon of Coral Springs, Fla., to win the Men's 50-over doubles title at the 2008 USPTA National Clay Court Championships.

Gill attended Carson Newman College in Jefferson City, Tenn., on a tennis scholarship where he studied Business Administration.

RAVI GILL has been teaching tennis since 1977, started with a program called "Recreation Tennis" under the supervision of Stanford coach Dick Gould. Ravi graduated from Columbia with MBA in business and has coached several state and nationally ranked junior players. He has been USPTA Certified since 1984, also a member of SAP Open Elite Staff and Team Prince as well as director of "Tennis For Fun" and "Youth League Tennis." Ravi played high school and

college tennis competitively and ran summer tennis camps at "Lake Owego Camp" and "Pine Forest Camp" back in the '80s. He coached Mission San Jose high school boys' tennis team to 1988 MVAL League, Singles and Doubles Championships. He also coached an USTA Boys' 18 & Under team to League, Nor-Cal and State Championships. Formerly ranked No. 2 nationally in Men's 40 Doubles and No. 5 nationally in Men's 45 Doubles, Ravi also played in Transamerica Open and Sybase Open Qualifying 1984-89.

WINIFRED C. GILLIFORD (1919–2001) was a prominent, well-respected name in Philadelphia, PA, area tennis circles. She taught individual players and coached teams of all sizes, ages and abilities for 57 years.

Winnie started life with Spina Bifida and took up tennis at age 13 for therapy.

Winnie joined the USPTA in 1963 and she was No. 19 in the organization.

She was at Martin's Dam Club for 16 years as the Head Professional. Upon leaving, she became Head Professional and Athletic Director at the Merion Cricket Club. After retiring in 1984 from Merion, she worked with disabled and wheelchair bound players. She also coached tennis at Villa Maria Academy, Linden Hall Academy and Radnor High School.

Her awards over the years go far beyond tennis. She was honored repeatedly for her civic work and physically challenged individuals.

She wrote a book called *Winnie's Wisdom (Great Tennis Truths From An 'Old Pro')*.

FLORIN GIUGLESCU has established a formidable reputation over the past 30 years as one of the leading tennis teachers in the New York City metropolitan area.

As head coach of both the Baruch men's and women's tennis teams, he has

compiled a record of success rivaled only by the star power of his client list.

He has been named the 2004, 2008 and 2012 City University of New York Athletic Conference (CUNYAC) Men's Tennis Coach of the Year for leading his young student-athletes to championship seasons.

His men's teams have won the CUNYAC Championships in 2000, 2002 and 2004 through 2009 in dominant fashion. They repeated as champions again from 2012 to 2014 and reached the second round of the NCAA Tournament in two of those years.

In addition, with the men winning the 2007 championship, they earned CUNY's first-ever berth to the NCAA Tournament. They made the most of their first NCAA appearance by defeating Alvernia, 5-4, in a first-round thriller played on the campus of Swarthmore College.

He was named the CUNYAC Women's Tennis Coach of the Year in 2015 and led the Bearcats to their first CUNYAC Championship since 1997, with an undefeated fall season record of 13-0.

In all, Florin has won a total of 13 CUNYAC championships (11 men, two women) at Baruch College. The success of the program has not only been on the court, but in the classroom as well, as a large number of his student-athletes have been named CUNYAC Scholar-Athletes.

The 2006 women's tennis team also featured a cumulative GPA of 3.44, and No. 1 singles player Kateryna Pylypyshyna (3.98 GPA) was twice named to the *ESPN The Magazine* District I - College Division All-Academic Second Team.

Giuglescu first came to Baruch in 1978, taking the reins of the men's tennis program until 1987. From 1980 to 1993, he was the sports director at Premier Vertical Club, where he worked with two former NCAA No. 1 players (Bill Scanlon No. 9 world, Tim Mayotte, No. 8 world). He returned to Baruch in fall of 1996 to coach both the women's and men's teams.

The accomplishments of the 2002 men's team earned them a full-page article in the *New York Daily News*.

A Life Member of the U.S. Professional Tennis Registry and a Master Pro with the U.S. Professional Tennis Association, Giuglescu has taught both top-notch pros and absolute beginners with equal enthusiasm and effectiveness.

His professional pupils have included the likes of Barbara Potter, Silvia Hanika, Tim Mayotte, Yannick Noah and Bill Scanlon. His list of amateur students, however, is still more impressive: Mike Lupica, Peter Jennings, Bill Cosby, Dustin Hoffman, Arnold Schwarzenegger, Harrison Ford and President George H.W. Bush have all taken past lessons from the Bearcat mentor.

He has also coached on the high school level at Dwight, Trinity and United Nations High School (UNIS). In 2013, he started the first men's varsity team at UNIS.

A native of Bolgrad, Romania, Giuglescu immigrated to the U.S. in 1973 and became an American citizen in 1979.

He is the holder of Bachelor of Science and Master of Science degrees in physical education from the University of Bucharest (Romania), and has also studied at NYU and Columbia University. He has a Ph.D. in Biomechanics Studies, Sports Psychology.

Florin is a lecturer in the department of psychology at Baruch College.

As a player, he was ranked between 28th to 36th in the U.S. and No. 3 in the USTA Eastern Over-40 Division between during 1983–1993. He won the Monte Carlo Doubles 35s in 1986 and reached semifinals for 40s Forest Hills Tournament in 2000.

Giuglescu speaks four languages fluently and can read in three others.

DALE GLAZE has been involved in tennis since 1964. He taught and managed at Brookhaven Country, Dallas in Dallas; Bossier City Tennis Club, Bossier, LA, and Spring Park Tennis Club, Garland, TX. He taught school (1964–1974) at East Wood High School in El Paso, TX. He produced six Jr. Wightman Cup and two Jr. Davis Cup players. He worked with three outstanding and well known players: Sal Castillo, Weston Reece and Susan Roberts. While teaching in Lubbock, TX, Dale worked with another outstanding

and well-known player, Kathy Vick, USPTA 2015 Senior Player of the Year.

Dale has a BA from Lubbock Christian University, BS from Texas Tech University and MA from Southeastern Oklahoma State University.

He played on three 4.5 Texas USTA League Sectional Championship Teams and the 1992 USTA National League 4.5 Championship Team. Dale won Mississippi Open 35 Singles Championship (1977) and ranked No. 1 in Texas in 45 Mixed Doubles (1986)

Presently he teaches privately.

WANDA GODFREY graduated from Great Bridge High School (1972), attended Norfolk State University-Bachelor of Arts (1976) and University of Virginia-Masters of Architecture (1978).

She was a volunteer at: Gaines Park Tennis Center, West Palm Beach, FL, (1980–1988), James Lewis Tennis Center, Birmingham, AL (1990–2005), and Fairfield Tennis Center, Fairfield, AL (2008–2011).

Wanda states, "During my entire career as a tennis professional, my passion has always been to engage children and youth in this sport. My time as coach, teacher and mentor has been devoted to children and youth tennis programming for excellence throughout a lifetime."

JEFF GOLDMANN, USPTA Elite Pro, is an independent tennis trainer in Talega-San Clemente area, Dana Point and Laguna Niguel, CA. He has established himself as a top teaching professional in Southern California.

Jeff has worked at more than 25 resorts and clubs in Europe and has taught tennis around the world. Since 1981, he has worked in the U.S., Dominican Republic, Bahamas, Mexico, Germany, Switzerland, Austria, Italy, Spain, Turkey and Greece.

As a player, Jeff was the 1975 South Coast Conference doubles champion at Fullerton College. From 1977-'81, he was on the All-Marine Corps tennis team, winning second place in the West Coast singles. In 1986, he played Verbands Liga Herren in Hamburg, Germany.

Jeff started teaching tennis after his service in the military. "I enjoy being able to travel all over the world using my talent in tennis, meeting people of all cultures and working outside," he says. His areas of expertise are stroke production and footwork.

Jeff enjoys fast cars, power boats, good food, wine and travel.

BARRY GOLDSMITH, USPTA Master Professional, USTA High Performance coach, member of the NJCAA Men's College Tennis Coaches Hall of Fame, 2009 US Masters Maccabi Tennis coach, a member of Who's Who in Tennis, coached tennis for 57 seasons – Kingsborough Community College (33 years, men's tennis and 10 years women's), LIU men's (one year), South Shore H.S. boys (three years) and Midwood H.S. boys (10 years). Author of "The The Wisdom of a Coach: Health, Wealth, Education, Athletics (Tennis and Basketball), A Game Plan for Life," published by Xilibris Press.

His teams at Kingsborough won the NJCAA Men's 1998 and Women's 2009 National Championship, producing 56 All-Americans and 17 National singles and doubles champions.

The Goldsmith family was the 1999 USTA Eastern Tennis Family of the Year. Rachelle Goldsmith coached the women's tennis team at Kingsborough Community College; Howard Goldsmith was captain of the Brandeis men's tennis team in 1999, an academic All-American and was nationally ranked in doubles, Division III; Robert Goldsmith, member of Phi Beta Kappa, was manager of Trinity College's (CT) tennis and squash teams, and in 2000, was the assistant men's tennis and squash coach, winning the NCAA Squash Championship.

DON GOMSI has been the Executive Director for the San Diego Division of the USPTA since 2009. He also serves as the Treasurer and previously as a Vice President of the Division. He has been a tester for the USPTA for the past 30 years having been a head tester for the California Division and now the San Diego Division. Don has the distinction of serving on the board of all three divisions in California. He was a vice president in Northern California and the president of the California Division from 1989-93 where he was awarded the pro of the year in 1993.

Along with USPTA work, he is an instructor at Carmel Valley Tennis located near Del Mar, north of San Diego. He currently coaches all levels of juniors and has had players previously ranked in the top 200 in the world.

GREGORY "SPIKE" GONZALES became a three-term President of USPTA Eastern. As Chairman of the National Nominating Committee, he helped transition USPTA to a modern and business-oriented organization. Spike is an inductee into the Eastern Division's Hall of Fame and the Rochester (NY) Tennis Hall of Fame.

Spike helped grow Tennis Corporation of America from one club to 30 in his 20 years with the Chicago-based company. During and after his TCA career, he developed and administered beginner programs for tens of thousands of new players throughout U.S. and Canada.

A key person in launching the National Tennis Rating Program in the late 1970s, he co-wrote the system's guidelines and promotional materials and brought together the USTA, USPTA and IRSA to adopt the universal program that became the cornerstone for USTA Leagues.

As a player Spike won western New York, Rochester and Eastern USPTA singles and doubles titles. He played four years on the World Professional Squash Tour.

An advocate for character development, Spike founded the Rochester Love-15 program, bringing free tennis instruction and tutoring to thousands of underprivileged youth. He has a 50-year history of teaching sportsmanship and mental skills to all ages.

ANNE GORDE has been a member of the USPTA since 1992. Started playing tennis at the age of 12, being privately coached by another USPTA professional Brian McCoy. Brian has developed and coached highly ranked juniors and collegiate tennis players throughout his teaching career. Anne represented the Northern section in several National tournaments and then went on to the University of Minnesota to play Big Ten tennis. Selected to the All Big Ten teams in singles and doubles. Big Ten Sportswoman of the Year for tennis in 1989. Continued to play tennis competitively for several years after college traveling with friends to USTA team tournaments. Now as a middle-aged player, prefers to play doubles with friends in a fun and relaxed setting. Currently teaches tennis to a small number of clients. Since 2012 has been the head coach for the Breck School girls tennis team. Married with three children, ages 18, 16 and 12.

Enjoys gardening, outdoor fitness activities and family vacations.

SYLVIA GOTHARD, originally from England, was an English County U21 Champion and Insurance Offices of Great Britain Champion. Her tennis career in the U.S. began in 1969 at the South Side Racquet Club in Dolton followed by manager of Park Forest Racquet Club. From 1976–1991 she served as Tennis Director at Ravisloe Country Club. She became a USPTA Elite Professional in 1972 and a Master Professional in 1996 along side of Nick Bollettieri.

Since 1977 Gothard has been at the H-F Racquet & Fitness Club in Homewood, IL. Under her leadership, the facility has won numerous awards, including the USTA/Midwest Section Organization of the Year (2001), USTA National Organization of the Year (1988, 2001), USTA/NRPA Excellence in Tennis Programming Award (2003), the USTA Chicago District's Facility of the Year (2000, 2008, 2011) and a facility of the National Recreation & Parks Association Gold Medal Award in 1991 and 2006.

Gothard, past Northern Illinois USPTA President, led a group of USPTA Professionals to an exhibition during the Avon WTA tour in Chicago. She has served as board member and past president of the USTA Chicago District Tennis Association, Chair of the USTA/Midwest Section Communications Committee, Chair and member of the USTA/Midwest Section Information Technology Committee, and member of the USTA/Midwest Section Tennis Industry Committee.

Gothard is the creator of the Homewood-Flossmoor Park District Tennisfest, a 10-day festival that started in 1988 with a 41-event tournament and free clinics. Since then, Tennisfest has expanded to a 12-day, 55-event tournament with free clinics, lessons, exhibits, Special Olympics tournament, Chicago District USTA Junior Team Tennis playoffs, book sales, pet contest and more which draws nearly 2,500 participants.

She remains a USTA Referee and ITF White Badge Referee, running tournaments from local to national levels.

Gothard's service has earned her numerous awards from the Chicago Community. She was presented the Senator Aldo DeAngelis Leadership Award from the Chicago Southland Convention & Visitors Bureau 1999, a Certificate of Recognition from the State of Illinois for her 35 years of service with the Homewood-Flossmoor Park District and Racquet Club in 2012, and two citations from the HF Park District honoring her accomplishments 1996, 2007.

Gothard also has been honored by the tennis community earning USTA and USPTA service awards. She was inducted into the USPTA Midwest Hall of Fame 1996, the Chicago District Tennis Hall of Fame class of 2014, is a recipient of the Billie Jean King Lifetime Achievement Award 2007, USPTA Midwest Pro of the Year 2006, USPTA Midwest State Pro of the Year 1994, 1997, Chicago Tennis Patrons Tournament Director of the Year four times, USPTA Midwest Nancy Mickler award three times and now the 2015 USTA Midwest Mel Bergman award.

DICK GOULD was men's tennis coach at Stanford for 38 years, where his teams won 17 NCAA team championships, 10 singles championships and seven doubles championships. Nine players he coached at Stanford have reached the top 15 in ATP world singles rankings and 14 top 10-ranked doubles players.

He was president of Professional Tennis, Inc. and an honorary member of the USPTA since 1981. He was named Coach of the Decade by the Intercollegiate Tennis Association in both the '80s and '90. Other awards received include the USTA Educational Merit Award (1983), the Kenneth M. Cuthbertson Award for Exceptional Service to Stanford University (2002) and the Positive Coaching Alliance's Lifetime Achievement Award in 2012. He was elected to Stanford Associates—an honorary society for service to Stanford University—in 2015.

Gould spearheaded a $20 million facility renovation drive that resulted in the Taube Center. The Stanford men's tennis program was completely endowed ($20 million) during his tenure as coach.

Gould retired from Stanford in 2004 and currently serves as John L. Hinds Director of Tennis.

MINOR DAVID GRAVES SR. was born to Ralph and Frances Graves in Jacksonville, FL, on Nov. 27, 1946. After graduation of New Stanton Sr. H.S., 1965, he was immediately drafted into the Vietnam War where he served one tour (two years). Afterwards, Minor was employed with CSX Railroad and retired after 38 years of service. During that period, Minor always had an interest in tennis and continued his interests by assisting the development of the Moncrief Adult Tennis League for Men/Women and later the NJTL Tennis League for the city of Jacksonville, FL. He later branched out, acquiring certification as a USTA umpire and in 2003 to present, became a USPTA coach. When asked what his greatest accomplishment is, Minor stated "working with his only son in coaching and support to the title of 'Top Junior Tennis Player' in the state of Florida." Minor has worked with numerous athletes in the tennis arena and several have acquired tennis scholarships to enhance their lifestyle and he is proud of the work he has accomplished personally and for the community.

MATT GRAYSON, Ansley Golf Club's Athletic/Director of Tennis, played most of his tennis career in Texas, but his family members are native Georgians. He is a graduate from Baylor University (1994).

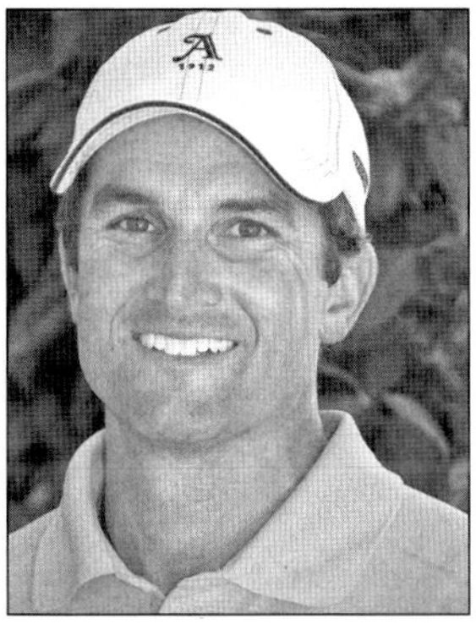

Matt spent his teaching career in the Atlanta area, beginning as an assistant tennis professional at Atlanta Country Club and Atlanta Athletic Club before moving to Laurel Springs as the head tennis professional in 1997. In 2003, Matt joined the Country Club of Roswell as head tennis professional, becoming director in 2004. In 2009, Matt restructured the club's management and took over as the Athletic Director. As of 2012, he coordinates the tennis, fitness, aquatic and youth care programs at the Ansley Golf Club in midtown Atlanta.

Matt is certified with the U.S. Professional Tennis Association as an Elite Professional and has served on many boards and committees on the local and Southern levels. Matt was honored as the Head Professional of the Year 1999–2002 by the Georgia Professional Tennis Association and as the Southern Professional of the Year by the USPTA in 2013.

ROBERT "BOB" GREEN, USPTA Elite Professional, has Top Ten rankings in all age groups through 65's. He taught at Forest Grove in Palatine, IL (1981–2005). Currently he has been Tennis Director, Pelican Preserve Country Club, Fort Myers, FL, for seven years.

Bob was Midwest Playing Pro of the Year, 45's, four times.

He and Carol have two sons, Robert Jr. and Darren Green.

ROBERT GREENE, 2009 USPTA National Pro of the Year and 2003 International Tennis Hall of Fame Educational Merit Award winner, played tennis and studied psychology and music at the University of Rochester in the early '70s. He served as the General Manager at the Worcester Tennis Club from 2010 to 2015 where he coached and provided community outreach programs for dozens of children. Prior to that, Bob served for 19 years as the Director of Tennis at the Balsams Grand Resort Hotel in New Hampshire.

Bob is an internationally recognized authority on player rating systems and sciences. He is an original architect of the NTRP. He has been a USTA volunteer since 1978 and has served on and/or chaired over 14 USTA National Committees including Olympic, Nominating, Strategic Planning, Budget, Leagues, Governance, Jr. Comp and Davis/Fed Cup also serving multiple terms as a President of USPTA and USTA New England. As a member of the Head/Penn Advisory Staff, Bob travels and shares his expertise with tennis teaching professionals across America. As a coach he has worked with many national and world ranked players. In 2014, he coached WTT Boston Lobsters. As a player he has and held a career-high No. 3 national ranking in USPTA Men's 50 Doubles in 2004 and several USTA section rankings. As former Chairman of Olympic Tennis, Bob accompanied Team USA to the Olympics in Beijing in 2008 and to the Pan-Am games in Rio de Janeiro in 2007.

Bob Greene with Venus Williams and Lindsay Davenport

Bob Greene with the WTT Boston Lobsters

Off the court, he likes to ski, snorkel, and plays several musical instruments.

MARIANN GODSICK GREENBERG has been a USPTA member for over 20 years. She played high school tennis at Columbia Grammar and was ranked in the ETA in the 15's.

She played college tennis at Syracuse University and Long Island University.

In the '70s Mariann was the men's and women's varsity tennis coach at Lehman College. She believes that she was the first female coach of a men's varsity.

Mariann was a panelist at the Research and Education Conference in NYC under Eve Kraft.

She was the head pro at the Fox Meadow Tennis Club in Scarsdale for 15 years.

Marian was head clinician for the ETA Caravan program, played in 35's in US Open at Flushing Meadow, ranked 1 in singles and doubles in 35's

IAN A. GRIFFIN, USPTA Master Professional, born Toronto, Oct. 14 1949. St. Michael's College School (Grade 13, Ontario Scholar) 1967, University of Toronto (B.A. Honours, Modern History) 1971, University of Toronto Law School (L1B./J.D.) 1974. Intercollegiate Champion tennis and squash teams. Following Law School spent one year travelling playing satellites, returned to do six interviews, realized preferred a career in tennis. Director of Tennis/Head Professional City of Beaumont Municipal Tennis Center (completed 1977) 1980–1994, The Oakville Club

Ian Griffin with children (L-R) David, Francesca and Danielle, 2007

(est. 1907) 1994–1999, La Crosse Country Club (est. 1900) 2000–2011.

In at ground floor/first year two major USTA programs: USTA (Penn) Circuit promoted with own funds event in North Tonawanda, NY 1979; later two other events Beaumont, TX, 1980, 1989. USTA Player Development Program, Houston ATC Head Scout 1988–1994. Developed on public courts as only professional coach several players who advanced from first formal instruction to No. 1 Sectional rankings, two won national tournaments. USTA Sport Science-certified Level II. Winner first-ever USPTA personal website contest 2008. At heart a public court-guy: wrote chapter "Negotiating a Contract for Yourself" for the "USPTA Guide to Municipal Operations;" led the discussion on this topic at the USPTA World Conference on Tennis 1988. Traveled to Rwanda at invitation of Ministry of Sport and Culture to work with Féderation Rwandaise de Tennis 2012; returned 2014, 2015 to teach children, distribute equipment, consult with coaches. Proud father of Dave (2001), Francesca (1998) and Danielle (1996).

DR. JACK GROPPEL, sport scientist, fitness and nutrition consultant, author, lecturer and coach, is a Co-Founder of the Johnson & Johnson Human Performance Institute, Inc. at Lake Nona in Orlando, FL.

Dr. Groppel served as Vice President on the National Board of Directors of the USPTA and served 16 years of chairman of the National Sport Science Committee. His "Ask the Professor" column in USPTA's *ADDvantage* magazine ran for 25 years.

As a professional tennis coach, Dr. Groppel is a certified Master Professional of the U.S. Professional Tennis Association and an International Master Professionals of the Professional Tennis Registry, the highest rating of each organization. He was awarded the USPTA's highest honor in 1987 as the USPTA Professional of the Year. He received the 1993 International Tennis Hall of Fame's Educational Merit Award and has been inducted into the Midwest USPTA Hall of Fame.

JAN GROVER, certified by the USPTA since 1987. She began her career as a teaching professional with the Virginia Beach Department of Parks and Recreation and later became head professional at Cedar Point Country Club in Suffolk, VA. Jan is also a former sports writer for the Virginian Pilot and Suffolk News Herald, and has written numerous articles published in the USPTA ADDvantage magazine, the USPTA Mid-Atlantic publication Service Lines, Virginiatennis.com, and USPTA newsletters. She wrote and published a tennis coloring book entitled "Color Me Tennis." Jan was a part of the Prince Advisory Staff from 1993 to 2000 and sponsored by the Prince Pro Team from 2001 to 2005.

She coached the 1990, 1991, 1992, and 1996 12 and under USTA Zonal Teams along with coaching in the 1990 and 1991 USTA National Challenge Cups. Jan also previously coached the JV girls tennis team at Nansemond-Suffolk Academy and the JV and varsity girls tennis teams at Norfolk Academy. She has served as the USTA Hampton Roads Coordinator of Junior Team Tennis in 1992, Head Scout at USTA Regional Training Center from 1990 to 1993, Chairperson of the USTA Mid-Atlantic Tennis Industry Committee in 1996, Chairperson of the USTA Virginia Tennis Council in 1996, and as USTA Virginia 2nd Vice President in 2005 and 2006. She also was a member of the 1993 and 1994 USTA Mid-Atlantic Schools Program and NJTL Committee, USTA Virginia Nominating Committee in 1994, 1998, and 1999, USTA Mid-Atlantic Junior Tournaments & Schedules committee in 1996, USPTA Mid-Atlantic delivery system coordinator in 1999, USTA Virginia Tournament Sanctions, Schedules and Ranking Committee in 1999, and USPTA Mid-Atlantic Nominating Committee from 2003 to 2006.

Jan has received numerous awards including: 1990 Mid-Atlantic Professional Tennis Association High School Coach of the Year, 1992, 1996, and 2004 USTA Virginia Tennis Association Family of the Year, 1992 USTA Schools Program Teacher of the Year Award, 1993 USTA Virginia Tennis Association Outstanding Service Award, 1994 USTA Mid-Atlantic Tennis Association Family of the Year, 2002 USTA Virginia Tennis Press Award, and 2005 USTA Virginia Tennis Volunteer of the Year Award.

JOHN (LARRY) GUEVARA coached the Lemoore High School boys' tennis team in California for over 20 years and retired from high school teaching in June 2014.

Larry played high school tennis and competed against Hank Pfister and Butch Walts. He teamed with Keizo Miamoto at College of the Sequoias in Visalia to win the Northern California Junior College Section Doubles Championships in 1975. He played for two years at California State University, Fresno, under Coach Duane Ballard.

Theris Brown, from Barstow, CA, sponsored Guevara to become a USPTA member in 1981. Guevara taught tennis at the River Island Club in Porterville, the Tulare Town and Country Club, and the Hanford Racquet Club before becoming a teacher at Strathmore High School, and started teaching business classes at Lemoore High School in 1987.

Guevara enjoys playing in local, sectional and national tennis tournaments, and is ranked in the top 10 in the Northern California section for 2015 in the Men's 60 division.

BILL GUILFOIL, age 93, is perhaps one of the oldest active professionals. A USPTA lifetime member, he came into the USPTA through membership in Texas Tennis Association. Besides being a tennis professional, he is also a table tennis pro at Overland Park Racquet Club in Overland Park, KS, a major tennis and table tennis club that he managed from its beginnings 40 years ago. Previously was a tennis and table tennis professional at Glenwood Manor Resort Hotel in Overland Park, KS.

Guilfoil participated in the 2012 and 2016 Olympic Trials for table tennis at ages 89 and 93, respectively, making him an Olympic athlete, even though he didn't make the team. He is a member of the USPTA and USATT halls of fame.

The former university and high school coach is presently on the staff of the Plaza Municipal Tennis Center. His four daughters all are accomplished tennis players and are on scolarships to major schools.

LORRAINE H. GUNTER won numerous tournaments in Illinois and St. Louis, MO. She taught high school English in Peoria, IL, and substitute taught, as well as teaching tennis.

Lorraine has been in the tennis industry for 52 years, teaching, organizing and directing junior and adult programs in Peoria; St. Louis, MO, and was summer Tennis Director in Minocqua, WI, in 2000 at Camp Cedar Ledge. She has done numerous volunteer work to promote tennis, including Play Tennis America.

Lorraine was USPTA, 2006, Missouri Pro of the Year.

Lorraine has one daughter, Corrina Van-Geison; one granddaughter, Caylee; one sister, Loretta and one brother, Lamont.

NEAL HAGBERG is Director of Tennis and Life Camps at Gustavus Adolphus College, which has been recognized as one of the top tennis camps in the country by Tennis Magazine. He is a USPTA Elite Professional and has worked for Tennis and Life Camps since 1981, and been director since 2010. Hagberg designed the "life" portion of TLC with legendary Gustavus coach and USPTA Hall of Fame Member Steve Wilkinson, who taught a radical, simple approach to winning more matches: take the focus off winning and who taught both tennis and life skills by focusing on the only things we can control: our attitude, our effort and our sportsmanship.

Hagberg is a 1981 graduate of Gustavus and was also a touring singer/songwriter for 25 years. He performed concerts in 45 states and Canada, in venues ranging from coffeehouses to Carnegie Hall and received two McKnight Fellowships for performing and composing.

CHRISTOPHER HAGMAN has been playing and teaching tennis for 40 years. He led Lakeland Santa Fe to a 23-0 match record and second place finish amongst all Florida High Schools. Chris was named MVP at FSU and won the GPTA Open Doubles. Since 1985 he has held a USPTA Elite Pro rating and was a USTA Player Development Coach. He has trained numerous players and Teaching Pros at clubs and communities in the Southeast. Mr. Hagman graduated from UF, is a member of ACE and also is a certified Fitness Professional. He founded Atlantic Recreation which does national fitness and tennis operations including amenity management, professional recruitment and program evaluations. Also, Chris represents Welch Tennis—the world's largest clay court builder. He invented the nSHADE court—a retractable shade for courts—and in 2015 was awarded patent. Chris likes playing competitive doubles, community service and travel with family.

J. CHRISTOPHER HALL was born in London, England, and grew up in Kingston, Jamaica W.I., where he first played tennis and soccer for Calabar High School. Moved to Toronto, Ontario, Canada, to continue schooling and graduated from the University of Guelph, Ontario, Canada, with a B.A. in Psychology and Recreational Planning. He was the Canadian National Collegiate and Open Champion in wrestling, representing Canada at the British Empire Games, the World Games in Moscow and the 1972 Olympic Games in Munich, Germany. He played collegiate tennis and soccer, and semi-pro soccer for the Toronto Falcons. Hall has been a nationally ranked USPTA playing and teaching professional for almost 40 years and served as the Director of Tennis at such premier clubs as the Wellington CC, Florida, Westhampton CC, Long Island, NY, and Candlewood Lake CC in Connecticut. He presently is the Director of New Development at Beacon College in Leesburg, FL. Beacon College is the only college in the country to offer a four-year accredited Baccalaureate degree to students with diagnosed learning disabilities. He has been at Beacon College the past eight years after resigning his position as the Director of Tennis, Fitness, Pool and Croquet at Mariner Sands C.C. in Stuart, FL, where he had been for 18 years. While at Mariner Sands he was the Tournament Director for the "The American Heart Open," raising $25,000 annually with over 230 participants from all over the country. Also as director of the tennis segment of Operation Outreach, along with the golf, raised almost $2,000,000 for several local charities in over seven years. Hobbies have been chess, scuba diving, and as a second love is also a piano player and singer and has entertained at country clubs and nightclubs in Canada, New York, and Florida, such as Burt Reynolds owned "Backstage."

SARA L. HAMILTON is a life member of USTA and National Senior Women's Tennis Association, USPTA since 1974. Sara received a 40-year Service Award from USPTA.

Amateur highlights include singles and doubles Girls 16S runner-up National Indoor Championships, MVTA Intersectional Team, National Jr. Tournaments Girls 14, 16, 18 Singles and Doubles, No. 4 Women's Singles and No. 1 Women's Singles and Virginia Slims event.

Sara graduated from Vic Braden Tennis College, Van Der Meer Tennis and Laver-Emerson. As Tennis Professional at Woodside RC, emphasis was on private lessons, junior program and pro shop merchandising. As Tennis Director at Round Hill Bath and Tennis club, pioneer of Tiny Tots program (ages 3-5). She has been Head Pro at Indian Creek CC, Walnut Creek CC, Oklahoma City Tennis Club, Oklahoma City CC, Wichita CC,

Wichita Advantage of World Team Tennis and Ariel at the Landings Yacht, Golf and Tennis Club.

JERRY HANKINS has taught and coached tennis at Harvest Racquet & Athletics in Rogers, AR since 2003. That's the year he and his wife, Mot, moved to NWA to be closer to their two granddaughters, Lauren and Emily, that live in Ft. Smith.

Jerry Hankins with future lefty-righty doubles team the Piech brothers, Alex (6) and Jason (8)

In Memphis, Jerry was Director of Tennis at Wooddale Tennis Center from 1975 to 1981.

From 1981 to 1999, he was head professional at Farmington C.C. in Germantown, TN. From 1999 to 2003 he taught as an independent contractor at apartment complexes and private courts.

Early influences on Jerry's teaching and coaching philosophies and methodologies include Harry Hopman, George Lott, Dennis Van der Meer, Vic Braden and more recently Brett Hobden and David Bailey. Jerry earned a BS degree from Memphis State in 1968. He served in the U.S. Army for two years that included a year in Vietnam.

An avowed lifelong student of the game, Jerry has witnessed a lot of changes as the game of tennis has evolved to its present form. After all these years, Jerry is still committed to helping his students discover and develop the fundamental skills and key tactics that make tennis easier and more enjoyable to play.

JONI HANNAH is the Director of Tennis at Westwood Country Club in Vienna, VA, since 1995 and is responsible for the development, implementation and oversight of all aspects of the club's tennis facilities and programs.

Joni is active in the USPTA and was named the first female president of USPTA Mid-Atlantic Division and currently serves as the Past President for the division. Joni has won numerous industry awards, including USPTA Mid-Atlantic Professional of the Year, NSWTA Margaret Russo National Sportsmanship Award, and USPTA and USTA Virginia Pro of the Year.

Joni earned top 10 national rankings in juniors and later played Division I tennis for Rollins College. As a senior player, Joni has won numerous national titles, earned the No. 1 ranking in the U.S. for the 40s in both singles and doubles, and was a four-time playing captain for USA Cup teams, winning two Young Cup international championships.

ROB HARDIN has been coaching high school tennis for 25 years in the State of Kentucky. He has been at Notre Dame Academy for 15 years as a head coach from 1997 to 2002 and 2007 to 2015, and as an assistant from 2003–2006. He also spent six years at Bellevue as the head boys and girls tennis coach before joining NDA. His NDA record includes three KHSAA State Team Championships and four KHSA State Team Finalists. He has been on the KHSAA Tennis Advisory Committee for over 20 years. In 1997, 1998 and 2010, Rob was voted Kentucky High School Tennis Coach of the Year. In 2010 he was a Semi-Finalist for the National High School Coach of the Year by the National High School Athletic Coaches' Association. Rob also coached at Northern Kentucky University as Head Coach for four years and Assistant for eight years.

CHRIS HARPER is 25 years old and from Lexington, NC. Chris graduated from Methodist University with a B.S. degree in Marketing and Professional Tennis Management and with a Minor in Business Administration. He is currently the Assistant Head Tennis Professional at North Shore Country Club in Portland, TX, which is near Corpus Christi. He has had a lot of success teaching at North Shore by leading junior team tennis champions and adult league champions. Before coming to North Shore, he was the Assistant Tennis Professional at Allegheny Country Club near Pittsburgh, PA; the Head Tennis Professional at Lake Owego Camp in Greeley, PA; and a Tennis Professional for RDU Tennis in various locations around North Carolina. Chris is an active member of the USPTA U30 Texas team and has been a member of the USPTA since 2011.

Chris Harper at the US Open

DARREN HARPER is a USPTA Elite Professional who lives in Jacksonville, FL. After graduating from the University of North Florida where he was a two-time All-American in Singles and Doubles, Darren started his teaching career at the ATP International Headquarters in Ponte Vedra Beach, FL, working under Brian Gottfried. From there, he took the Director of Tennis position at Timuquana Country Club in Jacksonville and was there for 16 years. Darren is currently the Director of Tennis at Queen's Harbour Yacht and Country Club in Jacksonville. Darren recently was inducted into the University of North Florida Athletic Hall of Fame.

MARK HARRISON currently teaches at the Bridge in Bridge Hampton, NY. He also is the head tennis coach at Holy Trinity Episcopal Academy and runs the Harrison Tennis Academy in Melbourne, FL.

Harrison is an active member of the USPTA for over 25 years and a member of the prestigious International Tennis Club of the U.S.

Mark has won 15 USTA National Championships, including the 2013 National Grass court Championships and regional tournaments including the 2014 USPTA Delray International. He has been ranked No 1 in both singles (in Florida) and doubles (nationally).

Mark was recently inducted into the Space Coast Sports Hall of Fame, which honors people from Brevard County, FL, who have accomplished highly significant achievements in sports.

Mark has also won the USPTA National Player of the Year (2004), the South Florida Championship and the All American Award, among other awards and accolades.

ROBERT "BOB" HAUGEN - Retired Faculty, Department of Kinesiology, The University of Texas at Austin. From 1983–2013 Bob was the Director of Instructional Tennis. He served as Assistant Women's Tennis Coach from 1983–1990. In 1986 he helped start the Longhorns Tennis Camp, which he then coordinated from 1986–2010. During his 30 years at UT Bob is very proud that he was involved with teaching and coaching over 20,000 students and campers. In addition to his work at UT, Bob has been involved in various junior development programs. From 1997–2012 he and his wife Judy directed a 10U tennis program throughout Austin, TX, called CenTex Scoop-It-Up Tennis. The program introduced over 8,000 juniors to tennis. From 2007–2013 he coached at St. Stephen's Tennis Academy in Austin, TX. In 1993 his work in the Austin Community earned him the award of CATA's Person Contributing the Most to Tennis. In 1995 he received the USTA Texas Lloyd Session Educational Merit Award. In 2002 the Haugen family was selected as USTA Texas Family of the Year. Bob has a Master's of Science degree in Sport Science from Utah State University. Currently he teaches independently and consults on programming, camps and the college recruiting process.

SHARON HAUGEN was introduced to tennis in high school and played at the Community College level before going on to earn a BS in Biology and a teaching credential from Cal Poly, San Luis Obispo. After arriving in the Bay Area, she became Assistant Director of the Exercise Physiology Lab at De Anza College for five years while also teaching tennis, aerobics, and wellness classes part-time for the college. For seven seasons, Haugen was the Assistant Coach for the girls' tennis team at Archbishop Mitty High School. After 10 seasons coaching the varsity girls' team (WBAL Skyline Division Champs in 2008 and 2013) and four coaching the varsity boys' team at The King's Academy, she still finds it exciting to begin each new high school season! Haugen's passion is to have her student-athletes improve their technique, strategy, fitness level and mental toughness in a competitive, yet encouraging atmosphere. All players are encouraged to reach their maximum potential as a tennis player and a Christian athlete. Certified by the USPTA since 2010, Haugen enjoys continuing tennis education through its workshops and conferences and enjoys competition through USTA leagues.

DARRELL HAWKINS, who has played tennis for more than 33 years, embarked on a tennis-teaching career in early 1997. Motivated by a desire to help beginning juniors and adults, he became a Professional member of USPTA.

In his playing career, he was a high school and college varsity letterman. His notable tennis accomplishments include: Men's 4.5 PNW Sectional Championship team (1995); third place Mixed Doubles 8.0 National Championships (1996); No. 1 35s PNW Doubles (2006-7); No. 10 35s PNW Singles (2008); No. 2 40s PNW Singles (2010); No. 4 40s PNW Singles (2012); Portland WTT Champions (2008); men's open doubles semifinalist Oregon Coast Tennis Classic (1996); and men's open singles finalist OSU Championships (1989-90).

His introduction to organizing tennis teams came when he was president of the Oregon State University Men's and Women's Tennis Club teams from 1988-91, and he started coaching the Corvallis High School boys' tennis team (1998–2000), winning the Valley League Championship in 1999. He was also site director for the USA Tennis programs during the summer. He continues helping juniors, coaching 10U and 12U JTT.

Darrell is currently employed as an Executive Consultant Program Director for IBM. He earned a B.S. in Finance from OSU (1992) and a M.S. in Management in Information Systems from CWRU (2001).

PATRICK "PATTY" RODGERS HAYES is a four time MVP, Augusta College (1982–1985). He was SAC Champion (1982) and PBC finalist (1985). Patrick had a No. 1 ranking in USTA Southern Men's (40) Doubles (2006, 2007, 2010 and 2011). He has been USTA Men's Doubles (40) Southern Champion – Clay Court (five times), Hard Court (four times).

From 1987–1991, he was Sports Instructor for Club Med Resorts. Patrick was Regional Sports Director at Asia-Pacific Club Med Resort (1991–2002), Director of Tennis at The Club at Rae's Creek (2004–2014) and Head Professional at various cities/clubs since 2014.

Patrick is a USPTA Elite Professional. As a member of Tennis Coaches of Australia, he is Certified 0-1. He is Coaching Certified in RPT Spanish Tennis Training.

Patrick and Ikuko Sugiyana have been married 25 years and have two children, Dallas Sugiyana Hayes and Adelaide Koeda Hayes.

E. DONALD "DON" HEBERT graduated from Union High School and Newark College of Engineering.

Don was associated with PSIN – Professional School of Engineering for 20 years. He spent 10 years of teaching tennis plus 25 years as a Professional Ski Instructor.

Don's professional highlights included teaching skiing at Bradly School of Skiing, helping with a handicapped tennis program.

ANNA VIKTORIA HEDDEN is a USPTA Elite Professional, 2013 USPTA Coach of the Year (San Diego, Imperial counties and Coachella Valley), Yonex Advisory Staff Member and a USTA selected High Performance Coaching Program Coach.

Anna Hedden (center) with Nick Bollettieri and Patrick McEnroe

Throughout her 18 years of teaching and coaching in San Diego, CA, she served as a Head Women's and Junior Development Professional at The Rancho Bernardo Inn and a High Performance Coach at the West Coast Tennis Academy at La Costa Resort and Spa.

Currently, she is director of her own Competitive Player Development Program and has trained, worked with and developed numerous top ranked juniors in Southern California and the nation. Among her students (whom she developed from beginners) are National and Sectional Champions in singles and doubles, multiple No. 1 ranked players in Southern California, third and 4th place finishes at the Easter Bowl, numerous players in top 10 and a host of NCAA scholarship players.

Anna has been a USTA and SCTA invited Coach for numerous Team USA training camps, as well as a multiple time Champion Coach of the Zonal Team Championships.

She has been featured in numerous publications and in 2014, was recognized by Patrick McEnroe, USTA's General Manager of Player Development and ESPN and CBS commentator, as one of "top developmental coaches of the highest-level juniors in the country" and "an integral part of Team USA."

Native of Tallinn, Estonia, Anna was a National Team player in the former Soviet Union and was ranked ninth in NCAA/Rolex ITA. She is a four-time Ohio Athletic Conference No. 1 singles and three-time No. 1 doubles Champion, having competed for the University of Mount Union in 1991–1994. Anna was a four-year MVP with a combined record of 106-7 and a 2010 inductee into the Mount Union Athletic Hall of Fame.

She earned Bachelor of Arts dual degrees in International Affairs and Economics and Political Science, and feels fortunate to have been able to use her love for the game to support a variety of charitable causes and after-school youth programs.

NORM HEGER started to play tennis after college over 50 years ago, a grassroots player who learned to play by reading books/magazines, watching professional matches and hitting against a wall. He played in tennis leagues, city tournaments and taught tennis as a hobby. He coached his oldest daughter in high school and college, where she earned State University of NY singles and doubles conference champion status. In 2010 his daughter became a USPTA Professional and recommended that he do likewise. Acquiring a USPTA membership as a corporate industry retiree inspired Norm to re-activate his teaching and coaching activity. Norm is the assistant USPTA pro at the Ebensburg Tennis Center, Head Coach of a high school varsity girls' team and assistant coach for the boys' varsity team. He also coaches two of his six grandchildren and in 2015 they acquired their first ever tennis tournament trophies.

BETSY HEIDENBERGER has been USPTA member since 1984. She has been named Maryland Pro of the Year in 2003, 2009, 2014 and Greater Washington Pro of the Year in 1995. After graduating from UNC-Chapel Hill in 1982, where she played top singles and doubles positions, Betsy turned professional, ranked No. 201.

In 1986 Betsy become Club Manager and Director of the National Cathedral School Tennis Club in Washington, DC, the club was honored as USTA District Club of the Year. Since 2004, Betsy has been the Tennis Director at the CCRA Swim and Tennis Club in Chevy Chase, MD.

Betsy is APTA certified and the Platform Tennis Director at the Chevy Chase Club, reached top five National Platform Tennis ranking.

Betsy is Vice President of the Mid-Atlantic USPTA Board, member of the Wilson Advisory Staff and has served as the Maryland District Representative for the Mid-Atlantic Tennis Association.

RICHARD B. "RICH" HENDERSON is still an active 50 year member of the USPTA (formerly the USPLTA).

He is a graduate of UNC Chapel Hill (AB English with graduate studies for MAT Class of '65). Rich was a four-year letterman of UNC Chapel Hill. He was a member of Four ACC Championship teams.

Rich Henderson with some young students

Rich was the first Tennis Director of Cape Fear Country Club in Wilmington, NC (six years). He was the first Tennis Director of North Ridge Country Club in Raleigh, NC (19 years). Currently he is Assistant Tennis Director of North Hills Club in Raleigh, NC (25 years to present).

MARY HERRICK, Elite Professional, has been involved in the tennis industry for 30+

years. She was Tennis Director at Fox Creek Golf and Racquet Club in Lorain, OH. She served as a coach for the USTA Midwest Section Girls Nationals Team, developed high school state champions and nationally ranked junior tennis players.

She served on the USPTA Midwest Board of Directors for 10 years and was President from 2002–2004.

Throughout her career, Herrick has received numerous awards including the USPTA Education Award, Ohio Professional of the Year Award, Midwest Pro of the Year Award and the USPTA National Industry Excellence Award.

A few of the most memorable accomplishments throughout her career were serving as USTA Midwest Chairman of the Marketing Committee when the name was changed from "Western" to "Midwest," serving as division president of USPTA when the Developmental Coach category was introduced to improve educational opportunities for high school coaches and the creation of Yellow Ball Tennis Camps, serving 8-college campuses throughout the State of Ohio.

Mary is a USPTA tester, a Wilson Advisory Staff Member and President of Team Safe Screening LLC.

TODD HICKS is the Oneida boys' and girls' varsity tennis coach in Oneida, NY. He has coached the girls' varsity tennis team for the past 14 years. He has compiled a record of 243 wins and 42 losses over 14 seasons. His girls' varsity team has won the New York State Section III Tennis Tournament for the past three years. Hicks' has led the boys' varsity team to a record of 134 wins and 22 losses over the past 11 years. He is the Tri-Valley League Chair and has been a Section III Committee Member for the past 10 years for both the girls' and boys' league. Hicks has advanced many players to the New York State Tennis Tournament. His biggest accomplishment was having the same girls' tennis team finish 4th, 5th and 4th place in three consecutive years.

Todd Hicks with his New York State Section III champion Oneida High School girls' team

RICHARD A. HILLWAY is an international tennis historian, author of 100+ historical tennis articles, collector of tennis books and letters and expert on inventor Wingfield and Bill Tilden.

Richard is founder and chairman Colorado Tennis Hall of Fame (2000–15).

He was tennis director/pro, Country Club of Colorado, C.S. (1981–2009); Head pro, Arapahoe Tennis Club (1968-'73); Head pro, Village Tennis & Swim Club (1974-'79); Instructor, Greeley Recreation (1961-'66 summers); High school coach of 46 boys' and girls' team state tennis titles; Head coach of Cherry Creek HS boys' team (1969–1980) that won first eight of 19 straight state team titles, first 115 of 316 straight dual meet wins; Asst. coach, Cheyenne Mtn. HS–boys won 17 state team titles, girls 19; three-time Colorado HS state champion, twice in No. 1 singles; University of Colorado–three years at No. 1 singles, Outstanding Senior Athlete-Scholar Award & Phi Beta Kappa 1965; All-Australian Universities Team 1967 at Univ. of NSW on Rotary Fellowship; ranked No. 1 men's open singles Intermountain section U.S. in 1966 and 1970, No. 2 in 1968.

He has been a USPTA member 30 years and served USTA/Colorado 40 years, Chairman Awards Committee 23 years, on the Board 12 years, Ranking 15 years. Richard was selected Colorado HS Tennis Coach of Year, (1976–1979).

W. GEOFFREY HODSON was No. 2 Junior, Western Australia, 1967. In 1970 he was Big 10 No. 2 Doubles Champion and Assistant Professional at Cleveland Racquet Club. In 1971 he was Big 10 No. 2 Singles and Big 10 No. 1 Doubles Champion.

Geoff was Head Professional at Middletown Tennis Club (1971–1973) and Denver Country Club (1973–1979). From 1979–1997 he was Director of Tennis at Pinery Country Club.

From 1977 to 1981, Geoff was President of the USPTA Intermountain Division and on the Executive Committee USPTA.

From 1981–1997 he was a USPTA National Tester and he is a National NTRP Verifier for the USTA.

Geoff has been chosen Divisional Professional of the Year twice and received the Colorado Tennis Association Bud Robineau Award.

Geoff's son is Joshua and grandson is Matthew.

DOUG HOFER played three years on his high school tennis team; undefeated league champions 1973, Most Valuable Player award 1973; two years with community college tennis team, Most Improved Player award, 1974; and two years with college tennis team. Most Valuable and No. 1 Player award 1977. He has held seven Adult Tournament Titles in singles, four doubles titles in men's and mixed.

He was Visalia Community Tennis Association Founder and Executive Director, 1989-present. Doug has owned Hofer Tennis, Professional Tennis Services since 1986.

He was Dunlop Advisory Staff Professional (2004–2014), USPTA member since 1981, USTA member since 1973, USRSA member since 1984, Certified Professional Racquet Stringer since 1985, USTA National Clinician 1992–1994, USTA Adjunct Faculty 1995–1997.

Doug received USTA/ITA Community Service Award 1991 and 1996, USPTA NorCal Independent Pro of the Year Award (2013), USPTA NorCal Regional Rep of the Year Award 1995 and 1998, USTA NorCal Section NJTL of the Year award 2006-Founder and Director, Visalia Community Tennis Association President's Award for Dedication to Tennis 1993 and 2004.

Doug and Kimberly have been married since 1987. Children are Megan Hofer and Madison

Hofer. Member of GateWay Church, Visalia, CA since 1981, Youth Lay Leader 1993–1996.

VICTORIA HOLLOWAY-BARTLETT was an All Region player at Glynn Academy for four years, received Coach's Award for three years, undefeated junior year at Glynn Academy and two year collegiate athlete at College of Coastal Georgia.

Victoria is a USPTA certified teaching pro, head teaching pro at Jekyll Island Tennis Center, owner of Southern Breeze Tennis and junior league coordinator for BGITA (Brunswick Golden Isles Tennis Association).

She is the daughter of Gary and Tina Holloway of Brunswick, GA and married to Spencer Bartlett. Also, proud dog mom of two golden retrievers, Crimson and Wesson Tide.

PETER HOLMES, a graduate of Urbana, IL High School (1973) and Connecticut State University in 1987 with a BS in Environmental Science, has been a USPTA Elite Pro since 1987. He was chosen USPTA Western New England Pro of the Year, 1991 and 1999.

In 1990, Peter was No. 4 New England Men's 35 Singles; in 1991 he was No. 1 New England Men's 25 Doubles and in 1992 No. 1 New England Men's 35 Doubles.

Peter was Tennis Director at Golf Club of Avon, CT, from 1992–2002. From 2001–2003 he was Head Tennis Coach at University of Hartford. Since 2007 he is the Tennis Director at Farmington Farms Tennis and Athletic Club.

HARLAN HOPCHIK was one of the top-ranked players in mens 50 singles in U.S. No. 2 in 2005, and No. 13 in 2004. He achieved a No. 50 ranking in the mens 60 division in 2015 and was ranked No. 4 in Texas the same year. His crowning achievement as a player was winning the men's 55 singles USPTA Championship in 2012.

Harlan Hopchik and Lisa

Hopchik has a successful coaching business in the Dallas Metroplex area.

ROB HORSCH has been a tennis coach for over 30 years. He is been with Laguna Niguel Racquet Club since 2007. He previously was employed with the Steve Johnson Tennis Academy in San Clemente, CA; Ritz Carlton Rancho Mirage, CA; University of Nevada Las Vegas men's and women's tennis programs and Director of Tennis at Club Mirage in Fountain Hills, AZ. He has been a certified USTA High Performance coach and with the American Council on Exercise.

As collegiate player, he was a member of Seminole Jr. College's national championship team in 1982, was an All American at UC Santa Cruz in 1984. After college he played and coached professionally in North America and Europe before settling in Laguna Niguel, CA in 1995.

CHRIS HOSHOUR graduated from Sumter High School 1985, attended Miami-Dade North Junior College, Coker College (1992) and holds a bachelor's degree in Exercise Science. Chris played No. 1 Singles and Doubles.

Chris has been teaching tennis since 1993. He was at Sunset Country Club (1993–1995) Sumter, SC, as assistant pro; Hartsville Country Club (1995–2001), Assistant Pro and at Charlotte Tennis Academy (2001-current) as Director of High Performance.

He coached Southern Zonals (2001, 2012–2015), Team Southern at National Hard Courts and Clay Courts (2001–2002, 2011–2012), was Lead Coach, Southern 10's Camp (2012), South Carolina Head Coach USTA CTC State training camps (1998–2000), Team North Carolina Coach (2012-Current), USTA Regional RTC Coach (2011- current).

Chris coached two players at the 2011 Junior US Open, in 2014 USTA North Carolina Pro of the Year, has coached two NCAA All-Americans and has coached on the USTA Pro circuit and ATP Challenger circuit.

GLEN HOWE, USPTA Master Professional, Superintendent of Tennis for the City of Tallahassee, has always said that ever since he tried the game in 1973, tennis is all he has wanted to do.

Glen has always worked in the tennis industry and has previously been employed at Quince Orchard Swim and Tennis Club, Potomac Tennis Club, the Paladin Club, Fry's Spring Beach and Tennis Club, Hercules Country Club, Delcastle Tennis Center, Braemar Country Club and Tuscawilla Country Club.

His playing experience includes the Christopher Newport University varsity tennis team and he was ranked nationally in the USTA 35's from 1995–1999. He held a USTA 35s sectional ranking for nine years and during this time, he was a top 10 interdistrict captain as well as an intersectional captain from 1995–2001.

Glen has also served as treasurer and president of the USPTA Middle States Division and was named Middle States Division Pro of the Year in 1998. He was twice named USPTA 35s Player of the Year and has received the USPTA National Facility Manager of the Year award. This former Wilmington Tennis Foundation vice president, USTA Middle States teaching professional liaison, USTA National Developmental coach and USTA Delaware District board member has an abundance of experience and energy both on and off the court. Glen is presently the Head Tester and an Officer of USPTA Florida Division.

"I enjoy all aspects of the game, but my most satisfying aspect of the profession is increasing the size of a facility. I also enjoy taking care of customers and giving them my best every day. My expertise includes the following areas: training professionals, facility ownership, directing programs, working with advanced players, managing large staffs at facilities, and pro shop operations," Glen adds.

Glen considers his greatest accomplishment as tennis pro to be that he still has a thirst to learn and is getting better as his career continues. He has withstood four ownership buyouts and he has bounced back and believes that he has ended up at a better facility. He is very proud of his USPTA Facility of the Year and USPTA Florida and Middle States Pro of the Year awards.

Among his personal accomplishments, Glen has been married to Cheri for 39 years. They have three children (Scott, Kristen and Glynda) and six grandchildren. It has been an incredible journey with many more adventures to come.

RICHARD C. HOWELL has taught and coached tennis since 1968 in Indiana, Wisconsin, Ohio, Michigan, Texas and North Carolina. Since 2012, as an independent contractor, he has taught in Fayetteville, Hope Mills, Raeford, Spring Lake and at Fort Bragg in North Carolina. In 1975 as assistant coach of the boys tennis team at Jefferson High School in Lafayette, IN, the team won the state championship and in 1976 was state runner-up. Richard attended the first USPTA Academy at Sapphire Valley in North Carolina and became a USPTA member in 1977.

Richard received B.A. in Social Studies Education from Purdue University in 1970, M.A. in History from Purdue in 1971 and M.S. in Physical Education from Purdue in 1982. His Master's thesis was "A Biomechanical Analysis of Flat and Topspin Serves in Tennis." His thesis was published by the University of Oregon on microfiche.

JERRY HUBBARD, the son of an Army officer, learned tennis from USPTA legend Clarence Mabry in San Antonio, was No. 1 in high school for the International School in Bangkok, Thailand, and a member of the University of Arizona team in college. After making Honolulu his home, he became a certified Elite Professional in 1977, starting at the Ilikai Hotel in Waikiki, but spending the bulk of his teaching and coaching career at Punahou School, the most successful junior tennis program in Hawaii.

Jerry has taught players of all ages and abilities, from beginners to top juniors. Jerry has trained players to the state, sectional, national and professional levels, including multiple state champions and several NCAA scholarship recipients. Now an ordained minister for Kaimuki Christian Church, Jerry still enjoys competitive singles and doubles in his age group.

MICHAEL E. HURLEY is Co-Director of Nashville Tennis Annual Special Populations Unified Doubles Tournament since 2014. He has been a USPTA member since 1979 with its highest rating, Elite Pro, and a USTA member since 1968. Michael has held dozens of rankings as a player in Ohio, Indiana, the Midwest Section, Tennessee and Southern Section.

From May 1991–present, Michael is Co-Director of the Tennis Venue for the Tennessee Special Olympics' State Games. June 1991–present, he teaches private and group lessons by appointment only. Fall 1997–present, he provides a FREE clinic for competitive high school junior players on Saturdays.

Michael has received: 2001—Midwest USPTA Hall of Fame; 1997—Jack Kramer Award from Wilson Sporting Goods; 1997—Special Olympics "Special Person of the Year;" 1984, 1987—Midwest USPTA Tennis Professional of the Year; 1981, 1984, 1985—Ohio Tennis Professional of the Year; 1986, 1988, 1989—United Cerebral Palsy NE Ohio Fundraiser of the Year.

Michael holds various district and state rankings in doubles and singles through the years. He has written and published several articles in professional newsletters and USPTA journals.

RAMONA HUSARU is the Education and Multimedia Manager for the USPTA. In her role, Ramona is in charge of overseeing the continuing education program and expanding its resources, including: the "On Court with USPTA" TV show that airs on the Tennis Channel, stroke analysis, conferences, workshops, webinars and TennisResources.com. She is also a USPTA Tester and part of the USPTA Under 30 initiative, developing opportunities through education and leadership for fellow young professionals. Ramona is a former WTA-ranked player and a two-time NCAA Division II National Team Champion with BYU-Hawaii, where she had a remarkable winning record of 45-0 in singles competition. She holds a bachelor's degree in Exercise Sport and Science and a master's degree in Sports Psychology.

GAIL INGIS, a USPTA member since 1977, devoted several years to teaching tennis. During the early years, she was invited to serve as the USPTA NJ secretary. Although she would have loved to serve, her busy schedule made that impossible. Gail was asked to do a painting that would depict the USPTA's 75th anniversary. The watercolor painting, 17"x22" was housed in USPTA headquarters in Houston, TX. She loves her tennis, and keeps her membership in USPTA to stay apprised of the industry and who's who. Here's what she's been doing in her design, art and writing careers.

Gail writes historical romance, loves history and romance, of course. Her weekly blog frequently covers historical content. A native of Brooklyn, NY, Gail's youth began and ended with writing, drawing and music. Her inspiration to write came from books gifted to her by an aunt. But life had other ideas.

After graduating from the New York School of Interior Design with a BFA in Interior Architecture and Design and master's studies in Architecture and Design Criticism at The New School (Parsons), she worked in the field. She founded a school of Interior Design and was twice asked by publishers to write a textbook, her efforts were thwarted by a heavy schedule. Gail resides in Connecticut with her scientist-writer husband. She and her husband love to travel, play tennis and ballroom dance. Currently, she sits on Lockwood-Mathews Mansion Museum Board of Trustees and serves as the curator of art exhibitions. Gail is also a professional artist. Having spent her youth dallying in Coney Island, she is doing historical and present paintings of Coney Island, for her upcoming exhibition in 2016 at the museum where she curates art.

TIM IRWIN is the past Executive Director of the USPTA Middle States Division. Tim has been teaching tennis since 1972 and has also served as the Assistant Coach of West Chester University, Head Tennis Professional of Radley Run Country Club, Frog Hollow Tennis Club, the Cynwyd Club and Director of Racquet Sports at Aronimink Golf Club. Tim has a Masters Degree in Educational Leadership from Neumann College. He is a certified facilitator of the "Seven Habits of Highly Effective People Signature Course," "The Leader In Me Operational System for Education" and is a domestic brother of the Brothers and Sisters of Charity. In addition Tim is a full-time health and physical education teacher in his hometown of Coatesville, PA. Tim is married to his wife Karen and they reside in Downingtown, PA.

SCOTT IRWIN, a native of Hollywood, CA was an active and successful player on the US national junior circuit and graduated from La Jolla High School in 1975, where he went undefeated in both singles and doubles during the regular season and state championships on the 1975 California Interscholastic Federation Championship (CIF) team, winning the CIF state doubles title that year with partner John Stout. Scott attended the University of Cincinnati from 1975–1977 and the University of Hawaii at Manoa in Honolulu from 1977–1979 on full athletic tennis scholarships. He was named Most Inspirational team member as a senior in 1978–1979 and then served as the Assistant Varsity Men's and Women's Tennis Coach at UH for the 1979–1980 season. Even today, Scott holds one of the highest victory percentages in UH school tennis history.

During and following college, Scott participated on the professional tennis circuit, competing in ATP and satellite events in 18 countries, winning one singles and two doubles titles. As his playing career wound down, Scott began directing tennis programs and eventually managing club operations at country clubs, resorts and racquet clubs in the Southeast US, California, New York, Michigan, Florida and Canada. Scott is a well-recognized hospitality and sports operations consultant and is a partner in several sports and hospitality management and consulting firms. Scott is a member of the Club Managers Association of America, the US Professional Tennis Association and the International Food Service Executives Association. He is a Life member of the US Tennis Association and has held a Community Association Manager license with the State of Florida. He was honored to be the recipient of the USPTA Club Manager of the Year Award for the nine Southeastern US states in 2002. In November of 2003, Scott was awarded his Certified Club Manager designation by the Club Managers Assn. of America, joining a select group of club managers throughout the world who hold this hallmark designation. In addition, in 2004 Scott was the first USPTA member and club manager in the U.S. to obtain not only the CCM but the prestigious Master Certified Food Executive designation as well.

RAJ H. JACKSON is an USPTA Elite Tennis Professional born in Hyderabad, India and lives in Las Vegas, NV. In 2007, he first became USPTA certified at the Billie Jean King USTA National Tennis Center in Flushing Meadows, NY. He achieved maximum tennis rating as an USPTA Elite Tennis Professional in 2016. He is unique as the only person in the world who is both an USPTA tennis professional and PGA golf professional.

Raj Jackson is a board-certified licensed Doctor of Chiropractic in California and Nevada. He received his Biology degree from West Virginia University and is a graduate of Life University Chiropractic College in Atlanta. He has been providing board-approved chiropractic continuing education courses about golf injuries and peak performance since 2014.

Raj Jackson is the only professional who is a member of both the PGA and the USPTA.

As a junior, he trained at the Nick Bollettieri tennis academy (IMG Academy) in Florida and attended various junior camps at the Dennis Van Der Meer tennis school in Hilton Head, S.C.

He grew up in southern West Virginia in a small coal mining town called Man.

Nicknamed "Hollywood" by his friends for his flashy style and big smile, he was the high school tennis star. Hollywood served as the captain of the Man high school tennis team for all three years. He played No. 1 singles and No. 1 doubles with a dominating record of 105 wins and seven losses and is a tennis legend in southern West Virginia.

Although his tennis career has been centered around teaching. Raj's highest USTA ranking came in 2012, when he was ranked No. 1 in USTA Open Men's Doubles in the Intermountain Section playing out of Las Vegas.

Raj Jackson's teaching career extends to many international destinations in the Caribbean as a resort tennis pro. He has worked at many 5-Star resorts in Mexico, Jamaica and Dominican Republic. His past teaching experiences include the Ritz Carlton, Iberostar Resorts, Grand Palladium Resorts, Now Jade, Now Sapphire, Grand Lido Negril, Hedonism, Couples Resorts, Dreams Resorts, and Crown Paradise Club.

In addition to his love for tennis, Raj has had a lifelong passion for golf as well.

Raj Jackson is a PGA Golf Professional who is an active member in Southern Nevada Chapter (Las Vegas) of the Southwest Section of the PGA.

The PGA of America currently has over 27,000 golf professionals around the world and less than 1% of them are Certified through the advanced professional program. Raj Jackson has successfully completed all four career tracks including Player Development, Teaching/Coaching, Golf Operations and General Management.

Raj is an expert in golf biomechanics and all facets of the golf instruction including the full swing, chipping, putting, bunkers and golf fitness. He has been a golf teaching professional at four country clubs in the U.S. in N.C. and W.V. In addition, he taught on four cruise ships while sailing around the world traveling to over 50 International countries in Europe, Africa, South America and Central America on Carnival Cruise Lines, Holland America Cruises, Celebrity Cruises and P&O Cruises Lines.

In 2015, his dreams came true. Raj Jackson was teaching golf on the PGA Tour for the Fidelity Investments Swinglab at eight different tour stops including the Waste Management Phoenix Open, LA Northern Trust Open, Valspar Championships, Arnold Palmer Bay Hill Invitational, Byron Nelson AT&T Championship, Tiger Woods Quicken Loans National, and Coca-Cola Tour Championship. In addition, he performed hi-def video swing analysis for the Golf Channel's Swing Fix.

GABRIEL B. JACOB, a tennis instructor for more than 34 years, holds an Elite Professional rating in the U.S. Professional Tennis Association (USPTA).

Gabriel previously coached the Cypress College men's tennis team and the San Bernardino Valley College women's tennis team, which ranked as high as second place in the Foothill Conference.

His formal education includes a bachelor of arts in business administration (management) from California State University at San Bernardino and a Master of Science degree in physical education from Azusa Pacific University.

Gabriel has served as the Inland Empire team coordinator for the USTA and as the commissioner for junior tennis in the Inland Empire for the Southern California Tennis Association.

Gabriel is currently Director of Tennis for Redlands Youth Tennis. He served as district president of the California USPTA, served as second vice president and Secretary of the Executive Board of the California USPTA.

DR. DAVID JACOME is CEO and Founder of Super Amazing Tennis. David obtained his BS in Physics and Mathematics and M.B.A. from Saint Peter's University. Thereafter, he received his MS in Physics from Stevens Institute of Technology. Lastly, he was awarded a Doctor of Divinity from Universal Life Church in Christianity and Catholicism. Currently, he's pursing a Doctor of Educational Leadership from Saint Peter's. David is Professor of Physics and Business at numerous universities in New Jersey. David has a Transitional G Physics K–12 Certification, Teacher of Physics Standard Certification in New Jersey, Recreational Coach with USPTA and certified Tennis Coach for MyTennisLessons.com. Besides his career as a tennis player, David is also CEO and Founder of Gateway 2 Science, a company started at the age of 18. David is also Director of the Hudson County New Jersey Tennis Network which has 115 active players.

THOMAS JAEGER, AIA, USPTA, USRSA, USTA, is a certified teaching member of the USPTA since 1995, achieving the Level IV Professional development award for 10 continuous years of professional commitment and achievement, certification as a USTA NTRP Verifier, 20 year member of the U.S. Racquet Stringers Association USRSA, and a member of the Professional Advisory Staff of Head/ Penn Racquet Sports. Currently tennis professional at The Racket Club in Crystal Lake, IL and The Judson University Division of Exercise Science and Sport, Elgin, IL. He has served as the Head Tennis Professional for the Tall Oaks Tennis Club, Del Webb Sun City Huntley, IL and The Minocqua Country Club, Minocqua, WI. He taught as tennis staff professional for the Horseshoe Bay Resort, Horseshoe Bay, TX, the Chicago District Tennis Association Junior Excellence Program, USTA Play Tennis America, USPTA Tennis Across America, Nike tennis camps for ages 6 to 17, and the USTA 10 and under Team Tennis Program. He has played on USTA state championship and regional teams out of River Trails Tennis Club in Arlington Heights, IL.

Born 1938 in Chicago, Master of Architecture degree from the University of Illinois Urbana Champaign. Emeritus Professor of Architecture, University of Illinois at Chicago and currently Senior University Lecturer and adjunct Professor of Architecture, Judson University. Recipient of the American Institute of Architects (AIA), Illinois 2014 Gold Medal for Outstanding Lifetime Service to the profession. This is the highest honor the AIA Illinois bestows and Tom is the sixth Illinois architect to have received it.

HUGO JIMENEZ, a USPTA certified professional since 1999, teaches with Denver Parks & Recreation's Star Search and Tennis in the Parks programs. He's a USTA School Tennis Specialist promoting tennis in schools K–12, at 9News Health Fairs and the Diversity-TennisFest Series. Hugo is a QuickStart and Cardio Tennis instructor and published in the USPTA Intermountaineer and CTA Tennis Newspaper for his article entitled Mini Tennis. He was awarded the USPTA Intermountain Star Award in 2010 for his grassroots work in Tennis. Hugo collaborated in the USTA Colorado "Vive tu Juego" TV Commercial with the Ricardo Flores Magon Academy where he taught for several years. He starred in commercial spots on the local Spanish TV station for the "Breaking the Barriers" series, "Vive el Ténis." Hugo's love of tennis shines through as evidenced in articles in the Summer 2012 Coloradotennis.com "High Five" issue and the Fall USTA School Tennis Newsletter.

MARY P. JOHNSEN, a protégé of Hazel Hotchkiss Wightman and Bill Hinchliff (Yale) tournament play resulted with a national ranking in the 1950s and USPTA membership in 1968. Degrees- B.A., M.A. Career highlights include pro at twelve facilities and operator of six (1955–2013); 1970 US Open doubles play; USTA Umpire, Board member and Executive Director National Tennis Ass'n; National Director IRSA; president, Racquet Sports Associates with numerous consulting assignments (1975–1989). Speaker USPTA- 1982 The Great Tennis Debates (with Hopman, Braden, Loehr, Bollettieri, Fox, Van der Meer, Schwartz, Tym), USTA, IRSA, Club Industry. Published or quoted- NY Times, Tennis, Tennis Industry,

World Tennis, IRSA News, The Wall Street Journal, Esquire, Club Industry, Inside Tennis, The Army Times. Member: USTA, NSWTA, USPTA. Awards: USTA Grass Roots Hero, 2003; US Olympic Committee Volunteer Coach of the Year, Tennis; USPTA NorCal President's and George Bacso Professional Achievement awards - 2003.

DICK "DJ" JOHNSON has long been a familiar face in Southwest tennis. Johnson grew up in Albuquerque's South Valley. He played tennis at Rio Grande High and at the University of Albuquerque, where he earned a B.S. in education in 1966 and was named Athlete of the Year twice. Later, he worked for the Rod Laver/Roy Emerson camps. Johnson has coached the La Cueva High School boys to 12 state championships in 15 years and enriched numerous young lives. His many honors include New Mexico High School Coach the Year four times, USPTA Southwest High School Coach of the year six times and national USPTA High School Coach of the Year in 2016. He has served three terms as president of the USTA Northern New Mexico Tennis Association and one term as president of the Southwest Professional Tennis Association. In 1998, Johnson was elected to the USTA Southwest Hall of Fame. He and Marcie have been married 43 years.

JAN "JJ" JOHNSON was a gymnast her college junior and senior years as there was no women's tennis. She moved to Minneapolis in 1989, joined Northwest Clubs and her tennis skills were picked up by Tennis Pro Jan Schissal. Jan loved the game and competition. She took the USPTA test in 1983 at 36 years old and passed with flying colors. She has taught ever since. Previously she taught Physical Education in Minnesota.

Jan has served all positions on NWTA (Northern) Board.

She has taken numerous players to national tournaments including her own daughters, teaching 16 years in Minneapolis, MN. She has now spent 16 years teaching in the Southwest.

Jan made a tennis video for Minnesota Sports Channel (May 1999) and put together a "Leadership Video" for Federated Insurance Co. using tennis as a model (1998).

Jan and D.J. have two daughters – Shanna was 1990 Singles State Champion and Heather was 1993 Singles State Champion.

ABDUL JORDAN was born Oct. 31, 1976 in Greenville, NC. He is one of five children (Joy, Newby, Omar and Patrick) of Charles and Linda Jordan. His older brother is also a tennis teaching pro in Charlotte, NC.

Abdul graduated from J.H. Rose High School (Greenville, NC) in 1995. He attended North Carolina Agricultural and Technical State University (Greensboro, NC), Bachelors of Science, Computer Graphics in 1999 University of Kansas (Lawrence, KS), Master's of Education in Sports Management (In Progress).

Amateur career highlights include Chancellor Academic Scholar, four-year full scholarship tennis player, four-year tennis team captain, four-time tennis letterman and three-time tennis MVP at North Carolina Agricultural and Technical State University (Greensboro, NC).

Professional highlights include Elite USPTA Teaching Professional since 2014. Owner/Operator, June 2008 to present Jordan Athletics Inc., Montgomery County, MD. Elite Professional Tennis Instructor, April 2010 to present Maryland-National Capital Park and Planning Commission, Montgomery County, MD.

Abdul is the proud father of David Jordan (14) and Bryan Jordan (10).

DAWN JUPIN, a USPTA Elite Pro since 1986, has been involved in tennis since the early 1970s. Since 2011 Dawn has been Director of Tennis & Croquet at The Chattooga Club in Cashiers, NC. Born and raised in West Sayville, NY, the daughter of Douglas and Judy Otto, Dawn graduated Sayville High School in 1979, and was inducted into the Athletic Hall of Fame in 2010.

Dawn's "tennis boom" began in 1972 when she and her father took their first tennis lesson together, and together that summer attended Harry Hopman's Tennis Camp in Amherst, MA, directed by Chuck Kriese. The following summer, as well as the next seven years, she was invited to all the USTA junior nationals. In the summer of 1974, Dawn represented the U.S. as the only girl on the "Tennis Europe" team.

From 1973-80, coached by Rick Elstein, Dawn acquired ETA top 5 and USTA top 10 rankings in the 12's–18's. Between 1981-83, Dawn played for the Lady Gamecocks at the University of South Carolina, coached by Jeff Kefalos, where they went on to post NCAA No. 12, No. 7 and No. 6 rankings respectfully. Playing No. 1 doubles for the Gamecocks, Dawn and teammate Ellen Oxreider, achieved All-American honors in 1982.

After receiving a BA degree from SUNY at Stony Brook in 1985, Dawn's career as a tennis teaching professional began, along with her most cherished personal highlight, her family. Dawn is the very proud mother of two sons, Richard Harenberg Jr. and Steven Harenberg. Dawn resides in the North Carolina mountains with her husband, George Jupin, also a tennis pro, and their black lab, Zelda.

JACK JUSTICE, USPTA Past President ('90-'92) member since 1969. A Southern Division Hall of Fame member, he has served in a variety of tennis positions throughout his more than 50 years in the industry. He authored the "USPTA How to Hire a Tennis Professional" manual and was a long time tester for the organization. An NJTL stalwart he worked to forward that program within USPTA. He served as Chairman of the Master Professional, Ethics, Archives/Hall of Fame, Long Range Planning, Club Relations, and USTA Relations Committees. He coached men's tennis at Austin Peay State University ('70-'71) while completing his BA in Health and PE. He was an All-Army player and retired in 1977 to begin a full-time career as a tennis teacher. Now retired from teaching tennis, he makes his home with wife Katie on Potato Creek in South Carolina.

DON KAISER started playing tennis at age 10. He had a very successful junior career being Kentucky State High School singles champion in 1946 and 1947. He was a member

of US Junior Davis Cup in 1948. Don was a member of the 1950 University of Miami tennis team which was No. 1 in the U.S. He was captain of that team in 1952. Don was Men's State Champion in Kentucky, Ohio, Alabama and Florida. Don won an all-Army tournament in Europe (singles and doubles) in 1955. He had a national men's ranking of No. 21 in 1951 and No. 27 in 1952.

Don worked four years for Kentucky Tennis Patron's Foundation, 10 years for University of Louisville and Louisville Country Club. He worked four years each at Bartlett Park in St. Petersburg and Treasure Island and 16 years at Shipwatch Tennis Club in Largo, FL, 10 years at the Longboat Club. He retired in Sarasota, FL, in 2003 at age 73.

Don was National Father and Son Champion in 1950 with Edward.

His best wins: USPTA 55 Singles (1982) and Doubles (1987) with Tom Barlett, USPTA National Ranking No. 1 singles and doubles, Semi-finals National 55, highest national ranking (1997) No. 3 65 singles. He won Orange Bowl Doubles and Southern Doubles.

RAY KEISER, a USPTA Recreational Coach since 2005, is also a PTR Professional, a USRSA member and field rep and high school coach. A retired schoolteacher, Ray is 71 years old and lives in Seekonk, MA. He was the Dighton-Rehoboth Reg. H.S. boys' coach (MIAA SCC Champions 1999) and has been the DR girls' coach since 2003. Ray was also the Tolman H.S. (Pawtucket, RI) girls' coach from 2000–2010; the 2000 RI Class C State Champions and Division Champions in 2000, 2001, and 2003. Inducted into the RI High School Girls' Tennis Coaches Hall of Fame in 2010, Ray has also been a part-time teaching pro at Fore Court Tennis and Fitness and Centre Court Tennis Club, both in Rhode Island. He was also fortunate enough to teach a clinic with Vic Braden (ForeCourt, 2003) and one with Tom Gullikson (CentreCourt, 2008). Ray currently teaches at the Indoor Court, a historic 100-year-old one-court facility featured in Tennis Magazine, located in East Providence, RI.

JOE KELLS began playing in college at Scottsdale, AZ C.C. and was Most Improved Player in 1980. He had Top 10 Rankings in Men's NCTA 35 and 40, No. 2 in 40 Singles in 1999. Joe and son, Drew (USC NCCA Champ 2009) were No. 2 Father-Son in NTA in 2012 and 2014 (No. 31 in U.S. in 2014).

Joe's first job was Assistant Pro at Mesa Country Club in 1983, moved to Bay area in 1984 and has been self-employed conducting clinics and lessons through the Rec. Dept. at Mill Valley and Tiburon for 30 years.

He was Head Varsity Tennis Coach for B&G in the late 1980s and early U's at Marin Catholic and Terpa Linda High Schools. He worked for USTA Player Development in its initial days in the late 1980s. Highlights have been coaching top kids on the local high school teams and watching several play in college.

Joe is divorced with a son, Andrew.

GARY L. KESL, Ph.D., BA Baylor University, Freshman Basketball, Varsity Tennis, Scholarship and Leadership Award; MS Southern Illinois University, Faculty appointment; Ph.D. University of Miami, Iron Arrow, OK, Phi Delta Kappa, President Graduate Student Government, Assistant Tennis Coach, Chairman Graduate Judicial Board, Associate Director Cuban Teacher Retraining Program.

Gary won Texas State TAAF Men's singles (ranked No. 6 in Texas '64-65); ranked No. 7 Florida singles, No. 1 doubles '70; won minor events while playing in 11 countries; direct acceptance US Open, Italian Open; consultant to *Seventeen Magazine*; host, Tennis Everyone TV show, 19 editions; owner, Deer Creek Racquet Club; founded Gary Kesl Tennis Academy; coach of four Junior Wimbledon winners including back-to-back winners; nine times Davis Cup coach, three times Sunshine Cup coach and developed numerous Orange Bowl and NCAA winners; charter member USTA High Performance Coaches; ATP Tour Elite Coaches Association; Vice President, USPTA of Florida; speaker, ITF Junior Tennis Conference, Paris, France; award for contribution to Mexican tennis, Merida, Mexico; 21 clinics in Mexico and Caribbean for Chevrolet Division of General Motors; coach, World Team Tennis, Florida Breakers (championship finalist, lost tiebreaker playoffs); guest clinician in Finland, Brazil, Costa Rica, Ukraine and Dominican Republic; two years WTA Appeals Board; guest on American Magazine TV show with NBA Dave Debusschere; numerous TV interviews, magazine articles and publications. Currently (2016) Director of Tennis at Boca Country Club, Boca Raton, FL.

EDWARD KEYSER'S expertise includes training and education effectiveness, personal productivity, innovation, team dynamics, empowerment and technology integration using tools to increase productivity and accountability. Catering to individuals' strengths, different learning styles and natural intelligences, Edward has developed and taught leadership, motivation, productivity and thinking skills to children and corporate CEOs. His experience and maturity moderate his high energy and excitement.

Edward "keeps the ax sharp" by taking part in activities that build physical strength and mental agility. He is an international ballroom dancer, sailing instructor and a USPTA-certified tennis professional. "I've learned from these activities that strength and agility come from periods of intense effort followed by sufficient recovery which promotes growth and stability," he says. "Learning involves the same process and I use it as part of my training methodology."

In the boardroom or on the court, Edward's sessions are intense and fun, the necessary ingredients for growth and learning.

ALLEN KIEL became a USPTA member in 1971, after playing tennis for DePaul University and the University of Northern Colorado and then graduating from UNC with a BS in Marketing. In 1973, George Bacso, Tim Heckler, Jack Barnaby and Allen wrote the first USPTA certification test.

During the 1970s in Illinois, he was the Head Pro and Manager at the Skokie, Oaklawn and Lincolnshire Racquet Clubs. Allen was USPTA Mid-West Division VP.

He moved to Colorado to get involved with real estate in 1978, but kept volunteering in tennis as President of the Colorado Youth Tennis Foundation, President of the Intermountain Tennis Association, ITA Delegate and Member of the USTA Executive Committee, and Chairman USTA Davis Cup, Learning & Leadership and NJTL committees among many other assignments. While Chairman of the Serve Committee, Allen led in the creation of USTA University. He is a member of the Colorado Tennis Hall of Fame and the DePaul University Sports Hall of Fame. Presently, Allen is a Board Member of Colorado Heights University and the Colorado Sports Hall of Fame and President of CRS at Citywide Banks.

Allen rejoined the USPTA as an Elite Pro in 2013 to take advantage of USPTA education programs, in order enhance his on-court teaching skills for volunteer work with top local minority juniors.

He is most proud of his 20 years of work to bring diversity and inclusion to the USTA and Colorado tennis.

TERRY KILLEN was inducted into the USPTA Mid-Atlantic Division Hall of Fame in March 2012 as part of the inaugural class of inductees and is the first Maryland tennis professional so recognized. A native of Baltimore, MD, Terry has lived in Darnestown area of suburban, DC since 1975. He is a certified USPTA Elite Professional and has been a member of the USPTA since 1973. He has developed numerous junior players who have achieved top state and sectional rankings. He was awarded the District of Columbia Association of Health, Physical Education, Recreation & Dance Outstanding Service Award for Coaching Excellence in 1984.

Terry presently serves as a USPTA National Certification Tester. He previously served as a USPTA Mid-Atlantic Divisional Officer. He has been a speaker at local conferences, has authored tennis articles for local and national magazines and has attended well over 30 national conventions, believing in the beneficial influence of the USPTA with its emphasis on continuing education.

The Mid-Atlantic Division of the USPTA has recognized Terry as the Maryland Professional of the Year six times, the Greater Washington, DC Professional of the Year three times, and as the Mid-Atlantic Coach of the Year. He was also selected as the USPTA Mid-Atlantic Division's Over 45 Player of the Year nine times. In addition, he received the USPTA's National Ranking six years in different age groupings in singles and doubles and held top five USTA Mid-Atlantic Sectional Rankings in 12 different age divisions in both singles and doubles. He has held two USTA National Rankings in Men's 55 Doubles (No. 12 in 2005, No. 38 in 2006). He has been a member of the USTA Mid-Atlantic Intersectional Team in the 45's, 55's and 65 men's divisions, serving as a two-year captain of the 55's Atlantic Coast Cup Team.

A former collegiate varsity basketball and baseball player at Frostburg State University, Terry was awarded the university's prestigious Jim Anderson Memorial Award in 2005 in recognition of his accomplishments as a teacher, coach and administrator in the fields of education and professional tennis. The award also cited his continuing success as a tennis professional, player and mentor. He is especially proud that his son Terence, also a USPTA Elite Professional, is following in his footsteps, serving the greater Washington, D.C. area.

Terry is a USTA lifetime member and a proud member of the Wilson Sporting Goods National Tennis Advisory Staff/National Team. He is semi-retired, spending six months of the year playing tennis in Bradenton, FL, and working the other six months as an assistant tennis professional in Potomac, MD. He is also proud to devote his time to worthy tennis foundations and fundraisers, such as Madisen's Match, an event sponsored by the Tim and Tom Gullikson's Pediatric Brain Tumor Foundation.

SKY KIM, Founder and CEO of Road to Pro, INC., has played on the professional tour and has been in the sport for more than 25 years. In 2011 he was the coach of the champion in the 16's Orange Bowl who is the top ATP player in Korea currently on tour, Hyeon Chung, and was the champion of the 16's Orange Bowl. From 2011 through 2013, he coached the members of the Davis Cup team in Korea and has Grand Slam coaching experience on the WTA tour.

As the founder of Road to Pro, he has created the Tennis Swing Training System that brings new and easy methods to teach and learn tennis swings and is working on a new book with a fresh new concept. He is located in Los Angeles, CA, teaching all levels from beginners to professionals.

DICK KING joined the Texas Professional Tennis Association in 1967 and has been a member of the USPTA since 1970 when the Texas section joined the USPTA. He started his professional tennis career as the Manager and Head Professional at Caswell Tennis Center in Austin, TX. Other professional stops included being the Director of Tennis at five other Texas clubs: Tarry House and The Courtyard Tennis and Swim Club in Austin; T-Bar-M Racquet Club, Amarillo; Walden on Lake Houston Country Club, Humble and Wildflower Country Club, Temple.

In 1976 King was the President of the Texas Professional Tennis Association and in 1983 he became a member of the first class receiving the USPTA Master Professional certification. He played college tennis at Southern Illinois University-Carbondale and held sectional and national rankings in open and senior tennis. His coaching experiences included coaching boys' tennis at Austin High School, Austin, being an interim Women's Tennis Coach at the University of Texas-Austin, and from 1992 until 2014, being the head men's and women's tennis coach at Temple College in Temple, TX. He was inducted into the NJCAA Men's Coaches Association Hall of Fame in 2000, the NJCAA Women's Coaches Association Hall of Fame in 2004 and the Texas Tennis Museum and Hall of Fame in 2015.

CHUCK KINYON, a native of Rochester, NY, graduated from The University of Louisville in 1997. Grad assistant at Penn State where he coached the Freshman Tennis and Soccer Teams, he moved on to Penn State Altoona Campus in 1969 where spent six seasons coaching tennis and soccer.

In 1975 he was hired by Phillips Exeter Academy (NH), where coached tennis and squash.

He was hired as Dartmouth's head squash coach and assistant men's tennis coach in 1980 and became the head coach to both in 1983.He coached both until 1990.

He began focusing solely on tennis for the last 20 years of his career before retiring in 2010. Along the way, he led Big Green to their first Ivy League tennis championships (1993 and '97). He was awarded Region 1 Coach of the Year and USPTA Pro of the Year.

He retired with more than 275 wins at Dartmouth. He was also named to the College Squash Hall of Fame and the prestigious Dartmouth Wearer's of the Green.

Bob Ceplikas said, "Thanks to Chuck's hard work, we built an indoor tennis facility that Billie Jean King later called 'the best college tennis facility in the country.'" The players' lounge is named in his honor.

In 1973 Chuck began what was to become the prestigious Junior Tennis Camp, KJTC.

As a teaching pro, Kinyon was the head professional at the Dublin Lake Club (1969-'89) and remains the Director of Tennis at the Quechee Club in Vermont.

KATHY KOLANKIEWICZ has been in the tennis industry for 30 years as a USPTA teaching professional, ITA Division I collegiate coach, Director of the Lobo Tennis Club, High School and Mid School coach. She led the Lobos to 24 successful years as Head Women's Coach at The University of New Mexico (356-236 record). Prior to that she was Assistant Coach at The University of Mississippi, '82-'85. Recently, Kathy coached the girls' high school and middle school teams at Bosque School, '12-'15.

As a player, she was Pennsylvania State Doubles Champion '76 and '77, AIAW Division II All American from The University of Tennessee at Chattanooga '78 and '79 and world ranked No. 249 in '82.

Kathy earned a B.S. from UTC and was inducted into their Sports Hall of Fame in '96, a M.S. from the UM in '85 and a Ph.D. from UNM in Sports Administration in '96.

ALAN L. KOTH was the Pennsylvania State Singles Champion in 1957, highly ranked (No. 3) Middle States single (late 1960s) and No. 1 ranked doubles Middle States for four years. Alan was No. 14 ranked Father-Son with father Earl (early 1970s) and No. 1 ranked with Earl eight years in Middle States. Alan and son Scott ranked No. 1 Nationally in Father-Son in 1983 and 1986.

He was No. 1 ranked, Men's 55 Doubles, Nationally USTA (1994) and No. 1 ranked USPTA Men 55 Doubles, nationally (1994–1999). In 1994 he competed on USTA Austria Cup Team in Ireland.

Alan was MSPLTA President in 1972. He was Head Pro at Merion C.C., Philadelphia (1973–1976); Highpoint R.C. (Calfont, (1976–1981); Head Pro and Owner, Winderest T.C. (1981–1984); and Head Pro at River Crest C.C., Fort Worth (1984–1992) and Bent Creek C.C., Lancaster (1992–2002).

Currently Alan is Instructor at Alamo T.C. in San Antonio.

Alan and Edith have two sons: Scott (wife Juanita, granddaughters Baylee and Jamie) and Shawn (wife Jodie, grandsons Ryan and Justin).

EON "SPEEDY" KOTZE was born in Klerksdorp, South Africa. He graduated from Boca Raton Community High School, class of 1997. Eon is a Certified Fire Fighter and EMT from Coral Springs Fire Academy 2011.

Eon holds a high ranking of 27 in Florida men's open division 2000.

He was a private touring coach in Europe in 2004, Tennis Operation Manager at Boca West Country Club and currently is Head Tennis Professional at Via Mizner Country Club in Boca Raton.

Eon learned to play tennis at age 6 from his dad, Ivan Sebborn.

He has been married for five years to Jillian and living in Boca Raton. When not playing tennis they enjoy running half marathons.

CHRISTINE "CHRIS" KOUTRAS was the top ranking Florida junior player (1961–1965). She received the Florida Lawn Tennis Association Sportsmanship Award (Girl's 18 and under division, 1964). Chris was top ranking Florida Intercollegiate player (1966–1969) and National Southeastern Intercollegiate Champion, singles and doubles, (1969).

Chris was included in the publications *Who's Who Among Students in American Junior Colleges* (1967) and *Outstanding College Athletes Of America* (1969).

Chris has been USPTA Elite Professional since 1971.

She was Head Tennis Professional (1970–1974), FIELD CLUB, Sarasota, FL, and Director of Tennis and Head Professional Plantation Golf and Country Club, Venice, FL, (1982–1994). Chris was selected Pro Volunteer of the Year, Florida District No. 8 (1993).

Chris had Florida Professional Tennis Association's No. 1 ranking, singles (1975) and USPTA National Champion, singles and doubles (1977).

As a USPTA Tennis Professional with over 40 years of teaching and playing experience, Chris is very proud and grateful to have the reputation as an accomplished club professional and innovative teacher of both adults and juniors.

KEVIN KOWALIK, Director of Tennis at Homestead Country Club. Kevin has been on the USPTA Missouri Valley Board of Directors and named Pro of the Year in 2010 and 2014. Homestead CC has won multiple awards including Lessons for Life and USTA 10 and Under organization of the year under his guidance.

He previously was employed as the Head Men's Tennis Coach at the University of Or-

egon and Wichita State University and as Associate Head Men's Tennis Coach at Baylor University.

Kevin holds a Master's Degree from the University of Kansas and was an All-American in tennis at the collegiate level.

BRIAN D. KOWELL joined the USPTA in 1975. He is currently on the staff at Towpath Tennis Club in Akron, OH. After playing varsity tennis at Baldwin-Wallace University, he taught at Manitou-Wabing tennis camp in Canada, joined Peter Burwash International teaching tennis at Midtown Tennis Club in Chicago and The Kaval Surf Tennis Club in Hawaii, and he also did clinics throughout Canada and the U.S. After a stint in Pharmaceutical Sales, Brian returned to teaching full time in Ohio at River Run Racquet Club, Peak Performance Tennis, as well as heading the tennis program at Cuyahoga Community College and the city of Broadview Heights.

DAVE "KOZ" KOZLOWSKI, one of the first 17 USPTA Master Professionals, has been lecturing at national and international conventions for the past three decades. Kozlowski is the creator of two instructional tennis videos: "Master Your Tennis Motor Memory" and "Fundamentally Sound Tennis." In 2001, he was named the USPTA national Pro of the Year. "Koz" was also named the 1999 USTA Broadcaster of the Year. In 2003, he was one of seven American journalists selected by the USTA to go to Moscow to cover the Federation Cup Final-Four. He is the executive producer and host of "Inside Tennis with the 'Koz,'" which aired for five years on the Tennis Channel as one of the network's "Original Series" and is now airing SNN TV and InsideTennisWiththeKoz.com.

He was the first American broadcaster to interview Maria Sharapova and Andy Roddick and has done anchor and play-by-play for The Sunshine/Connolly Continental Cup, The Owl Foundation (Venus vs. Serena Williams), The Eddie Herr Internationals, USTA Men's and Women's Challengers and The USPTA International Championships.

Kozlowski has interviewed the "Who's Who" in tennis and tennis fans, from Roger Federer to President Bush to Donald Trump.

He is the original coach of former WTA players Carling Bassett (former No. 5 WTA) and Shawn Stafford (former top 50 WTA). He has trained over 135 D-I level college players. He has guided his three children (Davidson, Kimberly and Carolyn Virginia) who have achieved tournament success nationally and internationally at the junior, college and professional level.

World Tennis Magazine recognized him as "A consummate professional with credentials and an ideal temperament" and cited his tennis programs as "one of the finest family tennis programs in any American tennis destination."

JERRY KRAESIG was born in Louisville, KY, and graduated from James Campbell H.S., 1977. He attended Leeward Community College, 1978–1980.

Jerry was a member of the Hawaii Junior Davis Cup Team in 1976–77. He was a player/coach of the Hawaii World Team Tennis Jr. League Runner Up Team. Jerry was a ball-person for the Hawaii Leis World Team Tennis Professional Team. He was Captain of the Leeward Community College Tennis Team and the Hawaii state community college doubles champion.

Jerry was certified by the USPTA in 1980 and began his teaching career at Barbers Point NAS Tennis facility in Hawaii. He was head tennis professional at Navy Submarine Base Pearl Harbor, Hawaii; Wheeler Air Force Base, Hawaii and the tennis director at Makaha Resort. Jerry was assistant pro at the JW Marriott Ihilani Resort and currently the tennis pro at the Ko'Olina Beach and Sports Club.

WHITNEY KRAFT has served as Director of Tennis for the USTA Billie Jean King National Tennis Center in Flushing Meadows, NY and the Director of Player Operations during the US Open since 2007.

Previously, Kraft served as Director of Tennis for the City of Fort Lauderdale Parks and Recreation Department (1997–2007), where he was tournament director for numerous national and world tennis tournaments including the ITF Worlds and National Public Park Tennis Championships. He has served on community boards such as the Broward Tennis Association and the Jimmy Evert Tennis Center Development Fund.

Kraft actively participates in, and promotes, beach tennis, cardio tennis, One-on-One doubles and platform/paddle tennis. He is a 2014 Guinness World Record Holder for conducting the largest simultaneous tennis lesson for 406 students.

A USPTA member since 1983, Kraft credits legendary coaches Jimmy Evert, Dr. Alex Mayer, George Bacso and Bill Murphy as valued mentors in guiding his career path.

After three years at University of Arizona, Whitney graduated from Florida Atlantic University with a B.A. in International Business. He was a 1983 All American and inducted into the inaugural Hall of Fame at F.A.U. for tennis.

JOHN KREIS has taught tennis since he was captain of the State Champion Brophy College Prep tennis team in Phoenix, AZ. He was taught and mentored by legendary pros including Tommy Bartlett, Gunter Polte, Jack Michalko, Ray Young, and Mike DePalmer. He has served as the Director of Tennis at the Norfolk Yacht & Country Club, Norfolk

VA, the Olde Providence Racquet Club, Charlotte, NC, and The Cloister, Retreat Tennis Center, Sea Island, GA. After playing college tennis John put together a distinguished collegiate coaching career at Tennessee (his alma mater), Alabama, and Mississippi State. Coach Kreis has been a finalist for National Coach of the Year honors while producing numerous All-Conference and All-America performers as well as National Doubles Champions and a National Team Championship in the Blue/Gray Team Tournament. He has also traveled as a coach on the ATP Tour, including trips to Wimbledon and the Australian Open. John and his wife Dottie have two daughters, Kirsten and Lindsey, and a granddaughter Adriana.

ALLEN KRISSMAN, USPTA Member since 1976, learned tennis in Los Angeles, CA, at parks and recreation level, age 10. His first organized team play was at Huntington Park High School.

Allen was hired as Head Professional and Manager for the Grand Island Tennis Club and took part in the complete planning/building/marketing process. As Director for State Junior Tennis Tournament, he developed seven state-ranked juniors. He became Head Tennis Professional for Cedar Rapids Racket Club (Iowa), stayed two years and went "international" as Head Professional for Sierra Madre Tennis Club (Monterrey, Mexico), where he coached for two years, and as Tournament Director for the "Pepsi Miestros," National Junior Championships of all Mexico (developed nine nationally ranked juniors), and the Monterrey ATP Professional Tournament.

In 1982 he relocated to Tokyo, Japan and trained Japanese Coaches as Head Trainer/Professional for American Tennis Schools in Japan. He umpired for Suntory Professional Tournament and controlled 12 Tennis Schools throughout all Japan.

In 1984 Allen opened Krissman International Tennis Schools LLC; the No. 1 English Language tennis schools operator in Tokyo for the last 30 years!

Allen is currently running School Locations including Tokyo American Club (TAC), American Embassy, Australian Embassy, American School in Japan (ASIJ) and other International Schools.

Allen has been married 30 years to Keiko, who runs three ballet Schools (Krissman International Dance Schools "KIDS"). During the summer they live in McMinnville, OR.

TOM KRUKIEL, Tennis Pro for the Jimmy Evert Tennis Center in Ft. Lauderdale, FL, since 1998. Previously employed with the Lauderdale Tennis Club for 15 years. He has been a USPTA member since 1996.

Best known for his role as a tournament director, Tom introduced prize money to the NJ State Championships in 1977. Moved to Florida in the '80s and became co-director of the USTA Boys' 14 National Clay Court Championships, which he still runs today. He has been the director of the USTA Men's and Women's National Open Championships since 2005.

Tom was the tournament director of the USPTA International Tennis Championships held at the now Miami Open for seven years. He ran the USPTA National Convention Individual and Team Championships for two years, and has run over 200 state and local tournaments.

An avid player, Tom still enjoys the thrill of hitting the sweet spot.

CHUCK KUHLE, born in Decatur, IL, graduated from MacArthur High School (Decatur, IL) in 1976, graduated from US International University (San Diego, CA) 1980 with a B.A. in Law and Human Behavior.

Chuck was ranked No. 1 Men's Singles three times in the Middle Illinois Tennis Association; played the Swiss Satellite Circuit in 1982 and was a finalist at the 1998 USTA Men's 40 National Singles Hardcourts in Tucson, AZ.

He has been Director of Tennis at the Decatur Athletic Club since 1980, President of the Decatur Community Tennis Foundation since 1993, Professional Tournament Director for the USTA Pro Circuit since 1999, and Director of Tennis at the Decatur Park District since 2007. Chuck has taught numerous nationally ranked juniors and Illinois State High School Champions.

Chuck is a USPTA Master Professional, USPTA Illinois Pro of the Year 2006, Racquet Sports Industry Junior Champion of the Year 2008, USTA/Midwest Cap Leighton Teaching Professional Award Winner 2013 and USPTA Midwest Pro of the Year 2014

Chuck and Terri Kuhle have three children who played college tennis (Patrick, Amy and Tracy).

NIKA KUKHARCHUK, born Feb. 8 1987 in Kaliningrad, Russia, currently teaches at Grand Slam Tennis Club, an Ivan Lendl Tennis Center in Bedford, NY.

She holds a BBA in Managerial Finance, The University of Mississippi, Ole Miss (2007) and MBA, The University of Mississippi, Ole Miss (2008).

Nika had a career-high WTA singles ranking of No. 456 (2013), and was the winner of four $10K ITF events (singles and doubles).

On a full scholarship to The University of Mississippi (Ole Miss) Tennis Team (2004–2008), she captained and played No. 1 singles and doubles her senior year. Nika was ranked 59 in singles and 26 in doubles in ITA collegiate ranking. She ranked No. 3 Nationally in Russia (16 and under). Nika was winner of 2012 USTA National Women's Open Singles Indoor Championship, gold ball. She is three-time winner of the US Open Qualifying Sectional Playoffs (2012, 2013, 2015).

Nika has seven years of full-time teaching/coaching experience and is USPTA/PTR certified (Elite Professional).

She is daughter of Valery and Larisa Kukharchuk (music teachers), sister to Alisa Kukharchuk (geo-physicist).

JACK LACKEY has been a USPTA member since 1980. He played tennis for California State University-Los Angeles. He has played in age group tennis tournaments in northern California.

For 21 years, Jack has organized tennis classes for the cities of Burbank, San Leandro and Concord, CA. He was Director of Tennis and head pro in Discovery Bay for two years. For two years he was Assistant Pro at the Modesto Racquet Club. He coached men's and women's tennis at California State for 10 years and coached high school tennis for 11 years.

Jack is a World War II Veteran, married with three children.

SHAREEN LAI, currently residing in Singapore, has been teaching professionally for 16 years. She previously taught in the U.S. and worked closely with NJTL of Trenton at the inner city schools of Greater Trenton and at

various clubs in the Northeast region.

As a high performance coach, Shareen has trained players to state, sectional, national levels. Her students have earned varsity positions at Boston U., Rutgers U., Syracuse U., Cornell U., Quinnipiac U., Penn State U.

Shareen was a top 5 junior in the Philippines. Originally born in Malaysia, played her junior career in the Philippines, participated in Fed Cup and South-East Asian Games for Malaysia. Played collegiate career at Syracuse University and ranked top 50 in singles. Won multiple USTA National Open category in singles, doubles and mixed.

PHIL LANCASTER, a native Australian, graduated from high school and played junior tennis there before receiving a BA in Sociology and Psychology from David Lipscomb College, where he also played tennis.

Lancaster has served as CEO/President of several oil and gas energy companies, but he has continued to be involved in tennis, holding the title of Master Professional since 1994. His activities within the USPTA include past service as a national board member and as Texas Division president. He was named Professional of the Year in the Texas Division in 1989.

His volunteer work has included service on the board of the Oklahoma City Tennis Centre's 1st Serve Program for underprivileged children. He started Texas Tennis Day, a precursor to Tennis Across America, and founded the Dallas Tennis Association Women's Indoor League.

Lancaster's family includes wife Irene and children Bernard, Peta Maree and Mia. All three children earned four-year tennis scholarships.

PATRICK LASALLE, New England Division Rhode Island Section President, has been a USPTA member and Elite Professional for over 30 years. His focus has been on growing the game of tennis in parks and recreation departments, first in Bedford, NY, and now in Coventry, RI. Working with all ages, Patrick has organized and participated in Tennis Across America Days, most recently at the International Tennis Hall of Fame. He has volunteered at Kid's Day and Military Appreciation Night at the Connecticut Open.

Collaborating with the USTA, Patrick procured grants for youth programs in Coventry and Central Falls, RI. Patrick believes in the professional development of USPTA members and in 2015 organized the first ever Rhode Island Section Clinic. Other USPTA positions he has held include Eastern Division Vice-President and President and Chairman of Developmental Coach and Education Committees.

LISA LEBOLD was a nationally-ranked junior and finished in the round of 16 in the National Clay Courts Girls' 16s. She was taught by her father, Richard Lebold. She was the Western Indoor Champion, Mid-American Junior Champion, Chicago Western Qualifier Champion, A.C. Nielson Junior Champion, US Olympic Trial participant and numerous other championships.

Lisa played Division I at Texas Tech. She was recognized by *Tennis* magazine for playing one of the longest matches, at five hours and 10 minutes. Lisa is known for winning one of the longest points estimated at over an hour.

Lisa has been ranked No. 1 woman in the Western Tennis Association and has numerous US National Public Park Championships. She has taught at a numerous Chicagoland clubs and high schools. She is currently at Beverly Hills Tennis Club and Evergreen Racquet and Fitness. The USPTA and competitive tennis has been beneficial to her teaching.

MICHAEL LEE'S interests are analysis, methodology, theory, new drill creation, systematic and scientific approach in fundamentals, shots, flows, strategies, and game.

JONY LEITENBAUER is the Head Tennis Professional at Windsor in Vero Beach, FL, where he has been employed for over 13 years. He is an integral part of the tennis curriculum, being involved in all aspects of the program including teaching lessons to all age groups and levels, organizing tournaments as well as court maintenance.

Jony is a certified USPTA Elite Professional. He has taught and played competitive tennis in Sweden and Austria and college tennis in the U.S. Language skills include Swedish and German in addition to English.

He has earned a high school degree from his native Sweden and has earned a B.S. degree in accounting as well as an MBA from Northwest Missouri State University. Jony is married to Shannon and they have three children who he enjoys spending time with in his spare time.

CYNTHIA "CINDY" LEPREVOST was Women's Coach at Central Florida Community College (1976–1978), Director of Tennis for Gainesville, FL, (1978–1980), part owner and director for Woodside Racket Club, Gainesville (1980–1983), Director Diplomat Hotel, Hollywood, FL, (1983–1984), Director of Tennis for Sunrise, FL, (1985–1987) and Tennis Director, Lauder-

dale Tennis Club (1999–2004) where she is still a pro and teaching part-time.

Cindy won a Silver Ball in Husband/Wife (1977), won a total of eight Gold Balls in W25 Doubles twice, W30D, W40D, W55D four times on clay, grass and hard courts. In 1998 Cindy was Florida Female Player of the Year and won the Petow Sportsmanship Award. She has captained the Florida Intersectional Team for over 20 years.

Cindy and former husband Dale, have one daughter and two grandchildren.

CHARLES LESSMANN, now living in Germany, was born in Omaha, NE. He graduated from Gustavas Adolfus College in 1998 with a B.A. and from Humbolt State University, Mississippi in 2003.

DOUG LEWIS, USPTA, at age 11 after watching Bjorn Borg play a match on television, began a tennis adventure from which he has yet to return.

Lewis played collegiate tennis at Ferris State University (ranked No. 4 in the nation during his tenure). He is a member of the first graduating class of Professional Tennis Management, at the time the only school in the world offering such a program.

Doug's first tennis job was working at Court One Athletic Club in Michigan. Court One was voted the No. 1 Tennis Club in the U.S. the following year.

Currently he is Director of Tennis at Quogue Field Club in the Hamptons area of New York (since 1994) and Tennis Director at The Healthplex Sports Club in Springfield, PA (since 1996).

Doug has worked with over 50 nationally-ranked juniors, two National Junior Champions, and many college players, including a former Harvard No. 1 and Ivy League player of the year.

He was USPTA Middle States Tennis Professional of the Year in 1999.

JEAN HENRI LHUILLIER, President and CEO of Cebuana Lhuillier, is considered as the patron of Philippine tennis, having supported it for more than two decades.

Lhuillier, who was a varsity player at St. Mary's College, USA during his playing days, has been the team manager of the Philippine Davis Cup Team since 2004 and has been instrumental in the rise of world-ranked doubles player Treat Huey.

Lhuillier is also the team manager of the Philippine Mavericks team in the International Premier Tennis League. As the Chairman of the Board of the Philippines Tennis Association, he has successfully organized international competitions such as ITF Men's Futures and ATP Challenger.

In the grassroots level, Lhuillier has been at the helm of the longest running age-group tennis circuit in the Philippines, spanning 10 years. This development program has produced national champions, most notably 2009 Australian Open Juniors doubles champion Francis Casey Alcantara.

YUHSIN AARON LI played tennis in college and worked as a part-time tennis instructor from 1990–1992. He was a Director of Clark Hatch Fitness Center in 1992–1995 and worked as College Instructor in Taiwan in 2000–2006.

Yushin joined USPTA in 2011 and has been coaching state ranked junior tennis players in Eastern Shores area in Alabama since then.

He works at the US Sports Academy as Doctoral Teaching Assistant and is also responsible for cooperation projects in China.

LEE LIBBY has been in the tennis business for 44 years and the last five years has been Head Pro at Minocqua CC in Minocqua, WI. Before moving to Minocqua CC he was Tennis Director at Camp Menominee for Boys in Eagle River, WI, for 18 years. He has always been active in promoting junior tennis and has worked with the boys' high school program at Lakeland HS in Minocqua.

Lee Libby (right) at Sweet Briar College, VA, with Dennis Van der Meer

Prior to retiring to the Northern Wisconsin area in 2001, Lee was HeadPro/Manager at numerous facilities in Racine, Kenosha, Milwaukee, WI, and Highland Park, IL.

Some of Lee's most satisfying achievements occurred when he took numerous high school teams and individuals from Horlick HS in Racineto to the Wisconsin State Tournament as their head coach. He was named Conference Coach of the Year twice.

Lee received a BA from UW Parkside in Secondary Education/English in 1971. After completing a tour in an Air Force Special Intelligence unit during Vietnam (1966–1970), Lee taught High School English in Racine. During this time he coached tennis and golf and worked as the Head Pro at Meadowbrook CC in the summer.

Lee has always valued his tennis involvement not only professionally, but also recreationally. At the age of 73 he continues to play at every opportunity and at one time was state-ranked in Wisconsin and the Midwest.

BOBBY LIGHT is a USPTA Elite Professional since 1999. He has taught tennis since 1981 in the south, including Kiawah Island and various communities in Atlanta over the last 25 years. He has coached top-ranked juniors to the beginner playing their first league match.

As a player he was fortunate enough to play for his dad at Appalachian State University, and was twice All-Conference, winning two doubles titles in 1979 and 1980. He won the South Carolina State Open Doubles title in 1984 and was ranked No. 1 in Georgia twice in men's 35 doubles.

He continues to teach, play on league teams and promote the game of tennis.

ROBERT GEORGE "BOB" LIGHT was a member of the USPTA in the 1970s. He was head coach in basketball and tennis at Appalachian State. His tennis teams won Southern Conference Championships and was SoCon Coach of the Year in 1978.

Light was inducted into the Appalachian State Hall of Fame in 1991 and HOF at Washington University in St. Louis in 1996.

As a player he won Saint Louis Men's City Championships, a Florida State Open Doubles Title and North Carolina State Championships. He was inducted into the North Carolina Tennis Hall of Fame in 1997.

He co-directed the Mountaineer Open Tennis Tournament in Boone, NC and served as Director of Tennis at Hound Ears Resort for over 30 years.

He served on tennis committees in North Carolina, the Southern Conference and the NCAA. And in 1975 co-produced an instructional video, *Bob Light on Tennis.*

LARRY LINEBERRY is a 40-year member of the USPTA and a Master Professional since 1990.

His tennis career has been primarily focused at a private tennis club in Roanoke, VA, and a semi-private tennis club in Sedona, AZ.

He was Virginia Professional of the Year four times 1981-85, Middle Atlantic Professional of the Year in 1986 and MAPTA president 1986-87. He was the Southwest Professional Tennis Association 2012 Star Award recipient and the Southwest Section (SWS) 2015 Volunteer of the Year both for his work raising funds for junior tennis across northern Arizona.

His students have earned over $500,000 in tennis scholarships since 1980. His tennis activities have earned over $350,000 for various charities since 1979. Larry has been USPTA nationally-ranked in singles and doubles.

He has promoted and directed 22 professional tennis tournaments, mostly USTA Women's Challengers and hundreds of amateur events since 1976.

PAM LIPPY graduated from Beachwood High School, Beachwood, OH, (1980), and Flagler College, St. Augustine, FL, (1985, BA degree).

Amateur highlights include a three-time USTA ADULT National Championship Qualifier 5.0 (1993 and 2009) and 4.5 over 40 (2014), two-time NAIA All American (1984 and 1985); FC HOF INDUCTEE (April 2007), GOLD MEDALIST MACCABIAH Women's Singles and Mixed Doubles (Winner 2009), APTA Platform tennis Region IV President's Cup (2015) and USTA life member.

Pam is a USPTA Elite Professional certified for 20+ years, Director of Tennis at New Albany Links Country Club since 2015, Creator and Director of MIGHTY MITE TENNIS COLUMBUS, OH, JCC preschool program (2000-present), junior high and high school coach for 22 years (Beachwood HS, Columbus School for Girls and Columbus Academy) (1986–2008), and Teaching Pro Olympic Indoor, Columbus and Racquet Club East, Cleveland.

Pam is married to David Lippy. She is the mother of four—Courtney, Carly, Harrison and Adam and grandmother of Marleigh.

LARRY LOEB, originally from Denver, CO, was the top-ranked Intermountain junior. At East High School he was undefeated all three years, and was captain and No. 1 player at the University of Pennsylvania. Larry was the top ranked player in Colorado in men's open and played the ATP circuit – career ranking No. 310. He won two Bronze Medals at the 1977 World Maccabiah Games in Israel, and won the USPTA Men's Open National Championships 1981, 1982, 1983, 1984. He is one of the top senior players in the U.S., ranked No. 1 in the U.S. Men's 40 Singles in 1992; No. 1 in Southern California Men's 60 Singles 2013, 2014. Larry was Director of Tennis at the Denver Tennis Club for 20 years and at Andulka Park Tennis Center, in Riverside, CA, for seven years. He was named USPTA California Divisional "Pro of the Year" in 2010 and "Player of the Year" in 2012.

PEG LONG was born in rural western Pennsylvania and attended a high school that did not have tennis courts. As an undergraduate major in physical education and health at Slippery Rock University, she developed a love of tennis and hasn't stopped learning and teaching others since. She began teaching at Lower Dauphin High School in 1979. During her tenure at LD, she coached the girls and boys tennis team and after retiring from teaching in 2013, she continues to coach both teams.

ANGEL LOPEZ, Director of Tennis/Head Tennis Professional, San Diego Tennis and Racquet Club, graduated from Montgomery High School San Diego, CA (1973), attended University Calif. San Diego (1974), attended San Diego City College (1975,1976 A.A. Degree) and University of Arizona (1977, 1978) - Full Ride Tennis Scholarship.

Angel played with Team WAC Conference Team Champions 1978, Conference Singles Finalist 1977, 1976 Team 2nd Place California Junior College, 1976 Southern Calif Team Champions and 1976 Ojai Tournament JC Doubles Champion. He competed on American Express Western and Eastern Pro Circuit, Southern Pro Circuit, Missouri Valley Circuit, ATP Qualifying.

Angel's professional highlights include: 1992-USPTA Master Professional Certified, 1993–1996 President USPTA San Diego Division, 1994 World Team Tennis Coach of the Year (Newport Beach Dukes), 1995-USPTA National Professional of the Year, 1999 US Olympic Committee/USTA Developmental Coach of the Year (Tennis), 2005 PTR International Professional of the Year, 2006 Member of ITF World Champion USA Fred Perry Cup Team, 2011-San Diego Tennis Hall of Fame and 2012 ITF World Champion 55 Mixed Doubles.

Angel has three daughters—Angelica, Daniela, Alexa.

OMAR S. LÓPEZ, Ph.D., a USPTA Elite Professional since 1981, has taught tennis at facilities in Mallorca, Spain and the U.S. His most notable teaching experiences were with Harry Hopman as a coach training advanced juniors and touring professionals and with Vic Braden as an instructor on weekends at Coto de Caza, CA, teaching students of all ages and levels. Dr. López' career includes working in different sectors as engineer, business consultant, and education policy researcher. He is presently an Associate Professor at Texas State University. Dr. López earned a B.A. from Trinity University, an MBA from the University of California at Irvine and an MSBA in Strategic Planning from the University of Southern California. He received his Ph.D. in strategy and educational policy from the University of Texas at Austin. Dr. López resides in Round Rock, TX, with his wife, Marta and they have two children, Gabriela and Diego.

BOB LOVE, tennis educator, is a Life Member of the USTA and was one of the first 18 USPTA Master Pros. He also served for six years as the chairman of the USPTA Master Pro Screening Committee. He has been a tennis educator for 48 years and is a 43-year member of the USPTA. Bob is a member of the USPTA Midwest Division Hall of Fame and Kentucky Tennis Hall of Fame, plus was the 2007 USPTA Southern Division Pro of the Year. Bob was born and raised in Port Huron, MI. He played varsity tennis at Alma College, Michigan, and then went into the U.S. Air Force and competed in Germany and Arizona. Following a medical discharge he began teaching public parks tennis in 1967. He taught mathematics and tennis and went "full time" in 1972 when named the Director of Tennis at the Toledo Racquet Club. He followed as General Manager of the division-winning Detroit Loves in World Team Tennis in 1974. His Junior Competitive Skills Program grew to over 350 participants before he left to be Director of Tennis at the East Hills Tennis Club, Grand Rapids. After helping develop the Minges Creek Racquet Club, Battle Creek, he went to Chicago and worked for the M. Putterman Company where he eventually became Vice President of Indoor Products marketing. For four summers he directed the tennis program at Camp Greylock, MA. He returned to Michigan to be junior development director of the Lansing Tennis Club, Okemos. He earned a master's degree from Michigan State University in psychology of sport. In 1976, Bob began to be invited to be a clinician and traveled coast to coast plus to Spain (1991) and Egypt (2011 and 2014). Bob has made invited presentations to five USTA national-level workshops, three USPTA World Conferences, nine USPTA divisions, and to high school coaches' workshops in 14 states. He created flow charting for analyzing momentum. He has published instructional articles in *ADDvantage, Scholastic Coach*, and the *Standard*, a publication of the USPTA Southern Division. Bob officiated at the first seven U.S. Opens and was presented the 2013 Kentucky Jr. Team Tennis Coordinator Award. He also taught high school mathematics for 30 years and is a Life Member of the Disabled American Veterans. He lives in Elizabethtown, KY, with his lovely wife, JoAnn.

Bob Love receiving the flag of the Egyptian Tennis Federation from Dr. Khaled Farouk, Technical Director, ETF. The flag was signed to Bob by the ETF Federation Cup team.

BRUCE LUM, USPTA Elite Pro member since 1984 and 31 year USRSA Certified Racquet Stringer member. Tennis instructor for Fairfield, CA, and Vacaville, CA, parks and recreation departments from 1975–1979. Head Tennis Pro from 1984–1986 at Vacaville Racquet Club in Vacaville, CA. Solano County Tennis Association board member in Northern California 1984–1986. USTA Schools clinician from 1984–1989 for Northern California Tennis Association. Head Women's Tennis Coach at NCAA Division II University of Hawaii-Hilo from 1990–1997. Head tennis coach for Hilo Junior Tennis Club from 1990–1998. Hawaii Pacific Tennis Association board member and certified tournament director/referee 1990–1998. Tennis pro and board member for the George McCall Youth Tennis Foundation in Las Vegas, NV from 1999–2007.

DR. JOY MACCI, CEO/Joy of Sport 20 years, USPTA Professional 30 years, PTR Pro/Advisory Staff. Spanning globe "Inner Winner" Success Sports Coach/Strategist/Speaker. She co-owned and directed w/ Rick Macci Int'l Tennis Academy & Superstar Tennis Protégés Serena and Venus Williams, Andy Roddick and Jennifer Capriati. Global Tennis Director w/ Peter Burwash Int'l U.S, Europe and Asia.

Dr. Joy's a headline speaker and on-court presenter at USPTA & PTR Int'l Tennis Symposiums, Global Clinics Austria, Tahiti and Japan, starred "Tele-Tennis" European Tennis TV Series. At 2016 Rio and 2012 London Olympics LWFCI Communications Director "Chaplains 4 World's Olympians" and co-host National Radio Show.

Currently, Joy's main focus is on giving back to the Great Sport of Tennis. She developed age-specialized program to grow and support global Baby Boomer Tennis community, gender-specialized training Women's Winning Bio-Mechanics and is University of Dallas, Adjunct Professor PAADS Leadership Academy training Sports Leaders-WTA, ATP, USTA, NFL, NBL, MLB, LPGA, NRL, NCAA and USOC. Inner Winner "Body/ Mind/Sport." Training to help everyone "WIN" in Tennis and the Game of Life!

RICK MACCI is one of the top coaches in the game today. He has coached five players who have been No. 1 in the world: Venus and Serena Williams, Andy Roddick, Jenni-

fer Capriati and Maria Sharapova. His tennis academy in Boca Raton, FL, has produced more than 134 national titles and has had students win all four major junior grand slam titles. The academy offers cutting-edge 3D analysis of stroke mechanics with an actual MRI of player strokes. He teaches more than 50 hours a week, working with beginner players as young as 4 to touring pros.

Macci is an instructional editor for *Tennis* magazine and has appeared on all major TV networks. He is a featured instructor in the award-winning television show "On Court with USPTA" for the past eight years on the Tennis Channel. He is a USPTA Master Professional and is in the USPTA Florida Division Hall of Fame and the Greenville, OH, Hall of Fame for tennis and basketball. He has been the Florida Division's Coach of the Year six times and was the 2005 USPTA Alex Gordon Professional of the Year.

Macci has been a consultant for Donald Trump Management and serves on the USPTA Player Development Committee. He also works with the USTA Player Development Program.

WILLIAM "BILL" MACOM has spent most of his career coaching college tennis, concluding 2015 with 394 career wins at Florida Tech and Jacksonville University.

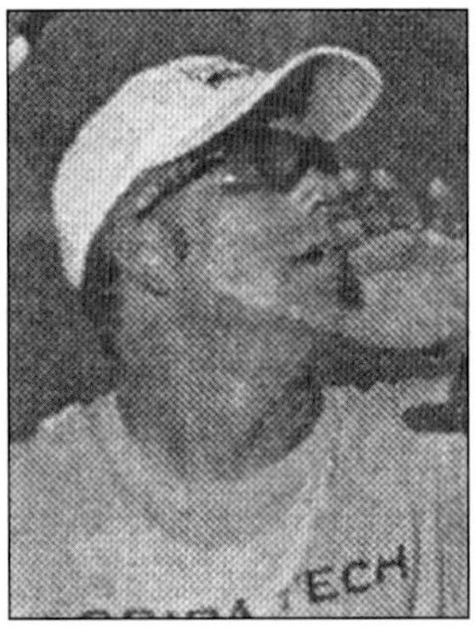

Macom was voted the 2015, 2013 and 2008 USPTA Florida College Coach of Year, the 2011 sectional winner of the USPTA/ITA Campus and Community Outreach Award, the 2009 USPTA/Florida-Melbourne District Tennis Professional of the Year and 2008 USPTA National College Coach of the Year.

He's served on the NCAA D-II Men's Regional Advisory and the ITA South Region Men's and Women's Ranking Committees, the NCAA Coaches Council and as a USTA Coach for Florida's 12 and14 Zonal teams.

He held Florida singles rankings of eighth in 2003 men's 35s, second in 2002 men's 30s, fifth in 2002 USPTA/FL, open and a 1999 USTA 25s national rank of 8. He played collegiately at Jacksonville University and graduated in 1990 with BA degree.

TIM MADDEN is the Director of Junior Tennis at Schwartz Tennis Center–Purdue University. Coach Madden has over 25 years of experience teaching youth and collegiate tennis athletes.

Madden coached the Purdue University men's tennis team from 1994 to 2009. One of the most respected coaches in the Big Ten, Coach Madden helped turn the Boilermaker program into a contender on the conference and national level. Madden was named Big Ten Coach of the Year (Purdue) and MCC Coach of the Year (Northern Illinois) in recognition of his successes.

Madden competed at the University of Wisconsin and became a three-time All-Big Ten player, NCAA Championships performer, and Big Ten Sportsman of the Year in 1987 and 1988. After earning his bachelor's degree in economics from Wisconsin, Madden served as the Assistant Coach at the University of Michigan where he earned a master's degree in kinesiology.

ROBERT "BOB" MADSON, member since 1981-Elite Pro level, left school to pursue tennis tour events and teaching.

Bob Madson's induction into the University of Minnesota Athletic Hall of Fame, 2011

Bob is ranked No. 1 in USTA singles, NWTA division, 30's; Top 10 NWTA Open Singles, Top 5 NWTA Open Doubles, No. 8 in USPTA Doubles and No. 38 in USPTA Singles.

He is a member of USTA Board of Directors, was for Director of Tennis for Golden Valley Country Club and Director of Tennis for Hyatt Hotels, North.

He is founder of High Tech Sports Tennis and Sports Psychology Services.

Bob was Head Coach at Wayzata High School (Minnesota AAA), State Championship Coach, Head Coach at Central Bucks South High School (Pennsylvania)-Conference Champions. He coached two state champs, five Division I players and dozens of D3 players.

Bob Madson after winning the Big Ten championship, 1981

He volunteers for USTA Schools Program, Arthur Ashe Youth Tennis and Education Center and continues to coach and teach.

Bob competes in USTA Father-Son (with Nicholas Madson) as well as USTA 50 and 55 National singles and doubles (with brother Brad).

Influenced very positively by fellow USPTA Pros Jerry Noyce (college coach) and Greg Wicklund (more talented college teammate). Special dedication and appreciation for high school coach, Jim Ryan at Benilde-St. Margaret's, who had a no-cut policy in 9th grade and gave Bob a chance to compete, ultimately helping him improve enough to play at a professional level. Thank you Coaches!

MARC MAJDICK, Tennis Professional, at Oakridge Athletic Club, Simi Valley, CA for 28 years. He also taught tennis at Northridge Park and Northridge Tennis Club. He is now teaching out of his home. Marc owes his success to his parents, who were avid tennis players.

His niece, Noelle Porter, inspired Marc through her junior and college tennis career! His breakthrough in teaching came from ski instructor Bob Smith, in Aspen, CO, who invited him into a ski clinic! Bob's kindness, on and off the hill, inspired Marc to get a degree in Physical Education and a Teaching Credential at California State University, Northridge. His college counselor suggested that Marc combine his "love for tennis" with education. He took her advice! Marc's most satisfying accomplishment was when Oakridge Athletic Club was awarded "Community Organization of the Year" in 2007 by the Countrywide Classic Tennis Championships in Los Angeles.

RAYMOND MAJOR played collegiate tennis at Methodist College from 1988-1989 and

posted the best overall record on the team his freshman year. He graduated from Illinois State University with a BS degree in Mass Communications in 1992.

After graduation he was an assistant pro at The Clubs at River City before becoming Pekin, IL, H.S. head tennis coach in 1994. He has also been Director of Junior Tennis at Knollwood Country Club and Director of Tournament Players at the South Bend Racquet Club.

He became Director of Tennis at Fretz Tennis Center in Dallas, TX, in 2001. He was Dallas Tennis Association Pro Volunteer of the Year in 2004 and was president and a member of the Dallas Tennis Association board from 2009–2013.

Major has been married to wife Theresa since 1998. The couple has a daughter, Lauren, born in 2004.

FARHAN MALIK has been a USPTA Elite Teaching Professional since 2004, competing in USPTA and USTA Men's 35 events, leading to a top 7 USPTA National Singles ranking and a top 10 USTA National Doubles ranking in 2009. He has been teaching at Pine Crest School in Fort Lauderdale since 2008, where, as the Boys' Varsity Coach, he led the team to several District and Regional Championships, winning the State Championship and earning third place at the Deco Turf High School National Championships in 2012. As the assistant coach to the Girls' Varsity Team (which included his daughter, Kaely), he led them to win the State Championship and earn second place at the Deco Turf High School National Championship in 2015. Prior to Pine Crest, Farhan taught at tennis academies, including Harold Solomon, Rick Macci, and Gary Kesl, where he also trained as a junior en route to representing Pakistan at the US Open Junior tournament in 1990. He has worked with many players who have gone on to be successful on the professional tour, both ATP and WTA.

L. PAUL MARCUM has a Bachelor of Science degree in Sports Recreation from Winona State University in Winona, MN, and had four years of training in the Ferris State University Professional Tennis Management (PTM) program in Big Rapids, MI. He has been an Elite Professional at The Sports Club of West Bloomfield in West Bloomfield, MI the last 14 years and also owns and operates Paul Marcum's Tennis Services, LLC during the summer months. Prior to The Sports Club, Paul was the Ferris State University Men's Head Tennis Coach and Head Tennis Professional for four years coaching two NCAA All-Americans.

Paul is the current USPTA Midwest Immediate Past President and has been a USPTA Tester the past eight years (three-time Midwest Tester of the Year). He became a USPTA Master Professional in 2016. As a player he has an extensive tournament background and was an NCAA All-American himself.

Paul is happily married to Lori Marcum Fedoronko, MD- Dermatology and they have two beautiful daughters, Kaitlyn, 12 years and Courtney, 10 years. They reside in Bloomfield Hills, MI.

LAURIE MARTIN is in her 11th year as head coach at Xavier College Preparatory in Phoenix, AZ. During her tenure, she has fought hard to run a No-Cut program for the freshman, JV and varsity teams. Coach Martin has an overall win/loss record of 397-21 with four State Championships and four State Runner-Up titles. As the USPTA representative on Central Arizona USTA, she continues to volunteer her time to help grow tennis in the Phoenix metropolitan area. Currently she is serving on the USTA National high school task force committee to help provide resources to high school coaches and is a member of the AIA tennis advisory committee in Arizona. One of her proudest achievements was getting rules changes passed in high school tennis that helped eliminate stacking of line-ups and locking them entering the state tournament.

She has been recognized for her efforts on and off the court by being named the 2015 *Tennis Industry's Magazine* National High School Coach of the Year, the 2015 National High School Coaches Association National Girls Tennis Coach of the Year and the 2008 USPTA National High School Coach of the Year. Her favorite pastime is spending time with her husband, Stan, who played one year of basketball and three years of football at Harvard, and her four kids, who all were college athletes in their various sports. Daughter Amanda (27) played tennis at Arizona State University and is now one of her assistant coaches, son Tanner (25) was the starting center at Carleton College for four years, daughter Courtney (23) was a softball pitcher at George Washington University and daughter Natalie (23) played tennis for Colorado State Mesa University.

ANGEL MARTINEZ is an Elite Tennis Professional from Arlington, TX. Angel was introduced to the game in high school. He did not play in college, but always was a student of the game. Upon graduation from the University of Texas at Arlington, he began coaching tennis at Cedar Hill High School in Cedar Hill, TX. Angel coached there for 15 years and built one of the most successful grassroots program in the state. After 15 years at Cedar Hill, Angel accepted a position at Grapevine High School. Grapevine High School had a rich tradition of success but had gone through four coaches in six years. Angel helped return the program to its former glory and take it a step further. During 16 years at Grapevine, Angel's team qualified for playoffs 15 consecutive years with his final team capturing the 2014 Texas State Championship. In his high school coaching career, he built a record of 638-105 with 19 District Championships while finishing as the runner-up on nine other occasions, two Area Championships and one State Championship. He has coached 344 All

District selections, 32 Players of the Year and 102 Regional Qualifiers. In 2002-03 Angel was named Wilson/Texas Tennis Coaches Association 5A Coach of the Year and the Fort Worth Star-Telegram Coach of the Year. He was named the USPTA Texas High Coach of the Year in 2005, 2009 and 2013, the 2011 Recipient of Texas Tennis Coaches Association Loretta Hrncir Award for the most dedicated coach in the state and was named USTA Starfish National Coach of the Year in 2009. While at Grapevine, Angel also transformed the facility into one of the top high school facilities in the state. Grapevine now has 12 lighted courts, covered seating viewing areas, locker rooms, concession stand, offices and meeting room, all housed in a building dedicated to the tennis team.

In 2015 Angel retired from high school coaching and accepted the Head Tennis Position at Texas Wesleyan University in Fort Worth, TX. In their first year, his team has a 10-6 record, and is the No. 2 team in the region. Angel's former players have played at Villanova, McMurray, University of Texas at Arlington, College of the Ozarks, Schriener College, Stevens College, St. Mary's University, Southwestern University and the University of Indiana-Indianapolis. Angel has also been a teaching professional at the Arlington Tennis Center in Arlington, TX, for the last 16 years as well. Angel was selected as 2001 Nike Team Texas Coach and a 2015 Zonals 14's Coach.

I, **JULIUS MASHONGANYIKA**, started to play the game of tennis in 1984 at Mufakose Tennis Coaching Agency in Harare, Zimbabwe. I am a Tennis Professional with both the USPTA & the PTR. I achieved 3 Certification in PTR Education Pathways in Adult Development, Junior Development, and Performance in May 2011. Also I am a Professional Tennis Coach with the Tennis Coaches Association of Zimbabwe. I started my tennis coaching career in 1995 at Mufakose Tennis Coaching Agency in Harare, Zimbabwe under the guidance of Mr. Albert Nhamoyebonde who is the Director of Coaching. I attended my High School at Mufakose High 2 School in Harare, Zimbabwe and played high school tennis. I have taught the game of tennis at Worldgate Athletic Club in Herndon, VA, from 2013 to 2015, and was responsible for teaching the 10 and Under Tennis, Club Coaching, Advanced Players, and a volunteer coach in Leesburg, VA.

I am a USTA High Performance Coach at Loudoun County School Tennis Initiative Program in County of Loudoun, VA, which provides non-profit tennis lessons to all beginner, advanced junior players.

I was a Development Coach for Tennis Zimbabwe from 1995 to1997. I was the former Director of Development at White Rhinos Tennis Club in Harare, Zimbabwe from 1998 to 2009.

I am an ITF Play & Stay Specialist and a Professional Coach with the Western Province Tennis Coaches Association in Western Province, Cape Town, South Africa.

Also I was the Secretary General of the Tennis Coaches Association of Zimbabwe from 2003 to 2009. I have attended some ITF & USTA, USPTA, USPTR, ZW & TSA tennis coaching workshops.

I was a Tennis Teaching Professional at Champs Tennis Academy in Cape Town, South Africa from 2009-2010. Also I was the Director of Tennis at Brookwood Camps in Glen Spey, NY, in 2011.

Also I am a holder of some Professional Tennis Management (PTM) Courses with the United States Professional Tennis Association & a USPTA/USPTR Specialist in Competitive Player Development through the United States Tennis Association (USTA) High Performance Coaching Program.

KEN McALLISTER took the USPTA Certification Test in Houston, December 1974 and was accepted in 1975. He attended 22 straight World Conferences plus another 11 since then.

He was elected to the Texas Division Board in 1975, becoming Texas Testing Chairman, a post held through 1990. Ken stayed on as a National Tester through 2008.

In 1976 Ken was selected Texas Pro of the Year and trained as a National Tester. In November 1976, he took the newly developed USPTR certification test and became a Charter member of Professional Tennis Registry (PTR).

In 1980 Ken was selected Texas Division Pro of the Year and in 1981 selected as USPTA National Pro of the Year. In 1981 he became Regional Vice President of Texas for the fourth time. Ken was elected Secretary of the Texas Division, (1985–1990).

He became a USPTA Master Professional in 1987.

In 1991, Ken became Executive Director of what is now USTA Texas, a post held for 24 years and became USTA Liaison for the Texas Division, 1991–2014.

In 2015 Ken received a 40-year USPTA pin and was elected USPTA Vice President (2016–2017).

DANIEL J. "DAN" McCORMICK graduated from Portsmouth Abbey School in 1979 and earned a BA from University of Rhode Island in 1983.

He held a ranking in singles and doubles in Boys 18's in New England. He played four years of college tennis at University of Rhode Island. As team captain, they finished No. 2 in the Atlantic 10 Conference in 1981.

From 1998 to 2009, Dan was Director of Racquet Sports at the Myopia Hunt Club, South Hamilton, MA.

From 2009 to present, he is Director of Racquet Sports at the Eastern Yacht Club.

BRIAN McCOY is tennis director of the Life Time Fitness in Fridley, MN (1988 - present). He manages a teaching staff of 18 tennis professionals. Brian was former general manager minority stockholder of the Arden Hills Club (1979–1988). He has been fortunate to work in just two buildings and one tennis community the past 37 years. Brian is past and current president of the USPTA Northern Division and current USTA Northern board member.

Brian has two sons who are teaching professional, Brody McCoy (Stone Creek Club) from New Orleans, LA, and Wyatt McCoy (Midtown Racquet Club) Chicago, IL, and wife Rene of 35 years who has a great forehand return and his partner for life.

Brian's main teaching focus has been training junior players with highlights that include coaching the 2005 and 2010 National Champions in the 14 and under Advanced Division of USTA Junior Team Tennis.

KENNETH D. McEWAN has an extensive playing, coaching and business background. He was former owner/developer of an indoor/outdoor tennis complex in Vermont. He was developer of an athletic com-

plex at Pico Ski Resort in Vermont.

Kenneth taught and coached in Alexandria, Egypt and Saudi Arabia as well as the USA.

He has been a member of the USPTA for 35 years. He was founder/director of Killington School for Tennis. The program gained worldwide recognition for excellence and voted "Top Ten Tennis Schools" in the Country by *Tennis Magazine*.

He has been a speaker for the Annual Conference of USTA in New York, and speaker at USPTA Conference in Palm Springs.

Kenneth was USPTA Professional of the Year, New England, 1986. He is a member of the International *Who's Who* in Tennis.

Kenneth and Cheryl have been married 46 years and have two daughters and four grandchildren. He is presently Senior Vice President-Wealth Management for UBS Financial Services.

HILARY PAUL McGUIRE, as a Benedictine Brother had three tennis teams: one at St. Gregory's HS and two (men and women) at SGC Shawnee, OK; taught two summers at The Kings Highway Tennis Club, Brooklyn; founded tennis program, Cantwell HS, Montebello, CA; taught tennis at Our Lady of Lourdes JH, LA. At the latter, he diverted Chicano youth from gangs using tennis, "the fun way to learn discipline." Wimbledon's Gussy Moran enlisted pros from the LATC to help. Story is in Hilary's books, "Hopie and the Los Homes Gang: A Gangland Primer" and "Homeboys in College," on Amazon. For his gratis tennis work he is Lifetime Honorary Member of the USPTA. Met Pat and Pam Stewart at San Diego's USPTA. Spent six years researching and writing their story, "Tennis Saves: Stewart Orphans Take World by Racket." Currently teaches gratis lessons through the San Diego Park Department at Challenger Middle School.

TAMARA McINTIRE graduated from Grove City College in 2009 with a BA in Christian Thought and minor in Exercise Science. She lettered four years at Grove City College.

She was Junior and Senior MVP of the PAC Conference and Junior Year Conference Player of the Week.

Tamar was USTA women's 4.5 participant in 2012 and 2013 Nationals. In 2012 she was in USTA 9.5 mixed sectionals.

Tamara is a USPTA teacher part-time and stay-at-home mom of three young children.

JIM McLENNAN was invited to "hit some balls" at Bluewater Bay with a close friend who was their tennis director (and became a Master Professional), Skip Singleton in the fall of 1987. When Jim arrived he realized he had been tricked into a testing session for USPTA membership conducted by Leo Katz. Skip had wanted Jim to join and he had resisted.

Moving to Northern California in 1988, Jim had the opportunity to join the NorCal board of directors.

Through the efforts and support of those board members, including Dave Houston, Bill Rapp and others, Jim was able to join the tennis community, meet so many friends and mentors, and experience the richness of working both sides of the street - meaning as a volunteer and as a tennis pro at a club.

The USPTA has done quite a bit for Jim, and he hopes to slowly repay.

MARK McMAHON is a USPTA Master Professional and has held a variety of professional roles in the tennis and club industry since 1981. He began his service to USPTA as a Florida Division board member in 1985 and served as President from 1988–1990. He served on many national committees and was elected to the USPTA National Board in 1994 and served until 2001. In 2000 Mark was recognized as USPTA Professional of the Year.

A native of Melbourne, Australia, Mark was introduced to tennis at an early age by his father, Des, who would hit with him while the adults enjoyed traditional afternoon tea. Having hit balls against the wall of the local Catholic Church while his parents played on weekend afternoons, Mark followed his two sisters and began weekly group lessons on Saturday mornings at the age of about 7. As a 10-year-old, he met Alistair Strong, the coach at Dendy Park Tennis Club, which consisted of public courts in a Melbourne suburb. In addition to teaching him the basics of the game, (which in later years he wished had not included a continental forehand grip!), Mr. Strong would remain a strong influence in Mark's life and career, particularly in terms of practicing good sportsmanship and the importance of hard work.

Mark played professional tennis from 1978–1980, traveling in Europe, the U.S. and Australia. He began his club career in Florida in 1981 and was hired for his first country club director of tennis position at Boca Lago Country Club in Boca Raton in 1984. After working in the same role at Boca West Country Club from 1991–1994, Mark moved to Atlanta and Dunwoody Country Club in 1995. He left the tennis teaching side of the industry in 2005 when he was hired by the USTA to launch and lead the new Tennis Service Representative Initiative where he managed a team of 90 TSRs deployed across the USTA's 17 sections.

Having previously delivered one-off consulting projects to tennis companies such as Prince while working as a tennis director, McMahon launched McMahon & Associates, a tennis consulting company in 2008. One of his first clients was in fact the USTA for whom he managed the launch of first Youth Tennis Registration Night as a part of Tennis Night in America. McMahon continues to consult for private club clients and is recognized as one private club industry's most accomplished tennis consultants.

Always the entrepreneur, McMahon's club management interests broadened, morphing with his passion for health and fitness in late 2015, when he purchased the rights to develop Koko FitClubs in South Carolina. Koko FitClubs are the world's first Digital Gyms, using patented technology to help people get fit and stay in shape and live a more active life.

HUNTLEY McNAB is the boys' tennis coach for Lutheran South H.S., and the girls' tennis coach for Nerinx Hall H.S. in St. Louis. When Huntley took over the tennis program at

Lutheran South three years ago, the team had a history of consistent losing seasons, pitiful, at best. He turned that program around 180 degrees and has now led them to three consecutive winning seasons.

At Nerinx Hall, Huntley took over the Head Varsity Coach position in 2007, after having spent several years as the assistant coach. He took over a team that, on paper, should have had a .500 season at best, due to losing half of the previous year's team to graduation.

However, Huntley saw things differently. He instilled a "can-do" philosophy in his players, and coached them to new heights, establishing several Nerinx Hall "firsts" along the way. A short list includes:

First place in League.

First Place in Parkway Doubles Tournament.

Qualified for Team Districts, finishing first overall as a team (first time in Nerinx Hall history).

First place in Team Districts Playoffs (first time in Nerinx Hall history).

First place in Team Regionals (first time in Nerinx Hall history).

First place in Team Sectionals (first time in Nerinx Hall history).

Went to State Championships as a team (first time in Nerinx Hall history) and finished in 4th place.

Coached Pam and Leslie Ganer to first place finish in individual districts in doubles in 2007. They finished fifth at state.

Huntley stresses the importance of academic excellence. The entire varsity team at Nerinx Hall made the Honor Roll, another first in the school's history. Most of them are straight A students, and most of them take honors classes.

2007 High School Coach of the Year, Huntley McNab.

JACK MICHALKO is a vice president on the USPTA National Board of Directors and current chairman of the USPTA National Membership Committee.

He was Director of Tennis at the Phoenix Country Club in Phoenix, AZ, for 39 years, retiring in 2009. Jack also served as Executive Director for the USPTA Southwest Division from 1990–2013.

Michalko is a former two-term USPTA Southwest Division President and was Southwest Pro of the Year in 1984 and again in 2004. Jack was inducted into the USTA Central Arizona Hall of Fame in 2010. He has served on the USPTA's National Awards Committee and was chairman of the USPTA National Nominating Committee. Michalko was presented *Tennis Buyer's Guide* "America's Best Retailer" award in 1989.

Jack has lectured at the 1998 and 1999 USPTA World Conferences in La Quinta, CA, and Miami, FL, the USPTA Northwest Division's Convention in Minneapolis, MN, the Intermountain Division's Convention in Vail, CO, New England Division Conference in Norwich, CT, and the Southwest USPTA/USTA Tennis Teacher's Conferences in Tucson and Phoenix, AZ. He and his wife Rita have been married for 46 years and have two grown children.

LYNN MILLER has been a career collegiate tennis coach, starting at Averett College (VA) then at Hofstra University (NY). She made her mark, however, when taking over the women's tennis program in 1980 at Wheaton College (Norton, MA) where she stayed for 35 years until her retirement in 2015. In 1989 Lynn was also named men's tennis coach when Wheaton went co-ed. Both teams have attained ITA East Region Rankings over the years and had individuals and/or teams qualify for NCAAs. Miller's teams have also consistently received ITA academic individual and team awards, plus she was several times named NEWMAC Coach of the Year for both men's and women's tennis. In addition, she has been inducted into the Plymouth State College (NH), the USTA/New England Tennis and Wheaton College (MA) Hall of Fame. Lynn continues to compete in USTA tournaments in her retirement and is the tennis pro at the Lake Sunapee Country Club in New London, NH.

Lynn is USPTA, PTR and USTA High Performance Certified.

Education: Oceanside High School, Oceanside, NY, class of 1970; Plymouth State College (now University), class of 1974 (BS-physical ed. major); Penn State University, Master of Science–1978 (sport psychology).

BRAD MINNS is the USPTA's first deaf tennis pro in its 90 year history. At age 3, Brad lost his hearing to a extreme high fever. His mother introduced him to tennis, hoping it would help him to become more focused. Brad went on the become one of Northwest Ohio's top junior tennis players, achieving No. 3 doubles ranking in the Western Tennis Association with Stan Oley. He placed third in the Ohio State Doubles Championships with partner Charles Ide while at Sylvania Northview High School. After high school Brad earned a tennis scholarship at the University of Toledo, playing line one singles and doubles for three of his four years of eligibility. While in college he won numerous awards, including the John Falvey Scholar Athlete of the Year Award and the Providence Speech and Hearing Centers Athlete Citizen of the Year Award. In 1985 Brad was the No. 1 ranked deaf tennis player in the world when he won his first Gold Medal in Los Angeles at the World Games for the Deaf. He also helped Team USA win its first Dresse Cup in history. As a coach he has worked at some of the top resorts in the world including Sea Pines RC at Hilton Head Island, Isleworth CC in Orlando, as well as some top city parks such as Flamingo Park, Miami and Sanlando, Altamonte Springs. He has served the Orlando area for nearly 30 years as a tennis coach. He is also the Boys and Girls Varsity Head Coach at Masters Academy in Oviedo. In 2013 he wrote his first book, *Never Give Up,* which highlights his career as a tennis pro, bodybuilder and model.

IVAN MOLINA, for 16 years on the Professional tour, reaching a career-high ranking of 22 and winning the 1974 French Open in mixed doubles along with Martina Navratilova. In 1977 he was the runner-up. Colombian Davis Cup Player for 12 years, with wins over USA and Mexico among others. He was 16

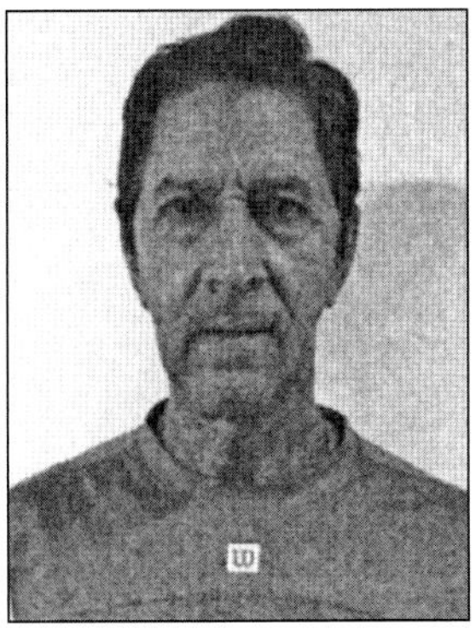

times the Colombian Davis Cup Captain. Since 1987 he has been a Touring Team Coach for the International Tennis Federation (ITF) juniors Internationals Teams, some of which have won, in Juniors, the French Open, the US Open and Wimbledon tournaments. Additionally, he coached the ITF Professional Team for four years and is currently an ITF Worldwide Speaker, tutor for the ITF Level 3 courses and ITF tutor for the Advance Coaches Manual with more than 40 courses. He has published several articles for the ITF coaches review. Certified as USPTA Elite Professional.

DR. BAL MOORE, PhD, is Director of Tennis at Northwoods Tennis Academy in Rhinelander, WI. He has coached Men's Tennis Teams at the University of Kentucky, Western Kentucky University and Jefferson State College for over 30 seasons. In addition, he has coached the USA Men's Wheelchair Tennis Teams to four world championships. For 12 years Moore was coach of the No. 1 wheelchair player in the world, Randy Snow, who was inducted into the International Tennis Hall of Fame in 2012. A Master Professional, the USPTA named him College Coach of the Year in 1992. In the same year he coached the USA Men's Wheelchair Athletes to gold medals in both singles and doubles at the Paralympic Games in Barcelona, Spain. He is a member of the Alabama Tennis Hall of Fame as well as the National Junior College Hall of Fame.

CHUCK MOORE, current USPTA Illinois Vice President, has been a member of USPTA since 1977. He provided tennis instruction on a part-time basis from 1977–2000 at the Evergreen Racquet and Fitness Club in Evergreen Park, IL, and the South Side Racquet Club in Dolton, IL. During his tenure, he provided instruction to over 2,000 club members.

Chuck's achievements in tennis include being voted 1983 Sponsor of the Year by the Midwest USPTA, profiled in *International Who's Who in Tennis*, 1983 and having an instructional article published in *Tennis* magazine, October 1981.

Chuck was employed on a full-time basis in the criminal justice field for over 34 years, retiring in 2010 as the Director of Investigations for the Chicago Public Schools Law Department.

Chuck earned Master's Degrees from Chicago State University and National-Louis University, a bachelor's degree from Iowa Wesleyan University and an Associate's Degree from Chicago City College.

BRIAN MORGAN was born in 1945 in Birmingham, UK. He graduated in 1972 from College of Estate Management in London, UK with a BSC in Real Estate.

Brian is a Teaching Pro at Crystal Lake Racket Club in Crystal Lake, IL. In 2015 he became a USPTA Certified Progressional.

Brian and Catherine have been married 45 years. They have two daughters, Louise and Jenny and four grandchildren.

WARFIELD MORSELL, tennis professional. Over 25 years of competing, teaching, and making contribution to the tennis industry, competed on the professional tennis circuits, trained players who competed and players who are attempting to break into the professional ranks.

He started Warfield T. Morsell International Tennis Incorporated in 1984. As president of Warfield T. Morsell International, with management experience and exceptional people skills, contracted with Guest Services Incorporated under the auspices of the Department of Interior, contracts to operate tennis programs at three locations in Washington DC: The Fitzgerald Tennis Center—24 tennis courts, 10 hard and 15 clay and one stadium; Haines Point Tennis Center—24 tennis courts, 14 hard and nine clay (a tennis bubble was put up for winter play at both facilities); and Rock Creek Park—five clay tennis courts. Keeping together a great staff, the programs ran at the three locations from 1984 to 1994. The client base ranged from congressmen, senators, king and queens from around the world, international dignitaries, movie stars and, most importantly, local juniors. For six months Warfield trained Malcolm Allen, who reached the third round of the Australian Open professional tennis tournament.

Warfield Morsell gets a hug from Billie Jean King

Warfield was the official racquet stringer for the Legg Mason professional tennis tournament for four years, stringing for tennis greats Bjorn Borg, Jimmy Connors, Rodney Harmon, Zina Garrison, Andre Agassi and many, many more of the top players in the world.

He was the official racquet stringer for the USTA Junior Nationals tennis tournament held in Scottsdale, AZ, in 2001.

While Director of Tennis at the Wig Wam Resort, Litchfield, AZ (2001 to 2003), he traveled occasionally to the Beverly Hills Country Club in Beverly Hills, CA, to do drills and exhibitions. From 2004 to 2007 he was a member of the professional teaching staff at the Arrow Head Country Club. There he created ladies tennis teams for women's team tennis team competition. He started and supervised the program to supervise practice and play for juniors preparing for high level competition.

In 2009 (to present), he started Warfield International Tennis Academy, featuring adult and junior training, training women's teams at the Trilogy Ccountry Club for ladies interclub competition and coaching even high school players (they each are playing No. 1 or 2 for their school).

Warfield began playing/teaching professional in December 1963. Before incorporating the Warfield T. Morsell International Tennis, he was one of the teaching professionals at the Arlington Y Tennis and Squash club in Arlington VA; President Bush frequented the club often. The club gave him the flexibility to travel to participate in tournaments. He also taught many Congressmen and Senators in Washington. DC on the fourth floor of the Hart Building.

He attained a high school diploma in Business Administration from Calvert County Senior, Prince Frederick, MD.

Warfield was a letterman all four years of high school in football/basketball/track/gymnastics. His senior year he was All Conference Guard in Basketball. He was in the first round tryouts for the Baltimore Bullets.

Warfield holds U.S. Professional Tennis Association Elite certification, is a member of U.S. Tennis Association and U.S. Racquet Stringers Association. He is a Penn Tennis Ball tester (play test occurred in match play) and Nike equipment tester (shoes).

JIM MORTON is in his 30th year of teaching tennis at the prestigious Ocean Reef Club in Key Largo, FL, the last 22 as their Director of Lawn and Tennis. A USPTA Elite Professional, he is the Florida District 19 President, was a national speaker at the 2013 World Conference on Tennis, achieved a top 10 national ranking in USPTA Men's 45 Doubles and hosted the 2010 Florida Divisional Convention. Originally from Geneva, OH, he has been the Head Tennis Professional at the Milbrook Club and the Belle Haven Club in Greenwich, CT. and was the Director of Tennis at the New Haven Lawn Club in New Haven, CT

JAMES A. "JIM" MOSS joined the USPTA in 1974 after playing varsity tennis at William and Mary and a three-year stint as an officer in the U.S. Army in Germany. He created the pro position at the Heidelberg American Tennis club in 1972 and taught and played around Europe for three years before becoming the men's and women's coach at the College of Santa Fe in New Mexico for 10 years, where he was named SWPTA Coach of the Year in 1984. In 1987, he moved back to Germany where his highlight was winning the All U.S. Armed Forces Tournament in the 40+ senior division three years in a row at the ages of 60-62 after suffering a near-fatal stroke at the age of 59 in 2003. His opponents were 52, 47 and 44! He is now Professor Emeritus at the University of Maryland.

DAN MOSTER began playing competitive tennis in middle school and continued through college. He transferred from Ball State University to Ferris State University and was a member of the first class of Professional Tennis Management students, graduating in 1988. (FSU's first class of PTM graduates.)

Upon graduation he began his teaching career as an assistant pro in northern Indiana. Later he began his team coaching career—high school tennis and volunteer assistant college coach. He started a parks and recreation tennis program and was hired to become the city's director of parks and recreation a year later.

More recently Moster has served as director of tennis for privately owned facilities and seasonal country clubs. In 2006 he started the men and women's tennis programs at Indiana Tech. In 2001 Dan created Geist Tennis Management, which provides a wide range of services to private and corporate facilities, country clubs, HOA's and schools.

Moster has served as President of the Indiana High School Tennis Coaches Association, VP and President of Indiana USPTA and served on USPTA Midwest Board of Directors. He was division president from 2008–2009 and sat on the USPTA Executive Committee from 2006–2009. Dan was elected twice by the USPTA membership to serve on the USPTA National Board of Directors. He served from 2011–2013 and 2013–2015.

RICHARD "LUCKY BANANA" MOUNT has played 27,365 sets since 1962!

Richard was the Head Professional, Quincy Tennis Club for 25 years. He introduced tennis to over 2,000 juniors (ages 5–16) in his summer program. For 19 years he coached Brookline High School Girls Tennis Team, with 282 wins and 72 losses, two state singles champions. Coached Men's 55 (NE) in Nationals. He started Close the Gap program. On the boards of four foundations. They give 20 grants each year to programs in six NE states to promote Jr. tennis. They have raised the money and coached inner-city kids in "Tenacity" for several years.

In 1989 he was given the William Friedman Award, in 2008 the Gardner Ward Chase Award (highest award NE can give), in 2009 the NED Weld Award (first recipient, life time achievement) in 2014 NE Hall of Fame-Newport. He was ranked No. 1 in NE in doubles three times.

PATTY OASTGER MRAZ played intercollegiate tennis and basketball at the College of St. Benedict, where she earned a degree in biology. Throughout more than 35 years as a USPTA member, she has coached high school and college tennis, served as a head tennis professional at resorts and country clubs, developed camps, and directed Parks and Recreation and Community Education programs. In all, more than 13,000 students have been impacted by her service. She volunteered for the USTA Northern Section for over 23 years as a key member of the Junior Tennis Council, a frequent clinician and workshop presenter, a sectional endorser and as one of the first pros in the Northern Section to coach Junior Team Tennis. She directed the first-ever Star of the North Tennis Tournament as part of the Minnesota State Games and served as volunteer director of the US Olympic Festival. Her teams competed in AAU Junior Olympic Team Ten-

nis National Championships six times, claiming silver medals in 1997. She developed novice tournament opportunities, hosted countless Regional Rallies and created a unique method to teach her students about the legacy of Arthur Ashe. Four of her students won the Arthur Ashe Essay Contest and three others were selected to attend NJTL leadership Camps. She has volunteered extensively for those with special needs. She also served as the USTA Player Development Director in her section, and provided Sports Science, local Excellence Training and College Night programs to many others in the section. She coached four national zone teams. Her emphasis on sportsmanship helped three player nominees receive national sportsmanship awards. She has been selected as the recipient of three national and eight sectional awards, including the Eve Kraft Community Service Award, the National Junior Tennis League Program of the Year, the Ward Burton Junior Development Award and USPTA Volunteer of the Year throughout her career. She was also chosen as a member of the All-American Team. She has competed in women's and mixed doubles national championship tournaments. She has earned two master's degrees and teaches middle school science.

BARB MUELLER, lifetime teaching, coaching and world class playing experience. Certified USPTA Elite Pro since 1975 with national singles and doubles titles, 1985–2000, named Midwest Playing Pro 1994, Senior Player of the Year 1990, San Diego Division.

Barb holds 55 USTA National Singles and Doubles Championships, ranked No. 1 ITF World Singles, holds four ITF Doubles Titles 1993-95. Selected member USA's International Cup Teams 1985–2004. USTA Midwest Hall of Famer 2008. Sportswoman of the Year Awards - 2006 Bunny Vostes, Merion Cricket Club, PA; 1989 International Senior Championships in Chile; Colorado YWCA 1984 and 1977. Top-ranked National Junior Player, alternate on National Jr. Wightman Cup Team.

Coached the Ohio State University Women's Tennis Team 1978–1985, Western Intersectional Team and Colorado's Wightman Cup Team in the 1970s.

Served on Wisconsin's Tennis Association Board, Chaired the Multicultural Committee, 2004-09.

First USPTA Pro to introduce tennis to Midwest Native American communities visiting 11 tribes 2001-03. 25th season as Head Pro Wisconsin Wheelchair and Adaptive Tennis Program. Worked with top wheelchair players in Ohio, Arizona, California and Wisconsin.

Former Director of Tennis Oconomowoc Lake Club, WI, 1994–2001, Rancho Mirage, CA and Denver, CO.

She begins 11th season as Head Tennis Instructor of Oconomowoc Park and Recreation Department, teaching tennis children and adults of all ages.

B.A. in Social Work and Theology, Valparaiso U., Indiana; M.A. Sports Science U. of Denver; Ph.D. coursework in Sports Psychology; US International University, San Diego.

ROLLIE MUELLER, a pioneer of tennis in Wisconsin was born in Milwaukee in 1918. Even though Rollie learned the game at a young age at a local park and went on to played on his high school team, Rollie's life was service to the game of tennis. At age 21 he became a tennis professional. In 1945 he bought and managed The Washington Tennis Club where he introduced the game to his two daughters and many others. He organized the County Parks Program, organized the first meeting of Wisconsin teaching pros and served on the USPTA Midwest executive board in the 1950s. He was president of the Wisconsin Tennis Association and was an active member for many years. Rollie was an active USTA umpire for more than 40 years. The Rollie Mueller family was USTA Midwest Family of the Year in 1978. In 1988 he received his 40 year USPTA service award, serving 42 years overall.

Daughter, Barbara Mueller, USPTA tennis professional for 40 years, is teaching at the Moorland Tennis Center and for the Oconomowoc Park and Recreation. Barbara was a highly ranked, international player with over 55 singles and doubles national titles. Barbara is a former coach of the Ohio State Women's tennis team. Barbara was the USPTA Midwest Player of the Year in 1994. She was inducted into the USTA Midwest Hall of Fame in 2008.

Daughter, Jackie Mueller Egelhoff, USPTA tennis professional is the Manager/Head Pro at the River Tennis Club in Milwaukee, WI. Jackie is the Homestead High School boys' and girls' varsity coach since 1980. She is co-director of Advantage Wisconsin Adaptive/Wheelchair tennis programs since 1990. Jackie received the USPTA National High School Coach award in 2011.

Grandson, Brian Egelhoff, USPTA tennis professional is a teaching pro in Mequon, WI. Brian is the co-director of The Advantage Wisconsin Adaptive/Wheelchair tennis programs since 1990. He received the Wisconsin Tennis Association Rollie Mueller Presidents award in 1997, the USPTA Midwest Fay Tooley award and the USPTA National Star award in 2009.

HERB MUNKS started tennis at age 10. Played in the South West African (Namibian) National under 19 singles and doubles finals at age 18. Played on the South African Pro circuit at age 20. Played in the Surbiton (led up to Wimbledon) tournament at age 24. Coached Grand Slam Clinics with Rod Laver at April Sound on Lake Conroe, TX, in 1979, prior to marrying an Australian and serving 11 years as resident pro/club manager (along with wife Eryl), at the Nottingham Forest Club in Houston, TX. Relocated to Australia in 1992 and coached at the Kalamunda and Maida Vale Tennis Clubs in Perth. Currently coaching at St Brigid's College, Lesmurdie in Perth along with 21-year-old son Rhett, which depicts the

Herb and Rhett Munks at the Maida Vale Tennis Club, Perth Australia

highlight of Herb's coaching career along with his association with Rod Laver, the ultimate tennis maestro and gentleman.

AVIS R. MURRAY, USPTA National Professional of the Year, USPTA Master Professional and member of PTR, has been Director of Tennis at Bass Rocks Golf Club since 1971 and in the winters Tennis Professional at Manchester Athletic Club since 1973.

As a member of USPTA she has served on many national committees as well as serving on the New England Board for 18 years and as president for two years, also chaired many committees. The USTA has offered her positions and she has served on the USTA Hall of Fame Committee since 1996, presently is treasurer of the USTA New England Eastern Board.

Avis has had courts named in her honor, both at the Manchester Athletic Club and Bass Rocks Golf Club; has been inducted in the USPTA New England Hall of Fame, Gloucester High School Athletic Hall of Fame and USTA New England Tennis Hall of Fame; received the New England Youth Tennis Foundation Ned Weld Award, USTA Gardner Ward Chase Memorial Award, and the Amvets Sports Award; and Gloucester Fisherman's Athletic Association has named an award in her honor to be given to an individual for extraordinary contributions to Gloucester Athletics.

Before joining USPTA, she served nine years in the Women's Army Corps.

SCOTT NAGLE, the son of Dash Nagle, was born in Hawaii and attained his BA at University of Oregon. He was a college team member at University of Oregon and a non-student member of University of Sydney, Australia.

He is Director of Tennis at Richmond County Country Club. Scott is a USPTA Head Tester, Pacific N.W.

Scott is a member of ITPA, PTR, USTA HP, NSWPTCA-I and II. He is a USTA umpire, member of USTA Schools Program, IC1 and USPTA Certified.

PHILIP "PHIL-NAP" NAPOLITANO is a USPTA Elite Professional. Amateur highlights include: Ranking-Eastern Section, NY 75 Singles No. 10, 65 Doubles No. 8 (2008; Senior Games (70-74), Singles-Gold (70-74), Doubles Silver (2003).

Professional highlights include: LaGuardia Community College-Forest Hills High School; NYC Parks, NJ JTL, USTA Clinician, Queens Hospital sponsor (Happy Hitters), Special Populations. He was mentioned in 1994 *US Open Magazine.*

He has been awarded Hero of the Month—*Queens Courier*, Tennis Coach Award—Young Adult Institute, Certificate of Appreciation—Claire Schulman; Borough President of Queens and NY Special Olympics, Inc. Certificate – Tennis.

DAVE NEUHART has trained beginners to tour players from North/South America, Mexico, Africa/Middle East, Asia/Pacific and Australia and at every instructional/business level for PBI, having received Pro of the Year in 2000. He received 2009 USTA/Georgia Tennis Professional of the Year, USPTA GA Professional of the Year and Georgia Volunteer of the Year in 2013. Dave is an Elite Professional and former tester for the USPTA and Certified Tester/Master Racquet Technician for the USRSA. He is currently PBI NA Eastern Regional Manager and past RM for Asia. He serves as EVP for USTA Georgia, Chairman - Southern Collegiate Committee and also USTA Southern and National Committees, and is listed in international Who's Who in Tennis.

Dave is based at Reynolds Lake Oconee, where awards include No. 1 PBI Facility for 2006, 2009 USTA Facility, 2009 RSI Private Facility of the Year and the Bliss Award for 2016 Best Tennis Community in America.

NICHOLAS NEWCOMB was a two-time state qualifier in high school (Ohio) in singles/doubles. His high school team finished second in Ohio and was three times Conference Champion. Nicholas was President of Wake Forest Club Tennis for two years. He was USTA 4.5 National Team Participant (Midwest) in 2013 with a 3-0 record at Nationals in doubles.

He was Camp Laurel Tennis Staff, Readfield, ME, summer of 2008; Assistant Pro at Swim and Racquet Club (2011–2013) and Elysium Tennis Club, Columbus, OH, (2013–2014). Nicholas was Hillard Bradley High School Assistant Coach, Boys and Girls (2011–2012) and coached girls state champion doubles team. Assistant pro at Park Crossing Tennis Club, Charlotte, NC (2015).

He currently enjoys playing tennis competitively in Southern USTA section while volunteering at youth tournaments and serving on USTA Southern Committees.

Both parents, Dr. Robert and Pamela, played tennis. Pamela was a varsity letter winner at Ohio State University and taught Nicholas tennis at age 3.

ROBIN SMILER NEWMAN, originally from Havertown, PA, holds a BS in Health and Physical Education and MS in Integrative Education. She taught middle school/high school physical education, 1972–2012; is an independent tennis teaching professional since 1985; USPTA Elite/PTR Professional, USTA/Lifetime; USPTA Florida Division Board Vice President 2003–2011. She was the liaison and expert advisor for the Broward County Schools tennis curriculum. During the 1997–1998 school year, she developed a teaching video and manual, "Teach Tennis … Who Me?

Teach Tennis to 40 Students Beginners Through Advanced Players in One Class?," distributed to Broward County schools. Robin has served on numerous committees, been published, contributed to curriculums, presented seminars/spoken at conferences and received numerous honors/awards from both the educational and tennis industry, the most prestigious, the 2006 Florida High School Physical Education Teacher of the Year. Her most memorable tennis event was coaching the 1990 International Special Olympic Tennis Team. "The most rewarding thing about teaching is seeing that ear-to-ear grin, a SMILE on the faces of my students!"

BRYAN NIBERT has been USPTA Midwest Pro of the Year and three-time Ohio Pro of the Year. Awards received as a coach include the Midwest Section Cap Leighton Award and the USPTA National Award for Industry Excellence. He is certified in high performance and sports science with the USTA and in competitive player development with the USPTA.

Bryan's coaching assignments have included head coach of the Columbus competition training center for 20 years, Ohio Valley team cup coach, Midwest zonal coach and Midwest regional camp coach. He has been Easter Bowl comp director for the Midwest, Florida and California.

Nibert has worked as a club pro include director of tennis at Portsmouth Racquet Club, owner/director of Chillicothe Swim and Racquet Club, tennis trainer a New Albany Country Club, owner/co-director of New Albany Tennis Center and head professional at Racquet Club of Columbus.

ENRIQUE "RICK" NINETE, has been teaching tennis for over 40 years, worked as Director of Tennis in California for Martinez, Piedmont and Pleasant Hill districts. He was featured in 1983's International Who's Who in Tennis. Rick returned to his native island of Guam in 1985. In 1986 he started a tennis program for the Department of Parks and Recreation where he continues working. He has worked for the ITF conducting workshops and tennis clinics in Micronesia. In 2004 the main tennis facility in Guam was renamed the Enrique R. "Rick" Ninete Tennis Center. He has received the following awards and recognition: 2011 Lifetime Achievement award from the Governor's Council on Health and Fitness, 2015 ITF award for service to the game, and 2016 service to Catholic schools for coaching and teaching (accredited PE course) tennis for the past 28 years. Rick has been a USPTA teaching professional for 30 years.

TODD NORTON, USPTA Elite tennis professional, has been in the tennis industry for 25 years. During this time he has served his communities well in a variety of roles such as country club tennis director, public tennis center head pro, entrepreneur and former USTA staffer. Before working within the industry for 25 years, he was a competitive tournament player with a career lasting about 14 years. Coach Todd (as his players affectionately refer to him) was born in Corpus Christi, TX, and comes from a tennis family where his father, Roger Norton, introduced tennis to him and his brothers. His two older brothers, Mike and Geoff, are also teaching professional and have been members of the USPTA for more than 60 years combined.

Norton has conducted workshops, clinics, and as of the year 2015, given general tennis lessons to more than 4,350 people and instructed over 40,000 hours on court including many internationally. While in Houston, TX, he was the USTA community development coordinator, a HPTA board member and President, the USPTA regional director, all the while serving as a full-time tennis director for a local country club. Also in Houston he focused his energy conducting USPTA/USTA workshops and trainings. After many years in Houston, Todd moved to the East coast to continue working for the USTA in South Carolina and continue developing his skills as a high performance coach. Shortly after serving in this role, Todd was promoted to be the Tennis Service Representative for the USTA Southern Section. Accredited to his tenure in the USTA are starting up multiple wheelchair tennis programs, USTA junior team tennis, coaching at All-Star camps and speaking at conferences and workshops to name a few.

Chasing his love to be on the court with as many players as possible, Todd moved back home to Texas where he delivers world-class instruction to players in South Texas. He continues to participate and be active at local, state, national and international events.

JOE "THE SHERIFF" NOTH spent four years of high school varsity tennis, played Methodist College men's varsity tennis and won USA SOUTH Conference Tournament. Joe gave instruction at Mercy Health Plex in Fairfield, OH, including teaching clinics of all ages, private/group lessons, racquet stringing/repair, answering telephones/court maintenance. He ran summer clinics at two outdoor country clubs including Weatherington Golf and Country Club.

From 2006–2011 he gave tennis instruction as Head Tennis Pro at Culpeper (VA) Sport and Racquet Club, including starting-developing-designing and teaching clinics for all ages and levels of players such as private lessons, junior and adult clinics, summer and cardio tennis classes. Running and developing adult and junior tournaments, Joe was added to USTA's list of tournament directors, started and maintained a successful pro shop and was head of indoor clay court maintenance. Captain of men's and ladies USTA teams, racquet stringing and repair, he ran clinics with Dr. Louie Cap. Joe received USPTR Professional certification from Dr. Cap in 2007, upgraded to USPTA Elite Professional and became USNTA and USATT certified.

In 2011 Joe was hired by Lifetime Tennis/Lifetime Activities as Tennis Director at Walnut Creek (CA) Tennis Center, home to the second largest public racquet club in California. WCTC membership/student participation increased, USTA teams rose and WCTC stands at nearly 1100 members. WCTC has sent multiple teams to USTA Nationals every year, with second place finishes by 2011–13.

MELVINA NOZICK has been in the tennis industry 50+ years. She has been an accredited tennis pro with USPTA since 1970.

From 1965–1976, in Massachusetts, she started a tennis program in Adult Education, was responsible for tennis in school-Physical Education curriculum and taught wives of faculty at Harvard University. She was Director of Racquet Club (all racquet sports – squash, racquetball and tennis) and Tennis Teaching Professional at Watergate Racquet Club, Alexandria, VA.

At North Virginia Community College (1990–1996), taught tennis as part of Adult Education and gave private lessons.

She was the Teaching Pro at Sun City H.H. (1998–2000) and gave private lessons from 2000–2008.

Melvina has played and captained tennis teams that have won at the local, state and sectional levels – Amateur level.

CRAIG NUNEZ grew up in Sulphur, LA, and competed in state, sectional and national tennis tournaments in the 1970s and 1980s.

He began teaching tennis in 1979 and served as a pro or visiting professional at various clubs and resorts over the next eight years, including Wild Dunes Resort, Isle of Palms, SC; Wimbledon U.S.A. Racquet Club, Palos Heights, IL; Bocage Racquet Club, Baton Rouge, LA; and Sherwood Forest Country Club, Baton Rouge, LA.

Craig transitioned from the tennis court to Wall Street in 1987 and later moved to the oil patch. He now enjoys playing tennis with his wife and two sons.

Craig holds a MBA (honors) from Duke University, JD from Louisiana State University Law School and BA, Louisiana State University.

BOOTS O'BRIEN, a member of USPTA since Jan. 1, 1971 has 45 years of service. Her tennis career started in Kansas City. She was voted Intermountain Pro of the Year numerous times. Boots was an editor on the Intermountain newsletter for 13 years and has published numerous tennis articles. She opened five tennis shops in Kansas City and was the official stringer for the Pro Tour. She was the tournament director for the Virginia Slims tournament. She produced a TV series, "Get a Kick Out of Tennis with Boots."

Boots O'Brien (second from right) with granddaughter Lillie Mehan (far left), daughter Bonnie O'Brien and daughter Bobbie O'Brien Mehan (far right)

Boots and Robert O'Brien (deceased) were married 50 years. They have four daughters: Bea Coleton, Barbi Dickison, Bonnie O'Brien and Bobbie O'Brien Mehan. Their granddaughters are Crissa Keen, Taylor Keen, Holly Keen and Lillie Mehan, who is playing college tennis at Belmont Abbey College.

STEVE O'CONNELL has been active in the tennis industry for over 40 years. Starting out as an assistant instructor for the fledgling Arthur Ashe National Junior Tennis League in Stamford, CT, (1976-78), Steve spent the next 35 years playing competitively, while coaching players and managing tennis programs across the country. Steve has served as USPTA/NE President and as a member of the USPTA National Executive Committee (2004-07). He is a certified USPTA Wheelchair Tennis Instructor, TIA Cardio Tennis Clinician, and a USPTA Tennis for the Health of it Ambassador. Steve has successfully coached regional and state championship high school teams for over a decade, sending many scholar-athletes to top athletic and academic universities. He is a former Director for the Connecticut Special Olympics Tennis venue (1993-98). Two proud achievements with the USPTA are helping develop a USPTA promotional broadcast commercial in cooperation with the USPTA national staff, the Boston Lobsters World Team Tennis franchise, and Comcast cable service that reached upwards of 3 million-plus viewers spreading a positive message of professionalism and high standards of the USPTA and directing a milestone 25th Anniversary USPTA Tennis Across America FREE Lesson for the general public at the tennis center at YALE University in August 2015. Steve has authored many articles and promotions for local newspapers and divisional newsletters as well as implementing and presenting at many seminars and meetings for the USPTA, APTA, and the Connecticut Interscholastic Athletic Association. He is a former USTA Schools Clinician. In addition to his tennis accomplishments, Steve has a degree in Marketing and a master's degree in Education. He is currently a Racquets Professional at The Patterson Club in Fairfield, CT, and coaches at other racquets facilities throughout Fairfield County, CT. Steve has raised four enthusiastic tennis-playing children and lives with his wife in Fairfield, CT.

DR. DESMOND OON, PH.D., is a longstanding member of the USPTA. He was accorded Master Professional title in the 1980s. Since 1983 he has been the de facto president of the SE Asia Div. of the USPTA and tester. He initiated USPTA certification in Singapore, Malaysia and S. Korea and maintains close liaison with countries in that division.

He is a former Davis Cup coach for Singapore who played on the international circuit in the 1960s. He has been involved in tennis at all levels for more than 60 years, coaching in 10 countries, speaking at conferences worldwide, and consulting with pro/amateur players, coaches, trainers and managers.

Dr. Oon specializes in the area of human potential and peak performance and has successfully blended Zen and The Tao with modern sport psychology and hypnotherapy, in his practice. Former USPTA president Ron Woods has called him "one of the foremost tennis teachers in the world in this area."

Today he is recognized by his peers and national tennis associations as the pioneer of Coach Education in Asia. Since 1965 he has personally trained, mentored and certified hundreds of coaches in his long career.

DR. HUGH R. PAGE, JR. has been a part of the tennis teaching community for more than four decades. An Episcopal priest and academic Ph.D., Harvard University–1990), he joined

the USPTA in 1989. His first instructional position was with All American Sports (AAS) at its Deerfield Academy junior camp in 1975. At various points throughout the 1980s and early 1990s, he directed junior camps at Amherst College (initially for AAS and later for the college itself) and Connecticut College (for AAS) and worked for a time as one of the assistant directors for the AAS adult camp at Amherst College. He was for many years—between 1993 and 2013—the volunteer assistant coach for the Men's Varsity Tennis Team at the University of Notre Dame, where he is currently a faculty member and administrator. He is also a certified member of the U.S. Professional Tennis Registry (USPTR).

CHARLIE PAINTER'S love affair with the sport of tennis was spurred by just that — a love affair. In hopes of improving the relationship with his wife-to-be, who just happened to be a local tennis pro, he became her eager pupil. Painter became a USPTA member in September, 1990 and currently holds the rank of Elite Professional. Now Painter is enjoying his 30th year of coaching tennis. This is Coach Painter's third year at Alter. He has been the Head Tennis Coach at Carroll High School, Franklin High School (one year), Wright State University (10 years), Oakwood High School (four years), and Beavercreek High School (10 years). He is currently the winningest tennis coach at Carroll High School (137), Wright State University (150 wins) and Beavercreek High School (235).

Painter received the OHSAA Sportsmanship, Ethics and Integrity Award in 2014. Painter was selected as Boys GWOC Coach of the Year in 2006 and 2011 and Girls GWOC Coach of the Year in 2009. He was GCCL Coach of the Year in 2004. He was selected as Midwest USPTA High School of the Year in 2012. He is founder of Miami Valley Coaches Association. Coach Painter has been inducted into Dayton Amateur Tennis Hall of Fame, MVTCA Hall of Fame, Dublin Coffman Athletic Hall of Fame and Dublin City Schools Hall of Fame. He is currently member of Ohio Tennis Coaches Association Executive Board and is tournament director of the OTCA Southwest District Team Tournament. In addition to his coaching chores, Painter is Endorser/ Director OVTA Girls 18 District Tennis Tournament and an OHSAA State Tournament Referee. He graduated B.S. degree in Physics and Mathematics from Wittenberg University and has a M.S. degree in guidance and counseling from Wright State University. Painter is currently teaching in the Mathematics Department at Sinclair Community College. He currently resides in Centerville with his wife, Karen, and has two children, Cristian and Tory (USPTA) who currently are pursuing careers of their own.

RANDY PAISLEY graduated from Dixon High School Dixon, IL; graduated from Sauk Valley College in 1976, Northern Illinois University with B.S. in Ed, 1979, and Middle Tennessee State University with M.S. in Ed, 1991.

Randy's amateur highlights include Illinois Junior College State Doubles Champion and MVP tennis team NIU Senior Year.

Currently he is Tennis Director of Midtown Athletic Club, Willowbrook, IL. He has spent 28 years teaching public school in Illinois and Tennessee and 18 years as head tennis professional in Brentwood, TN.

Randy has coached Brentwood High girls' tennis team to three state titles, Brentwood High boys' tennis team to one state title.

He has taught tennis professionally for 40 years and been a USPTA member for 20 years.

Randy feels very blessed to have been raised with three brothers in a loving household that promoted involvement in athletics and to set high standards in everything they did. He has been happily married to Katherine for 36 years, and they have three children (Meg, Carol, and Donny) whom they are very proud of and five grandchildren.

SAM THOMAS PARFITT is from Norfolk, England. He moved to the U.S. in 2009 to play Division I college tennis at the University of Tennessee at Chattanooga.

While at UTC he defeated several ITA-ranked opponents and won numerous awards, including the City of Chattanooga public service award. He was twice an All-American Scholar Athlete.

He is a USPTA professional and LTA tennis coach, and the director of athletics at St. Peter's School. He also assists the UTC women's tennis program.

In 2015 he founded The True Athlete Project, a non-profit organization that promotes the holistic development of young athletes. He has had the great fortune of presenting the project at the Muhammad Ali Center.

Sam loves coaching and is thrilled to be a part of the USPTA. He is inspired every day by his family! His favorite on-court moments were being coached by his father, Murray Parfitt, being cheered on by his mother, Imogen Parfitt and winning mixed doubles matches with his twin sister, Georgina Parfitt. He thanks 'Grangran' for her amazing support.

LINDA PARK, a native of San Marino, CA, was a top-flight competitor in USTA Juniors and was ranked 10th sectionally and 40th nationally. She and her partner were the top ranked doubles team in Southern California and 4th in the nation. Linda played her collegiate tennis at UC Berkeley and was the head women's tennis coach at Occidental College from 2006–2011. She was also the Tennis Director from 2009–2011, overseeing both the men's and women's programs. Currently, Linda works with junior players at Arroyo Seco Racquet Club in South Pasadena, CA.

Linda has a master's degree in Human Development and plans to teach in elementary school again in the fall of 2016. She taught in public school for four years in the '90s and will return now that her children are older. Linda currently resides in South Pasadena, CA, with her husband, three children and the family dog.

JIMMY PARKER, a member of the USPTA since 1972, has had a long and fulfilling career in tennis. He is a USPTA Master Pro, retired from the Houston Racquet Club after a 30-year stint as Director of Tennis and is currently the Pro Emeritus there and at the Santa Fe Tennis & Swim.

Early on, he was selected to the US Junior Davis Cup Team, was an All-American at Rice

University, and later its coach. He played the tour, and in fact played the opening match on Center Court of the first US Open in 1968, losing to Ken Rosewall. Other endeavors include a master's in Education, US Air Force jet pilot, U.S. State Department Emissary, newspaper columnist, television commentator, USPTA/Texas President, USTA/Texas Executive Committee, Tennis Channel instructor, USTA Junior Development Coach, and coach of hundreds of ranked players.

In the process, he accumulated numerous awards and records. He was named Coach of the Year, a 17-time Player of the Year, and has been ranked No. 1 in the U.S. in every USTA age category from the 35's to the 70's. Jimmy holds the American record for most ITF World Championship titles, most US World Cup Teams, and he currently is one away from holding the men's record for the most gold balls (USTA Nationals).

An inductee of four Halls of Fame, Jimmy is married to Ellen Hight Parker and has two sons, Chris and Ash, all tennis players.

GUY W. PARKS II is a USPTA Master Professional and has been the Director of Tennis at the Racquet Club of Columbus, Ohio, since 1998. In 2004 Guy was selected to the five-state USPTA Midwest Division Hall of Fame plus, in 2008, was named Pro of the Year. Guy was both the president of the Ohio Valley TA and the USPTA Midwest Division. He also was three-time Midwest Tester of the Year and the USPTA Midwest Faye Tooley Award winner.

Following service in Vietnam, Parks earned his bachelor's and master's degrees in Education (motor learning) at Ohio University. Guy is certified as a USTA high performance coach and has a specialist degree from the USPTA in competitive player development. He was the first Master Professional to earn certification by completing the USTA sport sciences program.

Guy start teaching at Lancaster (Ohio) Indoor and then directed programs in St. Joseph and Okemos, MI, plus was Owner/Director of Chillicothe Swim and Racquet Club. Guy has spoken numerous times at state, sectional, and international tennis seminars including the 2004 and 2009 USPTA World Conferences.

Guy, from Portsmouth, OH, was married to Jane, who passed away from pancreatic cancer in 2014. Their son Michael (Lt. Col. USAF) is a Squadron Commander in Third Air Force, 100th Air Refueling Wing, in England. Lt. Col Parks was awarded the "Bronze Star" medal for meritorious service in a combat zone, and served as an Instructor Pilot for C5 Galaxy, G37 and KC135. He lives in England with his wife, Allison and Guy's two grandchildren, Collin and Charlotte.

ENRIC PASCULADO, founder of CPRG Tennis based in Houston, TX, has been teaching tennis since 1995. A semi-retired Mining Engineer and Geologist, he has been promoting Quick Start Tennis since the program's introduction by USTA some years back and has been helping children develop to become competitive players, some of which are currently in the champs and super champs level. He has coached local private schools in Houston and Sugar Land. His teaching methodology has attracted young players as well as adults.

Enric is a certified ICI Assistant Coach and has successfully participated in the ICI Professional Coaching Course – Level 2 (Academia Sanchez-Casal and International Coaches Institute).

A USPTA Professional certified since 2006, Enric is also founder of College Planning & Research Group, a consulting entity helping families by tackling the high cost of college education since 1990. His service and expertise include helping competitive student-athletes get recruited to play collegiate level sports.

JOSE PASTRELLO is the tennis director at Collier's Reserve Country Club in Naples, FL. He was born and raised in Brazil and moved to the USA in 2001 to attend college. With knowledge in data analysis and business, he has been an active figure in the tennis industry in many levels. He was named USPTA Professional of the Year in 2015 for Naples, FL. Under his leadership, his district received the USPTA Florida District of the Year in 2015. He is currently the USPTA District President for Naples, FL.

Jose is also very involved with the community as he hosts fundraisers throughout tennis. Since 2012 he has been the tournament director of the Tom Manring Foundation Tennis Calcutta, which donates a scholarship to Florida Gulf Coast University, which he attended.

CHUCK PATE was born July 10, 1946 in Glendale, CA. He graduated from Santa Fe High School in 1964. Chuck attended Pepperdine (1964–1966), then transferred to Brigham Young University (1966–1969) attaining a Bachelor of Science Degree. He attained a master's degree from Chapman College in 1972.

Church was the USPTA California Singles Champion in 1972 and USPTA California Singles Champion in 1973.

Chuck is owner of Tustin Hills Racquet Club since 1976. He is the father of five children and grandfather of 10.

R.K. PATTON began a second career as a USPTA Pro (Elite), as Tennis Director for the Texins Association, a recreational facility for Texas Instruments in Dallas, after retiring from the corporate world in 1998. He assisted the junior program at Canyon Creek CC in Richardson, TX, and directed tennis at Spring Creek Swim and Tennis Club in Dallas. He spent a year in San Jose, CA, as head varsity tennis coach for Valley Christian High School. Returning to Texas in 2003, R.K. is currently a teaching pro at Oak Creek Tennis Center in Carrollton (since 2004). He directed a tennis program for the Spring Creek Tennis and Swim Club and assisted the junior tennis program at Twin Creeks Tennis Club in Allen. He worked with the Dallas Tennis Association, coordinating after school educational programs and tennis programs in 2004. His collection of early racquets and tennis memorabilia earned a nomination to represent the Texas Section USPTA in a National Competition for "Tennis Nut of the Year." R.K. no longer refers to his work as a "job," rather a labor of love.

VICKI ENGLAND PATTON took her USPTA test from Sheldon "Shelly" Caldwell at Cleveland Racquet Club in 1976. She played tennis with Panco Segura at the USPTA National Convention at Saddlebrook Resort in Tampa, FL, and played an exhibition match with Vic Braden in Akron, OH.

Vicki is Certified Elite Professional, Certified Tester for USPTA, and was Northern Ohio USPTA President for four years. She is a Midwest Division Board Member and Women's Liaison for the Midwest Division.

She has attended USPTA National Conventions and led meetings for Midwest Division.

Vicki has been a participant in USPTA National tournaments in women's singles and mixed doubles. She is an official stringer and practice partner for Virginia Slims Women's Professional Tournament. Vicki has coached and taught tennis for 39 years in the Akron/Cleveland area, with many students advancing to collegiate and national tournament levels.

Vicki is single, the mother of three highly successful children. Currently she is active in APA pool tournaments and has played in Las Vegas, has won multiple Top Gun awards in her category and plays on a league with her youngest son, who got her interested in the sport. Coaching and competition runs in the family!

MAX PAVON is a USPTA Certified Elite Professional Tennis Instructor with over 45 years of tennis teaching experience. Originally from Spain, Max was the Varsity Tennis Coach for six seasons at Harvard School in California. He taught all ages and abilities at Marina City Club for eight years and captained a 5.0 USTA League team there. Max has been a tennis professional and academy teacher at Punahou School since 1988. He is an active local, national and international player that has held No. 1 rankings in different age divisions for the last 20 years. He holds nine USPTA

Max Pavon, also known in Honolulu as "Rafael Nadal's grandpa"

Senior World Championship titles in both singles and doubles. Max has a Ph.D. in Spanish, speaks four languages and has taught Spanish language and literature at the University of Hawaii, Kapiolani Community College and Honolulu Community College for 10 years.

Max was the 2015 National Senior Olympics Gold Medal Winter, M70-74s in Minneapolis, MN.

ELLIE PEDEN, 40 years as member of USPTA, was born in Chicago, IL. She now lives in Forest Lake, MN. Ellie taught 35 years at Lilydale racquet club in Mendota Heights, MN. She was University of Minnesota Women's Tennis Coach, 1975–1983. Ellie was elected to Northern section Tennis Hall of Fame, 2001. She is married with four children and nine grandchildren. Ellie is now retired.

OLIVIA PEDRO has extensive playing and coaching experience. She was a finalist in the Pearson Ford Open, giving her a wild card into the Cincinnati ATP tournament. She played No. 1 singles and doubles for Butler University Division I tennis. As a junior player, she was highly ranked and received the CITA sportsmanship award. She continues to emphasize sportsmanship on and off the court.

Olivia has been a USPTA certified coach since 2006. She has coached all levels including elite juniors, USTA nationals players and Division I college tennis. Olivia was assistant coach for the Butler University Women's team for seven years and was league coordinator and director for an adult program in Indianapolis, IN. Olivia loves the game and continues to coach and support the growth of tennis in Northern Virginia. Olivia is thankful for her previous coaching and training experiences with Steve Contardi, Nick Bollettieri and Jason Suscha.

ANN (YOUNG) PELLOW was Intermountain section 12 and under champion, as well as Colorado High School State Champion in 1976 and 1977. She received Phyliss Lockwood Sportsmanship Award in 1976 and was a member of the 18 and under Whiteman Cup Team for Intermountain section.

She was a Pepperdine University Varsity Player (1978–1981) and held the No. 1 record for most career wins (82 career wins) at Pepperdine for 17 years.

Ann has competed in Team USA Player Maureen Connelly Cup Team 2015, USTA Northern California Intersectional Team Member 2015, Avery Cup Team (2015), German Club Tennis Blau-weiss Rostock (2003–2005), USTA National Senior Tournaments 30, 35, 40, 50, 55, Hawaii Grand Prix Circuit, Belgian Ladies Circuit (1982), Avon Futures Circuit (1982), and USTA National 21 and under circuit.

Ann was a tennis professional at John Newcombe's Tennis Ranch, New Braunfels, TX; Gates Tennis Center Denver, CO; Head Tennis Professional, Pearl Harbor Racquet Club. Honolulu, HI; and USTA Northern California National Girls 14 and 16 coach, Woodland High School Girls Tennis Coach.

EILEEN PERO'S journey to the USPTA will undoubtedly differ from most. Every year, she challenges herself to do something outside her comfort zone. Having played tennis for over 50 years, it seemed that passing the USPTA test was a good challenge. With encouragement from Steve Graves, Art/Laura Thomson, Joe Thompson, and Diane Selke, Eileen enrolled in the program, and ultimately, passed the test.

But what now? She taught a lesson to some friends, but knew that teaching wasn't going to be her fulltime job. Instead, she decided to contribute to the tennis world in different ways: as President of the Colorado Youth Tennis Foundation, Volunteer of the Year for Colorado and Intermountain, CTUA referee; Tournament Director–Denver City Open/Colorado State Open, host of the Annual CYTF Pro Am, creator of tennis yard art and promoter of tennis, 24/7.

Examples of Eileen Pero's tennis yard art

Ann says, "I am a tennis professional. I just don't teach."

FEMI "FEMMY" PERRY originally hails from Nigeria, West-Africa. She graduated from Shaw University with a B.A in Mass Communication in 2008. General Manager of TAG Consult Inc., a Business and Management Consulting Company in North Carolina.

She's won several state and national junior and adult championships, as well as toured in several junior ITF sanctioned tournaments and events while representing Nigeria.

"Femmy" toured Africa, Asia and Europe in the Women's Circuit (2000–2003), with a career high of 900s and 800s in the WTA Singles and Doubles ranking.

She was awarded 2013 USPTA North Carolina Public Facility Pro of the Year.

Femi has trained and developed junior players who have competed at the USTA state and national levels, some of which have acquired state and national ranking in the Southern North Carolina Section.

She is married with two wonderful children, who have developed an early interest in tennis.

DAN PETERSEN began playing tennis about 1969 in New Carrollton, MD. Wood racquets, white balls in metal cans. Tennis shorts, that earned their name. Every one sliced their backhands and came to the net. The first two handed backhands were scoffed at and considered weird. Then came metal, aluminum, fiberglass graphite and hybrid frames, which brought the first oversized racquets, a 95 square inch by Prince and Head. This caused an outrage with traditional tennis players. He remembers people refusing to play with people who used them. Let alone the first daring solos to use one and have a two-handed backhand. He's seen a lot of changes in the game along the way.

Dan played open level in the Mid-Atlantic Tennis Association tournaments through Maryland, Virginia, Delaware and Pennsylvania. He won the Regional Avis Challenge Series in Maryland.

He moved to West Palm Beach, FL, in 1985. In 2006 Dan wanted to share what he had gotten from the game that changed his life, and help others know the unbelievable joy from hitting a ball perfectly, nothing like it. He applied for membership in the USPTA. Took the test in 2008 and made a dream come true. After working at various clubs and academies, he works privately with aspiring juniors. The satisfaction he gets from their improvement is as rewarding as what he got from his own game. Dan loves to see his influence in their mechanics, and knowing this game will be a part of their life forever.

JAMIE PETERSON started his tennis teaching career while playing Division I for Towson State University. He got his start with the Steve Krulevitz Tennis Program and then as Assistant Pro at Eagles Nest Country Club. After graduating from TSU with the fourth highest winning percentage in the program's history, he worked as the Head Assistant Professional at L'Hirondelle Club. In 1997 Jamie moved on to be the head professional at the Homeland Racquet Club in Baltimore. He then became the Director of Tennis at Chartwell Golf & Country Club and served on the local USTA and USPTA boards. Some highlights of his 13-year stint were helping to double tennis memberships and helped introduce a new full service tennis pro shop in 2004. He also ran the highly competitive Chartwell Classic prize money tournament. In his time at Chartwell, his playing career highlights included nine Maryland State Doubles titles, a No. 1 ranking in the section for 35's and 40's. He is currently assistant women's tennis coach at Towson University, a teaching professional at Orchard Tennis Club and the President of Mid-Atlantic USPTA.

HANK PFISTER was born in Bakersfield, CA, where he and wife Kim live and have three daughters and seven grandchildren. He's a USPTA Elite Pro and has presented at USPTA regional, national and world conferences. He's the Director of Tennis & Fitness at Stockdale Country Club in Bakersfield since 1992. He's a past ATP TOUR player from 1976 to 1988, where he reached 19 in singles and nine in doubles with 10 singles finals (two wins) and 20 doubles finals (10 wins). He is a two-time French doubles champion and finalist at the US and Australian Opens. He's twice been the USPTA California Divisional and twice the District Pro of the Year.

He is a member of the Bob Alias, San Jose State and Bakersfield City Schools District Halls of Fame and the Ojai Libby Park Wall of Fame. He's a 20+ years SCTA Board Member.

FRED PFUHL graduated from Millbrook High School (Raleigh, NC) in 1978. He graduated from Appalachian State University in 1984 with a degree in Management.

Fred played varsity tennis at Appalachian State University. He has been ranked No. 1 or No. 2 in every adult age division (singles and doubles) 30 – 50 years.

Fred is presently Director of Tennis at Duck Woods Country Club (the premiere club of the Outer Banks). Formerly he was the head pro at high Point CC, Director at Goldsboro CC and the owner/director of the Westside Tennis Club for eight years. Previously he held the position of president for the USPTA's Central Penn division. Also a former head coach for USTA Area training centers. He has organized and presented at various conventions (regional/national). Fred has been a USPTA member since 1989.

Fred has been married since 1989 to wife Lisa and they have two children, Christian (24) and Jacklyn (20).

JOAO "JAY" PINHO is a former NCAA Division I player who is currently a Manager of Tennis Operations and High Performance Coach at Nassau Tennis Club, NJ. He was previously employed at the Intercollegiate Tennis Association and served as an Assistant Coach at Utah State University, The University of Toledo and Princeton University. Pinho has been recognized as one of the most complete professionals in the region and his background includes: USPTA Elite Professional, USTA High Performance Certified, PTR Master of Tennis: Performance, PTR Professional in 10U, 11–17 and Adult Development, GPTCA Level C Certified by the ATP Tour, Academia Sanchez-Casal Level 2 Professional, HPI Certified Specialist in Mental Toughness and Etcheberry Certified in Strength, Conditioning and Movement. Joao is a member of the USPTA Middle States Board since 2011 and was a speaker at the 2015 USPTA World Conference, as well as other regional conferences. Since 2010, Pinho was nominated Rookie of the Year, U30 Pro of the Year and Pro of the Year by the Middle States Division. He earned dual bachelor's degrees in Marketing and Human Resource Management from Utah State University, a Master of Business Administration, from The University of Toledo, and a Certificate of Sports Marketing and Management, from UCLA.

GARY "PIT" PITTMAN graduated from Sheffield High School in 1972. In 1976 he earned a bachelor's degree in Education at University of Tennessee at Martin and a master's degree in Athletics Administration from University of Memphis in 1986.

Gary has been a teaching professional at Colonial Country Club in Memphis, TN, since 2002. He has been the teaching professional for Bartlett Parks and Recreation since 2013.

Gary and Sandra have been married 35 years. They have two daughters, Chelsea and Shelby.

Gary Pittman working with young student Cody Goodnight, 2007

DR. JOSEPH "JOE" PIZZAT became a USPTA Master Professional in 1985. He was winner, National Ultra Senior Father and Son Clay Court, Saratoga, FL, (2008); winner, Singles South Dakota Open (1956) and semifinalist, PTA Singles Eastern Section (1963).

Joe was Kalamazoo Tennis Pro (1948); Montclair Beach Club Summer Tennis Pro (1962), Rock Spring CC Summer Tennis Pro (1964–1967), Faculty Adviser Tennis Club, Paterson State (1968), Lafayette CC Summer Tennis Pro (1969), Kahkwa CC Summer Tennis Pro and Westwood Racquet Club Senior Pro (1972), Mercyhurst College Tennis Learning Center (1971–1973), Lake Shore CC Summer Tennis Pro and Tennis Program Director (1975–1994).

"Joe" and Ruth have been married 62 years. They have two children, Michael Pizzat (USPTA Elite Pro) and Paul Tinnin (Ed.D.).

ANDREW POGONYI and his family immigrated from Hungary to the U.S. in 1956 when he was 2 years old. He learned to play tennis on the public courts of Philadelphia, PA, and won the Philadelphia Public Parks U-12 championship. Andrew was a highly-ranked junior in the USTA Middle States from 1968-1972.

He graduated from Cardinal Dougherty H.S. in Philadelphia in 1972. He played four years of varsity tennis before graduating with a B.A. in History in 1976 from West Chester University in Pennsyvania. He was the team's MVP in 1973 and the team won the East Coast Conference title in 1975.

Pogonyi enjoyed a long career at the Philadelphia Cricket Club as assistant pro from 1978–1985 and tennis director from 1985–1997.

Since 1997 he has served as tennis director at Kennett Square Golf and Country Club in Kennett Square, PA. He has been honored by the USPTA with the Middle States Pro of the Year Award in 1989 and the Middle States Norman Bramall Service Award in 1987.

MIKE POLLARD, Head Tennis Professional at Wexford Plantation in Hilton Head, SC, has been teaching professionally for 21 years. During these 21 years, he has held the title of both Head Professional and Director of Tennis in facilities in Florida, Kansas and South Carolina. USPTA Elite Professional Certified since 1995. As an adult doubles coaching specialist, Mike has coached numerous Adult USTA teams to state and sectional titles. Mike has been the head coach to three different high school teams. Mike is also currently the only member of the PTR to hold a Professional rating in all six career education pathways. Married 20 years to his wife Debi, they have two children, Sierra, 22, a University of Florida graduate, and Ryland, 11, an aspiring professional ice hockey player.

STANFORD POON is the Founder and Director of Tennis at Deuce Tennis in Santa Monica, CA, for 10+ years. He has been coaching tennis for 18+ years. Before forming Deuce Tennis, Stanford gained lots of experience and skills by working for many prestigious companies, such as The Riviera Country Club, UCLA Tennis, Beverly Hills Hotel and high school head coaching. He currently oversees and mentors junior tennis professionals that assist Stanford in junior tennis camps and adult and junior clinics. When he is not directing, Stanford loves being on the court coaching private students. Stanford's passion expanded to directing his own

USTA junior tournaments and forming team tennis clubs. He is skillful in racquet stringing and is an expert in social media and technology. He graduated from University of Arizona with a Business Degree focusing in Management Information Systems. Stanford is a New Balance Ambassador and USPTA Elite Professional.

GREG PREVETTE has been Director of Tennis at Barrington Golf Club in Aurora, OH, since 1999. As Racquet Club Manager since 2013, he oversees all of the club's tennis, fitness and aquatics operations.

He was previously employed as General Manager and Tennis Director at The Wembley Club in Chagrin Falls, OH, and an Assistant Tennis Professional at Cleveland Racquet Club in Pepper Pike, OH. He was also Assistant Men's Tennis Coach for The University of Akron.

Greg earned his BS degree in Business Administration/Marketing from The University of Akron. A varsity tennis player for all four years, he was captain of the tennis team for two years. In addition, he was chosen as MVP for two years and was voted to the All Conference Team. He continued to compete after college and he achieved the No. 1 Men's Doubles ranking in Northeast Ohio six times and No. 1 Men's Singles ranking twice. He was a Midwest Section Representative at the National 25 and Over Inter-sectionals, competed in the 30 and over National Clay court tournament and played on a 5.0 USTA Nationals qualifying team.

A USPTA Elite pro since 1991, Greg has been a USTA Adult League Verifier and USTA Area Training Center Coach. A member of the HEAD/Penn Ad Staff Team, Greg volunteers annually in the Victory Gallop Tennis Exhibition that benefits a local therapeutic riding program. He has served on the committee and participated in the Cystic Fibrosis Tennis Auction Ball. Greg currently resides in Twinsburg, OH, with his wife Maggie, and their three children—Rob, Olivia, and Virginia.

BENJAMIN PRICE has worked at Club Sport Valley Vista in Walnut Creek, CA, for 17 years, according to general manager Brian Amador. Ben is a tennis coach with all levels from 6 and under to mid-level adults. Ben also works at the Pro Shop and has been a certified racquet USRSA technician for 22 years. Before CSVV Ben was employed at Club Sport Pleasanton in California for six years, mostly working with children, youth, summer camps and beginning adults and stringing for all tennis members and racketball members. Joan Schnarr was head certifier time and Director of Tennis at CSP. Before that Ben, certified PTR instructor, started with summer camps at Walnut Creek Recreation Center and Club Sport Summer camps in Walnut Creek, CA.

Ben changed careers during his mid-30s and used an unorthodox approach to become a certified USPTA tennis professional. Suffering from major burnout in the computer technician industry and not having a background in college or high level competitive tennis, Ben took on the task of loving and playing the game of tennis since ninth grade to the next level of teaching and promoting the "game of a lifetime" to as many children and youth as possible to keep the game alive far into the future. It is very fulfilling to take a child from beginning to full-fledged tennis player. So many life lessons can be learned from this process. It is very fulfilling to make a difference in the tennis community.

CLIFF PRICE became a USPTA member in 1980.

Totally Tennis, Inc., owned and operated by Cliff and Sherry Price since 1975, is one of the oldest tennis shops in the USA. In its 25th anniversary edition, Totally Tennis was picked by *Tennis Industry Magazine* (now *RSI*) as one of the top three tennis shops in the USA.

Cliff Price (left) receives the Men's 55 National Player of the Year Award in 2010 from USPTA president Tom Daglis.

In 2012, Cliff was No. 1 in USTA Senior Father and Son with son, Nathan. He was elected into USTA/Missouri Valley Hall of Fame in 1999 and in 2010 inducted into MVTA Oklahoma Tennis Hall of Fame.

Cliff has been one of the top Money Singles and Open Singles in Oklahoma for four decades (late 1960s–1990s). He was USPTA 55 National Player of the Year (2009, 2010) and was USPTA 45 National Player of the ar (1995).

He holds nine USPTA National Championship titles in singles and doubles, ranked top 10 in USTA National Men's 35, 40, and 45 singles, was a singles finalist USTA Hardcourts Mens 45's (1993), singles finalist USTA Hardcourts Mens 40's (1989) and Big 8 Conference singles champ at No. 1 for Oklahoma State University (1968), runner-up at No. 1 (1967 and 1969).

Cliff and Sherry have been married since 1969. They have two children, Nathan and McKenzie.

O. CARL PROTHO is a USPTA Certified Professional at the Professional level.

Raised in Gary, IN, he has 30+ years of tennis involvement and is still loving it. He was first introduced to tennis at Morehouse College by Kappa Alpha Psi fraternity brother, Donald Hense. After moving to Los Angeles, CA, he was encouraged by Coach Richard Williams, RCTS, to join USPTA and become a certified professional.

Passing the USPTA Certification Exam was a huge achievement and one of the most satisfying moments for him, as well as his daughter, Nichelle, who provided constant unwavering support. He is very thankful to Richard Williams for encouraging him to join USPTA. He is also grateful to Lito Lasin, Josh Jergensen and Sam Freeman for immeasurable assistance during his preparation for the exam.

Another achievement in tennis was the awarding of certification as a USTA Certified Official in 2015. As a tournament official he has experienced many fulfilling moments throughout Los Angeles and Orange counties, umpiring sanctioned junior tournaments.

Carl has completed all of the courses at Tennis Teachers Institute with founder Don Henson as of December 2015. He has also completed courses in 10 and Under Tennis and Wheelchair Tennis.

JIM PROVINES, Colonel, US Air Force (retired) has been a USPTA-certified Elite Professional since 1973. Following his varsity tennis at the University of Oklahoma (OU), Jim served as Head Tennis Coach at OU prior to his 30-year Air Force career. He was inducted into the Dayton Tennis Hall of Fame (1997) and USTA Oklahoma Tennis Hall of Fame (2010).

Tennis wins include: US Air Force World-Wide Singles Champion (1967), Armed Forces

Doubles Champion (with Hank Jungle) (1967), Republic of the Philippines Doubles Champion (with Tok Butuin) (1978), USTA Men's 60 Doubles Clay Court Champion (with John Gorsky) - Gold Ball (2000), USPTA Men's 60 Singles and Doubles Category II USTA National Champion (with Jim Schwitters) (2000).

USPTA friends, mentors past and present include: Bill Bristow, David Bryant, Janet Bryant, Kathy Buchanan, Brian Chaney, Ken DeHart, Rich Fanning, Jerry Geyman, Dick Gilkey, Tim Heckler, Roger Jack, Dick Landenberger, Jason Morton, Bruce Nagel, Jim Parker, Colin Robertson, Fritz Schunck, Jim Schwitters, Arnold Short, Gary Trost, Bill Tym and Steve Wilkinson.

Most importantly, God's greatest blessing to Amy and Jim is the Lord's love for us all and our families.

PAT PURCELL, from her start in the public parks, became a nationally ranked junior player and the No. 1 St. Louis women's tennis player in the 1980s.

After graduating from Washington University, where she lettered two years on the men's team and two years on the women's team, Pat moved into the tennis business as a teaching pro. She was a tennis club owner, and built and maintains one of the largest recreational World Team Tennis programs in the country.

Pat returned to competitive tennis after a 20-year break and won USTA National titles in Women's 55 singles and doubles. She was a member of the US Women's 55 team that won the Maureen Connelly Cup at the 2013 World Competition in Antalya, Turkey.

Pat teaches at Chesterfield Athletic Club. She was inducted into the St. Louis Hall of Fame in April 2016.

LAURA PURYEAR joined the USTA Missouri Valley staff in 1996 and currently serves as the Tennis Service Representative for Oklahoma. In her tenure with the USTA Missouri Valley, Laura has managed School Tennis, NJTL, Junior Team Tennis, Adult Recreation, USA Tennis Pathway including Funded Markets.

Laura previously worked as a teaching professional at Babson Recreation Center in Wellesley, MA, from 1988–1992, where she taught group and private lessons, assisted with summer camps and pro shop sales. She was an Adjunct Faculty member at the University of Central Oklahoma in 2006, teaching beginning and intermediate tennis classes and was the Head Tennis Coach at Holland Hall from 2007–2013.

Laura served on the Missouri Valley Division board of directors from 2006–2013 as Director at Large and Secretary. Since 2000 she has served as the staff liaison to the USPTA. She is USTA National Trainer and a member of the USTA University Adjunct Faculty.

BRODY QUEAL is a member of Hutchinson High School Tennis Hall of Fame, was fourth in career wins at Hutchinson High School, a three-time State Medalist and on the State Champion (team) 2010.

Brody Queal (right) with Nick Saviano at a USPTA convention

Brody was certified in 2013 as a Elite Professional. He is on the USPTA U30 National Task Force (Missouri Valley) and with USTA Sports Science. Brody is also an Accredited Professional Coach.

He was Head Tennis Professional at Body First Wellness Center, Manhattan, KS, from 2013–2015. He is Junior Tennis Director at Milburn Country Club from 2015 to current.

MATT RAGAN has been the Director of Tennis at The Racquet Club at Scottsdale Ranch in Scottsdale, AZ, and The Stockbridge Golf Club in Stockbridge, MA, since 2005. He successfully coached the Scottsdale Christian Academy Tennis Team to back-to-back State Titles in 2004–2005. He was awarded the USPTA's Southwest Division High School Coach of the Year Award in 2005. Matt started teaching tennis in 1987 with the Phoenix Parks and Recreation Division and USTA National Junior Tennis League. Matt is an Elite USPTA Pro and has a B.S. in Finance from Arizona State University. He resides in Scottsdale, AZ, with his wife Katie.

BEN RAKUSIN, Elite Professional, is semi-retired, meaning he's very busy. He teaches at several clubs in both Broward and Palm Beach Counties in South Florida. A USPTA tester for over 20 years, Ben also continues to run the USPTA certification testing hub in Boca Raton. In his 35+ years in tennis, Ben has been a director of tennis, head pro, assistant pro, stringer, umpire, linesman, coach and shop owner.

Originally from Ohio, Ben's schooling and tennis included Cleveland Heights High School and Ohio State University. He is a three-time district professional of the year, four-time Florida division Tester of the Year and the 2011 George Bacso National Tester of the Year.

Ben has won numerous doubles titles including junior, college, open and senior divisions. He also currently serves on the national diversity committee.

Ben's great passions are the certification test and its improvement and giving back by way of numerous charity events. He has been married to Ingrid for 35 years.

RON REBHUHN was inducted as a member of the USTA Eastern Tennis Hall of Fame in April 2012 and just four months later he passed away, Aug. 26, 2012. He is missed. I met Ron through the USTA tournaments he organized. Our friendship began after he asked me my date of birth; this will not come as a surprise to those of you who knew Ron, a fellow Sagittarius, he called me for the next 20 years, I felt I was part of a private club with him. His tennis acumen was acute. I would ask what do you think of the opponent moments before playing and he would give a one line answer, continental grip hit high to the forehand, or stay out there as long as you can, but often he would just hand me the can of balls and point me in the direction of the court. Once out there I wanted to play well for him, I wanted his approval. I enjoyed the moments after a match and talking about the match and enjoying his presence, it was only a moment but he was generous with his knowledge and thoughts. He is missed. Submitted by Richard Callwood.

JOEL RECKEWEY is currently the head tennis coach at Concordia University for both of the men's and women's tennis programs. He is a high performing business graduate of the University of Nebraska and is an Elite USPTA certified teaching professional. Joel received his master's degree from Concordia University in Athletic Administration. In 1996, Joel was the class A Nebraska Boys' Tennis State runner up. In 2000 he was the Kansas 6A State High School Boys' Singles Tennis Champion and Team Champion. As a junior tennis player, he was ranked No. 2 in the Missouri Valley Boys' 16's and 18's divisions and was qualified to play at the National Boys' Hard Court Championships in Kalamazoo, MI, five years in a row. He posted a top No. 30 junior national ranking in the 18 and under division. Joel Reckewey was a four-year varsity letter winner for the University of Nebraska Men's Tennis Team and was awarded the weight lifter of the year in 2003. He was team captain in his senior season. He has tennis-teaching experience at the Lincoln Racquet Club, the Overland Park Racquet Club and the Mike Wolf Tennis Academy as a teaching pro and traveling coach. Joel has been the Co-Head tennis professional at the Abbott Sports Complex and Coach at the Nebraska Tennis Academy for more than 10 years. He is the former Head Coach for the Lincoln Christian High School Girls' Tennis Team. Joel is the Director of Tennis at Prairie Life Fitness in Lincoln, NE, for their outdoors tennis programs and he has served as a business service representative for Prince Global Sports. Joel now operates his own tennis business, "Reckewey Tennis" in Lincoln, NE, at the Abbott Sports Complex.

FERDINAND REDELIJK, a native from Breda, The Netherlands, left for the USA in 1977 to play college tennis for the University of Dallas, TX. Since 1987 he's a certified USPTA Elite Pro and a VNT Dutch certified professional. In 2015 he became a USPTA specialist in Competitive Player Development. Before enjoying coaching stints on the ATP/WTA and ITF tours, as a player he competed on several satellite and money tournaments in Europe. At present he's the Director of Tennis for over 25 years at Norwood Hills Country Club in St. Louis, MO. At this facility he owns and operates a pro shop and manages all tennis operations. In addition to tennis his interests include travel, soccer, the Internet and spending time with his family. Ferdinand's family includes his wife Lidwien, daughter Nikki and son Jordi. They reside in Orlando/Bradenton, FL.

ADAM REEB was a four-year member of the men's tennis team at Saint Louis University, served as team co-captain junior and senior year, finished career at SLU ranked seventh all-time for career doubles wins and tied for 18th all-time for career singles wins, named to the A-10's Academic All-Conference Team three times, named to the A-10 Commissioner's Honor Roll every semester, named an ITA Scholar-Athlete, received team's Spirit Award freshman and senior year, and received team's Most Improved Player Award junior year after leading the Billikens in doubles winning percentage and overall winning percentage.

Adam has been a college coach for seven years at DI, DII, and NAIA levels; DI head coach at the age of 28 at Seattle University, guided the McKendree University men's tennis team to its first NCAA DII Tournament appearance and first national and regional DII rankings in 2014. He has been an assistant coach at the DI and NAIA levels, was named the 2010 ITA NAIA Men's Region III Assistant Coach of the Year while at McKendree University. Adams has been teaching tennis for 12 years and has been USPTA certified since 2012. He was a National Team Coach for the USTA Missouri Valley section in summer 2015.

BRUCE REED is a full time Tennis Professional with Stafford Hills Club in Tualatin, OR. He's also the Tournament Director for the Baker City Grass Courts and a seasonal Tennis Professional with The Palm Desert Resort Country Club.

Prior to SHC Bruce was the Tennis Director for Club Green Meadows and Cascade Athletic Club.

He has been certified with the USPTA since 2001. Bruce has directed over 100 USTA Tennis Tournaments and has directed over 100 Tennis and Basketball Camps. He has coached over 50 USTA teams.

Bruce is currently endorsed by Prince and Adidas.

He won multiple 5.0 and Open USTA Singles and Doubles titles, and is currently rated 5.0 at age 49 (this year).

Bruce played Collegiate Tennis and Basketball from 1986–1992. He played Pro-Am Basketball in Phoenix and Seattle from 1992–2000.

He has a son, Colton (18) and daughter, Carlee (16). He's married to Tawnya (18 years).

Bruce loves tennis, snow skiing, mountain biking, and traveling.

JIM REFFKIN graduated from Bishop Noll High School in 1957 and obtained a bachelor's degree in 1962 from Marquette University.

He was the founder of the Southern Arizona Tennis Association, currently USTA Southern Arizona. Jim introduced

"Match Tiebreak" and "Collegiate" Scoring—eight-game pro set for doubles, "Super Sets" and "Shoot Outs."

Jim is in USPTA and USTA Halls of Fame. He has been Director of Tennis at Jim Reffkin Tennis Center for 40 years. He is a former National President of USPTA and National Pro of the Year. He was the first USTA National Chairperson of the USTA National Innovation Committee. Reffkin had tremendous success in changing tennis scoring rules but was responsible for implementing "Innovative Formats" to grow the game. He was an original member of Player Development Committee with Arthur Ashe, Cliff Drysdale and Stan Smith.

Jim and Lucille have a daughter, Amy.

EDWARD T. REID, son of Jimmy Reid, who was one of the founders of the present day USPTA. A Brooklyn, NY, native, Eddie became a top ranking junior player in the East and in 1936 was ranked 20th in USLTA Boys singles and ninth in doubles. Eddie turned pro at age 19 (before the days of "Open" tennis) and, after serving in the Coast Guard during the war, held positions at the Merion Cricket Club in Philadelphia and the Point Judith, Newport Casino and Agawam Hunt Clubs in Rhode Island. In 1947, he was named Head Tennis and Squash Professional at the Hartford Golf Club in West Hartford, CT. Eddie won the US Professional Squash Rackets Championship in 1947, 1949, 1950 and 1952 and was ranked No. 1 in the world in 1954. Eddie soon became recognized as one of the primary drivers of youth tennis development in New England and was awarded the NELTA Deitz Trophy in 1962 as the professional "who has done the most for the amateur game." Eddie pioneered indoor clay tennis in Greater Hartford with the opening of The Tennis Club in Bloomfield, CT, in 1963. He was a member of the winning New England pro team at the USPLTA's Intersectional Team Championships in 1965 and 1966. In 1969, Eddie was named Men's and Women's Tennis and Squash Coach at Bowdoin College in Brunswick, ME, where he introduced tennis as the first varsity women's sport. In 1977 Eddie was named USPTA Coach of the Year for his work with the men's team. Eddie was twice elected President of the USPTA-New England section in 1979 and 1980 and was inducted to the College Squash Hall of Fame in 1992, the Maine State Squash Hall of Fame in 2008 and the USPTA New England Division Hall of Fame in 2014. Eddie is a proud 60+ year member of the USPTA.

JAMES T. REID (1892–1993) was one of the founding fathers of Professional Lawn Tennis Association (PLTA), now USPTA. After emigrating from Greece as a teen, Jimmy came to the states via Ellis Island and settled in New York City with relatives. A gifted athlete, Jimmy originally took up boxing and won the Metropolitan Championships at the NY Athletic Club in 1913. He was introduced to the game of squash-tennis by Teddy Roosevelt, who helped him secure assistant pro jobs at the Harvard and Yale Clubs in New York City. In 1919, Jimmy reached the finals of the world squash-tennis championships. That same year, he was named Head Tennis and Squash pro at the Crescent Athletic Club of Brooklyn. In 1927, Jimmy was among a small group of tennis professionals who organized a national body whose mission was to further the best interests of the game of tennis through the professional players and instructors of the sport. In 1939 Jimmy moved to the Huntington Crescent Club in Long Island, where he remained until 1972. He also coached varsity tennis and squash at Wesleyan University in Middletown, CT, from 1940 to 1948. Jimmy's son, Edward, followed in his dad's footsteps, becoming a tennis and squash pro and ultimately earning the rank of the No. 1 squash player in the world in 1954.

ROB REIMER, USPTA Professional, prides himself on being a community servant, as well as a business owner.

Rob's goal is to increase community participation in tennis at both the junior and adult levels.

"I am proud that I was able to start a year-round program for the local high and middle schools where there was little participation before," he says. "Now the programs are full of junior players."

Rob is the owner and head pro of Reimer's Tennis Excellence in Rochester, N.Y.

"I most enjoy seeing student's progress and their excitement as they improve," he says. "Coaching many different sports for 30-plus years allows me to help newer players relate to the game."

Rob became a tennis pro "to help juniors and adults realize the joy of playing this sport well," he explains.

Rob himself has more than 30 years' playing experience, including on the high school and college level.

He earned a Bachelor of Science in Business Administration from Michigan Technological University.

Rob says he is proud to be a good father to his son, Eric, a good husband to his wife, Kathy, and a good citizen to the community.

JIM RICHARDS has been in the tennis industry for over 20 years. He came to Tampa, FL, from England in 1997 and was mentored by Carl Gavine, who owns a tennis management company "Tennis Heaven USA." He spent 15 years in Stuart, FL, as a Director of Tennis at various resorts, country clubs and public facilities before starting his own tennis school in 2006. He owes a great deal of his continuing education to Steve Smith and his current web site "Tennis Intelligence Applied" and has been fortunate enough to have had opportunities to work with high level players. In 2012 he spent a year in Dallas, TX, doing match and video analysis for Southlake Tennis Center before moving to Atlanta, GA, in the winter of 2013. He is currently the Head Pro at Smoke Rise Country Club in Atlanta, GA.

NICHOLAS RIGBY of Melbourne, Australia - USPTA member for 25 years. Tennis has been a lifelong enjoyment for him and as a coach, for 30+ years, he has found the profession to be an exciting, challenging and rewarding experience. Nicholas has travelled extensively and held a variety of roles within the profession. He has had considerable involvement

with local, state and national organizations/associations in several countries, including Australia, USA, Germany and Singapore, and has enjoyed these relationships immensely. Over the past decade his work has predominantly been coordinating and implementing advanced player training programs, both privately and in club/team situations and he finds working with high performance athletes both inspiring and motivating. During his residence in the U.S., Nicholas competed very successfully on the U.S. Collegiate Circuit, winning in consecutive years the Florida State Titles and still thoroughly enjoys the competitiveness that tennis provides.

JIM RITTER, USPTA Certified Professional, has been a part of the Round Rock Tennis Association for the past 35 years. Most recently a past vice president of the RRTA and currently serving on the Board of Directors.

As an independent coach working with all ages to improve their tennis game, efforts include working with local high schools, and 10 & Under Tennis. Currently, he is partnering with the USTA in Middle School Sponsorships in Central Texas. Ritter is a 1990 graduate of Saint Edwards University, Austin, TX.

KELVIN RIVERA, a certified teaching professional and tester with the U.S. Professional Tennis Association (USPTA) for 25+ years, has extensive coaching experience working with players ranging from touring professionals, top-ranked nationally and internationally junior players to teaching pros, adult and junior players. During his coaching career, Kelvin has developed numerous juniors into scholarship college players, novice adult players into successful league players and state ranked competitors and coached many league teams to division championships.

Kelvin earned the US Tennis Association (USTA) Specialist in Competitive Player Development degree in 2000. Kelvin has served on the USTA National Collegiate Committee, USTA National Hispanic Participation Task Force, USTA Florida Junior Competitive Council and USTA Florida Multicultural Committee. He was awarded USPTA Florida Division District 4 Volunteer of the Year and Tester of the Year.

Throughout his tennis teaching career, Kelvin has held positions at some of the nation's top tennis facilities, including the John Newcombe Tennis Ranch in Texas, Harry Hopman Tennis at Saddlebrook Resort in Tampa, FL, and the Human Performance Institute in Orlando, FL. He also served as Davis Cup Captain for Puerto Rico.

JULIUS ROBINSON began playing in the public parks of southwest Atlanta, GA, at age 14. He was tennis instructor for the City of Atlanta Department of Parks and Recreation at age 16.

Julius was a tennis instructor, South Atlanta Community Tennis Association's Summer Academy under the legendary William "Wink" Fulton.

He played Junior ALTA, captained his high school team at Benjamin E. Mays Academy and played varsity tennis for Morehouse College.

He was assistant tennis coach at Tri-Cities High School, tournament director for Verizon Wireless for three years and chairman of Shakerag Farms Tennis Association.

Julius was independent pro at Tennis Kids and Teens, Inc. and Double Aces, Inc. He led Autry Mill Lions to 2011 season championship.

He was Tennis Professional at Silvia Tennis Academy at Seven Oaks, Midtown Athletic Club at Windy Hill and Carl E. Sanders Family YMCA at Buckhead.

Julius is CEO of Atlanta Tennis Coach, LLC and Director of Junior Programs at The Falls of Autry Mill Tennis Club in Alpharetta, GA.

GARY C. ROCHE, USPTA Certified Elite Professional & Court Maintenance Supervisor, has been playing and competing in tennis for 29 years and teaching for almost 19 years. Gary is originally from Michigan. He has been with the Lost Tree Country Club Tennis Staff since 2004. He is a USPTA certified professional and a USPTA developmental coach. He also served as Tennis Director at the Chicago Club in Charlevoix, MI from 2006–2008. In addition, Gary was in charge of programming and instruction at Charlevoix Country Club and the Tennis Club of Charlevoix.

ANGEL RODRIGUEZ has been in the tennis industry for over 25 years. A native of Puerto Rico, Angel lives in Boca Raton, FL, and has worked as the Director of Tennis at The Club at Boca Pointe and more recently at The Moorings Yacht and Country Club (Vero Beach). Currently he is working at the Royal Palm Yacht and Country Club in Boca Raton, FL. Angel is a USPTA Elite Professional. He has received his share of awards, including the USPTA/USTA Florida State Service and Member Organization Award. As a player he attained the No. 1 ranking in the Men's 25-and-over doubles and the No. 6 ranking in the Men's 35-and-over singles, among other honors. He also became a Certified Personal Trainer in order to add another component to the development of players. He has worked with many junior players, including his daughter Alexis, who received a full scholarship for the University of Central Florida.

HANS ROMER, born and raised in the Netherlands, graduated from the prestigious CIOS Sport College with a bachelor's degree in Physical Education. In the Netherlands, Hans also obtained all three certification (A, B and C) levels with the KNLTB and

coached for their National Junior Development Program. After moving to the U.S. he fully embraced his USPTA membership by becoming a USPTA Master Professional and serving on the Board of Directors for USPTA California, New England and NorCal.

Hans has been a frequent speaker at Divisional and National Tennis Conferences and presented "On Court with USPTA" for the Tennis Channel. After hosting the 2012 USPTA World Conference in Monterey, CA, he received the USPTA NorCal "Pro of the Year" Award at Stanford University. As a player Hans held several USTA and USPTA Divisional/Sectional and National Rankings. Since 2001 he has been on the HEAD/Penn Advisory Staff.

Hans was active at the Vic Braden Tennis College, Pierpont Racquet Club, Portland Country Club, BallenIsles Country Club and currently serves as seasonal Director of Tennis at The Dunes Club in Narragansett, RI. In the winter season he coaches indoors in Maine, where he is also active as Board Member for the Maine Tennis Association.

JUSTIN ROMERO was born in Guam and graduated from West Mesa High School in 2008. He attended New Mexico Military Institute (AA Sports Management) and Western New Mexico University (B.S. Kinesiology).

Justin was raised in Albuquerque, NM, and was No. 2 Ranked Junior in the state. He played with NCAA Division II Team Conference and Regional Champions and was in NCAA Division II National Elite 8 Finish.

Justin is a USPTA Elite Professional, PTR Certified and Licensed Cardio Tennis Professional.

He is Head Tennis Professional at Ocean Reef Club in Key Largo, FL, and one of the starting members of the USPTA U30 initiative.

ROBERT RYLAND became a Life Member of USPTA in 1958 and in 1959 became the first Afro-American to play in a pro tournament when he joined Jack March's annual World Pro Tennis Championships in Cleveland.

Bob played No. 1 at Tilden Tech HS in Chicago and at Wayne State in Detroit. He was player coach at Tennessee A&I.

Bob won the ATA championships two times and was runner up once and was among the first black players to play at the USLTA championships in Forrest Hills in the early 1950s. He continued to play as a senior and won the USPTA National 65's in 1988 and the USTA Public Parks 85's in 2006.

Bob taught at St Albans, Washington, DC, and at Midtown, New York City, and coached players on the pro circuit.

Bob was inducted into the Wayne Athletic Hall of Fame in 1991 and the USTA Eastern HOF in 2002.

DEREK SABEDRA, head coach of both the men's and women's tennis programs at St. Mary's College of Maryland from 2006–2012, is the winningest coach in the history of that school. He previously spent 17 years coaching high school tennis at four schools, with teams accumulating 198 wins.

Sabedra received a BA from the University of Maryland in 1992, a MA from Bowie State in Massachusetts in 2000 and a Ph.D. in Psychology from Cabella University in 2015.

As a player, he was a top-ten ranked doubles player in Maryland in 2012 and 2013.

He served as secretary of the St. Mary's County Tennis Association from 2004–2012 and was named Maryland Tournament Director of the Year in 2011. Sabredra is a psychologist and has a son, Alex.

VYRON (BYRON) SACHARIDIS, a passionate tennis player for many years, came to the U.S. for graduate studies at Johns Hopkins and Georgetown University in 2012, receiving his coaching certifications by both the USPTA and the PTR in 2013. He has served the game of tennis in different capacities in the U.S. and overseas, in countries such as Italy, France and Greece. Byron specializes in adult development and has been delivering private lessons to players of varying levels in Washington, DC. He has competed in open tournaments achieving first and second place distinctions, but his greater joy remains to introduce people to the sport.

Byron Sacharidis officiating at a WTEF sponsored event, 2014

Byron Sacharidis with Nenad Zimonjic during a fundraiser prior to the Citi Open, 2015

As a holder of an ITF Level I certification, Byron has also assisted with officiating and fundraising, and as a USRSA certified stringer he has been offering highly specialized racquet customization services. Among his many students, wife Magda and daughter Marilyn-Athena stand out as clear favorites.

Byron Sacharidis with George Kalovelonis, coach of the Men's National Team of Greece

FRANK "SACH" SACHIRE has been P – USPTR since 1986 and USPTA Elite Pro since 1989. He did not do much tournament playing other than small local tournaments. Most of his time was spent teaching and coaching.

Frank was a high school English teacher for 35 years (1967–2002) and has been coaching 49 years, (1967-present). He was an assistant football coach for 18 years, assistant basketball coach for nine years and has been teaching and coaching tennis for 41 years.

"Sach" and Patty have been married 40 years. Their son, Ryan, is men's head tennis coach at University of Notre Dame. Ryan and wife Cindy have two daughters, Anna (7) and Emily (15).

MICHAEL SAINE is part of three generations of tennis coaching: father Joseph Saine, son Mike Saine and son/grandson, Quinn Saine. Joe is the father of the Indiana High School boys' state tournament. He coached four state team champions. Michael played on two of those teams. Both are IHSTeCA H of F members. Quinn was an all state and Western Kentucky player and has been on the professional staff for Peter Burwash International for several years. Joe started on the only undefeated football team in Ball State's history and returned to Peru to teach and coach. He was introduced to tennis and became an Indiana coaching legend. Mike Eikenberry, former USPTA president, was a force behind three of Coach Joe's state team champions. Mike followed his father as PHS coach and Miami County YMCA summer director. The Saine's have guided the local YMCA summer program for 61 straight summers.

CORY SANDGREN would like to thank those that have helped his tennis career. Cory has been teaching since 1989 and a USPTA professional for almost 25 years. He first started teaching tennis under Steve Wilkinson at Tennis and Life Camps at Gustavus Adolphus College. What an incredible mentor to learn about teaching tennis!! He was Cory's college coach for four years and summer employer for three years. Steve also got Cory his one and only full time job after college, teaching at the Decatur Athletic Club under owner Bob O'Connell and long time USPTA member Chuck Kuhle. Thank you all for such a wonderful opportunity in life!

CRAIG SANDVIG worked with Doug Smith and a cast of many to create a learning culture at Sunset Tennis Center in St. Louis. They worked with champions and life-long players at all levels; created, hosted and ran superior tournaments and shared the belief that tennis is a special game. All while having more fun than anyone should. Craig was a five-time State Champion in South Dakota. At the University of Iowa, he finished second at his flight twice and was awarded the University's Big Ten Medal as the top student athlete. Craig is a member of the South Dakota Tennis Hall of Fame and the St. Louis Tennis Hall of Fame. His mentors included Don Grebin, Don Klotz, and Steve Wilkinson.

THIAGO SANTOS has been the Director of Tennis of Genesis Health Clubs in Salina, KS, since June 2011. As a director, Thiago oversees all aspects of the tennis operations and serves over 2,000 members. Thiago's aspiration is to help continue to grow the game of tennis at all ages and levels.

Thiago has been a member of the USPTA since 2015.

As a tennis player, Thiago received a full scholarship to play college tennis at Wichita State from 2005 to 2009 and was one of the top junior players growing up in Brazil.

Thiago is currently ranked in the ATP doubles ranking and is the son of Gilberto and Marina Santos and the middle brother between Cinthya and Eduardo.

TOM SARSFIELD is the managing director of the Whitlinger/Sarsfield recreation tennis program that serves nine bay area cities in Northern California for over 25 years. A graduate of San Jose State University in Physical Education, Tom began his coaching/teaching career in 1981 with stints at the Almaden Swim & Racquet Club in San Jose, Saratoga High School, and has been involved with the Stanford Tennis Program since 1987. Stanford University currently employs him as a Physical Education Tennis Instructor. He was recognized in 2002 by the U.S. Tennis Association Northern California Community Tennis Committee for his outstanding contribution to the growth of the game.

MARK SAVAGE has been Director of Tennis at Sportsplex in New Windsor, NY, since 1999. During his leadership with Sportsplex, the club has been named USPTA Eastern Facility of the Year (2002) and USTA Member Organization of the Year (2005). In addition, Mark has been named USPTA Eastern Professional of the Year (2002) and USTA George Seewagen Eastern Professional of the Year (2010). A USPTA Master Professional, Mark is proud to be an active member of the USPTA, having served on the Executive Board as Eastern President from 2008–2009 and 2015–16.

Specializing in teaching high performance junior players, Mark has worked with two H.S. state champions and has produced nine years of girls and eight years of boys New York H.S. Section IX champions from 2003–2015. Mark has been married to his wife Jane since 1999. Mark and Jane have two girls, Emily and Erin, happily living in Wallkill, NY.

PETER C. SCALES, "Coach Pete," is a Ph.D. (Syracuse University, 1976) adolescent and child psychologist and the head JV tennis coach for girls and boys at Parkway South High, Manchester, MO, where he has coached for Parkway School District since 2008. Since 2008 he has also been a lead instructor in the annual Parkway Summer Tennis Program for players from 4th grade-college and in 2016 also joins the staff of the Washington University in St. Louis Junior Bears Summer Tennis Camp. He is a U.S. Professional Tennis Association-certified tennis teaching pro, and has published two articles in the USPTA magazine, ADDvantage, on positive coaching (2011) and mental toughness tips (2013). Coach Pete started playing tennis only at age 42. He played competitively for more than 20 years, achieving an NTRP rating of 4.0. He competed in numerous USTA singles and USTA mixed doubles leagues, World Team Tennis leagues, Interclub men's doubles and the West St. Louis County Tennis Ladder, the largest league in the metro area. He won four club league singles ti-

tles and reached five tournament finals, including the consolation final of the USTA Missouri Valley District championships in 2008. He finished No. 4 in Men's 55 singles in 2008 and No. 3 in mixed doubles with his wife Martha in 2006 in the West County Tennis Ladder, and won the bronze medal in singles at the 2007 St. Louis Senior Olympics.

CHUCK SCHUNK left a corporate business career in 1972 to build The Racket Club in Crystal Lake, IL, and was its General Manager for 10 years. After moving to San Diego, he was a teaching pro at Stoneridge Country Club in Poway. He was voted Most Improved Southern California Senior Player of the Year in 1991 and San Diego USPTA Pro of the Year in 2001. In 2011 he received the San Diego USPTA Lifetime Achievement Award. Chuck began playing tennis in 1932, organized the first tennis team at Chicago's Amundsen High School in 1939 and was its top player, captain and manager. He then played varsity three years for the University of Illinois. Until age 89, Chuck's competitive career earned him high age division rankings in singles and doubles in Chicago, the Midwest and Southern California. He served as a Marine in World War II and now lives in Decatur, GA.

MARK SCHWARTZ hit his first ball in 1957 at Camp Roosevelt in Monticello, NY. He dabbled during the summers through high school, then in college started to play seriously. He played No. 1 singles and doubles for LIU in the 1970s. Mark graduated in 1976 and began teaching tennis for one of the first USPTA members ever, Martin Buxby, in Florida. Taught many places including the NYAC Boca Raton Hotel Tennis Club of the Palm Beaches, The Breakers Sunningdale CC in Scarsdale, NY, as well as a few clubs in the Hamptons. He then shared time teaching tennis and umpiring tennis, getting to a very high level, chairing McEnroe 12 times and at present working 28 US Opens in a row—quite a number, only eclipsed by my 30th year as a member of the USPTA. It's been fun. Thank you.

ALAN SCHWIMMER is a tennis instructor at Glenview Tennis Club. He has been working with the Glenview Tennis Club since 2005. Glenview Tennis Club was selected as one of the USTA Tennis facilities of the year in 2009. He has also worked at numerous tennis clubs around Chicago including Poplar Creek Racquet Club, The Wright Club, Woodfield Racquet Club, as well as Ken Carrol Country Club in Colorado. He has been a member of the USPTA since the mid '70s.

Alan has always enjoyed the mental and physical aspects of the game and believes both are necessary to be successful. As a teacher, he finds great satisfaction from passing his knowledge on to others. He believes every student is different and their lessons should accommodate that fact. There is no better feeling than when a student learns something new or understands a new concept.

JOSEPH JAMES "JIM" SCHWITTERS was instructor in HPER Department at the University of Hawaii, 39 years; Men's Head Tennis Coach, University of Hawaii, 1966–2004-Record: 819-409-8; Women's Head Tennis Coach, University of Hawaii 1966–1971, 1980–2001-Record: 508-201-7. He retired as the tennis coach with most wins in NCAA history with combined record of 1327-610-15 and NCAA Region VII Coach of the Year 1990.

Assisted in establishing the USTA Hawaii-Pacific Section (1960s); Served as the second President (1965). He was trainer and coach of the French Polynesian (Tahiti) Tennis Team (1969) and founded the Hawaii Division of the USPTA (1974) and served as the first president (1974–1976).

Jim was inducted into St. Ambrose College Athletic Hall of Fame (1981), U.S. Professional Tennis Association Hawaii Hall of Fame (2004), Hawaii Sports Hall of Fame (2006), Hawaii U.S. Tennis Association Hall of Fame/Coach (2007), Hawaii U.S. Tennis Association Hall of Fame/Player and University of Hawaii Circle of Honor (2009), Intercollegiate Tennis Association Hall of Fame/Coach (2015).

He has won over 350 titles, competing in the U.S., Canada, Europe, Asia and South Pacific. Jim competed at US Open (Forest Hills, NY and Canadian Open, Vancouver, Canada-1966 and Toronto, Canada-1968). He was nationally ranked in singles and doubles over 20 times and named Player of the Decade (1970–1979) in Hawaii. In 2000, Jim was named in the *Top 10 Players of the Past Hundred Years* by the *Hawaii Tennis News*.

BUTCH SEEWAGEN was US Junior Runner-up No. 1 East all Divisions/All American Rice University two times. He was a member of US Jr. Davis Cup three times, Southwest Conference Singles one time, Doubles three times Champion. He was NCAA Team Runner-up (1968) and winner of US National Amateur Championships (1969). While coach for Columbia University, two times Ivy League Champions and Top 10 NCAA.

He played World Team Tennis for Detroit Loves (1974). He played US Open 13 times, Wimbledon five times, French Open two times. He was the 1976 Winner of American Express Challengers Circuit. Butch joined the Wimbledon boycott in 1973. He has played No. 1 singles for World Champion US Italia Cup Team and was US National 40 and over Champion (1986), ranked No. 1 US.

Butch and Christine (also USPTA member) have a son, Chad and grandson, Grant. Butch's father, George, is former two-time President of USPTA.

MATTHEW "COACH MATT" JOSEPH SEIDEMAN began playing tennis at the age of 6 and is a San Diego native. At 19 he began his tennis instructional career at the Rancho Bernardo Community Tennis Club in 1996. A year later, he was hired at the Rancho Santa Fe Tennis Club, where he successfully coached adults and juniors for over nine years. He was owner of the tennis pro shop in Rancho Santa Fe and ran popular club programs for the members.

Matt graduated from San Diego State University and is a former No. 1 Palomar collegiate singles player as well as recipient of the honorable student athlete award.

He is the founder of the STARS Tennis Academy in Poway and of MatchTraK Tennis.

In 2006, Matt became the Director of Junior Development at StoneRidge Country Club. He is currently a Yonex Team Member as well as an expert racquet stringer.

Matt currently enjoys competing in matches in Southern California and has played on numerous San Diego USTA Champion teams. He is married to his beautiful wife Sheila and has two sons, Easton Patrick Seideman and Garin Pierce Seideman.

DIANE SELKE has been a USPTA Professional for 31 years and USPTA Master Professional since 1996. Diane served on the Intermountain Board for 15 years and on the Executive Committee, twice as President and three times as Regional Vice President. She served as USPTA National Women's Chairperson twice and on the USPTA Master Pro Committee. Diane was the USPTA Intermountain Pro of the Year in 1989, 2003, 2006, and 2009. She is a USPTA Board of Director, Vice President and chairs the Convention, Awards, and Diversity and Inclusion Committees. Diane has been the Director/Head Tennis Professional at Valley Country Club, Centennial, CO since 1997. She worked for the Colorado Athletic Clubs – Monaco and Inverness, 1981–1989. Diane graduated and played for Michigan State University winning the Big Ten No. 1 Doubles, No. 5 Singles and Spartan Invitational No. 1 Singles. Diane received the Michigan State University Dr. Nell Jackson Lifetime Achievement Award in 2009.

SUE SELKE has been a USPTA certified Professional since 1976 and has achieved the status of Elite Professional. She worked for the Court One Athletic Clubs in Michigan for 40 years as Director of Tennis and Assistant Manager and now is the Executive Director since 2011. Sue was the Michigan USPTA Pro of the Year in 1995 and inducted into the USPTA Midwest Hall of Fame in 1999. She volunteered for the USTA and the USTA Midwest Section for 30+ years. Sue played for Michigan State University and won the Big Ten No. 1 Singles in 1973, 1974 and 1975. Her tennis teams were also Big Ten champions 1973 and 1974. Sue was the first tennis player, male or female, inducted into the Michigan State University Athletics Hall of Fame, 2014.

BILL SERUES played collegiate tennis at Navy and Umass and was a ranked USTA player as a junior and adult in New England and Middle States. He has been a USPTA member since 1973 and is a Elite Professional. He has served as a Division Officer for the Pacific Northwest and Middle States Divisions.

Bill has been head pro at Amherts (MA) Tennis Academy, Tacoma (WA) Lawn Tennis Club and Saucon Valley (PA) Country Club. He has the unique distinction of being one of the few (if not only) people to play tennis on all seven continents when he played in Antarctica in 2005 at the Chile Air Force Base, the only tennis court on the continent.

Bill's wife Jane was former women's tennis coach at Trinity, CT, College.

EDWARD SERUES, Master Professional, was born June 13, 1917 in Medford, MA, and died Aug. 4, 2004 at Naples, FL.

He graduated from Medford (MA) High School, attended Boston University (B.S. 1956) and Springfield College (M.A 1962).

Edward was the Massachusetts State Champion (1940), Hawaii Champion (1942), on the All Navy Tennis team numerous times, top ranked in many age categories as a senior in New England and USPTA Singles Champion in 55, 60, 65 and 70 age categories.

He served as President of New England USPTA division and National USPTA Officer as Secretary and President of New England Intercollegiate Tennis Coaches Assoc.

Edward spent 30+ years as Head Tennis and Squash Coach at Amherst (MA) College and was a member of New England Tennis Hall of Fame.

Edward saw US Navy action at Pearl Harbor on Dec. 7, 1941 and later was recalled to combat duty during the Korean War.

With wife Helen by his side, he spent many years keeping the New England branch of the USPTA going with their accurate recordkeeping, treasury and annual meetings.

New England USPTA Pro of the Year Award is named for Edward Serues.

MARK SHABAN, USPTA Elite Professional and PTR-Professional, has been teaching tennis for 21 years. He currently runs after-school programs for 1st thru 6th graders in Silicon Valley, CA.

He was previously employed at the Sunnyvale Municipal Tennis Center in Sunnyvale, CA, where he taught Adult/Junior Park and Recreation tennis lessons from 1994–2012. From 2001–2012 he also developed and ran a Tennis Specific Training and Conditioning Program.

Mark has been a certified Personal Trainer for 27+ years and holds multiple training certifications. He is one of only a handful of individuals in the world today to hold current certifications both as a USA Weightlifting Coach and a USPTA Elite Tennis professional.

His major career events are attending Nor-Cal Division conventions (Spanish Bay, Stanford) and the National Conferences at such locations as Las Vegas, La Quinta and Saddlebrook, but the most outstanding highlight thus far was attending one of the week-long teaching courses at the Tennis Teaching Institute in Southern California, conducted by USPTA Master Tennis Pro Don Henson.

CAROLYN STOWE SHANER has been a USPTA member since 1984 and a secondary school tennis coach and clinician for 30+ years in Ambler, PA. She first learned the game from USPTA pro (Joe Weaver) who created a summer tennis clinic for area students. USTA tournaments and team play followed during high school.

She earned her BS in Music Education from West Chester University where she also played on the tennis team. Summer jobs always included teaching tennis at area clubs and community programs. A MEd degree in Education was earned at Arcadia University where she has been an adjunct professor for the last 10 years. As a fulltime music teacher, Carolyn coached for 10 years at Wissahickon High School, proudly sending athletes to State competition and enjoying many league championship seasons. One of her achievements is the creation of a 'feeder' program at the middle school level where she continues to coach both the boys and girls teams. Earning the USPTA "Coach of the Year" award in 2015 was a career highlight.

DAVID SHAMBACH comes from a tennis playing family of six, playing high school tennis in Lockport, NY, and No. 1 singles at Division III Buffalo State College. He became USPTA certified in 1981 by the legendary Spike Gonzales as Dave began his high school English teaching and coaching career in LeRoy, NY. For the past three-plus decades, he has been the head instructor for the Summer Recreation Tennis Program in Lockport, NY. He has served as a volunteer coach for the Lockport High Girls' Tennis Team since their inception in 1982 and the head coach for the boys' team there since 1985. The two squads have earned or shared eight league titles. He served as league boys' tennis chair for many years and was selected as the Niagara Frontier League's Sportsmanship coaching recipient in 2009.

He was honored to receive the USPTA Eastern Division High School Coach of the Year in 2009 when the boys finished unbeaten in league play and sent two players (out of 10 since 1990) to the State Tournament at the US Open. He has served as a Western region advisor in helping nominate candidates for USPTA Eastern awards.

He retired from classroom teaching in 2013 but continues to do home teaching and college tutoring, as well as tennis coaching and instructing. His wife Nancy is an RN. Daughters Jennifer Lozano and Kim Lauta live in Albuquerque, NY.

BEN SHARPLES started playing tennis at age 6 and competing at age 8. He played for the Crossroads High School Boys' Tennis Team, where he was awarded Rookie of the Year as well as Most Valuable Player three years in a row. He finished his junior career ranked in the top 20 in Southern California and went on to play on the U.C. Berkeley Men's Tennis Team for four years.

Ben has been teaching tennis for over 15 years. He has instructed at UCLA, Manhattan Country Club, Jack Kramer Tennis Club, Pacific Palms Tennis Center, Brady Tennis Camp, Bassett-Martin Tennis Camp and he coached the Crossroads High School Boys' Tennis Team. In the summer of 2011, he had the opportunity to coach professional tennis player Zack Fleishman at the US Open.

Ben holds the USPTA's highest rating of Elite Professional.

STEPHEN SHORTRIDGE received a BS from Purdue University in 1974. He has been the head tennis pro at Colonial Country Club in Fort Myers, FL, for the past 10 years after working a various clubs in the Fort Myers area since 1978.

Shortridge has been a USPTA member for over 30 years. His playing highlights include a No. 1 national ranking in 55 singles in 2011 Player of the Year in the Florida Division in 55 singles the same year.

Shortridge is married and has two children.

JEROME SIMON, a graduate of Edinboro University with a PA, in Economics in 1974, has been a USPTA member since that year. He has built, owned and operated indoor tennis clubs in Pennsylvania, Ohio and Indiana. He established Fairview, PA, High School's tennis program, where he coached the no-cut program for 33 years.

At Edinboro he played on multiple PSAC championship teams and won individual conference titles. He is a member of the Edinboro all-time tennis team and Athletic Hall of Fame.

Currently Simon is coach of both the men's and women's tennis teams at Mercyhurst University. Many of his students at the high school and collegiate level have received all-state and all-conference honors.

His wife Lois is a retired teacher. They have two sons, Nicholas (Mercyhurst graduate) and Christopher (John Carroll graduate).

DAVE SIVERTSON, USPTA Master Professional, is a business management professional specializing in the sports club industry and recognized nationally for success in the tennis industry. He has extensive experience in planning, building, marketing, promoting and managing sports/tennis clubs. Dave is recognized for outstanding leadership, astute business judgement and innovative program development. His reputation has earned member and employee confidence through personal relationships and a commitment to service excellence. Dave is the author of "Net Profit: The Business Program for Club Tennis Professionals." Net Profit is a 400-page business program, training manual and reference guide designed to teach tennis professionals how to make their tennis operations more successful. He has spent more than 35 years in the club business, holding positions of Director of Tennis, Director of Sports and General Manager. Sivertson has been affiliated with top clubs including Westwood Country Club in Austin, TX, Mission Hills Country Club in Rancho Mirage, CA, and Braemar Country Club in Tarzana, CA. Sivertson has served as president of the USPTA Texas Division and twice was selected the division's "Tennis Professional of the Year." On the national level, he served on the USPTA Board of Directors for 10 years and was named USPTA's "Tennis Professional of the Year."

SEAN SLOANE has spent 35 years coaching tennis and squash at Williams College (1970–1987) and Haverford College (1997–2015) and earned national rankings as a player of both

sports. He has been an ITF Gold Badge Referee for many Davis Cup matches and the Volvo International/Pilot Pen (1975–1997) and Newport (1990–2015) ATP Tour tennis tournaments. In 1982 Sean coached Chris Mayotte on the ATP Tour.

A 50-year member of USPTA, Sean was President of USPTA/NE (1973-'74) and served on the USPTA Board from 1982–1987. In 1984 he edited *Tennis: A Professional Guide* (The Official USPTA Handbook), attained Master Pro status in 1985 and was named Pro of the Year in 1986.

Sean holds an undergraduate degree from Princeton (1964), an M.A.T. degree from Wesleyan (1966) and a Ph.D. from Umass/Amherst (1982).

A highlight of his coaching career came in 2005 when the College Squash Association renamed its Team Sportsmanship Trophy in his honor as the Sloane Award for Team Sportsmanship.

DARRELL R. SMITH attained a Bachelor of Science (1983) at Illinois State University. He has been a USPTA Elite Pro for 22 years. He was nationally ranked in Junior 16s and 18s, and No. 1 singles and No. 1 doubles at Illinois State University (1979–1983). He has ATP ranking of 616 singles and 727 doubles.

He began his career at the Wilmette (IL) Tennis Club in 1985 as a staff instructor, became the Head Professional in 1990 and the manager in 2006. The Wilmette Tennis Club is an eight-court indoor facility with a membership of 650 and one of the largest lesson programs in the Midwest, with over 1,000 students per session.

Darrell's partner is Barbara Jenkins. He has three adult children and one granddaughter.

DAVID HARLEY SMITH may be best known as a touring coach, but his knowledge and experience in the tennis industry reach far beyond coaching.

David Smith with Henry Lovett

Smith, who won the USPTA National Touring Coach of the Year Award in 1995 for his work with touring pro Chuck Adams, ranked No. 34 on the ATP computer, also has distinguished himself as a player and tennis program director.

This Elite Professional member of USPTA has put in 15 years playing, 25 years teaching and 20 years managing facilities. He has a bachelor of arts in business management from California State University–Long Beach.

David Smith with Alex Sarkissian

Smith has been Director of Tennis at Brentwood Country Club in Los Angeles, CA, for the past 12 years, where he has continued to develop juniors and professionals. To name a few, David coached Alex Sarkissian, Eric Taino, Michael Genender Stanford, Alex Wyman Princeton and Lester Cook. He currently has about 30 juniors that he trains, including Pam Shriver's son, George Lazenby and Henry Lovett.

He previously coached and trained touring pro Tom Shimada. Shimada has been a member of the Japanese Davis Cup squad since 1995 and has been competing in international ATP events. He is ranked in the top 40 in doubles.

Smith served as Director of Tennis at Tustin Hills Racquet Club from 1995 to 1997. He managed all aspects of the tennis program, including the pro shop, two assistant professionals, elite junior program, intra-clubs and all tournament and social functions.

Serving as coach and trainer to ATP touring pro Chuck Adams from age 15 until he achieved a career-high ranking of No. 34 in the world is a career highlight for Smith. Chuck was also the No. 1 junior in the nation in 1988 and '89 and won Kalamazoo in 1989. He had wins over Todd Martin, Mark Rosset, Michael Stitch, Ivan Lendl, Jonas Bjorkman and Thomas Enquist.

Smith held the position of Director of Tennis at La Canada Flintridge Country Club from 1988 to 1991. While there, he was selected as coach for the National Junior Training Centers of Southern California.

From 1987 to 1988, Smith was the personal coach and trainer to junior player Aila Winkler of Zagreb, Croatia, who achieved a world ranking of No. 10. The pair traveled to all international junior events throughout the year, including the Italian Open, Astrid Bowl, French Open, US Open and Wimbledon.

Smith was employed as assistant tennis professional at the Los Angeles Tennis Club from 1984 to 1987.

At California State University-Long Beach, Smith played on the men's varsity tennis team that won the PCAA championship in 1982. He played No. 3 singles and No. 1 doubles and was a Redlands Intercollegiate singles finalist and doubles champ.

He also was the Most Valuable Player on the men's tennis team and league champion at College of the Desert in Palm Desert, CA, where he earned an associate degree.

Smith went on to achieve a USTA Southern California Men's Open Singles ranking of No. 12 in 1984. Subsequent rankings included No. 27 and No. 19. He captured the USPTA national team title at No. 1 singles in 1986 and was a finalist in the USPTA National Team Tournament at No. 1 singles the following year.

Smith received the USPTA Touring Coach of the Year Award for the California Division in 1994, a year before he captured this award on the national level. In 1996, he won the USPTA National Team Title Open and 35 Doubles.

Smith is a member of the Adidas National Advisory Staff and Babolat National Staff.

PAUL SMITH won the Davis Cup Squad for New Zealand in 1979. He was winner of NCAA Indoor Doubles Title in 1983 and on the ATP tour from 1983 – 1985. Paul coached WTT Kansas City Explorers Franchise from 1993 to 2005. From 1994 to 2016 Paul won 15 USTA Gold Ball Doubles Titles and two ITF World Doubles Titles.

SCOTT SMITH has been Executive Director at Vineyard Youth Tennis for the past 10 years. This nonprofit facility on the island of Martha's Vineyard provides free tennis instruction to the youth of the island. Since Scott's arrival, he has been named New England Small Facility Manager of the Year, as well as Regional Pro of the Year and receiving the USPTA's Industry Excellence Award. Scott created the first Flex Tennis League on the island as well as founding the Martha's Vineyard Community Tennis Association and also hosting Tennis Talk with Scott, a local cable television show. Scott started his teaching career at the Nick Bollettieri Tennis Academy in the early 1980s and then branched out into the country club scene. Scott was previously employed as Director of Tennis at the Treasure Island Tennis and Yacht Club, as well as serving 10 years as the Club Manager and Tennis Director at the Cayman Islands Tennis Club in Grand Cayman, where he directed the largest junior program in the Caribbean. In Florida Scott also received a District Pro of the Year Award as well as serving as District President for two different counties. Scott is originally from Knoxville, TN and played collegiate tennis at Walter State College before transferring to the University of Tennessee. Scott is an avid runner, weightlifter and biker.

HELLE SPARRE, born in Copenhagen, Denmark, 1956, had won over 30 National Junior and Adult Championships in Denmark by the age of 18. Helle won the European Singles Championships at age 16 and turned pro in 1973.

Helle reached Round of 32 in Wimbledon 1978, played on WTA tour from 1973–1978 and reached a top singles ranking of 49.

Won US Clay Courts doubles in Indianapolis, 1978 with Swedish partner, Helena Anliot. From 1987–2015, Tennis Pro/Director at Scott Valley Swimming and Tennis Club in Mill Valley, CA.

Author of "Dynamite Doubles – Play Winning Tennis Today!" Published in 2004.

USPTA Elite Pro and member since 1987. USPTA specialty course presenter on Doubles Strategy including positioning, movement and shot selection.

In 1997 won the World Championships Doubles with Cherry Bronson and Bronze in singles. (40's)

Married Karin Lang in 2008 and moved to Arizona in 2015. Daughter Annika was born in 1981 and her children, Annika and Adrian in 2006 and 2009. Roger, the dog, was rescued and adopted in 2013.

TINA SPICHER is a physical education major from Keene State College in Keene, NH. She's been teaching tennis for over 20 years through the Keene Parks and Recreation Department and the Keene Racquet Club, Inc. She is an Elite member of the USPTA, joining in 1996 and mentored by her friend and colleague, Sue Doyle. Tina coached high school tennis, making it to their division finals four years in a row. She initiated and ran a world team tennis league in cooperation with the recreation department.

Tina L. Spicher with young student Teal Borden

Off and on, Tina has participated in USTA league play. In 1997 Tina and her doubles partner, Susan Fratus, were ranked No. 1 in 4.5 women's doubles, USTA New England. In 2001 her women's 4.5 USTA New England team won their districts and sectional tournaments to advance to the nationals held in Tucson, AZ. Tina still teaches and plays tennis in Keene, NH.

JOSEPH "JOE" SPURRIER, born May 29, 1953 in Baltimore, MD, graduated from Andover High School in 1971. He attended Towson University with a B.A. Business Administration (1973–1975) and University of Maryland Baltimore County (UMBC) (1971–1973).

Joe was a No. 1 singles player at Andover High School, UMBC and Towson University. In 1987 was the USTA League Mid-Atlantic National Champions (4.0).

Previously he was ranked top 10 in Maryland Men's singles, doubles, and mixed doubles.

Joe was employed by the Dept. of Defense for 19-1/2 years and Assistant Tennis coach at Andover High School (1979–1982).

Since joining USPTA in 1998, he has been providing private and group lessons on a personal clay hydro-court

Joe and Nannette have been married since 1984 and have four sons: Joseph, Jarrod, Trent and Troy. Troy played No. 2 doubles for St. Mary's College of Maryland Tennis Team 2016.

RON STEEGE, Director of Tennis, Greenwood Athletic and Tennis Club, has been in the tennis industry since 1983. He got his start with the prestigious John Gardiner organization and worked at various locations throughout the country including Keystone, CO, Scottsdale, AZ, Carmel Valley and Cupertino, CA, and Tampa, FL. He has served on numerous boards including the USPTA Intermountain Board, the Colorado Tennis Association Board and is currently the Colorado District rep on the USTA Intermountain Board.

Ron has been a USPTA certification tester since 1996 and named the Intermountain Tester of the year four times. He was Intermountain Pro of the year in 2001 and Facility Manager of the Year in 2006 and 2008. He is an accomplished speaker, having presented at numerous divisional conventions and twice at the USPTA World Conference. Next March Ron will be a guest speaker at the prestigious IHRSA convention in Orlando, FL.

BRETT STEPHENSON was born March 26, 1958. High School "All American" in three sports: Tennis, Swimming and Water Polo. Also, achieved "All American" in collegiate tennis. Nine year World Ranked Professional on the Association of Tennis Professionals (ATP) World Tour. Scored "Elite Professional" on first testing of the U.S. Professional Tennis Association (USPTA) certification exam. Appointed "Wellness" Advisor, NorCal USPTA Executive Committee, and USPTA member for 25+ years. Director

of Tennis/Head Tennis Professional for over two decades, coaching tennis for 42+ years and playing tennis for 50+ years. Coached state, sectional, national and world ranked players. Brought over 2,500 new players to the game of tennis. Other "long time" qualified skills (over 25 years): personal trainer, massage therapist, nutritionist, yoga instructor, lifestyle coach, vegetarian since 1978, and vegan since 1982. In 2006 Founder and Owner of Executive Wellness Services (EWS). EWS provides tennis, massage, personal training, yoga, meditation, and nutrition to corporations and private clients in the San Francisco Bay Area.

ROBERT STERK earned a B.S. in College Business Administration from University of the Pacific (1982) and Fifth Year Teaching Credential K-12 Business Education and Mathematics (1989).

Robert Sterk presents USPTA Intermountain Section College Coach of the Year Award to BSU coach Greg Patton.

Robert held a NTRP rating of 5.0 from 1982 to 2008. He was a Gold Ball Winner in USTA National Mixed 35s in 1999, and was Fourth Place Doubles in USTA National Men's 55s Indoors 2015

Robert has been a Professional with the USPTA since 1989, Professional 1 level and currently Elite level.

He has been Community/Grassroots teaching professional for Idaho (Treasure Valley) since 1995. Also working with the Idaho Tennis Association in varying positions – Senior and JTT league coordinator, Tennis 101 and TiE Instructor. Robert is a Junior Competition Committee member and participant in the 2.5 Incentive program. He has been Tournament Director for USTA National Men's 55 Indoors in Boise, ID, since 2007 and Tournament Director for over 100 other tournaments since 2001. As High School Head Coach at Eagle H.S. (2013 – 2015) led the High School Girls State Champion in 2015. Robert is a Wilson Team Advisory Staff member since 2009, previously certified as a USTA Official and the PTR and USPTA Idaho State Representative since 2010.

PAMELA STEWART was a Jr. Wightman Cup teammate of sister Pat Stewart and future Indianapolis tennis mogul Barbara Wynne. Pam (aka Billie Marie), ranked No. 3 in U.S. 16-and-under, did the adult circuit against the likes of Althea Gibson. Taught in NYC where she gave separate lessons to Oscar Hammerstein and Richard Rogers. She was pro and tennis director at the world's largest Jewish resort, The Concord Hotel in Kiamesha, NY. At the Doral Country Club she was the lone pro at Doral-on-the-Beach while her husband and fellow USPTA member, Edwin Kerr, manned the pro shop and gave lessons at the club. Then to The Fenway Golf Club in Scarsdale, NY, and to the famed Bishop's Lodge Santa Fe, NM. Her interactions with celebrities, including movie stars, NFL, players and the Kennedy clan provide good reading in the book "Tennis Saves: Stewart Orphans Take World by Racket," available on Amazon.

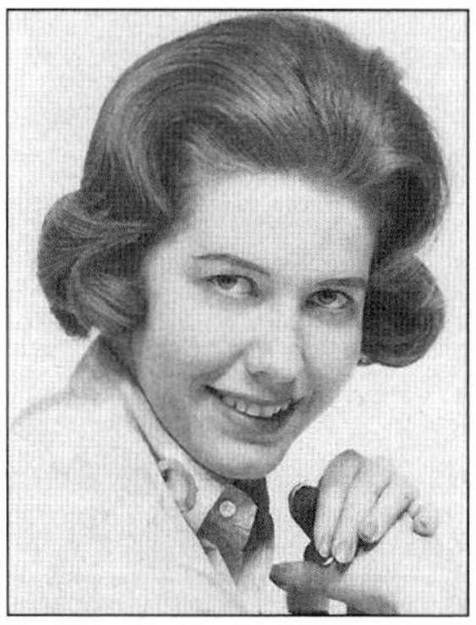

PATRICIA ANN STEWART-EDRICH-BELLIN was born in Indianapolis, IN, on Aug. 19, 1934. She played in the US Grass Court Championships from 1950 to 1958. Pat teamed with East German ace Eva Johannes to win the Polish Doubles Championship in 1959 in Katowitz, Poland. From 1959 to 1963, she played in the Italian Open, the French Open, and Wimbledon where she lost in quarter-finals of mixed doubles with Willie "Pato" Alvarez to Jeanne Arth and Bob Howe. She married John Hugh Edrich in September 1961. He was opening batsman at the Surrey County Cricket Club. Pat played 15 times at Forest Hills from 1951 to 1970. She taught tennis in New York City from 1969 to 1977. She has lived in San Diego since 1977. She is an honorary member of the Rancho Valencia Resort since 1991 as well as an honorary member of the Morgan Run Resort.

JACK STEYN, Tennis Director USPTA Elite Professional, was born in South Africa started his tennis teaching career in London, England.

Jack holds USPTA, LTA and USPTR teaching qualifications.

He has been head tennis professional in London, Miami and Bradenton, FL, and tennis director for Bradenton Country Club.

Jack was USPTA Florida President of District Eight for four years, USPTA District Eight Pro of the Year in 2012 and USPTA District President of the Year for the Florida Division in 2013.

He has competed in Wimbledon qualifying rounds in both singles and doubles. Jack has trained national and international juniors, college and ITF professional players.

In 2015, he was named the 40 and under USPTA national mixed player of the year.

Jack has ranked in the top five both singles and doubles in Florida for numerous years. He is certified in sports massage, Pilates, and has a diploma in sports psychology.

JIM STOCKER celebrates 42 years as a USPTA professional. Prior to turning pro, he was a highly ranked junior player in Chicago and the Midwest Section. He continued his tennis career at the University of Redlands, graduating in 1972 with a BS in Business.

From 1973–1980 he held Head Tennis Pro positions in Illinois and Tennessee. In 1980–1982 he established and directed the Nashville Junior Development Program in Nashville, TN.

In 1982 he returned to his hometown Hinsdale, IL, and served as Vice President of Stocker Hinge Mfg. Co., Brookfield, IL. Retiring in 2004 and moving to Amelia Island opened opportunities to coach local youth. In 2012–2014 he was head coach of the boys varsity tennis team, Episcopal School of Jacksonville, FL.

Jim is married 40 years to his wife Annette and they have one son, Jay.

DAN STOVER, born in Dallas, TX, grew up and attended the John Newcomb/Owen Davidson tennis academy. After a successful junior tennis career he played for the Univ. of Texas where he received such honors as NCAA Freshman of the Year and Second Team All Conference. Dan played for two seasons for the Longhorns before leaving on the pro tour where he received a career high finishing in the top 800 in the world. During this time Dan also had the benefit of coaching and playing with many world-class athletes finally ending him in a position in Timaru, New Zealand, where he was the director of junior tennis at the ASB Regional Tennis Facility and earned the privilege to participate in the coaching of the New Zealand Davis Cup team. Upon arriving back, Dan was pleased to call Florida home where he still mentors some of the county's top juniors and participate in many successful tennis programs such as the Jupiter Bay Tennis Club, PGA National Resort and Spa, Jupiter Country Club and now very pleased to call Willoughby Golf Club his home. He still loves to play competitive tennis and continues to finish top five in the country, has represented the U.S. in team competition and is on the Babalot Competition Team.

JASON STRONG - Since September of 1987, when Jason first saw that US Open final, his passion for this game has been growing. He loves the pro tour and especially seeing the newcomers there. He has been a fantastic high-energy coach since 1991. Whether it's adult group lessons, quality private lesson time with a USTA or high school junior, or cardio tennis, Jason can do it all pretty well. He is the "pied piper" of QuickStart level players as well. Kids love him. He has a great eye for stroke analysis and has several years director-of-tennis experience at a major metro NY tennis club. Full racquet stringing and pro shop/retail capabilities as well. Jason loves his family, his life and this great game. Oh, and Star Wars. May the force be with you!

JESSICA "JESS" SWANSON, graduated in 2011 from Mason High School, Mason, MI, and attended three years at Ferris State University Big Rapids, MI where she studied Professional Tennis Management and Marketing.

"Jess" spent two years playing varsity tennis and one year playing club tennis. Her club tennis team made it to the nationals in 2014. She was the Award recipient of the Wilson Most Dedicated and Most Improved Tennis Player in 2013 for the PTM Program.

She interned for three summers at the Little Harbor Club in Harbor Springs, MI (2013–2015). "Jess" landed her dream job at the Windsor Club in Vero Beach, FL, as a Tennis Professional in 2014-present and achieved USPTA certification in 2014. She joined the USPTA Florida U30 group in 2014-present and was awarded the USPTA Florida Division U30 Professional of the Year. "Jess" began teaching for the Mardy Fish Children's Foundation in 2014-present.

"Jess" is the eldest of three children and the only girl of Jennifer and Brady Harrington. Brothers are Jordan (19, active military serving in the U.S. Army) and Peyton (15). Her family is from Potterville, MI.

R.J. TESSIER, Master Professional, is the Tennis and Athletic Director at Dragon Ridge Country Club in Nevada. He was Director of Certification for the USPTA, and served as host of the award-winning "On Court with USPTA" on the Tennis Channel. As a speaker he presented workshops worldwide.

R.J. was the Professional Tennis Management Director at Ferris State University in Michigan and was the Racquet Sports Director at Bloomfield Open Hunt Club in Michigan, G.M. of the Club at Crested Butte, CO, and Director at the prestigious Boca Raton Country Club in Florida.

Tessier is a five-time recipient of the USPTA Tester of the Year, Southern Professional of the Year, two-time South Carolina Professional of the Year, and Midwest Professional of the Year.

With extensive coaching for the University of South Carolina, Coastal Campus he acted as captain of the USTA 18 Davis Cup squad representing the Midwest. He earned a degree from Western State College, Colorado. He is the founder/CEO of Resorts Consulting Internationale.

ART THOMSON (Feb. 10, 1947 – Dec. 19, 2015), a Colorado native, competed for George Washington High School. Graduating from University of Colorado-Boulder, at No. 1 singles position, finished third in the Big 8 Conference. Art captured the 1981 Colorado State Open singles title at age 34, holds three major Colorado open doubles titles – two Denver City Open crowns (1971 and 1972) and one Intermountain Championships (1973). He was runner up at the Denver City Open twice (1970 and 1973). Over a 30-year period, Art was named USPTA Intermountain Player of the Year in various age brackets, between 35–65. Art amassed 23 "triple titles" (singles, doubles and mixed) as well as numerous individual singles and doubles titles. In 1993, Art was named USPTA National 45+ Singles Player of the Year. In 2014, he was a Colorado Tennis Hall of Fame inductee. During his 50+ years as a USPTA Elite Professional he worked at Arapahoe Tennis Club, Mount Vernon Country Club, Vail Racquet Club and was owner/director for Loves Acre in Colorado. Art has shared his love and passion for the game of tennis with countless students.

MARK THOMSON was introduced to tennis at age 13 via the NJTL program and played tennis for George Washington H.S. in Philadelphia where he earned a Varsity letter and graduated in 1981. He received his USPTA Certification in 1982 and taught part time at several tennis clubs in the Philadelphia area while attending college.

In 1987 Mark earned a BBA from Temple University. That same year he accepted the position of Head Tennis Professional at Upper Dublin Tennis Club in Ambler, PA.

In 1988 Mark appeared in a Prince Manufacturing promotional video filmed at the Philadelphia Cricket Club, promoting the new Prince "Response" tennis racquet.

Mark currently works in the IT industry, coaches part time and competes in USTA Tournaments. He finished 2015 ranked No. 2 in the 50 and over Singles USTA Middle States Section. Married 24 years to wife Karyn and blessed with four sons who all play tennis recreationally.

HENRY TIBERIO was born in 1922, graduated from Wakefield High (class of 1940), attained a B.A. at Duke University (1948) and a master's degree (Child Welfare, Major) at Boston University.

Henry registered as a Teaching Pro in 1974. He has continued teaching and coaching from 1974 to the present.

From 1979–2009, Henry has been USTA New England No. 1 Singles 16 times and No. 1 Doubles 21 times. He won USTA National No. 1 Singles (grass court) and Doubles in 2012, 2013 and 2014.

Henry has four children, four grandchildren and five great-grandchildren.

NANCY TIELKE is the owner of the Rocking T Tennis Ranch in Needville, TX. She has been an active Elite Tennis Professional with USPTA for 20+ years. Nancy was the recipient of the Texas Proud Award in 2007 for her commitment to tennis at the community level, when she was an independent contractor for over 20 years at the Meadowcreek Racquet Club in Missouri City, TX. In 2011 at the World Conference on Tennis, she was the recipient of the Merit Award for 10 years of Continuing-Education Participation with over 90 hours of training. Nancy was the proud recipient of the Texas Star Award for 2014, honored for her commitment to 'grassroots' tennis in her rural farming community. In 2015, the Small Facility Tennis Manager Award was bestowed upon Nancy, reflecting her dedication to tennis as a USPTA professional.

JIM TIERNEY is Tennis Centers Administrator for the City of Boca Raton, FL. Jim has dedicated his career to public tennis for 30+ years. Since 2000, he has overseen the direction of the Boca Raton Tennis Center, Patch Reef Tennis Center, and the Swim and Racquet Center (53 total courts). Under his leadership the City of Boca Raton was selected "2014 USTA Florida Member Organization of the Year." The award's criteria included diverse and inclusive programming, contributions to the community and USTA involvement. Additionally, each center has individually been named "USTA Outstanding Facility of the Year." Jim became an advocate of wheelchair tennis in 2001 when he was named Site Manager of the Florida Open International Wheelchair Championships, for years the world's largest wheelchair tournament. Currently he organizes and hosts two annual wheelchair tournaments and he conducts a free weekly wheelchair clinic at Patch Reef Tennis Center. His professional associations include: USPTA, PRT, and USRSA – Master Racquet Technician and Regional Tester. A lifelong enthusiast of the game, Jim was half of a No. 1 doubles team in Florida and he set a world record by playing tennis for 110 consecutive hours while raising $25,000 for Cystic Fibrosis. Jim is grateful for the opportunities tennis has afforded him and strives to "play" it forward. He gives back to the game by volunteering and has served on the following USTA Florida committees: Community Outreach, Diversity, Nominating, and Volunteer.

JAMES R. TINDER maintains his historical Elite Pro status as a USPTA member with private lessons and an annual lesson demonstration for children at one of the largest tournaments in the world, the Miami Open. His forte is based around the "cosmetics of tennis."

Jim was introduced to tennis as a high school freshman by his parents. He joined the team and played No. 1 for Thomas Jefferson in Pittsburgh.

Later, he played "left out" at Penn State under the famous Coach Holmes. "Left out" is the individual who the walk-ons play, but then after defeating the walk-ons, would lose to the scholarship team. Lol! Penn State won two Eastern and one Atlantic 10 Championship while in attendance.

Professionally, Jim operates as a fractional CFO and business consultant. His specialty includes the migration of Family.Inc to Corporate.Inc. The resulting business is an entity that is prepared for improved profits, ownership transitions, as well as mergers, acquisitions or a total exit via a competitive bid sale.

Jim started teaching tennis at children camps within a year of learning the game. The summer camp teaching format supported Jim throughout high school and college. He learned the "cosmetics of tennis" through supporting the specific needs and dreams of the private lesson student.

KATHLEEN TORCH has been involved in tennis since adolescence, playing at Russell Park, Carbondale, PA. As there was no girls' team, she played on the boys' tennis team in high school. After playing many singles, doubles and attending camps, Marywood College offered her a full four year tennis scholarship. During her college years, she taught tennis to adolescents and adults.

Kathleen received a Bachelor of Arts Degree in Physical Education from Sonoma State University, Rohnert Park, CA, which opened many doors because she taught tennis at camps, parks, resorts and clubs.

Kathleen is a USTA Life Member and USPTA certified instructor for 22 years. She was Recreational Coach 2015 and 2014 USPTR.

She has taught tennis at several locations in Pennsylvania, Florida and California.

Kathleen was elated to attend a USPTA Conference at Stanford University. It was exceptional tennis at the Stanford Tennis Stadium. This event was the highlight of her tennis career.

DRU TORIAN was a member of the 1998 Tyler Jr. National Champs Women's Team, No. 4 in Women's Open for 2000–2001, 2014 Houston Open Women's 35 Singles winner and 2012 Bronze Ball Winnter in doubles at National 30s hard courts in Austin, TX.

Dru has been a USPTA member since 2001. She taught at several clubs and varsity tennis in Illinois, 2001–2001. She is currently assistant pro at a club at New Territory and Riverstone, both located in Sugarland, TX. Dru was the 2008 USPTA Women's Open Player of the Year.

LESLIE TRACY graduated from Corona del Sol High School in 1986 and attained a Bachelor of Science in Business Administration from University of the Pacific (1990). She competed in the SWTA section and nationally throughout the juniors. She played No. 1 and No. 2 singles for University of the Pacific with the highest national ranking, being No. 6 in doubles her senior year. She also qualified for the NCAA Championships in doubles in 1990.

Leslie was Associate Pro and Head Professional at the Carmel Valley Racquet Club from 1990–1996. She won a Golden Slam (USTA National Indoors, grass courts, clay courts and hard courts) in the Super Senior Mother Daughter (playing with her mom) in 2013.

She currently teaches (Associate Pro) at the Spanish Bay Club and The Beach and Tennis Club in Pebble Beach, CA.

Leslie and Jason married in 1991. Daughter Lauren was born in 1998 and son Scott was born in 2000.

ROY TRAFALSKI is the Co-founder and Executive Director of the DhhEAF Tennis Program.

In the history of the sport, DhhEAF is the only program in America which is specifically dedicated to teaching life's lessons to hearing impaired youth through tennis. He is a former university coach, nationally ranked senior tournament player, and in 2005 was the Coach of the USA Deaflympic Tennis Team where competition was held in Melbourne, Australia. His essays about teaching tennis to people who have hearing challenges have been translated and internationally distributed.

QUYNH TRAN has been an USPTA member since 2011. He has been Director of Tennis at Joel Ross Tennis Summer Camp in Kent, CT, since 2004 and Head Tennis Coach of Becamex Binh Duong Tennis Federation since 2007. As Director of Tennis of Joel Ross Summer Camp, he evaluates players, organizes ladder matches, runs single and doubles tournaments, manages other tennis instructors during teaching time and makes sure drills are run effectively and correctly for kids from 12 to 18 years old. As Head Tennis Coach of Becamex Binh Duong Tennis Federation, he coaches top junior tennis players in Vietnam and travels with them to play national tennis tournaments, ITF tours, ATP tours and Davis Cup. Quynh was also a Captain of Vietnam Men's Tennis Team to play Davis Cup in 2012. He is currently a Head Coach at Johnny Allen Tennis Academy. Quynh's biggest achievement is to coach Ly Hoang Nam to become the Vietnam Champion at age 15 in 2011, the youngest champion of Vietnam ever. Nam was also ranked 11 in ITF Junior on Aug. 31, 2015, and Nam won Wimbledon's Junior Doubles in 2015. Quynh also coached Thuy Dung Nguyen, who became Women's Single Champion in Vietnam in 2006–2009 and was ranked 612 in WTA. Quynh studied and played at Independent Community Colleges in Kansas in 2003–2004. He was Men's Singles Champion of Vietnam in 1994,1997,1998,1999, 2000. He played against Paradorn Srichaphan, ranked 10 in ATP at that time, at SEA Games in 1999.

BRENDON TRAVIS, owner B. Travis Tennis and Stringing. Has been in the tennis industry for 25+ years. He's been a teaching pro for almost 20-years and has been a member of the U.S. Professional Tennis Association (USPTA) Southern and Mid-Atlantic Division. He's also a Registró Profesional de Tenis (RPT – España Tenis Federación) Sanchez-Casal Tenis Academia. Travis has been a tennis coach since 1997 to present. He's coached at the high school level and all three of the National Collegiate Athletic Association (NCAA) Divisions, Div-I, Div-II and Div-III.

After a long break from competitive tennis, but a long time member of the U.S. Tennis Association (USTA), Travis got back into the swing of things as a USTA coach and player in 2009. Since then, he's help guide five teams to the USTA National Championships as a coach and was a participant at the 2013 USTA 40+ Men's National Championships at Indian Wells, CA.

He's been an active teaching pro and has taught for three years for The Columbia Association, nine years at Baltimore Fitness and Tennis and almost 20 years as the owner of B. Travis Tennis and Stringing. He's owned a tennis facility in Atlantic Beach, NC—Island Beach Racquet Club—and in 2011 became a Master Racquet Technician (MRT) with the U.S. Racquet Stringers Association (USRSA) and is a USRSA Official String Play Tester. That same year, he was the winner of the 2011 World's Fastest Stringer Competition, sponsored by Prince. Travis is a HEAD Penn Advisory Staff and Gamma String Advisory Staff member.

KEVIN TUFT, USPTA Elite Professional and CPA (Certified Public Accountant), has 15-plus years experience working as tennis professional and tax consultant (in banking and at Big Four accounting firm).

He was assistant tennis professional at the Glen View Club in Golf, IL, and the Onwentsia Club in Lake Forest, IL, which were ranked among the top 10 country clubs in the U.S. by *Business Week* magazine.

Kevin was head tennis instructor at Valley Lo Sports Country Club in Glenview, IL, and also tennis instructor at a junior college.

He was ranked in the top five in the men's open division of the Chicago District Tennis Association for five years.

Kevin has competed in professional tennis tournaments in Texas and Arkansas and played club tennis in Europe (Germany).

He was a member of nationally-ranked University of Arkansas tennis team, led high school team to the state championships three years, and also won national championship in Lutheran league church basketball.

Kevin holds a Bachelor of Science Degree in Business Administration, with a major in Accounting.

OLEG TUMASOV was born in Baku, Azerbaijan, in the former USSR. At the age of 9, he joined the Burevstnik Tennis Club in Baku, Azerbaijan. His tennis instructor was Oleg Speridonov, who was one of the best tennis players in the world. At the age of 13, Oleg was the national champion of Azerbaijan in both singles and doubles. Shortly thereafter, he was selected to participate in a professional tennis club, where he was able to interact and play with the best tennis players in the USSR. Oleg learned a lot from USSR champions Olga Merzova Zverev and Evgeniya Bereecova. From 1987 to 1989, he served in the Chemical Special Forces in the Nagorno-Karabakh Region in the USSR. In 1991, Oleg and family emigrated to the U.S. They left the night of the coup in August 1991. He continued playing tennis in the U.S. From 1999 to 2001, Oleg was a coach at the Daily City Tennis and Golf Club in Daily City, CA. From 2006 to 2008, he was a tennis coach at the Kim Grant Tennis Academy in Palo Alto, CA. From 2006 to the present time, Oleg is a tennis coach for son, Jonathan Tumasov, and other members of his community in Mountain View, CA. he owns an Art Gallery in Mountain View, CA, Tumasov Fine Art Studio.

LYNETTE TUREK, now 65, knows her most important Life Decisions were made at age 7: accepting JESUS CHRIST as Lord and Saviour, and allowing HIM to steer her into tennis, instead of other sports where she was also talented.

After playing Summer Jr. Tournaments, High School Varsity and at Trinity University, Lynette became certified with USPTA as Elite Professional in 1973. She served two years as Chairman of Texas Nominating Committee. In Dallas, she served as Brookhollow Country Club Assistant Professional, Maureen Connolly Brinker Tennis Foundation Tournament Director and Coach, and lead organizer for several "Texas Tennis Days." In Houston, she served as Brae-Burn Country Club Head Professional and Westwood Country Club Assistant Professional. As Head Pro at Westside Family YMCA for seven years, she built a nine-student program into 60+ junior and adult students each six-week session, expanding it to include summer tennis camps. She is Life Member of USTA.

As Certified USTA Clinician, Houston Tennis Association gave her "Sampson Memorial Award" for Outstanding Work with Junior Tennis, for starting "USTA Schools Program: Motivational Assemblies" in Houston-area schools.

In 1996 she moved to Lake Jackson, serving as Teaching Professional at Brazoswood Tennis Camp, Lake Jackson Intermediate School Assistant Tennis Coach, volunteer for LJI Tennis Team Try-outs, volunteer Site Director for Brazoswood High School Tournaments, Brazosport Christian School Tennis Coach, and now Tennis Coach for Our Lady Queen of Peace School in Lake Jackson.

From 2004 forward, she founded and serves as Tournament Director for four "MUDDY" Turek Memorial Doubles Tennis Tournaments per year, which honor her Mother ("MUDDY") who died from leukemia. Proceeds benefit Leukemia Society, local community needs, and Brazoswood High School Team. Lynette was named Brazoswood Tennis Booster Club - 2006 Honoree of the Year.

From 2012 to 2014, Lynette volunteered on Lake Jackson Parks and Rec Board, raising and donating her own personal funds to resurface and re-fence two city courts. This added to her earlier fund raising for intermediate school tennis court repair and resurfacing the high school courts.

Being self-employed for the last 20 years in Lake Jackson with only JESUS as her CEO, Lynette has taught a full load of private lessons, after-school camps and summer tennis camps. She also runs monthly game days and tournaments, and enjoys stringing rackets for her students. Her mission has always been to "Teach Tennis so her students can achieve their own physical, emotional, and spiritual health. And to use this tennis to build the Kingdom for her Lord, JESUS CHRIST." A wise man once said, "Do what you love and you will never work a day in your life." Lynette adds: "Do all this for GOD's Glory and you will never want for anything in your life." Lynette's personal goal is to keep teaching as she does now…running and playing against her students, until she is 84. We will see what JESUS will do with this desire of her heart, which HE put there in the first place.

JIM TURLEY – Teaching pro at Texarkana College in Texarkana, TX, now teaches where he learned to play the great game of tennis 39 years earlier. Playing in high school and college helped spark a lifelong love for playing that turned into teaching and developing other players. Started teaching tennis on a part-time basis 26 years ago helping develop junior tennis players.

In the past coached high school teams, tennis in several states in a church mission field as well as junior programs and players. Currently working at Texarkana College and with Arkansas Tennis Association as an area tennis coordinator for the USTA as well as running 10 under, Jr. programs, USTA leagues and college classes. Glad to be a part of the USPTA organization!

BILL TYM has been committed and dedicated to tennis for more than half a century. During this time he has made a positive impact throughout the U.S. and internationally as a player, coach, and administrator.

As a player he was a Southeastern Conference Champion at the University of Florida where he earned All-American honors and was inducted into the Gators Athletic Hall of Fame. He then competed on the world circuit (1965-70), winning 10 national/international championships. He has been ranked No. 1 in various age divisions by the USPTA and the USTA. He represented the U.S. in the Inaugural Fred Perry Cup.

As a coach, Bill has enjoyed success in developing home grown champions at the junior, interscholastic, intercollegiate, and professional levels of play. Bill is a former coach at the University of Tennessee (Chattanooga) and

Vanderbilt University. He also coached the Indonesian Davis Cup Team.

As an administrator, Bill served as Executive Director and President of the USPTA. He has also owned and operated several tennis clubs.

Bill has been recognized for his accomplishments in tennis by the USPTA/USTA many times, but his proudest moments came when he received the USPTA Lifetime Achievement Award in 2002 and was honored as a Grand Inductee into the USPTA Hall of Fame in 2007.

JEFF UNGER, a member of the USPTA since 1971, he was a four-year member and captain of the varsity tennis team at the University of Wisconsin, where he earned a bachelor's degree (history). He earned a master's in urban affairs at UW-Milwaukee. He was an assistant professional at South Shore Racquet Club, Lake Shore Club, North River Racquet Club and Le Club, all in Milwaukee. He was the head pro at Brynwood Country Club in Milwaukee, the director of the Milwaukee YMCA's summer tennis program and of the Nicolet High School summer tennis program in Glendale, WI. He was a journalist for United Press International in Milwaukee and Chicago, The Kansas City Star, and the Dallas Times Herald and, for 23 years, the director of the news service at the University of Illinois, where he has taught reporting in the journalism department. He is helping coach the tennis teams at Urbana High School in Illinois.

FRANK VALERIO is a USPTR/USPTA Elite Pro. He has coached at Trinity Christian Academy with two State Championships. Frank has coached for 18 years at Cooper Fitness Center in Dallas, TX, as well as at University of Dallas and East Texas Baptist University and Fritz Tennis Club. Frank has played in USTA tournaments through the years and at this time he is coaching at Trinity Christian Academy in Dallas, TX, and at Spring Creek Tennis Club in Richardson, TX.

TOM VAN DE HEY retired after 40 years as certified tennis professional. He now serves as the Executive Director of USPTA Intermountain Division.

During his career, he served on USTA Colorado Tennis Association Board of Directors and the USTA Intermountain for a combined 20 years. He was named as Volunteer of The Year by both organizations. He also received the Bud Robineau Award for Outstanding Contributions to Colorado Tennis.

Much of his focus over the years was on adult league tennis. His work in the verification program spanned some 20 years. He served on the National NTRP Advisory Committee, the USTA National League Committee (vice-chair) for six years each. In semi retirement, Tom continues to serve on USTA committees at the district and sectional levels and volunteers frequently.

VANCE VANPELT II grew up in Osborne, KS, where he first started his tennis career. He became the first player in school history to qualify for state all four years, winning regionals three straight years and finishing in the top four in the state tournament each of those years.

Vance attended Bethel College (KS) and was captain of a team that went to Nationals three times while finishing ranked in the top 20. He left BC with the third most wins in the program's history and was a two-time unanimous all-conference selection. Vance returned to BC in 2009 to be inducted into the Bethel College Athletics Hall of Fame.

As a player, in 2004, he won the Kansas Player of the Year Award. As a coach, he has won the Coach of the Year Awards for the Kansas Girls, Kansas Boys, Overall, and the Midwest Sectional Divisions. In 2010, he was selected the Missouri Valley USPTA Coach of the Year award, and later that year was honored as the USPTA National Coach of the Year. Since 2014, Vance has been a Missouri Valley Sectional Coach and a National Zonal Coach.

Vance is a USPTA Elite Professional who is currently head pro at the Jayhawk Tennis Center. He is USPTA certified in Competitive Player Development and holds a Sports Science degree and High Performance Coach certification from the USTA.

Vance resides in Lawrence with his wife Sommer and three children (all very active tennis players) Keegan, Kinley and Kale.

MARK VAN ORNUM has been teaching tennis for almost 30 years. He started as a helper at the age of 16, helping to teach junior clinics at Sierra Sport and Racquet Club in Fresno, CA.

He has continued to teach the game year round since that time and has gone on to working as a tennis pro at different clubs, a tennis director at residential camps, a high school tennis coach and a coach for the USTA's Player Development Program.

He is a former nationally ranked college tennis player, in NCAA Division II, at the University of California, Riverside and state ranked community college tennis player at Fresno City College.

He has a B.A. in Liberal Studies from the University of California, Riverside and a Teaching Credential from National University.

He lives in Fresno, CA, and is a self-employed tennis professional.

DUSAN VEMIC - Novak Djokovic was one of the first players Dusan has worked with (Andrea Petkovic and Ksenia Pervak, Pilip Krajinovic) after beginning his professional career.

Dusan's career spanned 17 years on the ATP World tour. He was a participant in the XXVII Olympic Games in Sydney (Yugoslavian national team). He was in two Grand Slam semi-

Coach Dusan Vemic (right) and physiotherapist Miljan Amanovic watch Novak Djokovic compete in the 2016 Miami Open. Djokovic won the tournament without dropping a set.

finals (Roland Garros 2008, Australian Open 2010), one quarterfinals US Open, 2008 and a final 16 at Wimbledon.

He was a Davis Cup member of Yugoslavia (Serbia) for 10 years, played 18 ties with a record of 20 wins and nine losses.

Dusan transitioned to coaching in 2011. During this time he has joined the Serbian Davis Cup team as a coach since 2013 and has become a consultant and adviser/mentor for countless top ranked junior ETA and pro tour ITF players.

ANDY VENTRESS says it all started when he was 11 years old. His uncle gave him an Ellsworth Vine autographed Wilson tennis racquet strung in gut. Andy thought this racquet was the greatest gift ever! Immediately, he began frequently making trips to Community Park in Effingham, IL, to practice his serve with balls lost by other players. (He kept the balls in a pillow case.) One accomplished player who helped him with some tips was the father of one of his friends. Andy's hero at that time was Poncho Gonzales.

His first love at that time was football, which greatly pleased his father, who played independent football back in the '30s and '40s. One was considered odd at that time if he played tennis. Andy played football as a corner and safety in high school and college at Eastern Illinois University, long before Tony Romo. While in college Andy admired many of his fraternity brothers who played on the EIU tennis team at the time.

After college graduation his interest turned fulltime to tennis after coaching football at the high school level for two years. Andy coached tennis at the high school level, both boys and girls, and taught mathematics. He played tournaments and earned some singles, doubles, and mixed doubles rankings in the Chicago District and Midwest USTA. The coaching was enjoyable and motivated him to become a teaching professional. In 1975 Andy, along with his wife, passed the USPTA test to become a certified USPTA professional under the sponsorship of Fernando Velasco. His coaching also included the high school coaching of daughter, Jody, who played at Ferris State University, earning her degree in Professional Tennis Management. She became a USPTA teaching professional in California, and, along with her mother and Andy, at some Chicago area tennis clubs, including Olympia Fields Country Club and Chicago's Beverly Tennis Club. Now has three grandsons who are also accomplished tennis players.

Andy's personal career in tennis includes certified pro status with the USPTA and PTR, membership in USRSA, and PTR 10 and Under instructor certification. At his present age of 71, his interest has turned to managing and directing numerous successful 10 and Under group lessons with SSTA, South Suburban Tennis Academy, Inc., of which he serves as president. SSTA has planned and conducted tennis programs in the Chicago area for the past 40-plus years at many tennis clubs, facilities and park districts.

Some of his service to the sport of tennis includes speaking at numerous USPTA conferences, including the USTA Teachers' Conference in conjunction with the US Tennis Open dealing with the use of the digital camera to teach tennis. One specific use of the digital camera he demonstrated was the dispelling of certain tennis myths, such as both feet touch the court at the same time with the completion of a split step.

All in all, Andy can say that, along with solving math problems, tennis has become his life interest.

JOHN VERDE, born July 19, 1947, in Beaumont, TX, graduated from Hardin-Jefferson High School in 1965, Sour Lake, TX. He graduated in 1970 from Lamar University, Beaumont, TX, with a B.S.

John was a member of the 1965 Class A Texas High School State Champs and a four-year letterman at Lamar University.

He is a Master Pro, (initial class) USPTA Member for 45 years. John has served on national, state and local committees. He is a professional speaker for USPTA divisional events and national conventions.

John has been with Strokemaster Tennis Co. since 1973. The company fabricates and installs custom windscreens to tennis clubs, horse and cattle ranches, private homes, industrial and other applications. Screens are used as a vision barrier, weather protection and privacy for people, livestock and equipment.

John's wife, Diane Verde, is the food service director - Grand Prairie ISD (30 years), active in USTA leagues and local tournaments. A son, Dr. Michael Verde, Ph.D., is founder of Memory Bridge Alzheimer Foundation.

RICHARD VERZAAL, Member, graduated from John T. Hoggard High School in 1969. He graduated from the University of North Carolina, Wilmington/Chapel Hill.

He is currently Tennis Director at Querbes Tennis Center, Shreveport, LA. Previously he was Tennis Director, City of Boynton Beach, Boynton Beach, FL, and Director of Tennis, Indian Spring Country Club, Boynton Beach, FL.

Richard was President, USPTA Florida Division (1983–1985), Louisiana Pro of the Year 2001 and 2002, Southern Pro of the Year 2002, a USTA Graduate of High Performance Program and has completed Sports Science 1 and 2.

Richard is past president of the USTA Community Tennis Association—Northwest Louisiana.

Richard and Kathy Verzaal have been married 25 years. Their son, Robert Verzaal, is a Top 15 US Junior Player, who played and graduated from Baylor University.

ALBERT VIAL, USPTA Certified Teaching Pro, has been a coach, mentor and friend to players of all ages and abilities wanting to take their tennis game to the next level since 1990.

He has helped many kids and adults through positive coaching, love and enthusiasm of the game to build self-confidence, culture a foundation of good sportsmanship and the value of effort, all while having fun!

He was a teaching pro at the Peninsula Tennis Club at Burlingame, CA under RS Tennis Academy since 1999–2013 and academy head pro 2009–2013.

In 2014, he trained and coached two singles women players to become No. 1 in Northern California in 4.0 and 4.5 level. He is currently an independent instructor.

DR. MARTIN VINOKUR founded Tennis: Europe in 1973, which takes junior tennis players to compete in international tournaments in Europe and on the West Coast. In the years since then, he has taken some 5,400 teenagers to 1,700 tournaments in 26 countries. Twenty-five of them have later gone on to the pro tour and hundreds have played college tennis.

Dr. Martin Vinokur at Trafalgar Square in London, 2014

A USPTA Elite Pro since 1964, he spent 10 years as New York State School Tennis Coordinator and coached boys' and girls' teams for 22 years. His Rye, New York girls' teams won four consecutive league titles and earned him "Coach of the Year" honors from his conference and the USPTA Eastern Division.

He received his master's in history from Columbia and his doctorate in political science from The American University. As an undergraduate, he played college tennis for Clark University in Massachusetts. He taught high school history in Plainview, NY, and is a certified guidance counselor.

LANCE VODICKA began playing tennis at 2-1/2, played his first tournament at the age of 7. He qualified from the St. Louis District for Missouri Valley Sectional competition at the age of 8. Represented the St. Louis District in sectional, zonal and national competition throughout his teen years from 1990–2001. He garnered numerous junior tournament titles and experienced many great moments in junior tennis!

In 2006, he began playing professional tennis overseas. His professional tennis journey has taken him to Spain, Thailand, China, India, Slovakia, Romania, Finland, Italy, Sardinia, France, Mexico, Hawaii, New Zealand, Australia, Japan and Norway to compete.

Currently he has 17 years of teaching experience and currently 10 years of service for the USPTA. He has received the Conference USA Sportsmanship Award Winner, NCAA Division I Tennis-2001, 2002, 2003 and 2004; Professional Level Teacher's Certificate, U.S. Professional Tennis Association–2005; St. Louis Adult Tennis Player of the Year, St. Louis District Tennis Association–2007; Missouri Valley Adult Tennis Player of the Year, USPTA-Missouri Valley–2009, 2011, and USTA St. Louis District Outstanding Contributor to Youth High Performance–2009.

Lance is currently teaching at the Miller Tennis Center in Williamsville, NY. He and Juliana have two children, Elijah and Anna.

HAROLD WALES was certified in 1996 and has over 38 years of playing, teaching and coaching experience. He coached West Chester University's women's tennis team for three fall seasons from 1997 to 1999. He turned around an ailing program by going from a record of two wins and 16 losses to a school record of 11 wins and four losses in 1998. In 1999 the team record was 10 wins and four losses.

He served as the head tennis pro at Valley Forge Mountain Racket Club for nine years and was Director of Tennis at the Brandywine YMCA for five years and associate pro at Pennypacker Country Club and Tennis Addiction Sports Club. He has coached various USTA tennis teams.

A 1969 graduate of Catawba College (NC), he earned his MBA in financial management from Pace University (NY) in 1978. He served in the U.S. Army from 1969 to 1971.

MIC WALLACE, Head Tennis Professional at Chapel Hill Country Club in Chapel Hill, NC, has been in the tennis industry for over 20 years. He has over 12 years' experience as a head pro working for different private and country clubs in Middle States and four years experience as a director of tennis. He has also successfully run his own business, focusing on competitive development camps and clinics. In 2013 He was named USTA Central Pennsylvania Pro of the Year. Wallace also has over 10 years experience coaching high school tennis. In 2005 he was named Baltimore Private School coach of the year and during his stint in Hershey, PA, his boys' teams won the Keystone Division three straight years, culminating with an undefeated season and conference championship prior to his departure. In 2014, his family relocated to North Carolina where he accepted his current position at Chapel Hill Country Club.

STEVE WALTERS began playing tennis at 14 with his father, Jim Walters and at Mount Rainier High under Coach Mel Command. At Seattle's Tennis World, he trained with top PNW juniors Erik Jacobsen, Becki Zier, Derin Riley, Mark Kovacevich and friend Matt Vercammen. He then played No. 1 for Highline College and No. 3 for Idaho St. University where he and partner Jeff Beckley set a school record for wins (20) in 1984.

Steve Walters (right) with NCAA singles champion and future Wimbledon doubles champ Jared Palmer, 1993

Steve has won prize money in 88 events and was ranked No. 1 in NE Ohio in singles (1992), No. 1 in the PNW in mixed doubles (with Jamla Kovacevich in 1985), and No. 1 in the PNW in men's doubles (with Rick Kovacevich in 2002, 2007, 2012 and 2013). Steve has taught at top tennis academies such as

USPTA Elite Pro Derin Riley (left) with Steve Walters upon returning from the 1986 USPTA National Convention in Palm Springs, CA

Steve Walters with students Anthony and Katie Thompson, children of Hopman head pro Tommy Thompson, Saddlebrook, FL, 1987

2008 Tennis World Academy Hall of Fame Induction Ceremony. L-R: David Miller, Rick Kovacevich, Steve Walters, Aaron Heier and Scott Sullivan.

Newks Tennis Ranch in Texas, the Manitouwabing Sports & Arts Centre in Ontario, Canada, and Harry Hopman/Saddlebrook International Tennis in Florida. At Saddlebrook, Steve taught with renowned Hopman pros Tommy Thompson, Roland Jaeger and Dr. Jack Groppel while training many top U.S. and ITF juniors. In 1988-89 he was personal trainer for U.S. No. 1 16s Jared Palmer on the ATP Tour including the 1988 US Open.

He was tennis director for four years at the Union Country Club in Ohio and taught for Pacific West/Bally Tennis in Washington for 10 years. From 1998–2012 Steve ran Tennis World Academy in Auburn and Kent, WA, and produced collegiate players David Miller (PLU), Dane Miller (Whitman), Alex Noyes (Whitman), Aaron Heier (Eastern WA), Sandy Dennett (Gonzaga), Mark Mettler (WSU), Scott Sullivan (Gonzaga), Alex VanDerschelden (Portland St.), Maggie Becker (Masters College) and Patrick Daly (Green River). Steve is now tennis director for Kent Parks/Recreation, the Meridian Valley Country Club and is a teaching pro at Tennis Center Sand Point in Seattle. In 2014 Steve went through the USTA High Performance training program in Norcross, GA and in 2015 served as USTA/PNW 16s boys' & girls' intersectional coach in Shreveport, LA.

MONIKA WANIEK, Director of Tennis at PEAC (Pennington Ewing Athletic Club) in Ewing, NJ, since 2005. As a director, she runs all aspects of youth and adult programs and assists in marketing and promoting tennis programs.

During the school season, Monika volunteers as an assistant coach for the girls' tennis team at Audubon High School, Audubon, NJ. She is also involved as a teaching professional with Green Wave Tennis association in Audubon, NJ.

Monika was previously employed as an assistant tennis coach at the College of New Jersey, Ewing, NJ, from 2005 to 2009. She was the head tennis professional at Jacksonville Golf and Country Club, Florida from 1992 to 2004.

She earned a bachelor's degree in Physical Education at Oklahoma State University and a master's degree in Sports Management from Neumann University, Aston, PA.

As a player, Monika was the former Women's Polish National Champion, Polish Federation Cup player, 1986, US Amateur Clay Court Champion 1989 and All-American at Oklahoma State University 1990–1991.

OLIVER NZABONIMANA WASHINGTON, USPTA Certified Professional, started tennis in his hometown, Kigali, the capital of Rwanda. Due to finances, he dropped out but came back to play in 1995 after the Rwanda genocide stopped. He survived but lost some family and tennis player friends. Oliver says coming back to tennis helped him stay calm and move on from his genocide experiences.

Oliver moved to the U.S. as a U.S. National Park Services' volunteer at Grand Canyon. He took The Tennis Tech program at Tyler Junior College, graduated in Professional Tennis Management (2014) and in May 2014 became a USPTA Certified Tennis Professional.

He is an assistant tennis professional at Rice University where he teaches tennis juniors. He's a tennis professional at Chancellor Family Center through King Daddy's Academy and The Striesfeld Group. Oliver teaches tennis in 10 and Under, Zat, Champs, Superchamps and adult clinics programs.

His tennis biography and career went through challenges and difficult times. "God was always with me and backed me up with the blessing. Without my mum's love and support I would not have made it into tennis. I wish she could have been alive to see what I have accomplished. I am happy that I have made it through and been able to get my degree in professional tennis management and my tennis teaching certification through USPTA."

HUGH WATERS III, USPTA Master Professional, is an inductee into the 1991 USTA Mid-Atlantic Tennis Hall of Fame, 2015 USPTA Mid-Atlantic Hall of Fame, 2013 Richmond Tennis Hall of Fame and his family received the 1999 USTA Family of the Year Award. He is a 1958 graduate of University of Florida, Captain of the Florida tennis team and author of the book, "A Better Mind Makes a Better Player." He joined the USPTA in 1963 and became the head pro for Orlando Tennis Center where he hosted five pro tournaments with Pancho Gonzales, Rod Laver and friends. Seven years later, he became Director of Tennis for the Westwood Club in Richmond, VA, where he hosted the first Virginia Slims Tournament with Billie Jean King and Margaret Court. He was founder of Richmond Tennis Teaching Academy with 600 players' lessons each week and was owner of Raintree Swim and Racquet Club in Richmond and owner of Trails Tennis Club in Ormond Beach, FL. Through the years, hundreds of his juniors received college scholarships and many played on the pro circuit. One year his group included 18 nationally ranked players. He produced the "World's Largest Tennis Tournament" with 2,032 players and 306 courts in Richmond and directed The KIDS-BASH for 1,500 fifth graders at the Daytona Beach Coliseum for multiple years. He was President of USPTA Mid-Atlantic, President of Richmond Tennis Association and served on the

USPTA National Board and USTA Mid-Atlantic Section Board. He served on the USTA National Junior and Adult Competition Committees. Hugh's love of tennis is contagious and his motto is: "To play is to win."

NANCY A. WATLAND, USPTA Elite Professional since 1992, Program and Team Tennis Coordinator for Homewood-Flossmoor Racquet and Fitness Club, Homewood, IL for over 23 years.

Nancy is a USTA Certified Referee, ITF White Badge Referee actively involved in running tournaments at USTA National, Midwest and Chicago District levels and MCB Little Mo Sectional and Regionals.

She has contributed to organizations as follows: Chicago District Tennis Association Board Member and Director at Large, Chicago District USTA Junior Team Tennis Coordinator, USTA/Midwest Adult Recreation Consultant, USTA Midwest Committee member for Adult Recreation and Adult Leagues.

Nancy has received recognition for outstanding service to the tennis industry and the community with the following: Chicago Southland Convention and Visitors Bureau Service Person of the Year 2002; Chicago Tennis Patrons CDTA Tournament Director of the Year 1996, 2004, 2009; USPTA/Midwest Nancy Mickler Award 1996 and 2002; CDTA Trudy Brahin Award 1995.

Greatest achievement, receiving the 2003 USTA/NRPA Excellence in Tennis Programming award, on stage in St. Louis.

DAN WATSON, a USPTA member since 1927, member for 65 years. Dan was an "Elite Professional."

Dan was Assistant Tennis Professional at Breakers in Florida in the '30s and protege of George Agutter (father of American tennis). Dan competed as a professional in the US PRO tournaments of the era, written up in newspaper of the day "as a hard hitter." Dan was head professional at Chevy Chase Country Club for 38 years, 1935–1976. Dan's tennis career was interrupted by World War II where he served as pilot trainer at flight school, suffering injuries in two crashes which limited his playing career but he returned to Chevy Chase Country Club as head professional.

Chevy Chase was prestigious country club hosting many international events including Davis Cup matches and national championships.

Dan is recognized in the Chevy Chase history for "his classic strokes, sportsmanship, and tennis etiquette." Dan was given a membership to the prestigious club when he retired. Born Oct. 2, 1909 and died May 26, 1996.

ED WATSON is owner and operator of Harbor Springs Tennis Co., a small business firm with roots in all aspects of the tennis industry from sales to construction designs to club direction and instruction. Ed has been a tennis professional since 1973 and has held numerous rankings in Florida, Indiana and Michigan.

Growing up in South America he was inspired by Davis Cup in various countries. He has been a Director of Tennis since 1983 having served at Little Traverse Racquet Club, Birchwood Farms Country Club, Wequetonsing Association of Harbor Springs, MI, and Aplex Tennis Center, Alpena, MI, and Indian Wells Racquet Club and Country Club, Indian Wells CA. Early teaching career began at Carmel Racquet Club, Carmel, IN. In 1997 he was named top five of America's greatest tennis heroes for involvement in fundraising and grassroots start up programs. He has held numerous USTA positions from verifier to rankings. A tennis club start up specialist, he has developed parks and recreation tennis and community homeowner tennis associations in both Indianapolis area and northern Michigan. A huge supporter of continuing education he has attended over 20 national and regional conventions to pursue continued excellence.

JOHN WEIL, aka "Mr. Peewee," Brand Manager, Prince Global Sports and 40+ years in the tennis industry. USPTA Elite Professional for over 35 years, Midwest Division Board Member/Divisional Tester, Head Tennis Professional, Pro Shop owner, Stringer for ATP/WTA Tournaments including the US Open. Consultant for developing the original USRSA Stringer Certification Test and Tester, Sales Manager for Babolat, Territory Manager/National Account Manager at Wilson Racquet Sports. Inventor/marketer of the "Mr. Peewee Tennis®" program which he developed in 1981. Authored/published a complete "how to" manual on utilizing the "Mr. Peewee Tennis®" program for tennis pros and tennis facilities. It is the first program designed to teach children 10 and under how to actually play tennis by utilizing a short court, lower nets, smaller rackets and sponge tennis balls. Wilson Racquet Sports leased the rights to market the equipment/program. It has become the basis for the USTA "Grow the Game" program.

BRUCE WESTRUM enjoyed an impressive amateur career in Minnesota, winning the Albert Lea City singles championship 12 times, the first in 1972. He won the doubles championship of the same tournament 41 years later in 2013. He also won multiple titles in Austin, MN. He rose to the No. 1 ranking in USTA's Northern Section 55 singles in 2013 and was in three Northern Section Finals. Westrum was six-time Star of the North singles gold medalist.

Westrum, who received an Associates Degree from Austin, MN Community College in 1972, has taught tennis with the Albert Lea Parks and Recreation Dept., Rochester Tennis Connection, Lilydale Club in St. Paul, Brook Park Tennis and West Hills clubs. He also was interim tennis coach at Macalester College in 1979-80.

BOB WHITEHOUSE'S dad exposed him to the game and they played father/son tournaments which led him to playing junior NE tournaments. At Plymouth State College he was undefeated in four years of singles and doubles, received the (1969) Varsity Club Award and was inducted into the Athletic Hall of Fame in 1987. A career change allowed him to teach and coach tennis at the Keene Racquet Club and Keene High School. He received the USPTA High School Coach of the Year in 2004. He continued to play New England mixed doubles, attaining the No. 1 ranking multiple times in

the 45's and 65's. Additionally he was a member of men's NTRP 4.0 teams that qualified for nationals four times, twice in the seniors (placing fourth in 2004) and twice in the super seniors. Retired in Florida, he plays in the Peace River Senior Men's League in Charlotte County.

NUNRY WILLIAMSON began learning tennis at an early age and has been a part of the tennis industry 30+ years as a player, teaching professional and personal coach. Nunry enlisted in the military in 1976 to serve his country and in 1977 he began playing open tournaments in the U.S. and abroad. Nunry started his teaching career in 1985 while stationed in Korea and during another assignment at the Pearl Harbor Racquet Club in Hawaii from 1986–1990 he supported USTA/NJTL programs. He became a member of the USPTA in 1990 and later was employed at Thousand Oaks Racquet Club 1991–1995 in San Antonio, TX. He feels his greatest reward has been the opportunity to work with the public and other professionals in growing the game. Currently he is a retired Air Force veteran and USPTA member in good standing. He continues to support our nation's defense and the tennis industry.

GERALD "JERRY" WINDER was born in Birmingham, England. He was a Regional High School Champion, College and Conference Finalist, and State Ranking in Men's 35 Singles.

He has been Director of Tennis in Louisiana, Tennessee, Vermont, Ohio, New York, Delaware, Massachusetts, Arizona, Virginia, Germany, Austria and Holland. He has coached in 20 states and six countries.

Winder is certified as USPTA Elite Professional; PTR, BTCA, USRSA, Level I and II Sport Science, Compu-Tennis; Finalist in USPTA-SW Community Service Award 1994; USPTA-SW Professional of the Year 1996 and 2009.

"Jerry" has been Team Captain for National Finalist USPTA-SW Team, Team Captain for National Consolation Finalist USPTA SW Team, served on every Divisional Committee USPTA-SW (1994-present), Divisional President USPTA-SW (2009–10), Served on USPTA Executive Committee (2004–2010), USPTA-SW Pro Emeritus (2011–12) and USPTA-SW Education Chairman (2005-present).

STEVE WINER, Elite Professional, has been a USPTA member since 1978. He was the Director of Tennis at the Wayside Racquet and Swim Club in Marlborough, MA, from 1987–2015, where he ran all club activities for adults and juniors. He is currently the Director of Junior Tennis and the USTA Tournament Director at the Marcus Lewis Tennis Center in Acton, MA. Steve has a BS degree in Psychology from Tufts University, where he competed on the Tufts tennis team all four years. He is a Pro Team member of the Babolat Advisory Staff and is currently the Varsity Girls' Tennis coach at Nashoba Regional High School in Bolton, MA. Steve has competed at top levels of play both in New England and nationally. He has received numerous awards including USPTA Eastern New England Professional of the Year. He is one of New England's premier USTA Tournament Directors and is a two-time winner of USTA/New England's Tournament of the Year Award.

TONY WILLINGHAM, Director of Tennis at Westside Athletic Club has over 20 years of experience as a USPTA professional. Tony currently holds a USPTA Elite Pro classification and has also served as a USPTA Official. He was selected as the USPTA NC Professional of the Year in 2013. He is tournament director of the largest charity tennis tournament in Northeast North Carolina that has raised over $200,000 for the local hospice agency.

Tony has been an incremental part of establishing USTA leagues including women's, men's, combos, tri-level, and junior team tennis leagues in Northeast North Carolina. He has coached over 30 women's and five men's district winning USTA teams, along with two national women's winning teams. He is a board member of the Outer Banks Tennis Association, a nonprofit committed to the development of recreational tennis. Tony volunteers at USTA youth events and host numerous local USTA play events.

Tony Willingham works with a young student on her forehand.

TED WITHALL was born nine days after the World War I Armistice on Nov. 20, 1918 in El Paso, TX. His dad got his discharge and they went home to San Diego, CA.

Tennis and baseball occupied Ted's time every day-all day with his best friend, Ted Williams. After high school Williams got tapped for the big leagues. Ted went to San Diego State College where he was No. 1 on the freshman tennis team and pitched for the freshman baseball team.

Ted went to San Diego State for four years and then transferred to University of California at Berkley (B.S. degree).

Between 1942–1946 he served in the Air Corps and between 1947–1948 enrolled at the University of Southern California for a year of graduate work. In 1948 he started to teach tennis in and around Beverly Hills and also had a radio show (singing) in Hollywood. In 1950 he decided to take a shot at New York.

In 1951 Ted succeeded Pancho Segura, who went on tour, at the Concord Hotel in upstate New York (summers-five years). In 1951 he also taught tennis in St. Thomas, Virgin Islands (winters-five years).

In 1956 he was teaching at the Maidstone Club in East Hampton, NY. He succeeded Fred Perry at the Boca Raton Hotel and Club in 1957 where he stayed for 13 years.

Ted left Boca for the Tennis Club in Fort Lauderdale because it presented a new concept in tennis clubs: condos surrounding tennis courts. He was there for two years when he was offered a vice presidency at the indoor Tennis Club of the Palm Beaches. The indoor tennis idea was not successful in Florida.

Ted joined the USPTA in 1950. He was the first President of the Florida PTA. He became President of the USPTA in 1972. He was among the first group of members to be honored as a Master Pro. He was also the first member to be inducted into the Florida PTA Hall of Fame. He has been a member for 64 years.

KENT WOMACK was born in Kansas City, MO; graduated from William Chrisman High School, Independence, MO (1964), and Central Methodist University, Fayette, MO, with a Bachelor of Music Education (January 1970).

Kent has participated in numerous tournaments with 11 wins, 16 runner-ups and four third places throughout various parts of the U.S. and Canada

He has been Tester for the MO Valley Division; "Tester of the Year" for MO Valley Division (2011); received the "Continuing Education Award" for MO Valley Division (2011); "High School Coach of the Year" for MO Valley Division (2006) and has been a member of MO Valley Division Board for 12 years (2002–2014).

Kent is married to wife, Carol, a violinist with the St. Louis Philharmonic.

KATHY S. WOODS served as President of the U.S. Professional Tennis Association (USPTA) from 1994–1996 and held the distinguished honor of being the first and only female to serve the Association in that capacity.

Currently she is the Manager and Director of Tennis at the Racquet Club of St. Petersburg, FL. Woods previously directed programs in Princeton, NJ; Key Biscayne, FL, and Westport, CT. Woods was also president of the Middle States Division of the USPTA.

Kathy has worked with the Tennis Industry Association, and has been a featured speaker at international and worldwide conferences and has served as a tennis club consultant in programming and staff training and corporate tennis entertainment.

In 1996, Kathy was the recipient of the International Tennis Hall of Fame's Tennis Educational Merit Award for outstanding service to tennis.

As a competitive player, Kathy earned a Gold Ball as the USTA National 30's Doubles Champion and has been ranked No. 1 in the nation by USPTA in both singles and doubles. She played varsity tennis for the University of Pennsylvania.

She lives with her husband Ron, co–author of their book, *Playing Tennis After 50*, in St. Petersburg, FL.

RON WOODS is past president of the USPTA and serves on the USPTA Executive Committee.

Ron and Loyce Woods

Ron was named 2010 USPTA National Pro of the Year and inducted into the Texas Tennis Hall of Fame in 2011.

Ron started as an assistant pro in 1965 after four years of collegiate play at the University of Houston. Woods has been a member of USPTA since 1966. During his 31 years as Director of Tennis at the Corpus Christi Country Club (1970–2001). Ron and wife Loyce administered one of the most successful tennis programs in Texas.

During his playing career Ron was the top-ranked junior in Texas, earning a full tennis scholarship at Houston. He was also a member of the victorious 2013 American Gordon Cup team, competing in the 70 and over division.

Ron is married to his lovely wife Loyce and has three children from a previous marriage, in addition to seven grandchildren and six great-grand kids. He serves as a volunteer in many tennis and recreation-related groups, while finding time to fish, golf and travel.

RONALD B. WOODS, Ph.D., has been a USPTA member for over 40 years which includes president of USPTA Middle States division, member of the national executive committee and frequent speaker at both national and division conventions. He was honored as national USPTA Coach of the Year in 1982 and as a Master Professional in 1984.

A graduate of East Stroudsburg University and an inductee into their Athletic Hall of Fame, Woods received his Ph.D. from Temple University in exercise science. For 17 years, he was a professor of physical education and men's tennis coach at West Chester University and was also inducted into their Athletic Hall of Fame.

Ron spent 20 years on the professional staff of the USTA and was the first USTA Director of Player Development charged with developing top junior players into professional players. He was inducted into the USTA Middle States Tennis Hall of Fame (2010) and USPTA Middle States Hall of Fame (2012). Ron was also awarded the educational merit award by the International Tennis Hall of Fame (1997).

Woods has authored, with his wife Kathy, *Playing Tennis After 50*, a college textbook *Social Issues in Sport*, now in the third edition, and numerous USTA publications.

He is currently an adjunct professor at the University of Tampa in exercise science and human performance and lives with Kathy in nearby St. Petersburg, FL.

SOPHIE WOORONS, Ph.D., is owner/Director of Brookstone Meadows Tennis, 12-court tennis facility, Anderson, SC. She obtained her Ph.D. in Sport Pedagogy from the University of Georgia.

Sophie was the 2015 USPTA Southern Professional of the Year. She has been a six times National Champion, women's for her age group.

She was a Bronze Medalist at Senior Fed Cup World Championships with Team USA. Sophie was a former All-American for Clemson University in both Singles and Doubles. She was ACC Player of the year and a member of the ACC 50 year anniversary team.

Sophie has made professional presentations at international, national and state conferences and published articles in *Tennis Pro, TennisWeek.com* and *Educational* magazine.

Playing professional team tennis, she was a teammate with Amelie Mauresmo and Pascale Paradis. She played in the European Pro Championships on professional team tennis with the country of Luxembourg.

Sophie is the mother of Noah Johnston.

DOUG WRIGHT, Director of Tennis at The Country Club of Petersburg, has been teaching professionally for 29 years. He has coached and directed at some of the most successful junior development Programs in the nation, including Houston, Philadelphia, Pittsburgh, Salisbury, MD, and now in the Greater Richmond, VA, area.

USPTA Elite Professional Certified since 1982, Doug was selected Head Coach for a USTA Area Training Center, USTA District "Teaching Pro of the Year," USPTA District President, NCAA Division I head coach and a two-sport MVP at St. Mary's College of Maryland.

As a High Performance/Junior Development specialist, Doug has trained players to state, sectional, national and professional levels. His students include five USTA State Champions, NCAA Scholarship and MVP players, earning varsity positions at Wake Forest, Florida Tech, Stevenson, U of Delaware, Salisbury University, University of Illinois and Pennsylvania.

JAMI YONEKURA-JONES grew up in San Diego as a top ranked junior player, earning national rankings of No. 17 in singles and No. 3 in doubles. She went on to attend the University of Miami on a tennis scholarship, where she was an All-American, reaching the finals of the NCAA doubles tournament in 1988. From 1993–1997, Jones was the Head Women's Tennis Coach at Long Beach State University. She has been a USPTA member since 1991 and is a USPTA Elite Professional, coaching both adults and juniors of all skill levels. In 1993, she was named the USPTA National Female Player of the Year. She was recently named the San Diego District Coach of the year for 2015. She is currently the Head Women's Tennis Coach at San Diego City College, and a teaching professional at Carmel Valley Tennis, where she coaches ladies league teams as well as USTA junior team tennis.

JIM YOUNG is an assistant professional at Harry Taylor Tennis Center in Pasadena, TX. He has been teaching tennis for over 30 years. Jim is a former teacher, coach and principal in public education. He has the privilege of teaching on the same courts that he took lessons on as a young tennis player. Jim wants his students to have the same positive experience that he had learning tennis. Jim enjoys playing tennis tournaments, playing ice hockey and playing guitar.

ANNE ZARRAONANDIA, a member of the USPTA since 1985. Taught all ages and levels at the San Rafael Recreation Department in Marin County, CA, with long time teaching partner, Teri Goodman. Coached Girls Tennis at Redwood High School in Larkspur for 23 years with many successful teams, league titles and a NCS championship. Inducted into the MCAL Hall of Fame (Marin County Athletic League) with over 300 wins as a Coach. North Coast Section Honor Coach, 2002. Coached Women's Tennis for 10 years+ at Dominican College. Played tennis at San Rafael High School, College of Marin and UC Davis in the 1970s. Played doubles with sister Carrie and won a few national titles on grass and hard courts. Ranked No. 1 in 30's and 35's WD in U.S. in the 1990s. Anne is a lefty with a love for the net, angles, spins and especially doubles.

CARRIE ZARRAONANDIA was 9 years old when she saw a strong, confident Billie Jean King play a tennis match. She knew then her life could be built around the game of tennis. She followed her passion, playing varsity tennis in high school and college. Carrie battled her way to seven national titles and is most proud of her No. 1 35's doubles ranking in the U.S. held with her sister Anne. After 45 years the "Sister Act" continues with a weekly hit and giggle game. As a USPTA Elite Professional member for over 30 years Carrie has enjoyed coaching all ages and abilities, from 4-year-old red ballers to university varsity tennis. She is currently on staff at The Rafael Racquet Club in California. While coaching tennis for 38 years Carrie has drawn insight from her students and fellow coaches and has been inspired by her many mentors.

DAVID ZEUTAS-BROER has been the director of Player Development for USTA New England since 2002. He oversees the competitive tracks available to junior players in the six New England states and promotes, organizes, facilitates, coordinates and runs a wide range of player development projects including high performance and educational events for players, parents and coaches.

Before this he was founder/director of Serious Fun® holistic tennis training for juniors, head tennis coach for men and women at Clark University and honored by USPTA New England in 2010 with the Joseph Dietz Bowl awarded, "to the professional who has done the most for New England tennis," in 2004 for "Professional of the Year" and in 1999 and 1997 for "Coach of the Year."

Zeutas-Broer is a USPTA Master Professional and a USTA Competitive Player Development Specialist and has served on the Boards of USPTA New England, Youth Tennis Foundation (YTF) of New England and ACLU Worcester County, MA.

BOB ZIPAY is the owner of Englewood Tennis Club. Originally from Massachusetts, he was a ranked junior player and his high school's No. 1 player for four years. He was an all-star in 1979 and 1980, and singles champion in 1980. After high school, and while attending Southeastern Massachusetts University, Bob played varsity tennis while earning a B.S. Degree in Mechanical Engineering. Eventually he decided the tennis world provided the lifestyle he preferred. He has been teaching for over 35 years and in 1990, Bob received his USPTA Elite Certification. He became a Certified Racquet Stringer in 1987, and Master Racquet Technician. As an adult player, Bob was ranked No. 8 in Florida, and currently has a National Father and Son Ranking with his son Benjamin. Bob currently donates much of his time on a project with his mother, Sue, in her quest to bring a Women's Sports Museum to Sarasota, FL.

Bob Zipay with son Ben

DENIS ZIVKOVIC competed and traveled as a ranked world-class tennis professional on the ATP World Tour, achieving highest ATP singles ranking of No. 292 in the world and ATP doubles ranking of 161 in the world. Denis earned three career professional titles in singles and 14 career doubles titles, with multiple grand slam appearances as a junior player, professional and coach. He is co-founder and Director of Tennis at Deni Sports Tennis in Miami, FL. He is extremely passionate, dedicated, vibrant and has a charismatic personality on and off the tennis court. Denis uses what he has learned as a tour professional covering six continents, 37 countries as a teaching tool to nurture and guide his tennis patrons to be better tennis players and individuals. Leisurely travel, boating sailing and spending time with his family are his passions.

BILL BEVERLY was born in Canton, OH, January 24, 1945. Bill began his tennis career at the age of 10, winning numerous junior titles in Kentucky, Ohio, and West Virginia. At age 18, he won the Kentucky State Boys singles title. In 1963, he graduated Paul G. Blazer High School in Ashland, KY. He received a full tennis scholarship and played 4 years for the nationally rated Western Kentucky University and graduated in 1967 with a Bachelor of Science Degree. From 1968–69 he suspended his tennis activities in order to serve in Vietnam in the U.S. Army. While stationed in Germany, he was selected to play The All Army Team-Europe. Winning singles and doubles titles, finishing two years as semifinalist in The All Army European championships, Garmish, Germany.

His long teaching and Directorship of Tennis started with The Continental Racquet Club, Columbus, OH, in 1972. In 1978, he was brought to FL, directing the Treasure Island Tennis and Yacht Club. Then later moving to Naples, FL, a to build the Wyndemere Country Club. Then for the next 20 years, he would be the Director of Tennis at The Legendary Naples Bath and Tennis Club, in Naples, FL. He co-directed The Registry Resort Hotel tennis program for a few years while preparing to build his next development, Sterling Oaks Tennis Club, in Naples, FL.

Bill is a natural showman, very energetic with an effervescent personality. He has produced and hosted his own tennis instructional TV show, "Racquet Talk," which aired across the state of Florida from the late '70s to the '90s. He created the Bill Beverly All American Sports Tennis Academy, which attracted groups from all over the world. Bill Beverly is a USPTA Elite Professional and is currently the Director of Tennis at The Club at Olde Cypress and resides in Naples, FL, with his wife Jane. He has two adult sons, Joshua and Jonathan, who reside in the state of Florida.

BILLY RAY JACKSON is in his 26th year on the Club Fit Staff.

He was born and raised in North Central Texas. Billy was a service brat and moved frequently in the States and Europe as his father, an Air Force Major, was a member of the famous Tuskegee Airmen. He attended Shaw University and received a M.A. degree in Sports and Fitness Administration. In October 2003 he was inducted into the Shaw University Hall of Fame for his achievements in football, baseball and tennis.

He is a life member of the Eastern Tennis Association, a USPTA Elite Professional and certified P-1 for PTR, and an MTM Tennis Coaching Professional. His accolades include: PTR Pro of the Year (1992), Eastern Section Pro of the Year (1998) and the Presidential Award for the Eastern Section (1996).

He is the former President the Eastern Section of the Professional Tennis Registry.

Billy is the former Athletic Director of the Abbott School.

He has worked with tennis legend Arthur Ashe and studied under world-renowned teaching professional Oscar Wenger.

Billy is on the cutting edge of tennis teaching and techniques. His programs are geared toward teaching the proper techniques and shot selection.

Billy lives in Ossining, NY, and has extensive contacts in the tennis industry.

MEMBERS OF THE UNITED STATES PROFESSIONAL TENNIS ASSOCIATION

The following list is based on records provided by the USPTA on Nov. 11, 2016. While every effort has been made to ensure that the list is a comprehensive list of USPTA members, neither the publisher nor the USPTA is responsible for errors or omissions.

Trent Aaron
Gary Aasen
Cedric Abalos
Darrell Abang
Hisham Abaza
Jeff Abbey
Steven Abbondondelo
Laila Abdala Saad
Gregory Abe
Kazuhiro Abe
Yoshimasa Abe
Yuuki Abe
Mark Abel
Fredrik Aberg
Albert Ablorh
Carl Abraham
Ernie Abraham
Henry Abrahams
D A Abrams
Larry Abrams
Troy Abrams
Patrick Abshire
Michael Ach
Mauricio Achondo
Frank Acierno
Alina Ackenbom
Dru Ackert
Antonio Acosta
Ralph Acosta
Scot Acre
Janina Acri
Eddie Acuna
Francisco Acuna
Rafael Acuna
Wesley Adam
Andrew Adams
Bucky Adams
Christopher Adams
Ed Adams
Gregory Adams
James Adams
John Adams
Joseph Adams
Judy Adams
Katie Adams
Katrina Adams
Lee Adams
Neil Adams
Orville Adams
Scott Adams
Susan Adams
Sylvia Adams
Tony Adams
Jonathan Adamson
Steve Adamson
Mason Addison
Michael Addison
Terry Addison
Frank Adinolfe
Arthur Adkins
Brian Adkins
Janet Adkisson
Mitchell Adler
Paul Adler
Peter Adler
Benjamin Adrian
Avinash Advani
Georgi Adzhikov
Eduardo Afini
Gary Agardy
Arnulf Agbunag
Chong Yew Ager Chiew
Marcel Agnolin
John Agori
Juan Agostini
Pharis Ahmed
Troy Aiken
Kip Aitken
Hideo Aizawa
Hiroshi Aizawa
Yoshi Akabane
Vanne Akagi-Bustin
Brian Akers
C Akers
Karina Akhmedova
Ty Aki
Sho Akiba
Osamu Akimoto
Tomoko Akino
Yuichi Akita
Ikuo Akiyama
Jill Akiyama
Kunihiko Akiyama
Tiffany Akiyama
Karl Akkerman
Senem Aktuccar
Saeed Al Askari
Imad Al-Suki
Tania Alaby
Vel Alahan
Nelson Alapi
Felipe Alarcon
Fatema Alawadhi
Paul Albares
Valerie Albaret
Benjamin Albers
Janna Albers
Ron Albers
Brad Albert
Caroline Albertsma-Rivera
Michael Albrecht
Jerry Albrikes
Pablo Albuja
Omar Alcaino
Jocel Alcedo
Nathan Alcocer
Chanon Alcon
Cindy Alcorn
Mike Alcott
Alfonso Aldana
David Alden
Barbara Aldorisio
Richard Aldrete
Corey Aldridge
Natalia Alekhova
Dallas Aleman
Jimmy Aleman
Ron Alessi
Glen Alex
Greg Alexander
Keely Alexander
Matthew Alexander
Susan Alexander
Lazaro Alfonso
Nancy Alfonso
Clinton Alford
Jason Alfrey
Mario Algarra
Paul Algate
Don Alger
Raya Alher
Clint Ali
Francis Ali
Gregory Alice
Zahra Alijani
Darya Alikhver
Pedro Alipio
Peter Alkhazov
Paul Allam
Patricia Allar
Bunnie Allare
Vincent Allegre
James Allemby
Chris Allen
Courtney Allen
Eric Allen
Jason Allen
Jim Allen
Mark Allen
Mark Allen
Sally Allen
Susan Allen
Allison Allen-Gillespie
Robert Allensworth
Franco Aller
Angela Allin
Patricia Allison
Art Allmond
Susan Allshouse
Glenn Allsop
Tracy Almeda-Singian
William Almeyda
J D Almond
Jose Alonso
Loreto Alonso
Maria Del Mar Alonso
Julian Alonso Pintor
Steve Alonzi
David Alonzo
Byron Alp
Gary Alpert
Kenneth Alrutz
Rikki Alrutz
Adrienne Alteri
Jayne Alterman
David Altshuler
Carlos Alvarado
Abraham Alvarez
Gilberto Alvarez
Guillermo Alvarez
Mario Alvarez
Mike Alvarez
Francis Alvir
Alan Alvistur
Randolph Alvut
Gary Amadio
Kazuhiko Amano
Masaki Amano
Nuno Amaral
Rodrigo Amaral
Steve Amaro
Greg Amaya
Romain Ambert
Molly Ambrose
Brandon Ambroske
Marco Ambu
Derek Ameel
Orlando Amen
Gregory Amerson
Sophie Amiach
James Amick
Joseph Amoroso
Paul Amrein
Jeff Amurao
Frank Anania
Matthew Anastasi
Angelo Anastopoulo
Arthur Anastopoulo
Alan Anastos
Bob Anderman
Ray Anders
Scott Anders
Lance Andersen
Blake Anderson
Bradley Anderson
Brent Anderson
Brian Anderson
Brian Anderson
Chad Anderson
Chris Anderson
Dana Anderson
David Anderson
Eric Anderson
Erik Anderson
Greg Anderson
Guy Anderson
Kirk Anderson
Maureen Anderson
Pam Anderson
Patricia Anderson
Raymond Anderson
Reed Anderson
Roger Anderson
Ross Anderson
Scott Anderson
Sherwin Anderson
Todd Anderson
William Anderson
Anna Andersson
Jonas Andersson
Mikael Andersson
Kazuhiko Ando
Luke Andreae
Giancarlo Andreani
Dusko Andreic
Antonio Andreon
Jorge Andrew
Deborah-Rose Andrews
Donald Andrews
Jonathan Andrews
Mercedes Andrews
Michael Andrews
Mick Andrews
Rich Andrews
Todd Andrews
Kenneth Andriano
Collin Andry
Krista Andry
Adrian Ang
Bruce Angeli
John Angelino
Russell Angell
Carmine Angeloni
Peco Angjeleski
Adam Angle
Steve Annacone
Jim Annesi
Hiroaki Anno
Scott Ansay
Nancy Ansboury
Sarah Ansboury
Philip Ansdell
Erich Anspach
Saby Antal
Alan Antolic
Michael Anttila
Alex Antunes
Gustavo Anzola
Hiromichi Aoki
Yoshihiro Aoki
Akira Aono
Yuji Aoyama
Frank Apecechea
Taylor Apostol
Alexandra Apostu
Bill Appelt
Christian Appleman
Daniel Aquila
Chad Arado
Hideki Arai

Yuji Arai
David Araiza
Osamu Arakawa
Kenjiro Araki
Makoto Araki
Yukiko Araki
Dennis Aran
Anibal Aranda
Jeffrey Aranda
Jordan Aranda
Stan Aranda
Cougar Arande
Bill Araneo
Pablo Araujo
Gilberto Arcay
Alexandra Archer
Neil Archer
Cameron Archie
Samantha Ardenfriend
Luis Ardila
Ricardo Arenas
Bill Arfsten
Javier Arias
Joe Arias
Bill Arick
Juntaro Arimura
Mert Arinc
Hibiki Arita
Richard Arlindo
Claudio Armandi
Alex Armstrong
Duane Armstrong
John Armstrong
Lance Armstrong
Michael Armstrong
Norm Armstrong
Yon Armstrong
Phillip Arndt
E. Shawn Arnette
Marie Arnold
Tina Arnold
Christopher Arns
Howie Arons
Michael Aronson
William Aronson
Akshay Arora
Ankit Arora
Kelly Arp
Brandon Arradaza
Gonzalo Arriagada
Rafael Arribas
Michael Arrigo
Paul-Henri Arrigoni
Glenn Arrington
Jonathan Arrington
Kristin Arrowsmith
Jeri Arts
Yasunori Asagi
George Asato
Arletta Asatrian
Kevin Asbell
Michael Asfeld
Ari Ash
Michelle Ash
Ashlee Ashba
Richard Ashby
Roger Ashcroft
Steven Asher
Fred Ashhurst
Geoffrey Ashley
Saad Ashraf
Kaleb Ashton
Gerhard Asiedu-Ofei
Jess Asper
Elaine Asplundh
Vic Assad
Marc Assaraf
Marcos Asse
Todd Assini
Alejandro Astiz
Miguel Astorga
Vasil Atanasov
Gregory Aten
Scott Atkin
Jonathan Atkins
Adri Atkinson
Asa Atkinson
Doug Atkinson
Jeff Atkinson
Marc Atkinson
Christopher Atzet
Jennifer Aubin
Rick Aubin
Patrick Aubone
Dan Aubuchon
Darby Auerbach-Morris
Brittany Augustine
Bryn Auld
Suzi Aulicino
Grant Aungst
Alan Aure
Damon Austin
John Austin
Pamela Austin
Tracy Austin
William Austin
John-Paul Austrew
Cory Avants
Henry Avants
Sharon Avants
Hratch Avedissian
Antonella Avena
George Avery
Tom Avery
Martin Aviles
John Avolio
Gergana Avramova
Clifton Awuy
Brian Axelrod
Keith Axelrod
Yushi Ayabe
Diego Ayala
Juan Ayala
Luis Ayala
Peter Ayers
Reda Azagar
Philippe Azar
Na'im Azhar
Attila Azucki
Toshihide Azuma
Tammy Azur
Takeshi Baba
Yamato Baba
Elizabeta Babb
Clay Babcock
Reese Babcock
Meike Babel
Michaela Babicova
Julie Babler
Phil Baboulis
Alfonso Bacalja
Larry Bach
Cris Bacharach
Lewis Bachetti
Jill Bachochin
Wayne Backman
Elizabeth Bacon
Matthew Bacon
Natalie Bacon
Sebastian Bader
Amy Badger
Charles Badger
Sandra Badillo
Bogdan Badiu
Veronica Badon
Martin Badt
Andrew Badura
Chang-Kyu Bae
Ian Sungkwon Baek
Beth Baer
Dan Baer
David Baer
Erick Baer
Luka Bagos
Afshin Bahrami
Mohamad Bahrami
Vlad Bahrencu
David Baier
Chris Baile
David Bailey
Jack Bailey
Jackson Bailey
Jacquelyn Bailey
John Bailey
Rod Bailey
Steve Bailey
William Bailey
Jonathan Bailin
Philip Baillos
Carol Baily
Trevor Bain
Jed Bair
Jonathan Bair
David Baird
Cheryl Baker
Dirk Baker
Erik Baker
Jeff Baker
Kelly Baker
Mack Baker
Marilyn Baker
Mark Baker
Sheldon Baker
William Baker
Ingrid Bakke
Nicholas Bakos
Rajan Balachandar
Bernard Balagula
Isriz Balase
Bala Balasundar
Michael Baldemor
Chris Baldwin
Jaclyn Baldwin
Jessica Baldwin
Michael Baldwin
Mike Baldwin
Mike Bales
Charles Ball
Corey Ball
Mark Ball
Syd Ball
Richard Ballantine
Louis Ballantyne
Dennis Ballard
John Ballard
Michael Ballard
Debbie Ballerino
Quacey Balleste
Daniel Ballesteros
Dale Balun
Greg Bamford
Edward Banach
Brian Banas
Piotr Banas
Henry Banaszak
Zenon Banawa
Alex Bancila
Todor Bandev
Meg Bandy
Corey Banghart
Sekou Bangoura
James Banks
Thomas Banks
Deborah Banks Kristoff
Mike Bannister
Margit Bannon
Bernardo Baptista
Mani Barajas-Alexander
John Barbagallo
John Barbaria
Chris Barbe
Shawn Barbee
Amy Barber
Bill Barber
Devin Barber
Michael Barber
Sarah Barber
Tim Barber
Thiago Barbosa
Davi Barbour
Roland Bardony
Robert Bareford
Rosie Bareis
Trey Baring
Emre Baris
Carri Barish
Amanda Barkema
Christopher Barker
Francis Barker
John Barker
John Barker
Scott Barker
Greg Barkley
Ed Barksdale
Keith Barksdale
Timothy Barlow
Bryce Barnard
Tim Barnard
Andrea Barnes
Brian Barnes
Jefferson Barnes
Kathy Barnes
Katrina Barnes
Michael Barnes
Mitch Barnes
Ronald Barnes
Tim Barnes
Brett Barnett
Cheryl Barnett
Julie Barnett
Chris Barnhart
Robert Barnick
Jim Barnish
Martin Baroch
Benjamin Baron
Bernard Baron
Chad Baron
Ivan Baron
Anna Baronayte
Nick Barone
Shawn Barone
Bruce Barr
John Barr
Scott Barr
Francie Barragan
Miguel Barranon
Jeffrey Barrera
Aubrey Barrett
Drew Barrett
Wesley Barrett
Mario Barrette
Girin Barretto
Dan Barrie
Woodrow Barrie
Francisco Barrientos
Ernest Barriga
Amy Barrington
Paulo Barros
Lenka Barrow
Patrick Barrows
Ed Barry
Eric Barry
Kelly Barry
Van Barry
Lisa Barry Berg
John Barston
James Bartell
Adam Barth
Doug Barthel
Carl Barthold
Paul Bartholomai
Bill Bartlett
Claire Bartlett
Dennis Bartlett
Sue Bartlett
Lindsay Bartlett-Montero
Todd Bartolomeo
Glenn Barton
Tut Bartzen
Brian Bascome
Lee Basey
Josh Basha
Beau Basham
Mark Basham
Jerry Baskin
Monty Basnyat
Brian Bass
Theron Bass
Brice Bassett
Kim Bastable
Alexandra Bastock
Rene Bastres
Janan Batchelor
Jason Bates
Paul Bates

Rob Bates
Georgy Batrakov
Brad Batstone
Charles Batt
Fortunato Battad
Thomas Battaglia
Luciano Battaglini
Graham Battle
Vincent Baudat
Maxwell Bauer
Ted Bauer
Michael Baugh
Steven Baum
Ryan Bauman
Thomas Bauman
Bryan Baumann
John Baumgartner
Hans Baumstark
Rich Bausch
Deepak Bawa
Hemant Baxi
Dominic Baxley
Rill Baxter
Ryan Baxter
Scott Baxter
Dahu Bayaer
Zhalagen Bayaer
Bob Bayliss
Darryl Baynes
Jeremy Bayon
Jason Bazinet
Geza Bazula
Elliot Beam
Ryan Bean
Scott Bean
Mark Bearby
Richard Beard
Jason Beardslee
Jak Beardsworth
Donna Bearup
Jeff Bearup
Betsy Beasley
Barbara Beattie
Brett Beattie
John Beaube
Matt Beavers
David Bebout
Vasile Beches
John Bechtel
Brian Beck
David Beck
Jeremiah Beck
Jim Beck
Michael Beck
Donald Becker
Eric Becker
Jonathan Becker
Kendra Becker
Rainer Becker
Ricky Becker
Lisa Beckett
Lanell Beckles
Mario Beckles
Darren Beckman
Martin Bedecarratz
Andrew BeDell
Jim Bedilion
Sherry Bedingfield
George Bedrosian
Earl Beebe
Kenneth Beebe
Jeffrey Beecher
Mark Beede
Dan Beedle
Jennifer Beekman
Ron Beekman
Dave Beerman
Ryan Beeson
Branden Beets
Jennifer Beets
D'Wayne Begay
Alexi Beggs
Viktoria Beggs
Justin Behm
Stephen Behmlander
Sheryl Behne
Krisi Behrens
Joseph Behson
Richard Beijer
David Beilinson
Erich Bein
Luke Beling
Viktoria Belinsky
Lou Belken
Craig Bell
David Bell
Dudley Bell
Greg Bell
Jamie Bell
Melinda Bell
Nathan Bell
Sandra Bell
Sherri Bell
Ted Bell
Wesley Bell
Zachary Bell
Steven Bellamy
Virginia Bellis
Joan Bellissimo
Kahree Bellow
Mark Belman
Ray Belmudez
Daniel Beloso
William Belser
Louis Belt
Lorenzo Beltrame
Denis Belusic
Lukas Beman
Henry Ben
Kim Bender
Lynn Bender
Tom Bender
Andy Benedict
Charles Benedict
John Bengston
David Benjamin
J P Benjamin
Steven Benjamin
Peter Benko
Andrew Benner
Brent Bennett
Chris Bennett
Christina Bennett
David Bennett
Don Bennett
Lindsay Bennett
Michael Bennett
Mike Bennett
Mitchell Bennett
Neil Bennett
Terry Bennett
William Benoit
Andy Benson
Jeff Benson
Mary Bente
Christopher Bentley
Miles Bentley
Nigel Bentley
Lindsay Benton
Michael Benton
Seth Benton
Malik Benyebka
Marvin Benzing
Cindy Benzon
David Berens
Jill Berg
Randy Berg
Allen Berger
Jay Berger
Nicole Berger
Roland Berger
Michael Bergeron
Anders Bergkvist
Bernie Bergman
Mark Bergman
Nicholas Bergman
Carl Bergquist
Gerry Berkheimer
Jeremy Berlin
Ken Berlin
Jay Berman
Nestor Bernabe
Jeffrey Bernales
Peggy Bernardis
Turhan Berne
Mark Berner
Roy Bernhardt
Lee Ann Berning
Bart Bernstein
Bobby Bernstein
Buck Bernstein
David Bernstein
Robert Bernstein
Mark Bernstine
James Berrigan
Bradlee Berry
Brian Berry
Dan Berry
Eileen Berry
Jay Berry
Chad Berryhill
Ryan Berthod
Gary Bertoldo
Jeff Berumen
Benjamin Berven
Clifford Berwald
Neil Bessent
David Best
Alvaro Betancur
Jon Betts
Daniel Bettwy
Bill Beverly
Jay Bewley
Mark Bewsey
Adrian Bey
Mark Bey
Tim Beyer
Taras Beyko
Ed Beyster
Jerko Bezelj
Ana Bezjak
Happy Bhalla
Himanshu Bhardwaj
Jaideep Bhatia
Tushar Bhosle
Juan Bianchi
Tanda Bianco
Charles Bibbee
Ronald Bick
Daniel Bickett
Steve Bickham
Benjamin Bicknese
Debbie Bickoff
Joe Biedenharn
Anna Bielen-Zarska
David Bier
Joseph BierFauble
Bryan Biever
Rifat Biktyakov
Joshua Bill
Peter Billingham
Ray Bilsey
Beth Bilyeu
Joseph Binder
Carl Bindlechner
Jeff Bingo
Jean Binkovitz
Stephanie Bird
Leigh Birdsong
Asher Birnbaum
David Birnbaum
Michael Birnbaum
Jeff Biro
April Bisharat
Ben Bishop
Mark Bishop
Skip Bishop
Charles Bison
Brian Bixler
Carl Bjerregaard
Ernest Blachowiak
Brandon Black
Jeffrey Black
John Black
Kristin Black
Paul Black
Rob Black
Scott Black
Shawn Black
Debby Blackburn
Dustin Blackburn
Kyle Blackburn
Robert Blackburn
Martin Blackman
Miles Blackman
Philip Blackwelder
Phyllis Blackwell
Oscar Blacutt
David Blagden
Christopher Blair
David Blakeley
Creighton Blanchard
Zak Blanchard
Grayson Blanchette
Louis Blanchette
Ryan Blanchette
Ismael Blanco
Ernie Blando
Oscar Blando
Adam Blanford
Bill Blankenbaker
Jack Blankenhorn
Paul Blankenship
Michael Blass
Jennifer Blassingame
Jamie Blatman
Bob Blazekovic
Dean Bleazby
Charles Bleckinger
Joanne Bleckinger-O'Bryan
Tim Blenkiron
Timothy Blessing
John Block
Pat Block
Gina Bloemers
Jeffrey Bloomberg
William Bloomquist
Kurt Blorstad
Marc Blouin
Gwen Blount
Sasha Bluestone
Jason Blum
Scott Blumberg
Bradley Blume
David Blumeris
Donald Bly
James Boardman
Lisa Bobby
Craig Bobo
Riki Bocchini
Grace Bociccio
Alden Bock
Jace Boda
Josiah Boda
Jim Boden
Gary Bodenmiller
Bill Bodie
Cameron Bodily
Nicholas Bodley
Daniel Bodner
Steven Boeder
Cynthia Boehler-Walsh
Chrisann Boehm
Sergiu Boerica
Bo Bogardus
Antonio Bogat
Steven Bogdanoff
Alex Bogdanovic
Chris Bogdanovitch
David Boggs
Matthew Boggs
Richard Bograd
Trey Bogue
John Bogusewski
Elizabeth Bohac
Alan Bohane
Jacqueline Bohannon
Andrea Bohn Eisinger
Mark Bohren
David Bohrnstedt
Richard Bohrnstedt
Ron Bohrnstedt
Tom Boice
David Bojalad
Bruce Boland

Pamela Bolduc
Charles Bolender
Lee Boles
Michael Boles
Lewis Bolin
Charles Boling
Steven Boll
James Bollettieri
Nick Bollettieri
Nathan Bolling
Brian Bollman
Kathryn Bolstad
Ralph Bolton
Krysta Anne Boltz
Iztok Bombac
Joyce Bonasera
James Bond
Donnia Bondallian
Nataliya Bondarenko
Matthew Bonds
Matthew Bong
James Bongiovi
Michael Bonnell
Chico Bonner
Rebecca Bonner
Rick Bonner
Jamie Bonter
Rick Bontrager
Catherine Boomer
Dave Boon
Steve Boone
Andrea Booth
Andrew Booth
Charlie Booth
Douglas Booth
Kenneth Booth
Teri Boragno
Jane Borden
Will Borders
James Borell
Dave Borelli
Barry Boren
James Borendame
Mark Borgiasz
Tim Borick
Steven Bork
Desislav Borov
Scott Borowiak
Eva Borras
Carlos Jonathan Borras Estevez
Kara Borromeo
Maureen Bortscheller
Roman Borvanov
German Boryachinskiy
Jerry Borysko
Lucile Bosche
Andrew Bosco
Alex Bose
Paul Boslet
Beat Bossart
Stanford Boster
Mary Boston
Blake Boswell
Doug Boswell
Deon Botha
Christopher Botsford
Lynn Bottger
Adam Bottorff
Yuri Boudagian
Matthew Boughton
John Bougon
Stephen Bouis
Thomas Boulay
Philip Boulter
Kai Renee Boulware
Joe Bouquin
Edward Bourchier
Gary Bourgeois
Lloyd Bourne
Jamie Bourquin
James Boustany
Bob Boutin
Steve Bova
Chris Bovett
John Bowbin
Emily Bowden
Stuart Bowden
Warren Bowden
Jack Bowe
Michael Bowen
Steven Bowen
Bret Bowers
Daniel Bowers
Beverly Bowes-Hackney
Elizabeth Bowker
Todd Bowlby
David Bowman
Stacie Bowman
Greg Bowser
Aisling Bowyer
Brendan Bowyer
Shaun Boyce
David Boyd
David Boyd
Greg Boyd
Jeanette Boyd
Roger Boyer
Scott Boyer
Steven Boyer
Paul Boykin
Sue Boyle
William Boyles
Rick Boysen
Don Bozarth
Maury Bozman
Juan Bracho
Jeffrey Brack
Jack Bracken
David Brackett
Ian Bradburn
Joseph Braden
Carey Brading
Amy Bradley
Andy Bradley
Chris Bradley
Christie Bradley
Doug Bradley
Gordon Bradley
Harvey Bradley
Kevin Bradley
Milo Bradley
Arnold Bradshaw
Benjamin Bradshaw
Gavin Bradshaw
Paul Bradshaw
Jessica Bradu
Barry Brady
Brad Brady
Christopher Brady
Cindy Brady
Kip Brady
Pam Brady
Steve Brady
John Bragg
William Brahler
Jeff Brainard
Alicia Bramhall
Mark Bran
Ronny Bran
Michael Branan
Allyson Brand
Cassandra Brand
Kevin Brandalik
Mitchel Brandell
Mark Brandenburg
Jeff Brandes
Andy Brandi
James Brandon
Michael Brandon
James Brannon
Eddie Brantley
Sydney Brass
Roger Brasseaux
David Braswell
Nina Bratchikova-Kur
Dan Bratetic
Phil Brauer
Collin Braun
Kevin Braun
Michael Braun
Carol Braunstein
Grete Bravo
Milvia Bravo
Stephen Brawley
Dawn Bray
James Bray
Brad Breakstone
Tom Breece
Patrick Breen
Patrick Breen
John Bregin
David Breitkopf
Scott Brekken
Michael Breler
Robert Brenes
Frank Brennan
Gayle Brennan
Jaylen Brennan
John Brennan
Kevin Brennan
Tom Brennan
Charles Brenner
Christine Brenner
Hank Brenner
Jeff Brenner
David Brent
Paul Bress
Chris Bretoi
Bob Brett
Patrick Breuer
Arthur Thomas Brevick
Christopher Brewer
Lewis Brewer
Matt Brewer
Nestor Briceno
Jeffrey Bricker
David Briddle
Mitchell Bridge
Bob Bridges
Charles Bridges
Kirby Bridges
Randy Bridgman
Tim Brielmaier
Robert Brierley
Anthony Bright
Steve Brillhart
Paul Brinda
Thomas Brinkhoff
Lori Brinson
Glenn Britzius
Aaron Brock
Tony Brock
Steve Brockriede
Alanna Broderick
David Broderick
Jerry Brodt
Alan Brogan
Jan Brogan
David Bromberg
Harold Bromer
Cheryl Bromley
Peter Bronson
Ayako Brooks
Brian Brooks
Chip Brooks
David Brooks
Derek Brooks
Jimmie Brooks
Norward Brooks
Ronald Brooks
Denise Brosseau
Don Brosseau
Andrew Brothers
Matt Brothers
Jack Broudy
Jason Broussard
Clete Browder
Aaron Brown
Amy Brown
Bailey Brown
Baraka Brown
Brian Brown
Chris Brown
Chuck Brown
Curtis Brown
Dale Brown
Dante Brown
Dave Brown
David Brown
Deborah Brown
Doug Brown
Evan Brown
Jeff Brown
Jim Brown
John Brown
Kelvin Brown
Larry Brown
Larry Brown
Marcia Brown
Mark Brown
Matthew Brown
Melburn Brown
Michael Brown
Michelle Brown
Nigel Brown
Norvell Brown
Peter Brown
Richard Brown
Rick Brown
Russell Brown
Scott Brown
Stacy Brown
Stephen Brown
Susie Brown
Suzy Brown
Tara Brown
Tyler Brown
Wade Brown
William Brown
Jane Brown Grimes
Christopher Brown-Borden
Kelly Brown-Cobbs
Doug Browne
Federico Browne
Geoff Browne
Roger Browne
Meredith Browning
Renee Broxson
Charles Bruce
Marcy Bruce
Lloyd Bruce-Burgess
Tami Bruce-Romero
Arne Brudner
Tim Brueggeman
Mark Bruflat
Duane Bruley
Erik Bruley
David Brummitt
Kevin Brundle
Ed Brune
James Brunetti
Diego Brunicardi
Bunny Bruning
Juandell Brunner
Mark Brunner
Matthew Brunner
Mason Brunson
Steven Brunstein
John Brvenik
Bill Bryan
Danielle Bryan
Merle Bryan
Michael Bryan
Roy Bryan
Charles Bryant
Robert Bryant
Stephen Bryant
William Bryant
Chuck Brymer
Gordon Brynildsen
Mike Brzoska
Mickey Brzov
Ana Brzova
Igal Buberman
Tomas Bubilek
Michael Bucar
Steve Bucar
Dominick Bucca
David Buchheim
Laura Buchholtz-Belardinelli
Andrew Buchholz
Taylor Buchholz
Trey Buchholz
Gregg Buchko

Scott Bucic
Cari Buck
David Buck
J. Page Buck
Jim Buck
Lulu Buck
Gary Buckhalter
Beverly Buckley
Brant Buckley
Andrew Buckner
Robert Budacsek
Nancy Budde
Karen Buddenborg
Troy Budgen
Joshua Budler
Kevin Budrawich
David Budway
Nathaniel Buechler
Scott Buell
Tom Buell
Andrew Buensalida
Regi Buenviaje
Carlton Buerger
David Buerkle
Richard Buerkle
Ernest Buff
Brooks Buffington
Barrett Bugg
Heidi Buggele
Vicki Buholz
Wesley Buhr
Trung Bui
Vu Bui
David Bukowski
David Buksa
Adriana Bule
Carol Bulfer
Nancy Bulkley
Bob Bull
Chris Bull
Kyle Bull
Leighton Bull
Will Bull
Matthew Bullock
Wayne Bullock
Peter Buntemeyer
Danny Buongiorno
Gennady Burakovsky
Adam Burbary
Dan Burch
Lori Burdell
Fred Burdick
Frank Bures
Aldo Burga
Elizabeth Burger
Lukas Burger
Vaclav Burger
Daniel Burgess
Daniel Burgess
Luis Burgos
Douglas Burhanna
Abigail Burke
Kathy Burke
Philip Burke
Susan Burke
Tim Burke
Tim Burke
Greg Burks
Johnny Burks

Herman Burkstaller
Jesse Burleson
Lisa Burleson
Peter Burling
Stephanie Burnam
Howard Burnett
Cordie Burnette
Brian Burns
Kenneth Burns
Mary Burns
Patrick Burns
Patti Burns
Paul Burns
Michael Burnstein
Celina Burris
Paul Burrus
Adam Burt
Gerard Burt
Michael Burt
Rose Burtnett
Doug Burton
Scott Burton
Peter Burwash
James Busby
Bill Bush
C G Bush
Charles Bush
George Bush
Sean Bush
David Bushnell
Bill Busiek
William Bussey
Andrew Bustamante
Michael Bustamante
Rich Bustamante
Barry Butcher
Trish Buterbaugh
Bekky Butler
Kimberly Butler
Leslie Butler
Richard Butler
Tom Butler
Tim Butorac
Ed Butterworth
Leland Buttle
Suzie Butts
Sommer Butz
Stephen Butzlaff
Thaddeus Buurkarl
Kevin Buyse
David Bvunzawabaya
Lynn Bybee
Kelly Bylciw
Bob Bynum
Mark Byrd
Rick Byrd
Thomas Byrne
John Byron
Matthew Cabana
Michael Cabana
Chris Cabanban
Rodrigo Cabato
Ben Cabell
Lindsey Cable
Mike Caboy
Leonard Cabrera
Dean Caccamo
Kevin Caccia
Sandy Cadel

Collin Cadwell
Michael Caeg
Rodrigo Cagide
Christopher Cagle
Sean Cahill
Thomas Cahill
Tom Cahill
Ying Zhan Cai
Tracy Caillaud
Athena Cajas
Vilis Cakans
Willie Cakans
Chuck Calar
Quinn Caldaron
Dale Caldwell
Paul Caldwell
Rob Caldwell
Tom Caldwell
Michael Calkins
Jonathan Call
Thomas Callahan
Lester Callaway
Robert Callaway
Jennifer Callen Beveridge
Kenny Callender
John Callicutt
Jonathan Calloway
Richard Callwood
John Calton
Rick Calton
Mark Calvert
Andrea Calvert-Sanders
Manuel Calvo
Peter Camenzind
Andrew Cameron
Rob Cameron
Anthony Cammarata
Caleb Camp
Bobbie Campanaro
Mark Campanile
Anni Campbell
Cliff 'Levi' Campbell
Colin Campbell
Dale Campbell
Grady Campbell
John Campbell
Julie Campbell
Matthew Campbell
Philip Campbell
Robert Campbell
Timothy Campbell
Todd Campbell
Travares Campbell
Walter Campbell
Jessica Campbell Batchelor
Benton Camper
Enrico Campi
Aldrin Campos
Joe Canada
Richard Canales
Miguel Cancel
Adrian Canencia
Thomas Cangelosi
Paige Cangialosi
Katelyn Caniford
Pedro Caniza
Steven Cannavale
Shelby Cannon
Arturo Cano

Melissa Canowitz
Rose Cantlin
Daniel Cantu
David Cantu
Guadalupe Cantu
Sabrina Capannolo
Jerry Cape
Rory Capener
Jorge Capestany
Martha Capestany
Eymard Capinpin
Eric Caplan
Joe Capobianco
Philip Capozziello
Michael Capozzoli
Joe Cappellino
Don Caprio
Tin Capulong
Joseph Caputo
Dan Caragata
Wendy Caragher
David Carberry
Margaret Card Beckmann
Fredy Cardenas Reyes
Mary Lou Cardie
Richard Cardiff
Javier Cardona
Danilo Cardoso
Martin Carenko
Anthony Carey
Tom Carey
William Carey
Mary Carillo
Jevgenij Cariov
Jeremy Carl
Robert Carlbo
Frank Carleton
Howard Carley
Andrew Carlos
Andrew Carlson
Brandon Carlson
Brian Carlson
Danny Carlson
Hans Carlson
Mesa Carlson
Robert Carlson
Ted Carlson
Todd Carlson
George Carlsson
Robert Carlton
Sean Carlton
Steven Carman
Evan Carney
Katherine Carnohan
Teresa Caro
Gino Carosella
Dan Carozza
Elizabeth Carpenter
Jeff Carpenter
Kathryn Carpenter
Marshall Carpenter
Anthony Carpio
Devin Carr
Haven Carr
James Carr
Lancy Carr
Michael Carr
Michael Carreno
Carlos Carrillo

Gabriela Carrillo
John Carrizosa
Ben Carroll
Keith Carroll
Patricia Carroll
Grace Carruthers
Mark Carruthers
Richard Carson
Scott Carson
Jared Carstenn
William Carte
Andrew Carter
Claire Carter
Greg Carter
Jamie Carter
Kris Carter
Margot Carter
Mike Carter
Molly Carter
Ryan Carter
Stan Carter
Tim Carter
Christopher Cartwright
Mikolaj Caruk
James Caruthers
Cid Carvalho
Frederique Carver
Rob Carver
Farren Casad
Vincent Casale
Pam Casale-Telford
Christopher Casanova
Gigi Casapu
Billy Casas
Georg Casas Hoelscher
Tom Cascarano
Rick Case
Ross Case
Rebecca Case-Lawler
Peter Caselton
Carlos Casely
Daniel Casesa
Lillo Casesa
Brett Casey
Chris Casey
Kendra Casey
Mike Casey
Robert Casey
Alan Cash
Doug Cash
Bobby Cashman
Joseph Casper
Marc Casperino
Jason Caspers
Miranda Cass
Paul Cass
John Cassas
Neal Cassidy
Rob Cassidy
Ryan Cassidy
Jeremiah Casson
Ernesto Castanares
Cesar Castaneda
Francois Castejon
Rodney Caster
Keith Casterlin
Gary Castillo
Luis Roberto Castillo
Michael Castillo

Neale Castillo
Ruben Castillo
Sal Castillo
Skye Castle
Rob Castorri
Andres Castro
Danny Castro
Patrick Castronovo
Ron Catano
Steve Catapano
Tomas Catar
Byron Cato
Bruce Caton
Steve Cattani
Humberto Catter
Travis Cattron
Jerry Caulfield
Cassie Causey
Rachel Causey
Rich Causey
Giancarlo Cava
David Cavalcanti
Robert Cavanagh
Tiernan Cavanna
John Cave
Vincelle Caviness
Hunter Cawley
Philippe Ceas
Rebecca Cecere
Michal Cech
Christopher Cecil
Guillermo Celard
Mario Celarie
Philip Cello
Mario Celso
Tyler Cempre
Greg Center
Michael Center
Richard Centerbar
Mark Centrella
Maria Cercone
Leon Cerdena
Rodrigo Cerdera
Debbie Cerell-Weinberg
Zdenek Cernoch
Jesus Ceron Garrido
Jeff Cervantes
Jorge Cervantes
Manuel Cervantes
Miguel Cervantes
Sheen Cesare
Adrien Chabria
Raul Chacon
Umang Chadda
Sam Chadwell
Barney Chadwick
Billy Chadwick
Brent Chaffee
Walker Chaffin
Michael Chaho
Kandy Chain
Lloyd Chaisson
Veronique Chalhoub
Kent Chalmers
John Michael Cham-A-Koon
Gary Chamberlain
Michael Chamberlain
Philip Chamberlain
Nicole Chambers
Shelley Chambers
Terry Chambers
Chris Champ
Bill Champion
Gail Champion
Melissa Champion
Victor Champion
Chun Lung Chan
Francois Chan
John Chan
Ricky Chan
Ryan Chan
Shu Yin Chan
Thomas Chan
Chip Chandley
Jeff Chandley
John Chanfreau
Andy Chang
David Chang
Hon Chin Cy Chang
Weylu Chang
Sithiphon Chantos
Yang Chao
Casey Chapa
Cody Chapman
Courtenay Chapman
Jaime Chapman
John Chapman
Mayela Chapman
Richard Chapman
Robert Chapman
Steve Chapman
William Chapman
Rich Chappuis
Bruce Charity
Ed Charles
Margot Charlton
Jared Chase
John Chase
Linda Chase
Neil Chase
Robert Chase
Albert Chassard
Anthony Chatfield
Amy Chatoff
Bhuvan Chaturvedi
Arnab Chaudhuri
Carlos Chaumer
Dennise Chauvet
Fernando Chavez
Mark Chavez
Raul Chavez
J. Dean Chavooshian
Sheldon Chazen
Tom Cheatham
Mark Chellas
Chung Hsiu Chen
Dan Chen
Jason Chen
Li Chen
Png Chen
Wei Jie Chen
Xiaoming Chen
Xiu Qin Chen
Yang Chen
Ye Chen
Brian Cheney
Christopher Cheng
Danny Cheng
Tech Cheng
Marco Cheng Wai Kuen
Jacky Cheong
Sorin Cherebetiu
Dana Cherebetiu Potts
Anthony Cherone
Leigh Cherveny
Curt Chesley
Mukesh Chetan
Thiroshan Chetty
Waip Ip Cheung
Brice Chevalier
Mike Cheves
Jonathan Chew
Vivian Chhetri
Poon Chi Kwong
Chris Chiang
Darren Chiao
Kaori Chiba
Masayuki Chiba
Taizo Chibana
Masashi Chida
Robert Chiene
Manju Chikkappa
Barbara Childers
Robert Childers
Jamie Childree
Keith Childree
Gary Childress
Tammy Childs
Zoe Childs
Edmund Chilton
Robyn Ching
Todd Ching
Tokiharu Chino
Jose Chipe
Catalin Chira
Sheila Chiricosta
Kendall Chitambar
Gheorghe Chitu
Linda Chitwood
Tommy Chiu
Wing Shun Chiu
Jason Cho
Howard Chodak
Junne Choe
Jung Ho Choi
Ming Fai Choi
Young Kee Choi
Holly Chomyn
Hyun Jin Chong
Javier Chong
Matthew Chong
Chris Chopra
Doneta Chorney
Tom Chorney
Dave Chover
Alvin Chow
Stevie Chow
Sam Chow Chak Chung
Ruslan Chowdhury
Salim Chraibi
Brian Christensen
Paul Christensen
Corbett Christian
George Christian
Kevin Christian
Paul Christian
Virgil Christian
Eric Christiansen
Jeff Christianson
Ronald Christman
Jerry Christoforatos
Alan Christopher
Mingyang Chu
Wesley Chu
Sasha Chuchkovich
Jonathan Chui
Edwin Chukwurah
Kourtney Chumbley
David Chun
Cheng Chun Sing
Gavin Chun Suen
Chan Chun To
Danny Chung
David Chung
Henry Chung
Kristin Chung
Nate Chura
Bob Cianchetti
Franklin Ciano
John Ciarleglio
Greg Cicatelli
Jerry Cifuentes
Craig Cignarelli
Paola Cigui
Bertan Cikigil
Gary Cimperman
Harry Cinnamon
Emma Cioffi
Agata Cioroch
Mark Cipollini
James Ciuffo
Sam Ciulla
Mike Claiborne
Jon Clair
Bill Clark
Bobby Clark
Bonita Clark
Brian Clark
Brian Clark
Carl Clark
Catherine Clark
Christian Clark
Clayton Clark
David Clark
Eric Clark
Jacqueline Clark
Jeff Clark
Jessica Clark
Justin Clark
Kathy Clark
Kevin Clark
Kim Clark
Michael Clark
Michael Clark
Natalie Clark
William Clark
Clinton Clarke
Corey Clarke
Mary Clarke
Brian Clary
Marc Claude
Adam Clauson
Bob Clauson
Christian Clauson
Beth Clay
Brian Clay
Eric Clay
Christopher Clayton
Noel Clayton
John Cleary
Scott Cleere
Dwayne Clegg
Sharon Cleland
Scott Clemens
Robert Clement
Delric Clemmons
Kurt Clemmons
Gary Clermont
Pierre Clermont
Don Cleveland
Will Cleveland
Jill Cleverdon
Paul Click
Gabriel Clinger
Penny Clinger
Ernie Cloer
Herminio Closas
Dale Closi
Patti Clousing
Dean Clower
Eric Clowers
Stephen Cluse
Gregory Coache
Rex Coad
Andrew Cobb
Lillian Cobb
Stephen Cobb
Tom Cobb
Tyler Cobb
Sean Cobble
Miguel Cobbs
George Cobia
Mario Cobo
Carlos Cobos
Robert Coby
Joseph Coccimiglio
Dennis Cochran
Charles Cochrane
Park Cockerill
John Anthony Codomo
Joseph Codomo
Bob Cofer
Lowell Coffman
Anders Cohen
Bob Cohen
Ernest Cohen
Issa Cohen
Jason Cohen
Jay Cohen
Jeff Cohen
Jeff Cohen
Stacey Cohen
Steve Cohen
Ali Colak
Catherine Colarossi
Ricardo Colberg
Pat Colbert
Chad Colby
Bill Cole
Carla Cole
Elizabeth Cole
Paul Cole
Troy Cole
William Cole
Scott Colebourne

Chuck Coleman
Claudia Coleman
Garry Coleman
Jeffrey Coleman
Keith Coleman
Keith Coleman
Michael Coleman
Ron Coleman
Tweet Coleman
Arianna Colffer
Erick Collas
Leoncio Collas
Isabel Collas-Banis
Jose Collazo
Aredi Colletti
Frank Colletti
George Collier
Kevin Collier
Cary Collins
Ed Collins
Gene Collins
Glen Collins
Gordon Collins
Kathryn Collins
Kevin Collins
Larry Collins
Marjorie Collins
Mark Collins
Mike Collins
Scot Collins
Todd Collins
Marquel Collins-Gray
Courtney Collins-Guentner
Scott Collinsworth
Kurt Collis
Brian Collison
Daniel Colon
Kevin Colozzi
Pablo Colvee Nebot
Maryann Colville
Meaghan Colville
Dennis Combs
Gregory Combs
Jeff Comer
Jared Compton
Rocco Cona
Gregory Conaway
Ivan Conchar
Joe Concialdi
Jim Concotelli
Callee Conda
James Conda
John Condreay
Andrew Conley
Kevin Conlogue
Michele Conlon
Casey Connaway
Deborah Connell
John-Paul Connell
Karen Connell
Tommy Connell
Frances Connelly
Katherine Connelly
Kevin Conner
Tad Connerton
Barrett Connolly
Kevin Connolly
Susan Connolly
Matt Connor
Cheryl Connors
Christian Connors
Jack Conrad
Jerry Conrad
Linda Conrad
Janusz Conradi
Dennis Conroy
Koach Conroy
Michael Conroy
Shane Conroy
Ellen Considine-Miller
Calin Constanceanu
Steve Contardi
Steven Contardi
Leonardo Contini
Bryan Conway
Harold Conway
John Conway
Loretta Conway
Shawn Conyers
Anne Cook
Brian Cook
Christy Cook
David Cook
Jack Cook
Jennifer Cook
Jim Cook
John Cook
John Cook
JonMichael Cook
Justin Cook
Lloyd Cook
Matthew Cook
Robert Cook
Steve Cook
William Cook
Yvette Cook
Jonathan Cooke
Shawn Cooke
Richard Cooley
Karl Coombes
Andrew Coon
Jordan Coons
Bob Cooper
Brittany Cooper
Charles Cooper
Chucky Cooper
Greg Cooper
Jack Cooper
Jon Cooper
Kenneth Cooper
Shelby Cooper
Joshua Cooperman
Christopher Cooprider
Norman Copeland
Peter Copeland
Michael Copenhaver
Eddie Copete
Matt Copland
Kandace Copley
Marius Copos
Rafael Corazza
Dave Corbin
Julie Corcoran
Chris Cordano
Nicholas Cordes
Andrew Cordova
Rodolfo Cordova
Diana CordovaElliott
David Cordrey
Krista Corette
Clark Corey
Glenn Corey
Craig Corfield
Russell Cormier
Jim Corn
Eric Cornejo
Daniel Cornelison
Hilary Cornelius
Mary Cornell
Rob Cornell
Juan Coronel
Michael Corpening
Juan Cristobal Correa
Natalia Correa
Jeffrey Corson
Sana Cortas
Nelson Cortes Anderson
Anthony Cortez
Jaime Corteza
Trenton Corvino
Timon Corwin
Brian Cory
Kevin Cory
Matthew Cory
Francis Coryell
Frank Cosentino
Colleen Cosgrove
Greg Cosgrove
Roy Cosio
Ransom Coslett
Brian Cosma
Erica Cossairt
Josh Cossitt
John Cost
Arturo Costa
Gavin Costanzo
Jan Costello
Will Coston
Nicholas Cote
Richard Cote
Alesia Cotman
Annabelle Cotten
Daniel Cotton
Lee Couillard
Paula Coulter
Brian Counts
Jill Counts
Charles Courtney
Jeffrey Courtney
Julian Cousins
Dany Couture
Chloe Couture-Chrislock
Duane Covell
Richard Covell
Robin Coverdale
Fabrizio Coviello
Joel Coville
Dennis Covington
Matthieu Covizzi
Conrad Cowan
Polo Cowan
Susan Cowan
Brian Cox
Dee Cox
Joan Cox
John Cox
Nancy Cox
Robert Cox
Tyler Cox
Kristen Coy
Stephen Coyle
Jim Coyne
Malachy Coyne
Megan Cozad
Sean Craft
Glenda Craig
John Craig
John Craig
Shawn Craig
Trent Craig
Corky Cramer
Eric Cramer
Art Cramp
Jim Crane
Patti Crane
Adam Cranford
Paul Cranis
Devin Crawbuck
Carl Crawford
Collin Crawford
David Crawford
Geoffrey Crawford
Randy Crawford
Steve Crawford
Tamara Crawford
Leonard Credeur
Ian Creighton
Robin Creighton
Annette Cremin
Walter Crenshaw
Andrew Cretella
Thatcher Cribbs
Scott Crichlow
Nathan Crick
Petra Crimmel
Christopher Cring
Julie Criscoe
Michael Criscoe
Ryan Criscoe
Henry Crocker
Debbie Croft
Bay Croitoru
Tobias Croke
Gregory Cromwell
Craig Cronrath
Al Crook
Gregory Crosby
Tom Crosby
Cody Cross
Derik Crosser
Monte Crosswhite
Perry Crosswhite
Devin Crotzer
David Crouch
Glenn Crouch
George Crouse
George Crouse
Jim Crouse
Matthew Crouse
David Crouzet
Jeff Crowne
Karen Crumpton
Dion Crupi
Rick Crutcher
Antonio Cruz
Emerito Cruz
Liz Cruz
Mirian Cruz
Carlos Cruz-Aedo
Joe Csandli
Kris Csandli
Regina Csibi
Bill Csipkay
Rex Cuajunco
Jose Cubillos
Zhenhui Cui
Keith Cullen
Chris Culley
Chip Cullison
Lisa Culp
Steven Culver
Tom Cuming
Chris Cummings
Darryl Cummings
Kevin Cummings
Windy Cummings
Anthony Cunha
Bryce Cunningham
Patrick Cunningham
Steve Cunninghame
Rick Cuny
Patrick Cupo
Julien Curatella
Rafael Curbelo
Joseph Curcio
Barry Curley
Sean Curley
Michael Curran
Travis Curran
Tracie Currie
David Currier
Robert Currier
Patrick Curry
Jade Curtis
Melissa Curtis
Todd Curtiss
Liam Cushing
Ken Cussick
Mike Custer
Steve Cutchin
Alan Cutler
Mark Cutter
Toby Cuttriss-Curtis
Gerard Cuva
Roger Cypriano
John Cyrus
Miguel Cysneiros
Carla Czaja
Cami Czech
Joseph D'Aleo
Ammon D'Alessio
Ralph D'Ambrosio
Paul D'Amico
Anthony D'Angelo
James D'Angelo
Lori D'Antonio
Louie Da Silva
Neil Da Silva
Breita Daavettila
Rajnish Dabkara
Chris Dabrowski
Ben Dabush
Houshang Dadfar
Rich Dadich
Shervin Dadkhahipoor

Andrei Daescu
Austin Daglis
Thomas Daglis
Tom Daglis
Tony Daharsh
Jacob Dahl
Peter Dahlborg
Brian Dahlstrom
William Dahm
Samual Dahmer
Mary Dailey
Yasuyuki Daimon
Hasan Dajani
Julie Dale
Milton Dalida
Chris Dallas
Bob Dallis
Rosalee Dallman
Cory Dalos
Christopher Dalton
Daniel Daly
James Daly
Jeffrey Daly
John Damgaard
Boris Damjanovic
William Damron
Sachiyo Dan
Brad Dancer
Ed Dancsak
Timothy Dancy
Andre Danford
Mark Dang
Scott Daniel
Corey Daniels
Diane Daniels
Terri Daniels
Paul Danielson
Scott Danielson
Dan Dao
Long Dao
Jaime Dapper
Kethan Darbar
Nicholas Dargene
Clement Darko
Charles Darley
David Darling
Gloria Darling
Vincent Darmohusodo
Roger Darrohn
Curtis Darrow
Gregory Dart
Hakan Darud
Naveen Das
Melkon Dasnabedian
Tracy Daspit
Michael Date
Gabrielle Datlow
Rajeev Datt
Phillis Dattilo
Peter Daub
Michael Daugherty
Steve Daugherty
Peter Dauphinee
Aaron Davenport
Mike Davey
Jean David
Kristopher David
Mitchell David
Sylesh David
Bill Davidson
Debra Davidson
Michael Davidson
Owen Davidson
Tracy Davies
Alexander Davis
Anne Davis
Bud Davis
Carling Davis
Corey Davis
Curly Davis
Daniel Davis
Donald Davis
Eddie Davis
Glenn Davis
Jeff Davis
Jesse Davis
Jim Davis
Jonathan Davis
Jonathon Davis
Kim Davis
Kimberly Davis
Lavonne Davis
Leslie Davis
Lori Davis
Mark Davis
Mark Davis
Mark Davis
Mark Davis
Mary Davis
Mason Davis
Matthew Davis
Max Davis
Paul Davis
Randy Davis
Raymond Davis
Ricky Davis
Robert Davis
Robert Davis
Robert Davis
Scott Davis
Seth Davis
Tim Davis
William Davis
Rick Davison
Anoosh Davoudzadeh
Sara Davy
Karleen Dawson
Arlon Day
Kenny Day
Matt Day
Reginald Day
Chris Dazet
Job De Boer
Jaime De Carvalho
Emile de Cuba
Carlos de Cubas
Matias De Genaro
Brent De Groot
Jeremiah De Jose
Christian De Los Rios
Jose de Moura
Rohan De Silva
Rik de Voest
Cullen De Windt
Cedric De Zutter
Jay Deacon
Mark Deaderick
Brian Dean
Chip Dean
Kimberly Dean
Jack DeAndrade
Diana Deaver
Miki DeBaise
Runumee DeBerry
Elliot DeBolt
Jimmy Deboo
Dominick DeCarlo
Anthony DeCecco
Andrew Decker
Chris Decker
Robby Deckert
Scott DeCoste
Conray Decuba
Raymond DeCuba
Brett DeCurtins
Jan Deener
Donna DeFrances
Lewie DeGeneault
Steve Deggelman
Ruzie Degirmenci
Doug DeGroot
Ken DeHart
Rosemary DeHoog
Victor DeHoog
Gregg Deinhart
Matthew Deitch
Robin Deitch
Joe Deitchler
Davor Dekaris
David Dekeersmaker
Matthew Dektas
Moses Del Bosque
Jorge Del Moral
Michael Del Priore
Jill Del Rio
Angel Del Valle
Gerald Del Valle
Jamie Dela Cruz
Bill Delaney
Cathie Delaney
Christophe Delavaut
Jimmy Delevante
Olivia Delfausse
Justin Delgado
Robert Delgado
Bob Deller
Stephen Deller
Katie Dellich
John Delloiacono
Arch Delmarsh
John Delong
Joe DeLuna
Diane DeMartini
John DeMartini
Lisa DeMasi
Robin Demasse
Jeanne Demer
Brook Deming
Leonardo DeMiranda
George Demmas
Brian DeMontfort
James Demos
Gregory DeMoustes
Jim Dempsey
Jim Dempsey
Ryan Dempsey
Larry Dempster
Jennifer Demsey
Yasen Deng
David Denham
Kim Denig
Allison Denike
Linda Denis
Lansing Dennett
Susan Dennett
Elaine Denney
George Dennis
George Dennis
Patrick Dennis
Marvin Dent
Phil Dent
Taylor Dent
Ivaylo Dentchev
Douglas Denton
Steve Denton
William Denton
Nitin Deodhar
John DePew
Justin DePietropaolo
Royce Deppe
Bill DeRango
Michael Derby
Anthony DeRitis
James Derrick
Elizabeth Derry
Jean Desdunes
Shirish Deshpande
Michael DeSimone
Sam DeSimone
Maxime Desmars
Becky Desmond
Bailey Desormeaux
Denton Desquitado
Gale Desrosiers
Charles Dess
Trimmer Dettor
David Detwiler
Melissa Detwiler
Brian DeVilliers
Brian DeVirgilio
Kyle Devlin
Marty Devlin
John DeVorss
Stephen DeVries
Madhusudan Dewan
Brad DeWitt
Michael DeWitt
Doug Dexheimer
Lee DeYoung
Gino Di Giacinto-Hillis
Carlos Di Laura
Francis Di Menna
Elena Diaconu
Dmitri Diakonov
Stephen Dial
Jonathan Diamond
Steve Diamond
Angel Diankov
Joseph Dianna
Alex Dias
Brent Dias
Francisco Diaz
Jesus Diaz
Juan Diaz
Maureen Diaz
Stephen Diaz
Thomas DiBartolomeo
Samuel Dibbins
Colin Dibley
Jerri DiCamillo
Mark DiChiara
Dave Outback Dickenman
Mike Dickens
Janna Dickerson
Scott Dickey
David Dickinson
Ruth Dickinson
Mark Dickson
Joseph DiCosola
Millie Didio
Tricia Diebner
Andrew Diefenbach
George Dieffenbach
William Diehl
Kristen Diels-Flagler
Khanh Diep
Peter Dietrich
Tim Dietrich
James Dieveney
Steve diFeliciantonio
Jeff Diggs
David Dilettuso
Claudia Dill
Kenneth Dill
Kim Dillard
Zachary Dillard
Ewell Brent Dillon
Mario DiLonardo
Jai DiLouie
Justin Dilts
Justin DiMaio
Milos Dimic
Marc Dimino
Thomas Dimitry
Tom Dimofski
Radu Dina
Tony DiNardo
Joseph Dinoffer
Nicholas DiNubile
Michael Dinubilo
Stephen Dionne
Natalie Diorio
Tricia DiPalo
Bryan Dirk
Natalie Diroma
Douglas DiRosario
Gerrit Disbergen
David DiSesa
Keith Dismuke
Todd Dissly
John Dister
Butch Dixon
Jason Dixon
Jim Dixon
Stephen Dixon
Tom Dixon
Sean Dizon
Thomas Dizon
Javier Djeu
Khoa Do
Vinh Do
W. Dobbins
Eric Dobsha
Kevin Dobyns
Chad Docktor

Tonia Dodd
Michelle Dodier
Pam Dodman
Edward Dodson
Lisa Dodson
Cynthia Doerner
Jim Doessel
Hiroshi Doi
John Dokken
Stephanie Dolence
Cameron Doles
Eugene Dolgovykh
William Dollard
Dave Dollins
Jeff Dollins
Kimberly Dollins
Michael Dolph
Michelle Domanico
Mike Dombrowski
Mollie Domian
Craig Domingues
Macky Dominguez
Mark Dominguez
Jesus Dominguez Guerrero
Daniel Dominguez Lario
Arlen Domoney
Bill Donahoe
Douglas Donald
Larry Donaldson
Matthew Donaldson
Troy Donato
Teodora Doncheva
Michael Donchey
Haolei Dong
Gary Donnelly
Patrick Donnelly
Peter Donnelly
Matthew Donnett
Edwin Donoso
Raymond Donovan
Scott Donovan
Dave Dooley
Mark Dooley
Samantha Dooley
Terry Doran
Alex Dorato
Conor Dorian
Alex Dority
Chase Dority
Richard Dorn
Ryan Dornier
Frank Dorsky
Tamir Dossiea
Eliot Dota
Mary Doten
Daniel Dotsey
John Dotson
Rita Dotson
Debbie Dotson Swindoll
Mike Doty
Bryce Doubrava
Brian Dougherty
Deborah Douglas
Gordon Douglas
Jennifer Douglas
Pharrington Douglass
Alexander Dove
Eric Dove
William Dow
Jacob Dowdell
Rodney Dowell
Daniel Downing
James Downing
Martha Downing
Matt Downing
Mike Downs
Michael Dowse
Emma Doyle
Steve Doyle
Susan Doyle
Andrea Drabenstott
Marta Drane
Landon Draper
Paulina Dreaden
Whitney Dreaden
Ronald Dredge
Scott Dredge
Madeleine Dreith
Reggie Drew
Fred Drilling
Nancy Driscoll
Tim Driscoll
John Drnec
Mark Drons
Stephen Drosdick
Glidden Droz
Gary Druckman
Beth Druffel
Ralph Drumheller
Bradley Drummond
Cliff Drysdale
Johan Du Randt
Paul du Toit
Thiago Dualiby
Alfonso Duarte
Kris Dubach
Jeanne Dubin
Ross Dubins
Michael Dublin
Allen DuBois
Mait DuBois
William DuBois
Ted Ducary
Christopher Dudeck
Blake Duden
Chris Dudley
Julie Dudley
Marcus Dudley
Waylon Dudley
Carol Duffy
Edward Duffy
Kevin Duffy
Shelby Dufrene
Chris Dugan
Rod Dulany
Jacques Dumais
Jeff Dumansky
Pierre-Henri Dumas
Emily Dumelle
Arnold Dun
Maxim Dunaev
Ralph Dunbar
Vic Dunbar
John Duncan
Karen Duncan
Kayla Duncan
Kyle Duncan
Mike Duncan
Stuart Duncan
Chris Dundas
Tom Dundis
Timothy Dunford
Peter Dungca
Robert Dunkle
William Dunkle
Jonathan Dunlap
Andrew Dunleavy
Laird Dunlop
Steven Dunmore
Grace Dunn
Joseph Dunn
Tara Dunne
Rod Dunnett
Joseph Dunphy
James Dunseith
Harry Dunstan
Timothy Dunville
Larry Dupleich
Guillaume Dupont
Matthew Dupont
Petra DuPont
Victor Dupre
Lary Duque
Raymond Durack
Gilbert Duran
Andres Durandegui
Andy Durham
Carolyn Duronslet
Brian Dushock
Jacques DuToit
Jacqueline Dutot
Arup Dutta
Ron Dutton
Andrew Duvall
Aaron Dvorak
David Dvorak
Urska Dvorsek
Joan Dwyer
Oleg Dyachenko
Jakub Dybala
Jacek Dybas
Julie Dybendahl
Aaron Dyer
Joshua Dyer
Rusty Dyer
Joseph Dyser
Ron Dyson
Natallia Dziamidzenka
Leng Ea
Patrick Eagan
Cameron Eagle
Carly Eagle
Robert Eanes
Sen Eapen
Fred Earle
David Earlewine
Shane Earley
Michael Early
Ramsey Earnhart
Louis Eason
Brad Easterbrook
Brendan Easterling
Glen Eastridge
Delores Eaton
Ross Eaton
Jonah Ebenhoeh
Doug Ebenstein
Warren Eber
Caitlin Eberle
Kevin Eberwein
Kevin Eby
Zachary Eccher
Erica Echko
Michael Eck
Kreg Eckert
Peter Eckhardt
Jason Eckles
Laura Ecton
Bob Ecuyer
Jacob Eddins
Christine Eddy
Kurt Edelbrock
Anna Edelman
David Edgar
Linda Edgar
Michael Edghill
Steve Edgington
Katie Edin
Matthew Edin
Joe Edles
Becky Edles-Rye
Derek Edmonds
Thomas Edsall
Dai Edwardes-Evans
Blake Edwards
Brian Edwards
Cherise Edwards
Conner Edwards
Crandall Edwards
David Edwards
Jamie Edwards
John Edwards
Regina Edwards
Todd Edwards
Spencer Eells
Ko Egashira
Brian Egelhoff
Jacqueline Egelhoff
Christopher Eger
Dieter Ehlermann
Richard Ehrenreich
Kurt Ehrhardt
Ruya Eichelberger
Larry Eichenbaum
Jeff Eicher
Patrick Eichhorn
Charles Eidenschink
Tim Eiff
Mike Eikenberry
Polly Eilers
Jack Einbinder
Taylor Eisemann
Charles Eisenberger
Tony Eisiliones
Bassel Eissa
Nicholas Ekern
Patrik Ekstrand
Abdellah El Farissi
Naser El-Amad
Mehdi El-Kheddiwi
Amir Elbayoumy
Aaron Elbert
John Elbogen
James Elder
Wayne Elderton
Svetoslav Elenkov
Ibrahim ElGazaery
Lionel Eli
George Elias
Kerner Elie
Ronald Elizondo
Henri Elkins
Todd Ellenbecker
Sean Ellerbrock
Carl Ellerson
Bonnie Elliott
Erik Elliott
Heath Elliott
Jeffrey Elliott
Mark Elliott
Sam Elliott
Todd Elliott
Bryan Ellis
Charles Ellis
Charlie Ellis
Marlene Ellis
Debra Ellsworth
Doug Elsass
James Elwing
Christopher Elwood
Lloyd Emanuel
Rudolph Embernate
John Embree
Wayne Emerick
Brett Emerson
Jim Emerson
Roy Emerson
Nelson Emery
Daniel Emmerson
Martin Emmrich
Joseph Emond
Masanori Emori
Chad Empey
Manuel Encalada
Roy Encarnacion
Kunio Endo
Ryan Endraske
Betsy Endres
Doug Eng
William Eng
Guy Engbino
Arin Enge
Charles Enge
Scott Enge
Allison Engel
Tom Engel
Nico Engelbrecht
Eric Engelsgjerd
Zubin Engineer
Claude England
Vicki England Patton
Elana Engleman
Nathaniel Engler
Jeff English
Tommy English
Anthony Enlow
Bill Ennis
Yasuyuki Enoki
Isao Enomoto
Takuya Enomoto
Yuki Enshu
Stephen Ensor
Steffi Entzminger
Tarik Enustun
Robert Eppsteiner

Joshua Epstein
Robert Epstein
Benjamin Erickson
Eric Erickson
Lynn Erickson
Nina Eriksson
Eric Erlandsen
Eric Ernstrom
Jacques Ertel
Patrick Escalambre
Richard Escalante
Dale Eshelbrenner
Hideo Eshima
Juan Manuel Esparcia Clemente
Paige Esparza
Elvis Espinal Acevedo
George Espinosa
Hugo Espinosa
Michael Espinosa
George Esqueda
Michelle Esquivel
Kevin Essary
Stephan Esser
Joseph Estacio
Eduardo Esteban
Maxx Esteves
Pedro Estrada
Yale Estrin
Rick Etchells
Steve Ethier
Jeannie Etra-Latuga
Jeffery Etterbeek
Timo Ettore
Brian Etzkin
Caerwyn Evans
Chase Evans
Craig Evans
Dave Evans
John Evans
Lane Evans
Mike Evans
Pride Evans
Susan Evans
Chris Evert
Drew Evert
John Evert
Laura Ewert
Tom Ewert
Chayenne Ewijk
Jeff Ewing
Lawrence Eyre
Marcus Eyth
Frederick Faber
Mark Faber
Manuel Fabian
Constantino Fabros
Peter Fagan
Douglas Failla
Barbara Fain
Daniel Fair
Jason Fairbrother
Joseph Fait
Mary Pat Faley
Steven Falk
Heather Falkin
Brandon Fallon
James Falvo
Kevin Fane
Glen Fanelli
Brian Fankhauser
James Fannin
Frank Fanning
Jose Farias
Julia Farina
Ernesto Farinas
Danny Fariss
Dave Farmer
John Farmer
Paige Farmer
Pam Farmer
Scott Farnham
Pamela Farnsworth
Eric Farran
Brian Farrell
Mike Farrell
Terry Farrell
Margaret Farris
Fredrick Farrokhi
Bjorn Farrugia
Sheri Fasbinder
Michael Fash
Christoffer Fasth
Toby Fasth
Melanie Fauchet
Margaret Faughnan
Jacques Faulise
Hayden Faulkenbury
Brooke Faulkner
Steve Faulkner
Tom Faulkner
Trish Faulkner
Christopher Faulman
Patricia Faust
Richard Faust
Matthew Fawcett
David Fay
Peter Fazekas
Chip Fazio
Jamie Feagan
Vicky Feaman
Andrew Fearnside
John Fears
Leonard Fechter
Mike Fedderly
Roy Fedelem
William Federhofer
Ryan Feenick
Jill Feher
Lajla Feichter
Paul Fein
Marilyn Feinstein
Edward Brittin Feldhausen
Jil Feldhausen
Brandon Feldman
Erik Feldman
Joe Felice
Nick Felice
Manrico Feliciano
Tracy Fenelon
Zhu Feng
Tucker Fenske
Elyse Fenton
Jeffrey Fenton
Robert Fenton
Markham Fentriss
Byron Ferguson
Doug Ferguson
Lavenia Ferguson
Mickey Ferguson
Roger Ferguson
Mark Ferlazzo
Richard Ferman
Ernie Fernandez
Gigi Fernandez
Isabel Fernandez
Manuel Fernandez
Mercedes Fernandez
Robert Fernandez
Roberto Fernandez
Robert Ferrante
Bernard Ferrao
Andre Ferreira
Brad Ferreira
Luiz Ferreira
Sean Ferreira
Charles Ferreira Da Silva
Colleen Ferrell
James Ferriero
Jorge Ferrin-Kranewitter
Brandon Ferris
Michael Ferriss
James Ferry
Boris Fetbroyt
Barbara Fetter
Sterling Fetty
Matthew Feury
Eric Fey
Tom Fey
Paul Fiala
Andre Fick
Mark Ficks
Scott Ficks
Luis Fidalgo
Julie Fidler
Travis Fields
Jennifer Fiers
Ricardo Fiestas Iglesia
Joann Figueroa
Reinaldo Figueroa
Alvaro Figuerola
Ryan Fike
David Filhart
Michael Filipek
Roderick Filipinas
Igor Filipovic
Lisa Filpi
Ron Filstrup
Victor Fimbres
Tina Fina
Gay Finch
Douglas Finck
Andy Findlay
Paul Findlay
Yann Findlay
Michael Findling
Amanda Fink
Mary Fink
Zach Fink
John Finkel
Richard Finn
Lynn Finnell
Robert Finney
Peter Fiore
Charlie Fischer
Lowell Fischer
Michael Fischer
Milan Fiser
Tom Fish
Barbara Fisher
Dale Fisher
Daryl Fisher
Howard Fisher
Jessica Fisher
Roger Fisher
Shane Fisher
Todd Fisher
Steve Fiske
Tony Fittipaldi
Andy Fitzell
Maureen Fitzgerald
Michael Fitzgerald
Mike Fitzgerald
Patrick Fitzgerald
Timothy Fitzgerald
Gilma Fitzgibbon
Richard Fitzmaurice
Tom Fitzmaurice
Jim Fitzpatrick
Kristopher Fitzpatrick
Mike Fitzpatrick
Luke Fitzsimons
Peter Fiumefreddo
Marco Flacco
Rick Flach
Randall Flachman
Robert Flader
Kaitlin Flaherty
David Flakoll
Brandon Flanagan
Philip Flanagan
James Flanigan
Roald Flater
Karen Fleissner
Jim Fleming
Mark Fleming
Scott Fleming
Jim Flesch
Andrew Fletcher
Bill Fletcher
Christopher Fletcher
Ian Fletcher
Dave Fleury
Lori Flick
Craig Fligstein
Ann Flint
Craig Flint
Marilee Flint
Dusan Flok
Tony Floreno
Francisco Flores
Mary Ann Flores
Renato Floresca
Robert Florian
Mike Flowers
Brooks Floyd
Marcus Fluitt
Justin Flynn
William Flynn
Daniel Fogel
Jeff Foley
John Foley
Chadwick Folger
Roger Follmer
Kevin Folse
Maxsim Fomine
Dexter Fong
Kar Chun Fong
Kuang Fong
Scott Fong
Patrick Fontana
Paul Fontana
Kris Foote
Adam Ford
Frank Ford
Scott Ford
Merlene Forde
Bill Foreman
Brett Foreman
Kie Foreman
Rex Foreman
Scott Foreman
William Foreman
David Forman
Dustin Forman
Darryl Fornatora
Jayner Foronda
Christopher Forrest
Gregory Forrest
Keith Forrester
Gregory Forster
Tracie Forsythe
Stephen Fortson
Paul Fortunato
Jaime Fortuno
Steven Fosdick
Alan Foster
David Foster
Ed Foster
Jack Foster
John Foster
Kevin Foster
Shawn Foster
Trey Foster
Vicki Foster
Kathy Foulk
Frank Fourgeau
Thomas Fowkes
Jeff Fowle
Barbara Fowler
Charles Fowler
David Fowler
Harry Fowler
Jeff Fowler
Jim Fowler
Richard Fowler
Bryan Fowlkes
Allen Fox
Connie Fox
Dainyell Fox
Keith Fox
Peter Fox
Regis Fox
Tamara Fox
Rayni Fox-Borinsky
Christopher Frageman
Imelda Frail
Fernando Fraile Salgado
Jerry Frain
Mark Fraley
Jonathan Fralick
Sally Frame
Mark Frampton
Carolyn Franca
Peter Francesconi

Joseph Francis
Neville Francis
Christer Francke
Anthony Franco
Briana Francois
Steve Francour
Barbara Frank
Steven Frankel
Joanne Franklin
Martha Franklin
Steve Franklin
Bruce Franks
Amanda Frantz
Wendy Franz
Dustin Franzen
Joseph Franzen
John Fraser
Patricia Fraser
Ryan Fraser
Jason Frausto
John Frausto
Claude Frazer
J. Howard Frazer
Shaun Frazeur
Ray Frazier
Jim Frederick
Joy Frederick
Lee Fredricks
Nicole Fredricks
Mark Fredriksz
Ashley Freeman
Dorothea Freeman
Marcus Freeman
Mark Freeman
Billy Freer
George Freije
David Freiman
Peter Freischlag
Anne French
Janet French
Robbie French
Tory Fretz
Warren Frewer
Robert Frey
Kenneth Friar
Susan Frieder
Barry Friedman
Barry Friedman
Jaynes Friedman
Michael Friedman
Michael Friedman
Ross Friedman
Jennifer Friend-Kerr
Peter Friesen
Jeffrey Frischman
John Fritts
David Fritz
Frank Froehling
Robert Fronauer
Jose Frontera
Bill Frost
John Paul Fruttero
John Fry
Kevin Frye
Rafael Fuentes
Marcus Fugate
Keiichiro Fuji
Yuko Fujiki
Kenji Fujima
Kimitaka Fujimoto
Akihisa Fujino
Toshinori Fujinuma
Tomokazu Fujishige
Akira Fujita
Hidemaru Fujita
Miwa Fujita
Hiroaki Fujiwara
Kazuhisa Fujiwara
Shohei Fujiwara
Norio Fukaya
Yasuo Fukui
Tetsuya Fukumoto
Toru Fukumoto
Yoshio Fukuoka
Jun Fukushima
Makoto Fukushima
Warren Fulgenzi
Anthony Fuller
Jeremiah Fuller
Ty Fuller
Thomas Fulmer
William Fulton
Zane Fulton
Dean Funabiki
Jack Funcik
Jose Funes
Christy Funk
Kim Funk
Tom Funk
Joseph Furioso
Karol Furmaga
Roger Furman
Maja Furniss
Susan Furtney
Shoji Furukawa
Satoshi Fushita
Julia Fusik
Steve Futchko
Steve Futchko
Kim Fyfe
Megan Gaard
Elad Gabay
Sara Gabbard
Sarah Gabel-Hall
Laura Gabella
Philippe Gabler
Stefan Gabler
Seth Gabriel
Elizabeth Gabrielle
Linsey Gabris
Sotera Gacad-Cowan
Umesh Gadasalli
Greg Gadoua
Bonnie Gadusek
Samuel Gaeddert
Emmanuelle Gagliardi
Mario Gagliardi
Paul Gagliardi
Adam Gagnon
Larry Gagnon
Paul Gagon
Matthew Gahan
Kelly Gaines
Aleksandar Gajic
Sabrina Galan
Tom Galbraith
Simon Gale
Ginifer Galey
Bambi Gallagher
Karen Gallagher
Ned Gallagher
Steve Gallagher
Steve Gallagher
David Gallardo
Donald Gallardo
Dennis Gallas
Hans Gallauer
Hunter Gallaway
Brian Galle
Chris Galle
Derek Galli
Michael Galli
Devin Gallo
Joseph Gallo
Mariano Gallo
Yvonne Gallop
Tracy Galongo
Daijiro Gamachi
Mary Gambale
Leslie Gambee
Bruce Gambill
Derek Gamble
Mandy Gamble
Anna Marie Gamboa
Kristine Gambrell
John Gambucci
Adolfo Games
Michael Gan
Spencer Gander
Zachary Ganger
Craig Gansen
John Gant
Raj Ganti
Zhengyang Gao
Angelina Gaponova
Greg Garancovsky
Matt Garavaglia
Carmen Garcia
Ed Garcia
Gonzalo Garcia
Ivan Christopher Garcia
Jesus Garcia
Juan Garcia
Kayla Garcia
Mario Garcia
Robert Garcia
Sam Garcia
Hernan Garcia Vivot
Bogdan Gard
Jake Gard'ner
Sue Gardiner
Ashlee Gardner
Jason Gardner
Michael Gardner
Sanford Gardner
Teresa Gardner
Mary Lynn Garger
T J Garin
Steve Garman
John Garnett
Michael-John Garnett
Sig Garnett
Spence Garo
Augie Garofoli
Johan Garos
John Garr
Javier Garrapiz
Kyle Garretson
Clay Garrett
Kevin Garrett
William Garrett
Amy Garrity
Robert Garrucho
Gary Garver
Lucy Garvin
David Gary
Connor Garyotis
Rosie Garza
David Garzia
Martha Garzon
Ed Gaskell
Perry Gaskell
Terri Gaskill
Donald Gaskins
Tim Gasko
Alexandra Gaspar
Mark Gasper
Michael Gaston
Chuck Gately
Bill Gates
Gary Gates
Jack Gates
Julianna Gates
Kirkland Gates
Richard Gates
Scott Gates
Bill Gatlin
Shannan Gaudette
Gary Gaudio
William Gauditz
Lisa Gauff
Richard Gaulieder
Guillaume Gauthier
Angelica Gavaldon
Laramie Gavin
Dudley Gayle
Benton Gaylor
Matthew Gaynor
Gerard Gbedey
Michael Gealer
Diane Geater
David Geatz
Adam Gebeau
Johan Gedlitschka
Darryl Gee
John Gegenheimer
Russell Gehring
Geoff Gehrke
Ted Geier
Lindsay Geiger
Nathan Geigle
Susan Geist
Michele Gelfman
James Gelhaar
Jennifer Gelhaus
Marc Gelina
Tom Gellner
Mark Gelsinger
Paul Gemborys
Kelly Gemmiti
Kenyon Generette-Oliver
Marion Gengler Melton
Asaya Genka
Mike Gennette
Gina Genovese
Ron Gentner
Tommie George
Zorana George
Andrea Georgian
Walter Geraghty
John Gerard
Michael Gerard
Glenn Gerbino
Stuart Gerechoff
Jeff Gerhart
Jerry Gerig
Jens Gerlach
Peter Gerstenfeld
John Gervasio
Steven Gervickas
Ben Clifford Gerwick
Eric Gessner
Patricia Gessner
Vernon Gettone
Nicolaus Getz
Mark Geyer
Christopher Geyman
Jerry Geyman
Nancy Ghantous
Abbas Ghasemi Hesar
Paul Ghayad
Florica Gheorghe
Tommy Ghosn
Sam Giammalva
Sam Giammalva
Frank Giampaolo
James Giancola
David Giannandrea
Kerry Giardino
Kenneth Giavara
Dennis Gibbens
Jackie Gibbins
Tim Gibbon
Paul Gibbs
Rhonda Gibbs
Carri-Ann Gibson
Elton Gibson
Kathy Gibson
Laurence Gibson
Peter Gibson
Robert Gibson
Tom Gibson
Kim Gidley
Edgar Giffenig
Brian Giffin
Reiko Giffords
Abbas Giha
Eduardo Gil
Harry Gilbert
Jason Gilbert
K Napoleon Gilbert
Keith Gilbert
Laura Gilbert
Pamela Gilbert
Lisa Gilbride
Geoff Gilchrist
Diane Gildemeister
Fritz Gildemeister
Marissa Gildemeister Chapin
Jason Gilkey
Bryon Gill
Chuck Gill
Dana Gill
David Gill
Golden Gill

Paul Gill
Ravi Gill
Patrick Gillant
Damian Gillespie
Robert Gillespie
Roy Gillespie
Tom Gillespie
Damon Gillette
Kevin Gillette
Joseph Gilliam
Patricia Gilliam
Jay Gilliford
Katherine Gillis
Courtney Gilman
Malcolm Gilreath
Chris Gilroy
Virginia Gilroy
Regan Gin
Clifton Gingerich
Deborah Ginn
Keith Ginnetti
Claudio Giraldi
Leo Giraldi
Carlos Girola
Adam Gislason
Bill Gist
Moses Gittens
Steve Gittleson
Florin Giuglescu
Iddan Givon
David Giza
David Glackin
Kasey Gladding Hamaway
Andrew Gladstone
Rita Gladstone
William Glasgow
Karen Glaus
Dale Glaze
Alyssa Gleason
Michael Gleason
Kevin Glenn
Matthew Glennon
Joshua Glick
Robert Glickman
Brett Glidewell
Geoffrey Gluck
Lisa Gnann
Keva Godfrey
Wanda Godfrey
Eric Godin
Marlin Godown
Julio Godreau
Martin Godwin
Neville Godwin
Joshua Goff
Carlos Goffi
David Gold
Jonas Gold
Michael Goldammer
Dolly Goldberg
Lisa Goldberg
Marc Goldberg
Dermott Golden
Jason Golden
Jeffrey Golden
Richard Golden
Dustin Goldenberg
Tim Golder
Dean Goldfine
Marty Goldhaber
Mark Goldin
Darryl Goldman
James Goldman
Sally Goldman
Steve Goldman
Jeff Goldmann
Barry Goldsmith
Jonathan Goldsmith
Adam Goldstein
Bernice Goldstein
Drew Goldstein
Ralph Goldstraw
Jenna Gollub
Charles Golphin
Robert Golsmith
Juan Gomez
Robert Gomez
Ruben Gomez
Don Gomsi
Gustavo Goncalves
Lakshman Gonela
Chris Gonzales
Claudia Gonzales
Edward Gonzales
Leonardo Gonzales
Manuel Gonzales
Mark Gonzales
Phillip Gonzales
Spike Gonzales
Benjamin Gonzalez
Eddie Gonzalez
Emilio Gonzalez
Erasmo Gonzalez
Francisco Gonzalez
Gilberto Gonzalez
Hiram Gonzalez
Ivan Gonzalez
Mark Gonzalez
Max Gonzalez
Nikolas Gonzalez
Sandra Gonzalez
Alberto Gonzalez Villodas
Terrie Gooch
Douglas Goodall
Ronnie Goodall
Paul Goode
Jenni Goodling
David Goodman
Michael Goodman
Susan Goodman
Teri Goodman
Michael Goodrich
Ian Goodwillie
Lawrence Goodwyn
Trish Gooley
Rena Goolsby
Shigeaki Gorai
Craig Gorbach
Jason Gorchow
Anne Gorde
Bill Gordon
Brian Gordon
Edward Gordon
Kwame Gordon
Matthew Gordon
Theodore Gordon
Todd Gordon
Shannon Gordon Carney
Kenneth Gore
Jim Gorman
Joseph Gorman
Susan Gorman-Smallman
Sam Matthew Gornez
Christopher Goroleski
Anne Gorrell
Sergey Gorshenin
Mary Gorton
Bob Goss
Sylvia Gothard
Junko Goto
Mariko Goto
Yoshitaka Goto
Brian Gottfried
Larry Gottfried
Jan Gottlin
Bruce Gould
Dick Gould
Ronald Gould
Sharon Gouse
Marcelo Gouts
Jay Govan
Frank Governor
Megan Govi
Jagadish Gowda
Allen Gowin
Yuu Gozawa
Erich Grabowski
Chris Gracey
Ron Gracey
Andrew Graczyk
Kim Gradoville
Kristen Grady
Joy Graeff
Bob Graf
Isabella Graf
Marilyn Graf
Mike Graff
Rusty Graff
Edward Grafilo
Alan Graham
Harold Graham
John Graham
M Allan Graham
Mark Graham
Philip Graham
Ross Graham
Deborah Graham Shaffer
Dennis Grainger
Genevieve Gramatica
Nestor Gramatica
Adam Grandstaff
Marco Grangeiro
Borden Granger
Aaron Grant
Michael Grant
Pat Grant
Sheldon Grant
Austin Grantham
Michael Grantham
Tony Grassadonia
Terry Gratz
Hali Grauvogel
Antwan Graves
Farrell Graves
Minor Graves
Minor Graves
Bo Gray
Charles Gray
Daniel Gray
David Gray
Jeff Gray
Jenny Gray
Jim Gray
Kathy Gray
Susan Gray
Tommy Gray
William Gray
Matt Grayson
Kimberly Greason
Joseph Grech
Robert Greco
Tony Greco
Alex Green
Bob Green
Brock Green
Brooks Green
Cecil Green
Denny Green
Hallet Green
John Green
Peter Green
Phillip Green
Robert Green
Tracy Greenbaum
Mariann Greenberg
Michael Greenberg
Morton Greenberg
Stuart Greenburg
Michael Greene
Robert Greene
Stephen Greene
Jason Greenspan
Doug Greenwald
Jeff Greenwald
Rocky Greenwood
James Greer
Robert Greer
Scott Greer
Bill Gregg
Keithan Gregg
Mike Gregg
Miha Gregorc
Renee Gregorio
Matthew Gregory
Tom Greider
Genevieve Greiwe-King
Christopher Grennen
Debbie Gresh
Noel Gressner
Matt Greteman
Matt Gribbin
Zenda Griebenow
Mark Griep
Laura Griesinger
Jon Griesser
Jamie Grieve
Alexandria Griffin
Geoff Griffin
Ian Griffin
John Griffin
Madison Griffin
Michael Griffin
Nate Griffin
Noah Griffin
Page Griffin
Kenneth Griffith
Mike Griffith
Walter Griffith
Rene Grifol
Jason Grigg
James Grigo
Gevorg Grigoryan
Steve Grill
Jarred Grimes
Christy Grisham
Anne Griswold
Charl Grobler
Jacob Groce
Russell Grogan
Jay Grollman
Brian Grooms
Jack Groppel
Jared Grose
Jason Grose
Nathan Gross
Tom Gross
Allan Grossman
Bob Grossman
Montgomery Grout
Cory Grove
Jennifer Grove
Janice Grover
Wendy Grover
Jason Grubb
Kyle Grubb
Ann Grubbs
John Gruberg
Branislav Grujic
Myron Grunberg
Arthur Grundy
Dave Grzelak
Jakub Grzeslo
Jeanne Guanzon
Fernando Guarachi
Aggie Guastella
Noel Gubatan
Michael Gucciardo
Frank Guengerich
Linda Guentert
Artie Guerin
Jeff Guerin
Kent Guerin
Fred Guerra
Pat Guerry
Kamel Guessoum
Fernando Guevara
John Guevara
Joseph Guglielmi
Sabine Guibal Britt
Michael Guice
Marco Guida
Henry Guignet
Bill Guilfoil
Michael Guill
Angela Guillette
Patrick Guion
Agustin Guirado
Dayna Guizzetti
Gregory Gull
Bruce Gullikson
Tom Gullikson
Don Guluzzy
Isin Gumuscu
Andrew Gunberg
Charlie Gundi

Michael Gunsallus
Lorri Gunter
Xingpeng Guo
Prem Gupta
Rick Guralski
Cem Gurkaynak
Spike Gurney
Ron Guse
Bernard Gusman
Tim Guss
Magnus Gustafsson
Carolyn Gustavson
Donna Sue Gutierrez
Leandro Gutierrez
Len Gutin
Matthew Gutkin
Jacqueline Guy
Traci Guy
Radek Guzik
Ron Gwyn
Jeff Gwynne
Katalin Gyulai
Iva Gyurgina
William Haardt
Cornelius Haarmann
Heinz Haas
Prycen Haas
Bruce Haase
Herbert Haase
Lauren Haase
Jim Hackett
Christina Haddad
Tanner Haddon
Daniel Haertl
Lance Hagan
Mark Hagan
Trent Hagan
Neal Hagberg
Edward Hagens
Alexander Hager
Jane Hagerty
Mary Hagerty-Severns
Benjamin Hageseth
Ted Hagey
Holly Haggerty
Yuki Hagimori
David Hagler
Christopher Hagman
Jeffrey Hagman
Doug Hague
Kavan Hahn
Phillip Hahn
Brooke Haifley
Sue Haight
Robert Hailer
Darrell Haines
Jonathan Hains
Siamak Hajarizadeh
Farid Hajebi
Lars Hakansson
Robert Hakobyan
Renish Halani
Allison Halbert
Dustin Hale
Kendell Hale
George Haley
Raymond Haley
Ryan Haley
Michael Halisky
Biljana Hall
Brett Hall
Carlin Hall
Danielle Hall
J D Hall
Jaclyn Hall
Joey Hall
John Hall
Kenyon Hall
Kristen Hall
Lisa Hall
Megan Hall
Michael Hall
Michelle Hall
Mike Hall
Richard Hall
Steven Hall
Ted Hall
Mike Haller
Monica Haller
Charles Halm
David Haluska
Steve Halverson
Dan Halvorsen
James Ham
Hiroshi Hamada
Shigeru Hamada
Tadaaki Hamaguchi
Taichi Hamaguchi
Yasutoshi Hamaguchi
Mike Hambrock
Owen Hambrook
Kelly Liggan Hamidi
Clayton Hamilton
Harry Hamilton
Jonathan Hamilton
Kevin Hamilton
Sara Hamilton
Eric Hamlin
Kendal Hammel
Laury Hammel
Kevin Hammell
Bob Hammerlee
Kurt Hammerschmidt
Gordon Hammond
Paul Hammond
Tonya Hammond
Loni Hammons
Devin Hampton
Joel Hampton
Courtney Hance
Ken Hance
Clark Hancock
Craig Hancock
Michael Hancock
Peter Hancy
Robert Hand
Sean Handy
Gregory Hanessian
Sally Haning
Florentina Hanisch
Barry Hankel
Jerry Hankins
Benjamin Hanks
Shishaldin Hanlen
Matthew Hanlin
Mark Hanna
Molly Hannagan
Joni Hannah
Jake Hannas
Bill Hannigan
Rick Hanover
Chris Hansen
Jacob Hansen
John Hansen
Mark Hansen
Jason Hanson
Katie Hanson
Mark Hanson
Calle Hanssen
Patrick Hanssen
Tore Hanssen
Zhengdong Hao
Steve Happe
Simbarashe Happy
Hiroyuki Hara
Hiroshi Harada
Andy Harader
Hiroyuki Harazono
Paul Harclerode
Jerry Hardacre
Sarah Hardacre
Duane Hardek
Daniel Harden
John Harden
Craig Hardenbergh
Keith Hardie
Robert Hardin
Robert Hardin
Erika Harding
Lisa Harding
Charles Hardman
Jay Hardman
Jon Hardman
Byron Hardy
David Hardy
Richard Harfst
Robert Harjes
Thomas Harker
Sarah Harkins
Donnie Harlan
Cathrine Harless
Matt Harless
Jason Harman
Troy Harmon
Jason Harnett
Chris Harper
Darren Harper
Michael Harper
Scott Harper
Tim Harper
Chris Harradine
Keith Harrietha
Craig Harrington
Robert Harrington
Scott Harrington
Simon Harrington
Casey Harris
Clayton Harris
David Harris
Hank Harris
Henry Harris
Irene Harris
Jason Harris
Kristen Harris
Mike Harris
Nancy Harris
Robin Harris
Scott Harris
Sean Harris
Seth Harris
Shawn Harris
Todd Harris
Tumeka Harris
Ursula Harris
Alison Harrison
Kristen Harrison
Mark Harrison
Mark Harrison
Mary Harrison
Nora Harrison
Patricia Harrison
Shane Harrison
Tom Harrison
Shaun Harrop-Keenan
Ryan Harry
Matthew Harse
Jeff Harst
Lisa Hart
Roger Hart
Geoff Harte
Larry Harte
Joseph Hartkemeyer
Carol Hartmann
Kevin Hartmann
Artak Harutyunyan
Douglas Harvey
Tim Harvey
Jim Harwood
Ahmed Hasan
Janonn Hasan
Masahiro Hasegawa
Shinya Hasegawa
Junko Hashimoto
Shinji Hashimoto
Tsuyoshi Hashimoto
Ronnie Hass
Feisal Hassan
Carlos Hassey
Roberto Hassey
Scheraq Hassim
Chris Hastings
Jim Hastings
Shinji Hata
Masakiyo Hatamori
Michael Hatcher
Jerry Hatchett
Sarah Hatgas
Mark Hathorn
Anthony Hatori
Josiah Hatt
Yoshinao Hatta
Frank Hatten
Hironari Hattori
Tomokazu Hattori
Tim Hauge
Robert Haugen
Sharon Haugen
Larry Haugness
Brandon Haus
Tim Haus
Tom Hauser
Karen Hausman
Carol Hauspurg
Gavin Havrilenko
Jeff Hawes
Kevin Hawke
Claudia Hawkes
Charles Hawkins
Darrell Hawkins
Donald Hawkins
Gia Hawkins
Jeff Hawkins
Kathy Hawkins
Tom Hawkins
Ryan Hay
William Hay
Nobuyuki Hayama
Hideki Hayashi
Hiroshi Hayashi
Kenichi Hayashi
Naoaki Hayashi
Yosuke Hayashi
Steve Hayden
Bettie Hayes
Keith Hayes
Linda Hayes
Michael Hayes
Patrick Hayes
Scott Hayes
Angela Haynes
Jason Haynes
Mark Haynes
Nicholas Haynes
Ron Haynes
Christi Hays
Michael Hayter
Trenton Hayward
Paul Hazell
Anna Hazlett
Stephanie Hazlett
Jason Hazley
Jim Heacock
Paul Healing
Craig Healy
Patrick Healy
Mark Hearing
Gregory Hearn
Gregory Heartt
Brandon Heath
Joshua Heath
William Heath
Andrew Heatherly
Gary Heatwole
Will Heaven
C. Kent Hebdon
Melissa Heberle
Chad Hebert
John Hebert
Robert Hebert
Karin Hechenberger
Eric Hechtman
Darren Heck
Rod Heckelman
Peter Heckler
Jeff Hedberg
Anna Hedden
Mark Hedden
Geoff Hedges
Shawn Hedrick
Jim Heebner
Peter Heffernan
Lauri Hegarty
Norman Heger
Wendy Heger
Carol Hegranes

Robert Heideman
Josh Heiden
Betsy Heidenberger
Cindy Heidkamp
Ken Heidman
Russell Heier
Brian Heil
John Heim
Kevin Heimann
John Hein
Craig Heinberg
Shawn Heinchon
James Heinecke
Jane Heintzman
Dennis Heinz
Bob Heiser
Julie Heitman
Jordan Helderman
Joshua Heller
Robert Heller
Walter Hellriegel
Matthew Helm
Henry Helmers
Matt Helsel
Bob Helton
Andrew Hemings
Susan Hemphill
Elizabeth Henderson
Gary Henderson
Gerald Henderson
Harold Henderson
Kendra Henderson
Marvin Henderson
Mike Henderson
Richard Henderson
Thomas Henderson
Todd Henderson
David Hendricks
John Hendrickson
James Hendrix
Ned Henize
Damon Henkel
James Henkelman
Mitchell Henkin
Kristi Henn
Bill Henness
David Hennessee
Marty Hennessy
Pat Hennessy
Teri Hennessy
Jonathan Henning
Cathleen Henrich
Mike Henrich
Dee Henry
Elvis Henry
George Henry
Milton Henry
Richard Henry
Steve Henry
Robert Henshaw
Dennis Hensley
Patrick Hensley
Don Henson
Michael Henty
Haryeol Heo
Hyojoon Heo
Greg Herbert
Leslie Herbert
Lester Herbert
William Herbert
Dennis Herendeen
Sean Hergert
Dierdre Herman
Lauren Herman
Thomas Herman
Patric Hermanson
Alex Hermeto
Julio Hermosillo
Brent Hermsmeier
Al Hernandez
Felipe Hernandez
Hector Hernandez
Jacobo Hernandez
Joe Hernandez
Stefan Hernandez
Jefferey Herr
Debra Herrell
Marco Herrera
Han Herrick
John Herrick
Mary Herrick
Peter Herrmann
Dale Hersch
Sean Hersey
Jeff Hersh
Jonathan Hertlein
Alexander Herwig
Jenna Hessert
Pete Hessert
Ruth Hessert
Jason Hester
Benjamin Hestley
Jackie Heston
Jane Hetherington-Rauth
Cole Heule
Julie Heussenstamm
Alan Heverly
Jamie Hevron
Bevan Hewett
Paulo Hexsel
Joseph Heydt
Christine Heynysh
Anthony Hiatt
Shawn Hiatt
Steve Hibben
Kendall Hibbs
Soichi Hibi
DeDe Hibinger
Tony Hicklin
Johnna Hickman
David Hicks
Duaine Hicks
Emery Hicks
Haley Hicks
Shaun Hicks
Todd Hicks
William Hicks
Daniel Hiddleson
Greg Hiers
Sheri Hiester
Jun Higaki
Yasuaki Higaki
Billy Higgins
Kevin Higgins
Mike Higgins
Zachary Higgins
James Higgs-Horwell
Greg High
Joel Higham
Terrance Highfield
Clay Hightower
Jim Hightower
Ron Hightower
Ron Hilburn
Kristen Hildebrand
Mark Hilderbrand
Blake Hilgenkamp
Matthew Hilkey
Christina Hill
Cindy Hill
Glen Hill
Gregory Hill
John Hill
Mary Hill
Matthew Hill
Robert Hill
Steven Hill
Thomas Hill
Tom Hill
Waverly Hill
Catherine Hills
Greg Hills
Richard Hillway
Aboud Hilo
Eric Hilpert
Kevin Hilpert
Rudolf Hilpert
David Hilton
Jon Hilzendeger
Yukihiro Himeda
Adrin Himmelheber
Frederick Hindle
Ken Hine
Bryan Hiner
Alvin Hines
Luis Hines
Paul Hing
Monica Hinkamper
Andy Hinkle
Scott Hinkle
Frank Hinkley
Chris Hinson
Jim Hinson
Ian Hintz
Arnel Hipolito
Haruya Hirai
Haruyuki Hirai
Takashi Hirai
Yoshinori Hirai
Takahiko Hiramatsu
Taku Hirano
Daisuke Hirao
Yusuke Hirasawa
Patrick Hire
Masaru Hirohashi
Takamichi Hirooka
Kaori Hirose
Futoshi Hirota
Chris Hirst
Chris Hirtler
Mark Hirtler
Todd Hiscox
Robert Hislop
Jay Hitchcock
Christina Hites
Susan Hites
Kei Hitomi
Lau Hiu Wai
Yasuhito Hiyoshi
Tom Hlavacek
Zina Hlobil
Chi Hang Ho
Steve Ho
Ryan Hoag
Will Hoag
Anhtu Hoang
Charles Hoang
Brett Hobden
Jimbo Hobson
Robert Hochstadter
Laurie Hock
Andrew Hocker
Michael Hoctor
Bryan Hodge
Andrew Hodges
Anne Hodges
Cary Hodges
Janan Hodges
Allison Hodges Bravo
Ferenc Hodosy
Geoff Hodsdon
Dean Hodsman
Doug Hofer
Anne Hoffman
Christopher Hoffman
Jamie Hoffman
Margery Hoffman
Sandra Hoffman
Rick Hoffmann
Justin Hogh
Eric Hogue
Hisanobu Hojo
Christi Hoke
Nicole Hola
Paul Holbach
Bruce Holbrook
Cullen Holbrook
Ross Holesinsky
Delia Holguin
Hannah Holladay
John Holladay
Jason Holland
Joseph Holland
Randolph Holland
Layne Hollander
Cynthia Hollenbeck
Adam Holley
Darclyn Holliday
Robert Hollis
Lori Hollister
Mariana Hollman
Marne Holloway
Victoria Holloway
Ross Hollowell
Brant Holman
Dan Holman
Becky Holmes
Danard Holmes
Joseph Holmes
Neal Holmes
Norman Holmes
Peter Holmes
Robert Holmes
Waldemar Holowetzki
Sue Holroyd
Chieko Holt
Darren Holt
Matthew Holt
Scott Holub
Lee Holyoak
Adam Holzman
Shawn Holzmann
Alvin Hom
Mike Hon Chi Man
Masamitsu Hondo
Chris Honeycutt
Jiang Hong
Scott Honig
Hisayoshi Honma
Sasao Honma
Stephanie Honsberg
Robert Honzo
Brandon Hooker
Mark Hooper
Peter Hoopes
Aziz Hoosenally
Andreae Hoosty
Christopher Hoover
Heath Hoover
Richard Hoover
Harlan Hopchik
Meredith Hope
Paul Hope
Thomas Hopewell
Dan Hopkins
Philip Hopkins
Allen Hopp
Rick Hoppe
Anne Hopson
Morgan Hopson
Robert Hopson
William Hopson
Angela Horacek
Andrew Horen
Kenneth Horgan
Yoshiharu Hori
Kazuhiro Horie
Kenichi Horii
Shotaro Horiuchi
Chuck Hormann
Timothy Horn
Chris Horne
Jay Horne
Victor Horne
Kevin Hornik
Jennifer Hornsby
Barry Horowitz
Nancy Horowitz
Rob Horsch
John Horsfall
Alec Horton
Rodney Horton
Tom Horton
Gary Horvath
Joseph Horvath
Don Hosch
Hiroshi Hoshi
Chris Hoshour
Scott Hosick
Jim Hoskins
Tina Hoskins
Mototsugu Hosoda
Shinichi Hosoda
Henry Hostetler
Joel Hostetler

Derek Hostetter
Sharif Hotaki
Jim Hotsinpiller
Guangyu Hou
Gregory Houck
Frederic Houdaille
Cameron Houghtaling
Tracy Houk
Justin Houle
Renee Houle
Denise Houriet
Pablo Hours
Brenton House
James House
Marcella Houseal
Matthew Houser
Paul Housholder
Leslie Housman
Dave Houston
Randy Houston
Samvel Hovhannisyan
Stepan Hovhannisyan
Chris Howard
Curtis Howard
Daniel Howard
Dwayne Howard
Jerry Howard
Julie Howard
Ken Howard
Matthew Howard
Michele Howard
Nolie Howard
Renee Howard
Ryan Howard
Scott Howard
Skip Howard
Stephanie Howard
Steven Howard
Todd Howard
Jared Howat
Glen Howe
Bob Howell
Clark Howell
David Howell
David Howell
Dick Howell
Duncan Howell
Johnathan Howell
Peter Howell
Richard Howell
David Howes
Jance Hoy
Thomas Hoyle
Daniel Hoyme
Sheldon Hseih
Ken Hsieh
Chiou Kuo Hsu
Jason Hsu
Thiha Htwar
Charles Huang
Ching Huang
Meng Huang
Shuai Huang
Zhuanxi Huang
Chris Hubbard
Jerry Hubbard
Keith Hubbard
John Hubbell
Ed Hubbs
James Huber
Lysle Huber
Stephen Huber
Martin Hublitz
Adam Huch
Kristy Huck
Shawn Huck
David Huckaby
Adolph Huddleston
Clark Hudson
John Hudson
Kathy Hudson
Kevin Hudson
Les Hudson
Adam Huebner
Chase Huebner
John Huebner
Carlos Huerta
Brent Huesman
Marie-Pier Huet
Candace Huetteman
Patrick Huewe
William Huffman
Emily Hufnagel
Nathaniel Huggett
Jason Huggins
Gregory Hughes
Hank Hughes
John Hughes
Kelli Hughes
Thaddeus Hughes
Ray Hugill
David Hugues
Barry Hui
Chuen Yun Hui
John Hui
Tang Hui Yin
Hassan Humayun
Alain Humblet
Mark Humes
Nick Hummel
William Hummel
Michael Humphrey
Brad Humphreys
Edward Humphreys
Evan Hundley
James Huneke
Melissa Hunfalvay
Andrew Hung
Roger Hung
William Hung
Ashley Hungerford
Bradley Hunt
Conner Hunt
Daniel Hunt
Howard Hunt
James Hunt
James Hunt
Benjamin Hunter
Brent Hunter
Cody Hunter
Jane Hunter
Larry Hunter
Michael Hunter
Terry Hunter
William Hunter
William Huntington
Eric Huntley
Jay Hurd
Walter Hurd
Michael Hurley
Robert Hurley
Mark Hurvitt
Paul Hurwitz
Laura Husaru
Lauren Huse
Anne Hussey
Andrew Huszar
Dalton Hutchins
Charles Hutchinson
Kim Hutchinson
Louis Hutchinson
Renga-Moi Hutchinson
Scott Hutchinson
Sue Hutchinson Carson
Jason Hutchison
Jean Huttepain
Jim Hwang
Judith Hyde
Kenneth Hydinger
Tim Hynes
Dale Hyska
Stefano Ianni
Alessio Iannozzi
Chieko Ibaraki
Fernando Ibarrola
Brad Ibbott
Eric Ice
Takeshi Ichikawa
Hiroo Ichinose
Yasuyuki Ichinose
Masashi Ida
Takeshi Ide
Yohei Ide
Ryan Ideta
Abdul Idi
Nikhil Idnani
Louis Iglesias
Takashi Iguchi
Suzanne Ihnat
Masaki Iinuma
Hidenori Ikeda
Hitomi Ikeda
Shigeki Ikeda
Ryouji Ikehata
Masafumi Ikeshiro
Branimar Ilic
Ksenija Ilic
Martin Illuzzi
Naoto Imai
Toshiaki Imano
Noboru Imasaka
Carlo Impeduglia
Marco Impeduglia
Masayuki Inagaki
Wataru Inagami
Bob Ingersole
Gail Ingis
John Ingles
Gary Ingram
John Ingram
Tom Ingram
Fernando Iniestra
Frank Inn
Gary Innes
Noel Inniss
Keiko Inoue
Kunio Inoue
Ryouichi Inoue
Takeshi Inoue
Yoshihiro Inoue
Yukiko Inoue
Felix Insaurralde
Meg Inscoe
Mike Insko
Fabio Intriago
Keiji Inuzuka
Andrei Ionescu
Florin Ionescu
Heung Yan Ip
Ka-yee IP
Mikk Irdoja
Andre Iriarte
Lauren Irick
Masakazu Irie
Sakae Irisawa
John Irish
Hank Irvine
Helen Irwin
Joel Irwin
Mike Irwin
Scott Irwin
Tim Irwin
Sandi Irwin-Rosato
Jennifer Isaac
Tom Isaac
Evan Isaacs
Robert Isaacs
Yoshiharu Isawa
Joseph Isenhour
Kevin Isenhour
Ronald Iseri
Greg Isermann
Toshinori Ishibashi
Emi Ishida
Junzo Ishida
Ryo Ishigaki
Hideki Ishii
Hiroshi Ishii
Yasuyuki Ishiwata
Yuta Ishizaki
Tsukasa Ishizu
Ali Ismail
Jordan Isom
Dale Israelson
Ippou Itami
Masafumi Itaya
Meiko Ito
Ren Ito
Satomi Ito
Tatsuya Itoh
Chris Ivanov
Andre Ivarsson
Darius Ivaska
Allan Iverson
Dean Ives
Alyssa Ivey
Tomotaka Iwahase
Takahiro Iwamoto
Tetsuya Iwasaki
Katsuji Iwata
Makiko Iwatsuki
Shunji Iwatsuki
Matt Iwersen
David Izumi
Brian Jaaksi
Greg Jablonski
Jeremy Jack
Jeffrey Jacklich
Nathaniel Jackmon
Anna Jackson
Billy Jackson
Cameron Jackson
Carrie Jackson
Curtis Jackson
Donnie Jackson
Eric Jackson
Jimmy Jackson
Kenneth Jackson
Kevin Jackson
Kevin Jackson
Lamar Jackson
Lisa Jackson
Preston Jackson
Raj Jackson
Skip Jackson
Steve Jackson
Gabriel Jacob
Nick Jacobs
Erik Jacobsen
Eugene Jacobsen
Eric Jacobson
Ivona Jacobson
Jeff Jacobson
John Jacobson
Jon Jacobson
Mark Jacobson
David Jacome
Ed Jacques
Eddie Jacques
Kathy Jacques
Mark Jacques
Mike Jacques
Jonathan Jaeger
R. Jaeger
Liz Jaffe
Geoffrey Jagdfeld
Colby Jager
Jumanne Jahi
Carlos Jaik Meillon
Joseph Jaindl
Tom Jaklitsch
Mario Jakovljevic
Susana Jalali
Edmund Jalinske
Edward Jalomo
Mustapha Jamal
Brenton James
Douglas James
Elliott James
Jarvis James
Joe James
Mike James
Tony James
Rebecca Jameson
Jimmy Jamie
Jason Jamison
Renata Jancikova
Jonathan Janda
Karel Jandus
Karel Jandus
John Janes
Zachary Janes
Susie Jannach
Mohammed Jannif
Paolo Jannuzzi

Andy Jansen
Brian Jansen
Darrell Janssen
Tanja Janssen
Kenneth Jantz
Rich Jantzi
Paulina Janus-Titterington
Michael Janz
Javier Jaramillo
Eric Jarkowski
Christopher Jarrell
Howard Jarvis
Adam Jasick
Marius Jaskowski
David Jasmin
Paul Jasperson
Daniel Jauregui
Daria Javid
Edward Javornik
Neeru Jayanthi
Raman Jayapathy
Lahiru Jayasuriya
Judy Jeanette
Lizzie Jeffcoat
Cynthia Jeffcott
Brinton Jefferis
Jason Jeffers
Pavle Jefferson
Stan Jefferson
Kristal Jeffrey
Mark Jeffrey
Mary Jeffries
Ylia Jelali
Karim Jelassi
Jan Robert Jendelund
Michael Jenders
Scott Jenkin
David Jenkins
Pat Jenkins
Paul Jenkins
R Quentin Jenkins
Charles Jenks
Randy Jenks
Justin Jennings
Lee Jennings
Tom Jennings
Allan Jensen
Hans Jensen
Rich Jenson
Teri Jenson
Bryan Jeong
Karen Jeppson
Dale Jerden
David Jerden
John Jerome
Robert Jessen
Michael Jessup
Arun Jetli
Porus Jetli
James Jetton
Trey Jewell
Chaoying Ji
Yongcheng Jia
Yu Jiang
Barbora Jilkova
Russell Jilot
Alberto Jimenez
Hugo Jimenez
Jorge Jimenez
Jorge Jimenez
Richard Jimenez
Tylir Jimenez
Audrey Jin
Baochun Jin
Makoto Jinno
Mike Jizmejian
Allison Joanlanne
Ikaika Jobe
Randall Jobson
Alexander Johansson
Anders Johansson
David Johansson
Erik Johansson
Hakan Johansson
Emmanuel John
Alex Johns
Michael Johns
Mary Johnsen
Benjamin Johnson
Bob Johnson
Bobbie Johnson
Bud Johnson
Bunmi Johnson
Carl Johnson
Christopher Johnson
Chuck Johnson
Clint Johnson
David Johnson
David Johnson
David Johnson
Dencil Johnson
Dick Johnson
Edwin Johnson
Franklin Johnson
Freddie Johnson
Gordon Johnson
Greg Johnson
Jackie Johnson
Jacqueline Johnson
James Johnson
Jan Johnson
Jan Johnson
Jason Johnson
Jason Johnson
Karl Johnson
Kent Johnson
Kerry Johnson
Kyra Johnson
Lance Johnson
Leonard Johnson
Lynda Johnson
Madeline Johnson
Marc Johnson
Marisa Johnson
Michael Johnson
Michael Johnson
Michael Johnson
Nick Johnson
Otis Johnson
Patrick Johnson
Richard Johnson
Shane Johnson
Steve Johnson
Terry Johnson
Timothy Johnson
Travis Johnson
Walter Johnson
William Johnson
Zack Johnson
Adam Johnston
Andrew Johnston
Bill Johnston
David Johnston
Merritt Johnston
Michelle Johnston
Nadia Johnston
Thomas Johnston
Barbara Johnston Hill
Wade Johnstone
Lennart Jonason
Andy Jones
Arthur Jones
Beau Jones
Benny Jones
Brannon Jones
Cameron Jones
Carlton Jones
Craig Jones
Craig Jones
Dave Jones
Dial Jones
Gary Jones
Gordon Jones
Greg Jones
Jack Jones
Jacquelyn Jones
James Jones
Karl Jones
Kimberly Jones
Lawrence Jones
Lianna Jones
Linda Jones
Liz Jones
Mark Jones
Martha Jones
Marvin Jones
Matthew Jones
Michelle Jones
Mike Jones
Rose Jones
Rusty Jones
Spencer Jones
Thomas Jones
William Jones
William Jones
William Jones
Abdul Jordan
Anthony Jordan
Charles Jordan
Keith Jordan
Marc Jordan
Michael Jordan
Josh Jorgensen
Bob Joseph
Ray Josephs
Charles Joslin
Robert Joslin
John Joyce
Cyrus Joyner
Joe Jozefczyk
Maciej Jozwiak
Albert Juaneza
Peter Juarez
Bill Juberian
Terry Juchartz
Bradford Judson
Chris Juergens
Heidi Juhl
Bryan Juinio
Robb Julian
Christopher Juneau
Anna Jung
Daniel Jung
Hyeoncheol Jung
Min Chul Jung
Penny Jung
Roger Junge
Algis Juodikis
Dawn Jupin
Amy Juppenlatz
Stephanie Jurgensen
Mikael Jurkovic
Charles Justice
Jack Justice
Kyle Justice
Peter Jutras
Mike Juul
Kohichi Kabasawa
Rhona Kaczmarczyk
Christopher Kader
Dean Kadera
Michal Kadlacek
James Kaedden
Shinichi Kaga
Masataka Kageyama
Amadi Kagoma
Rachel Kahan
Scott Kahler
Adam Kahn
Larry Kahn
Roger Kahn
Ronald Kahn
Hi Tak Ernest Kai
Takeshi Kaifuku
Don Kaiser
Yoshiaki Kajishita
Junpei Kajiyama
Shigeru Kakita
Takahiro Kakiuchi
Nipun Kakkar
Carrie Kalapala
James Kalenak
Taylor Kalister
Norman Kalkhoff
Jared Kalpin
Lanny Kalpin
Chow Kam Fai
Henry Kamakana
Martin Kamara
Dan Kamerman
Takao Kameyama
Hiroo Kamide
Takashi Kamishima
Hiroshi Kamiya
John Kamosa
Kurt Kamperman
Yuki Kanamaru
Mike Kanapeaux
David Kane
Jason Kane
Kevin Kane
Richard Kane
Takanobu Kaneda
Akihiro Kaneko
Naoyuki Kaneko
Tomoyo Kaneko
Yoshitsugu Kaneko
Tokinari Kanemaru
Kyle Kaneshiro
Petar Kanev
Hyung Seok Kang
Max Kangasniemi
Frederick Kangwa
Patrick Kangwa
Sibongile Kangwa
Yukiko Kankawa
Chris Kannenberg
Keith Kanner
Yoshio Kanno
Daniel Kantar
Elianna Kantar
Robert Kantner
Eric Kantor
Jeff Kantor
Marc Kantor
John Kanyo
Steven Kapaun
Arthur Kapetanakis
Jill Kaplan
Jenna Kappel
Stephen Kappes
Michael Kapsemalis
Larry Karageanes
Craig Kardon
Brad Karen
Christopher Karen
Steven Karendal
Eugene Karimov
John Karle
Christian Karlovits
Janette Karner
Gil Karni
Zsolt Karosi
Kevin Karoub
George Karr
James Karr
Kaptan Karsolia
Jahan Kashani
Yoshiki Kashitani
Yukio Kashiwadani
Kiyotada Kashiwagi
Masaki Kashiwai
Chris Kaskow
Ed Kassatly
Keith Kassouf
Larry Kast
Olivia Kasten
Kirstin Kastor
Carolyn Katayama
Masataka Katayama
Masaki Kato
Takumi Kato
Yutaka Kato
Taroh Katoh
Sota Katsuno
Keizo Katsuragi
Emilie Katz
Larry Katz
Leo Katz
Marilyn Katz
Maurica Katz
Marna Katzel
Dave Kaufman
Richard Kaufman
Ryan Kaufman

Eric Kave
Nicholas Kavelaris
Takami Kawabata
Yukitoshi Kawabata
Jackie Kawahakui
Chad Kawahara
Naoto Kawai
Jun Kawamura
Kenji Kawamura
Hiroto Kawasaki
Tomomi Kawase
Masahiko Kawashima
Kazuhiro Kawauchi
Matt Kay
Yuhta Kayama
David Kayatta
Chris Kayes
Sandra Kazanjian-Gostanian
Douglas Kazarosian
Randy Kazdan
Timothy Kealy
William Kealy
Joseph Keane
Kevin Kearns
Patrick Kearns
Daniel Keating
Jason Kedzierski
Stephen Kee
Chelsea Keefe
Matthew Keefe
Timothy Keegan
Robin Keener
David Keeney
Jerry Keever
Jeff Kefalos
Doug Kegerreis
Manolito Kehoss
Raymond Keiser
Sean Kelleher
Kirk Keller
Steve Keller
Derek Kellermann
Casey Kelley
Levander Kelley
Joe Kells
Anderson Kelly
Catharine Kelly
Charlotte Kelly
Derek Kelly
Ed Kelly
Frank Kelly
Laura Kelly
Lyndsey Kelly
Pete Kelly
Sean Kelly
Thomas Kelly
Tracy Kelly
William Kelly
Dallas Kelsey
Jill Kelsey
Dan Kelton
Amy Kelts
Michael Kember
Wessel Kemp
Amy Kemper
Lisa Kempton
Tyler Kempton
Mary Anne Kendall
Kerry Kendrick
Barbara Kennedy
Bart Kennedy
David Kennedy
Russ Kennedy
Sam Kennedy
Samuel Kennedy
Steve Kennedy
Marsha Kennedy-Horton
Sheldon Kennell
Yu-Hsien Kennell
Neil Kenner
Alex Kenney
Brendan Kenny
David Kensler
Eric Kent
Gordon Kent
Steven Kent
Kimberly Kenwell
Randy Kenyon
Rick Kepler
Jonathan Kerch
Sam Kercheval
Anthony Kerin
Tom Kern
Deanna Kernan
Miikka Keronen
Glenn Kerr
John Kerr
Ivi Kerrigan
Mary Kersey
Punam Kersten
Thomas Kersten
Gary Kesl
Betsy Kessing
Bob Kessler
Keith Kessler
Rajan Keswani
Nicholas Ketcham
Kimm Ketelsen
Linda Kettell
Stephen Keung
Mark Kevorkian
Adam Kework
Edward Keyser
Lynn Khaing
Seyed Ali Khalili Kashani
Ilyar Khammadov
Anwar Khan
Rahim Khan
Patrick Khandroo
Vigen Khanlarian
Harout Khatchatrian
Iryna Khatsko-Scott
Olga Khitrova
Kostyantyn Khodirev
Hyung-Moon Ki
Wailey Kiang
Alexander Kiblin
Paul Kid
Byron Kidd
Scott Kidd
Allen Kiel
Michael Kiewiet
Brian Kiggans
Shunichi Kikuchi
Taisuke Kikuchi
Yoshio Kikuchi
Yumi Kikuchi
Satoshi Kikuzato
Daniel Kilen
Mary Beth Kilian
Tony Kille
Dennis Killelea
Leah Killen
Terence Killen
Terence Killen
Todd Killen
Kieran Killigrew
Patsy Kilmartin
Walt Kilmartin
Eugene Kim
Jae Kyung Kim
Jimmy Kim
Joseph Kim
Scott Kim
Sky Kim
Stephen Kim
Tae Kim
Wonkyoung Kim
David Kimball
Henry Kimmel
Robert Kimnach
Akihiro Kimura
Fuminobu Kimura
Hiroyuki Kimura
Shigenobu Kimura
Elissa Kinard
Judith Kinasewitz
Kimberly Kinberg
Joel Kincaid
David Kincheloe
Jason Kinder
Shelly Kindig
Lew Kiner
Billie Jean King
Bob King
Charles King
Chip King
Cyrus King
Dick King
Doug King
Hannah King
Heidi King
James King
Jamie King
John King
Jordan King
Lisa King
Matthew King
Michelle King
Nancy King
Richard King
Richard King
Riley King
Timothy King
Travis King
Chuck Kingman
David Kingsbury
Jack Kingsbury
Christine Kingsley
Harry Kingsley
Jeff Kinlaw
Kent Kinnear
Akemi Kinoshita
Sho Kinoshita
Takeshi Kinoshita
John Kinsella
Wes Kintner
Charles Kinyon
Gregory Kipnis
Donald Kirby
Susan Kirby
Patricia Kirch
John Kircher
J F Kirk
Joanne Kirk
Steve Kirk
Wesley Kirk
Robert Kirkendall
Drew Kirkley
Jamie Kirkman
Stoyan Kirkov
Bill Kirsch
Glen Kirstine
Sally Kirstine
Clare Kirwan
John Kirwan
Rudolf Kischel
Charles Kiser
Lori Kiser
Matthew Kiser
Mike Kiser
Joseph Kissel
Andrew Kissick
Barbara Kissick
Atsushi Kitano
Gary Kitchell
Cheryl Kitley
Rodney Kitner
Steven Klaas
Jonathan Klampe
Joshua Klapow
Aaron Klapper
Mike Kleban
Cindy Klebe
Aaron Kleefield
Jonathan Kleeman
Zach Kleiman
Art Klein
Daniel Klein
Jim Klein
Francis Klemser
Patrick Klett
Alisa Kleybanova
Drew Kline
Larry Kline
Matt Kline
Robert Kline
Susan Kline
Rick Klingbile
Donald Klinge
Kyle Klinge
Larry Klingenberg
Jared Klose
Andrew Klug
Kris Kluis
Bob Klyce
Corey Knapp
Ralph Knapp
Ryan Knarr
David Knaszak
Bryan Knehr
James Kneussl
Zeljko Knezevic
Dan Knight
Dick Knight
Thomas Knights
Matt Knoll
Devin Knox
Rob Knox
Marc Knutila
Brad Knutson
William Ko
John Koahou
Kenichiro Kobayashi
Masaaki Kobayashi
Yoshito Kobayashi
Yugo Kobayashi
Yuuki Kobayashi
Yuuki Kobayashi
Paul Kobelt
James Kober
Richard Kobleur
Zlata Kobzantsev
Aaron Koch
Robert Koch
Donna Kocyba
Peter Koekkoek
Erin Koenig
Courtney Koenigsfeld
Craig Koessler
Mark Kofman
Toshihide Koga
Barbra Kogan
Jeremy Kogen
Hiroki Kohara
Takuya Kohara
Chris Kohl
Jeff Kohl
Cody Kohlmoos
Yohei Koide
Yoshinori Koide
Michio Koizumi
Satoru Koizumi
Yukie Koizumi
Yoshihisa Kojima
Kenta Kokumai
Dorukcan Kokver
Kathy Kolankiewicz
Erin Kolar
Robert Kolb
Fred Kolehmainen
Michael Kolendo
Paul Kolenich
Thomas Kolenich
Peter Kolifrath
Keith Kolke
Paul Kollmorgen
Tom Kollock
Katya Kolodynska
Aaron Kolz
Norikazu Komaki
Jack Komar
Andrew Komarov
Tom Komassa
Daisuke Komatsu
Tomohiro Kometani
Junpei Komiyama
Glenn Kommer
Mamiko Komoriya
James Konarske
Karel Konderla
Maxim Kondrasov
Maria Kondratieva
John Konecne
Che Wah Kong

Ling Xian Kong
Siow-Kee Kong
Slava Konikov
Paul Kononenko
Kevin Koo
Myongyong Koo
Mark Koons
Thomas Koopsen
Randy Kop
Candice Kopetzki-Girdler
Dimitri Kopilashvili
Ted Kopren
Tijana Koprivica
Zoran Korac
Moe Koregaokar
Alfred Koripamo
Igor Korogodskiy
Yana Koroleva
Boniface Koross
Erik Kortland
Marcin Kosakowski
George Kosanke
Lew Kosich
Michael Koslik
George Kosloff
Adam Kossak
Paul Kostin
Alan Koth
Shubrick Kothe
Yasuhiro Kotobuki
Eon Kotze
Angela Koumaris
Atsushi Kounosu
Glenn Kouns
Adi Kourim
Max Kourim
Diane Koury
Ivaylo Koutlov
Christine Koutras
June Kovach
Keith Kovach
Krisztina Kovacs
Mark Kovacs
Michael Kovar
David Kovas
Kimberly Kovasala
Robert Kowalczyk
Kevin Kowalik
Brian Kowell
Kayne Kowis
Noriyoshi Koyama
Takuro Koyama
Toshiyuki Koyama
Viktoriya Kozachuk
Pawel Kozak
Neda Kozic
Dave Kozlowski
Davidson Kozlowski
Christopher Kraemer
Jerry Kraesig
Brett Kraft
Jonathan Kraft
Whitney Kraft
Rox Ann Krahn
Harry Kraly
David Kramer
Donald Kramer
Karyle Kramer
Suzzanne Kramer
Ryan Krane
Lina Krasnorutskaya
Ed Krass
Michaela Kratochvilova
Toby Krauel
Michele Krause
Kirby Krauter
Jerry Krawchuk
Martin Krbec
Mark Krebs
Michael Kreider
Jacob Kreimer
John Kreis
Lisa Krekeler
Michael Krenz
Robert Kresberg
Daniel Kresh
Chris Kretchmer
Steven Krieger
Steven Krieger
Pieter Kriek
Jim Krimbill
Allen Krissman
Robert Kronauge
Stephan Kronseder
Niclas Kroon
Steve Kroupa
Bob Krueger
Marla Krueger
Scott Krueger
Dawn Kruger
Stefan Kruger
Tom Krukiel
Lille Krukrubo
Steve Krulevitz
Lynne Krulich
Lisa Krupp
Oksana Krutiyenko
Donald Krzan
Urszula Krzyzowski
Milan Kubala
Edward Kubick
Christopher Kubicka
Kohei Kubo
Michitaka Kubo
Yohei Kubota
James Kucera
Halina Kucharski
Mark Kucharski
Joey Kuchler
Kamil Kuchta
Blair Kuckie
Steven Kuechel
Chuck Kuhle
David Kuhlman
Jenna Kuhlman
David Kuhn
Iveta Kuhnel
Kurt Kujawa
Kazuhito Kuji
Nika Kukharchuk
Naresh Kulendran
Cindy Kullman
Eiji Kumagai
Yukiko Kumakura
Praveen Kumar
Sunny Kumar
Masahiro Kumazawa
Chris Kuna
Hisao Kunisaki
Shoji Kunitoshi
Ryuji Kuniyoshi
Nathan Kunnen
David Kunselman
James Kuntzi
Tomoko Kuramori
John Kuramoto
Takeshi Kurano
David Kuras
Michael Kuriniec
Yukihiro Kurita
Victoria Kuritsyna
Masanori Kuriyama
Jeff Kurnik
Shirley Kurnoff
Shogo Kuroda
Yoshihide Kuroda
Shintaro Kuroiwa
Sheila Kurosu
Dusan Kurta
Bill Kurtain
Arthur Kurtz
Brett Kurtz
Bruce Kurtz
David Kurtz
Kevin Kurtz
Marc Kurtz
Ron Kurtz
Rishan Kuruppu
Jo Ann Kurz
Brian Kuscher
Robert Kuseski
Yuri Kusina
Thomas Kuskowski
Joel Kusnierz
Oksana Kusyo
Bradley Kutcha
Takashi Kuwahara
Anna Kuykendall
Ray Kuzava
Sam Kwak
Ralph Kwilosz
Eric Kwok
Kevin Kwon
Richard Kynast
Brandon L'Heureux
Arnaud L'official
Tom La Fountain
Gregory Labanowski
Patricia LaBat
Suzanne LaBelle
James Labinski
Alain Labrecque
Massimo Lacarbonara
Aldene LaCaria
Tod Lacey
Radka Lacjak
Jack Lackey
Kim Lackey
William Lackie
Cary LaCouture
Katherine LaCroix
Kyle LaCroix
Alejandro Lacruz
Charles Lacy-Thompson
Debbie Ladig
Robert Laemel
David LaFevers
Karen Laflin
Laurent Lafontant
Calvin LaForrest
Frederick Lageman
Angelica Lagrange
Ron Lague
Shareen Lai
Siu Fan Derek Lai
Andrew Laing
Barry Laing
Jacqueline Laird
Roy Laird
Andrew Lake
Shibu Lal
Claudette Laliberte
Deepak Lall
Niren Lall
Nancy Lally
David Lam
Hon Kuen Lam
Jony Lam
Man Wing Lam
Randy Lam
Sam Lam
Samantha Lam
Wai Yin Lam
Sujay Lama
Richard Lamb
Scott Lambdin
Arthur Lambert
John Lambert
Laurie Lambert
Barb Lamkin
Griffin Lamkin
Mike Lammens
Ruben Lamothe
J R Lampley
Michael Lanahan
Joseph Lanave
Kerry Lancaster
Phil Lancaster
Marcos Landavazo
Greg Landesman
Jenna Landis
David Landoch
Dawn Landon Boice
Richard Landry
Alexander Lane
Johnny Lane
Joseph Lane
Pippa Lane
Richard Lane
Ronald Lane
Peter Lang
Stephen Lang
Tessa Lang
Tucker Lang
Dennis Langdell
Chris Langdon
Greg Langdon
Kelly Langdon
James Lange
Mike Lange
Steven Langenbach
Eric Langenkamp
Bob Langer
Susan Langford
Leon Langley
Joseph Langlois
PJ Langone
Scott Langs
Erich Langston
James Lankey
Robert Lansdorp
Stephanie Lansdorp
Thomas Lapenna
Aaron Lapkin
Barbara Laporte
Stefan Laporte
Greg Lappin
John Lara
Laura Laramee
Michael Lardino
Rebeca Larios
Amelia Larkin
Vincent LaRocca
Mike Larscheid
Deanne Larsell
Scott Larsen
Tom Larsen
Darryl Larson
Emma Larson
Kristian Larson
Sean Larson
Shannon Larson
Toby Larson
Tony Larson
Vic Larson
Patrick LaSalle
Gene Paul Lascano
Walt Lasek
Katherine Lashbrook
Joselito Lasin
Nicholas Laskaris
Ewa Laskey
Lukasz Lasota
Matthew Lasprilla
Robert Last
Herbert Lato
Joseph Laubie
Debbie Lauer
Ryan Lauer
Theodore Lauer
Jim Laughlin
Jim Laughlin
Rebecca Laughton
Clint Laukhuf
Michael Laurel
Judith Laursen
Domagoj Lausic
Paul Lauterbach
Darren Lavallee
Greg LaVelle
Rod Laver
Chantalle Lavertu
Alan Laveson
Dina LaVoe
Chase Law
Craig Law
Elliott Law
Kwan Law
Sai Yu Law
Wai On Law
Emily Lawent
Howard Lawpaugh
John Lawrence
Michael Lawrence
Pamela Jill Lawrence

Dennis Laws
Carolyn Lawver
Michael Lawver
Nancy Lay
Aaron Layman
Fred Layman
Kip Layman
Alberto Layrisse
Michael Layton
Peter Lazansky
Brad Lazaro
Glenn Lazenby
Dan Le
Thomas Le
Tony Le
Christy Le Duff
Jason Le Duff
Erwan Le Ridant
Gwendal Le Tutour
Colin Lea
Carolyn Leach
Michael Leach
Amy Leahy
Benjamin Leahy
Brian Leahy
Jim Leahy
Kevin Leahy
Wade Leake
Daniel Leal
Kerry Leander
David Leatherwood
Jason Leavitt
Jerry Leavitt
Donald Leavy
Donni Leaycraft
Lawrence Lebatique
Michael Lebeau
Peter Lebedevs
Rolland LeBlanc
Lisa Lebold
Jon Lebon
Hannah Lebowitz
Laurent Lecellier
Scott LechugaDiSalvo
Ashley LeCorgne Burris
Morton Lederman
Paul Lederman
Ed LeDuc
Andrew Lee
Christopher Lee
David Lee
David Lee
Deborah Lee
Hoyoung Lee
Hyoungtae Lee
Jay Lee
Jean Lee
JoAnn Lee
John Lee
Karl Lee
Martina Lee
Michael Lee
Paul Lee
Sperry Lee
Steve Lee
Venton Lee
Vicky Lee
Wayland Lee
Wei-Feng Lee
Youngdai Lee
Debbie Leecock
Shane Leeder
Kara Lees
Nathan LeFevre
Sophie Lefevre
Christy Leggett
Christiaan LeGrand
John LeGrand
Mary Lehman
Thomas Lehman
John Lehmer
Elizabeth Lehnen
Kevin Lehr
Stuart Lehr
Lauren Lehrner
Seth Leichtfuss
Scott Leifer
Duncan Leiggi
Mallory Leighty
Cody Leimback
Darrel Leimback
Stefan Leiner
Jony Leitenbauer
Laszlo Leiter
Tiago Leivas
Warren Lem
Barbara Lemberg
Matt Lemery
Suzanne Lemery
Craig Lemley
Brandon Lenfert
Frederick Lenhard
Henner Lenhardt
Matthew Lennox
Joseph Leo
Susan Leo
Dan Leon
Gavin Leon
Ricardo Leon
Roberto Leon
Royce Leon
Timmy Leon
Todd Leone
Angela Leong
Chee Wai Leong
Christopher Leong
Stuart Leong
Tim Leos
Danut Lepadatu
Paul LePera
Jim Lepping
Cindy LePrevost
John Lerch
Steven LeRoy
Ruthly Lesane
Debbie Leslie
Vern Leslie
Gregory Lesser
Charles Lessmann
Jacob Lester
Jayson Lester
Jenell Lester
William Lester
Mike Letcher
Jim Leto
Edward Letteron
John Letts
Bradley Leu
Steve Leube
Kin Ming Tony Leung
Siu Wun Leung
Lam Leung Fat
Jim Leupold
Karl Levanat
Rob Leventhal
Julia Levering
Alexander Levie
Dominique Levin
Reid Levin
Stephen Levin
Brad Levine
Bruce Levine
Carol Levine
Thomas Levine
Elizabeth Levinson
Dory Levinter
Adam Levitt
Robert Leviyev
Jaime Levonian
Joanne Levy
Michael Levy
Samuel Levy
Kim Lewers D'Amico
Anne Lewis
Barbara Lewis
C W Lewis
Dan Lewis
Darryl Lewis
Doug Lewis
Jeff Lewis
Larry Lewis
Linton Lewis
Mark Lewis
Michael Lewis
Mike Lewis
Patrick Lewis
Taffy Lewis
Stephen Lewis-Driver
Christopher Lewit
Mike Lewitt
Samuel Lhotak
Jean Lhuillier
Guipeng Li
Hua Li
Jin Lu Li
Peng Li
Qian Li
Wei Li
Wei Gang Li
Weiqiang Li
Wentong Li
Xiao Li
Xuemin Li
Yu-Hsin (Aaron) Li
Zhengjun Li
Karen Li-Jensen
Elliott Liardo
Lee Libby
Mary Liberatore
Brandon Lichtman
Adrian Lie
Rick Liebman
Linda Lied
Chip Liefert
Rachelle Lifpitz
Bobby Light
Dale Light
Jo Lightsey
Wade Liles
Marc Lilley
Ben Lilly
Thomas Lilly
Erik Lim
John Lim
Wee Yeow Lim
Yeow Choon Lim
Marcel Lima
Raphaela Lima
Robert Limpias
Gang-Wei Lin
Tsung Ho Lin
Maxwell Linder
Clifford Lindsay
Brady Lindsley
Larry Lineberry
Derek Ling
Larry Link
Tim Linn
Richard Lipinski
Bruce Lipka
Keith Lipp
John Lippman
Pam Lippy
Hunter Lipscomb
Jonathan Lipsit
Nathan Lipson
Benjamin Lisai
Joseph Lisi
Alex Lisica
Mike Lissner
Jarrod Liston
Walt Listuon
Cheryl Litle
Bob Litrich
Enrico Litterini
Debra Little
Bob Litwin
Chang Liu
Hongjie Liu
Jian Liu
Park Liu
Roland Liu
T Solomon Liu
Vincent Liu
Xiaoni Liu
Xinyu Liu
Yi Liu
Yong Hong Liu
David Livengood
Matthew Liverman
Jimmy Livesay
Greg Livingston
Rob Lizares
Sam Lizzul
Ivo Ljubibratic
Joan Llado Socias
Mario Llano
Jovito Llevares
Greg Llewellyn
Kirsty Llewellyn
Matt Llewellyn
Cody Lloyd
David Lloyd
Hank Lloyd
Peter Lloyd
Ted Lloyd
William Lloyd
Dree Lo
Joey Lo
Meri Lobel
Luiz Lobo
Jonathan Lockeretz
Bruce Lockette
Paul Lockwood
Geoffrey LoConte
Ben Loeb
Justin Loeb
Larry Loeb
Kelly Loehe
Alan Loehr
Jim Loehr
Bill Lofgren
Nicholas Logan
Toni Logan
Michael Logarzo
Max Loguirato
Bernard Loh
Mark Lohan
Carl Lokko
Michael Loleng
Rodger Lolley
Jordan Lomas
Brian Lomax
Kyara Lombre
Oscar Lomeli
Jeffrey Lonczak
Stephanie London-Krogius
Allen Long
Christopher Long
Jeff Long
Kevin Long
Mark Long
Peggy Long
Scott Long
Zach Long
Mike Longanecker
Todd Longfellow
Stephen Longley
Rodrigo Longo
William Longua
Johan Loo
Patrick Loo
Matthew Look
Brian Loomis
Myke Loomis
Zach Loomis
Angel Lopez
Cristian Lopez
Francisco Lopez
Leonard Lopez
Omar Lopez
Luis Lopez-Alejandre
Conan Lorenzo
Richard Lorenzo
Kay Lorrain
Cary Lothringer
Nino Louarsabishvili
Mimi Loucks
Nick Loudermilk
Judy Louie
Chad Loup
William Loupe
Orlando Lourenco
Bob Love
James Love

Jason Love
Jeffrey Love
Susan Lovejoy
Ann Lovell
David Lovell
Kenneth Lovett
Elliot Lovi
Marko Lovrinovic
Joseph Lovullo
Michael Lowdermilk
Garry Lowe
George Lowe
Robert Lowe
Ronald Lowe
Dianne Lowings
Allison Lowry
Anne Lowry
August Lozano
Victor Lozano
An Lu
Ling Lu
Paul Lubbers
Edward Lube
Robert Luby
Brett Lucas
Christopher Lucas
Christyn Lucas
Paul Lucas
John Lucchesi
Adam Lucero
Marc Lucero
Lance Luciani
Miro Lucic
Jan Lucky
Timothy Ludeke
Chris Ludwig
Dave Luebbe
Kevin Lueck
David Luedtke
Robert Luedtke
Jean Luetschwager
Alfred Lui
Shing Fung Lui
Al Luistro
Victor Luk
Patsy Lukas
Sarge Luke
Katsiaryna Lukomskaya
Bruce Lum
Daniel Lum
Brad Lum-Tucker
Carolyn Lumber
Tony Lumsden
Mark Luna
Xavier Luna
Thomas Luncford
Rick Lund
Bryan Lundberg
Jessica Lundberg
Jonas Lundblad
Anne-Marie Lunde
Mark Lundgren
Giau Luong
Gregg Luongo
Marc Lupinacci
Gordon Luscombe
Brian Lusson
Michael Lustig
David Lutes

Jennifer Lutgert
Bob Lutz
Brian Lutz
Eric Lutz
Karen Lutz
Jeff Luxenburger
Chan Ly
Joe Lyden
Elizabeth Lyle
Brendan Lynaugh
Ann Marie Lynch
Brad Lynch
Peggy Lynch
Sandy Lynch
James Lynn
David Lyon
Kendall Lyon
Taryn Lyon
Christine Lyons
Georgia Lyons
Jennifer Lyons
Jennifer Lyons
Kevin Lyons
Christopher Ma
Esu Ma'at
Michael Maarup
John Maas
William Maas
Dixie Mabe
Kyle Mabe
Linda Mabe
Jennifer MacAlister
Cyril Macasero
Ted MacBeth
Dexter MacBride
David MacBurnie
Daniel Maccanello
Joy Macci
Rick Macci
Doug MacCurdy
Steve MacDermut
Daniel MacDonald
Mary MacDonald
Paul MacDonald
Itamar Macedo
Frank Maceira
Jim MacGibbon
Cammy MacGregor-Ward
David Mach
Steven Machen
Gary Machholz
Shingo Machida
Belinda Machiela
Azusa Machii
Miguel Maciel
Gene Macion
Cassie Mackell
Robert Mackey
Walter Mackey
Harold Mackin
Kyle-Cameron Mackintosh-Lewis
Angus MacLean
Therese MacLeod
William Macom
Ellen MacPherson
Carol Macpherson Caldwell
Christine Macur
Kyle Macy

Patricio Madariaga
Karim Madatali
Tim Madden
Bill Maddock
Douglas Madeux
Michael Madorna
John Mario Madrigal
Chris Madsen
Bob Madson
Kelly Madson
Theresa Madson
Akihiro Maeda
Masahiro Maeda
Shuichi Maeda
Eleazar Magallan
Alejandro Magana
Deb Magarrell
Junie Magbag
Daniel Magee
Leilani Magee
Anne Magellan
Rai Magendra
Kenneth Maget
Deborah Maggio
Brett Maginn
Dan Magnuson
Tsutomu Magome
Chris Magyary
Joseph Mahaffey
Gewan Maharaj
Michele Maharaj
Sabita Maharaj
Saisnarine Maharaj
Sewsankar Maharaj
Vishnu Maharaj
Thomas Maher
Bruce Mahler
David Mahoney
Michael Mahoney
Spencer Mai
Harold Maier
Mike Maier
Reiny Maier
Richard Maier
Travis Maike
Peter Mainelli
Gerry Maingot
Barbara Maitland
Marc Majdick
Andrew Majett
Akiyoshi Majima
Raymond Major
Po Yee Mak
Terry Mak
Richard Makepeace
Kenichi Makino
Brian Malcolm
Maurice Malcolm
Carlos Maldonado
Keyvan Maleki
Louis Malfait
Sharla Malfait
Farhan Malik
Gary Malin
David Malinowski
Vladimir Malkin
Ken Malley
Blake Mallick
Annette Malloy

Zachary Malmgren
Ola Malmqvist
Allison Maloney
Matthew Maloney
Vetu Mam
Alim Mambetov
Cecil Mamiit
Nicholas Mamula
Whitney Man
Ko Man Hon
Todor Manchev
Max Mancini
Tim Mangan
Barbara Mangan DeLaney
Karen Manger-Zupp
Anthony Mangiafico
Jean Max Mangones
Damon Mangual
Hilde Manhardt
Wasyl Manko
Maria Manley
Chad Mann
Dave Mann
John Mann
Morgan Mann
William Mann
Gregg Manning
Melanie Manning
Steven Manning
Frank Mannix
John Mano
Anish Manrai
Luis Fernando Manrique
Alex Mansfield
Matthew Mansfield
Carol Manso
Jayant Manthripragada
Edmond Manuel
Tyler Mappes
Thomas Mar
Charl Marais
Haley Marais
Matthew Marceau
Alex Marcial
Rick Marcotulli
Paul Marcum
Jeanette Marcus
Harvey Mardyks
Jeff Maren
Tyler Marengo
Timothy Mares
Pierre Mareschal
Alan Margot
Manny Mariani
Ryan Marick
Matias Marin
Svetozar Marinkovic
Viktor Marinkovic
Louis Marino
Michael Marino
Tony Marino
Will Marino
Donald Marinoni
James Marion
Mathew Marion
Kenneth Marisseau
Roger Mark
James Markert
Kyle Markham

David Markin
Aleksandar Markov
Sinisa Markovic
Israel Markovitz
Sara Markowitz
Vicki Markowsky
Christopher Marks
Donna Marks
Daniel Marquart
Juliana Marques
Chris Marquez
David Marquina-Maldonado
Shelly Mars
Jaime Marsella
David Marshall
Gary Marshall
Jason Marshall
Kelly Marshall
M. Damian Marshall
Wayne Marshall
Lester Marston
Camelia Marta
Jody Marten
Robert Martens
Alina Martin
Andrew Martin
Butch Martin
Don Martin
Glenn Martin
James Martin
Jennifer Martin
Jeremy Martin
John Martin
Jonathan Martin
Joshua Martin
Kelly Martin
Laurie Martin
Lorena Martin
Lucas Martin
Mickey Martin
Miguel Martin
Paula Martin
Rawleigh Martin
Rick Martin
Roger Martin
Samuel Martin
Todd Martin
Wayne Martin
Wesley Martin
James Martineau
Angel Martincz
Brian Martinez
Dimitrio Martinez
Erick Martinez
Geoff Martinez
Jim Martinez
Lazaro Martinez
Michael Martinez
Robert Martinez
Alfonso Martinez Magan
Francisco Martinez Tovar
Juan Martinez-Arraya
Terrence Martino
Olga Martinsone
Bill Martire
Tigran Martirosyan
Marco Martizi
Jake Martyn
Joe Masaki

Drew Mascarin
Dominick Masciantonio
Sam Mascitti
Mike Masemore
Julius Mashonganyika
Sheryl Maskell
Cathy Maso-Giannelli
Bill Mason
Jeff Mason
Jim Mason
Larry Mason
Louis Mason
Patrick Mason
Thomas Mason
Trey Mason
Troy Mass
Jay Massart
Amit Massey
Michael Massie
Stephen Masso
David Mast
Delaine Mast
Bradley Masters
Thomas Mastromarino
Yoshitaka Masuda
Yuji Masuda
Franco Mata
Margie Mateljan
Fernando Mateu
John Matheny
Dave Mathews
David Mathews
John Mathews
Nicholas Mathews
Sidnei Matias
Tina Matis
John Matkulak
Sveto Matovic
Molly Matricardi
Jordee Matson
Keisuke Matsuda
Kouhei Matsuda
Yoshio Matsuda
Yoshiomi Matsuda
Kiyohiro Matsui
Sadataka Matsui
Bret Matsumoto
Minoru Matsumoto
Satoshi Matsumoto
Shigeo Matsuo
Atsushi Matsuoka
Tadao Matsushima
Takuma Matsushima
Tadashi Matsuyama
Tomohiro Matsuyama
Masaaki Matsuzawa
Gabriel Matteazzi
Daniel Mattera
Jonathan Matthews
William Matthews
Eric Matthewson
Creig Matthieson
Brendan Mattingly
Mike Mattingly
Gabriel Mattos
James Mattson
Douglas Matuska
Janis Mauldin
LeGeorge Mauldin
Mika Maunula
Louis Maunupau
James Mauri
Kyle Mauro
George Maurtua
Suresh Maurya
Eric Maust
Giampaolo Mauti
Norman Mauz
Shelby Mavis
Anton Mavrin
Vlade Mavropoulos
Stoliarenko
Jack Maxwell
Rob Maxwell
Lamar May
Margaret May
Mike May
Chris Mayer
Courtney Mayer
Peter Mayer
Rachel Mayer
Sandy Mayer
Sean Maymi
Doug Maynard
Lyndsey Maynard
Fernando Maynetto
Clayton Maynor
Tom Maynor
Derek Mayo
Sarah Mayo
Sean Mayo
Chris Mayotte
Alison Mays
Cason Mays
Dean Mays
Pavel Mazaev
Stephen Mazak
Vasileios Mazarakis
Julie Mazinova
Mark Mazique
Brent Mazza
Robert Mazzanti
Pete Mazzella
Tita Mba
Robert McAdoo
William McAdoo
Ken McAllister
Jody McBain
Darvin McBrayer
Brad McBride
Maja McBride
Isaac McBroom
Jim McCabe
Kevin McCadams
Sean McCaffrey
Raleigh McCammon
Robert McCammon
Kim McCann
Jeffrey McCardle
John McCarthy
Kevin McCarthy
Sean McCarthy
Mindy McCarthy-Oki
Harvey McCartney
Kieran McCartney
Matt McCaskill
Matthew McCauley
Bill McClain
Layne McCleary
Jeremy McClelland
Daniel McClintic
Casey McClure
Dennis McClure
Kevin McClure
Mark McClure
Matthew McClure
Marina McCollom
James McCollum
Jeff McConkey
Bill McConnell
Melissa McCorkle
Peter McCorkle
Thomas McCormack
Bill McCormick
Dan McCormick
Daniel McCormick
Matthew McCormick
Matty McCormick
Brian McCoy
Broderick McCoy
Buster McCoy
Diana McCoy
Steven McCoy
Wyatt Mccoy
Fred McCracken
James McCready
Irene McCullagh
Chris McCullar
Robert McCune
Ian McCusker
Gregory McDaniel
John McDaniel
Ron McDaniel
Ryan McDaniel
Adrian McDermott
Drew McDermott
Michael McDermott
Tina McDermott
Alex McDonald
Jordan McDonald
Liz McDonald
William McDonald
Michael McDonnell
J J McDonough
Paul McDonough
Marcus McDorman
Michael McDowell
John McElroy
Zach McElroy
Parker McElveen
Steven McElwain
Klint McEnery
Patrick McEnroe
Will McEntire
Joseph McEntyre
Ken McEwan
Brian McFadden
Chauncey McFarland
Patrick McFarland
Richard McField
Dominic McGann
Jim McGarry
Steven McGary
Gail McGavock
Matthew McGee
Thomas McGee
Eugene McGeehan
John McGeehan
Tim McGettigan
Fred McGill
Lacey McGill
Johnny McGinn
Jason McGinnis
Mike McGinnis
Darlene McGlone
Rebecca Mcglothlin
Kevin McGlynn
Matthew McGowan
Bill McGrath
Molly McGrath
Tom McGraw
Kevin McGuffie
Tyson McGuffin
Daniel McGuire
Hilary McGuire
Mark McGuire
Mike McGuire
Ruth McGuire
Wade McGuire
Alyssa McGurk
Joseph McGurrin
Connie McHugh
James McHugh
Bob McInerney
Matthew McInerney
Sheila McInerney
Conrad McIntire
Tamara McIntire
Gregg McIntosh
Jesse McIntyre
Scott McKay
Bryant McKee
Grady McKee
Richard McKee
Roger McKee
Bob McKeegan
Bob McKenna
Kevin McKenna
Robert McKenna
Vesna McKenna
Carla McKenzie
Stephen McKibbin
Timothy McKimm
Billy McKinney
Dave McKinney
David McKinney
Stefan McKinney
Valerie McKinney
Martha McKinnon
Cleon McKnight
Nate McLauchlin
Jonathan McLaughlin
Sandra McLaughlin
John McLean
John McLean
Jim McLennan
Thomas McLeod
Martin McLernon
Edward McLorie
Robert McMahan
Angela McMahon
Mark McMahon
Philip McMillion
Russell McMindes
Troy McMullen
Glen McMurdo
Huntley McNab
Lynn McNally
David McNamara
Karen McNamara
Torrey McNeal
Paul McNulty
Paul McNulty
Vanessa McPadden
Paul McPherson
Mark McPhillips
Billy McQuaid
Deborah McQueen
Stephen McQuillen
Ed McQuillin
Dane McQuivey
Mel McRee
Caleb McReynolds
Sean McRoberts
Hillary McSpadden
John McSween
Dennis McWilliams
Russ Meadows
Teddy Mebounou
Bill Mecca
Tomas Mecho Ruiz
Nelson Medders
Jaroslav Medek
Greg Medford
Luis Mediero
Steven Medoff
Mark Medow
Jesse Medvene-Collins
Sara Meehan
Daniel Meek
Christopher Meeker
Denny Meelarp
David Meharg
Jerry Mehciz
Romy Mehlman
Maxwell Mehren
Grace Mehrizi
Scott Meier
Anne Meigs
Ira Meiling
John Meincke
Leif Meineke
Allyson Meister
Bouavone Meksavanh
Joan Melahn
Benjamin Melancon
Nicole Melch
Simon Melendez
Julio Melgarejo
Chuck Melkent
Christine Mellon
Horace Mells
Jeffrey Melnick
Victor Melo
Morris Melotti
Glen Meloy
Ben Melvin
Richard Mendell
Armen Mendelyan
Tom Mendenhall
David Mendez
Gerson Mendez
Ricardo Mendivil
Carl Mendoza
Hector Mendoza

Shirley Mendoza
Carol Menefee
Grace Menna
Emmanuel Mensah
Angus Menzies
Cherise Meoli
Eduard Merc
Nicholas Mercado
John Mercer
Tom Mercer
David Mercier
Michael Mercier
Paul Mercury
Jennifer Meredith
Roger Meredith
Virginia Merrell
Bridget Merrick
Suzanne Merrick
Kevin Merrigan
Rob Merriman
Jim Merritt
Brenda Mertz
James Mertz
Charles Merzbacher
Bostjan Merzdovnik
Bruce Mesches
Joseph Mesmer
Oliver Messerli
Ron Metcalf
Ty Metcalfe
John Metz
Mike Metz
Eric Metzger
Barb Meyer
Brian Meyer
Ean Meyer
Eric Meyer
George Meyer
John Meyer
Nancy Meyer
Riley Meyer
Robert Meyer
Ted Meyer
William Meyer
Andrew Meyers
Bob Meyers
Eric Meyers
Rick Meyers
Walt Meyers
Perry Meyers-Sinett
Michael Meza
Jose Meza Ramos
Liping Miao
Jason Michael
Jack Michalko
Christopher Michalowski
Michael Michaud
Matthew Micheel
Connor Michelich
Nony Michulka
Paul Mick
Michael Mickelson
Carl Mickler
James Middleton
Todd Middleton
Martin Miedzowicz
Julian Mielniczuk
Grant Migita
John Miglionico
Florian Mihai
Dalibor Mihajlovic
Leo Mihalkovitz
Trude Mihalovich-Pletcher
Adam Mihok
Morry Mikesell
Yasuyuki Mikoshiba
Landis Milam
Steven Mildon
Justin Miles
Lori Miles
Philip Milford
Biljana Milicevic
Nikola Milinkovic
Peter Militzer
Jeff Millaire
Alex Millar
Allen Miller
Allen Miller
Anni Miller
Charles Miller
Craig Miller
Dale Miller
Daniel Miller
Derek Miller
Doug Miller
Elizabeth Miller
Jack Miller
James Miller
Jason Miller
Jeff Miller
John Miller
John Miller
Lawrence Miller
Lewis Miller
Lindsay Miller
Lynn Miller
Mark Miller
Mark Miller
Michael Miller
Mike Miller
Paula Miller
Rex Miller
Rick Miller
Rick Miller
Roy Miller
Ryan Miller
Scott Miller
Sean Miller
Seth Miller
Theodore Miller
Jerome Millet
Thomas Millet
Barry Mills
Chelsea Mills
John Mills
Kate Mills
McKenna Mills
Mark Milner
Tiffany Milner
Kevin Milton
Joy Minaai
Hiroaki Minami
Katsuyoshi Minami
Naoki Minami
Bond Minard
Peter Minarich
Ian Mindell
Katherine Miness
Ming Ming
Dejan Minic
Chris Minihan
David Minihan
Andrew Minnelli
Brad Minns
Shusaku Minoda
Allan Minter
Bryan Minton
Meg Minton
Oleg Mironchikov
Hamid Mirzadeh
Vahid Mirzadeh
Aurelija Miseviciute
Shivang Mishra
Edward Misiolek
Patricio Misitrano
Zack Miskel
James Misner
Gaurav Misra
Bob Mitchell
Fulton Mitchell
Kerry Mitchell
Matthew Mitchell
Scott Mitchell
Scott Mitchell
Timothy Mitchell
Todd Mitchell
Daniel Mitha
Kristijan Mitrovski
Junichi Mitsuhashi
Katsuhiko Mitsui
Koji Mitsumori
Akio Mitsuwa
Michael Mitzell
Naoki Miura
Bradley Mixson
Kazumichi Miyachi
Keitaro Miyake
Takuya Miyamoto
Masahiro Miyashita
Yasushi Miyata
Tae Miyazaki
Clay Mize
Kenneth Mize
Andy Mizell
Takako Mizoguchi
Kei Mizuguchi
Masazumi Mizuno
Kazumasa Mizusawa
Lon Mlnarik
Innocent Modika
Ryan Modri
Jeffrey Modrow
Leslie Moe
Jim Moellering
Andrew Moffat
Adrian Moghina
Brian Mogus
Shabir Mohamed
Haruka Mohri
Kevin Moir
Robert Mojica
Jeremy Mokry
Adam Molda
Lisa Moldrem
Ray Molhem
Andres Molina
Chris Molina
Fernando Molina
Ivan Molina
Joey Molina
Alessio Mollo
Molly Molony
Kara Molony-Hussey
Brent Molyneux
Irene Mombach
Severino Mon
Tom Monahan
Annie Moncada
Lenin Mongerie
James Monk
John Monnier
Don Monroe
Jacob Monroe
Leslie Monroe
Richard Monroe
Felipe Monroy
Karl Monson
Tina Montagnet
Jaxon Montague
Terry Montague
Timothy Montague
Michael Montalbano
Matt Montana
Patrick Montane
Ricardo Montanez
Mary Monteiro
Victor Monteiro
Al Montemayor
Gabriel Montenegro
Alejandro Montes
Domingo Montes
Adrian Montgomery
Geoff Montgomery
James Montgomery
Javon Montgomery
Patrick Montgomery
Res Montgomery
Martin Montigel
Gabriel Montilla
George Montoya
Maria Mood-Brown
Donald Moody
Walter Moody
Damian Mooney
Alec Moore
Bal Moore
Bob Moore
Cameron Moore
Cathy Moore
Charles Moore
Cheryl Moore
Christopher Moore
Curtis Moore
Darryl Moore
Derek Moore
Geoffrey Moore
Howard Moore
Jason Moore
Jim Moore
Joshua Moore
Kevin Moore
Matthew Moore
Peter Moore
Phillip Moore
Ric Moore
Robert Moore
Scott Moore
Tom Moore
Heiki Moorlat
Jim Moortgat
Albert Mora
Cesar Morales
Dencil Morales
Eddie Morales
John Morales
Miguel Morales
Raymond Noel Morales
Guillermo Morales-Rubert
Eric Moran
Marc Moran
Michael Moran
Rodney Morasch
William Moravec
Adam Morehart
Bill Morehouse
Christopher Morehouse
Todd Morelle
Rafael Moreno Higueras
Benny Morentin
Jaime Moretti
Kirsten Morey
Adam Morgan
Bob Morgan
Brian Morgan
Chad Morgan
Greg Morgan
Jay Morgan
Joe Morgan
Kris Morgan
Nick Morgan
Seth Morgan
Shauna Morgan
Timothy Morgan
Carl Morgenstern
Daisuke Mori
Jiro Mori
Nanami Mori
Ryoichi Mori
Marvin Moriarty
Michael Moriarty
Taichi Morikawa
Matthew Morillo
Masatake Morimoto
Kiyoshi Morioka
Yasufumi Morise
Hiroyuki Morishita
Yasushi Morishita
Brien Morissette
Naoki Morita
Taihei Morita
Tsuneki Morita
Yuuki Morita
Tomoko Morito
Kirk Moritz
Katlyn Morley
John Morlidge
Thomas Morlock
Linda Mormile
Julio Moros
Ekaterina Morozova-Pomier
Marilyn Morrell-Kristal
Aaron Morrill
Dural Morris
Gene Morris
Jacqueline Morris

Rusty Morris
Tammy Morris
William Morris
William Morris
Alyssa Morrison
Charles Morrison
David Morrison
Frank Morrison
Maureen Morrison
Brian Morrissey
Richard Morrissey
Ronald Morrow
Sara Morse
Jerry Morse-Karzen
Warfield Morsell
Jenno Morson
Ricardo Morte
Kate Mortensen
Ainslie Morton
James Morton
Thomas Morton
Anthony Moschetto
Danny Moscovici
Paul Moseby
Blake Mosley
Kirk Mosley
Caryn Moss
Denis Moss
James Moss
Jim Moss
John Moss
Peter Moss
Michael Mossburg
Daniel Moster
Matthew Motil
Elly Motloch
Seijiro Motoda
Ryo Motooka
Kyle Motoshige
Kevin Motoyasu
Craig Mott
Janice Mott
Mickey Mott
Kevin Motta
Zen Mottershead
Mary Mottola
Steven Motyka
Ricky Moua
Jerome Moukouanga
Frankie Moulton
Julie Moultrie
Richard Mount
William Mountford
Lucila Moure
Arthur Mourjan
Craig Mours
Larry Mousouris
Greg Moussette
David Moyer
Jonathan Moyer
Mike Moyer
Jack Moynihan
Thomas Mozur
Patricia Mraz
Christine Mroz
Fengchun Mu
Mark Mudra
Peyton Muehlmeier
Barbara Ann Mueller
Chris Mueller
Jason Mueller
Jean Mueller
Kathy Mueller Rohan
Paul Muesing
Michael Muffoletto
Dave Muir
Rob Muir
Timir Mukherjee
Paul Muldoon
Michael Mule
Tony Mule
Majorie Muller
Maria Muller
Martin Mulligan
Michael Mulligan
Dale Mullin
Andrew Mullins
David Mullins
Joseph Mullins
John Mullman
Gardnar Mulloy
Kelly Mulready
Steve Mumford
Paul Munafo
Marcus Muniz
Herbert Munks
Pamela Muno
Greg Munoz
Michael Munoz
Steven Munro
Dennis Munroe
Ian Munroe
Jim Munsil
Floyd Munson
Mark Muntifering
Samantha Munze
Katsunori Murahashi
Nobuhiro Murakami
Yoshiyuki Murakami
Naoto Muraki
Shigeo Murakumo
Takaaki Muranaka
Albert Murata
Kazuya Murayama
David Murillo
Chet Murphy
Colbert Murphy
Erin Murphy
Jerry Murphy
Jerry Murphy
Jonathan Murphy
Kenny Murphy
Michaela Murphy
Scott Murphy
Sean Murphy
Terry Murphy
Kim Murphy-Francis
Avis Murray
Gaston Murray
Jim Murray
Jim Murray
Lisa Murray
Phillip Murray
Richard Murray
Stacy Murray
Ted Murray
Tetsuhiko Musashi
Jim Musgrave
Justin Musgrove
Admire Mushonga
James Musil
Wayne Muskievicz
Jenna Musolino
Takura Musungwa
Matthew Muszala
Allington Mutimer
Andrew Myer
Andrew Myers
Andrew Myers
Benjamin Myers
Derek Myers
Joel Myers
Phil Myers
Randy Myers
Tye Myers
Claudia Myers-Whiteley
Bob Myerson
Moe Moe Myinttun
Yuyu Myinttun
George Mykkanen
Christopher Myrold
Fabrice Myrtil
Daniel Nabedrick
Jeffrey Nabity
Garry Nadebaum
Ingrid Nadell
Mia Nadler
Yoshihiro Nagao
Junichi Nagasako
Maki Nagasawa
Mamoru Nagasawa
Shinji Nagasawa
Shoichi Nagasawa
Kenichi Nagashima
Brad Nagel
Bruce Nagel
Courtney Nagel
Edward Nagel
Donald Nagle
Keith Nagle
Scott Nagle
Glenn Nagorski
Daniel Nahmouli
Kazuyoshi Naito
Vlatko Najdek
Karim Najdi
Kris Najdovski
Jack Najjar
Hirokazu Nakagawa
Seigi Nakagawa
Galen Nakahara
Norikazu Nakaima
Keiji Nakajima
Yasuhiro Nakajima
Yuji Nakajima
Atsushi Nakamoto
Sean Nakamoto
Masami Nakamura
Sanae Nakamura
Shinji Nakamura
Taito Nakamura
Yukie Nakamura
Yusuke Nakamura
Fumiya Nakano
Yoshitaka Nakano
Yukihiko Nakano
Atsuko Nakashima
Paul Nakatsuka
Shin Nakaya
John Nallon
Jonathan Nam
Patrick Nam
Takuya Namekawa
Toru Nanba
John Nance
Santiago Nanez
Gail Nankervis
Reynaldo Nantuna
Phil Napolitano
Yuji Nara
Kent Naraghi-Grcich
Akio Naraki
Susan Nardi
Daichi Narita
Matthew Narr
Pat Narvaiz
Chuck Narvin
Khayot Narzikulov
Glauco Nascimento
Brian Nash
Novak Nash
Roosevelt Nash
Mark Naslund
Chris Nasrallah
Todd Nassief
John Natolly
William Nau
Ritesh Nautiyal
Shashank Nautiyal
Miguel Navarro
Arturo Navarro Guzman
Diana Navrotska
Nesar Nayak
Trevor Ncube
Gabriel Neacsu
Don Nead
Douglas Neagle
Billy Nealon
William Nealon
David Neel
Marcela Negrete
Kathy Neil
Tiiu Neiland
Jim Neitzel
Jana Nejedly Welt
Blair Neller
Andrea Nelson
Andrew Nelson
Anthony Nelson
Bob Nelson
Charles Nelson
Charles Nelson
Christopher Nelson
Craig Nelson
Dick Nelson
James Nelson
John Nelson
Josh Nelson
Joshua Nelson
Linda Nelson
Thomas Nelson
Ronald Nemchock
Nicholas Nemeroff
Aurae Nemesis
Yukihide Nemoto
Jon Neri
Ulysses Neri
Scott Nesbit
Dean Ness
Jing (Amy) Nestle
Scott Nestor
Jai Nettimi
Hans Neufeld
David Neuhart
Helen Neuhoff
Jeffrey Neuman
Karen Neuman
Donald Neuner
Bill Neuschafer
Abbi Neuthaler
Brandon Nevel
Ben Neveras
Vadim Nevsky
Rick New
Luke Newbold
Linda Newby
Nicholas Newcomb
Sidney Newcomb
Sidney Newcomb
Brian Newhall
Edgar Newlin
Brian Newman
Jack Newman
Judy Newman
Noah Newman
Robin Newman
Taylor Newman
Woody Newson
David Newton
Sean Newton
Adrian Ng
Victor Ng
Aime Ngounoue
Anh-Steve Nguyen
Anhtuan Nguyen
Bao Nguyen
Charles Nguyen
Courtney Nguyen
David Nguyen
Hai Nguyen
Hung Nguyen
Hung Nguyen
Huong Nguyen
Huy Nguyen
Jade Nguyen
Luan Nguyen
Pete Nguyen
Richard Nguyen
Thao Nguyen
Vi Nguyen
Viet Nguyen
Vinh Nguyen
Bryan Nibert
Margaret Niccolai
Scott Nichols
Stephanie Nichols
Kate Nicholson
Matthew Nicholson
Holger Nickel
Danielle Nickerson
Anne Nicksick
Zuzana Nicoletti
Cathleen Nicoloff
Jacob Nicolussi
Angelo Niculescu

Gabriela Niculescu
Sue Nidzgorski
Matthew Nielsen
Thomas Nielsen
Adam Nielson
Brent Nielson
Dennis Nielson
Brenda Niemeyer
Alyssa Niemiec
Rafael Nieto
Alessandro Nieves
Manabu Niikura
Hiroshi Nikadori
Artemiy Nikitin
Igor Nikitin
Youlian Nikolov
T A Niles
Per Anders Nilhagen
Greg Nilsen
Rick Ninete
Felix Ningas
Masato Nishi
Toshihiko Nishikimura
Airi Nishimura
Shuji Nishimura
Junpei Nishiura
Bill Nissley
Timothy Nissley
Kermit Nixon
Nenad Njegovan
James No
Crystal Noble
Dean Noble
Kristi Noble
Mark Noble
Heather Nobler
William Noblitt
Kenichiro Noda
Joseph Noecker
Corey Noel
Ken Noel
Michael Noel
Patrick Noelke
Masahiro Noguchi
Jose Nolasco
Steve Nolen
Alison Noll
Rebekah Noll
Makoto Nomura
Masato Nonogawa
Ronald Noon
Jason Noonan
Timothy Noonan
Waseem Noor
Derek Nordentoft
Leif Nordlund
Lois Nordman
Mason Norman
Simon Norman
Whitnie Norman
Jeffrey Normile
Ken Normoyle
Thomas Norrell
Chuck Norris
Michael Norris
Ned Norris
Sheri Norris
Cecil North
Rupert North
Franklin Northcott
Bob Northcut
Claire Norton
Joe Norton
Robert Norton
Todd Norton
Bryan Norville
Philip Norville
David Nostrant
William Notar
Joseph Noth
Brian Notis
Jaroslav Novak
Scott Novak
David Nowak
Jonathan Noyes
Melvina Nozick
Benjamin Nuger
Jeffrey Nuhfer
Katsumi Numaguchi
Chris Numbers
Craig Nunez
Eric Nunez
Gonzalo Nunez
Juan Nunez
Louis Nunez
Mark Nunez
Nestor Nunez
Fabian Nunez Seixa
Donald Nush
Ross Nwachukwu
Shingirayi Nyagura
Fredrik Nyborg
Steven Nycum
Thomas Nygaard
Rex Nyquist
Dirk Nyren
Jerry O Hara
Boots O'Brien
Charles O'Brien
Cory O'Brien
Craig O'Brien
Joe O'Brien
Kelly O'Brien
Meagan O'Brien
Michael O'Brien
Tom O'Brien
Wesley O'Brien
Mark O'Bryan
Mark O'Bryan
William O'Bryant
Dan O'Connell
Jim O'Connell
Mike O'Connell
Steven O'Connell
Gregory O'Connor
John O'Connor
Matthew O'Connor
Sean O'Connor
Sean O'Daniel
Jenna O'Dell
Rodney O'Dell
Brian O'Donnell
Jamie O'Donnell
Shaun O'Donovan
Terry O'Grady
Michael O'Keefe
Stephen O'Keefe
Gillian O'Kelley
David O'Meara
Leaf O'Neal
Tim O'Neal
Greg O'Neil
Sean O'Neil
Wayne O'Neil
Kevin O'Neill
Gordon O'Reilly
Shane O'Reilly
Nigel O'Rourke
Craig O'Shannessy
Kevin O'Shea
Frances O'Sullivan
Chris Oakes
Rob Oakes
Todd Oaks
Tim Oberhelman
Kenneth Obermeier
Vladimir Obradovic
Rudy Obregon
Juan Ocampo
Albert Ochoa
David Ochotorena
Geoffrey OConnor
Walter Oden
Mark Odgers
Anders Oding
Tiffany Odlum
Leslie Oduwole
Jacob Oehser
Jim Oescher
Benjamin Oestreich
Donny Offerle
John Officer
Henry Offner
Chigozie Offor
Warner Offord
Ethan Ogard
Takuya Ogasawara
Higashi Ogata
Kimio Ogata
Koichiro Ogawa
William Ogene
Daisuke Ogiwara
Bob Ogle
Chihiro Ohashi
Hayato Ohashi
Akinori Ohgi
Takanori Ohkoshi
Kazuo Ohmori
Hiroaki Ohmura
Koji Ohnuki
Jacob Ohrman
Masakazu Ohsaka
Takeru Ohshima
Kozo Ohta
Yasumasa Ohta
Christopher Ojakian
Tadahiro Okabe
Yukihito Okabe
Morihiro Okada
Yasuhiro Okamoto
Kent Okamura
Yoji Okawa
Ryo Okazaki
Toshiya Okazaki
Naoya Oki
Tatsumi Okuda
Robert Okuly
Katsumi Okuyama
Jess Olavarria
Michael Olds
Dennis Olenik
Phillip Olesen
Stan Oley
Joe Olfindo
Andris Olins
Corey Oliphant
Steven Olivas
Dan Oliver
Steve Oliver
Tomas Ollestad
Mark Olman
David Olmedo
Luis Olmedo
Robert Olmstead
Sandy Olney
Hans Olsen
Matthew Olsen
Jack Olson
Kathryn Olson
Matthew Olson
Michael Olson
Michelle Olson
Ristine Olson
Christer Olsson
Leif Olsson
Dominika Olszewska
Rafael Omana
Samuel Omoile
Paul Onac
Martina Ondrejkova
Suk Ong
Takanori Onguchi
Allen Oni
Kentaro Onitake
Akira Ono
Eiko Ono
Mineki Ono
Shushichiro Ono
Takahide Ono
Takayuki Ono
Celso Onofre
Patrick Onoro
Kei Oofuji
Desmond Oon
Ernest Oon
Yuusuke Oowaki
Dustin Opalka
Matthew Opilo
Rebecca Opoien
James Opondo
Keith Orahood
Kirk Orahood
James Orange
Mike Oransky
Andrew Orban
Sandor Orban
Jon Orellana
Joshua Oremland
Singo Oribe
Dennis Oricchio
Tomohiko Orikasa
Katie Orlando
Suzanne Ornstein
Guillermo Oropez
Ricky Ortega
Jose Luis Ortega Vaquero
Noah Orth
Juan Ortiz
Randy Ortwein
Mark Orwig
Lisa Osborn
Sheryl Osborn
Kathryn Osborne
Tom Osborne
Kendall Osbourne
Frances Osei
Randy Osga
Yoshihiro Oshima
Miguel Osio
Vasil Osipenko
AnneClaire Osman
Andres Osorio
Diana Ospina-Taylor
Anabel Ossombi
Joshua Osswald
Daniel Osterman
Mitsuteru Osugi
Rick Oswald
Masato Ota
Francisco Otalvaro
Hideaki Otokita
Mitsuo Otsudo
Hayato Otsuka
David Ott
Jeffrey Otterbein
Ken Ouellette
Debra Ouye
Tom Over
Dustin Overbeek
Allan Overland
Jason Overland
John Owen
Michael Owen
Pamela Owen
Peter Owen
Wendy Owen
Winston Owen
Angela Owens
Charlie Owens
Mike Owens
Steve Owens
Tyler Owens
Chad Oxendine
Joshua Oxendine
Larry Oxford
Brian Oxley
Jose Oyco
Bill Ozaki
Nobuo Ozawa
James Paajanen
Ashley Pace
Steve Pace
Marie-Josee Pachl
Mark Pachtner
David Pack
Kenny Pack
Lisa Packard
Marshall Packowitz
Jeanette Paddock
Brandon Padgett
Gus Padilla
Simon Paek
Brian Page
David Page
David Page

Hugh Page
Jason Page
Kevin Page
Meghan Page
Patrick Paggeot
Charles Painter
Karen Painter
Stephen Painton
Christopher Paish
Randy Paisley
Don Paitrick
Valter Paiva
Cristian Paiz
Jerome Pajot
Hanna Pajunen
Alex Palladino
Michael-Ray Pallares
Marihelen Palmer
Mary Palmer
Richard Palmer
Tom Palmer
Federico Palombo
Peter Paltsios
Daryl Paluch
Duke Paluch
Mark Palus
BJ Pammit
Anne Pamplin-Evenson
Krishn Panchal
David Panconi
Craig Panhofer
John Panizzo
Richard Pannomarew
Ajay Pant
William Pantsari
Charlie Panui
Gregg Paolini
Kevin Pape
Steve Paper
Ryan Papiernik
Christopher Pappas
David Paradzik
Nelly Pardo
Sam Parfitt
Joe Parish
Ben Park
Daniel Park
Heungseo Park
Hung Soon (Brian) Park
Jihyun Jade Park
Linda Park
Nicholas Park
Seon Young Park
Barry Parker
Barry Parker
Cecilia Parker
Christine Parker
Eddie Parker
James Parker
Jeff Parker
Jim Parker
Jim Parker
Larry Parker
Matthew Parker
Michael Parker
Morio Parker
Murphey Parker
Rob Parker
Timothy Parker
Thomas Parkes
Barry Parks
David Parks
Guy Parks
Jonathan Parks
Peggy Parks
Ron Parlman
Kasey Parmelee
Lucas Parrau
Chris Parrish
Clay Parrish
Phillip Parrish
Kent Parrot
Evan Parry
Christopher Parsons
Tony Parzanese
Daria Pascale
Gary Paschal
Jason Pascua
Enric Pasculado
Craig Pasqua
Tom Pasquale
Robert Pass
Eddie Pasternak
Roger Pastore
Brahna Pastorini
Jose Pastrello
Andrew Pate
Chuck Pate
Harshul Patel
Jay Patel
Pintu Patel
Ravi Patel
Sumeet Patel
Vimal Patel
Khan Pathan
Mikhail Don Patria
Daniel Patrick
Dan Patterson
Don Patterson
Joan Patterson
Lindsey Patterson
Steve Patterson
Jason Patti
Bill Patton
Gail Patton
Greg Patton
Levi Patton
R K Patton
Stephen Patton
Charlie Paukert
Gregory Paukstis
Aaron Paul
Adam Paul
Erin Paul
Gordon Paul
Todd Paul
Vijay Paul
Linda Paulding
Steve Paulsen
Pamela Paun
Paul Pautsch
Lucy Paux
Khrystyna Pavlyuk
Max Pavon
David Pawid
Jessica Paxman
John Paxton
Jack Payne
Melinda Payne
Randall Payne
Virginia Payne
Walter Paz
Mike Pazourek
Jesse Peach
Jerry Peacock
Brad Pearce
Brent Pearce
Craig Pearce
James Pearce
Joseph Pearce
Paul Pearce
Roger Pearce
Christopher Pearson
Greg Pearson
Lisa Pearson
Michael Pearson
Rodney Pearson
Eric Pease
Kara Pease
Kevin Pease
Jim Peavy
Matthew Peck
Eleanor Peden
Fred Pedersen
Brian Pederson
Dilcia Pederson
Jonathan Pedoulas
Candace Pedro
Margaret Peeling
Mirko Pehar
Garrett Pekar
Steve Pekich
Murillo Pelegrino
John Pelkey
Steve Pelletier
Dennis Pelley
Ann Pellow
Adrian Pelmus
David Pena
Juan Pena
Adam Penar
Bernard Pence
Susan Pendo
Craig Pendrys
Dean Penero
Cheng Peng
Thomas Penner
Wayne Penniman
Gordon Pennington
Scott Pennington
Steve Pennington
James Penny
Cristian Pensavalle
Lisa Pento
Jack Pepiot
Mike Perales
Petr Perecinsky
Melwin Pereira
Michael Pereira
Yevgeny Pereverzin
Alberto Perez
Craig Perez
Marco Perez
Philip Perez
Rosa Maria Perez Domenech
Alvaro Perez Garcia
Pablo Perez Gras
Maria Pergamalis
Darlene Pergola
Jerome Peri
Serge Peri
Adam Perkins
Anthony Perkins
Bruce Perkins
Cristopher Perkins
Elizabeth Perkins
Stephen Perkins
Todd Perkins
John Perkison
Jeffrey Perlman
Kerry Perlman
Scott Perlstein
Klara Permenter
Mikael Pernfors
Eileen Pero
George Perrego
Vince Perri
Terri Perrin
Micah Perron
Neil Perron
Joseph Perrone
Joseph Perrone
Brian Perry
Femi Perry
Gerry Perry
Jack Perry
John Perry
Joseph Perry
Ronald Perry
Hunter Person
Armor Persons
Ross Persons
Paul Pertile
Ira Peskowitz
Jon Pesnell
Kurt Pessa
Arnaud Petel
Brian Peters
Joel Peters
Nathaniel Peters
Aaron Petersen
Dan Petersen
Scott Petersen
Terry Petersen
Adam Peterson
Adam Peterson
Bob Peterson
Erica Peterson
Glen Peterson
Jamie Peterson
John Peterson
Mark Peterson
Pete Peterson
Rob Peterson
Robert Peterson
Terry Peterson
Tom Peterson
Craig Petra
Jay Petrich
Nicholai Petrick
Donald Petrine
William Petro
Andrew Petrone
David Petros
Dubravko Petrovich
Robert Petrovski
Hillary Petruska
Charles Petrusky
Narelle Pettee
Kim Petterson
Brent Pettersson
Paul Petticrew
Craig Pettigrove
Leroy Pettis
Elliott Pettit
Judith Petty
Tanya Petty
Filippo Pezzoli
Jason Pfannschmidt
Catherine Pfarrer
John Pfeiffer
Lauren Pfeiffer
Allison Pfeifler
Ed Pfenninger
Hank Pfister
Mike Pfisterer
Katherine Pfordt
Fred Pfuhl
Anthony Pham
Brian Pham
Eric Pham
Tuan Pham
Hung Phan
Pat Phanthanusorn
Chris Phelan
Jenny Phelps
Miguel Phelps
Raith Phelps
Laura Pheneger
Steve Phifer
Bob Phillips
Byron Phillips
Claudia Phillips
Dave Phillips
Ginger Phillips
John Phillips
Margaret Phillips
Mark Phillips
Mike Phillips
Patty Phillips
REB Phillips
William Phillips
Phoutthasack Phimvongsa
Chris Phua
Wayne Pickard
David Picker
Marc Picker
Jeffrey Pickering
Jonathan Pickett
Martin Pickup
Jose Pico
Andy Picon
Jason Picone
Jared Pieper
Richard Pier
David Pierce
Robert Pierce
Roger Pierce
Wendell Pierce
Desi Pierre
Keith Pierson
Fausthyara Pietersz
Jill Pietrowsky
Ben Pigorsch
Brandon Pike

Todd Piker
Alina Pila
Bill Pilardi
Keri Pilkey-Thompson
Chip Pill
Shaun Pilling
Marcus Pillion
Pamela Pillo
Steven Pillon
Adrian Pina
Zachary Pine
Marco Pineda
Maxher Pineda
Monica Pineda
Fred Pinho
Joao Pinho
Jimmy Pinjuv
Janet Pinkett
Samantha Pinnell
Kuan Pio
Edward Piorkowski
Deborah Piper
Wilson Pipkin
Gregory Pipkins
Bradley Pippin
Richard Piretti
Elisaveta Pironkova-Petrov
Albert Piscitelli
Gianni Piseddu
Andrea Piski
Eric Piskura
Jimmy Pitkanen
Anthony Pitt
De'Vonte Pittman
Gary Pittman
David Pitts
Daniel Pitz
Jonathan Pivor
Joseph Pizzat
Michael Pizzat
Anthony Pizzulli
Gary Plank
Tracey Plascencia
Richard Plasschaert
Benjamin Platt
Michelle Plattel
Eric Plaushines
Peter Plaushines
Darin Pleasant
Sonia Pleasant
Tim Pleasant
Pete Ploog
Becky Plowman-Hahn
Lori Plum
Oksana Plutchok
Kimberly Po
Andrew Pogonyi
Erik Pohls
Dophie Poiset
Pedro Pola
Marcin Polak
Michael Polasek
Leann Polen
Jan Polhamus
Frank Polito
Tomislav Poljak
Sean Polk
Pete Polkinghorn
Sylvia Poll
David Pollack
Jonas Pollack
Meredith Pollack
Keith Pollak
Michael Pollard
Jonathan Pollare
Christie Pollin
Kevin Pollock
Paolo Polloni
Alejandro Polo
Bert Poole
David Poole
Pete Poole
Stephan Poole
Stanford Poon
Wilston Poon
Octavian Popaluca
Jared Pope
Kevin Pope
William Popejoy
Laurentiu Popescu
David Popiel
Michael Popienko
Chris Poplin
Peter Popov
Doron Popper
Dorian Porada
Leonardo Porcella
Rocco Porreca
Alexander Porter
Butch Porter
David Porter
David Porter
Derek Porter
Ellen Porter
Richard Porter
Robert Porter
Steffen Porter
Carl Poske
Kathleen Post
Doug Potkay
Loraine Potochick
Andy Potter
Jay Potter
John Potter
Roseann Potter
Scott Potter
Sean Potter
Chris Potthast
Leesa Potts
Matt Potts
Stephen Poulos
Bill Pound
Iain Pound
Paul Pound
John Pouzzner
Bryn Powell
Carey Powell
Dana Powell
Evan Powell
Kenneth Powell
Billy Power
Dave Power
John Powers
Samantha Powers
Shawn Powers
Brian Poynter
John Prachar
Daniel Prado
Jaime Prado
Paul Prah
John Pratt
Celeste Pregracke
Gayle Prejean
Kris Premo
Mike Premo
Keri Preng
Aleco Preovolos
Tara Pressley
Brian Preston
Dave Preston
Warren Pretorius
Greg Prevette
Matthew Previdi
William Previdi
Nicolas Previte
Aland Price
Benjamin Price
Christina Price
Cliff Price
David Price
Howard Price
Loydd Price
Nate Price
Robert Price
Cameron Prichard
John Prickitt
Charlotte Primer
Dennis Prinos
Roy Prior
Peter Pristach
Jim Prittinen
Jorge Privat
Salvatore Procacci
Richard Prochaska
Josef Prochazka
Bruce Proctor
Mike Prokopik
Bjorn Propst
Steve Prosowski
Timon Prosper
Orlando Protho
Matthew Prouatt
Doug Proudian
Xavier Proulx
Jim Provines
Brian Prudhomme
Edward Prudhomme
Greg Prudhomme
Mandy Prudhomme
Steven Prueter
Kristen Prunier
Richard Prybell
David Przystasz
Karin Ptaszek-Kochis
Mike Puc
Christopher Pucci
Ivan Puchkarov
Kathleen Pudlo
David Pugh
Mike Pugh
Nigel Pugh
Lisa Pugliese
Scott Pukys
Joey Puleri
David Pulis
Andy Pullen
Ellen Pulsinelle
Robert Pulver
Prachark Pumpuang
Alan Punke
Hoku Purcell
Patricia Purcell
John Purdon
Rob Purdy
Betsy Purpura
Vija Purs
Laura Puryear
Raymond Puryear
Kristina Pusateri
Myron Pushyk
Corey Putchel
Kenneth Puvogel
Bienvenido Puyat
Paul Puz
Qiuchen Qin
Yun Qin
Jim Quagliana
Stephanie Quan
Gary Quandt
Serena Quarelli
Bill Quario
Valerie Quarles
Kevin Quay
Brody Queal
Stephen Queenan
Justin Quest
Noel Quevreaux
Carlos Quijano
Ann Quinn
Arthur Quinn
Brian Quinn
Airam Quintero
Luis Quintero
Eric Quiroz
Ralph Rabago
Rhonda Rabanal
Michelle Rabatin
Cliff Raben
Eli Rabin
Melinda Rabinowitz
Shane Racine
Christopher Racz
Frank Raddi
Shane Rader
Andreas Radermacher
Jovana Radmanovic
Zoran Radosevic
Margaret Radtke
Bob Raedisch
Jack Raftery
Matt Ragan
Denny Rager
Marc Raggenbass
Joe Ragland
Mike Ragland
James Ragsdale
Mike Rahaley
Mir Rahim
Ittaro Rai
Michael Raikhlin
Adria Raines
Andrea Rains
Angie Rains
Ron Rainyn
Dinesh Rajagopalan
Chandra Rajakar
Neil Rajapakse
Ben Rakusin
Thomas Ralph
Richard Ralston
Heidi Ramaekers
Suresh Ramakrishnan
Suresh Ramamurthi
Mai Ramey
Alice Ramirez
Crisanto Ramirez
Antonio Ramos
Antonio Ramos
David Ramos
Eduardo Ramos
Lenoir Ramos
Nathan Ramos
Raul Ramos
Mahendra Rampersaud
Bill Ramsay
Charlie Ramsay
John Ramsey
Paul Ramsey
Russell Mark Ramsey
Dave Randall
Jarrod Randle
Bob Randolph
Kevin Randolph
Marc Randolph
Patti Randolph
Shannon Randolph
Gabriel Raneses
Trevor Rankow
Nithi Ranonda
Greer Ransom
Julia Ransom
Dipesh Rao
David Rapp
Herb Rapp
Felicia Raschiatore
Ryan Rasco
Ivan Rashkov
Anup Rashtrawar
Kevin Rasmussen
Kyle Rasmussen
Aziz Rasool
Charles Rasor
Hall Ratcliffe
Paul Ratcliffe
Elaine Rathgeber
Dhiren Rathod
Adrian Rattenbury
Jeff Ratthe
Brian Ratzlaff
Robert Raub
Mario Rauch
Eric Rauschenberger
Lindsay Rawstorne
Bill Ray
David Ray
Judith Ray
Kevin Ray
Mark Ray
Robyn Ray
Rod Ray
Joshua Raymond
Mike Raymond
Mike Raymond
Raul Raymundo
John Reade

Alyce Reames
Mark Rearden
Alex Rebeiz
Dennis Reblin
Sergio Rebolledo
Becky Recavarren
Felix Recavarren
Ryan Recht
Samuel Rechtin
Joel Reckewey
Jon Reckewey
Devin Reddick
David Redding
DandaVijaya Reddy
Seth Redelheim
Ferdinand Redelijk
Chris Redman
Wayne Redman
Michael Redmond
Francois Redondo Cordero
Clay Redwood
Adam Reeb
Bill Reed
Bruce Reed
David Reed
Jensen Reed
Joe Reed
Karen Reed
Kristin Reed
Robert Reed
Setsuko Reed
Shari Reed
Thaddeus Reed
Alice Reen
Chris Rees
Doug Rees
Shanna Rees
Thomas Rees
Ted Reese
Weston Reese
Virginia Reeter
Bobby Reeves
Erin Reeves
John Henry Reeves
Melanie Reeves
Tommy Reeves
Jim Reffkin
Colleen Regan
Daniel Regan
Peter Regan
Lucas Regas
Rebecca Reger
Lori Reich
Andy Reid
Ed Reid
Gordon Reid
Justin Reid
Kristie Reid
Mike Reid
Chris Reiff
Katherine Reigelman
Peggy Reilly
Mike Reily
Robert Reimer
Victor Reimer
Jennifer Reinbold
Joseph Reiney
Josh Reinhard
Steven Reiniger
Scott Reinmund
Alexander Reinsch
Luis Reis
Martin Reisert
Charles Reisig
Karen Rembert
Zachary Remis
Shen Ren
Bryan Renaud
Alexander Renauldo
Luke Rencher
Denis Rende
Cindy Rendel
Charles Renfrew
Peter Reni
Susan Renick
Brian Renvall
Jonathan Renwick
Frances Resha
Julee Reslewic
Jody Resmondo Garner
Alvaro Restrepo
Claudiu Retean
Kurt Retzler
David Reuben
Cindy Reuter
Clay Reuter
Whit Reutlinger
Wendy Revak
Joseph Reveteriano
Rafael Rexach
Ivette Reyes
Steve Reyes
Tony Reyes
Anne Reynolds
Jeffery Reynolds
Keith Reynolds
Lincoln Reynolds
Randy Reynolds
Thomas Reynolds
Kristie Reynolds-Gipe
Andrew Reynoso
Eligio Reynoso
Fabiana Rezak
Will Rhame
Sherry Rhoden
Corey Rhodes
John Rhodes
Scott Rhodes
Denis Riabuchin
Paulo Ribeiro
Seth Ribnick
Michael Ricci
Donna Ricco
Jeff Rice
Laura Rice
Ron Rice
Tim Rice
Justin Rich
Albert Richards
Dan Richards
Jeff Richards
Jim Richards
John Richards
Joseph Richards
Leon Richards
Mike Richards
Daniel Richardson
David Richardson
Dennis Richardson
Ed Richardson
Keith Richardson
Paul Richardson
Scott Richardson
Tim Richardson
Gary Richey
Jason Richey
Peter Richman
David Richmond
Alan Richter
Bryan Richter
David Richter
Kelley Rickard
Scott Rickel
Jill Rickey
Michael Ricks
Mike Ridaoui
Trish Riddell
Barry Riddle
Bill Riddle
Suzette Riddle
Mike Ridener
Malcolm Ridenour
Timothy Ridge
James Ridgley
Julie Riely
Marty Riessen
Lori Riffice
Joshua Rifkin
Nicholas Rigby
Lindsay Riggenbach
Marsh Riggs
Derin Riley
George Riley
Jack Riley
Mark Riley
Roy Riley
Kathy Rinaldi
Daniel Rinchuse
Donald Rinchuse
Edmundo Rincon
Gilberto Rincon
Jose Rincon
David Rindo
Mario Rindone
David Rineberg
Alex Ringwald
Raquel Rinn
Andrew Rios
Juan Rios
Tom Rios
Guillermo Ripoll-Brenot
Brie Rippner-Parsons
Robert Risboskin
Kevin Riser
Bob Risinger
Matthew Risoldi
Magali Risoleo
Andreas Riss
Bobby Ritacco
Gwendolyn Ritchie
Pat Ritchie
Tim Ritchie
James Ritter
John Ritucci
Thomas Ritz
Allie Ritzenberg
Joey Rive
Alfredo Rivera
Anthony Rivera
Charlie Rivera
Julio Rivera
Kelvin Rivera
Lilivette Rivera
Raul Rivera
Dennis Rizza
Clifford Rizzi
Larry Rizzo
Laura Rizzo
Bill Roach
Jack Roach
Phyllis Roach
Thomas Roach
Chris Robb
Jenny Robb
Mason Robb
Julius Robberts
Emily Robbins
Mark Robbins
Ralph Robbins
John Roberge
Mike Roberson
Mimi Roberson
Bill Roberti
Beverly Roberts
Carol Roberts
Coby Roberts
Mark Roberts
Pat Roberts
Paul Roberts
Steven Roberts
Tyler Roberts
Colin Robertson
Fitzroy Robertson
Lori Robertson
Michael Robertson
Christian Robichaud
Paul Robin
Angela Robinson
Carl Robinson
Christopher Robinson
Clay Robinson
David Robinson
David Robinson
Drew Robinson
Julius Robinson
Ken Robinson
Kurt Robinson
Lisa Robinson
Marina Robinson
Randy Robinson
Stephen Robinson
Tara Robinson
Terrence Robinson
Troy Robinson
James Robison
Bob Robles
Michael Rocca
Patrick Rocca
Fausto Rocha
Gary Roche
Geoff Roche
Spritely Roche
Timothy Roche
Mike Rocheleau
Merissa Rock
Cory Rockow
Mark Rodel
Marcela Rodezno Hernandez
Bob Rodgers
Sarah Rodgers
Philippe Rodrigue
Raphael Rodrigues
Adriana Rodriguez
Angel Rodriguez
Bruno Rodriguez
Ivan Rodriguez
Jose Rodriguez
Kristian Rodriguez
Miranda Rodriguez
Phillip Rodriguez
Raul Rodriguez
Rodolfo Rodriguez
Ronald Rodriguez
Mauricio Rodriguez Ramirez
Jackie Roe
Austin Roebuck
Joe Roediger
James Roesch
Kyle Roeser
Don Roesler
Ryan Roeth
Bryan Rogers
David Rogers
James Rogers
Jason Rogers
Kathryn Rogers
Kip Rogers
Mike Rogers
Pat Rogers
Philip Rogers
Seth Rogers
Skyler Rogers
Weldon Rogers
Chuck Rogge
Claudia Rohaly
Frank Rohenes
Warren Rohmfeld
Nick Rohner
Michael Rohrbach
James Rohrbacher
Tom Rohrbacher
Donna Roisom
Christian Rojas
Rick Rojas
Andy Roland
Carlos Roldan
Joie Rolf-Switzer
Marieke Rolland
Thomas Roller
Grant Rolley
Lynne Rolley
Ashlie Rolley Miller
Lee Rollins
Wayne Rollock
Ross Roloff
Chris Roman
Jeff Roman
Allison Romano
Ron Romano
Tonya Romanowski
Eric Romasanta
Dave Romberg
Christina Romeka
Derek Romer
Hans Romer

Robert Romer
Damon Romero
Deborah Romero
Justin Romero
Michael Romisher
Shaun Romisher
Bill Rompf
Mary Rompf
Callie Ronkowski
Karen Ronney
Travis Rood
Kathleen Rooney
Brent Root
Patrick Root
Vanessa Roper
Matthew Rorech
Jose Rosa
Luis Rosado
Kurt Roschauer
Matthew Rose
Sandra Rose
Kin Roseborough
Joe Rosell
Evan Rosen
Jenny Rosen
Marisa Rosen
Paul Rosenbaum
Barry Rosenberg
Leo Rosenberg
David Rosenfeld
Christopher Rosensteel
Terence Rosenthal
George Roser
Doug Roseth
Scott Rosewarne
Farhad Roshanaie
John Rosini
Matthew Rosner
Adam Rosow
Joel Ross
John Ross
Kenny Ross
Mario Ross
Randy Ross
Robert Ross
Shawn Ross
Angelo Rossetti
Ettore Rossetti
Brandt Rossi
Gagik Rostomyan
Matthew Roszkowski
Christine Roth
Jennifer Roth
Karen Roth
Nicole Roth
Todd Roth
Martin Rothfels
Kurt Rothman
Naomi Rothring
Jeff Rothstein
Lauren Rothstein
Matt Rotter
Richard Rottkamp
Lynn Rottschafer
Frederic Rouault
John Rountree
Moira Roush
Sina Roushan
Dave Rowat
Brad Rowe
Robert Rowe
Ryan Rowedder
Dennis Rowen
Charles Rowley
Neeladitya Roy
Dennis Royal
Jimmy Royalty
Stephen Royalty
Shawn Roybal
Roderick Royer
Richard Rozell
Marcin Rozpedski
Kiki Rozwadowski Lopes
Yevgeniy Rozygrayev
Julie Ruamthong
Lin Ruan
Karla Ruaya
Barry Ruback
Paul Rubas
Robert Rubel
David Ruben
Todd Ruben
Mitchell Rubiano
Edward Rubin
Harvey Rubin
Marlin Rubin
Todd Rubinstein
Bill Rublee
Michal Rubner
Arron Rucks
Susan Rudd
John Ruder
James Rudolph
Kelly Rudolph-Rohrbach
David Rudrud
Dean Rudrud
Todd Ruedisili
Chuck Rueff
Jose Ruelas
Nick Ruess
Barbara Rueth
Arlene Ruffin
Don Ruffin
Doug Ruffin
Jeff Ruffin
Brian Ruffner
Tiago Ruffoni
James Rufiange
Ronald Rugimbana
Rainer Ruhland
Luis Ruiz
Richard Rumble
Jane Rumiano
Willis Runck
Ellen Runda
Scott Runda
Kenneth Runyan
Matthew Runyan
Robert Runyan
Brian Ruppel
Brian Rusche
Gretchen Rush
Robert Rush
Justine Rusk
Chuck Russell
Gregory Russell
James Russell
JoAnne Russell
Michael Russell
Rhett Russell
Robert Russell
Robert Russell
Robyn Russell
Scott Russell
Wyatt Russell
Anthony Russo
Eugene Russo
John Russo
Mark Russo
Pablo Russo
Vincent Russo
Kevin Rust
Theodore Rust
Fern Ruth
Gregory Ruth
Chad Ruthig
Marcus Rutsche
Allan Ruttley
Patrick Rutz
Margit Ruutel
Robert Ruzanic
Ryan Ruzziconi
Gregory Ryan
John Ryan
Kevin Ryan
Patrick Ryan
Robert Ryan
Hilary Ryan-McCarthy
Robert Rye
Bob Ryland
Duane Ryman
Jeffrey Ryman
Mark Ryman
Michael Ryon
Heather Rytting
Steven Ryuse
Donald Saab-Alvarez
Muhammad Saad
Raul Saad
Ricardo Saad
Roberto Saad
Marc Sabas Montoro
Derek Sabedra
Maria Sablina
Vyron Sacharidis
Jyotin Sachdev
Ankur Sachdeva
Frank Sachire
Lester Sack
Mark Sack
Jennifer Sackman
Franklin Sacks
Roman Sada
Otis Sadler
Thomas Sadzeck
Shigeo Saeda
Seizo Saeki
Fred Safipour
Lawrence Sagel
Christopher Sagers
Edmond Sahag
Larry Saheim
Stuart Saiki
Michael Saine
Pathorr Saini
Jiro Saito
Yoshinori Saka
Hiroki Sakaguchi
Shuhei Sakaguchi
Motonari Sakai
Takayuki Sakai
Teruaki Sakai
Kenji Sakamoto
Masato Sakamoto
Shiniti Sakashita
Keisuke Sakata
Brian Sakey
Brock Sakey
Ross Sakey
Hayato Sakurai
Hirotoshi Sakurai
Miwako Sakurai
Michael Sakvarelidze
Jose Salas
Carlos Salazar
Ron Salazar
Stephen Salazar
David Salemi
Robert Salerno
Joseph Salinas
Jason Sallin
Danny Salloum
Lawrence Salmon
Tom Salmon
Lisa Salo
Marty Salokas
Max Salonga
Ninka Salopek-Paunovic
Karen Salter
David Saltman
Trevor Salton
Leonard Saltzman
Rod Saludo
Robert Salum
Paul Salvador
Wilfredo Salvador
Philippe Salvat
Paige Salveter
Jeffrey Salzenstein
Diaguely Tamba Samassa
Jody Sambrick
Andrej Samets
Amy Samons
Timothy Samons
Teresa Samstag-Haug
Christine Samuel
Steven Samuel
Dessie Samuels
Bonnie Samuelsen
Alek Samuelson
Erik Samuelson
Kristen Samuelson
Chuck Sanchelli
Andres Sanchez
Anthony Sanchez
Carlos Sanchez
Daniel Sanchez
Frederic Sanchez
Johnny Sanchez
Michael Sanchez
Roderic Sanchez
Marco Sanchez Hernandez
Emilio Sanchez Vicario
Jaime Sanchez-Canamares Rios
Madeleine Sanchez-Petel
Damian Sancilio
Steven Sand
Christina Sanders
John Sanders
Josephine Sanders
Michael Sanders
Shearline Sanders
Peter Sanderson
Cory Sandgren
Charles Sandomenico
David Sandoval
Michael Sandoval
Carol Sandoz
Adrian Sands
Trevor Sands
Carol Sandvig
Craig Sandvig
Marvin Sanemitsu
Charles Sanfilippo
Michael Sanford
John Sangveraphunsiri
Bill Sanis
Michael Saniuk
Christopher Sanni
John Sanny
Domenico Sano
Thomas Sansonetti
Eduardo Santana Cardenes
Alejandro Santiago
Ronald Santiago
Anthony Santonastaso
Arthur Santos
Fernando Santos
Patience Santos
Thiago Santos
Steven Sapolsky
Paul Saputo
Eusebio Sarabia
Christine Sarandopolis
Brett Sargeant
Sona Saringulyan
Gerald Sarmiento
Hector Sarmiento
Michael Sarney
Kenneth Sarnoff
Jonathan Sarosiek
Tom Sarsfield
Shawna Sarson
Mark Sarver
Steven Sarver
Mikolaj Sarzynski
Akira Sasa
Gen Sasaki
Hiroto Sasaki
Yoji Sasaki
Bob Sassano
Barbara Sasser
Robert Sasseville
Ricky Sasso
Kimihito Satake
Mari Satani
Akihiro Sato
Akira Sato
Hisashi Sato
Katsuki Sato
Naoko Sato
Tetsuya Sato
Takao Satoh
Cyril Saulnier

Lea Sauls
Mark Saunders
Peter Saunders
Richard Saunders
Johann Saurbier
Juan Sauri
Lawrence Savage
Mark Savage
Nick Saviano
Makoto Sawada
Tomohide Sawamura
Tsubasa Sawamura
Ken Sawer
Steve Sawer
Ted Sawyer
Jack Sayers
Stephen Sayoc
Ted Sayrahder
Frank Sberno
Robert Scale
Peter Scales
Larry Scalia
Andre Scarlett
Kirk Schaaf
Leigh Schachter
Luke Schachter
Robb Schachter
Denny Schackter
Christy Schaefer
Curt Schaefer
Emily Schaefer
Jim Schaefer
Kalla Schaefer
Lyle Schaefer
Stephanie Schaefer
Glennon Schafer
Richard Schaffer
Payne Schanski
Peter Schaper
Katelyn Schaub
Paula Scheb
Daniel Scheider
Wendy Schenk
Timothy Scheuerman
Lenny Scheuermann
Robert Schewior
Adriano Schiavo
Annette Schiavone
Scott Schibig
Peggy Schick
John Schildt
Jodi Schiller
Natalie Schiller
Bill Schillings
Bobby Schindler
Stephen Schkade
Tylor Schlader
Stephan Schlagenhauff
Anne Schleicher
Ian Schleif
Scott Schlesinger
Linda Schley
Robert Schlink
Lenny Schloss
Mark Schlossenberg
Dane Schmidgall
Andrew Schmidt
Guy Schmidt
Mara Schmidt
Nina Schmidt
Richard Schmidt
Steve Schmidt
Vincent Schmidt
Mark Schminke
Joseph Schmulian
Tim Schnaible
Diana Schnakenburg
Joan Schnarr
Beth Ann Schneider
Dick Schneider
Jack Schneider
Jorge Schneider
Kristen Schneider
Nicholas Schneider
Scott Schneider
Tobias Schneider
Dave Schobel
Doug Schoelzel
Thomas Schoen
Douglas Schoenly
John Schoenmakers
Gira Schofield
David Scholl
Eric Scholl
Gary Scholl
Rick Scholl
Joseph Scholtens
Neil Schonfeld
Chris Schoop
Jesse Schouten
Matthew Schrader
Joshua Schraeter
Bret Schrama
Lisa Schreiber
Emily Schreur
Logan Schreur
Bud Schroeder
Carl Schroeder
Rod Schroeder
Svetlana Schroeder
Tina Schroeder
Tracy Schroeder
Drew Schrum
Brian Schubert
Laurie Schubert
Randall Schubert
Tony Schubert
Fred Schuchert
Mark Schuering
Tom Schuett
George Schuldberg
Frank Schuler
Kenneth Schuler
Brad Schulte
Gary Schulterbrandt
Scott Schultz
Scott Schultz
David Schumacher
Elizabeth Schumacher
Gregg Schumacher
Fritz Schunck
Chuck Schunk
Jim Schutty
Russell Schutzman
Scott Schutzman
Andrew Schuyler
Fred Schwan
Josh Schwanger
Jeffrey Schwankl
Alan Schwartz
Anne Schwartz
Brett Schwartz
David Schwartz
Jason Schwartz
Mark Schwartz
Michael Schwartz
Ari Schwarz
Caesar Schwarz
Bob Schweid
Ken Schweitzer
Zachary Schwenning
Paul Schwerdtfeger
Alan Schwimmer
Jim Schwitters
Jim Sciarro
Daniel Scopp
Andrew Scorteanu
Bill Scott
Bob Scott
Courtney Scott
David Scott
James Scott
Janet Scott
Jeffrey Scott
Julia Scott
Matthew Scott
Matthew Scott
Michael Scott
Rob Scott
John Scrivani
Kimberly Scullion
Lois Sczepaniak
Geoffrey Seagram
Joshua Searle
Elizabeth Seay
David Secker
Jonathan Sedgmore
Fred Sedillo
Mike See
Terry See
Bradley Seegert
Butch Seewagen
Aaron Segal
Ryan Segelke
Patrik Segfeldt
Armand Segodo
Paul Segodo
Luis Segovia
Vince Segovia
William Segraves
Pancho Segura
Neil Sehgal
Rasim Sehovic
Jessica Seibert
Trey Seibold
Walter Seidel
Matthew Seideman
Erik Seifert
Jane Seiffert
John Seiter
Frank Seitz
Juraj Sekera
Kenichi Sekiguchi
Namiki Seko
Carmen Selaru-Stewart
Abbe Seldin
Dawn Selindh
Diane Selke
Susan Selke
Michael Sell
Juan Pablo Selle
Jayson Sellers
Thomas Seltzer
Todd Seltzer
Tiffany Selvaggio
Kim Selzman
Albert Semaan
Richard Seman
Mike Sember
Chirajeet Sen
Miyuki Sena
Asim Sengun
Ognjen Senic
Donavan September
Leonard Serafino
Juan Serna
Eliseo Serrano
Pat Serret
Elvi Serrot
William Serues
Delia Sescioreanu
Robin Sessions
Jonathan Sessom
Yuji Setou
John Setticerze
Paul Settles
Jason Seufert
Katerina Sevcikova
John Sevely
Marie Seward
Bernard Sewell
Adam Sexton
Ai Sexton
Brad Seymour
Garry Seymour
Trey Seymour
Mark Shaban
Louis Shackelford
Paul Shacklock
John Shade
John Shade
Robert Shafer
Patricia Shaffer
Ryan Shaffer
Abraham Shagoury
Jay Shaheen
Ilan Shaltuper
Gary Shamaly
David Shambach
Timothy Shambaugh
Tim Shanahan
Edward Shanaphy
Carolyn Shaner
YunJiao ShangGuan
Darryl Shanholtz
Vijay Shankar
Kent Shanks
Brian Shanley
Arthur Shannon
Christopher Shannon
Dan Shannon
Gregory Shannon
Scott Shannon
Genie Shapiro
Julie Shapiro
Max Shapiro
Roger Shapiro
Ron Shapiro
Wilbur Shardlow
William Shardlow
Ishant Sharma
Sagar Sharma
Michael Sharp
Ron Sharp
John Sharpe
Ben Sharples
Lonnie Sharrock
Jim Sharton
Richard Sharton
James Shaughnessy
Bill Shaw
George Shaw
Jon Shaw
Joshua Shaw
Ross Shaw
Steven Shaw
Timothy Shaw
Victoria Shaw
Richard Shawfrank
Amy Shay
Thomas Shea
Tom Shea
Jill Sheahan
Patrick Sheahan
Christopher Shearburn
Alan Shearer
Lesley Sheehan
Jack Sheehy
Steven Sheer
Robert Sheets
Amy Sheetz
Wesley Sheffy
Barry Sheiber
Kenneth Sheiffele
Amjid Sheikh
Alexander Shek
Sirsa Shekim
John Shelander
Chris Sheldon
David Shell
Tyler Shelly
Darla Shelton
Edgar Shelton
Leigh Shelton
Ronald Shelton
Wendell Shelton
Ryan Shelven
Simon Shen
Zi Tian Shen
Ming Sheng
Skip Shephard
Paul Shepherd
Annette Sheppard
Mark Sheppard
Crystal Sher Yat Sze
Stephen Sherba
Gary Sherby
Mike Sherer
Warren Sherman
David Sherry
Ryan Sherry
Bradley Sherwood
Dave Sherwood
John Sherwood
Jaideep Shetty

Masato Shibahara
Mizuki Shibahara
Tetsuya Shibayama
Kazuyoshi Shibuya
Timothy Shideler
Daniel Shidler
Andy Shields
Burrell Shields
Ron Shields
Scott Shields
Doug Shifflett
Eric Shih
Yoshiyuki Shiji
Fumio Shima
Dean Shimada
Katsunori Shimamura
Ryo Shimaura
Ken Shimizu
Manabu Shimizu
Shinsuke Shimohata
Masayuki Shinohara
Ken Shioi
Kazunari Shiomi
Denee Shipley-Massie
John Shipman
John Shipstedt
Hidenori Shirakawa
Masaaki Shirakawa
Larry Shireman
Michael Shires
Bill Shivar
William Shivar
Riaz Shivji
Jake Shoemake
Adam Shoemaker
Kirk Shoemaker
Peter Shoemaker
Scott Shogreen
Takahiro Shoji
Brian Shoman
Daniel Shoop
Matthew Shoop
Scott Shope
Hazel Shore
Jennifer Shorr
Jeff Short
Stephen Shortridge
Anthony Shortt
Sue Shrader
Jeffrey Shrager
Stephen Shreiner
Pam Shriver
Cheryl Shrum
Alexander Shubny
Lorie Shuck
Eric Shulman
Lori Shulman
Kent Shultz
Tara Shultz
Venant Shum
Elizabeth Shumway
Kristopher Shumway
Alex Shusis
Ilan Shvartz
Liz Shweky
Chenwei Si
David Siddons
Darren Sidney
Kathrin Sieberth
Gene Siegel
Matthew Siegel
Samantha Siegel
Linda Siegel-Splivalo
Suzanne Siegler
Brandon Sieh
Gordon Siek
John Siemens
Mark Sieving
Beka Sikharulidze
Jason Sikola
Brian Sikorski
Kamil Sikorski
Fabio Silva
Juan Pablo Silva
Scott Silva
Dawn Silverberg
Joshua Silverman
Adam Silverstein
David Silvia
Heather Silvia
Yong Sim
Len Simard
Mark Simcina
Goran Simic
Ed Simko
Roseann Simko
Bill Simmers
Sabina Simmonds
George Simmons
James Simmons
Kyle Simmons
Angela Simon
Ben Simon
Bill Simon
Jerome Simon
Spencer Simon
Danielle Simone
Anthony Simonelli
Joshua Simonetta-Lee
Kelly Simons
Cathy Simpson
Chad Simpson
Russell Simpson
Scott Simpson
Thomas Simpson
Evan Sims
Niza Simunyola
Leung Sin Him
Andy Sinclair
Christopher Singer
Daniel Singer
John Singer
Michael Singh
Pravin Singh
Shikhagr Singh
Nathan Singleton
John Sinkins
Jason Sinkoff
Paul Sinuk
Philip Siordia
Christopher Siragusa
Nicole Sire
Chase Sires
Cristina Sirianni
Joseph Sirianni
Gofur Sirojiddinov
Andrew Sirota
Frank Sisinni
Michael Sitter
Dave Sivertson
Brian Sivinski
Joe Sivley
Kenneth Sjoberg
Clifford Skakle
Stanley Skakle
Charles Skalsky
Edward Skarwecki
Stephanie Skarwecki
Dylan Skeffington
Patricia Skelly
William Skiendiel
Mark Skillicorn
Alexander Skinner
Kailyn Skjonsby
Kevin Skousen
Ashley Skrabut
Mary Skubik
Barbara Skurdall
Matthew Skwaruzynski
Cindy Slachta
Bob Slack
Roderick Slack
Marc Slama
John Slavin
Richard Slaymaker
Evgeny Slesarev
Richard Slick
Mike Slipyan
Richard Slivocka
Andrew Slizeski
Ron Sloan
Sean Sloane
Scott Slobin
Susan Sloboth
Glen Slonac
John Slootweg
Gabriel Slotnick
Pavel Slozil
Wayne Sluice
Douglas Small
Alan Smallwood
Brian Smallwood
Basarab Smarandescu
Kaysie Smashey
Jesse Smatt
Brent Smiga
Alyson Smith
Bill Smith
Brad Smith
Bret Smith
Brian Smith
Bryan Smith
Byron Smith
Carolyn Smith
Chad Smith
Chris Smith
Christopher Smith
Christopher Smith
Cody Smith
Colin Smith
Connor Smith
Cori Smith
Craig Smith
Curtis Smith
Cy Smith
Darrell Smith
David Smith
David Smith
David Smith
David Smith
David Smith
David Smith
David Smith
David Smith
Ed Smith
Greg Smith
H A Smith
James Smith
Jamie Smith
Jamyl Smith
Jarrod Smith
Jeff Smith
Jeff Smith
Jeffrey Smith
Jennifer Smith
Jermaine Smith
Jesse Smith
Joseph Smith
Kelly Smith
Kent Smith
Leonard Smith
Lindsay Smith
Lynne Smith
Martin Smith
Michael Smith
Michael Smith
Michael Smith
Mike Smith
Nicholas Smith
Oliver Smith
Patrick Smith
Patrick Smith
Paul Smith
Paul Smith
Peter Smith
Peter Smith
RaFeael Smith
Ray Smith
Ray Smith
Raymond Smith
Raymond Smith
Reginald Smith
Ronnie Smith
Scott Smith
Scott Smith
Scott Smith
Sean Smith
Shannon Smith
Stan Smith
Steve Smith
Tim Smith
Tim Smith
Tim Smith
Timothy Smith
Timothy Smith
Todd Smith
Todd Smith
Tosha Smith
Travis Smith
Walter Smith
Wesley Smith
William Smith
Woodie Smith
Zakkary Smith
Richard Smithers
Jack Smithheisler
Jay Smithley
Dan Smithyman
Kirill Smolkin
Vladimir Smolkin
Michael Smookler
Eugene Smotkin
Anne Smudz
Peter Smythe
Joe Snailum
Lilia Clare Snape
Sean Snee
James Sneed
Jonathan Snell
Tim Snell
Jeff Snelling
Jordan Snider
Steve Snider
Arthur Snow
David Snow
Scott Snow
Dean Snyder
Todd Snyder
Whitney Snyder
Chun Yip So
Keith Soanes
David Sobel
Chuck Sobers
Mark Sobieralski
Karin Sobotta
Paul Sochin
Niurka Sodupe
Hideki Soga
Suzuo Soga
Ashvin Soin
Pete Sok
Chisato Sokai
Norman Sokalski
Douglas Sokol
Jonathan Sokol
Renie Sokolowski
Fernando Sol
Augusto Solano
Jonathan Solari
Jannine Soldan
Amyn Soldier
Bryan Solem
Arturo Solis
Austin Soliz
Harold Solomon
Jeff Solomon
Spencer Solomon
Manuel Solorio
Jon Solow
Ladislav Soltes
Sutirapan Somabut
Laurence Sombito
Hilary Somers
Barry Somerville
Henry Somerville
Karl Sommer
Robert Soneru
Kai Song
Luiza Sonnervig
Mariana Sonnervig
Manabu Sonobe
Sue Sookiasian
Will Sophiea
Marc Sophoulis
Joseph Sopko

Terry Sorensen
John Soriano
David Sornberger
Oleg Sorokin
J M Sorrell
Andrew Sorrentino
Elizabeth Sortland
William Sosebee
Richard Sotelo
Mathieu Soto
Barbara Sotura-Tscherne
Yuka Soule
Yuichiro Souma
Skip South
Lia Southwick
Lucas Souza
George Sowards
Dananja Soysa
Kim Spaccarotella
David Span
Robert Spann
Eugenio Spano
Stephen Spano
Collin Sparks
Jennifer Sparks
Reed Sparks
William Sparks
Helle Sparre
Daniel Spatz
Tara Spaulding
Jonathan Spear
Scott Spearman
Amanda Speegle
Jeremy Speicher
James Speir
Jason Speirs
Julise Spell
Len Spencer
Mary Spencer
Nancy Spencer
Fred Sperber
Dylan Sperry
Tina Spicher
Sharon Spiegel
Jeffrey Spiers
Paul Spies
Bob Spilman
Jim Spindler
Aris Spirtos
Edward Sposa
Trevor Spracklin
Hugo Spratley
Bryant Springer
Clara Springer
Matthew Springer
Richard Spurling
Joe Spurrier
Stephen Squire
Andre Squires
Tikky Srieud
John Sruk
Ivan Srut
Heather St. John
Ron St. John
Victoria St. John
Eugene St. Martin
Gregory St. Van
Mark Staats
Dan Stablein
Brandon Stacey
Greg Stacey
Barbara Stack
Jeffrey Stack
Kent Stadum
Joseph Stafford
Les Stafford
Bob Stafutti
Robert Stahl
Kelly Stahlhuth
Bill Stahr
Shane Staley
Richard Stall
Michelle Stallard
Susie Staloch
Robert Stambaugh
Eric Stampfl
Michael Stamps
Shaun Stamps
Marius Stan
Jack Standifer
Jeremy Standiford
Katerina Stanford
Stewart Stanger
Elizabeth Stanis
Jason Stanislaw
Alan Stanley
Brian Stanley
Todd Stanley
Silvana Stans
John Stanton
Taylor Stanton
Addison Staples
Butch Staples
Bruce Stapleton
Ben Stapp
Peter Stapperfend
Greg Star
David Stark
Larry Stark
William Stark
Michael Starke
Blake Starkey
Derek Starleaf
Bob Starr
Larry Starr
Jeff Stassen
Chip Staton
Peter Staub
Dean Stavri
Ioannis Stavridis
Sally Stead
Brian Stead-Dorval
Chip Stearns
Suzanne Stebbins
Preston Steblein
Mark Steeds
Bill Steege
Ron Steege
Kevin Steele
Margie Steele
Paul Steele
Jan Steenekamp
Therina Steenkamp
Russell Steere
Steve Stefanki
Milos Stefanovic
Anthony Stefanski
Armand Steger
Donald Stein
Jonathan Stein
Michael Stein
David Steinbach
George Steinemann
Andy Steingold
Aaron Steinhauser
Sidney Steinour
Frederick Steiwer
Tom Stem
Sue Stemmler
Pavlos Stephanides
Andrew Stephen
Carlene Stephens
Jason Stephens
Milena Stephens
Oliver Stephens
Randy Stephens
Robert Stephens
Brett Stephenson
Greg Stephenson
Barry Sterett
Robert Sterk
William Stern
Christopher Stevens
Don Stevens
Mark Stevens
Jamie Stevenson
John Stevenson
Matt Steverson
Buster Stewart
Forrest Stewart
James Stewart
Jeri Stewart
Pamela Stewart
Patricia Stewart
Robert Stewart
Scott Stewart
Scott Stewart
Sean Stewart
Taylor Stewart
Jack Steyn
Ryan Stickley
Judith Stiff
Christopher Stigum
Shelly Stillman-Scott
Matt Stiltz
Arthur Stilwell
Graham Stilwell
Brad Stine
Conni Stinek
Tony Stingley
Jesse Stirnemann
Jon Stitt
Sonia Stock
Jim Stocker
Susan Elizabeth Stocker
Michele Stockman
Dick Stockton
Elizabeth Stockton
Kristine Stofey
Lisa Stoica
Roman Stoisavljevic
Dennis Stojewa
Jason Stokes
Jay Stokes
Teresita Stokes
Fred Stolle
Daniel Stone
Eck Stone
Marisa Stone
Mike Stone
Rachael Stone
Robert Stone
Stephanie Stone
Terry Stone
Andy Stoner
Natasha Stoop
Stephen Storey
Peter Storm
Richard Storr
Susan Storrer
Michael Story
Barry Stout
Daniel Stover
Michael Strahan
Hollister Strain
Harrison Straley
Sean Straley
Richard Strandskov
James Strassle
Mark Stratos
Wendy Strauss
Buddy Strawn
David Strebel
Wayne Street
Nicholas Streibick
Eric Striesfeld
Steve Striffler
Ronald Stroia
Christine Stromberg
Adrian Strong
Jason Strong
Karin Strong
Jason Strother
York Strother
Nicholas Stroynick
Winston Strozier
Adam Struble
Carrie Strum
Bob Stubbs
Scott Stubbs
Steven Stuckenschneider
Stefan Studer
Rachel Stuhlmann
Carol Stuller
Joshua Sturgis
Doug Stursma
Nick Stutsman
Jerry Styer
Cynthia Stys
Susanna Styve
Henry Su
Kwok Fung Su
Owen Suagee
Jamie Suard
Rodrigo Suarez
Eric Subirats
Arun Subramanian
Jerome Subtil
Jordan Sucamele
Susan Suddeth
Nicholas Sudol
Alex Sugai
Masakazu Sugai
Aya Suginouchi
Yuji Sugita
Akira Sugiura
Shigeki Sugiyama
Takako Sugiyama
Gerard Suhor
Shawnie Suica
Mark Suiter
Peter Sukalo
Akira Sukegawa
Irene Sukner
George Sulc
Beverly Sullivan
Brad Sullivan
Courtney Sullivan
Diane Sullivan
Dillon Sullivan
Joseph Sullivan
Paul Sullivan
Kyoichiro Sumimoto
Stephen Summer
Carl Summerlin
Ray Summers
Steven Summers
Harold Sumner
Phillip Sumner
Blaine Sumpter
Tiffany Sumpter
Clint Sumrow
Ken Sumrow
Jonathan Sun
Justin Sun
Tim Sunderland
Stephen Sundra
Scott Sundstrom
Matthew Sunter
Marilyn Superville
Igor Supica
Arumun Surma
George Surratt
Steven Surtman
Seth Sushinsky
Mark Susser
Kyle Sutherland
Julie Sutherlin
Robyn Suto
Lee Sutor
John Sutter
Earl Suttle
Justin Suttle
Astrid Suurbeek
Mitsunobu Suwa
Rick Suydam
Satoshi Suzawa
Akihiko Suzuki
Hironori Suzuki
Masaaki Suzuki
Masaru Suzuki
Toshifumi Suzuki
Thomas Svajda
Tobias Svantesson
Miloslav Svec
Johan Svensson
Jekaterina Svirina
Ben Swain
Tex Swain
Skylar Swall
Casey Swan
John Swan
Kevin Swank
Carl Swanson
Harold Swanson

Jason Swanson
Jessica Swanson
Mark Swanson
Melvin Swanson
Scott Swanson
Sarah Swanston
Andrew Swart
Paul Swartwood
Dan Swartz
Sylvia Swartz
Shelly Sweeney
Drew Sweet
Tom Sweitzer
Audrey Swift
Matt Swigart
Jim Swiggart
Stacy Sue Swiggart
Keith Swindoll
Paul Swink
Vern Swisher
Andrea Swope
Frank Swope
Pamela Swords
Andrew Swortfiguer
Bellary Syamasundaram
Saif Syed
Temujin Sykahua
Chris Sylvester
Alan Sylvia
Logan Symes
Hadley Syverud
Knute Syvrud
Beatrix Szalay-Klein
Joseph Szucs
Jimy Szymanski
Tony Szymczyk
Shadi Tabatabai
Matilde Taborda
Titus Tabotabo
Hiroshi Tabuchi
Marco Taccalite
Yuji Tachimi
Howard Tacub
Aaron Tada
Hakop Tadevosian
Samuel Tadevosian
Melissa Tafoya
Peter Taggard
Jerald Taggart
Alireza Taghizadehafshari
Nobuyoshi Taguchi
Zhichun Tai
Eric Taino
Mary Tait
Junya Taka
Kazunori Takagi
Kazuki Takahashi
Kazuya Takahashi
Kenji Takahashi
Masato Takahashi
Mitsuharu Takahashi
Nobumasa Takahashi
Satoshi Takahashi
Tomonori Takahashi
Kazuhiko Takai
Shoko Takai
Toshihiro Takaishi
Kazuto Takakusa
Atsushi Takamiyagi
Junichi Takamoto
Kenji Takao
Yosuke Takaoka
Katsumi Takasawa
Kazuhisa Takase
Kimiyuki Takase
Shunji Takasuka
Mariko Takata
Aki Takayama
Hideki Takayama
Masami Take
Jungo Takeda
Nobuhiro Takeda
Tadashi Takeda
Ikuko Takemura
Ichiro Takeuchi
Koh Takeuchi
Yoshino Takeuchi
Charles Talbert
Jan Talian
Emily Talley
Luis Tama
Masakatsu Tamai
Tetsuya Tamai
Barry Tamarkin
Mike Tammen
Hidekazu Tamura
Kenji Tamura
Naoki Tamura
Stan Tamura
John Tan
Eiji Tanaka
Emi Tanaka
Gakuya Tanaka
Hideyuki Tanaka
Katsunori Tanaka
Kazuhiro Tanaka
Norihisa Tanaka
Toru Tanaka
Yoshiaki Tanaka
Yumio Taniguchi
Dustin Tankersley
Velton Tankersley
Jaime Tannenbaum
Garrett Tanouye
Lance Tanouye
Bill Tanurchis
Tao Tao
Ramon Tapia
Russ Tapper
George Tarangioli
Mark Tarentino
William Tarnasky
Danny Tarpley
Jack Tarr
Jon Tarr
Patrick Tarrant
Michael Tarsha
Douglas Tarter
Dave Tarwater
Michael Tasi
Elizabeth Tassone
Brad Tate
Darrell Tate
George Tate
Terrilee Tatum
Mark Tatusko
Wendy Tauscheck
Anthony Taverna
Fabiana Taverna Saballos
Kay Gim Tay
Kinde Taye
Andrea Taylor
Benjamin Taylor
Benjamin Taylor
Bryna Taylor
Chris Taylor
Clark Taylor
Daniel Taylor
David Taylor
David Taylor
Donald Taylor
Eric Taylor
Frank Taylor
Jamie Taylor
Jenny Taylor
Joel Taylor
Kyle Taylor
Marc Taylor
Mark Taylor
Mark Taylor
Mary Taylor
Matthew Taylor
Max Taylor
Norma Taylor
Peter Taylor
Phyllis Taylor
Robert Taylor
Taylor Taylor
Todd Taylor
William Taylor
William Taylor
Elsa Tchourumoff
Brian Teacher
Joan Teaford
Steve Tebeau
Lisa Teer
Larry Tegtmeyer
Wilson Teixeira
Roland Tekenbroek
Alan Telfer
Markus Tell
Stefan Tell
Scott Teller
Pete Tellijohn
Yukitaka Temma
Greg Temofeew
Orlando Temple
Tig Templeton
Joel Tennison
Mary Taylor Tepper
Yoshinari Teranaka
Andrea Terrill
Jason Terry
Michael Terry
Naoki Terui
Theodore Teryazos
David Terzaghi
R J Tessier
Fumio Tetsuyama
Konstantin Teverovskiy
Hirotada Tezuka
Vinh Thai
Mark Thalhofer
Jawahar Thangavelu
Cristine Tharrington
Alan Thatcher
Michael Thatcher
Brian Theberge
Yann Thefaine
Kurt Thein
Kevin Theos
Patricia Theriault
Johan Theron
Frank Theveny
Carolyn Thibault
Trae Thibodeaux
Rick Thiel
Dave Thies
Daniel Thiets
Stephen Thirolle
Michael Thoeresz
Rich Thom
Stephen Thom
Albert Thomas
Andre Thomas
Bill Thomas
Brad Thomas
Brian Thomas
Brian Thomas
Bruce Thomas
Buck Thomas
Catherine Thomas
Chase Thomas
Donald Thomas
Dwayne Thomas
Harrell Thomas
J. Chad Thomas
Jeffrey Thomas
Jerry Thomas
John Thomas
Kellen Thomas
Linda Thomas
Marie Thomas
Michael Thomas
Paul Thomas
Paul Thomas
Rebecca Thomas
Tim Thomas
Zachary Thomas
Ann Thomas-Beery
Jerome Thomas-Bunkley
Anne Thompson
Arnold Thompson
Barbara Thompson
Bill Thompson
Calvin Thompson
Catrina Thompson
Corey Thompson
Craig Thompson
Dale Thompson
David Thompson
Frank Thompson
Graham Thompson
H'Cone Thompson
Jack Thompson
James Thompson
James Thompson
Joseph Thompson
Justin Thompson
Kristin Thompson
Patrick Thompson
Ryan Thompson
Tony Thompson
Jeff Thomsen
Adam Thomson
Dane Thomson
Ian Thomson
Laura Thomson
Linda Thomson
Mark Thomson
Sonthana Thongsithavong
Matthew Thormahlen
James Thormann
Lee Thornburg
Kyle Thornhill
Matthew Thornton
Raymond Thornton
Scott Thornton
Jennifer Thorpe
Carl Thorsen
James Thortsen
Terry Thrash
Travis Threadgill
Stephen Thuot
Christin Thurston
Brad Thyroff
Hong Liang Tian
Christopher Tibbetts
Dan Tibbetts
David Tibbetts
Michael Tiberg
Henry Tiberio
Avery Ticer
Steve Tidball
Craig Tidwell
Nancy Tielke
Jim Tierney
Allen Tieu
Craig Tiley
Gundars Tilmanis
Jeff Timmer
James Tinder
Ashley Tindle
Steven Ting
Toy Tingsombutyout
Clay Tinham
Jerold Tinjaca
Laurie Tinnell
Mark Tiu
Gerald Tjon-A-Joe
Paul Tobin
Andrew Todd
Murray Todd
Konstantin Todorov
Behrooz Tofighrad
Erik Tofteland
Anna Maria Toker
Takashi Tokida
Yasuhisa Tokunaga
Susan Toler
Lori Tollberg
Donna Tollefsen
Scott Tolliver
Richard Tom
Ivana Tomaic
Calvin Tomaschko
Vladimir Tomasevic
Kyle Tomaska
Yasuo Tomatsu
Hiroshi Tomii
Kohei Tomioka
Shinya Tomioka
Hirohiko Tomitsuka
Akihiro Tomiyama
Robert Tomiyasu

Nobuyoshi Tomizawa
Aavo Tomkov
George Tompkins
Cliff Toms
Noah Tondre
Andrej Tonejc
Jill Toney
Reedy Toney
Chi Fai Tong
Raymond Tong Chun Man
Jeff Tonjes
Tracy Tooke
Kathy Toon
Gabriel Topor
Mark Toppe
John Topper
Andrew Toprak
Mark Torbert
Kathy Torch
Pete Torgrimson
Dru Torian
Sadanori Torigata
Yoshitaka Torii
Nenad Toroman
Susan Torrance
Guillermo Torres
Jerome Torres
Jose Torres
Mark Tortolani
Claudio Toscano
Eric Toth
Laura Toth
Justin Touchstone
Chie Tougas
Abdoulaye Toure
Penny Tourtellot
Harold Toussaint
Michael Towne
Byron Townsend
Mark Townsend
Joseph Townshend
Shinya Toya
Takumi Toyoda
Toshiaki Toyokura
Shunichi Toyotome
Anna Tozin
Mike Trabert
Tony Trabert
John Tracy
Leslie Tracy
Ryan Tracy
Roy Trafalski
Richard Trager
Phil Trahan
Christopher Tran
Cody Tran
Desiree Tran
Eric Tran
Patrick (Thanh) Tran
Quynh Tran
Sang Tran
Thanh Tran
Viet Tran
Byron Trapp
Skip Trapp
John Trask
Brendon Travis
Laura Travis
Tim Travis
Robert Travnicek
Terrance Treber
Scott Treibly
Bill Treise
Richard Treiss
Edwin Trellue
Jim Tressler
Nathan Tretsven
August Treyz
Carlos Triana
Tim Trigueiro
John Trimp
Daniel Trinh
John Trinity
Chris Trinkle
Robert Trinley
Ed Tripp
William Tritt
Christopher Trizzino
Robert Trogolo
Todd Trombetta
Genya Trosman
Gary Trost
Gail Trostel
Alvin Trotter
Mark Troutman
Keena Trowbridge
Rob Trowbridge
Rene Troxler
Wendell Troy
Dennis Troyke
Mario Trstenjak
Robert Trujillo
John Trump
Tracy Trunck
Do Duc Trung
Franklin Truong
Khoi Truong
Paul Trupia
Michael Trupiano
Daniel Trusca
Dean Tsamas
David Tsang
John Tsang
Terry Tsang
Philippe Tsangarides
Stephen Tscherne
Patrick Tse
Shing Lam Tse
Thomas Tse
Edward Tseng
Katsuaki Tsubura
Shinichi Tsuda
Frank Tsui
Kent Tsui
Kouichi Tsukada
John Tsumas
Tetsuya Tsuzaki
Naomasa Tsuzuki
Daniel Tu
Eve Tubman
Michael Tucci
Rick Tucker
Scottie Tucker
Steven Tucker
Tracy Tucker
Kevin Tuft
Jack Tulatammagul
Shannon Tully
Oleg Tumasov
Lori Tunnell
Leonie Turack
James Turbervill
Christi Turdo
Lynette Turek
Jim Turley
Karen Turman
Arthur Turnbill
Brian Turnbull
Don Turner
Jacqueline Turner
Jeffery Turner
John Turner
Michael Turner
Wakana Turner
Wayne Turner
Erik Turnquist
Jacquelin Turpie
David Turrin
Bryan Turunen
Larry Turville
Cory Tusler
Daria Tuzhikova
Thomas Tvedt
Jacek Twarowski
Bryan Twente
Julius Twyman
Matthew Tyler
Bill Tym
Marilyn Tynes
Tony Tynes
Rick Tyng
Shane Tyree
Nicholas Tzekos
Alexis Ubiera
Rei Uchida
Shinji Uchihashi
Aurelie Udall
Kazuo Ue
Lars Uebel
Kokichi Ueda
Nobukazu Ueda
William Uelze
Masanori Uesugi
Kim Uhlik
Vladka Uhlirova
Kenso Ukon
Mark Ullman
Daniel Underkofler
Chelsea Underwood
Christine Underwood
Renee Underwood
Timothy Underwood
Cheryl Unger
Jeff Unger
Joey Unkenholz
Hiroki Unno
Naoki Uno
Katherine Unsworth
Jennifer Untermeyer
Lisa Upchurch
Todd Upchurch
Josh Uran
Chase Urban
James Urbelis
Christine Uriarte
David Urich
Jeffery Urie
Phillip Urrutia
Fujio Uruma
Victor Urzua
Toyohiko Ushiyama
Efe Ustundag
Vance Usui
Akihiro Usukura
Craig Uttley
Kathleen Mae Uy
Tom Uyehara
Allen Uzzell
Christopher Uzzi
Mehrdad Vahabi
Debby Vakauta
Dan Valbak
Albert Valbuena
Luis Valdez
Hector Valentin
Glenn Valentine
Ryen Valentine
Evan Valeri
Frank Valerio
Mark Valladares
Louis Vallejo
Cristobal Valverde
Jason Van
Clint Van Aswegen
Linda Van B Stafford
Natalie van Blerk
Tom Van De Hey
Bill Van Deinse
James Van Deinse
Joseph Van Deinse
Thomas Van Deinse
Danie van den Heever
Dennis Van der Meer
Peter Van Der Schans
Robert Van Der Schans
Brendan Van Der Weide
Michael Van Dusen
Anousjka Van Exel
Bill Van Glabek
John Van Handel
Peter Van Lingen
David Van Ness
Woodrow van Ommeren
Mark Van Ornum
Andre Van Rensburg
Frank van Riggelen
Devin Van Treeck
Jesse Van Wagner
Carrie Van Wert
Charles Van Wynbergen
Mike Van Zutphen
Robert Van't Hof
John VanAlst
Andrew VanCott
Anthonius Vandepieterman
Cynthia Vander Berg
Grant VanderHayden
Brian Vanderheiden
Jeff VanDis
Brian Vandor
Kevin VanHaitsma
John VanLokeren
Brandon Vann
Michael Vann
Alexa VanOsdol
Vance VanPelt
Don VanRamshorst
Jason Varela
Herbert Vargas
Jaime Vargas
Nestor Vargas
Rolando Vargas
Alvin Varnado
Al Varoski
Fabio Vasconcellos
Vitali Vasileuski
Milos Vasovic
Raymond Vassas
Whitney Vasu
Jordan Vaughan
Stephen Vaughan
Steve Vaughan
Steve Vaughan
Brad Vaughn
Ethan Vaughn
Gary Vaughn
Jean Vaughn
Kevin Vaughn
Les Vaughn
Sheryl Vaughn
Taylor Vaughn
Ali Vaziri Hamedani
Carlos Vazquez
Juan Vazquez
Nicolas Vazquez Fazio
Andrew Veal
Norma Veal
Jay Veazey
Andrew Veeder
Jon Vegosen
Jodi Veillette
Fernando Velasco
Manuel Velasco
Michael Velasco
Robert Velasco
Jon Velasquez
Lars Veldheer
Mick Veldheer
Roberto Velez
Dusan Vemic
Anthony Venable
Ken Veney
Joe Venezia
Anand Venkataramani
Kasey Vens
Carien Venter
Andy Ventress
Tena Ventress-Soller
Ritush Venugopal
Timothy Ver Hoeven
Emma Verberne Collins
John Verde
Noel Vere
Marc Verebey
Robert Verkins
Yvonne Vermaak
Frank Vermeer
Courtney Vernon
Dax Vernon
Collin Vero-Casavant
Julien Versailles
Richard Verzaal
Eric Vescuso
Roman Veselinov
Julian Vespan

John Vest
Rick Vetter
Tamara Vezina
Albert Vial
Fred Viancos
Rubens Vianna
Gerri Viant
Eduardo Vicencio
Jan Vick
Jeffrey Vick
Kathy Vick
Samuel Vickroy
Samuel Vickroy
Gary Victor
René Vidal
Victor Vidal
Rafael Vieira
Vinicius Vieira
John Vigil
Jorge Vila
Emillia Viljoen
Eduardo Villagomez
Martha Villalobos
William Villalobos
Jose Villaluz
Jeff Villano
Israel Villanova
Juan Villanueva
Cesar Villarroel
Fausto Villarroel
Andrea Villasana
Jonathan Villegas
Abigail Villena
Thibault Villeneuve
Valerie Villucci
Robert Vinal
Trace Vincent
Joe Vincler
Jeffrey Vine
Mark Vines
Martin Vinokur
Jack Vinson
John Vinson
Susan Vinton Chandler
Andrew Violette
Anjan Viplav
Christopher Visconti
Joshua Vissman
David Vitanovec
Leigh Vitasek
Andoni Vivanco Guzma
Gonzalo Vivas
Stephen Viviano
Brad Vo
Lance Vodicka
Waldemar Vogelgesang
Eric Voges
Judith Vogt
Milena Volkova
Veng Vollavanh
Andrey Volotskov
Ali Von Kennel
Amar Vora
Stephen Vorhees
Kieron Vorster
Oliver Vorwald
Leo Vorwerk
Alex Voss
James Vouvakis
Helaine Vrana
Bud Vredeveld
Evan Vrsaljko
Hank Vu
Otis Vu
Sam Vuille
Karl Vukobrat
Yan Vulitskiy
Aleksandar Vulovic
Frederick Vulpio
Katherine Wacnik
Hiromasa Wada
Tadao Wada
Noel Wadawu
Heidi Waddell
Brent Waddle
Christopher Wade
Eric Wade
Tommy Wade
Charles Wadlington
Drew Wager
Sarah Waggoner
Aaron Wagner
Bob Wagner
Chris Wagner
Dennis Wagner
Harold Wagner
Lorna Wagner
Mark Wagner
Matthew Wagner
Samantha Wagner
Jonathan Wagshul
Bob Wagstaff
Jeff Wagstaff
John Wahlborg
Carol Wahlstrand
Ip Wai Lam
Carole Waite
Jack Waite
Kelsey Waite
Shun Wakabayasi
Keiko Wakasa
Katsumi Wakatsuki
Lanny Wake
Laura Waldon
Andrew Waldrop
Harold Wales
Mark Wales
Kyla Walgren
Benjamin Walker
Bobby Walker
Buddy Walker
Colleen Walker
Deb Walker
James Walker
James Walker
John Walker
Katherine Walker
Matthew Walker
Patrick Walker
Rich Walker
Ross Walker
Rusty Walker
Scott Walker
Stephen Walker
Tom Walker
Tom Walker
Wendall Walker
Christopher Wall
Eric Wall
Justin Wall
Spencer Wall
Barbara Wallace
Brad Lee Wallace
Mic Wallace
Michael Wallace
Timothy Wallace
Tom Wallace
Valerie Wallace
Joanne Wallen
Vane Waller
William Walling
Donnie Wallis
Mikael Wallman
Limual Walpole
Betty Walsh
Henry Walsh
Medina Walsh
Michael Walsh
Benjamin Walter
Christine Walter
Jeff Walter
John Walter
Michael Walter
Brian Walters
Jeff Walters
Matt Walters
Ronnie Walters
Steve Walters
Pancho Walthall
Charlie Waltman
John Walton
Ralph Walton
John Waltz
Paul Waltz
Stephen Walz
Eric Wammock
Richard Wamsley
Changsheng Wan
Bin Wang
Dachun Wang
Doanh Wang
Emily Wang
Fang Wang
Jian Wang
Jiaxu Wang
Jingyu Wang
Joseph Wang
Philip Wang
Siqi Wang
Wilma Wang
Yue Wang
Zheng Wang
Zilong Wang
Tom Wangelin
Monika Waniek
David Wanja
Christopher Wann
Gregory Wanner
Andrew Wapowsky
Andre Ward
Brenda Ward
Brian Ward
Christy Ward
Houston Ward
Jared Ward
Lee Ward
Lincoln Ward
Marty Ward
Michael Ward
Rod Ward
Stephen Ward
Stephen Ward
Terry Ward
Brick Warden
Laurie Warder
Brian Wardhammar
Ray Wardlaw
David Ware
Jared Ware
Kevin Ware
Mike Ware
Eric Warm
Tomm Warneke
Charles Warner
Christopher Warner
Christopher Warner
Jennifer Warner
Kyle Warner
Lois Warner
Matthew Warner
Russ Warner
David Warren
Kendon Warren
Michael Warren
William Warren
Gareth Warrilow
Bill Washauer
Herman Washington
Oliver Washington
Masaya Washisu
Jason Wass
Atsushi Watanabe
Kazuki Watanabe
Takashi Watanabe
Tyler Watanabe
Dick Waterfall
David Waterman
Kilmeny Waterman Connor
Hugh Waters
Jeff Waters
Stephen Waters
Stuart Waters
Bradley Watkins
Clint Watkins
Todd Watkins
Horace Watkis
Nancy Watland
Teri Watland
Ashley Watling
Bradley Watson
Carol Watson
Charles Watson
Christopher Watson
David Watson
Ed Watson
Matt Watson
Maxwell Watson
Roger Watson
Ted Watson
Alan Watts
Campbell Watts
Dave Watts
Jessica Watts
Joshua Way
Timothy Way
Christopher Waychunas
Michael Wayman
Richard Wayman
Daniel Weant
Patrick Weant
Jeff Weaver
Ryan Weaver
Chris Webb
David Webb
Michael Webb
Rachel Webb
Randy Webb
Thomas Webb
Chip Weber
Christine Weber
David Weber
Gideon Weber
James Weber
William Weber
Christopher Webster
Daniel Webster
Samuel Webster
William Webster
Kim Wedige
Robert Weer
Jim Wegener
Oscar Wegner
Shannon Wegner
Steven Wegner
Dai Wei
David Weibel
Randy Weidemann
Darin Weidenheimer
Mike Weidl
Paul Weighell
Dennis Weikel
Jerry Weil
Mark Weil
Philip Weil
James Weinacker
Jimmy Weinacker
Matthew Weinapple
Julie Weinberger
Eddie Weiner
Gary Weiner
Marci Weiner
Phil Weiner
Mindy Weiner-Horne
Marc Weinstein
Sheila Weinstock
Amir Weintraub
Benay Weintraub
Ilene Weintraub
Karen Weir
Mark Weir
Thomas Weir
Jason Weir-Smith
Maxwell Weishan
Lorinda Weiss
Matthew Weiss
Alan Weissbaum
Roberto Weissmann
Holly Weitendorf
Maria Jesusa Wekow
Gregory Weksel
Betty Sue Welch
Marissa Welch
Nathan Welden
Brent Wellman
Craig Wells

Shane Wells
Doug Welsh
Stephen Welt
W Welty
Lydia Wen Li Yuan
Tzu Ting Weng
Bob Wenger
Douglas Wenger
Jim Wenger
Erika Wentz-Russell
Clarence Wenzel
Marianne Werdel
Michelle Werkema
Bud Werner
Dean Werner
Jeffrey Wernick
Hal Wernik
William Wert
Jill Wertenberger
Jodi Wertenberger
Kristen Wertenberger
Chris Wertz
Joe Wesson
Aaron West
Avery West
Erik West
Gay West
Logan West
Robert West
Rupert West
Terrell West
Tom West
Yelena West
Carey Westberg
Julie Westercamp
Ken Westerfeld
Lisa Westergard
Dan Westerhaus
Rick Westhoff
John Weston
Patric Westoo
Colton Westran
Bruce Westrum
Harold Wetzel
Andreas Weyermann
Steven Weyhing
Craig Weymer
Carol Weymuller
Marnie Whalen
Dee Wharton
Rob Wheatley
David Wheeler
Keith Wheeler
Marvin Wheeler
Nancy Wheeler
Scotty Wheeler
Rachel Whelton
David Whetstone
Edward Whetton
Matthew Whicker
Kevin Whipple
Ken Whitaker
Christian White
David White
Donnie White
Jay White
John White
John White
Lee White
Lisa White
Luke White
Mackenzie White
Marc White
Melinda White
Michael White
Michael White
Michael White
Robin White
Roger White
Roy White
Teddy White
William White
Jordan Whitehead
Ryan Whitehill
John Whitehurst
Susan Whiteside
John Whitlinger
Tate Whitlinger
Wendy Whitlinger
Daniel Whitlock
Tollan Whitlock
Barbara Whitman
Josh Whitman
Greg Whitmire
Gregory Whitmore
Chuck Whitnell
Marceil Whitney
Larry Whitson
Bryan Whitt
Steven Whitted
Thomas Whitten
Richard Whittington
Wendie Whitton
Pat Whitworth
Ted Wiard
William Wickenheisser
Harry Wickes
Greg Wicklund
Kishan Wickramasinghe
George Wideikis
Martina Widjaja
Chris Widney
Jeffrey Wiedemann
Joshua Wiedenfeld
Sam Wiener
Dave Wiest
Susan Wiet
Gwen Wiggins
Stephanie Wiggins
Scott Wightman
Lisa Wilcott
John Wilcox
Kenneth Wilcox
Bruce Wild
Rochelle Wild
Steve Wild
William Wild
Val Wilder
Pamela Wildt
Jennifer Wilent
Scott Wiles
Theo Wiles
Jennifer Wiley
Cindy Wilfong
Joseph Wilkerson
Rusty Wilkes
Brooke Wilkins
Chris Wilkins
Sion Wilkins
Jana Wilks
Jason Wilks
Larissa Will
Frank Willard
Craig Willeford
Broc Willems
Chuck Willenborg
Lawrence Willens
Rick Willett
Glenn William
Alan Williams
Ben Williams
Brad Williams
Bret Williams
Darrio Williams
David Williams
Derek Williams
Donald Williams
Donald Williams
Duane Williams
Eddie Williams
Elizabeth Williams
Francisco Williams
G Williams
Glenn Williams
Gordon Williams
Janet Williams
Jeffrey Williams
John Williams
John Williams
John Williams
John Williams
Kara Williams
Kathy Williams
Kim Williams
Lee Williams
Mark Williams
Mary Beth Williams
Michael Williams
Michelle Williams
Monte Williams
Noel Williams
Rachel Williams
Richard Williams
Robert Williams
Rodney Williams
Ron Williams
Ryan Williams
Scott Williams
Stephen Williams
Steve Williams
Vatrice Williams
Walt Williams
Jose Williamson
Kevin Williamson
Mace Williamson
Mike Williamson
Nunry Williamson
Phillip Williamson
Shane Williford
Bill Willing
Todd Willing
Tony Willingham
Scott Willinsky
Nicholas Willis
Richard Willis
Daniel Willman
Reagan Willman
Brian Wills
Scott Wills
Robert Wilner
Angela Wilson
Aoife Wilson
Brian Wilson
Brock Wilson
Clay Wilson
Dan Wilson
Danny Wilson
Derrick Wilson
Eric Wilson
George Wilson
Grady Wilson
Helen Wilson
Jamey Wilson
Jason Wilson
Jeffrey Wilson
Jeffrey Wilson
Jody Wilson
Kimberly Wilson
Kristen Wilson
Kyle Wilson
Phillip Wilson
Rick Wilson
Stephen Wilson
Walter Wilson
Tricia Wilstead
Bo Win Tin
Gerald Winder
Caroline Winebrenner
Jason Winegar
Steven Winer
DeDee Winfield
Newlyn Wing
William Wing
Jacqueline Wingard
Eric Winn
Alexander Winslow
Katharina Winterhalter
Matthew Winters
Ryan Winters
William Winzeler
Lincoln Wirgau
Shelley Wirt
Robert Wirth
Steven Wise
Todd Wise
Kate Wiseman
William Wiseman
Amy Wishingrad
Agnes Wiski-Pagnotta
Darryl Wisner
Jed Wisniewski
Ross Wisser
Rick Wissig
Donna Wissinger
Ted Withall
Ryan Witham
Neil Witherow
Victor Withers
Jeff Witmer
Daniel Witt
Taylor Witt
Gregory Witta
Kim Wittenberg
John Witter
Craig Wittus
Michael Wojtkowski
Jim Wolavka
David Wolden
Mark Woldmoe
David Wolf
John Wolf
Tina Wolf
Ed Wolfarth
Jeffrey Wolfberg
Chris Wolff
Meghan Wolfgram
Ryan Wolfington
Joshua Wolfson
Jacek Wolicki
Ed Wolin
Brandon Womack
Brett Womack
Kent Womack
Aaron Wong
Erik Wong
Frederick Wong
Gary Wong
Lamson Wong
Man Lung Wong
Ming Wai Wong
Sai Lee Wong
Sai Wah Wong
Silvio Wong
Wing Ming Wong
Kitty Wong Lai Kuen
David Woo
Adelaide Wood
Christian Wood
Clark Wood
Griffin Wood
Jeff Wood
Jon Wood
Patrick Wood
Rory Wood
Samuel Wood
Shane Wood
Stacy Wood
Carol Woodard
Darren Woodford
Mark Woodforde
Brett Woodmansee
Richard Woodroof
Angella Woods
Benjamin Woods
Harold Woods
Kathy Woods
Kira Woods
Marley Woods
Michael Woods
Oliver Woods
Ron Woods
Ron Woods
Sarah Woods
Mark Woodson
Mike Woody
Jorge Woog
Kevin Woog
Wayne Wookey
Matt Wooldridge
Shawn Wooley
David Woolf
Lucien Woorons
Sophie Woorons
Daniel Wooten
Jessica Worden

Rick Workman
Rod Workman
Scott Works
John Worley
Kaleen Worley
Herbert Wormser
Mark Worsham
Paul Worstell
Julian Wortelboer
Alex Worth
Courtia Worth
Shawn Worth
William Worth
Martin Wostenholme
Jeff Wrage
Thomas Wride
Cynthia Wright
Damita Wright
Doug Wright
Ernest Wright
Jarett Wright
John Wright
Lee Wright
Steve Wright
Thomas Wright
Aleksander Wrzeszcz
Amanda Wu
Dan Wu
Minghui Wu
Samson Wu
Thomas Wu
Robert Wuhrman
Matthew Wuller
Ann Wunderlich
Marc Wurtzman
Daryl Wyatt
Russell Wyatt
Tim Wyatt
Charlotte Wylie
Mark Wylie
Larry Wyman
Austin Wynne
Tim Wynne
Tom Wynne
Brian Wyrick
Jeffrey Wyshner
Kyle Wyszynski
Gregory Wyzykowski
Zhijia Xie
Da Xu
Zikang Xu
Ed Yablonski
Takashi Yagi
Ryousuke Yaginuma
Greg Yahia
Craig Yahne
Joann Yakscoe
Kiwamu Yakugawa
Kazuhiko Yakushiji
Mamoru Yamada
Masayuki Yamaguchi
Tadashi Yamaguchi
Riki Yamakami
Yoshiaki Yamakawa
Hiroshi Yamaki
Glenn Yamamoto
Naohiro Yamamoto
Norifumi Yamamoto
Ryota Yamamoto
Yoshikata Yamamoto
Hideyuki Yamanaka
Kaz Yamanoha
Akira Yamasaki
Hidemi Yamashita
David Yamauchi
Yuma Yamazaki
Kenta Yanagibashi
John Yancey
John Yandell
Alesya Yanez
Ruben Yanez
Victor Yaneza
Anna Yang
Joshua Yang
Morisa Yang
Nan Yang
Susan Xia Yang
Tony Yang
Tony Yang
Steve Yankello
Yukihiro Yano
Gerald Anthony Yanson
De Min Yao
Jun Wang Yap
Reagan Yap
Justin Yarbrough
Kristen Yarbrough
Mehmet Yargici
Zehra Yargici
Ross Yarlott
Alfredo Yarur
Masayuki Yashima
Tsuyoshi Yashiro
Sandra Yaskow
Takehiko Yasu
Tatsuo Yasugi
Hiroya Yasukawa
Mitsuru Yasumoto
Michio Yasuna
Kiyoshi Yasuno
Keiichi Yasuoka
Barbi Yates
Micheal Yates
Richard Yates
Miranda Yates-Steg
Samuel Yau Tow Yong
Zachary Yeadon
Graham Yeager
Ronald Yeaton
Steve Yedinak
Anthony Yee
Danny Yee
Michael Yeh
Peter Yellico
Collette Yelverton
Bryden Yemm
Andrew Yenawine
Eddie Yeo
Justin Yeo
Steven Yeong
Kari Yerg
Troy Yerian
Charles Yerrick
David Yett
Alan Yeung
Misha Yevtich
Yorgo Yfantopoulos
Aron Yingling
Wing Yip
Hau Man Yiu
Lup Whung Yiu
James Yoakum
Greg Yocum
Kotaro Yoda
Chris Yoder
Toshihiko Yogo
Manabu Yokota
Akitoki Yokoyama
Kazuo Yokoyama
Cynthia Yonathan
Rio Yonathan
Masako Yonehana
Jami Yonekura-Jones
Hak Soo Yoo
Joo Yoon
Ron York
William York
David Yorks
Maksim Yorsh
Fumitoshi Yoshida
Masahiko Yoshida
Nobuyuki Yoshida
Taira Yoshida
Tomoaki Yoshida
Masashi Yoshiike
Tadasu Yoshikai
Hitoshi Yoshikawa
Yoshimi Yoshimura
Yuuki Yoshinaga
Hiroshi Yoshino
Shunsuke Yoshioka
Ray Yost
Eugene You
Farley Youman
Brian Young
Brian Young
Butch Young
Christopher Young
Dana Young
Donald Young
Gerald Young
James Young
Kwong Young
Thomas Young
Timothy Young
Wendell Young
George Youssef
Aaron Yovan
Jerry Yu
Renjie Yu
Steve Yu
Xue Long Yu
Yang Yu
Shogo Yuasa
Jason Yue
George Yuen
Vania Yui-De Los Reyes
Rie Yukihiro
Naohiro Yukita
Darrick Yun
Song Chol Yun
Shchukin Yuriy
Jicham Zaatini
Paula Zager
Vazghen Zaghiyan
Karim Zaher
George Zahorsky
Adnan Zaidi
Boris Zaitsev
Ali Zalat
Jon Zalinski
Steve Zalinski
Vladimir Zaltsman
Michal Zaluski
Dave Zamarripa
Ernest Zamora
Roger Zamudio
June Zanchelli
Afshin Zand
Madeline Zanfardino
Telly Zangas
Thomas Zapp
Job Zarate
Paul Zaretsky
Susan Zaro
Anne Zarraonandia
Carrie Zarraonandia
Marie Zassoda
Adam Zastempowski
Eric Zatman
Michael Zavacky
Paul Zavala
Christen Zawatsky
Gordon ZawTun
Jack Zdvorak
Matthew Zedler
Charlie Zeigler
Glendale Zell
Brent Zeller
Marla Zeller
Mitch Zenaty
Gwinyai Zengeni
Jeff Zenisek
Sevan Zenopian
Scott Zent
Jon Zepp
Rod Zerni
David Zeutas-Broer
Anzela Zguna
Adrians Zguns
Bin Zhang
Chuanguo Zhang
Hao Zhang
Huanyu Zhang
Lei Zhang
Mingzhe Zhang
Shuai Zhang
Yanfei Zhang
Zhao Zhang
Han Zhao
Mingzhen Zhao
Xin Song Zhao
Xuanqi Zhao
Yakun Zhao
Yansong Zhao
Aleksey Zharinov
Chao Zheng
Jian Zheng
Yu Zheng
Ni Zhou
Xuanzhi Zhou
Xufan Zhou
Junfeng Zhu
Zurab Zhvania
Jonathan Zielke
Brian Ziemba
Kevin Zimmaro
Nick Zimmer
Charles Zimmerman
Leigh Zimmerman
Wade Zimmerman
Aidan Zimmermann
David Zimmermann
Dean Zimmermann
Kathleen Zingler
Ben Zink
George Zink
Nick Zinsmeister
Robert Zipay
Daniel Zirolla
Denis Zivkovic
Andy Zodin
Nikolas Zogaj
Zachary Zola
Jason Zoladz
Jonathan Zolin
Mark Zolman
Jiazheng Zou
Julia Zubkova
Kacie Zuck
Melissa Zuiderveen
Lisa Zuk
Ana Zuleta
Martin Zumpft
Yang Zuo
Anna Zurek
Michael Zury
Bob Zysk

INDEX

The roster of the USPTA members is not included in the index since it is in alphabetical order on pages 152-187.